A LIBRARY OF LITERARY CRITICISM

A Library
of Literary Criticism

MODERN SPANISH AND PORTUGUESE LITERATURES

Compiled and edited by
Marshall J. Schneider
Baruch College,
City University of New York

Irwin Stern
Columbia University

A Frederick Ungar Book
CONTINUUM • NEW YORK

1988

The Continuum Publishing Company
370 Lexington Avenue, New York, NY 10017

Printed in the United States of America

Library of Congress Cataloging-in-Publication Data

Modern Spanish and Portuguese literatures.

(A Library of literary criticism)
Includes index.
1. Spanish literature—20th century—History and criticism. 2. Portuguese
literature—20th century—History and criticism. I. Schneider, Marshall J.
II. Stern, Irwin. III. Series.
PQ6072.M57 1988   860   87-13754
ISBN 0-8044-3280-5

CONTENTS

PREFACE

Modern Spanish and Portuguese Literatures presents a selection of critical opinions about some eighty twentieth-century authors of the Iberian Peninsula, writing in Spanish, Catalan, Galician, and Portuguese. Originally prepared for publication in 1979, the volume's selections were updated beginning in 1984.

Writers chosen for inclusion in this volume have been the leading figures of their literatures. Our goal was to present an overview of critical opinions since the beginning of a writer's career, highlighting distinctive aspects of their works, their lives, and their interaction with their contemporaries. In most cases we were able to obtain, through the generosity of authors, periodicals, and book publishers, selections that we considered of great consequence. Owing to the lack of a significant body of critical evaluations of writers whose careers began during the last ten years, none of these could be included.

Several procedures have been adopted to facilitate use of this volume. Following the Introduction, which offers a survey of the literary situation of the Iberian nations in the twentieth century, a general alphabetical listing of authors included under the headings Spain and Portugal, appears. The organization of these alphabetical listings merits special note. Authors writing in Spanish (sometimes called Castilian), Catalan, and Galician are listed by their traditional last names, quite often a composite name (e.g., García Lorca, Torrente Ballester). Portuguese writers are listed by their very last names, in accordance with a practice adopted by the Library of Congress. Thus, José Cardoso Pires appears under "P" rather than under "C." The exceptions are hyphenated names, such as Sá-Carneiro, and pseudonyms, such as Teixeira de Pascoaes, listed under "S" and "T" respectively. A list of periodicals used, with an explanation of abbreviations, is also provided.

The main body of the text is divided into two parts: Spain and Portugal. Sections on writers once again appear in alphabetical order, with cross references in the Portuguese sections as necessary. In the critical selections themselves, however, the form of the author's name used by the critic is maintained. The dates in brackets following critical selections indicate the year of its original publication. The † following page numbers indicates that this is the first English translation of that text prepared by the editors.

A listing of Works Mentioned at the back of the book provides information about titles in the original language, publication dates, and published English translations. The volume concludes with an index of critics cited.

The editors would like to express their gratitude to all copyright holders—critics and publishers—who have so generously offered their material for use in this volume. In addition, we owe many thanks to Rita Stein, senior editor at Frederick Ungar, who put it all together.

M.J.S.
I.S.

INTRODUCTION

SPAIN

Even the most abbreviated study of Spanish history and literature during the twentieth century can reveal why the ad-campaign slogan of the 1960s encouraging tourism—"Spain is different"—is an apt one. Spain is a country in western Europe that had to struggle to westernize itself; for which democracy has never been a given; and to which industrialization has come tardily and with great difficulty. It is a country that was severely wounded by a tragic civil war that managed not only to isolate it from the rest of the world for several decades but also to estrange Spaniards from each other and from their own artistic and literary achievements of the past.

In spite of the success of the tourism ad, which helped to attract millions of people to Spain, it is not exactly clear why Spain's history and literature have remained relatively unknown. This situation of neglect is unfortunate, and it is to be hoped that within the very near future it will all change as Spain joins the community of Western nations.

The predicament in which Spain found herself at the beginning of this century presaged the turbulent history that afflicted her in the ensuing years. The Spanish-American War of 1898, a war that Spain chose to fight against all odds because of a misguided sense of honor, resulted in total catastrophe: Within less than a year, Spain lost all her remaining colonies—Guam, Puerto Rico, Cuba, the Philippines, and the Marianas. Spain's predictable defeat by the United States occasioned deep moral disgust, painful embarrassment, and thorough disillusionment in Spain. This loss of power was, however, stunningly compensated for by a group of writers, the Generation of 1898, who were responsible for a second Golden Age of literature. Out of the ashes of defeat came a sparkling and insightful literature.

The wars in Morocco, where Spain held two garrison towns—Ceuta and Melilla—soon led to another major national humiliation. Once again, Spain acted out of honor and with intransigence. Instead of abandoning Morocco, the Spanish government, headed by Alfonso XIII, the new Bourbon king, committed its army there more and more deeply. The government asserted that it was protecting Spanish nationals and stubbornly continued to invoke some vague notion of manifest destiny. Finally, in the summer of 1921 at Annual, Abd-el-Kim, a skillful military leader, ambushed Spanish troops who were about to carry out a major offensive, which was, according to the plans of the king, to coincide with both the day of Saint James Matamoros ("Kill-Moor") and the celebratory removal of the mortal remains of the Cid, Spain's most famous Moor-Killer, to the Cathedral of Burgos. Eight thousand Spanish soldiers perished in this travesty of history and tradition. Spain's army was proven worthless, and it was now only a matter of a few years until the government and parliamentary rule would fall. On September 23, 1923, Miguel Primo de Rivera became dictator. As promised, he created some semblance of order and national pride, even if it was only temporary, and in May 1926 finally defeated Abd-el-Kim.

Even though there were impingements on free expression during the dictatorship, censorship of literature was relatively benign. Both Miguel Unamuno and Ramón del Valle-Inclán, beloved public figures now, were at one time either exiled or imprisoned; for the most part, however, the business of literature went on. In fact, it flourished. A writer could attack neither Primo de Rivera personally nor his pompous military complex. Other matters, though, were fair game. All the venerated writers of the Generation 1898 continued their acerbic criticism of Spanish institutions, and a new generation of writers—the Generation of 1927—was born. Although Primo de Rivera mistrusted writers, he grudgingly allowed them to work in relative peace.

Against a background of violent strikes, student unrest, widespread clamoring for democracy, economic instability, political ferment, and regional demands for autonomy, the tottering dictatorship of Primo de Rivera ended, and on April 14, 1931, the Second Republic began. Alfonso XIII abdicated and sought refuge in Paris. The new age of republicanism brought forth a change in literary attitudes. The Generation of 1936, which tried to rehumanize and radicalize literature politically, appeared.

The Republican years were not halcyon, but on the contrary, were marred by violence and utter turmoil. To understand exactly what had gone wrong would be a herculean task that would far exceed the scope of this introduction. Suffice it to say that an "antidote" to Spain's sickness was discovered and administered under the rebellious leadership of Generalísimo Franco. On July 18, 1936, the Spanish Civil War began. It lasted for three years, and almost a million Spaniards perished in it. The war caused such deep wounds among the populace and such a thorough discontinuity in Spanish institutions that now, fifty years later, Spain still finds herself recovering from Franco's "antidote."

The ironies of Franco's rebellion abound and replicate the Spanish predilection for tradition and the abstract hazy notion of honor, already seen in the Spanish-American War and in the Moroccan wars. With the support of wealthy landowners, of the omnipotent Catholic Church, of eager monarchists, of the bulk of the military, of Hitler's and Mussolini's manpower and weaponry, of the Falangist party, led by Antonio Primo de Rivera, son of the erstwhile dictator, and even of Spain's traditionally hated enemies, the Moors, Franco embarked upon a Christian crusade to give back to the Spanish people their inviolate values: Catholicism and traditionalism. Franco's simplistic and Manichean vision of the world created, at his victory in 1939, an "officialism" that stifled his country's creativity and growth for the thirty-nine years he ruled. It is hard to evaluate the full extent to which his regime curtailed the quality of literature, but some general observations can be made objectively.

That literary activity practically came to a halt during the bloody war and for several years after was the least of the injuries, and was to be expected. There were, however, more serious indictments against the authoritarian regime that defined by fiat the practices and limits of authority and what constituted proper public expression. Not only did the best and most important writers and thinkers leave Spain, but the rigorous and capricious censorship laws further abetted the erosion of the quality of Spanish literature. Until the 1960s, the books of most writers who lived in exile could not be sold in Spain or published there. This was also true of certain "subversive" foreign writers. In general, drama, a performance art, was hit harder than poetry, which was least scrutinized by the state. In 1966 the censorship laws fortunately became looser, but brought a new twist: Excepting performance art, there would be precensorship by the authors themselves of their own works; submission of a manuscript to the board of censors, which over the years had become controlled by lay members, was not necessary. In other words, censorship by the state would be *post facto*. As a result many writers chose to publish abroad. There were, however, accommodations made to foreign writers and Spanish exiles, whose books, with certain exceptions, were now allowed to be read and published.

Censorship, though, was only one arm of the Franco regime that dampened literary energy and intellectual activity within the country. Franco's officialism was almost all-inclusive. Because he mistrusted other Western nations and even Spaniards themselves, he created an autarkical and highly interventionist government during the first years of his rule. He promulgated the idea that the national political health could be attained only through political apathy and an absence of political parties; he allowed the arch-conservative Church to oversee all educational activities. Therefore, together with strict censorship, these factors effected a blandness of spirit and isolated Spain from the rest of the world. These conditions lasted well into the 1950s and produced, as will be seen, a literature that responded quite appropriately to this unique political reality. Writers who grew up in Spain during the early Franco years were markedly different from other European writers.

Franco's death in 1975 marked the beginning of Spain's rebirth and reentry into the world as a free nation. Under King Juan Carlos (the grandson of Alfonso XIII), who was reared and groomed for the job—oddly enough, by Franco—Spain has become a constitutional monarchy, fully dedicated to democracy. For almost a decade now national elections have been the rule; censorship ceased in 1978; literature and the other arts receive the full benefits of being in free and open contact with the creative ideas and energies of other countries; officialism is a thing of the past, and subsidies for writing and other creative endeavors, which are now widely available, are based on merit and not on knee-jerk responses to governmental dicta. It is to be hoped that foreigners will not only rush to Spain's shores because "Spain is different," but that they will come to know the literature of Spain because it is intrinsically interesting and worthy of careful attention.

The development of Spanish literature during the twentieth century, while difficult to pigeonhole neatly and characterize precisely, can generally be likened to the movement of a pendulum. Literary generations, that is, groups of writers loosely connected to each other by age and spirit, alternate their manner of response to their immediate reality by being referential—reacting directly to the problems of their day—or by being figural—producing a literature that is concerned with aesthetic and creative processes. At times groups or individual writers can create literature that is both figural and referential. Writers often change their approach in order to join or herald the spirit of the next turn in literary fashion. The general rule of thumb is that authors concerned with Spain—the reality of the moment—are less influenced by foreign literary currents than those whose interests are more literary and aesthetic. The Generation of 1898, brought into being, as has already been seen, by Spain's humiliating defeat at the hands of the United States, is an example of a group of writers whose interests were both Spain and the discovery of a vibrant language that could create a new literature. The writings of Miguel de Unamuno, José Ortega y Gasset, and Antonio Machado, for example, were meditative and philosophical, keeping alive the legacy that the late-nineteenth-century writers Ángel Ganivet and Benito Pérez Galdós left behind. Influenced by the Modernism of the Nicaraguan poet Rubén Darío (1867–1916) and the French Symbolists, the works of Ramón del Valle-Inclán and Juan Ramón Jiménez, on the other hand, were more stylized and aesthetic. Unamuno and Machado felt that a writer was just a man of flesh and blood and that literature was communication, while Jiménez, the supreme aesthete, promulgated symbolist ideas: Literature for him was a type of religious undertaking; the writer had special knowledge and a privileged position. It is curious that these two different schools of thought—literature as communication and literature as epistemology—will characterize the ebb and flow of the literary generations throughout the century.

The novelists of the Generation of 1898 gave new vitality to the genre. Unamuno, Pío Baroja, Azorín, and Valle-Inclán all took up the innovating spirit of Pérez Galdós and were intent on shaping a novel that dealt adequately with the rapid changes of the new century. Unamuno stripped his novel bare, exposing the raw bone of being and existence; Azorín experimented with lyricism and painted with impressionistic brushstrokes subtle states of being; Baroja, from whom Ernest Hemingway claimed to have learned his craft, wrote turgid, sprawling novels that indicted Spaniards and all of humanity for their sins of passivity and inauthenticity; Valle-Inclán, an elegant stylist, started by borrowing from the end-of-century decadents and ended up by being an experimentalist and acute critic of Spanish society. He created the *esperpento,* which he defined as a grotesque reflection seen in a distorting concave mirror.

Drama also enjoyed a renaissance, and like the novel, was influenced in no small way by Pérez Galdós, the so-called Ibsen of Spain. Eschewing the excessively melodramatic plays of the Nobel laureate (1904) José Echegaray (1832–1916), Jacinto Benavente—also a Nobel laureate (1922)—arrived at natural dialogue and psychological verisimilitude. The brothers Machado—Antonio and Manuel—along with Azorín cultivated an interesting poetic and lyrical theater. Valle-Inclán, though, was perhaps the most talented, although undervalued dramatist of the moment. His dark "esperpentic" visions are more appreciated and studied today than is the drama of Benavente, whose plays dominated the Spanish theater almost until the time of his death in 1954.

Literary experimentation and anti-bourgeois writing did not escape Spain during the 1920s, an era in which literary playfulness was in the foreground. This exciting period saw the birth of a new group of writers, the Generation of 1927, that differed greatly from the preceding Generation of 1898. Taking their cue from a somewhat less than impartial reading of Ortega y Gasset's *La deshumanización del arte* (1925; *The Dehumanization of Art,* 1948), Pedro Salinas, Federico García Lorca, Luis Cernuda, Rafael Alberti, Vicente Aleixandre (Nobel laureate of 1977), Jorge Guillén, and Dámaso Alonso created a literature that remained aloof from social urgencies and immediate human concerns. In the footsteps of the French symbolists, they believed that the purpose of words was not communication. To name a thing was to kill it; the effects of phenomena were important. These writers fostered a myriad of literary movements, thereby creating the "Age of Isms." The creative act was sacrosanct and special for them; they chose not to view themselves as ordinary mortals but as superior beings who brought back news from some secret place. The group rallied around the tricentenary of the death of the Baroque poet Luis Góngora (1561–1627), and at least in the beginning, remained true to him by supporting vanguardism, love for poetic purity, and innovative language.

The writers of the Generation of 1927 remained for the most part on track well into the 1930s. Many of the novels and plays that were written by writers from the group or their epigones were difficult and intended for only a small minority of the reading public. Even the early plays of García Lorca, which attacked bourgeois values, were not well received or understood. It took his trilogy of rural Andalusia—*Bodas de sangre* (1935; *Blood Wedding,* 1939), *Yerma* (1937; *Yerma,* 1941), and *La casa de Bernarda Alba* (1945; *The House of Bernarda Alba,* 1947), in which there was a blending of folk and vanguard elements, to make him a more accessible and popular writer.

The literary pendulum swung once again after the crash of the stock market in 1929. Amid the strong currents of "dehumanized" literature, Ramón Sender's novel about the disaster at Annual, *Imán* (1930; *Pro Patria,* 1935), announced the new spirit of the 1930s, which brought forth a rehumanization of the arts, an appropriate expression of a tumultuously political decade marked by optimism and violence, despair and bloodshed. The jubilation and new affirmation of the dignity of man and of liberty occasioned by republicanism soon turned into tragic violence in 1936 at the onset of the civil war, and then, in 1939, into gloom when Franco set into motion his repressive regime.

The Generation of 1936, who were by and large committed politically and socially, represented both factions of the civil war, a struggle that has often been called the last great ideological encounter of our century. During the Republic the agenda of this troubled but spirited group had a different purpose from that of the preceding generation. Their political milieu had changed, offering them an opportunity to criticize freely and to broaden the social consciousness of the people. Novelists like Sender, Francisco Ayala, and Max Aub, who would later write in exile, published agit-prop novels that were militant and reflective of the unstable times. Miguel Hernández, the tragic victim of Franco's postwar vindicativeness, who died in prison, wrote resonant social poetry and political dramas, imbued with lyricism and sensitivity, which communicated a love of freedom and a call to vigilance. Alejandro Casona, who would soon spend most of his life in Argentina, wrote social plays that oscillated between journalistic truth and lyrical fantasy. He also collaborated with García Lorca in bringing Spain's theatrical legacy to the small and isolated villages of the nation; both were dedicated to the enlightenment of the people of the Spanish Republic.

During the civil war literature in Spain came virtually to a halt. Perhaps, the only good "literature of the trenches" was written by Hernández. It was inevitable that the turn of events in Spanish history took a toll on Spanish literature. At the beginning of the war Spain lost through death—natural or otherwise—Antonio Machado, García Lorca, Valle-Inclán, and Unamuno. Some writers and intellectuals perished in prison or in actual combat. Some of the very best, however, left Spain and continued to write in exile, thereby destroying the continuity in Spanish letters. Those who stayed—Aleixandre, Alonso, Camilo José Cela, Blas de Otero, Miguel Delibes, and Carlos Bousoño (b. 1923)—wrote in spite of the regime in a sort of "inner exile," to use a phrase of the hispanist Paul Ilie.

The years immediately after the war were difficult, if not exasperating, for literary activity. Poets turned their verses toward God, and poets who wished to accommodate to the cruel dictatorship or who were too tired to carry on the fight against it in their work affected a rather anachronistic type of formalism, using the rhythms, language, and versification of Spain's great Renaissance poets, especially those of Garcilaso de la Vega (1501–1536). Thus, the movement "Garcilasismo" was born. It evaded the depressing reality of the day, supporting Spain's old glory during her hegemony in the sixteenth century. The embedded ideology in the work of these poets was pro-Franco. By imitating the poetic style of the Renaissance, they affirmed that Francoism represented historical continuity and the proper values of a former age that was truly "Spanish." In the areas of the novel and theater, things worked in a similar fashion. Much of the output was either pure Francoist propaganda or sterile pastiches of old forms.

There were, however, bursts of hope on the literary horizon during the 1940s. There was for example, Dámaso Alonso, who wrote the scathing and highly personal *Hijos de la ira* (1944; *Children of Wrath,* 1970), which was an indictment of not only the poet himself but of all Spaniards who had brought upon themselves the civil war. Alonso broke with the vacuous formalism of his contemporaries; his book was an existential assertion of social and moral commitment.

In this regard, the first novels by Cela and Carmen Laforet—*La familia de Pascual Duarte* (1942; *The Family of Pascual Duarte,* 1964) and *Nada* (1945; *Nada,* 1958) respectively, can also be viewed as honest literature that was committed to a profound and intelligent exploration of the human condition in a universe almost completely defamiliarized by the ravages of cruelty, death and war. These novels, characterized the decade of the 1940s, in which "tremendismo," a literary movement indigenously Spanish that combined the existential notion of absurdity and the graphic depiction of gratuitous violence and grotesqueness of naturalism and of expressionism also, had come into vogue.

The mood of literature changed during the 1950s. Writers grew weary of their anguished, existential writings about the alienated and tragic psyche of Spain and turned to a literature dedicated to social commitment and direct communication. They insisted that good literature must seem objective and must report without heroics what was happening in a country where newspapers were filled with soft news and self-congratulatory pieces of empty rhetoric. The officialism fostered by the Franco regime encouraged political apathy and a delusive sense of well-being that was clearly contrary to the reality of Spain's sociopolitical situation.

In each literary genre the response was forthright. The social poets, headed by Gabriel Celaya, rallied around the humanistic concerns of Machado and Unamuno; they believed that life was an ongoing chore and ought to be described in a clear and colloquial language capable of being easily comprehended. They thought that poetry must be able to transform society. Since they did not search for God but for social justice, their poetry opposed the literary objectives of the pseudoreligious state.

Likewise, the novel became an instrument for reporting the silenced thoughts and behaviors of the Spanish people. It too served social ends by combining the techniques of Italian Neorealism, which was socially motivated, and those of the French New Novel of the 1950s, which although more theoretical than the Spanish novel, also rejected conventional psychology and sentiment by attempting to be objective and distant.

In Cela's *La colmena* (1951; *The Hive,* 1953) and in Rafael Sánchez-Ferlosio's *El Jarama* (1956; *The One Day of the Week,* 1962), two of the leading so-called objectivist novels in Spain, the authors were little more than witnesses, unwilling to see below the surface. They used the impartial eye of the camera and the unprejudiced ear of the tape recorder. Their novels were filled with little action and with faceless group-protagonists. Writers became documentarians, quasi-journalists, and some used the format of the newspaper exposé. Others like Ana María Matute and Miguel Delibes still gave primacy to the inner world of the individual protagonist who had to confront an objective reality.

Drama also made a commitment to the "objective" communication of truth and exposed Spain's social reality. Whether it was Antonio Buero Vallejo's *Historia de una escalera* (1949; story of a staircase) or Alfonso Sastre's *Escuadra hacia la muerte* (1953; *Condemned Squad,* 1961), the theatergoing public experienced something more honest and revealing than the usual boulevard drama. Both Buero Vallejo and Sastre, the founder of "Theater of Social Agitation," portrayed the sickness of Spain and the Spanish people who were immobilized on their "stairwells," to use the central image of Buero Vallejo's seminal play.

The 1950s also saw an important development in Spanish literary criticism that had previously been characterized by an overabundance of Life and Works-type studies, taxonomic and tediously classifactory investigations, propaganda pieces of the "achievements" of the Franco regime, and impressionistic and bombastic essays of personal praise or scorn. Dámaso Alonso's publication of *Seis calas en la expresión literaria española* (1951; six soundings in Spanish literary expression) transformed literary criticism in Spain. Rather than relying on positivistic historicism, Alonso's work fostered a science of literature based on linguistic models. Carlos Bousoño also contributed, and together they opened up Spanish criticism for the theoretical pluralism of different critical schools that would soon come into vogue: Marxism, structuralism, deconstruction, semiotics, reader-response, etc.

During the next two decades Spanish writers began to reject literature that was predominantly social and bent solely on communication. They believed that the literary output of the 1950s was uninteresting; it had become stale. Poets, led by José Angel Valente (b. 1929), Francisco Brines (b. 1934), and Claudio Rodríguez (b. 1934) contended that poetry was an epistemological endeavor that highlighted the creative process itself. These writers arrived at their aesthetic theories in a more opened and prosperous Spain.

Just as poetry demanded more active participation by the reader because of its imaginative use of language and of cultural artifacts, recalling the difficult Neo-Baroquism of the Generation of 1927, so did the novel. The publication of Luis Martín-Santos's *Tiempo de silencio* (1962; *Time of Silence,* 1964) marked the beginning of a new approach to fiction, rigorously complicating the neorealism of the fifties with what critics have called "dialectical realism," a method of transmitting a multifaceted reality. Martín-Santos presented an external narrative sequence simultaneously with an internal reality that has symbolic and allegorical resonance.

Tiempo de silencio led to the structural or "nueva novela" (not to be confused with France's New Novel of the 1950s). Juan Benet's *Volverás a Región* (1967; *You Will Return to Región,* 1985) is one of the first manifestations of the Neo-Baroque New Novel. Benet's work is dense, plotless, difficult; it experiments with syntax, punctuation, chronology, and point of view. Similarly, Juan Goytisolo's recent novels are labyrinthine linguistic experiments that fragment reality and experience. Goytisolo also plays with chronology, perspective and characterization, necessitating that the reader be a co-creator of the text. The creative impetus seen in the novel was a reflection of the freedom that Spain experienced in the 1970s, especially after Franco's death.

Drama also turned toward experimentation. Social drama became more textured, and writers like José Ruibal, the most well-known dramatist of the *Teatro Subterráneo* (Underground Theater) embraced absurdist techniques that mocked and criticized harshly the Franco regime and all imperialist powers, the steadily growing materialism in the world, and the robotization of human experience. Café-theaters, which produced experimental plays for small audiences, began to flourish.

It is not easy to characterize accurately the decade of the 1980s. Eclectism and artistic plurality seem to be the rule in Spain's newly found age of democracy. Perhaps because literature had become so difficult and demanding during the seventies, there was a return to the lyrically personal memoir on one hand and to both the political exposé and historical narrative on the other hand. Creative vitality and excellence, though, are present, and perhaps Spain will soon have a literature that will be as vibrant and far-reaching as it once was at the turn of the century.

M.J.S.

CATALONIA

The immense creativity and originality of Catalan literature can be gleaned from the fact that it produced one of the most important literary works of the Renaissance, *Tirant lo Blanc,* by Joanot Martorell (1413–1468). Catalonia defended its integrity despite its absorption into the Kingdom of Spain in 1492 and the subsequent imposition of Castilian culture and language. In the late-eighteenth century, the incipient romantic movement, with its nationalistic thematics, led to the Catalan *Renaixença,* which flourished into the early twentieth century.

In the pre-civil-war period, new thematic voices were heard, most notably Joan Maragall (1860–1911) and later Josep Carner (1884-1970), both of whom brought the region's sociopolitical reality into poetry. Carner, along with Eugeni d'Ors (1882–1954), founded *Noucentisme,* a "twentieth-century poetry movement" that rejected the "rustic" themes typical of poetry of the earlier centuries. Rather, these poets sought inspiration in the medieval Catalan writers, such as Ausiàs March (1397–1459). Cubism, futurism, and dadaism also influenced poetry, the literary genre that has dominated Catalan literature.

The Franco dictatorship brought an end to Catalonian political autonomy and also to its cultural life in the Catalan language. Many writers were forced into or sought exile. Through the mid-1950s, there was little activity. Gradually there emerged several streams of writers, as in other regions of the peninsula burdened by the dictatorship: those who accepted the status quo; those who spoke out against the regime and risked persecution; and those who dedicated themselves to expanding the limits of the culture through contacts with Spanish and foreign literatures and writers. Catalan fiction based on the events of the civil war or grounded in the contemporary situation began to appear in the mid-1950s. With the end of the Franco regime, Catalonia has regained much of its political autonomy, and its culture and literature have attracted substantial interest and attention from the rest of the peninsula as well as from many foreign nations. Castilian acceptance of Catalan culture was recently highlighted by the publication of Salvador Espriu's complete works in bilingual editions, and, in 1984, by the awarding of the Spanish National letters Prize to J. V. Foix.

Although at a more sophisticated level than Galician literary criticism, commentary on Catalan literature, until the last few years, was
sparse and limited to but a few general or highly specialized literary
reviews. The writers presented in this volume reflect various phases in
the development of twentieth-century Catalan literature: Carles Riba
was an adherent of the *Noucentisme* movement who adapted its principles to serve his own poetic needs; J. V. Foix was associated with the
surrealist movement in Catalan letters, but he was also concerned with
the philosophy of art; Salvador Espriu is considered the most significant voice of the post-civil-war period; and Manuel de Pedrolo is a
prolific writer whose works, owing to the dictatorship, were published
in their original language long after they were written and often after
they have appeared in English-language translations.

Owing to the dearth of criticism, several distinguished Catalan
writers are omitted from *Modern Spanish and Portuguese Literatures,*
including d'Ors, Carner, Pere Quart (Joan Oliver, b. 1899), Joan Vinyolí
(1914–1984), the recently rediscovered novelist Mercè Rodoreda (1909–
1983), a novel of whose has appeared in English translation, and contemporaries, such as the dramatist Jordi Teixidor (b. 1939), the novelist
Terenci Moix (b. 1943), and the poet Pere Gimferrer (b. 1945).

I.S.

GALICIA

Galician is spoken in the province of Galicia in northwestern Spain.
During the medieval period, its predecessor, Galician-Portuguese, was
the peninsula's main poetic language. With the development of Spanish
and Portuguese, however, its reign was eclipsed.

A literary renaissance of Galician took place in the mid-nineteenth
century. This *Rexurdimento* was led by the poets Rosalía de Castro
(1837–1885) and Curros Enríquez (1851–1908). Writing in Galician flourished through the early years of the Spanish Republic and was mildly
influenced by the avant-garde movements of the early 1900s. The major
themes, nonetheless, were the regional and folkloric aspects of Galician
life, as exemplified by the work of [Alfonso Rodríguez] Castelao.

The success of General Franco's military campaign during the civil
war and the resultant centralization of political and cultural life brought
an end to the use of Galician as an official and literary language. Franco,
himself a native of Galicia, caused the self-exile of many of the
province's leading intellectuals to Argentina, Cuba, and the United
States, where they organized social and cultural organizations to preserve and promote Galician culture.

Those writers who remained in Galicia or who began to write
during the years of the dictatorship were obliged to choose Spanish as
their literary language. Others, for example, Álvaro Cunqueiro, whose

literary career began before the civil war, continued to write in Galician and translated their own works into Spanish, the language in which they gained national fame. Still others adopted different literary names and personalities for each language.

During the late 1960s, a muted Galician literary voice began to be heard once again, with *Grial,* a Galician cultural review, spearheading the revival. Since the end of the Franco regime, Galicia has been granted autonomous status in Spain, and Galician is now taught in the schools. A great expansion in literary and cultural production has begun. Most notable, perhaps, is the desire to develop strong cultural relations with the Portuguese, whom the Galicians consider as spiritually closer to them than the Castilians.

Critical commentary on Galician literature has been very limited and is of a thoroughly impressionistic vein. For this reason only two Galician writers are presented here: Alfonso Rodríguez Castelao, who wrote prior to the civil war; and Álvaro Cunqueiro, who began to write in the early 1930s and continued his career in Galician and Spanish until his death. Several other writers of note are omitted owing to the lack of viable commentary. These include Eduardo Blanco Amor (1897–1970), Ramón Otero Pedrayo (1888–1976), Vicente Risco (1884-1963), and Celso Emilio Ferreiro (1914-1979), known as the "Patriarch of Galician Poetry," as well as the significant younger writers Xosé Neira Vilas (b. 1928), Xohana Torres (b. 1931), and Xosé Méndez Ferrín (b. 1938).

I.S.

PORTUGAL

Modern Portuguese culture is an inheritance of more than eight centuries of national existence encompassing daring maritime explorations in the late fourteenth through late sixteenth centuries followed by centuries of despotism and insular chauvinism, all tinged with a bizarre fatalism.

The twentieth century in Portugal might be said to have actually begun with the British Ultimatum of 1890, when the British demanded the withdrawal of Portuguese forces from inland territories in Africa claimed by Portugal. Faced with a break in diplomatic relations and even a threat of war, the powerless Portuguese yielded. National decadence had already been recognized by the distinguished writers and intellectuals of the Portuguese Generation of 1870: Eça de Queiroz (1845–1900), Antero de Quental (1842–1891), Joaquim Pedro de Oliveira Martins (1845–1894), and others. They all commented on the nation's unhappy present and dismal future from various perspectives—socioeconomic, political, and cultural—and hoped for the "Europeanization" of Portugal to remedy her desperate ills. Public events, however, frustrated their desires.

With the assassination in 1908 of King Carlos and his eldest son, Prince Luís Felipe, by republican supporters, a younger prince, Manuel, assumed the throne. The end of the Bragança dynasty came quickly however. A Republican revolt in October 1910 displaced the monarchy and established one of the first modern European parliamentary republics. Continual instability characterized the nation between 1910 and 1926.

In 1926 a military junta easily took power from the civilian government. Thus began a repressive regime which endured for forty-eight years and which was led for thirty-six of those years by António de Oliveira Salazar (1889–1970). Salazar had been a professor of economics (accountancy his detractors say) at the University of Coimbra. Although he had modest roots in rural central Beira Alta province, in the wine-growing village of Santa Comba Dão, he managed to obtain his education through the support of the local clergy. In 1929 he entered the government as Finance Minister, and within three years he assumed dictatorial powers as Prime Minister. Salazar established his "Estado Novo," the New State, whose program and policies were put into force within eighteen months of his ascension. His belief in the so-called "traditional values" of Portuguese society—ruralism, simplicity, the Roman Catholic heritage—led him to defend the interest of the traditional rural oligarchy and thus denied the common Portuguese education, a political life, and access to foreign trends and ideas. His secret police monitored everyday life and persecuted anyone guilty of the slightest transgression, above all political activity. His tight-fisted economic policies brought surpluses to the national treasury at the expense of the social advancement of the Portuguese.

Throughout his dictatorship Salazar tacitly supported his Spanish counterpart, General Franco, in his totalitarian policies, and this support was reciprocated. During the 1940s and 1950s, their relationship was particularly close, owing to a mutual defense pact, their declared neutrality during World War II, and their staunch, fervent anticommunist stands of the cold-war years. Franco had greater foresight about the future role of Spain and allowed foreign multinational corporations to industrialize the country. Salazar always preferred the go-it-alone philosophy in order to shelter his people from foreign influences and values, and to maintain his entrenched political and social system.

By the late 1950s, however, the situation in Portugal had changed dramatically. The 1961 hijacking of the Portuguese luxury ocean liner the *Santa Maria* by Salazar's old ally Henrique Galvão (1895–1970), Nehru's military annexation of the Portuguese territories of Goa, Damão, and Diu in 1961, the beginning of guerrilla warfare in the African colonies between 1961 and 1963, and the assassination of Humberto Delgado (1906–1965), who had been the opposition candidate for President in the mock elections of 1958, all brought Portuguese life to the front pages of newspapers throughout the world.

The African colonial wars had extremely serious consequences for the nation and the dictatorship. One half of the yearly budget was used to fight the wars. Demoralization and despair overwhelmed the Portuguese people as well as the Portuguese army, which saw no possible successful conclusion to the campaign. Emigration out of Portugal increased dramatically during the war years, as Portuguese sought better living and working conditions and educational opportunities—denied them in their homeland—abroad.

Salazar suffered a debilitating stroke in 1968 and was replaced by Marcello Caetano, a University of Lisbon law professor and a long-time adviser to him. Salazar died in 1970, never having been told that he had been supplanted as prime minister. Caetano presented a program of "evolution through continuity," which allowed for some liberalizations. Rightest forces sought to curtail any changes. The case of the "three Marias" is most representative of this moment of conflict. In 1973 *Novas cartas portuguesas* (*New Portuguese Letters,* 1975) was published. The three authors, Maria Teresa Horta (b. 1937), Maria Isabel Barreno (b. 1939), and Maria Velho da Costa (b. 1938), presented the plight of women in Portugal in a collection of pieces that ranged "from the erotic to the pornographic." After publication under new censorship policies, the book was removed by the censor and the three Marias were prosecuted for "moral offense to the nation." An international furor developed. The Portuguese revolution of 1974, however, precluded any disposition of the case.

In fact, while there had been several unsuccessful attempts at revolution during Salazar's years (the most daring in 1964), in March 1974 there was another abortive attempt, followed by the revolution of April 25, 1974, which brought the dictatorship to an end. The coup had its roots in Africa. Military officers serving in the colonial wars had read essays on warfare and national self-determination by Lenin, Che Guevara, Agostinho Neto, et al.—works of writers forbidden in Portugal—and had become convinced that the Portuguese presence in Africa was wrong. The colonies finally took "revenge" on the mother country.

The years since the revolution have left Portugal still searching for its role in Europe in the late twentieth century. Great hope was expressed for a better economic future as Portugal joined the European Economic Community in 1986.*

The sixteen Portuguese writers presented in *Modern Spanish and Portuguese Literatures* are representative of literary trends of this century. The dictatorship's effective censor kept Portugal a cultural

*For an excellent overview of modern Portugal, see Tom Gallagher, *Portugal: A Twentieth Century Interpretation* (Manchester: Manchester University Press, 1983).

backwater. In fact, with the demise of the members of the Generation of 1870 and the impact of the British Ultimatum of 1890, Portuguese literature (which had been under the influence of French culture since the eighteenth century) became rather insular. Raul Brandão's fiction dwelt on the misery of the rural masses. It radiated the pessimism of the decadentist writers and employed Dostoevsky's approach to psychological portraits of human relations. Teixeira de Pascoaes attempted to present a philosophy of the Portuguese existence. He called it *saudosismo,* a nebulous form of mystical nostalgia for a long-gone past.

The avant-garde movements related to Futurism influenced a small group of Portuguese writers and intellectuals, most notably the poets Fernando Pessoa and Mário de Sá-Carneiro. Sá-Carneiro produced emotionally charged poetry and fiction but was overcome by fits of depression and committed suicide. Pessoa led a rather obscure life. In fact, it was not until the 1940s, some ten years after his death, that his works became widely known even in Portugal. Today, Pessoa is recognized internationally. He has been enshrined, along with Luís de Camões (1524–1580), as the great symbolic figure of modern Portugal.

Fiction of the 1920s and 1930s described living conditions in Republican Portugal. José Maria Ferreira de Castro's autobiographical novel *A selva* (1930; *The Jungle,* 1935) lamented the plight of Portuguese emigrants to Brazil, while José Rodrigues Miguéis doted over the Lisbon of his childhood, although he soon emigrated to Brazil and then the United States, where he became a permanent exile. Aquilino Ribeiro narrated the hard life of the rural folk; his participation in Republican and anti-dictatorship activities led to his repeated exiles. Following the publication of his novel *Quando os lobos uivam* (1958; *When the Wolves Howl,* 1963), which attacked government rural policy, he was prosecuted by the Salazar regime.

José Régio's poetry and drama have a religious focus of an ecumenical rather than sacred nature, while his fiction describes student life at the University of Coimbra. He was one of the founding members of the Presença group of poets in 1927. Miguel Torga and José Gomes Ferreira wrote militant poetry and prose in favor of democracy in Portugal and were often targets of the regime's censors. Similarly, the rise of the neorealist movement, indebted to North American and Brazilian social novelists of the 1930s, brought António Alves Redol, Vergílio Ferreira, Fernando Namora, Fernando Monteiro de Castro Soromenho, Jorge de Sena, and José Cardoso Pires into direct conflict with the authorities. Alves Redol wrote about the desperate conditions imposed on day workers in Portugal's breadbasket, the Alentejo province. Vergílio Ferreira touched on similar themes, but he later turned to existentialist fiction and most recently has written memoirs which have led to heated debates. Castro Soromenho was one of the very few Portuguese writers to describe life in prewar Portuguese Africa. His portraits of the colonial administrators' relationship with the Africans in Angola were hardly flattering, and he, like many other writers, had to publish his works in Brazil. Namora has described life in small towns of Portugal's interior from the point of view of a doctor competing with centuries-old superstitions. As a poet, fiction writer, and literary critic Jorge de Sena is ranked very highly in Portuguese letters of the last decades. In his masterful fiction, Cardoso Pires has attempted to discover the key to the national psychology and to explain the reason for the docile acceptance of years of dictatorship and repression.

Literary criticism as an objective forum for evaluation was almost nonexistent in Portugal prior to the 1960s. The years of censorship discouraged literature from being read and thought about. Very few literary critics presented more than simple comments, most often personal, vehement impressions. From the 1930s to our own day, João Gaspar Simões (1903–1987) dominated the critical scene with a very personal style of criticism indebted to the Presença school, of which he was a founder. Yet another important name in criticism of the time is Adolfo Casais Monteiro (1908–1972), another *presencista* and poet who fled in exile to Brazil in the 1950s. Franco Nogueira (b. 1918) was a government figure during the dictatorship whose hobby was literary criticism. He did produce a valid corpus in the 1950s. Since the 1960s, Portuguese criticism has fallen under the direct influence of recent critical approaches—semiology, deconstructionism—which has oftentimes resulted in rather incomprehensible critical tracts. Today, *critificção*, criticism-fiction, is a very common phenomenon in Portugal.

Owing to the absence of sufficient criticism of quality, many Portuguese writers of note are regrettably omitted from *Modern Spanish and Portuguese Literatures*. These include the novelists José Saramago (b. 1922), whose recently translated novel, *Baltasar and Blimunda* (1987), received rave reviews in England and the United States; Nuno Bragança (1929–1985); Olga Gonçalves (b. 1929); Almeida Faria (b. 1943); António Lobo Antunes (b. 1944); Lídia Jorge (b. 1946); and Mário Cláudio (b. 1947); the poets Eugénio de Castro (1869–1944); António Gedeão (b. 1906); Sophia de Melo Breyner Andresen (b. 1919); Eugénio de Andrade (b. 1923); and António Ramos Rosa (b. 1924); and the dramatists Luiz Francisco Rebello (b. 1924); and Bernardo Santareno (1924–1980).

I.S.

AUTHORS INCLUDED

SPAIN

Alberti, Rafael
Aldecoa, Ignacio
Aleixandre, Vicente
Alonso, Dámaso
Álvarez Quintero, Serafín and
   Joaquín
Aub, Max
Ayala, Francisco
Azorín
Barea, Arturo
Baroja, Pío
Benavente, Jacinto
Benet, Juan
Bergamín, José
Blasco Ibáñez, Vicente
Buero Vallejo, Antonio
Casona, Alejandro
Cela, Camilo José
Celaya, Gabriel
Cernuda, Luis
Cunqueiro, Álvaro (writing in
   Galician and Spanish)
Delibes, Miguel
Diego, Gerardo
Espina, Concha
Espriu, Salvador (writing in Catalan)
Felipe, León
Foix, J. V. (writing in Catalan)
Ganivet, Ángel
García Hortelano, Juan
García Lorca, Federico
Gironella, José María
Gómez de la Serna, Ramón
Goytisolo, Juan
Guillén, Jorge
Hernández, Miguel
Jarnés, Benjamín
Jiménez, Juan Ramón

Laforet, Carmen
Machado, Antonio
Machado, Manuel
Martín Gaite, Carmen
Martín-Santos, Luis
Martínez Sierra, Gregorio and María
Matute, Ana María
Miró, Gabriel
Ortega y Gasset, José
Otero, Blas de
Paso, Alfonso
Pedrolo, Manuel de (writing in
   Catalan)
Pérez de Ayala, Ramón
Pérez Galdós, Benito
Quiroga, Elena
Riba, Carles (writing in Catalan)
Rodríguez Castelao, Alfonso (writing
   in Galician)
Ruibal, José
Salinas, Pedro
Sánchez Ferlosio, Rafael
Sastre, Alfonso
Sender, Ramón J.
Torrente Ballester, Gonzalo
Unamuno, Miguel de
Valle-Inclán, Ramón del
Zunzunegui, Juan Antonio de

PORTUGAL

Brandão, Raul
Castro, José Maria Ferreira de
Ferreira, José Gomes
Ferreira, Vergílio
Miguéis, José Rodrigues
Namora, Fernando
Pessoa, Fernando

Pires, José Cardoso
Redol, António Alves
Régio, José
Ribeiro, Aquilino
Sá-Carneiro, Mário de

Sena, Jorge de
Soromenho, Fernando Monteiro de
Castro
Teixeira de Pascoaes
Torga, Miguel

Sections Compiled and Edited by Marshall J. Schneider

Alberti
Aleixandre
Álvarez Quintero
Aub
Ayala
Barea
Benavente
Benet
Blasco Ibáñez
Buero Vallejo
Casona
Delibes
Diego
Espina
Felipe
Ganivet
García Hortelano
García Lorca
Gironella
Goytisolo

Guillén
Hernández
Jiménez
Laforet
Machado, M.
Martín Gaite
Martínez Sierra
Matute
Ortega y Gasset
Paso
Pérez Galdós
Quiroga
Ruibal
Sánchez Ferlosio
Sastre
Sender
Unamuno
Valle-Inclán
Zunzunegui

Sections Compiled and Edited by Irwin Stern

Aldecoa
Alonso
Azorín
Baroja
Bergamín
Brandão
Castro
Cela
Celaya
Cernuda
Cunqueiro
Espriu
Ferreira, J. G.
Ferreira, V.
Foix
Gómez de la Serna

Jarnés
Machado, A.
Martín-Santos
Miguéis
Miró
Namora
Otero
Pedrolo
Pérez de Ayala
Pessoa
Pires
Redol
Régio
Riba
Ribeiro
Rodríguez Castelao

PERIODICALS USED

Listed below are their titles, their abbreviations, if any, and current or last place of publication.

	A águia (Oporto, Portugal)
	Accent: A Quarterly of New Literature (Urbana, IL)
	Agenda (London)
TAH	The American Hispanist (Cleer Creek, IN)
ASch	The American Scholar (Washington, DC)
ALEC	Anales de la literatura española contemporánea (Boulder, Colorado, formerly *ANP:* Anales de la novela española de posguerra, Lincoln, NE)
ANP	Anales de la novela española de posguerra (Lincoln, NE)
AR	The Antioch Review (Yellow Springs, OH)
	Arbor: Ciencia, Pensamiento y Cultura (Madrid)
	Archivum (Oviedo, Spain)
ArQ	Arizona Quarterly (Tucson)
	Asomante (Río Piedras, Puerto Rico)
	Atlante de la cultura (Mexico City)
AtM	The Atlantic Monthly (Boston, later *AT:* The Atlantic, New York)
	Bandarra (Oporto, Portugal)
BMtr	Black Mountain Review (Black Mountain, NC)
	Boletín de la Academia Cubana de la Lengua (Havana)
BkmL	The Bookman (absorbed by the London Mercury, London)
BA	Books Abroad (later *WLT:* World Literature Today, Norman, OK)
BUJ	Boston University Journal (Boston)
	Brotéria (Lisbon)
BEPIF	Bulletin des études portugaises et brésiliennes (Paris)
BH	Bulletin Hispanique (Bordeaux, France)
BHS	Bulletin of Hispanic Studies (formerly *BSpS:* Bulletin of Spanish Studies, Liverpool)
BSpS	Bulletin of Spanish Studies (later *BHS:* Bulletin of Hispanic Studies, Liverpool)
CRB	Cahiers de la Compagnie Madeleine Rénaud-Jean Louis Barrault (Paris)
CS	Cahiers du Sud (Marseille)

CdA	Camp de l'Arpa: Revista de literatura (Barcelona)
	Ciclón (Buenos Aires)
	Clavileño (Madrid)
Colóquio	Colóquio/Letras (Lisbon)
CL	Comparative Literature (Eugene, OR)
ConP	Contemporary Poetry: A Journal of Criticism (Bryn Mawr, PA)
ContempR	Contemporary Review (London)
CritI	Critical Inquiry (Chicago)
	Critique: Revue générale des publications françaises et étrangères (Paris)
CA	Cuadernos americanos (Mexico City)
	Cuadernos de ágora (Madrid)
	Cuadernos de literatura (Madrid)
CHA	Cuadernos hispanoamericanos: Revista mensual de cultura hispánica (Madrid)
	Destino (Barcelona)
	Diacritics: A Review of Contemporary Criticism (Ithaca, NY)
TDR	The Drama Review (New York)
DR	The Dublin Review (Dublin, later The Wiseman Review, London)
	Encounter (London)
	Estreno: Cuadernos del teatro español contemporáneo (Cincinnati)
	Filología (Buenos Aires)
FMLS	Forum for Modern Language Studies (St. Andrews, Scotland)
	Free World Review (New York)
Grial	Grial: Revista galega de cultura (Vigo, Spain)
	Harper's Magazine (New York)
	Haz: Revista nacional (Madrid)
	Hispania: A Journal Devoted to the Interests of the Teaching of Spanish and Portuguese (Los Angeles)
HR	Hispanic Review (Philadelphia)
	Hispanófila (Chapel Hill, NC)
	Horizon: A Review of Literature and Art (London)
HudR	The Hudson Review (New York)
Ibero	Iberomania: Zeitschrift für die iberoromanischen Sprachen und Literaturen in Europa und Amerika/Revista dedicada a las Lenguas y Literaturas iberorrománicas de Europa y América (Kuhardt, West Germany)
I&L	Ideologies and Literature: A Journal of Hispanic and Luso-Brazilian Studies (Minneapolis)
	Índice (Madrid)
	Ínsula: Revista bibliográfica de ciencias y letras (Madrid)
IFR	International Fiction Review (New Brunswick, Canada)
IJWS	International Journal of Women's Studies (Montreal)
	Jornal de letras (Lisbon)

JAAC	Journal of Aesthetics and Art Criticism (Philadelphia)
JAPS	Journal of the American Portuguese Society (New York)
JSSTC	Journal of Spanish Studies: Twentieth Century (Lincoln, NE absorbed by *ALEC:* Anales de la literatura española contemporánea, Boulder, CO)
KRQ	Kentucky Romance Quarterly (Lexington, KY)
LATR	Latin American Theatre Review (Lawrence, KS)
	Lectura: Revista de ciencias y artes (Madrid)
LyP	El libro y el pueblo (Mexico City)
	Living Age (Boston)
LBR	Luso-Brazilian Review (Madison, WI)
MHRev	Malahat Review: An International Quarterly of Life and Letters (Victoria, Canada)
MTQ	The Mark Twain Quarterly (later, Mark Twain Journal, Charleston, SC)
MdF	Mercure de France (Paris)
MD	Modern Drama (Toronto)
MLJ	The Modern Language Journal (Columbus, OH)
MLN	*MLN* (formerly Modern Language Notes, Baltimore, MD)
MLQ	Modern Language Quarterly (Seattle)
MLS	Modern Language Studies (Providence, RI)
	Mosaic: A Journal for the Interdisciplinary Study of Literature (Winnipeg, Canada)
Nation	The Nation (New York)
Neophil	Neophilologus (Groningen, Netherlands)
NR	The New Republic (Washington, DC)
NY	The New Yorker (New York)
NYHTB	New York Herald Tribune Book Review (New York)
NYT	New York Times (New York)
NYTBR	New York Times Book Review (New York)
NorthAR	North American Review (New York)
	Nosotros (Buenos Aires)
NL	Nouvelles littéraires (Paris)
NRF	Nouvelle revue française (Paris)
NE	Nueva Estafeta (Madrid)
Obs	The Observer (London)
	Ocidente (Lisbon)
PSA	Papeles de son armadans (Palma de Mallorca, Spain)
PLL	Papers on Language and Literature: A Journal for Scholars and Critics of Language and Literature (Edwardsville, IL)
	Parnassus: Poetry in Review (New York)
PR	Partisan Review (Boston)
PhQ	Philological Quarterly (Iowa City)
PP	Philologica Pragensia (Prague, Czechoslovakia)
	Poetry (Chicago)
PrA	Primer Acto (Madrid)
	PMLA: Publications of the Modern Language Association of America (New York)
RyF	Razón y Fe: Revista hispanoamericana de cultura (Madrid)

	Realidad: Revista de ideas (Buenos Aires)
REH	Revista de estudios hispánicos (Poughkeepsie, NY)
	Revista de las Indias (Bogotá, Colombia)
RdL	Revista de letras (Mayaguez, Puerto Rico)
RL	Revista de literatura (Madrid)
RO	Revista de occidente (Madrid)
RHM	Revista hispánica moderna: Columbia University Hispanic Studies (New York)
RLC	Revue de littérature comparée (Tours, France)
RH	Revue hispanique (Paris)
BRMMLA	Rocky Mountain Review of Language and Literature (Tempe, AZ)
RomN	Romance Notes (Chapel Hill, NC)
RR	Romanic Review (New York)
SR	Saturday Review (Washington, DC)
SeN	Seara nova (Lisbon)
	Serra d'Or (Barcelona)
SinN	Sin nombre (San Juan, PR)
	Sixties (Madison, MN)
SAB	South Atlantic Bulletin (later South Atlantic Review, Chapel Hill, NC)
SpanR	Spanish Review (New York)
Spec	The Spectator (London)
StTCL	Studies in Twentieth Century Literature (Manhattan, KS)
	Sur (Buenos Aires)
SYM	Symposium (Syracuse, NY)
	Teatro (Bogotá, Colombia)
TPr	Tempo presente (Lisbon)
TLS	The Times Literary Supplement (London)
	Topic: A Journal of the Liberal Arts (Washington, DC)
Torre	La Torre: Revista general de la Universidad de Puerto Rico (Río Piedras)
	Twice a Year: A Semi-annual Journal of Literature, the Arts and Civil Liberties (New York)
UMHAS	University of Miami Hispanic-American Studies (Coral Gables, FL)
UObs	University Observer: A Journal of Politics (Chicago)
UWSLL	University of Wisconsin Studies of Language and Literature (Madison, WI)
	Vértice: revista de cultura e arte (Coimbra, Portugal)
WVUPP	West Virginia University Philological Papers (Morgantown)
WLT	World Literature Today: A Literary Quarterly of the University of Oklahoma (formerly *BA:* Books Abroad, Norman, OK)

SPAIN

A la memoria de Josefina Romo Arregui
Querida maestra e inspirada poeta

M. J. S.

To F.E.R.

I. S.

ALBERTI, RAFAEL (1902–   )

For Alberti, what is basic is what is of the greatest value; what is basic is what is humble—the humble in things and men. All of Alberti's poetry is summed up in a passionate love for what is scorned, what is forgotten, for what is outside human esteem. . . . And, ineluctably, the poet arrives at a special realism. It is not the realism of the naturalists, which has been passé for quite some time already, but a love of things independent of all societal ends. Neither a system nor a teleology. Things disdained for themselves; humility in one's own life without relation to the world. And since Alberti is a great lyric poet, time has him caught in its iron grip. . . . And that is why Alberti, with great feeling, falls back on the elegy. The elegy is the poetry of the great lyric poets. . . .

Truly, Rafael Alberti is a rare kind of poet, one of those who comes along every eighty or one hundred years. [Jan., 1930]

Azorín. In Manuel Durán, ed., *Rafael Alberti*
(Madrid, Taurus, 1975), pp. 36–37†

Rafael Alberti is a great poet. He represents the sincere effort, quite successful in his case, of a bourgeois writer who has identified himself with the class struggle and who is enthusiastically helping the workers in their courageous fight. . . . [These poems] show the application of a highly sophisticated virtuosity (rich metaphors and images, complex vision, juxtaposition of lyrical planes) to present revolutionary conditions—a T. S. Eliot or a Hart Crane who had read with understanding the *Communist Manifesto*. . . . We find, above all, a keen satirist—the bourgeois poet evoking his bourgeois background and exposing its deadly elements and corruption. . . .

Alberti, the true revolutionary poet, rises to address the exploited and oppressed, summoning them to arms. . . . Alberti has swayed the working class with poems in the traditional vein, reminiscent of popular ballads and folk poems, which, unfortunately, defy translation; and, then again, with poems in free verse, easy to grasp, convincing, robust. The toiling masses . . . have rightly appropriated them and recite or sing them throughout Spain. Alberti has become *the* Revolutionary Poet of Spain.

Ángel Flores. Introduction to Rafael Alberti, *A
Spectre Is Haunting Europe: Poems of
Revolutionary Spain* (New York, Critics Group,
1936), pp. 10–11

Concerning the Angels is in the first place a poet's confession of a tremendous crisis in his life. What Alberti records with such power and insight is by no means unique to him. The struggle and the agony which he has to face in his transition from the dreams of youth to a rigorous grasp of reality is known to other poets. . . .

Just as Eliot in *The Waste Land* depicts the crisis of the modern spirit which has lost the dignity and style of the past, so Alberti is above all the poet of those who have been forced to recognize the imperfections of existence, but, instead of complaining about it, have decided to face it with courage and candour.

In *Concerning the Angels* Alberti shows how an experience which might seem to be depressing and devitalising can be turned into the highest poetry. No doubt part of this success comes from the fighting spirit which Alberti shows in his war with circumstances, but part also comes from his masterly management of a modern technique. If this experience had been expressed in a more regular and more harmonious form, it would have lost its most essential qualities. Just because it is so chaotic and so devastating it falls perfectly into an art which responds exactly to disordered states of mind and soul. And more important than this is the way in which Alberti's technique enables him to extract the last drop of poetry from each moment in his crisis. . . .

By following his sure instinct for what is really poetry Alberti gives its special splendour to *Concerning the Angels,* but hardly less important in the final result is the intellectual passion and passionate desire for the truth which accompanies the creative instinct. Through this Alberti both makes his poetry relevant to the experience of other men and gives to it a strength which nothing can shake. In every poem we feel this solid foundation of fact, this determination to portray experience as it really is, and not to make concessions to any romantic or sentimental outlooks. In this Alberti takes his place with the best poets of his time.

C. M. Bowra. *The Creative Experiment*
(London, Macmillan, 1949), pp. 250–53.

In human nature, Alberti is very different from García Lorca; Alberti lacks the humility that the poet from Granada has. He knows what is of value, and by understanding all that there may be of it, he imitates it, improving upon it with full knowledge of cause. . . .

Spanish dualism—which García Lorca learned how to amalgamate on more than one occasion—remains alive in [Alberti]. He is learned or popular as the occasion requires. But popular in his own way, without ever picking up the music of the people. . . . Alberti is, before all else, a learned poet, who always knows what he is doing. He succeeds with a virtuosity that can be equaled, but not surpassed.

Max Aub. *La poesía española contemporánea*
(Mexico City, Imprenta Universitaria, 1954),
p. 169†

Rafael Alberti: a friend of García Lorca and a more intellectual poet who underwent the same influences, is more easily placed in relation to tradition and in his political sympathies. His protest is much simpler than García Lorca's; it is, in fact, the age-old protest of Spanish liberalism against the selfishness of landowners and the obscurantism of churchmen. If he has lived a *saison en enfer* its causes lie in the outside world, in the destruction of war and the long years of exile from his own corner of Andalusia, which he loves as dearly as García Lorca loved Granada. . . .

Alberti's subjects were of two kinds, one drawn from the memory of his own childhood on the seacoast near Cádiz, and the other modish in its references to such familiar idols as Charlie Chaplin and Buster Keaton. In 1927, however, in a book entitled *Concerning the Angels,* Alberti developed his own mythology. It is no simple matter to decide what significance these angelic figures had for the poet. Certainly they are unrelated to the angels of theology, and are not readily to be associated with Rilke's, yet they too in a sense were transforming the visible into the invisible. They represent not qualities of inspiration, but mental or psychological states. . . .

Alberti's symbols present none of the difficulties of Breton's or even of Éluard's; they divide simply into those which record the shock of betrayal. Alberti's imagination has some of the freshness of Pasternak's. But although Alberti too has some skill as a painter, his vision is far less complex. He is also readier than his Russian contemporary to see situations in black and white. Intellectual though the organization of his poetry may be, he has still accepted some inheritance from the Romantics. Like Aleixandre, he moves from a private to a social vision. His angels are not only embodiments of his own moods and states of mind but are also active on the social plane.

J. M. Cohen. *Poetry of This Age* (London,
Hutchinson, 1960), pp. 190–92

It would appear that, with his very first book, Alberti was already a craftsman in total command of his medium, writing with effortless grace and impeccable versification, in brilliant and controlled imagery: a poet at the peak of his form. There is not a false note or a wavering line in the whole of *Sailor Ashore* (1925)—as though, literally born to the art, he was incapable of poetical error. What is admirable, among other things, is the extent to which a youth of limited formal education appears to have pondered and assimilated the great lyric tradition of his country, the popular along with the learned. Here was the spectacle of a twenty-two-year-old sufficiently schooled in the poets most admired by a generation before him—Baudelaire, Verlaine, Mallarmé, D'Annunzio, Darío—to profit by their example and supersede it; of a provincial intelligence drenched in the dialect of West Andalusia, commanding a lexicon that would ravish the heart of a purist. . . .

To be sure, there are a number of pieces in *Sailor Ashore* in which

Alberti pays his respects to the symbolists; even here, however, the skill with which formulas imported from abroad have been used in the service of personal experience is impressive. Along with his borrowed appurtenances we find, in sharp contrast, a poetical language which leaves symbolism far behind. For even where symbols abound, the Albertian image shows a precision that the symbolists (obsessed with *la nuance, le sugérer*) would never have sanctioned; and metaphorical epithet in the hands of Alberti is as indelibly precise as it is in the classical Spanish tradition.

Luis Monguió. Introduction to Rafael Alberti,
Selected Poems (Berkeley, University of
California Press, 1966), pp. 13–14

The Uninhabited Man shares the same preoccupation and uses similar techniques to the philosophical novelists. We have the seriousness of intention, of a journey of self-discovery that accompanies the presentation of the autobiographical hero, a single character, through whom this ideological seriousness can be systematically followed. We also have the one central preoccupation with the problem of authenticity and the separation of the hero from his fellows. This is consonant with the concept of tragedy that pervades this type of investigation that Unamuno, Gide and Camus along with Alberti declare to be a part of their "tragic sense of life" in the widest meaning. It is this implication of dramatic tragedy and the art of understatement in general that leads to a further technique that Alberti also shares in common: the technique of allegory. As in the philosophical novel so in Alberti's *auto* we are given a picture of modern man preoccupied with his ontological status, the question of ethics and his eschatological position. The awareness and depiction of the "nothingness of life" by definition precludes the direct realist method. Allegory serves to allude to another set of circumstances, another state of mind or experience that does not belong to the expressive canon of previous novelistic tradition. In *The Uninhabited Man* the structure, the settings of the symbolic Hell of the "road-up" or of the Eden of the walled garden, the horrible parody of God and the senses are not so much concerned with the portrayal of a real character or situation as with the evocation in physical terms of man's spiritual bankruptcy and the awareness of the nothingness and absurdity of existence. Alberti is using for his own ends the traditional allegorical form.

Richard Cardwell. *Ibero.* Aug., 1970, p. 131

There seems no real reason why the much more stimulating drama of Rafael Alberti should not one day be accorded the recognition it deserves in Spain. Alberti has not relented in his opposition to the present Spanish government, but most of his plays are not political, and they are more entertaining than much of the avant-garde theatre of his European contemporaries. Alberti and García Lorca are alike as dramatists in several ways. Alberti was already a mature and established poet when he turned his attention seriously to the theatre in the early days of the Republic. Like García Lorca, he saw an urgent need to reform it. . . . Like García Lorca, Alberti . . . transforms all this [traditionalism] into highly original works of theatrical art, which invariably depend for their dramatic force on the presence of an inescapable tragic fate. This is particularly prominent in Alberti's first and in some ways most interesting play, *The Uninhabited Man*. . . . It is an imposing, disturbing creation, spun in part from the fearful imagery of *Concerning the Angels,* and reflecting the awful sense of inner void which afflicted Alberti and García Lorca in the late twenties. But it ran for a month on the Madrid stage. *Fermín Galán,* on the other hand, caused such a furor that the safety curtain had to be lowered to protect the actors from the public. But this second work was calculated to arouse political passions. Alberti commented sarcastically that his mistake had been to show it to a bourgeois public instead of peasants, but this was a political comment, not an artistic one. The considerable success of *The Uninhabited Man* with the bourgeois public suggests that Alberti and García Lorca were beginning to have some effect on public taste. . . .

Alberti's plays are spectacular, powerful plays of great formal beauty and poetic elegance. They stimulate the imagination and set it moving along paths of its own—sometimes by baffling it, it is true, but never gratuitously so. Although they are dramas that repay careful, unhurried reflection, it is easy to see when reading them that their immediate effect on a theatre audience would be exciting. They are not merely the by-products of a fine poet, but excellent plays in their own right, which deserve to be better known.

G. G. Brown. *A Literary History of Spain: The
Twentieth Century* (New York, Barnes & Noble,
1972), pp. 130–32

Alberti is both a difficult and accessible poet. He is endlessly inventive, yet his themes are recognizably simple. One reads him and feels that he is among the most effortless of poets. Gongoristic [from Góngora, a Spanish baroque poet of the seventeenth century] sonnets seem written with the same ease as Jiménez-like fragments of song, and lamentations with the same energy as celebratory odes. Whatever he does seems touched with originality and grace. . . .

The poems of *Concerning the Angels* and *Sermons and Dwellings* are a far cry from the early folkloric poems in *Sailor Ashore* (1925) or the attempts at baroque elegance *Lime and Stone* (1929). The vision is more anguished, more central in its mythology, and not as dependent on the nuances of nostalgia or the rhetoric of embellishment and contrivance.

Mark Strand. Preface to Rafael Alberti, *The
Owl's Insomnia* (New York, Atheneum, 1973),
p. vii

I would say that Alberti has good taste. I have never been quite sure what good taste is in Spain, but I am fairly sure that where it ends the *duende* [charm] begins, and García Lorca. A Spanish formulation of good taste in dress is "never call attention to yourself but make everybody stare." Which is funny, but indicates that a very quiet perfection can be as impressive in Spain as the gaudier manner which strikes us more. At any rate, some are so impressed with Alberti's formal clarity and perfection that they think and say there is no emotion in his poetry. . . .

The trouble with Alberti—and it would be no trouble at all if he were not associated with García Lorca—is that he is a perfectly civilized poet, exquisitely cultivated, a man of the city, including the museums. Not that García Lorca was a peasant, but his work stays pretty close to the land, to rudimentary passions, folklore, and balladry. I once heard Auden dismiss him as "agrarian," which at the time (the end of the Spanish war) I found infuriating. . . .

It would be nice if one could also forget García Lorca when reading Alberti, and perhaps, with concentration, one can. He is rich enough and brilliant enough to be absorbing on his own. And evidently, since the death of García Lorca in 1936, Alberti's work has ranged far and wide and developed well beyond anything they had in common—the generation of 1927, their Andalusia, their laments for the death of the same bullfighter [Sánchez Mejías]. What I know of this later work seems to me more interesting than what I know of the earlier work, which is full of the fashions of its time. Still, the Twenties are back in fashion, and one can enjoy being introduced to poems Alberti published in 1924.

Donald Sutherland. Parnassus. Fall–Winter,
1974, pp. 53, 56–57

[The Generation of '27 is] unlike no other group I can think of; it seemed to be made up entirely of exuberant virtuosos. None seemed more of one than Alberti, even when it came to displaying facility with both the learned baroque modes and the oral popular traditions which Alberti and García Lorca managed to revive so brilliantly and turn into a valid modern idiom. Like Alberti, they all took to their craft with a kind of Adamic ebullience, as if poetry had just been invented, or at least rediscovered—to the irritation of their elders. They took to experimenting with images, metaphors (especially metaphors), levels of diction, subjects, even entire traditions, often, it seemed just for the pleasure of making them stand on edge, to be played with most untraditionally. . . .

Like García Lorca, Alberti is a fish in water within the idiomatic ambit of popular poetry and in what is most alive in his contemporary language and its traditional presentations of reality. And, like García

Lorca, he is very much a child of this century. It was not for nothing that he once said, describing himself, "I was, please respect me, born with the movies."

J. M. Alonso. *Nation*. Jan. 11, 1976, pp. 22, 24, 26

There is an infinite variety of angels in [*Concerning the Angels*]. Most of them seem to be fallen angels, representing different stages of anguish and inner crisis. Some correspond to the traditional angelology (angels of fury, revenge, evil, etc.). Many others are entirely of Alberti's invention. For example, the Dumb Angel, the Ugly Angel, the Angel of Numbers. Some are connected with disintegrating matter: the angels of coal, ashes, mildew. Or with hell itself: sulphur, darkness, fire. Seldom, very seldom, the Good Angel makes a few short appearances: once, he comes down to bring a letter from Heaven. For an instant, there is harmony and light. But not for long. Soon, the bad angels attack again, on foot or on horseback. The sour fires and sulphur winds renew their strife. Alberti's angels are essentially choleric ones. What they have kept from heaven is their spiritual substance and superhuman strength, often associated with swift flight and light or fire. But they are also what remains of a lost heaven. . . .

Man's task in *Concerning the Angels* . . . is the endeavour to remember, to recapture the vision of a lost paradise. Yet, what he describes again and again, is a chaotic world, abysmal and cruel. But near the end of the book, three poems appear, "three recollections of heaven," in which we are confronted with a most tenuous, beautiful, delicate new world, a world in the process of creation, where man himself is dreaming his own possible advent. . . .

Besides, the angels have not entirely abandoned man. The book had begun with a dead one. It ends with a wounded one, wing clipped, but alive. The originality of Alberti's vision is that it leaves us, at the end, with something more than just a crumbling world. In such contemporary poets as William Butler Yeats and T. S. Eliot, obsessed with the vision of chaos, the result is much more devastating. Alberti has a certain advantage: he is working with traditional images, which ultimately point to a cosmic order. He has found a familiar system to objectivize his internal strife. And as we said before, the angels have not entirely forsaken the poet. *Concerning the Angels* is, after all, a continuation, a reflection of the angelic world. In it, Rafael Alberti creates a sense of mystery akin to religious experience.

Solita Salinas de Marichal. *MHRev*. July, 1978, pp. 23–24

It seems to me that an interesting and elucidating comparison can be made between Pablo Picasso and Rafael Alberti. There is a torrential quality about Rafael Alberti's creative activity which is clearly to be found in the works of Pablo Picasso, and it was not merely coincidence nor the circumstances arising from the Civil War in Spain which brought these two very Spanish artists together in friendship. The Spanish critic Manuel Durán has written about the inevitability of comparing the poetic style of Rafael Alberti with the painting techniques of Pablo Picasso. For Manuel Durán, Pablo Picasso and Rafael Alberti are both moralists of our time who have been able to domesticate their own personal demons, thus leading the way for others to do the same. To my mind, it is the almost constant display of exuberant vitality, the sense of never being at rest, which makes it inevitable that a reader of Rafael Alberti's poetry would compare it to the works of this other prolific Andalusian artist. . . .

There is an immediacy and poetic agility present in most of Rafael Alberti's compositions, qualities consistently discovered in much of Pablo Picasso's art. At the very center of the artistic philosophy of both men, no matter how protean their stylistic inventions seem to be throughout their long lives, we readily find the need to maintain an innocence and almost primitive open-eyed wonder toward the world, and to express the novelty of this vision in the playful, imaginative and naturally graceful ways of a child. Mixed in with this childlike freshness and abandon, however, is a sense of mischief, of precociousness and even some compulsion to "impress."

> Gabriel Berns. Introduction to *The Other
> Shore: 100 Poems by Rafael Alberti* (San
> Francisco, Kosmos, 1981), pp. 3–4

Alberti experienced in Spain the same Wasteland that T. S. Eliot had confronted in England and America, but Rafael Alberti's response to it was different. It would be wrong to accuse T. S. Eliot of having no "spirit" and no "interiority," but the mysticism of *Four Quartets* remains distinctly sober, objective, barely hinted at in spare and traditional austerities of roses and flame, ashes and dark explosions and silences, frost, and stone, a bell in the sea. Rafael Alberti (struggling as did Gerontion with what has since become fashionable as the "death of God") created or rather discovered the depths of his subjective struggle and came to spiritual terms with himself in a world of disconcerting forces which he called angels. His poems *Concerning the Angels* are most powerful in their controlled anarchy and their sustained ironies which plunge much further than T. S. Eliot into the hidden dynamism of our extraordinary world and of our own predicament in it. . . .

The *Angels* of Rafael Alberti belong to a period of personal crisis in the late twenties, followed by a time of objectivity, recovery, and political consciousness during the Spanish Civil War. The latter poems are by far less interesting: Rafael Alberti having become a success on the Left and having enjoyed the usual free trips to Russia was now well-to-do—a member, in fact, of a particular poetic establishment in which there was no more place or need for angels. . . .

The angelic poems of Rafael Alberti are prophetic "burdens" like the burdens of Isaiah and the laments of Ezekiel over Babylon and Tyre, and as such they can be attended to with a certain pity and fear appropriate to the awareness of tragedy and accursedness—an awareness to which our own poets have seldom been attuned though a few of our prose writers—William Faulkner above all—certainly have. One can agree with the translator [Geoffrey Connell] of these poems that this book can be considered one of the greatest poetic works of the twentieth century. [1967]

Thomas Merton. *The Literary Essays of Thomas Merton* (New York, New Directions, 1981), pp. 314–15, 317

ALDECOA, IGNACIO (1925–1969)

Aldecoa's stories, without losing the qualities of that genre, are short novels, or lesser novels structured around a smaller cosmos, but in their reduced scale they involve the same proportions as his longer books. . . .

Aldecoa has published two volumes of stories: *Vespers of Silence* and *Third Class Waiting Room*. The first one has five narrations, three of which are rather extensive, while in the second there are ten stories, generally short, and thus closer to the characteristics of the genre as we know it today. . . .

Vespers of Silence is a model book of its genre, as well as evidence of Aldecoa's virtues of listening to and describing life. In two of the stories . . . Aldecoa follows the technique of interweaving in a counterpoint two parallel actions, which correspond to different social worlds. . . . One could not doubt the presence of a social concern that distinguishes the author. In any case, the result is excellent, and the impression of authentic, sharply captured life is evident from this crossing of two planes. . . .

All these narratives are made up of small daily events, without recourse to excessive strokes of the brush nor violent events . . . but neither do they ever consist of minutiae that melt away or impalpable subtleties; rather they are common facts, but powerfully significant ones, which are chosen with great care and rigorously assembled. Few authors achieve the impression of truth and life that Aldecoa attains with his narrative art.

José Luis Alborg. *Hora actual de la novela española,* Vol. I (Madrid, Taurus, 1958), pp. 293–94†

Some critics have compared *Great Sole* to *The Jarama* [by Sánchez Ferlosio]. Indeed, both novels, in addition to being two outstanding works of their epoch, have points of contact. Both, for example, lack anecdotes and are, above all, written starting from a very strict concept of narrative objectivity. The curve of interest in Sánchez Ferlosio's novel increases with the death of Lucita (an apparent end). In Aldecoa's novel the point of climax occurs with the death of Simón Orozco. While Aldecoa intends fundamentally to describe work (leaving other elements aside), the details of a job, Sánchez Ferlosio, through a very similar process, narrates the small diversions, the trivial conversations of some guys who spend a summer Sunday afternoon at the shore of Madrid's river. Both novels have been called slow and boring; this is a superficial and hasty evaluation of the works. The two novels are, in reality, key works of the epic of commonness, two irreproachable testimonies of emptiness, of the world of work, and the foolish amusements of a social class.

On the other hand, both novels open avenues in the objective tendency for what will later, unfortunately, be called "literature without an author". . . .

Julio M. de la Rosa. CHA. Jan., 1970, p. 195†

[Aldecoa's] last book is *Part of a Story* (1967). Written ten years after *Great Sole,* this new work continues, nonetheless, his cycle about sea life. . . . According to the plan that the novelist announced in 1958, *Great Sole* is dedicated to long-term fishing; *Part of a Story* to short-term fishing. The action takes place in a little fishing village situated on a small island to the north of Lanzarote . . . to which the narrator—the novel is told in the first person—returns, after a long time, with the aim of recovering his spiritual equilibrium. In this work Aldecoa attains the peak of his art as a writer. The expressive exactness, the ability to suggest with veiled references without getting bogged down in detailed explanations, the subtle yet never forced incorporation of dialectal linguistic forms are some of the elements that make *Part of a Story* an absolutely perfect work in certain aspects.

Here too, as in *Great Sole,* the plot line is very slight. The daily routine of the fishermen of the island is broken by a fortuitous event: a yacht runs aground on the coast, with three men and a woman, American tourists, whose arrival constitutes a strong shock for the village fishermen. The tourists, while waiting for their boat to be repaired and to get underway, spend time with the island people, although in a very superficial way. The proof of this is that the narrator sees them from afar, without really wanting to get to know them. . . . In *Part of a Story* all of Aldecoa's virtues become clearly evident, but so also do his voluntary limitations: the lack of inventiveness, the excessive fidelity to a concept of narrative realism that can hold back—or even cut off—

many of the elements that the novelist considers semantically accessory. What remains, nonetheless, is new evidence of an exceptional prose writer, perhaps more gifted than any other contemporary writer for creating atmospheres. . . .

Ricardo Senabre. *PSA*. Jan., 1970, pp. 15–16†

Aldecoa has an uncommon facility of observation which allows him to perceive the beauty of humble, even "ugly" things, and the ability to translate that observation into art, an intense expression which may even provoke shame in the reader who is suddenly brought face to face with his own relative insensibility. . . .

Lightning and Blood . . . , Aldecoa's first published novel, was a "finalist," or runner-up, for the Premio Planeta, today Spain's most highly endowed prize for fiction. The initial volume of a projected (and apparently truncated) trilogy on the *Guardia Civil* [the Civil Guard], this severely simple novel is classical in its observance of the unities of time, space and action. The novelist reproduces Castile's stark, austere landscape as the backdrop for the internal dramas of a handful of women, wives of the *Guardia Civil,* who have heard that one unidentified man in their troop was killed that afternoon. The helplessness of those who can only wait—one of Aldecoa's most insistent themes—is masterfully presented, with the suspense maintained until the final moment.

The second volume of the trilogy, *With the East Wind* . . . , an independent but related sequel, recounts the flight and pursuit of the gypsy guilty of the homicide of the first part. . . . This is a novel of solitude, the solitude of Cain after the death of Abel, or the loneliness and isolation of [Camus's] *The Stranger,* pursued and surrounded by an accusing society. . . .

While no explanation has been offered regarding the missing third volume, the most common cause for non-appearance of announced books in Spain is the censorship. . . . It seems logical that the projected third part might have focused on specific police agents, or might have treated some case of injustice. . . . The first two works may have been approved largely because in them the *Guardia Civil* is almost an invisible presence, never in the center of the stage.

Janet Winecoff Díaz. *RomN*. Spring, 1970,
pp. 477–78

On a fly-leaf immediately prior to the first page of text of *With the East Wind,* Ignacio Aldecoa makes two references to the Old Testament. Citing Haggai and Amos, he quotes: "Os herí con el viento solano" ("I smote you with east wind"). . . .

The east wind of Amos and Haggai which brought suffering to the Israelites serves Aldecoa as more than a thematic adumbration. . . . Its use in the Bible suggests the stylistic structure of the novel, as well. In quoting Amos and Haggai, Aldecoa reverses the order, citing Haggai first. Perhaps Aldecoa purposely changed the order of these books to draw attention to them in more than a casual manner. Amos, the first book in Biblical order and the last to be considered in Aldecoa's arrangement, contains not only the thematically important east wind phrase, but also a structural model for Aldecoa's prose style in *With the East Wind*. The key passage [is from Amos 4:6–9].

The stylistic structure of *With the East Wind* parallels this passage in two ways. First, the repetition of the phrase *"no os volvisteis a mí"* ["you did not return to me"] figures forth the litany-like repetitions found throughout Aldecoa's novel. Secondly, the catalogue of punishments sent by God is like similar catalogues found in great variety throughout the narrative of *With the East Wind*. . . . The effect of Aldecoa's borrowing of the east wind motif is to enhance the lyrical quality of the prose with its refrain and to clarify the extent of [the character] Sebastián Vásquez's alienation.

Charles R. Carlisle. *BRMMLA*. Fall, 1972,
pp. 83–85

Man and his personal adventure form the nucleus of [Aldecoa's] interest, on a social as well as an existential level. His preoccupation with the "social" question is not limited by the rules of critical realism, which is the predominant current among the majority of the novelists of his generation. His concern for the status of the collective unit, a sector or group, goes along with his concern with the individual and his personal situation. . . .

Aldecoa believed that the novelist's mission was to bear witness to the moment in which he lives, and that is exactly what he did. His view of the surrounding reality was melancholic and pessimistic for the destiny of man in his dimension as a social being and in his existential dimension. The contemplation of this reality caused him to arrive at the discouraging conclusion that no one gets anywhere in this life.

The concern with the social theme, seen in its collective meaning and through the existential theme, or seen in the case of a particular person, is linked with the aesthetic concern in his work. His novels reveal his preoccupation through a careful structuring and manipulation of language that is both lyrical and functional at the same time. The balance he achieved between content and form evidences the responsibility that he, as a creator, took in presenting the contemporary problems of Spanish society in his novels, recreating them in a work that was "well made" from an aesthetic point of view. His contribution to the novelistic genre is found in this duality of having blended with felicity and skill the right proportions of theme and artistic expression.

Drosoula Lytra. *Soledad y convivencia en las
novelas de Ignacio Aldecoa* (Madrid,
Fundación Universitaria Española, 1978),
p. 164†

ALEIXANDRE, VICENTE (1898–1984)

If in [*Swords Like Lips*] there was a clear budding of surrealism, *Destruction or Love* is now completely liberated surrealistic poetry, a much more definite surrealism than that of any other of the present-day Spanish poets. Love, hate, and death are the dominant themes in this fervent and despairing poetry; but love, hate, and death are not felt or expressed like an intimate subjective emotion, or like an experience or a longing, but rather like acting forces in the universe . . . a universe in which the poet is only one more object, a sensitive object that collects anguish and participates in the drama. The poet looks for and at the same time expresses his own soul through Nature, a telluric and profound nature, whose disordered reality, made symbol or myth, is the mirror of his own inner disorder. Besides these dominant themes, two other factors closely tie the poetry of the book with [surrealism]: the prophetic tone of the verse and above all the dreamlike subconscious character of the images, which, as much as in their monstrous forms . . . as in their other more lyrical and pleasant ones, ceaselessly recall the paintings of artists of the same movement.

Ángel del Río. *RHM*. Oct., 1935, p. 21†

The lyrical world of *Shadow of Paradise* is, as already defined by its title, a paradisiacal world, where the elements of Nature—the river, the sky, the sea, the night, the island, the inhabitants, and love itself—radiate their purest and most pristine beauty, like naked creatures of a world newly created, which receives the kiss of light for the very first time. In these poems, the poet seems to remember with nostalgia the radiant beauty, the heavenly light of that evoked world. To remember? Won't that nostalgic flavor of many of Aleixandre's poems, that melancholically pining voice deceive us? Won't that paradisiacal world be only a creation of the poet, a beautiful and complete image of his own desire? If we listen to the poet himself, we will see how that world of beauty was inhabited by him one day, and in what manner it lit up his heart, intoxicated his veins so gently with an intense fire, who now, exiled from that light for so long a time, orphan of that beauty, will want to evoke it all in his poetry in order to experience it once more, in order to feel its heavenly transparency, the caress of the pure white birds again. [1945]

José Luis Cano. *La poesía de la generación del 27* (Madrid, Guadarrama, 1970), pp. 137–38†

Each of [Aleixandre's] principal books is held together by a single theme. *Destruction or Love* . . . presents a vision of nature as a physical whole in which violence and love are contrasting aspects of the same force, and man's spirit lives only through his body. *Shadow of Paradise* . . . introduces the theme of time and transience, of the poet's childhood in a newly created world, and of his subsequent exile from it, and not till *History of the Heart* . . . do man and his destiny become detached from the context of nature in which the poet has hitherto exclusively seen them. In this last book love is no longer an impersonal creative force, but also includes a responsibility for the poet's fellow men, and a sense of personal affection. Man is here, for the first time, seen as a creature with spiritual possibilities. Señor Aleixandre's evolution over thirty years and more has been deflected by no passing fashions. . . .

Señor Aleixandre has stuck to his own line, the detailed features of which can hardly have been clear to him before they were isolated by the critics. What is most remarkable about his poetry is its persistent rhythms; it is as if words had been added at a late stage to perceptions that first announced themselves in musical form. Here there is a parallel, which cannot, however, be carried farther, with Mr. Eliot's *Four Quartets*. But Señor Aleixandre's intricately cadenced *vers libre* is technically closest to that of Dame Edith Sitwell, and it was already perfected in *Destruction or Love*. His metaphors, once abrupt and violent, are now simpler and more human but are still elemental; they owe very little to the poet's reading.

Señor Aleixandre is principally moved by shapes and textures, by physical sensations, by the warmth, brightness and colour of things recalled from the past and reassembled in a visionary dream.

J. M. Cohen. TLS. May 17, 1957, p. 306

Vicente Aleixandre descends to the deepest levels of his life or ascends to the paradisiacal, like a man who is hallucinating or like a soul filled with grace, without ever feeling the satanic joy other creators feel. And his vision is perfect without much calculation or meditation. He is a *visionary*. With diamondlike wit, he surprises the mysterious origins of all phenomena, of weather, of love. He is, in part, a man who dreams, and in part a man illuminated by that wit and natural wisdom. His poetic light has gone beyond the brevity of life, in order to draw from it the fluidity of its sap.

In general, [*Shadow of Paradise*] is inscrutable, like the soul within the boundaries of its corporeality, and hostile to all comparison in the dominion of artistic forms. Here, there is no room for comparison; only admiration is possible for this art, for such natural mastery goes beyond all standards and schools. And the more we enter in *Shadow of Paradise*, the more potent and inconceivable does his greatness appear to us, as it loses us in its infiniteness.

Concha Zardoya. Poesía española
contemporánea (Madrid, Guadarrama, 1961),
pp. 443–44†

Aleixandre had been the greatest poetical rebel of the Republican period. He seems to have been the only poet definitely to set out [in Aleixandre's words] to write under the "influence . . . of a psychologist who caused vast literary repercussions," that is to say, of course, of Freud. Aleixandre was thought of in early life as a revolutionary in every way. . . .

In the prose-poems of *Passion of the Earth* he wrote in dream-symbols. His other poetry, in a highly rhythmical free-verse, used the same sort of symbols but subordinated them to some theme, usually of love, interspersed with clear statements about his emotions and thoughts. Aleixandre does not induce in himself the trance Surrealists require; instead, he voluntarily creates a pleasing though rather stark pattern with unusual images. . . .

If some historian, in a very distant future age, is left with Aleixandre's books as the only record of the present age he will probably assume that nothing of note took place in the times through which this poet lived. There is only a gradual change in Aleixandre's style, of a kind we might have expected in all the poets of his generation had there been no Civil War. Yet the young were looking for something new in poetry and this was where they found it.

Charles David Ley. *Spanish Poetry since 1939*
(Washington, D.C., Catholic University of
America Press, 1962), pp. 37, 41

This vast dominion that Vicente Aleixandre summarizes in one of his most extensive and complete books [*In a Vast Dominion*] is that of man. Or better, that of humanity, what men alone are capable of experiencing according to Goethean affirmation. It is the dominion, the world of human matter, the unique cosmic matter complete in its constitution of human life. Because the whole world, that cosmic unity explored by the poet in his previous great books, is nothing but unique matter that is *incorporated*—that's it; it becomes embodied—in different forms of life: a gigantic geology, a jungle vastness, an immense sea, an enormous or diminutive zoological throbbing. And man.

This book is the *incorporation* . . . of matter into human life. And the incorporation of the material into the social and historical life of man.

Leopoldo de Luis. *Vicente Aleixandre*. (Madrid,
ESPESA, 1970), pp. 162–63†

In his erotic poetry, Aleixandre sought, through a fusion with the flesh of his loved one, to capture the light of unattainable passion and happiness; he broadened his psychoanalytic and surrealistic base for more human and social themes in his later work. Most critics recognize at least two stages in the poetry of Aleixandre. Starting off with a highly individualistic and irrational view of the cosmos, the poet makes of love the beginning and end of all things. In love with the cosmos, the stars, the sea, and the moon, Aleixandre seeks to fuse with his loved one because the only perfect love possible is a complete identification with the universe. Aleixandre equates thanatos with eros, for only through death and a return to the earth can one destroy the bodily limits which keep one from his love. Thus the final perfect love must be death. In his early works man, for Aleixandre, ranked last in the mineral, vegetable and animal universe. Later, from his own present, the poet tried to escape from the cruelties of civilization by returning to a kind of Paradise before the creation of man, a primitive world of innocence in which, of course, he could not permanently reside. The poet, in his universal love, which formerly put man on the periphery, concentrates in his second period, whose first real high point is *History of the Heart* (1954), on man's existential and social problems, views man as a historical and temporal being, and feels a communion with all of humanity. Turning his eyes from cosmic love to that of man, Aleixandre sings for everybody and not just for the telluric elemental creatures. If Aleixandre's poetry of the thirties stressed the idea of cosmic fusion with the material universe through love, and in the forties and fifties examined humans, their childhood, their fleeting existence and the poet's own identification with the many, finally in 1962, with the publication of *In a Vast Dominion,* it achieved a final reconciliation of man and creation. *History of the Heart* ended with a stoic acceptance of death. *In a Vast Dominion* also sorrows at man's demise but at the same time sees the universe, composed of one single material which may undergo temporal and physical changes, as eternal. A formless creation awaits fruition in the flux of time through the shaping and order of love, Aleixandre adds a new dimension to the poetry of the day, as did his destructive love and provocative Paradise, and preaches the universal communion of all matter.

Kessel Schwartz. *Vicente Aleixandre* (New
York, Twayne, 1970), pp. 1–2

Aleixandre's . . . *Destruction or Love* (1935), *World Alone* (1950; but written before the Civil War), and *Shadow of Paradise* (1944) have the maturity and control which were needed to turn his vivid poetic imagination to the production of interesting poetry. All three books were conceived as unities, and their poems make much more sense in the context of the whole book than if they are read separately. Their themes are mythical, in the primary sense that they offer poetic, non-rational accounts of why the universe is as it is. *Destruction or Love* speaks of an elemental natural force which unites all living things, and here the "or" of the title is not gratuitous. In his own way Aleixandre is observing, as psychoanalysts and laymen have done before and since, the real relation between love and destructive violence, and expressing it in vivid images which challenge, but this time also reward, the imagination. The jungle ruled by this elemental force is real up to a point, for Aleixandre is considering its actual revelation in beasts of prey and their victims. But the jungle and its inhabitants also take their symbolic places in a mythological cosmogony, and are bounded on one side by the cold, black depths of a loveless, lifeless ocean, and on the other by an azure heaven to which the denizens of the forest reach up in hope, as they shrink from the dead sea. Without being an allegory of human life, the book is rich in compellingly allusive images of the human condition. The other two books relate more specifically to man's place in the cosmos. Their main myth, more human but less potently expressed in both books than in *Destruction or Love,* is that of paradise lost, and they present a bleak vision of human desolation and despair in a worn-out, corrupt, ephemeral world, where only the searching eye of the poet can perceive the faint relics of the marvellous dawn of creation.

> G. G. Brown. *A Literary History of Spain: The Twentieth Century* (New York, Barnes & Noble, 1972), p. 98

The problem . . . with calling Vicente Aleixandre a pantheistical mystic or simply a pantheist is that such terms suggest a Christian position which is not borne out by an examination of the poet's texts. To be a mystic, one must believe in God. And to be a pantheist, as the very root meaning of the word implies, one must be able to see the presence or know the spirit of the Godhead in all things. Now Aleixandre's method is to spiritualize some factor of nature (the earth, the sky, the sea, etc.) by mingling his desire and his sense of identity with that element. All aspects of nature for him are potentially part of the same ongoing sense of matter. The forms of matter are created and destroyed but matter itself remains constant. This primal sense of the continual dying and rebirth that goes on in nature, not only of the cycle of the seasons, but of the appearance and disappearance of plants, animals and men, is the basis for the poet's communion with the outward world and the means of his fulfillment. Aleixandre sees the natural world most often like a pre-Socratic philosopher's (Leucippus' or Democritus') plenum: the world is full of interacting matter, and the process of death cannot diminish it. Such an idea has its formulation in the second law of thermodynamics, the law of the conservation of matter.

> Louise M. Bourne. *RevL.* June, 1974, pp. 170–71

All of [the work of Aleixandre], in its broad unfolding, forms a single body of vast proportions, where the different limbs are irrigated by a common circulating blood that gives life to the single structure. Each one of his books has an individual meaning; but this individual meaning does not exhaust its total meaning, since, besides it, there is another superimposed meaning which the other volumes of the poet are entrusted with giving it. Therefore whoever has not read *Shadow of*

Paradise, Final Birth and *History of the Heart,* and later, *In a Vast Dominion, Poems of Consummation* and *Dialogues of Knowledge,* cannot completely understand *Passion of the Earth, Swords Like Lips, Destruction or Love* or *World Alone.* Nor does each one of the later poetic realities become completely intelligible without our having previously gone through the experience which the reading of the others assumes. All of them emanate from a single center at which they all converge, and which consists of a vast exercise of communion and solidarity with respect to Creation in its double aspect, cosmic and human: communion and solidarity with elemental nature (from *Passion of the Earth* to *Final Birth*); and also (*History of the Heart* and *In a Vast Dominion*) communion and solidarity with men, with their tasks (life as effort), sorrows (existence within the temporal framework) and hopes (the human solidarity itself which the poet proclaims). The theme of *History of the Heart* and of *In a Vast Dominion* is not, then, nor even partially, love lived for its own sake; it is rather the appetite for communion with which the poet approaches his fellow men, except that, in a number of pieces, this communion is revealed as assumed and represented by the human couple, whose two members mutually offer each other warmth and company.

Carlos Bousoño. *RevL.* June, 1974, pp. 195–96

Vicente Aleixandre is one of the most original Spanish poets of this century. In his poetry of two major periods he created an original and coherent vision of the universe based upon the amorous solidarity of humanity. Rejecting (or going beyond) the culture around him, he sought a perfect fusion with the elements of nature, expressed with the images of erotic love. Through this fusion, love becomes destruction, destruction becomes death as the final liberation. In his second period, he attempted to break out of his cosmic isolation and to approach mankind directly, still rejecting culture. As any great poet must, he expressed his vision in an original style of surrealist, Freudian, and neo-Romantic elements. He is the acknowledged master of free verse in Spain, surpassing both Jiménez and García Lorca. His development of the visionary image and symbol, a technique also used by García Lorca and Cernuda, added a new dimension to Spanish poetry. Aleixandre's poetry is extremely difficult (even hermetic) in his first period, surprisingly clear and simple in expression in his second; both manners have been deemed fitting for our complex times. Like Jiménez and Guillén, Aleixandre offers an extensive and complete metaphysical structure in his poetry, in which all the parts combine and complement each other. With his poetry and presence, he has exerted a major influence upon the Spanish poets since 1939.

Carl W. Cobb. *Contemporary Spanish Poetry*
(1898–1963) (Boston, Twayne, 1976), p. 132

Mr. Aleixandre has described his poetry as "a longing for the light." The early poems are often opaque and difficult. They were written with "black light," he says, as if the approach to the unconscious had dragged far under the sea where no light can penetrate and the fish must attract each other with their own luminescence.

But even in his early work, Mr. Aleixandre had begun to rise. He is one of the few pessimistic poets of this century who manage to emerge and find something above the darkness.

The shift was quite dramatic. It came with *History of the Heart,* a book published in 1954. Death and loss still hover over these later poems but they seem accepted now, passed over to something else. The book affirms human fellowship, a spiritual unity, friendliness. The poems are social, the style is narrative, almost talky. There are real people all around and he pays attention to them, to friends and lovers, to strangers and dead heroes, to his dog.

Where before he had been attentive to nature and longed to join it, now nature is just the background for the lives of human beings. . . .

Vicente Aleixandre deserves the honor that the Swedish Academy has given him [the Nobel Prize]. He is a poet of intellectual vigor, spiritual depth and tenacity. He did the work. He went far down into the soul and brought back pieces of life as a gift for the rest of us.

Lewis Hyde. *NYT.* Oct. 7, 1977, p. 12

How fitting it is that Vicente Aleixandre has won the Nobel Prize! He is one of the greatest poets alive and his work stands for endurance, the roots under the tree of consciousness, the slowly growing trunk. He receives the prize for all the others of his generation in Spain, especially Jorge Guillén and Rafael Alberti. . . .

In his work you can see more clearly than in any poet in English the impact of Freud. The civilized Western man and woman had produced for several centuries a poetry that resembled a formal dance in a ballroom. [Pablo] Neruda, not being a European, had his dances outdoors, so it was left to Aleixandre to feel the full clash of Freud inside a drawing room. He evokes what it was like for a Westerner to read Freud's testimony of the immense and persistent sexual energy trying to rise into every vein and capillary of life and then go to a formal ball. . . .

For the Nobel Prize to come to Aleixandre now is fitting not only because of the energy and intensity of his own poetry, but because it comes at this moment in Spanish history. Spain is waking up after years of sleep, and Aleixandre's poetry and stubborn presence have a strong part in that awakening.

Robert Bly. *NYTBR.* Oct. 30, 1977, pp. 3, 52

History of the Heart is the one book of Aleixandre that I re-read most often: in it are many of my favorite poems. Perhaps the reason for this is that as the years pass by, I feel an ever-increasing affinity between my essential temperament and the one that is revealed in the book. There are no hard contrasts between the blazing sun and complete shade in it, but there is a filtered light that is projected upon the resignations of a declining life. . . . Our existence is a flash between two dark voids, but in that flash there is room for love, communion with all of humanity; and lastly, mystery and death possess the virtue of consolation. . . .

Love is not the only theme of this book, but it is its axis. It is the total love of the human couple—in body and soul. . . . Thematically the construction of the book is perfect; and it is also perfect in its progressive refinement and transcendence of love. In this sense, Aleixandre coincides . . . with the Neoplatonism of the Renaissance.

Rafael Lapesa. *Ínsula.* Jan.-Feb., 1978,
pp. 1, 10†

Aleixandre realizes, as most surrealist poets did, that the conventions of the rational world, as opposed to the desires and visions of the subconscious world of dreams and fantasies, tend to split into two mutilated halves what for primitive man was a whole and sound universe; hence the cult of voluntary hallucination and the sudden changes of subject and perspective, which can be baffling indeed to the average reader. There can be no doubt that Aleixandre is one of the most difficult poets ever to use the Spanish language. More than García Lorca, Guillén and even Cernuda, in his generation, he employs every device that can free the mind of its rational categories. He wills a new reality whose truth is poetic rather than scientific, universal rather than particular. His main tool is his uncommon imagination, which faces the ordinary world and "derealizes" it. In other words, the conventional boundaries between ordinary perception and delirious hallucination are broken down, and every conceivable approach to experience becomes permissible. . . .

[Aleixandre's] poems are above all noble, "large," uplifting: we are always facing giants, a larger-than-life vision of the landscape and the figures in it. This feeling of *grandeur* can be attributed in part to some of the subjects; the sea, for instance, is a recurring theme. Yet there is more: Aleixandre has created, out of the influence of surrealism, a multi-layered style, one in which symbols are hidden behind words, and each line calls to mind a new group of symbols, flying through the air toward the reader. For example, many of his nature poems can be read three ways, the first interpretation being that of a dream, a vision. And then the symbols begin to appear, both the Freudian and Jungian variety. The poem unfolds, new dimensions are added to it: it is a poem about a visionary poet, who at the same time is a child looking for his mother—and afraid of his parents—and a whole people remembering its past and the origins of the world.

Manuel Durán. *WLT.* Summer, 1978,
pp. 204, 206

In *Poems of Consummation* Aleixandre has had the daring to enter, with no attenuating illusions, into the dramatic problem which tears apart an old man still anxious to prove his love of life. And upon doing this, he may well have provided an escape for his present inner demon in a kind of poetic-moral exorcism which will leave him cleansed and prepared for the new and more audacious adventures in thought of which his next book, *Dialogues of Knowledge,* is the best proof. On turning to this theme, what Vicente Aleixandre does in *Poems of Consummation* is articulate this poetry of his maturity congruently with that of his earlier maturity: *In a Vast Dominion,* or with the earlier *Shadow of Paradise,* or even with the poetry of his shaken youth, *Destruction or Love*. Throughout all of his works, he had enthusiastically sung the identification of man with natural reality; to achieve this in all of its intensity required that it be intuited in terms of energy, force and brilliance: attributes exclusive to youth. Nature, as a moral lesson to be imitated or as an attracting force to any dream of pantheistic union, manifests itself solely in the form of vital force, operative, perpetually renovated and totally free of any sign of decadence or annihilation. What happens now is that the poet, because of his personal circumstance and moment (present old age, lost youth), has decided to treat historically what has always been the core of his poetry; although certain earlier periods, like the one of *History of the Heart,* responded to a projection of meaning analogous to what is suggested here. These circumstances will determine the inevitable elegiac tone, since the one who suffers them cannot forget that at one time his own youth and the plenitude of nature were the same thing and this explains the heart-rending side of many of these poems. But the years have also brought serenity, that is, the state of mind necessary to examine what is remaining of human existence, what of him will remain as true substance and singular destiny. This examination, calm and melancholy, reflective and pathetic, will reveal the other face of the book, constructive and enriching, and will give it its depth and universality.

José Olivio Jiménez. In Vicente Cabrera and
Harriet Boyer, eds., *Critical Views on Vicente
Aleixandre's Poetry* (Lincoln, Neb., Society of
Spanish and Spanish-American Studies, 1979),
p. 72

Although man is part of [the] cosmic unity and as such will be fused with all creation, Vicente Aleixandre believes that man has little knowledge of his predicament and needs a way of becoming aware of it; thus poetry, which is the "clairvoyant fusion of man with creation, with that which perhaps has no name." The poet, then, is seen as a possible receptive "magnetic pole" of all the forces coming from the mysterious cosmos with which he becomes one. It is natural that Vicente

Aleixandre should declare that "poetry is not a matter of words." What really matters for him is, paraphrasing his terms, not the false luminosity emanating from the crystal of poetic language, but the real light of knowledge. Language is unable to make this light visible if it has to conform to established patterns of expression; and since it has always been used under control, language has never had enough power to signify the profound and mysterious luminosity of true reality. The poet has to disregard the regular forms of poetic writing and creating his own, in a daily effort to produce the "light of the poem." He runs away from the well-known toward the spheres of absolute truth.

As in *Passion of the Earth,* Vicente Aleixandre is still driven by the desire for authenticity and looks for revelation on the level of the surreal, where words change their everyday meaning to make manifest in the poem the revealed truth. The poet is listening to the messages of the cosmos and makes of them a sensitive and communicating expression completely different from the normal aesthetic form of speaking. It is a form of surrealism, except that in this case the author no longer writes the utterances of an unconscious self, a first-person individuality, but becomes the voice of all life and matter expressing itself through the unconscious of someone who acts as a sibyl, a point of fusion between man and cosmos.

Santiago Daydí-Tolson. Introduction to
Santiago Daydí-Tolson, ed., *Vicente Aleixandre:
A Critical Appraisal* (Ypsilanti, Mich., Bilingual
Press, 1981), pp. 11–12

ALONSO, DÁMASO (1898–   )

Sr. A[lonso] continues to add solid contributions to his already long list of interpretations of [Luis de] Góngora. The present volume [*The Poetic Language of Góngora (First Part)*] is devoted to a study of the vocabulary and a few striking stylistic and syntactic mannerisms of the poet. Its purpose is to demonstrate that all the linguistic elements which characterize his typical later style are to be found in his earlier works and that it is therefore improper to divide his creative activity into two chronological periods; his later work is marked by an intensification and densification of the methods used already in his earliest writings. . . .

There is a danger that in the attempt to rehabilitate Góngora, devotees will merely establish a cult, worshipping his defects as blindly as his gifts. Sr. A[lonso] is not one of these. He recognizes clearly the excesses of which the poet is guilty. But he insists, and properly, that these very excesses are part and parcel of the whole Renaissance movement which culminates in Góngora. . . . Sr. A[lonso]'s study brings a wealth of specific data to illustrate the process by which the greatest of the Baroque poets evolved his linguistic medium.

Hayward Keniston. HR. Oct., 1937, pp. 353, 356

As a theoretician of style Dámaso Alonso starts from the positions of [Ferdinand de] Saussure and [Charles] Bally. He denies, however, that language in practice can ever be separated from speech, or that the affective element alone can be a criterion for establishing the domain of style versus the domain of grammar. The only worthy object of stylistic study is the language of the literary artist. . . .

As an interpreter of texts, Dámaso Alonso represents the most objective imaginable type of scholarly scrutiny and pedagogical ability. He moves easily from strophic structure, metrics, accents, caesura, smooth or rough enjambement to word order, moderate and exaggerated hyperbaton, aristocratic or popular selection of vocabulary, particular figures of style and last, but not least, imagery. He is more concerned with exact description than with explanation at all costs. But the explanations are always convincing. . . .

With Alonso . . . we are safe in saying that a science of stylistics exists, not a science for determining "affective speech," but rather of the artistic grasp on poetry, not of subjective intuition, but of objective proof, not of personal lucubrations but of communicable and teachable procedure. The limitations of this new science in the making must be compensated, Dámaso Alonso thinks, with [Leo] Spitzer, by a constant shifting of method, dealing individually with individual authors. Alonso is, as far as method is concerned, even ready to leave the *ergon* in order to reconstruct the poet's probable *energeia* in creating it. Thus, apparently falling back to the fallacy of [Pierre] Audiat, he actually attains at least what [Benedetto] Croce and Spitzer meant by the poetical (rather than the historical) personality of the poet. He sees four Lopes [de Vega] at different epochs rather than one. . . .

Helmut Hatzfeld. CL. Winter, 1952, pp. 87–89

Dark Message, as Dámaso Alonso published it, is a book of alluvium. I mean that he has added other poems of other periods and origins to the sixteen poems of the first part. But in the first part of the book, in the poems that make up his real *Dark Message,* all the existential themes, which he will bring to their ultimate consequences in *Children of Wrath* through a more rigorous and imaginative construction, are already evident. Although many of the poems in *Dark Message* are sonnets, they have a disorganized, even chaotic, strength; the sonnets of *Children of Wrath* reveal more concentration and symbolic invention.

In *Dark Message,* the sonnets alternate with other poetic forms; the sonnets are the most tormented and fierce. On the other hand, in poems like the one called "To Those Who Will Be Born," a more tender and loving expression is evident through the free verse. . . .

In the sonnets that are of classical Spanish origin—i.e., baroque—poetry as an exercise is compatible with poetry as an authentic revelation. The greater the demands for a closed form, on one hand, the greater the need for a, on the other, stormy word. . . . The baroque form of the grand style is converted into a recipient of a vital desperation with all its impotency. This last thing, impotency, is the most decisive. As if it were dealing with an adolescent's poem, the word establishes a reality in which the poet cannot live. Some tercets of the poem "Love" are examples. . . . The poet's stylistic tendency to accumulate many definitions of the same reality is noted here. It is a tendency that will be perfected later in *Children of Wrath.*

Luis Felipe Vivanco. Introducción a la poesía
española contemporánea (Madrid,
Guadarrama, 1957), pp. 274–75†

Dámaso Alonso must be chronologically placed in the between-the-wars generation, call it the generation of 1925 . . . the generation of the Dictatorship . . . or the generation of 1927, as is most frequently heard, owing to the date of the tricentenary of [Luis de] Góngora, an extremely opportune commemoration that permitted this group of poets a more defined and concrete external projection. . . . From that period there is only his first book *Pure Poems: Short Poems of the City,* dated 1921. . . . One particular note places it in the general attitude of the time . . . the search for poetic purity. But the word "purity," in this sense, had its special implications. . . . The between-the-wars artist desired to flee from the ugliness and the impurity of life and, with this aim, the untouched, autonomous, very pure field of Art and Poetry, both with capital letters, offered him the bridge for flight, the goal of escape.

One must understand that the qualifier "pure," as applied by Dámaso Alonso to his first poems, does not exactly fit with the ideal. There is, in them, a note of purity, but in the sense of tenderness, delicateness, and the finely human. A human adolescent . . . without the extreme violence or pain of the future adult. But never the "extra-human principle," never outside of feeling. To the contrary, *Pure Poems: Short Poems of the City* puts a note of exceptional and tranquil trembling into the young poetry of that historical moment. And that is already an index that permits the spiritual connection of this book . . . with all Dámaso Alonso's later poetry.

José Olivio Jiménez. Boletín de la Academia
Cubana de la Lengua. Jan.-June, 1958,
pp. 81–82†

After Azorín and after Ortega, only Dámaso Alonso has exercised and is exercising such a real and profound influence on our literature. His personality is always the same (except in his rigorous and entertaining phonetic and dialectal diversions), and it is present in every one of his works. . . .

And even in his strictly scientific entertainments . . . what pushes him on and enlivens him with no diminution of rigor . . . is horseback riding on the roads from Lugo to Asturias and León, wisely conversing with a shepherd or farmer, picking up a pure vowel sound from the lips of a child or from a servant at an inn, linking their personalities to his own.

> Leopoldo Panero. *PSA.* Nov.-Dec., 1958,
> pp. 366–67†

And now we come to the great autobiographical poem that ends *Children of Wrath:* "Final Dedication (The Wings)." In spite of this progressive impulse toward God, Dámaso Alonso never feels himself possessed by angelic qualities. . . . It is inhuman to separate oneself from the miseries of man. For this reason we do not find the culmination or the "height" of *grace,* that dynamic and amplifying power that radiates and spreads with subjugating drive in all directions, in this last poem. On the other hand, neither is there a frustration of this ascensional impulse, this hunger for God. No. After many days of effort and struggle, the spirit must achieve some consolation or award—mere exaltation or even victory, something that we might call liberation of the will or the birth of wings. Something that is a surpassing of the purgative state on the mystic road, and the attainment of a type of illuminated happiness. That prize is obtained on a simply human level, in which the poet at the end recognizes God's grace: in the gifts that God has given him in this world—his mother and his wife. They are his wings, the pure strengths that carry him from the earth and elevate him to God. They are the wings of love, which are born not from within, but from without, but which penetrate him, pierce him, and finally enlighten him benevolently, beautifully, and redeemingly. The final lesson that perhaps one gets from this poem is that the kindness of God permits the human creature always to be saved by something or someone. [1959]

> Concha Zardoya. *Poesía española*
> *contemporánea* (Madrid, Guadarrama, 1961),
> pp. 422–23†

Man and God is the most meticulously structured and planned book by Dámaso Alonso. It consists of a prologue, five commentaries, and an epilogue. Seven splendid sonnets are intercalated between the commentaries (all in free or measured verse); another serves as prologue; the text proper begins with yet another one, which has the same title as the book. The first commentary is divided into three palinodes (one, dedicated to intelligence, another to spilled human blood, the other to *logris,* or man's formal appearance.)

That "Man and God" is placed between the first and second commentaries is not a caprice; rather, this placement is determined by the book's conceptual structure. What he wants to signify is that the intention of the book is not, as its title might suggest, the mere sum of man and God, but the simultaneous residence in man of both the human and the divine; simultaneity, not the contiguous presence of man and God. For this reason, the prologue—gratitude to God for having watched over the structure of things through his myopia, and praise for his vague cottonlike beauty—is followed by three palinodes. . . .

With this begins the dissatisfaction with imperfection—that is, with the "myopia"—and the statement of Man-God or God in Man.

José Luis Varela. *Arbor.* April, 1960,
pp. 497–98†

In Dámaso Alonso's poetry, starting with *Man and God,* common vocabulary exists, but it loses its emotive violent character. It is a transformation that once again proves the validity of Dámaso Alonso's innovation. The poet shows us how, for example, a repugnant vocabulary, previously used to produce violent jolts, can, in the hands of an artist, express other spiritual realities, including tenderness. . . .

Another aspect of the common or nonpoetic vocabulary . . . is that which represents daily realities or that of purely utilitarian value. I once discussed the relative arbitrariness with which certain words are accepted as poetic and others are rejected. . . . Some words possess a rich literary tradition, while others belong to the category of contemporary inventions, about which we think only in terms of practical use.

Dámaso Alonso also enters this field and creates some examples in which the arbitrariness of such a situation is seen. If other poets throughout Spanish literary history described their contemporaries with all kinds of details, Dámaso Alonso can justly write poems that define modern man. . . . In the same way we discover that within Dámaso Alonso's poetic language, disseminated in his books, there is room for all types of images of the immediate reality. . . .

The examination of man and his destiny in the world, the serious observation about evil and its causes, and, later, the affirmation of the central position that man has in the universe logically produce a conceptual and philosophic language that culminates in *Man and God.* We have already noted the condensation of these concepts in this volume and in *Pleasures of Sight.* Without doubt, we are dealing with brilliant samples of intellectual precision, in which the poet makes an effort to find the exact word—an impossible task, as he himself admits. . . .

Miguel J. Flys. *La poesía existencial de
Dámaso Alonso* (Madrid, Gredos, 1968),
pp. 38–40†

But is *Children of Wrath* a dialogue or a monologue? Sometimes the protagonist finds himself completely alone: he calls on God, and there is no answer. At other times he thinks he hears God's call, but he cannot reply. The whole book is in effect the prolonged monologue of a semi-atheistic psalmist. For one cannot understand God's purpose, that is, the naming of cosmos, if in fact it does have some sense of direction. This solitude and abandonment is very clearly expressed in the book's first poem, "Insomnia," in which the protagonist "Dámaso" becomes the spokesman of humanity accusing a silent God.

While in a few poems we have this cosmic, quasi-religious perspective, in most of them the perspective is rather more earth-bound. And the two basic attitudes possible among earthly beings are hatred, or alienation, and love. The protagonist resists hatred with horror. In several poems ferocious images express the irruption of human barbarity into a lost paradise. It is this paradise, related to childhood innocence, that heightens the more odious aspects of human existence. The nostalgically remembered landscape of Eden makes more sharply perceptible the immediate anguish of present existence. The dead too belong to a similar distant world of essences.

But the possibility of love within existence has not been entirely lost. There is a series of poems in which the protagonist explores affective comprehension; here there are even touches of humor.

Elias L. Rivers. Introduction to *Hijos de la ira/*
Children of Wrath (Baltimore, Johns Hopkins
University Press, 1970), pp. xii–xiii

It might do well to note . . . that satirical references of diverse types appear throughout Alonso's creative work. His "Songs for Solo Whistle," never published as a book, contain humoristic poems written between 1919 and 1967; some of them satirize the speaker, the modern world, even the use of abbreviations in our society. At least two poems from *Pure Poems* . . . satirize the bourgeois world and the worn imagery of earlier poetic styles. Two short stories of Alonso published in the late 1920s contain pedestrian but illusion-seeking protagonists and deal with the conflict between a limited reality and higher aspirations. Satire seems to be, then, a constant if at times minor note in Alonso's creative work. It attains frequency and importance in his post-Civil War poetry, offering Alonso a technique through which to underline the limitations of the world portrayed and above all to cast these limitations in effective dramatic monologues. Satirical references and dramatic monologue allow the poet, as we have seen, to govern our reactions to his protagonists and thus give vivid expression to his meanings. They prevent his works, based as they are on philosophic themes and built around specific attitudes to the world, from seeming either arbitrary or didactic. (Paradoxically enough, satire permits Alonso to present his negative visions and yet avoid a simplistic dogmatic attack.)

Andrew Debicki. *BA*. Spring, 1974, p. 285

In modern poetry, unlike its sixteenth-century counterparts, metrical organization is at once problematic: metrics is no longer a convenient critical handle with which the reader may grasp the organizational devices in poetry. From the point of view of metrics, an obvious starting place for the analysis of Petrachists, a poem such as "The Obsession" presents several key literary problems. I wish to suggest here that where metrics seems inoperative or unsystematic, syntactic patterning may provide a critical tool for delving into poetic structure.

Dámaso Alonso himself refers to his collection *Children of Wrath* as "una protesta literaria" [a literary protest], and in this protest he isolates three major areas of inquiry: metrics, poetic diction, and content. . . .

Critics of Alonso attempt to systematize his poetry along traditional lines of metrical organization, as one might analyze a Petrarchan sonnet. Yet the results invariably amount to metrical inconsistencies, with half-glimpsed hendecasyllables or an occasional heptasyllabic combination. In "The Obsession" the reader looks in vain for rhyme words, assonance, consistent line length, or rhythmic pattern. Line length can vary from three syllables to twenty-six. Of the fifty-seven lines, there are six stanzaic units: nine lines, plus twelve, plus ten, plus four, plus eight, plus fourteen. Alonso's poem then obliges the reader to examine its internal structure as a means of comprehending its ordering devices, lest these stanzaic divisions appear incoherent. The reader can no longer use the *hic-est* method of identifying metric type and then consider the task of analyzing organizational devices completed.

In addition, Alonso's poem challenges the reader on another traditional level of poetic analysis: that of diction or word choice.

Sharon Ghertman. In Lisa E. Davis and Isabel
C. Tarán, eds., *The Analysis of Hispanic Texts:
Current Trends in Methodology* (New York,
Bilingual Press, 1976), p. 183

ÁLVAREZ QUINTERO, SERAFÍN 1871–1938) and JOAQUÍN (1873–1944)

Personally, I do not believe that the Álvarez Quinteros have tried to be innovative about anything, since they hold little respect for plot, the art of elaboration, all that constitutes, in a word, "theatrical carpentry." Judging by their works, what must have instinctively attracted them was the description of types and manners, where this kind of writing must have arisen; among other merits, this has the one of being entirely their own. They have not changed anything. In order to behave as moderns they needed to return to the true canons of classicism, and in many of their plays one can see confirmed the precept in which Horace tells us, "Let the character be at the end as he was at the beginning." . . . The Álvarez Quinteros—from what can be deduced from their productions—have studied and admired the masterpieces of the classics. Here lies their true strength.

The Álvarez Quinteros guessed that characters can be anti-evolutive within their own complexity, because in life, even within those moments that we could label as conflicting because of the multiple tendencies that the characters manifest, there is an implacable logic. The colossal error of the majority of playwrights lies in not having foreseen such a possibility. Analyze any of their plays—The *Galley Slaves*, for example, where drama is combined with comedy in a pleasing proportion, and if you excuse me for seeking out complicated phrases that are an expression of what I simply believe, I will say to you with an apriorism free of all partiality that for me such a work is truly remarkable.

Pedro González Blanco. *Lectura*. Dec., 1902,
pp. 319–20†

The drama may be a vehicle for any mental concept: satire, ethics, cynicism, philosophy, realism, poetry, social problems, melodrama. Sane optimism and realism suffused with poetry are inspiring forces of the brothers Quintero. They have no thesis to prove, except that life is sweet and worth living; no didactic aim, except to show that human nature is still sound in the main. It is a distinct relief to read plays so natural and serene, after one has surfeited upon the products of many contemporary continental playwrights, the monotony of whose subject-matter is so obvious that not even supreme technical skill can conceal the sterility of the authors. The eternal triangle, the threadbare motivation into which true affection never enters for a moment, have been ridden to death, and even a French critic is led to comment with resignation upon "this completely unmoral world which is almost the only one we are permitted to see upon the stage. . . ." There has never been an age nor a place where average life did not contain potential material for a creative writer. The Quinteros have undertaken precisely to present the average existence of the bourgeois and lower classes in an interesting way, instead of racking the audience with problems that to at least nine people out of ten are no problems at all. Like Dickens, they touch the comedies and tragedies of daily life with a poetic light, and the revelation of Spanish character reminds us once more of the saying that Spaniards, more than any other European people, resemble Americans. It was William Dean Howells who said, in writing of one of the later novels of Palacio Valdés, that he found in it "a humanity so like

the Anglo-Saxon." He would surely extend the statement to the Quinteros comedies.

S. Griswold Morley. Introduction to Serafín and
Joaquín Álvarez Quintero, *Doña Clarines y
Mañana de sol* (Boston, D. C. Heath, 1915),
pp. xii–xiii

From their very first works, the Álvarez Quinteros have been in control
of dramatic structure. . . . Their masterpiece, a true technical marvel, is
The Women's Town. The two brothers have not surpassed—nor is it
possible to do so—that labor of dramatic structure. There is nothing
superfluous in *The Women's Town;* there are neither remnants of exposition from the first act found in the second act, nor false tracks, nor slow-
downs in the action. The dialogue—devoid of eloquence—glides along
naturally, clearly, and directly. And another perfect example of exposition is the first act of *The Happy Nature.* . . .

The Álvarez Quinteros put care into the observation of the surrounding reality; they study it from up close; they are scrupulous and
precise in the brush-strokes with which they paint reality; they describe
in minute detail male and female characters. And after all, in their
perpetual doubt, in their eternal vacillation between society and the
individual, they end up by being a little skeptical, but gently so; they are
skeptical with care and kindness. And that is the prevailing trait in the
theater of the Álvarez Quinteros: kindness. Away from the literary
clamor, life does not hold for them—they who are so quiet and discreet—painful stings. They do not lose their spiritual serenity. . . .

All is silence, spiritual withdrawal. When the misfortune has ended,
the gentleness and peace of the scene reject to the very depths of the
heart the sob that rises up and was to become a cry of pain. And
perhaps, having been muted and contained, the pain is more lasting and
intense. Such is the feeling in *The Flowers, Cancionera, Fortunato,* and
Concha the Pure.

Azorín. *Los Quinteros y otras páginas* (Madrid,
R. Caro Raggio, 1925), pp. 13, 15–16, 23–25†

When one has said of [*A Hundred Years Old*] that a certain delicacy in
the writing does as much as could possibly be done to make tolerable
its unrelieved sweetness, one has said about all that can be said in its
favor. . . . Servants are loyal and masters are kindly. The priests are
good and so are the freethinkers. In fact, everybody is good, and even
those who seem least promising are only waiting for a favorable opportunity to demonstrate at what a low temperature their hearts will melt.
Occasionally frail? Yes. Wicked? Never! And of course, enough forgiveness to go all the way around is constantly on tap.

"Anything that has its foundation in happiness and success must
be allowed to be the object of comedy; and sure it must be an improve-

ment of it to introduce a joy too exquisite for laughter." These words were not written either by Martínez Sierra or the Quinteros. As a matter of fact they were written just a little over two hundred years ago as part of the preface attached by Richard Steele to his sentimental comedy *The Conscious Lovers,* and were intended as a kind of proclamation in favor of a certain kind of play. But so constant is the type that they might serve our Spanish authors just as well. They express the philosophy behind a kind of drama which aims at only one kind of effect—that produced by scenes of repentance, reconciliation, forgiveness, and general benevolence. . . . The author is so anxious to get at the repentance or the reconciliation that he can hardly spare the time to allow anybody to sin or quarrel. The whole thing is one long happy ending, and there is no cloud to sew the silver lining to.

The appearance of such a play is always the occasion for various people to ask why, after all, there isn't a legitimate place for what they call "wholesome sentiment," but the answer is not so difficult as they seem to imply. Sentimentality has been well defined as the attitude which arises in those who are so anxious to believe that things are what they ought to be that they pay no attention at all to what they are. It means the end not only of drama but of every vestige of the critical attitude toward persons and events.

Joseph Wood Krutch. Nation. Oct. 23, 1929,
p. 474

Genial and delightful as writers of comedy are the Quintero brothers. . . . Their boyhood was passed in the capital of Andalusia [Seville], where, in their teens, they saw performed their first farce, *Fencing and Love.* Encouraged by its success, the young men went to Madrid, worked in and for the theater, and, after various experiments, won popular approval by another farce, with incidental music entitled *The Good Spirit.* Thereafter, they produced with apparent ease many delightful airy plays which exhibit life as they have observed it with piquant local color and fine good humor. They are most at home in revealing the manners of the middle or the lower classes and in depicting character. There is nothing profound or unduly subtle about their work. They create the illusion of a world darkened only enough to throw into relief its high lights. For nicely woven plots, they care little. They are content to take the simplest situations, to develop these in one or two acts, and to send their audiences home smiling and confirmed in the belief that a tender heart is the best of human possessions. Even in the three-act form, they remain essentially anecdotal.

The plays of the Álvarez Quinteros bear some resemblance to those of [James M.] Barrie. Sentiment colors all. The mood of optimism is saddened only by wistful regret. Many of their sketches for the stage remind one also of the short pieces of Lady Gregory. Here are *sainetes* [short dramatic compositions] like *The Mad Muse* and *The Happy Nature,* recommending laughter as a cure for every evil. . . .

Best known of all the plays by the Álvarez Quinteros is *Malvaloca,* a delicate plea for indulgence toward one guilty of a slip from virtue. . . . In place of the harsh code of honor so often emphasized in earlier Spanish literature, we find here a tender sympathy that is broadly human, the same indulgence that marks such American plays as *Anna Christie* and *They Knew What They Wanted.*

The Spanish critic Manuel Bueno declares of the Álvarez Quinteros that all Spanish ladies over forty like to regard themselves as mother to the pair, and that all young folk look upon them as boon comrades. In a given case, everybody thinks that he or she would have said or done just what the characters of these dramatists say and do. Hence they feel themselves to be collaborating with the Álvarez Quinteros, and are edified without being preached to, and amused without being made to puzzle their heads over problems. Certainly, the Álvarez Quinteros deserve the recognition they have received. Their work may be sentimental and pretty rather than great, but it satisfies a need of the heart and exhibits the new tendency to make the drama pictorial rather than theatrical.

Frank W. Chandler. *Modern Continental Playwrights* (New York, Harper & Brothers, 1931), pp. 487–88, 492, 494

The Álvarez Quinteros learned how to oppose the hatred of Mankind, for which they had great compassion and love. . . . Their works, like the brothers themselves, are very polite. There is no acrimony or bitterness to be found in their works. Nor does evil ever turn into perversion, or silliness into scorn in their characters. The bad and the foolish are capable of improvement; they are not those bad and ignorant people for whom salvation is not possible. There is in all the work of Álvarez Quinteros's something like an endearing expression of indulgence for all concerned; this represents the highest level of understanding. In writing dialogue, they were masters; spontaneous, always generous, never professorial or pedantic. They were inimitable in the liveliness of their repartee.

The Álvarez Quinteros never cheapened the language by giving it too much naturalness or making it seem too real. Even though they were Andalusians, and Andalusians from Seville, which is like being Andalusian twice over, . . . nobody could brand them as regional authors. Even in the works set in Seville, they are not entirely regional, nor could it be said of these works . . . that they are written with more love than the plays about Madrid. *The Daughters of Cain* is a play set in Madrid, and in my opinion, if in the extreme case of a catastrophe only one work of each author could be saved, I would always save *The*

Daughters of Cain among all the plays of the Álvarez Quinteros, so admirable has the play always seemed to me. [ca. 1950]

Jacinto Benavente. *Obras completas,* Vol. XI
(Madrid, Aguilar, 1958), pp. 258, 261†

The theatrical world of the Álvarez Quinteros is a world that redeems itself by irony when it is just at the point of condemning itself by corniness. And here it is that suddenly this commemoration of the Álvarez Quinteros acquires an unexpectedly timely tone, all the suggestive timeliness of kitsch. If what is corny is often what is beautiful seen with the perspective of time, and this temporal relativity of corniness is ironically emphasized by diluting the emptiness of its contents into pure decorative form, we are one step from the aesthetics of "camp." This aforementioned vein of ingenious irony from Seville purifies the Álvarez Quinteros of that decorative and facile artificiality of their works, and it converts the centennial of Serafín Álvarez Quintero into an authentically camp centennial. . . .

Perhaps irony, as attitude and as style, is the most interesting and original contribution of the Álvarez Quinteros. . . . The entire theater of the Álvarez Quinteros is impregnated with this irony, a subtle and playful irony that—as I have said—redeems it to a great extent from its corniness. *The Patio, The Happy Nature, Doña Clarines,* or *The Daughters of Cain* are—precisely because of that diffuse spirit of authentic irony—unique works of the Álvarez Quinteros, superior to the facile melodramatic ploys of *Malvaloca* or *The Galley Slaves* or to the botanical and talky short farces. And it is here, in this manner purified by irony, where friendly humanity is enriched and refined—the kind and laughing affection by which Serafín and Joaquín Álvarez Quintero have passed into the history of our literature.

Florencio Segura. *RyF.* July-Aug., 1971,
pp. 18, 20–21†

AUB, MAX (1903–1972)

Botany [in *Green Fable*] for Max Aub is more than a guide to different types of plants; it is a difficult grid on which he traces with the quickest and boldest lines the tapestry and arabesque of colorful threads of metaphors, a fine spinning of wit and poetry.

Aub's *Green Fable* is similar to another of his books, *Geography.* . . . Like *Geography,* it is arbitrary but with a studied arbitrariness that is, nevertheless, present from the beginning of the work. This arbitrariness is born from an initial metaphor, which when it is deciphered by turning in on itself, infuses the whole game, whose power is the root of the work, with its creative impetus.

In Max Aub's literary production, *Geography* and *Green Fable* are really only diversions. The two works are written out of pure pleasure in literary exercise and out of a desire to avoid the principal and lasting work of the writer: his work for the theater, which we already know— we await the production of several plays collected in the volume *Narcissus* and some farces published in *Incomplete Theater.*

In all of these plays, Max Aub reveals the essential qualities also present in *Green Fable:* a lyric inventive facility and sweet, humanistic humor, coupled with qualities of intelligence and the subtle delicacies of a fluid art.

The prose of *Green Fable* is rich and succulent, pure, full of color, like the myriad plants that he describes. But like them, it is also, at times, unripe. It is more than stupidity or carelessness. It seems that Max Aub intentionally disdains persistent patience, which is the honest virtue of any writer. And if in this way he gains in freshness what he loses in perseverance, he does not attain in perfection what he doubtlessly and continually does in clear and spontaneous naturalness. It would not be difficult for Aub to reach rigorous perfection along with graceful agility.

Juan Chabás. *RO.* Jan., 1933, pp. 104–5†

For Max Aub, the novel is fundamentally a reflection of life, and, moreover, of the agitated and tumultuous life of our times. This concept leads the author to look for the subject matter of his works—the fiction as much as the drama—in the burning issues of the moment. Among these themes there is none that is more intense and tragic—especially for a Spaniard like Max Aub—than that of the war against the Spanish Republic, which bloodied Iberian soil for about three years. The political and social milieu of Spain in the years before this war is recorded with a dextrous hand in *Closed Battlefield,* one of the best novels published by a Spanish exile in the Americas. The book is divided into two very distinct parts: one that unfolds in the Valencian province of Castellón de la Plana, and the other in the city of Barcelona. The first enables Max Aub, who used to live in Valencia, to give us a lively view, with firm and bold strokes of the pen, of his adopted homeland, which he knows and loves so well. In the second part there is a drastic change of scenery: the monotonous tranquility of the Castilian life in which the hero, Rafael Serrador, feels more and more stifled each day, is replaced by the social agitation of the great Catalonian metropolis with its violent political battles. A great variety of Barcelonan characters file through these pages: militant syndicalists, theorizing socialists, activist communists, aggressive Falangists—people from every corner of Spain who make up the masses of the Catalonian metropolis. There is an absolute sincerity in the characterization of all these human types; there is the sincerity of an artist who knows how to separate himself from his own political convictions in order to serve truth exclusively.

Emilio González López. *RHM.* Jan.–April, 1945, pp. 251–52†

Dear Max:

A formidable book, this "biography" of *Jusep Torres Campalans*, which I have finally had a chance to see. It is a surprising book, and, in a certain sense, "unique." You have created an unexpected figure, with a vigor and an inspiration (I refuse to call him a fantasy) and at the same time with an insistent vigilance that seem to me incomparable, for various reasons. Your book reads like a prodigious pursuit and admits the power of that intuition of a Hispanic type that is entirely your own: the development and reconstitution of his life (yes, yes a reconstitution: one must so label that inlaying in reality of a piece that is . . . magical) by converting his discovery and detailed initiation into a fabulous adventure.

Because Jusep's life, since it is an incredible adventure, is in tune with the life of the author who "re-encounters" him, not in Mexico, but across a bygone world, yet one that is near, in its multiple and unknown attestations that are so, so "difficult." Thus, along with being other things, you are the living investigator—that is the word—guided by an extremely complex instinct, made up of the sense of smell and super-knowledge, illumined by the light of a refined irony, difficult to describe to the reader. (Your book could be subtitled: *An Expedient to Reality* or *A New Optical Illusion*). And that is how you are, with your received cultural values; the novelist (now there is the right word) who gives life to a being, to his milieu, to his history, creating him totally from top to bottom. . . .

I would keep on talking about you, but let me add only that I have enjoyed your writing. It is a prose that is direct, endowed with power, flowing with life in its rich fullness; a muscular prose with sensitive sinews within at all times; a prose that one must call supervital and that announces the hand, the arm, the entire being of the writer who produces it. Do not smile: but it is a prose that "nourishes."

Marvelous painter Torres Campalans. It must have been a passion that made you compose and complete this book. You have "brought back" (I refuse to say invented) to our twentieth century a painter who had sunk in the waters, throwing himself into the sea. And one has to see with what substance you have brought him back to us. What a novelist . . . even with your painter's hands!

And let Picasso say (if he dares) that he did not know Torres Campalans. Sure he knew him . . . he just does not remember.

Vicente Aleixandre. *Ínsula.* Oct., 1959, p. 2†

On some occasions, as in *Desired,* Aub will attempt a dehistoricized theatrical piece, in which he is able to give himself over freely to the needs of his characters, who become the center and axis of the action. Sometimes, as in *Married Life,* he allows his characters and their conflicts to have their own lives without having to depend on the political event that had stimulated the author in the first place. But we must admit that this is the exception, because in Aub's theater there is always a tension between him and dramatic "objectivity," between his political stance and the situation of the characters, a tension that is often resolved in only one act, perhaps because the work's structure— generally of one situation—permits the author to free his characters from the servitude that is characteristic of a long work. The one-acter permits a "compact" between the tyranny of the author and the needs of the characters, which becomes a lot more difficult to sustain in a long work, where the author is obliged to "hide" himself much more. . . .

Even in *San Juan,* the author speaks more about "what he sees or what he reads," than about "what is happening." In fact, it will be here where his work assumes a much more committed posture, and even the works of his youth acquire, in contrast, a new and expressive meaning. . . .

There are certain elements of Brecht in the work, but Aub avoids any one interpretation that is politically identifiable with one party, in order to raise his play to the level of humanistic protest, as a defense of all the persecuted of earth. From this commitment comes the essential trait of *San Juan:* its choral force, the wise harmony between the individual needs of the character and their communal situation as victims.

José Monleón. El teatro de Max Aub (Madrid,
Taurus, 1971), pp. 25, 55–56†

[Aub's] writing before the war shows him to have been faithful to the principle that art is an ingenious game which may distract us from a drab reality. Since the war, in exile in Mexico, Aub's enormous literary energy—which shows no sign of flagging as he approaches his seventies—has produced a torrent of plays, stories, novels, and essays on a rich variety of themes. But as a novelist, his central achievement is his great cycle of books about the Civil War, beginning with *Closed Battlefield* (1943; dated 1939) and ending with *Battlefield of Almond Trees* (1968), collectively entitled *The Magic Labyrinth.* . . . A fragmented technique of short passages—conversations, encounters, flashbacks, anecdotes—weaves the stories of many hundreds of characters into a dense and varied tapestry. Some of the characters appear briefly in a single scene or anecdote; others occupy the foreground for long periods; a few reappear repeatedly throughout the series, so that we come to know them well. Some are historical, some fictional, but most are both, for as Aub says in a direct authorial intervention in *Battlefield of*

Almond Trees, as far as his memories and his novels are concerned, the difference between real people and characters who have lived beside them in his imagination during the thirty years he has devoted to the cycle is a meaningless one. Moreover, the novels have no protagonist. The characters who appear most frequently are simply the ones whom Aub chooses to observe most closely as representative of attitudes and mentalities which offer insights into what the war was about. . . .

The Magic Labyrinth is not only indispensable reading for anyone who wants to fathom the psychological origins of the Spanish Civil War; it is also indisputably the most impressive work of literary art among the host of novels produced by the war.

The Magic Labyrinth is the finest achievement in Aub's immense literary output, but its fame has been at least temporarily eclipsed by that of *Jusep Torres Campalans* (1958). . . . It is an absorbing book, with detailed documentation, reproductions of some of the paintings, and serious reflections on art. But in spite of a photograph of Torres Campalans and Picasso together, it is wholly the product of Aub's own imagination and ingenuity. There was never any such painter. The book naturally led many people to believe that he had existed, and even, it is said, elicited reminiscences from some who claimed to have known him; but it is more than an elaborate hoax. In the first place it presents an extremely interesting account of the psychology of an unusual artist. Then its serious meditations on the function of art—which are not confined to painting—provide some indication of why Aub chose to write the book as a biographical study. If a Torres Campalans had really existed, his biography would still be a book, a work of literature, which is something quite different from the life of a man. The point is relevant to Aub's methods, and his interpolated comments, in the novels of *The Magic Labyrinth:* as many writers have realised since Aristotle, if a fiction contains a human truth, it may matter little whether or not the characters who embody it *also* lived real lives in the real world.

G. G. Brown. *A Literary History of Spain: The Twentieth Century* (New York, Barnes & Noble, 1972), pp. 136–38

[Aub's] theater, like Valle-Inclán's, has seen itself condemned to pallid readings. The present revival of Valle-Inclán's theater comforts us and gives us hope, but it is an overdue event that resolves nothing on the personal level. And that agonizing, personal area continues to be important to me: the bitter zone of suffering that is supposedly—and this I doubt—necessary. Although Aub's theater may achieve a brilliant vindication tomorrow, many of those who may praise him and many of those who do praise him now—will offer belated reparations. To have insulted yesterday in order to praise today . . . an old story.

What has happened? A theater that is difficult, too advanced for its times? A theater that has a theatricality unacceptable to most audiences until many years after the writing? Has that also been the problem of Max Aub?

Ahead of his times, like any worthwhile writer—it is undeniable that he has been so. But it is doubtful that this is the reason scarcely any of his works have been performed. Aesthetic daring more radical than his has succeeded in conquering the countercurrent of the prevailing taste. And even today, if the majority of the public do not yet accept the most excessive attempts of the new theater, numerous experimental groups force public opinion to acknowledge the quality of the oddest works. But the works of Max are not included in the repertory, because they are not known or because, perhaps, their rewards are still too subtle. . . .

But hesitant Europe has also missed the theater of this Spaniard, who ought to figure on the list of the most important writers of our time. And if Europe would recover him it would likewise do it belatedly. Let us not be disturbed by this: in this infinite wait there is an infinite benefit for anyone who is perceptive. We are not going to stop admiring or rereading the plays of Max Aub.

Antonio Buero Vallejo. CA. March–April, 1973,
pp. 65–66, 70†

The past, present and future will be an endless source of preoccupation for the characters in Aub's dramas. It is this preoccupation which will lend a nostalgic and reflective character to his work. However, the past, present and future are not disparate points on the scale of time, but, rather, form a continuum. The memories of the past which are continually present with the individual will determine his projection into the future. . . . It will become evident in Aub's plays, however, that a character's conception of the past, present and future depends on his attitude of commitment toward life. For one not committed, one unmoved to act upon his environment, "living memory" will be transformed into "dead memory." The past will be either a cause of paralyzing remorse, or else a comfortable haven in which to dwell inertly. For the committed person, on the other hand, the past, no matter what its content, will be a source of action, his raison d'être. . . .

This ambivalence in the perception of time is curiously matched by a seemingly imminent paradox within time itself. In an illusory fashion, it seems to pass quickly and at the same time, not pass at all. This particular idea is found in the return of a prisoner or exile. After being away from his normal environment for a lifetime, he must have the years reconstructed for him, yet in reality, nothing has actually changed. Very often the drama will impart the idea that time has stopped, that life has become paralyzed and its people incapable of moving just as a tree cannot free itself from its roots, in short, that life has become death. Time is involved in the debate between instinct and reason, intuition and history. The question will be raised as to whether it is wiser to approach the problems of humanity through intuition and instinct, attacking the situation at hand, rebelling against existing evils, or through a more intellectual approach wherein history, culture and tradition are taken into account.

In Aub's dramatic works there are nuances of the sense of time that escape definition. If a generalization were to be made, however, it would be that time, in its rigidity and resilience, invites man to contend with it. He attempts to fight its passing, yet resists its confinement and oppression. In brief, he wishes he were able to manipulate it.

Ángel A. Borrás. *Mosaic*. No. 3, 1975,
pp. 209–10

In *Major Theater* [a title given by Aub to the six works mentioned below], there is a constant concern for regaining a sense of dignity and for achieving a measure of freedom, no matter how small, in a senseless world. Aub, like Albert Camus, believed that man's greatness lies "in his decision to be stronger than his condition," and he brings before us an ethic of revolt in each of his plays. Carlos in *San Juan,* Samuel in *Married Life,* Margarita in *The Rape of Europa; or, Something Always Can Be Done,* Juan in *To Die By Closing Your Eyes,* Molina in *Heads and Tails,* and finally Hermann in *No* represent different manifestations of this ethic. Each of these personages achieves a degree of freedom by confronting his/her circumstances with the will and commitment necessary to overcome it. Each is free or liberated because he or she is a reflective, conscious individual of good faith who is aware of his or her personal and social responsibility. Aub contrasts these positive characters with the refugees who wander without purpose and with those individuals of bad faith. . . .

Aub's "historical dramas" call our attention to many who acquiesced to the forces that dehumanized, humiliated, and destroyed them and to the few who found meaning in their lives while contributing to the betterment of mankind by assuming full responsibility for their acts. Thus, *Major Theater,* much of which was published years before the existentialist playwrights began to write their plays, is both a condemnation of the self-defeating fatalists and a paean to those who call for action and show the way to personal liberty.

Eliot Glass. *LATR*. Autumn, 1978, p. 69

AYALA, FRANCISCO (1906–   )

Francisco Ayala's "The Bewitched" is something like a silent nightmare. Or better, it is something like an inextricable dream that is about to become a nightmare. . . . This story details a history of the useless, labyrinthine goings-on . . . in the court of Charles the Bewitched, the successor of Philip IV. . . . The worlds of Kafka and of Herman Melville are full of anguish; in Ayala's we perceive, under the wormlike agitation of its multitudes, a quiet and savage desperation. The silent scene that crowns the tale—the meeting with Charles the Bewitched, in a hidden chamber of the palace—is seen in the final pages and likewise in one of the first few pages; in this repetition there is something of the infinite mirror.

For its economy, its creativeness, the dignity of its language, "The Bewitched" is one of the most memorable stories in Hispanic literature.

Jorge Luis Borges. Sur. Dec., 1944, pp. 58–59†

When one finishes reading *Don Quixote* or *Moby Dick,* one begins to notice the directions taken by the *meaning,* and that they are independent from the original and essential line of the narrative. These books have a second life or larger meaning, defined by how much they *say* after the fact rather than what they actually did say. It is the halo or supernatural aura of truly lasting books. All this suggests to me Francisco Ayala's short novel [*The Tagus*]. . . . Lieutenant Santolalla, during the Spanish Civil War, in the middle of a routine search for grapes, comes face to face with a soldier from the opposing forces, whom he kills. All the absurdity, monstrousness, and stupidity of the war are latent in the telling of this casual episode, out of which will remain, like a payment due, the death of a man, his horrible rotting and post-mortem stench, which will pursue the gentle young lieutenant like an accusing shadow. Obsessed by the idea of that man killed by his hand, Santolalla goes about with his days of peace clouded by the memory and burned by the red-hot coal of the identity card of the soldier he killed, and who was, by chance, his countryman. . . . Once the narrative is over, its more important meanings begin to take over: this human life whose elimination was enough to poison with horror and guilt Santolalla's life had no importance for the dead man's family, whom the lieutenant assumed would be pained and aggrieved; true life shows its lack of accommodation to our false and sorry scale of values; and a character—much more broken than Santolalla—begins to emerge at the end of the narrative: the death itself of the dead man, a wandering ghost that now will never find a niche outside of the place where he lives in the conscience of the one who killed him. Many other consequences come to mind after finishing this admirable short novel; among others is a quotation from Mauriac: "It is out of habit that one gives infinite importance to the existence of a man."

Eduardo Mallea. Notas de un novelista (Buenos
Aires, Emecé, 1954), pp. 110–11†

The structure [of *A Dog's Death*] is that of a series of private pieces of correspondence and personal memoirs of the principal characters which have been acquired by Luis Pinedo, a crippled historian with great insight into the ills of his country. He is very conscious of the importance of the notes that he collects, and as he collects them he presents them to the readers of the novel in a consciously haphazard manner, reminding us from time to time that he is awaiting the occasion when he will be able to synthesize them in a coherent work.

This structural device of a historian putting notes together for his future use was an apt choice for Ayala; for to a great extent it blended his view of his society with a distinctive literary form. The apparent looseness of construction is in itself an imitation of the chaotic atmosphere out of which the book grew—a reflection of the state that it describes. The novel itself can thus be seen, as far as its construction is concerned, as an expression or a symbol of the reality that it represents.

Again, this mode of construction allows the author to remain entirely separated from his work and makes it stand by itself. The novel consequently gives an illusion of spontaneous creation: of being a loosely arranged compilation of incidents without the author's intervention.

Further, many of these letters and notes have been written by the characters themselves either as private pieces of correspondence or as personal memoirs. These writings serve as forms of interior monologues in the novel, providing access to the inner workings of the minds of the characters. This device, then, enables Ayala to present his characters fully and make them completely revealing of their thoughts. The contemporary Spanish-American novel has sometimes been criticized for a lack of sustained development and analysis of characters. Ayala, by a technique such as he uses here, brings a fresh and advanced contribution to the trend of the psychological novel in Spanish America. . . .

A Dog's Death is an important novel. More than a mere presentation of a society under a Spanish-American dictatorship and an implicit condemnation of the evils of dictators and dictatorships, it is a significant examination of a state of the human condition. The results of Ayala's study are alarming for their revelation of an absence of values that we are likely to regard as worthwhile in the very real society that the author has presented to us. Further, as far as its structure is concerned, it is an important Spanish-American novel since it is exemplary in effectively blending its psychological subject matter with an advanced and highly appropriate technique.

Keith Ellis. *Hispania.* May, 1960, pp. 223–25

It may be conceded that Mr. Ayala does not traduce reality, but will it be believed that *Death as a Way of Life* [*A Dog's Death*] is a comic novel? It is, though. Horribly comic, implacable, fascinating. The story is an imaginative paradigm of the fall of a dictator, and the coming to power in his place of the usual obscurely connected junta of military and civil personalities. It is told by a cripple whose infirmity has kept him out of harm's way, free to pursue his self-imposed task of collecting documents for an eventual history of his era. The narrator's malice and literary pedantry tell us as much about the state of the nation as the documents he quotes, and prepare us for the *coup de théâtre* that, occurring on the very last page, gives a final ironic twist to the Dostoevskian succession of crises that makeup the tale.

The comparison with the Russian writer is a measure of the intensity of imagination displayed in *Death as a Way of Life*. Francisco Ayala chooses in this novel to work on a narrower compass than we think of in connection with Dostoevsky, but the shock of his breathless peripeties, managed with the same uncanny stagecraft, and the strain of brutal and despairing humor, suggest an unexpected affinity between the Spaniard and the Slav. The comparison, of course, has its limits. For one thing, Mr. Ayala is sane. His conceptions, for all their complexity, are articulated with a Latin clarity; in this sense, he could offer no greater contrast to the creative madness and muddle of Dostoevsky.

In any case, *Death as a Way of Life* seems to me to represent quite astonishing literary powers. . . . Mr. Ayala's wit transmutes itself naturally into style, for his gifts include the linguistic ones that we have almost given up hoping for from our writers. Even his meditated grossness is graceful—as when he sums up by *"sursum corda"* the reaction of a young arriviste to the proffered charms of his leader's wife. And this example of politico-sexual insight is one of the keys to Ayala's literary imagination, for he is preoccupied with the way in which appetites relate to action, and desire takes its crooked course toward realization.

Emile Capouya. *SatR*. June 13, 1964, p. 31

The novel of Ayala is fundamentally an intellectual novel, in the fullest sense of the word. This does not presuppose, as many assume, a coldness, a lack of life, dehumanized abstraction, etc. In the novels of Ayala, there are passions, dramas, flesh and blood, pained or hope-filled humanity. But there is also a conscious, reflective, fully human vision; a richness of techniques and of perspectives; in short, an opening onto the general human themes . . . that gives his narratives a very full dimension.

All this makes the tone of Francisco Ayala's works different from the usual tone of the postwar Spanish novel. . . . Because of his intellectual makeup and his biographical circumstances, Ayala clearly escapes its limitations. . . .

The novelist does not operate in the abstract, but with his eyes fully open to the reality of the contemporary world. Therefore, he is preoccupied with eroticism, for example. . . . In this "world of degeneration," the only salvation possible is "the moral revolution." This is the great theme of the narrator Francisco Ayala: *the human condition, today*. . . . Or if you prefer, moralization by means of tragicomedy. To this theme he dedicates himself with all his intelligence, his lucidity, and his creative capacity. . . . In the deepest part of his work, there is, of course, corruption, but there is also a possibility (in spite of everything) of purity, a possibility of a little bit of a fresh, tremulous, and weak hope.

Andrés Amorós. Prologue to Francisco Ayala,
Obras narrativas completas (Madrid, Aguilar,
1969), pp. 89–90, 92†

Far from being "odd pieces from a broken mirror," as the author claims in an editorial postscript, these narrative sketches [in *The Garden of Delights*] have been disposed in a structurally cohesive whole through which Ayala presents us with the two sides of his world-vision.

Part One, "The Devil World," is a bitter satire of an absurd and cruel world, evoked in literary equivalents of Hieronymus Bosch or Goya's pictorial nightmares (the book's general title is borrowed from the Bosch triptych reproduced on its cover). . . .

The book's second part, "Happy Days," represents the positive side of life seen through the wisdom of maturity. It is clearly auto-biographical, beginning with distant childhood evocations, memories of student days in Munich, glimpses of a few passionate love affairs and more serene present-day tableaux with emphasis on the small pleasures of everyday life. Love is presented throughout as the only real, if fleeting, value, and the constant focus on familiar works of art as the only means to recall and relive past happinesses.

The Garden of Delights is a nostalgic but deeply human book. Its thematic content is adequately summarized on the cover's flyleaf as "crepuscular disillusionment before the seduction of earthly appearances." Above all, the book offers varied examples of Ayala's extraordinary prose. The author is, along with Camilo José Cela, Spain's most accomplished stylist of today. One marvels at his versatility and complete mastery of his medium. Some of these sketches are only half a page long, yet, in just one paragraph, Ayala can create a convincing atmosphere which totally captivates the reader.

John Crispin. *BA*. Summer, 1972, pp. 452–53

[Ayala's] pre-war writing is characterized by a dedicated aestheticism subjected to a keen intelligence, and the result is fiction similar to that of Jarnés, of minimal anecdotal or descriptive interest, pursuing brilliant metaphors with tireless ingenuity. Such writing is out of fashion, and Ayala himself has spoken unkindly of this early work in retrospect. But *Hunter at Dawn* is a very impressive achievement for a twenty-three-year-old. Ayala, however, spent 1929 and 1930 in the sinister atmosphere of the Berlin of those years. What he observed there, and in Spain and the rest of the world in the dark years that followed, changed his attitude to art sharply. His fiction struck him as frivolous, and he wrote no more of it for nearly twenty years, turning his talents instead to what remains an important part of his writing, essays and books on sociological, philosophical, and literary topics. Like most of his fellow-writers in exile, he has earned his living principally as a university teacher.

When he returned to creative fiction with *The Usurpers* (1949), it was a different kind from his pre-war work. . . . The "usurpation" in question is that which always occurs, according to Ayala, when one man seeks to subjugate another to his will. Ayala treats this universal immortality from different points of view in finely written fables, writing now out of indignation and pessimism, but still with intelligence and artistry.

G. G. Brown. *A Literary History of Spain: The Twentieth Century* (New York, Barnes & Noble, 1972), pp. 140–41

[Ayala] examines the passions that come into play in man's conduct toward his fellow man. His fictional characters find themselves situated in a world of values in crisis, troubled by social pressures, the lust for power which curtails freedom, the weight of time and the certainty of death, and by their own human weaknesses. Man's vulnerability is communicated by the practical jokes and deceptions to which his characters often fall victim. Man is also the victim of his physical demands which betray him, sometimes with comic consequences, but the reader senses the author's commiseration with his creatures even though the world around them may seem cruel and insensitive. There is an atmosphere of timelessness in Ayala's fictions, enhanced by his consistent utilization of literary precedents in the form of explicit or veiled allusions to Spanish and universal masterworks or by the re-working of "borrowed" themes previously exploited by authors of past ages. Thus, the novel inevitably acquires novelty in the original configuration of essentially limited plots determined by each author's circumstances, experience, purpose, and style.

Ayala favors the first-person narrative in most of his fictions and he enjoys teasing the reader into suspecting autobiographical implication which may indeed be there. It becomes virtually impossible to determine the degree to which actual experience has been artistically disguised or to find the real "I." The only alternative is to accept the narrator as fictitious, thus allowing the author to protect himself from the probing reader. Many of his narrators tend to be callous or of negative traits, which in itself discourages ready identification with the author.

The stories and novels . . . are open-ended in that they are deliberately ambiguous. Like life itself, Ayala's inventions present puzzles and enigmas which cannot be considered fully resolved even after critical analysis.

Other constants in these fictions are the use of negative and occa-sionally scabrous materials with moral connotations such as frequent animal imagery suggestive of man's degradation in certain situations; the presence of humor, not gratuitous, but rooted rather deeply in irony; and constant allusions to Spanish and universal art, including literature, painting, sculpture, and music.

In Ayala's works, the reader finds himself confused by multiple perspectives of events and by the direction of vision vertiginously up, down, and around, close up and far away. Our author's expert manipula-tion of point of view is just one facet of his very polished narrative technique. Proper names and word play are vehicles of subtle com-ments, and it is this attention to detail that makes even the briefest selection extremely dense and open to intensive analysis. It is apparent that for Ayala the creative process involves careful artistic elaboration, in part representing conscious awareness of his craft, but in large measure depending upon sheer natural talent.

Estelle Irizarry. *Francisco Ayala* (Boston,
Twayne, 1977), pp. 147–48

The entire second part of *The Bottom of the Glass* consists of news-paper clippings, whose thematic function is to accuse the protagonist of a crime he has not committed by means of an insidious manipulation of public opinion. Parts I and III of the novel form two ironic and par-odistic perspectives of the narrator in as much as he is (1) an observer of the world around him and (2) an explorer of his own inner self (in reality a parody of the confessional and self-revelatory genre). If within these perspectives there prevails the focus of a stunted intelligence guided by self-serving, vain, and pathetic sentiments, the journalistic discourse is enlivened by the calculated and deceiving objectivity of the impersonal language. The voice of the protagonist emits the com-monplaces of daily speech and of popular traditional topics (apoth-egms, proverbs, clichés, etc.), while a formalized, pseudorational, and diabolical language takes over in the journalistic prose. The personal formulaic speech of José Lino clashes with the impersonal, institu-tionalized rhetoric represented by the daily press. The language of Lino as well as that of the newspaper *El Comercio* are formulaic and inauth-entic, incapable of capturing and transmitting reality, such as it is, or as the author permits us to glimpse it. José Lino's distortion of reality is due to vanity and stupidity; that of the newspaper to the conscious Machiavellian manipulation of the group with its vested interests that publishes it. Both languages, hollow and false, mask the moral emp-tiness of society.

Thomas Mermall. *Las alegorías del poder en
Francisco Ayala* (Madrid, Fundamentos, 1984),
pp. 106–7†

AZORÍN (pseudonym of José Martínez Ruiz, 1873– 1967)

The Confessions of a Little Philosopher is . . . like an ablution and purification of the literary *I*, like a baptism of a catechumen who hesitated a long time on the threshold, held back by old prejudices, before penetrating into the interior of the temple. . . .

In *The Confessions of a Little Philosopher* the evocative power and the facility for reproducing the unequivocal vision of daily life . . . are achieved in all their splendor. One might say that this most recent and admirable work of the analyst of *The Will* is outstanding for two reasons: the complete possession of a style and the faithful reproduction of reality. . . .

To achieve [these], Martínez Ruiz has used the last [literary] resort that remains after everything else has been used up: simplicity. . . . Upon reading this work, I think that the ideal of the modern artist should be to say complex things in a simple language. . . . Martínez Ruiz possesses this secret of simplicity.

Andrés González Blanco. *Los contemporáneos,*
Vol. I (Paris, Garnier Hermanos, [1907]),
pp. 7–8, 11–13†

In Azorín appears more starkly than in the other individualists the dreary philosophical background of the end of the century. It was overlaid by idealism in [Ángel] Ganivet, by spiritual aspiration in [Miguel de] Unamuno, and in [Pío] Baroja by a passion for action which revealed itself to him first as man's natural participation in a world of struggle, and afterwards as a means of escaping the importunities of thought. Azorín has not even this recourse. In him, furthermore, the power of philosophy is reinforced by the fact that he, far more than the others, lives his real life in books, and has developed a curious dualism of thinking and then finding his thought in some past writer. . . .

Most of Azorín's contribution to the literature of the will is found in a series of novels: *The Will, Antonio Azorín,* and *The Confessions of a Little Philosopher,* which form a detailed study of the *abulia* [lack of will], characteristic of youth of Azorín's own time and type, an *abulia* . . . less purely Spanish, of less exaltation and more depression, most of all, an *abulia* proceeding from an excess of rather than a lack of thought.

One fact which the course of Spanish will, both individual and national, seems to have impressed itself upon Azorín from the first: its tendency to anticlimax.

Doris King Arjona. *Revue Hispanique*. Dec.,
1928, pp. 632–33

Félix Vargas begins a new trajectory in the usual aesthetic orbit of Azorín. This book resembles his earlier ones very little. In *Félix Vargas* that lyrical plasma that nourishes, with elegant romanticism, the author of *The Villages* and *The Castilian Soul* is not lacking. The solitary tone of the text is, as it could not help but be, very like Azorín. But its structure, its plan, the psychological development of the topic, and, above all, the incorporation of certain extra-literary elements into the novel, give this work the unquestionable air of something very new. It is something that has been long sought after in the laboratories of the Vanguard, and which Azorín is able to bring into his book.

It is evident that Azorín does not propose to definitively resolve what we might label the "cinematic-imagist" question of modern literature in *Félix Vargas*. . . .

The whole novel appears to be made up of movable pieces: characters, topics, descriptions, and dialogues. These pieces never maintain a permanent position in the architectural space of the novel, but, rather, they vary at each climax of situation and rhythm, becoming dissolved in shadows or in touches of light; or rather suddenly taking on form with photogenic energy in a tangible body. . . . The trick consists of a clean visual maneuvering of distances and foci, of planes and volumes.

Nevertheless, after "attending" the complete showing of *Félix Vargas,* one does not remember the purely external optical effects and fleeting richness of the screen, but rather the solid sensation of reality: reality (in literature) with all its consequences of argumentation, direct vision, and possibilities of prose.

Antonio Espina. RO. Jan., 1929, pp. 114, 116†

The psychological and artistic duality of love of the old and eager interest in the modern prevents the definitive affiliation of Azorín with André Breton's group—even though one of Azorín's books is entitled *Surrealism*.

Of course we comprehend the atmosphere of pure imagination, of dreams, of intuitions and fantasies in that work, which Azorín called a pre-novel. But Azorín would not admit—nor would he be able to share—the work of those who intended to "désensibiliser l'univers" [desensitize the universe]. Neither does it appear to me that he hands himself over to "automatic writing," as the surrealist revolutionists did—even though he frequently excludes the verb from the sentence in *Surrealism,* or puts in just the infinitive form. Azorín does not let his mind rest in a passive state so that images may float up spontaneously from the subconscious. To the contrary: he appears to be dominated by reason.

José A. Balseiro. Nosotros (Buenos Aires).
Aug., 1937, p. 371†

In *Castile,* the predominant theme—the eternal return—is of a Nietzschean origin, and Azorín repeatedly employs the technique of describing the same scene at different times; sounds play an important role in the scene. The sound of the clapper of the windmill and the flute music are repeated through the generations. . . .

This theme of eternal return appears again when the bells of an old Castilian city ring in the silence of the night; the city's voice, which is expressed in them, proclaims the same things now that it has said centuries ago and that it will say in the future.

Time's continuity is expressed not only through the bells, but also in the old clock. The clock has belonged to the family for six generations, and its tick-tock has sounded impassively while children were born and old people died, thus uniting in time, as a symbol of continuity, all these beloved beings. But the old clock had stopped working; the hours no longer sounded, and it had to be sent to be fixed, thus breaking the sense of historical continuity.

Nonetheless, the continuity of the bells does not end. The Spanish bells are not subjected to the limitations of time or space. When Azorín hears the bells of Monóvar, he is uncertain about their identity. They could be the bells of any Spanish city. The chain of bells unites him with the chain of ancestors who created Spain. Since the thirteenth century, the crystalline bells of the convents have been ringing in the silent night. . . .

Marguerite C. Rand. *Castilla en Azorín*
(Madrid, Revista de Occidente, 1948),
pp. 710–11†

The novelistic substance of *Doña Inés* is very small. Basically, it is the story of a kiss: the one that Doña Inés and the poet Diego give each other at the door of the Segovia Cathedral in 1840. That kiss . . . is a cosmic event. All the previous slow pages [of the volume] have been leading up to it. . . . And that kiss provokes magical commotions in Segovia, in the book, and in Azorín's writings. Owing to it . . . Azorín discovers nothing less than movement and with it the fullness of the novel.

The internal movement is understood. When the four lips touch . . . all Segovia is excited in a violent swirl, a furious and captivating wind. The rhythm of the work accelerates. Azorín's prose abandons its slow pace and becomes electrified. . . . Isn't this like a film? Azorín, scriptwriter and film director, discovers movement at the age of fifty-two.

What can he do next? . . . A ballet in Azorín? There it is . . . in chapter XXXIX of *Doña Inés,* and all it needs is music and feet eager to dance.

Julián Marías. *Ínsula.* Oct. 15, 1953, p. 9†

The theme and ending of *Old Spain* are analogous to those of Azorín's later play, *The Guerrilla:* love is the force which can unite a couple if they are willing to modify the beliefs that they have formulated as citizens of different nations with conflicting ideas. . . . *Old Spain* must be regarded as a series of evocations in which the author once again brings forth his subjective treatment of "el paisaje" [the landscape], his love for Spain, his "ensueño" [dream] and "quijotismo" [Quixotism], his hope for Spain's future progress, and his conception of time—all of these characteristics of the members of the Generation of 1898. . . .

Joaquín represents the author's quixotic, ideal aspiration to bring material advancement to Spain. Likewise, Azorín's portrayal of Castilian landscape is an element of his "ensueño," his dream of what Spain might be in the future.

Old Spain, then, is mainly the continuation of themes which run throughout our author's works, and is, again, an excellent example of the essential unity in Azorín. There is, however, one instance wherein Joaquín's words are indicative of the concept which surrealist dramas present—the significance of dreams. . . .

In *Old Spain* the author has followed closely the dramatic credo expressed in his articles of criticism. In this play everything depends upon dialogue. Very few stage directions are given—in fact the stage appears almost bare in all three acts. He has given the actors and the director ample opportunity for individual interpretation. Each actor must find motivation for his personal art in the dialogue. The director must formulate his own scenic recourses. All of this is consistent with his idea that actors and directors must study a play thoroughly in order to give an effective performance to an audience. The author also leaves the lighting to the discretion of the director.

Lawrence A. LaJohn. *Azorín and the Spanish
Stage* (New York, Hispanic Institute, 1961),
pp. 113–15

The treatment of the problem of time-space supplies the key to the trajectory of Azorín's novels. First, he faces the problem of evolving a synthesis out of a world in chaotic conflict, of creating form out of a time-space which has no form. With this heterogeneous material he proceeds through chronological retrogression to the attempt to balance finite and infinite. In the second stage space-time is counterposed to space-timelessness, the sensory worldly to the mystic other-worldly. This all-embracing span cannot be achieved literally, since it is interminable in its extent, but only schematically, by an elliptical method that dispenses with detailed transitions. This is . . . the elimination of logical concatenations rendered possible by the suppression of reason. The bracketing of real existence, now transcended into the psychically uninhibited, alogical fusion of all possible planes of time and space, including the infinite, results in a space-time conscious of itself, as the novel is conscious of its own elaboration. Finally, in the third stage, a new time-space continuum is *created*. It is no longer the revivification of past time retraced in memory nor the elliptical bracketing of time and space, but a purely esthetic elaboration, neither real nor unreal, yet both, wrought out of the artistic material provided by the two preceding experiences. It is the hypothetical, verisimilar world of time-space that is art, that simulates reality while retaining the purely virtual quality of ideality that it inherits from its earlier emancipation from contingent reality, a time-space that has both the dimensions of apparent actuality and the unreal, ethereal atmosphere of the oneiric.

The evolution of the changing concept of time-space is confirmed by a significant stylistic detail: the variance in the predominance of certain verb tenses. In the initial stages of retrogression in which the author seeks to capture the past in the present the most characteristic tense is the present perfect in a particular use which Azorín has made so much his own that it has become a sort of trademark.

Leon Livingstone. *PMLA.* March, 1962, p. 129

The evaluation of a writer is complete only when the critic has found the theme that underlies the whole literary production—the vital theme. In the case of Azorín it seems as unjust to condemn his critical work for its lack of facts or objectivity as it does to criticize his novels for the lack of plots, since it tends to overlook an explanation of his vital theme. After the analysis of his critical production, it is clear that he was trying to do the same thing in, let us say, *Castile* as he was in *Spanish Readings*. Yet one is a collection of descriptions of *paisaje* [landscape] and the other is a collection of essays on Spanish literature. The theme of all of Azorín's production, it is now obvious, whether he is writing novels or evaluating literature, was a definition of the Spanish spirit. And we find this spirit either by seeking the elements and sentiments that occur over and over again in the national literature or by extracting the essence of the environment which has been a determining factor in the formation of his spirit.

For Azorín, then, the true *castizo* [pure spirit] is a love for the concrete realities of daily existence and the melancholy that results from the consciousness that time destroys these realities. No writer in the history of Spanish literature . . . has been able to escape the *dolorido sentir* [painful feeling]. This is, for Azorín, the "tragic sense of life," and it is what forced him from the political and social struggle. It is the cause of the Spanish *abulia* [lack of will].

E. Inman Fox. *Azorín as a Literary Critic* (New
York, Hispanic Institute, 1962), pp. 161–62

Structurally and stylistically *The Nonpresent Gentleman* depends on the struggle of the creative artist to write and the ensuing psychological and technical problems. Through the creative powers of effective memory, evocative imagination, and his creative sensitivity, Félix Vargas struggles ceaselessly to counteract the ravages of time, the inevitable loss of memory and images. By his self-abandonment to his work, Félix, at the risk of insanity, achieves a strange form of existence beyond the ordinary bonds of time and space, thus becoming a *caballero inactual* [nonpresent gentleman]. The story of Félix Vargas and all his psychological and technical problems is enclosed with in the larger scheme of his creator, Azorín. . . . For Azorín, the complex amalgam of old and new techniques in *The Nonpresent Gentleman* grew naturally out of his successfully attained goals, which were: (1) to depict the creative process in its formative stages (the struggle); (2) to depict thought in its raw, formative state; (3) to seize the inner essence of things; (4) to capture the fleeting sensation of the present; and (5) to create the illusion of *inactualidad,* or timelessness, which was achieved through the registering of Félix Vargas' supra-temporal, supra-spatial, and, at times, even supra-sensory thought processes.

Robert E. Lott. The Structure and Style of
Azorín's "El caballero inactual" (Athens, Ga.,
University of Georgia Press, 1963), p. 70

From *Tomás Rueda* and later statements, we get a clear enough idea why the Licenciate Vidriera became not only Azorín's preferred Spanish myth among those that he chose to remodel, but also a genuine motif, or rather, a bundle of basic motifs. Tomás is the contemplative little boy that Azorín was in Monóvar and at the school in Yecla. He is the industrious student that Azorín was in his youth, an unceasing reader, a tracer of old books, a defender of justice and the regeneration of the homeland. He is the one who is dubious of indirect learning from books and becomes, as Azorín did, set on direct, vital learning: trips to Spanish villages and the countries of Europe. And if Tomás, upon falling ill, changes into the Licenciate Vidriera, distant and clairvoyant, Azorín at the time he was writing *Tomás Rueda* was increasing his own sensitivity to such an extreme withdrawal that Ortega in 1924 would refer to his "crystalline shell." . . .

If the mythic character can be defined as a fictional figure who embodies a fecund human truth, or rather, one that is susceptible to variations in form but that in its basic aspect has a universal and constant importance, Tomás Rueda was, for Azorín, a mythic character to whom he felt the closest. . . .

Of the five motifs that are joined in the mythic character Tomás Rueda (boy, student, traveler, sick man, the separated one) the only one that Azorín invents and adds to Cervantes's text [of *The Licentiate Vidriera*] is the first: the boy. It is the one that receives the greatest amount of space, if we except the fifth one, which exists through almost all of the story.

Gonzalo Sobejano. CHA. Oct.-Nov., 1968,
pp. 244–45†

Azorín's fascination with the concept of "accident" is clearly expressed in the prologues to *White on Blue* and *To Ponder and Consider,* as well as in a great number of other stories that are equally representative of all his literary stages. Life presents a series of coincidences that have a profound and decisive meaning. Thanks to a coincidence one can become rich, fall in love, or save a life. But at the same time, Azorín shows little faith in accidents: something seems to be an accident to us only because we cannot examine it in depth. There are mysterious and impenetrable areas in which the threads of human destiny are spun and woven, but our limited senses cruelly prevent us from capturing these realities. Our universe is closed, and we are enchained by our incapacity to cross its boundaries. One of Azorín's characters expresses the same thing when he says, "My power of imagination does not go beyond perception!" What seems to us a mere coincidence is, in reality, something preestablished by unknown forces. Thus, our lives conform to a plan that is already determined and over which we have no control. Azorín's philosophical perspective and his acceptance of the complexities and demands of life are strongly marked by [this] fundamental belief, which is repeated over and over again. . . .

But Azorín does not limit himself to abstract statements or generalizations. On the contrary, he attempts to show the intervention of these forces in specific lives. Thus, his belief in a preestablished destiny has a romantic interpretation in "The Butterfly and the Flame." . . . Blanca Durán, his sensitive protagonist, is destined to find death in a silent plaza in León, and any resistance to her fate will be useless. . . . A series of coincidences delay her trip to León, in an attempt to impede the course of her destiny. . . . Blanca sets out and takes her trip to León, and, with it, her prescribed destiny.

Mirella Servodidio. *Azorín, escritor de cuentos*
(New York, Las Américas, 1971), pp. 163–64†

It is not without significance that Martínez Ruiz, who as an angry young man had not been a favourite of the public, was not long after the publication of *The Confessions of a Little Philosopher* to become so popular that he was actually to complain about his newly gained popularity—a popularity derived perhaps from the public's weariness at the soul-searching of intellectuals in the years immediately following the disaster of 1898. After the anguished and angry cries proffered by Martínez Ruiz and some of his companions, it is not surprising that they took to Azorín's benignly ironic love of Spain and its culture.

But it would be a mistake to over-emphasize the change that took place in Martínez Ruiz. Though he might seem in *The Confessions of a Little Philosopher* to have become a transformed person . . . this is not completely true. He may no longer have pined for "la gloria" [glory], but then, as he had it, it was only natural that his preoccupation with it should disappear. It is interesting to remember his epilogue to *The Villages,* "Epilogue in 1960" . . . where Azorín describes ironically how a certain man one day comes across a book which once belonged to Azorín and wonders who this unknown person could possibly have been. . . . If Azorín ceased being worried about being famous, he never altogether relinquished his preoccupation with social reform. He continued to indulge in politics and from time to time he still protested against conditions in Spain. Finally, he never rid himself of the moods of pessimism which had beset him so violently at the turn of the century; the only difference is that these moods became milder and were sometimes tinged with ironic resignation.

M. D. van Biervliet. FMLS. Oct., 1972, p. 303

Concomitant with his readings of the eighteenth century, Azorín was engaged in the problems of his own time. He did not fail to see that unique parallelism existing between the two centuries, which, of course, further increased his interest and his selectivity with regard to eighteenth-century writers and their writings. Azorín perceived in both centuries politico-socio-economic and cultural retrogression. He saw groups of men in the two eras, superior to the mediocrity about them, who preached a reform movement which involved education, the sciences, liberalization of Church and government, and openness to foreign influences as the principal means for achieving their goals. He witnessed the beginnings of a renaissance in both centuries not only in the social, but in the cultural as well. Because of his perception of this parallelism between the two centuries, he began to use the eighteenth century as an inspiration and as a call to arms for reform. He quoted eighteenth-century authors as authorities on twentieth-century subjects, seeing them as meaningful, and even more meaningful, for today as they were in their own time. He even perceived a cause-effect of evolutionary relationship between the two centuries, claiming that seeds planted in that era were only now beginning to bear fruit. Motivated by this mutual reflection of himself, his generation, and his century, in the eighteenth century, he explored at some length and with some detail certain aspects of [Nicolás] Moratín, [Padre] Isla, [Fray] Feijóo, [Gaspar Melchor de] Jovellanos, and [José] Cadalso.

John A. Catsoris. Azorín and the Eighteenth
Century (Madrid, Plaza Mayor, 1972),
pp. 112–13

Cervantes; or, The Enchanted House (1931) also emphasizes the relationship between the Quijote theme and Pirandellism. The play-within-the-play represents the delirium of a poet, except for the first scene and the epilogue which treats the manner of preparing the audience for a play based on the subconscious adventures of a poet. The poet, Victor, is the protagonist of the play-within-the play and he drinks a potion to increase his imaginative power, which in act 3 enables him to visit Cervantes. Don Quijote also arrives. . . . "Don Quijote," however, is only a neighbor, Jacinto, who has served as a model for Cervantes's creation and who has also taken on some of Don Quijote's characteristics through force of suggestion. . . .

Thus, several of Pirandello's techniques and ideas appear, but they are transformed into something quite different—the poet's illness caused him to withdraw into himself, enabling him to discover in his subconscious the true essence of his being. He has found a synthesis of the past and the present and the end of the play calls for a forward surge toward a new world. . . .

Angelita (1930), a manifestation of Azorín's preoccupation with time, is his most completely Pirandellian play—it is almost a sampler of Pirandello's techniques and ideas. Azorín calls attention to the theater as such through the use of theater-within-the-theater methods. After Angelita has turned her magic ring twice to make two years pass, she suddenly finds that she is the wife of a playwright, Carlos, who raves about the difficulties he is having in producing his play. In *Angelita,* as in Pirandello's plays, the simultaneous presence of several planes of reality is an indispensable element. Carlos complains that the leading lady is not interpreting properly a scene in which she is to pretend she does not know her husband. The situation in Carlos' own life (although he does not know it) is similar to the scene in the play.

Wilma Newberry, *The Pirandellian Mode in*
Spanish Literature (Albany, State University of
New York Press, 1973), p. 107

Azorín found support for his own ideas and some literary stability in his readings of French publications, which began early in his life and continued until his death in 1967. The formative period of his activity thus offers abundant material about French culture that permits a much more complete comprehension of his later works. The literary style, structure, technique, and ideology of the works written after 1901 stand out in higher relief against the background of his early readings in French; ideas and techniques that might appear incidental acquire their true importance only in relation to Azorín's absorbing interest in France and its civilization. . . .

This obstinate and singular interest in France gives him a unique place among the members of the Generation of '98. No other author of this group appears to have turned to France, as he did, in a relationship of creative tension that served to strengthen and define his literary ideology. Azorín's contribution to the Europeanizing tendencies of his generation is almost completely limited to his contact with France, and the awareness of this contact is, in turn, essential for a complete comprehension of his works.

James H. Abbot. *Azorín y Francia* (Madrid,
Seminarios y Ediciones, 1973), pp. 197–98†

During the years 1925 to 1931, José Martínez Ruiz . . . experienced a cycle of renewal in his creative life. Certain themes which had previously appeared in his works became more prevalent and better developed. New ones appeared. It is highly possible that Azorín's esthetic theories may have been influenced by his reading of Marcel Proust's *À la recherche du temps perdu,* a work which the Spanish novelist read and which he significantly commented on in "The Art of Proust" from *Walking and Thinking.* Through their narrators both Proust and Azorín ponder the question of what a novel is and what it should attempt to do. In the case of Azorín there is no single aesthetic theory which prevails. Advancing first one and then another, he experiments with the form of the novel. His basic plan during his experimental period seems to be to reveal the creative act in its unfinished state and to provide an opening through which the reader may observe the novel in the process of becoming.

Lawrence B. Joiner. *SAB.* May, 1974, p. 42

Salvadora de Olbena reaffirms the superior truth of fiction. In Chapter 3 the author announces that up to this point he has been a historian, but from now on he will be a novelist, for the novel is the domain of the "true truth." He warns the reader not to be surprised by certain peculiarities of language and action which he will encounter in the pages that lie ahead, explaining that the artist's view of what is "natural" is quite different from the historian's.

Azorín utilizes narrative perspectivism to demonstrate the limited nature of human intelligence and the relativity of knowledge. The fact that man cannot decipher the enigma of the universe is symbolized by the author's inability to determine the reasons for the supposed falling-out between Salvadora and her relative Don Juan Pimentel.

Recognizing the limitations of the intellect, Azorín's attitude is one of skepticism with regard to the possibility of absolute knowledge. Man, he concludes, is condemned to partial vision, limited to his own particular viewpoint. Amid "universal uncertainty," the most he can achieve is the knowledge that he knows nothing.

It is only in recent years that Azorín's importance as a novelist has begun to be recognized, and there is still a tendency on the part of a number of critics to regard his novels with a certain disdain. Implicit in much of their criticism is the notion that a work which does not adhere to traditional narrative formulae is undeserving of the term "novel." Azorín, however, deliberately rejected the nineteenth-century canon. For him the novel is not a closed but an open form in which discussions of intellectual and aesthetic questions play an important role. As a matter of fact, theorizing about the novel, reflections on the problems of literary creation, and views of the artist at work—often seen conceiving or elaborating the very composition we are reading—are fundamental components of his narratives.

Kathleen Glenn. *Azorín (José Martínez Ruiz)*
(Boston, Twayne, 1981), pp. 132, 133, 136

BAREA, ARTURO (1897–1957)

If some Russian writer were at this moment to produce a book of reminiscences of his childhood in 1900, it would be difficult to review it without mentioning the fact that Soviet Russia is now our ally against Germany, and in the same way it is impossible to read *The Forge* without thinking at almost every page of the Spanish Civil War. In fact there is no direct connection, for the book deals only with Señor Barea's early youth and ends in 1914. . . . One seems to hear the thunder of future battles somewhere behind Señor Barea's pages, and it is as a sort of prologue to the civil war, a picture of the society that made it possible, that his book is most likely to be valued. . . .

There are no half-tones in the Spain that Señor Barea is describing. Everything is happening in the open, in the ferocious Spanish sunlight. It is the straightforward corruption of a primitive country, where the capitalist is openly a sweater, the official always a crook, the priest an ignorant bigot or a comic rascal, the brothel a necessary pillar of society. . . .

The Forge is not primarily a political book, however. It is a fragment of autobiography, and we may hope that others will follow it, for Señor Barea has had a varied and adventurous life. He has travelled widely, he has been both worker and capitalist, he took part in the civil war and he served in the Riff War [in Morocco] under General Franco. If the Fascist powers have done no other good, they have at least enriched the English-speaking world by exiling all their best writers.

George Orwell. *Horizon*. Sept., 1941,
pp. 214–17

The twentieth-century writers hover over their work like nervous mothers, and if they write about themselves, they hover over their own personalities. They exert ruthless control over their work, and allow it little spontaneity or internal development. . . .

To this contemporary tendency, Arturo Barea is a refreshing exception. Though he has written an autobiography, in which form one expects the writer's personality to be central, the I of *[The Forging of a Rebel]* is its least important figure. Things happen to him; his senses register; but he neither manipulates his past nor attempts to give it retrospective order. He merely allows his laden memory to flow freely. The center of the book then becomes a city, Madrid; and since the twentieth-century history of Madrid reflects the transformations of Spanish civilization—the never completed transition to modernity so

painful in backward countries—what would otherwise be a mere atom-
ized and indiscriminate sequence of recollection acquires more general
validity.

Even when writing about his private concerns, as in the movingly
scrupulous description of his neurotic paralysis before the issues thrust
upon him by the 1936 civil war, Barea succeeds in making them seem a
symbolic fraction of the tragedy which struck Spain and Europe. The
result is a book fringeing on the first rate, a work of social autobiography which, if not history itself, contains the ores from which history is
fused, and which bears a palpable, sensuous quality seldom present in
formal historical writings. . . .

Reading this massive work, one is reminded of an Elder Breughel
with its movement of differentiated but not thoroughly individualized
figures in which no attempt is made to accentuate but in which the
action is so inviting and warm that the spectator finds himself merged
with its context. Much of the same sympathetic inclusion is effected by
Barea's book, which lacks only that sense of purposeful control that
gives a Breughel its unity. And that is where Barea pays for his greatest
weakness: his lack of concern with ideas. Absence of self-consciousness permits a rich recollection, but the selectivity essential to
form demands a highly trained intelligence as well.

If Spain is vivid in the book, Barea is dim. Between his personal
history and the movement of the book there is a disturbing lack of
harmony. At each crucial juncture of his life, the book blacks out. At
one moment a child, the next a man; at one moment apolitical, the next
a socialist. The personal biography is like a series of jerky slides from
which the decisive ones have been omitted. But the book is redeemed
by its vision of Spain's tragedy, by now a symbol of our age.

Irving Howe. *PR*. Summer, 1947, pp. 310–11

The Broken Root deals with a modest Spanish bank clerk, a refugee in
London, who returns to Madrid after ten years. . . . Neither the family
nor the country are what they used to be to the hero. The disillusionment is painful but the exile has had so many in his life that he is not
surprised and hardly complains. He realizes that his conscience has
matured in contact with a liberal culture while his family has been
degenerating in the atmosphere of abjection. That is all and it is enough
to create a dramatic tension which covers up the trivial in the way the
author chooses such and such a fact with allegorical intention. The best
quality in the book is its simplicity and absence of sophistication.
Facing the horror of the facts the narrative has soothing and calming
innocence which makes the argument more persuasive. The fusion of
the autobiographical with the imaginary raises problems which Barea
solves decorously.

In the narrative rather than in the description—and in the realistic plasticity of the dialogue—the novel occasionally maintains the vigor of *The Forging of a Rebel,* a previous book by Barea. I prefer other works of the author, but *The Broken Root* is the first about living conditions in the Spain of today and it deserves more consideration than that of the ample priority in time. I am sure that Americans will agree.

Ramón Sender. *NYTBR.* March 11, 1951, p. 4

The reading of the Spanish edition of this novel *[The Forging of a Rebel]* easily confirms the laudatory opinions of foreign critics. Barea is an excellent novelist; he has marvelous talents for being an observer; he knows how to choose with skill the world that he observes in order to give us from it a vision of humanity, in this case Spanish humanity; and he possesses the difficult art of a narrator who is capable of reproducing with vigor and energy what he has seen. . . .

The Forging of a Rebel is an authentic document of the contemporary history of Spain, of its political and social tragedies, written by a witness of singular artistic capabilities for reproducing on each page, in each character and incident, the bitter and painful reality of life and homeland, while being able to maintain within this pain an attitude of consolatory compassion toward all things and human beings.

Emilio González López. *RHM.* Jan.–Dec.,
1953, pp. 103–4†

The Forging of a Rebel is a shocking book. Its clear crisp prose, rapid action, concise character portrayals, and accurate historical recall make it easy to read. It is a book that is "hard to put down." On the other hand, the bare realistic narration of terrible but real history combined with the bitter rebellious and revolutionary reaction to that same reality could well cause a person to put the book down quickly—unfinished. Within that paradox lies its value. Beneath the vinegar, there is a warmth and a value structure that is bedrock in the ideology of Catholicism or any western religion, for that matter. The frequently tragic turns in Barea's life symbolize the tragedy of many other Spanish liberals who became embittered lapsed Catholics.

John Devlin. *Spanish Anticlericalism: A Study
in Modern Alienation* (New York, Las
Américas, 1966), p. 168

In [*The Forge*], there are brilliant, self-confident pictures of Barea's family, all, as it were, peering over the edge of the giant cauldron of Spanish working-class feelings to see what sort of mixture will result. Don Luis, the blacksmith of Brunete, with his breakfasts of rabbit and brandy, is a particularly compelling figure. These 200 or so pages seem to me to be among the two or three best pieces of writing ever done which are inspired by working-class life. Or can one call that world of craftsmen about to sink, or about to rise, as fate determines, really "working-class"? I think not: indeed, the whole sweep of this section of Barea's work reminds one of the diversity of the class whom some would quite neglect in their efforts to reach a simple and stark interpretation of politics. Priests and engine drivers, lion tamers and cashiers, matadors and beggars—all live forever caught by one short sentence or anecdote, thanks to Barea's acute and selective memory. A particularly important function of these pages is that they show, through the analysis of relations between men and women, just how authoritarian modern Spain was—perhaps still is. . . .

Barea's [*The Forging of a Rebel*] gives a fine picture of an old society in decay. It is no less compelling because, from the standpoint of the much more conventional, clean, characterless Madrid of today, one cannot help a certain nostalgia for the fascinating slum life of Barea's childhood: poor, often wretched, but what vigor, what eccentricity! It seems, nevertheless, and taking everything into account, that some sort of authoritarian structure was inevitable. What of the future? The marked change in both the Church and the women (matters to which Barea devoted a tremendous amount of attention) suggests that optimism is possible.

Hugh Thomas. Nation. May 3, 1975, pp. 535–36

In his narrative [*The Flame*] of life in besieged Madrid, Arturo Barea succeeds—as in *The Forge*—in converting the city into a character acting as background, forming itself into an autonomous entity in the story. He does not construct his personages by forcing their character nor by forcing the description of the surroundings within which they move. The relevance of the language is tied to the minimal distancing necessary for an omniscient narrator to allow his creations to define themselves and for the memories, with what they involve about knowledge of all the keys and all results of what is narrated, to be a pretext for him to novelize his own life without it ceasing to be a necessary objectivization of the narrative flow. Arturo Barea knows his characters, but does not manipulate them whimsically. They are a part of his own life; they are not literary means or functionally usable beings. . . . I do not share the opinions that have pointed out the partisanship of [Arturo Barea] as one of the characteristics of *The Flame*. That he narrates passionately does not mean that his theses are partisan or that he tries to justify his position by distorting the reality of the facts.

Another fundamental trait of these memoirs of Arturo Barea is its deep tenderness toward the innocent victims of the civil war. He is a born pacifist who knows that the war inevitably arose because of the danger that the right had sensed of losing its privileges.

Luis Suñén. CdA. March, 1979, p. 63†

BAROJA, PÍO (1872–1956)

There is something painful, a certain cruelty in the detailed observations, in the tales that make up *Somber Lives,* and there is something Dostoevskian in some of them. Indeed, some aspects remind us of Dostoevsky while others remind us of Poe. Read "Hidden Kindness" and you will think of the Russian; read "Medium," a narration whose greatest beauty lies in its offering scarcely any meaning, and you will recall the Yankee. You will be reminded of them, of course, but you will see that these stories have not been taken from them, but rather from Baroja's own experience, his own heart, his own mind, which is in a state between somnolence and anxiety. I have said somnolence and anxiety because it is thus that Baroja's spirit appears: troubled in dreams and dreaming his anxiety. His tales have the liveliness of brief and vague details of certain dreams, and their lack of clarity, and at times their incoherence. [1900]

> Miguel de Unamuno. In Fernando Baeza, ed.,
> *Baroja y su mundo,* Vol. II (Madrid, Arión,
> 1961), p. 11†

Instead of solving his own problem with . . . pharmaceutical death, Baroja has written twenty-six or twenty-eight volumes, which open up like so many yawns of transcendental boredom before a world where everything is insufficient.

The feeling of insufficiency which plagues the ideas and values of contemporary culture is the mainspring which moves Baroja's whole soul. The present war has revealed to the less perspicacious not a few of the hypocrisies, deceits, disloyalties, torpid utopianisms, and pathetic frauds in which we are living. . . . Nothing more natural, then, than the effect produced by Baroja on the majority of readers. This effect is indignation. Because Baroja is not content to differ on one or two points in the system of commonplace topics and conventional opinions but, rather, makes protest against the conventional way of thinking and feeling the very fiber of his production.

In this longing for sincerity and loyalty to self I know no one, in or out of Spain, comparable to Baroja. I was speaking earlier of a certain incorruptible reserve there is in us. . . . Only a few men endowed with a rare energy are able to glimpse at certain instants the attitudes of what [Henri] Bergson would call the "profound self." From time to time the latent voice of consciousness will come to the surface. Baroja, then, is the very strange case, unique in my experience, of a man made up almost exclusively of that incorruptible reserve and completely exempt from the conventional self that usually envelops it. . . .

In such a man nothing can be indifferent. His ideas may seem absurd to us; but since in him they are pure and spontaneous reactions of the most inalienable part of man, they gain value in relation to reality in proportion to what is lacking or superfluous to them in logical consistency. [1916]

José Ortega y Gasset. *Crit I.* Dec., 1974, pp. 428–29

The present book, *Youth and Egolatry,* was written at the height of the late war, and there is a preface to the original edition, omitted here, in which Baroja defends his concern with aesthetic and philosophical matters at such a time. The apologia was gratuitous. A book on the war, though by the first novelist of present-day Spain, would probably have been as useless as all the other books on the war. . . . Baroja, evading this grand enemy of all ideas, sat himself down to inspect and co-ordinate the ideas that had gradually come to growth in his mind before the bands began to bray. The result is a book that is interesting, not only as the frank talking aloud of one very unusual man, but also as a representation of what is going on in the heads of a great many other Spaniards. . . . Baroja is more interested in a literary feud in Madrid than in a holocaust beyond the Pyrenees. He gets into his discussion of every problem a definitely Spanish flavour. He is unmistakenly a Span-iard even when he is trying most rigorously to be unbiased and interna-tional. He thinks out everything in Spanish terms. In him, from first to last, one observes all the peculiar qualities of the Iberian mind—its disillusion, its patient weariness, its pervasive melancholy. . . .

Baroja, then, stands for the modern Spanish mind at its most enlightened. He is the Spaniard of education and worldly wisdom, detached from the mediaeval imbecilities of the old régime and yet aloof from the worse follies of the demagogues who now rage in the country. Vastly less picturesque than Blasco-Ibáñez, he is nearer the normal Spaniard—the Spaniard who, in the long run, must erect a new struc-ture of society upon the half archaic and half utopian chaos now reigning in the peninsula.

H. L. Mencken. Introduction to *Youth and Egolatry* by Pío Baroja (New York, Alfred A. Knopf, 1920), pp. 18–20

Baroja has scandalized the orthodox and the academicians by saying openly that he cannot read the Spanish classics—his tastes are not unlike those of the Englishman in his early novel *The Lord of La-braz.* . . . What he means is probably that he never read them with any great enjoyment, and does not read them now; his favorite authors, he says, are Stendhal and Dickens, both of whom he reads solidly. Yet it is curious that he has something of the same view of life as Cervantes and the old novelists, who wrote the kind of stories which have been called "picaresque." . . .

Baroja is more interested in people than in culture, in the Spanish character than in the Spanish classics; but in spite of that, he is as full of the spirit of wandering as any of the old Spanish writers. And it is this quality which makes his work so attractive. . . . Baroja feels a *Sehnsucht,* a longing for a life which is not ordered and pre-established. He seeks it on the margins of society, among those who are commonly said to be failures; for those lives, he would say, though practically they are defeated and broken are morally victories and an ascent to something higher. . . . Baroja's *Sehnsucht* has led him to wander over Spain and the rest of Europe in search of the stimulus to make him feel at home in the world. The solution when he found it was not very new, to be sure, and only works with temperaments like his own, and those he contemplates. It was a life of action; and Baroja's apple of contentment has been not to live a life of action, but to contemplate it.

J. B. Trend. A Picture of Modern Spain: Men
and Music (London, Constable, 1921), pp. 71–74

Baroja's most important work lies in the four series of novels of the Spanish life he lived, in Madrid, in the provincial towns where he practiced medicine, and in the Basque country, where he had been brought up. The foundation of these was laid in *The Tree of Knowledge,* a novel half autobiographical describing the life and death of a doctor, giving a picture of existence in Madrid and then in two Spanish provincial towns. Its tremendously vivid painting of inertia and the deadening under its weight of intellectual effort made a very profound impression in Spain. Two novels about the anarchist movement followed it, *The Wandering Lady,* which describes the state of mind of forward-looking Spaniards at the time of the famous anarchist attempt on the lives of the king and queen the day of their marriage and *The City of Fog,* about the Spanish colony in London. Then came the series called *The Quest,* which to me is Baroja's best work, and one of the most interesting things published in Europe in the last decade. It deals with the lowest and most miserable life in Madrid and is written with a cold acidity which Maupassant would have envied and is permeated by a human vividness that I do not think Maupassant could have achieved. All three novels, *The Quest, Weeds, Red Dawn,* deal with the drifting of a typical uneducated Spanish boy, son of a maid of all work in a boarding house, through different strata of Madrid life. They give a sense of unadorned reality very rare in any literature, and besides their power as novels are immensely interesting as sheer natural history.

John Dos Passos. Rosinante to the Road Again
(New York, George H. Doran, 1922), pp. 96–98

Deprived of a religious explanation of the world, Baroja turns toward science. . . . His *Paradox, King* is nothing more than the humorous expression of his faith in science as the organizing element of the world.

Silvestre Paradox, the protagonist whom he has taken from an earlier novel, is basically a more or less transfigured incarnation of the author. . . . Silvestre Paradox is an unhappy man, affable and unsociable at the same time, a loner who loves children and animals, who hates hypocrisy and believes that it is easier to conquer the blacks of Africa through showing them in practice the advantages of civilization rather than shooting them down under a decree of martial law. This is the critico-political lesson that one gets from the entertaining story about an expedition of Spanish, English, and French adventurers who fall into the hands of a tribe of cannibals and go from the chief's larder to the highest positions in the state, owing to their mental and moral superiority. This idea of reason, man's light and guide through the world, is here extended by Baroja to all of Nature, so that every being—stone, tree, animal, star, man—expresses his own point of view, *his own reason*. Yet nonetheless, here as a philosopher, as before a creator, Baroja does not manage to unite, to make a whole out of a cacophony of separate words. The thinker in him, like the artist, remains in the first phase: the perception of unconnected events.

Intellectually, this is due to the lack of what the French call *esprit de suite*. Creatively, this is explained by the more serious deficiency that Baroja presents as an artist, that is, his complete lack of lyric sense. [1924]

Salvador de Madariaga. In Fernando Baeza,
ed., *Baroja y su mundo,* Vol. II (Madrid, Arión,
1961), pp. 127–28†

The Tree of Knowledge is the story of an embittered young intellectual, told in his own vivid and individual manner by Spain's foremost contemporary novelist. Its pessimism is intellectual, decadent, material; between it, and the gloomy depths of, let us say, the Russians, lies the difference between a skeptical and a mystical outlook upon life. Beyond the dark of Baroja's picture of meanness and selfishness there appears no vision of the soul. Not only is the world lost; there is no new world, within oneself or without, to be gained.

Pío Baroja is a master of the Spanish scene: set his acid-etched figures of Madrid's lower life against, for example, Blasco Ibáñez's, and there are whole lives lighted up from behind instead of a mere picture, excellent enough as journalism, of slum life. An insight tempered with skepticism has caught the debased conventions of society, sounded out the lives of Church and State, the incompetence of the professional world, the petty jealousies and dishonesties of men thwarted in their conflict with life. In Baroja's record of the career of Andrés Hurtado we are shown, not merely his own failure and unhappiness, but the circumstances and environment which brought them about. . . . Before our eyes is reared a world of poverty and insufficiency, the cause of most of what's wrong. From out of them comes a degenerate and corrupt life, an absurdly blind defense of Spain in relation to the rest of the world which leads to meanness and intolerance. . . .

The Tree of Knowledge is too determined an effort to expose a condition at the expense of a character. There is too propagandistic a quality to its pessimism; the defeat of Andrés is used to illustrate the unhappy state of Spain.

NYTBR. July 22, 1928, Section 3, p. 4

The novelist Pío Baroja has included . . . the events of 1931 and the preceding years in his trilogy "The Dark Jungle," which includes *The Errotacho Family, The Cape of Storms,* and *The Visionaries.* . . .

The interest of the three books by Baroja is found, above all, in the swift and violent narration, which is like the events in Spain during the last few years. The great topic for Baroja's characters is to work. In order to reconstruct their existences, the author has undertaken detailed investigations, read diaries, held conversations, above all with the eye witnesses to the events recounted, and recorded personal observations, anecdotes, and popular though short-lived expressions. . . . All of Spain comes to life . . .—the life of the workers, the bourgeoisie, the farmers. We also enter into an aristocratic family that is stricken with a very comical terror, a veritable gallery of grotesques, unintelligent and maladjusted, drawn with a sharp sense of caricature. . . .

Numerous ideas of a more serious nature confer distinction upon "The Dark Jungle." His tone appears at times more pathetic than previous works. His observations are never coordinated or systematic. . . . They are scattered about throughout the three volumes. We are not referring to the very violent satire about the fallen king and his family, but rather to the dialogue about sedition, in which Baroja develops his ideas about relativism in politics and the notion of law. We must also point out the parallel between "Mediterranean" and "Atlantic"; in literature, Mediterranean is equivalent to trite and Atlantic to complications and interest. In politics it is the opposite. [1933]

Jean Sarrailh. In Fernando Baeza, ed., *Baroja y su mundo,* Vol. II (Madrid, Arión, 1961), pp. 184–86†

Neither Benavente nor Baroja were liked in the beginning; Benavente was liked by neither the actors nor the public. Baroja was not liked by the older writers nor the readers. However, the most important fact is that Benavente, who was rejected by Madrid society, is now, and was since he began, the finest and most elegant, faithful, and detailed portrayer of the society that repudiates him. And Baroja, rejected by the older writers and the general public, was already the most profound, most intense, and most complex representative of the new spirit that was born in 1900; throughout all his writings, Baroja was to be, parallel to Benavente, a historian of his epoch. I have cited the year 1900; that year, more or less, is the dividing line for two epochs or two tendencies in Spanish aesthetics. What Baroja and Benavente achieved at the beginning of the twentieth century is exactly what Lope and Cervantes achieved at the beginning of the seventeenth century: a desintegration of the old and an integration of the new. . . .

In 1898 [Benavente's] *The Wild Beasts' Banquet* opened. . . . This work is a complete break with the old aesthetics. . . . The essential point of this work, as in Baroja's novels, is that nothing happens. The audience or the reader, conditioned for things to occur in novels or dramas, waits for something to happen . . . and nothing does. . . .

If we compare Pérez Galdós's *Doña Perfecta* with Baroja's *Road to Perfection,* we notice almost immediately the radical difference that already exists between the old novel and the new one. Everything in Pérez Galdós converges, and in Baroja everything is dispersed, without a focal point. In both the theater and the novel, a new aesthetic phase has begun; in literary evolution we have arrived at an unknown region. [1944]

Azorín. Ante Baroja (Zaragoza, Librería
General, 1946), pp. 256–57†

Action . . . as Baroja interprets it, is primarily the restless movement of one who longs for an unknowable something and yet scarcely ventures more than the satisfaction of curiosity with respect to things close at hand. Zalacaín [of *Zalacaín, the Adventurer*] with all his restlessness, is really a bystander who watches his earthly destiny transpire in a rapid succession of casually related happenings, and then faces suddenly an immensity that fuses all fleeting events in one vast stream of memory. As though playing a dual role, he is the illusory reality of successive moments and the vague constituent of an endless duration. . . .

Zalacaín's history can quite justifiably and pleasurably be viewed as materializing on a plane of action, that is, movement, and then fading into the realm of pure memory on the plane of dream. Linkage between the two planes in the form of a recollection partially perceptual and partially dreamlike is indicated by a nostalgic tone in reference to concrete places, by the youth's dreams of freedom and heroic deeds, and by the delicate evocation of heroic personality from the past—the allusion, for example, to Ulysses when Zalacaín is detained in the home of Linda and, again, at the time of Zalacaín's death, the reference to the horn of Roland. The dreamlike quality overwhelms all else in the conclusion; but before this we witness—on the plane of action—the steady rhythm of time marking off the passage of life as perceived and rationalized by intellect. The incidents, large and small, sprinkled along the hero's path and held together by little more than chronological relatedness, are like the ticking of a clock marking off minutes of a life span. Chance happenings and passing acquaintances . . . take their place alongside love, marriage, and death and contribute with equal magnitude to the impression of a moving chain of independent objects forcefully speaking for the extended world of matter. . . . In Zalacaín's life they constitute a kaleidoscopic panorama of things, from which the individual remains detached, knowing that his reality cannot be identified with them.

Sherman H. Eoff. *The Modern Spanish Novel*
(New York, New York University Press, 1961),
pp. 180–82

When Baroja speaks about women in literature, he says that men generally invent types of women not as they are in reality, but as they dream them to be. . . . María Aracil [of *The Wandering Lady* and *The City of Fog*] is one of the most successful types in our literature, and if it is true that the feminine character created by men is the projection of the author's dream, María Aracil indicates Baroja's ideal of respect, comprehension, and admiration of woman. . . . María Aracil is an intelligent, sensitive woman. At difficult moments, it is she who resolves the situations. . . . She is able to understand the men around her and appreciate them as friends, while the young fellows who pursue her say that she has no heart because she doesn't like stupid games. When, while in London, she has to fight alone, it never occurs to her to find a sensual and easy solution to her problems—not even owing to curiosity. She believes in love, in friendship, in the purity of acts and feelings. She is brave enough to suffer hunger in order to enjoy the small things in life. She becomes ill when she sees that the man with whom she is in love has neither courage nor moral strength. . . . Pío Baroja, this brilliant unknown, branded a misogynist, presented one of the purest visions of womanhood, one of the most divine, most truthful and tender of our literature in 1908. [1961]

Carmen Laforet. In Fernando Baeza, ed.,
Baroja y su mundo, Vol. II (Madrid, Arión,
1961), pp. 384–85†

It seems strange to talk about a philosophy influencing the structure of a novel but curiously enough this is almost what happened in *The Tree of Knowledge*. We must begin with the assumption that Baroja's inspiration as a novelist was never aesthetic or literary but rather philosophical and social. In novels of the kind that Baroja wrote form and content tend to become fused. The novel in question is a study of the inability of the protagonist, Andrés Hurtado, to adapt himself to the surrounding circumstances (Spain at the turn of the century) and his attempt to come to terms with the vicissitudes of life. . . . We come one step closer to a total understanding of this novel when we realize that it is more autobiographical than others of Baroja and that it actually reveals the author's own philosophy of life. Baroja also classifies it as his most accomplished philosophical treatise. . . . Thus the essence of this novel is Baroja's personal philosophy and the mark of Schopenhauer is clear, for the framework of the novel is nothing more, nothing less, than an outworking of Schopenhauer's principal work *The World as Will and Idea*—a work read and digested many times by Baroja. . . .

[Andrés Hurtado] passes from being caught up in the blind current of life to the complete boredom of *ataraxia* obtained through contemplation: that is, from the world of Will to the world of Idea. The fact that Hurtado gained this euphoric state (even though he lost it later) made him a precursor of the understanding of life. It is probable that later in his life Baroja found the affirmative philosophy of Nietzsche to be more consoling but it remains without question that his affinity with Schopenhauer was the controlling factor in his artistic and ideological production during his formative years. One can also guess that it was acceptance of this pessimistic philosophy that made him popular with the disillusioned Spaniards of the period.

E. Inman Fox. RLC. July–Sept., 1963,
pp. 355, 359

César or Nothing is Baroja's longest novel and for that reason alone technically interesting. . . . In the text as a whole dialogue is fairly evenly distributed, occupying about two fifths of Part I, with concentrations when César engages Preciozi and Kennedy in discussion, and falling to approximately one third in Part II. Some eighty-seven personages actually appear in the narrative, with reference to a score or more of other. One character (Yarza) reappears from previous novels. . . .

César remains on stage continuously from his first entry until practically the end, except for a few instances when the narrative halts for formal description or summary. In contrast, the heroine, Amparito, enters the novel only at a point rather later than two thirds of the way through, and then receives only passing mention. The courtship is telescoped into a meagre score or so of pages sandwiched in, in three brief scenes, among accounts of César's political activities. In spite of the importance of her role in the final determination of César's character, Amparito has no independent existence, no appearances except in his company, and thus no development except in relation to him. Like his sister Laura, she is simply one of a circle of interlocutors and foils, including Alzugaray, Preciozi and Kennedy, each of whom draws him out in a given direction, so that the reader gathers a series of impressions which establish his character. In spite of the satirical intention of the novel, one of its most obvious features is the absence of satirical situations as such, practically the only exception being the visit to the Catacombs. Baroja prefers caricature. Hence the essential members of the heterogeneous group of bit-parts and extras who follow on after César and his immediate circle are grotesques who fill out the general satirical picture, and especially the notables of Castro Duro. For the rest, of the people whom César meets, those who are not knaves are generally fools. *César or Nothing* is therefore a typical Barojan novel: a monolinear narrative, dominated by the hero and his ideology, enlivened by its settings, by observed detail and by lavish use of dialogue. There is little love-interest. The tempo is markedly irregular. None of the subordinate characters achieves independent existence.

D. L. Shaw. *BHS.* July, 1963, pp. 155–56

Baroja's interest in painting and painters, though hardly overwhelming and seldom kindly, is well known. There are several references to and discussion of artists, Picasso among them, in his *Memoirs.* And in *Road to Perfection* (1902) there are mentions of Santiago Rusiñol, Ignacio Zuloaga, Darío Regoyos, all Spanish painters of the epoch. There is a long episode involving Ossorio's reaction to El Greco's "Burial of Conde de Orgaz." . . .

There was also a brief but concrete encounter between Baroja and Picasso in 1901 when both were associated with the short-lived Madrid journal *Arte joven*. This is the period, for Picasso, of poverty and Bohemian living. . . .

For Baroja, as for Picasso, these years and these experiences provide material for later works. A comparison of Picasso's sketches in *Arte joven* or the figures of the following Blue Period (1901–1904), with the figures and ambiance of Baroja's early novels, reveals an obvious community of experience in the two artists. For Baroja also haunted the *barrios bajos* [lower-class neighborhoods], the bullfight arenas, the cafés, the circus, etc., sometimes to haul a wayward worker back to the family bakery, sometimes as part of what [Eugenio de] Nora calls the *de rigueur* Bohemianism of the young intellectual of the epoch. And such is the similarity of their interests, that Picasso's beggars, the blind, the drunks, the circus personnel, the old Jew . . . might well serve as illustrative material in, for example, Baroja's *The Quest* (1904).

The contact between the two artists was neither prolonged nor profound. Although Picasso did a well-known sketch of Baroja on one occasion, and also created some illustrations to accompany Baroja's literary productions, Picasso left shortly for Barcelona, Paris, and another cultural world.

Charles Olstad, *RomN.* Spring, 1964, pp. 124–25

Baroja believed in the "realism" of the [English] adventure novels. He did not necessarily believe that "those" specific adventures about which he read had occurred; but rather, he believed that other adventures, which were very similar but no less marvelous, had taken place. The adventures in these novels did not take place, but it is "as if" they had taken place, and they are, in fact, inspired by real events. The novelist thus, although not a historian, is a spectator of his own creations.

It seems unquestionable to me that Baroja believed that this was the mission of the writer and that he understood "realism" in this way, since there are many passages where he talks about the idea that "the novel took from life what life gave to the novel." According to this idea, a literary hero cannot emerge from a common person. Balzac's and Dickens's adventurers were possible thanks to the immense, dark, and mysterious cities of Paris and London, where a criminal or a conspirator was able to hide for months and mock his pursuers, owing to the incompetence of the police. . . . And the same thing is true about the literature of the sea. The pirates, buccaneers, smugglers, whalers, slave traders, or simply the daring seamen in the era of the sail, provided a great deal of material for the novelist, in particular the English novelist. . . . But, since the adventure novel makes a spectacle of human vicissitudes, as soon as adventure ends so does the adventure novel.

Such a concept of adventure as a desubjectivized intellectual spectacle . . . fits perfectly well with the structure of many of Baroja's favorite [English] novels and with his own novelistic ideal.

José Alberich. Los ingleses y otros temas de
Baroja (Madrid, Alfaguara, 1966), pp. 112–13†

Baroja's first books attest to the constant preoccupation with verisimilitude in what is invented. In his last books this disappears almost completely, since he brings to the texts real events and characters. . . . The narration changes focus: instead of concentrating interest on the development of the plot, he gradually is drawn toward digression. Thus, from a certain period on, the author appears to be more interested in *revealing himself* than in *telling,* which causes a more frequent repetition of themes, situations, and even of types. Through the years, the echoes of his readings of serials and books of adventures diminish, and are replaced by philosophy. . . .

The novels of the intermediate period show greater concern for structure and for interior unity, although the basic techniques can be found right from the start: the change in point of view in *Road to Perfection;* the synthetic or symbolic summaries at the head of each chapter in *The Lord of Labraz;* the alternation of the dynamic and the humoristic with lyrical passages in *Somber Lives* and in *The Fair of the Discreet,* the technique of rapid notation, like that of fragmentation, is found in all; the almost always linear development—he never presents complicated schemes. . . . Baroja did not essentially change during his lifetime. Upon becoming more oriented to and involved with ideas, the bitter "inflection" became more intensified in him. Since the novel represents for him, above everything else, a faithful expression of man, he continued through some evolution, without showing any radical transformations except for greater mastery of structure.

Biruté Ciplijauskaité. *Baroja, un estilo* (Madrid, Ínsula, 1972), pp. 246–47†

The first two novels of [the series] "Basque Land," *The House of Aizgorri* and *The Lord of Labraz,* have a stronger relationship to each other than with the other two of the series of four: the two deal with the same theme, that of the crises that the noble Basque families suffer as a result of the problems of modern daily life, dominated by capitalism, and the ambitions of a bourgeoisie without ideals and without scruples, which is only preoccupied with satisfying its desire for wealth.

Baroja's preoccupation with the fate of the noble families of the Basque villages, which are the symbol of his land's traditions, brings his novels closer to the *Barbarous Dramas* of Valle-Inclán, which, like *The House of Aizgorri* and *The Legend of Jaun de Alzate,* are composed in dialogue form. But it is necessary to point out a profound difference between the treatment of the crisis of the noble families in Valle-Inclán's works and in Baroja's. In the first case the destruction of the Montenegro family, a symbol of the agonizing feudalism of Galicia, is produced by its own vices, with the aid of the curse cast on the family by the abbot of Brandeso, while in Baroja the decline of the noble family and in one case its destruction *(The Lord of Labraz)* is a result of the plots planned by the workers (in *The House of Aizgorri*) and the ambitious bourgeoisie alone *(The Lord of Labraz)* or the two groups together, a theme that never appears in Valle-Inclán's *Barbarous Dramas.*

Emilio González López. *El arte narrativo de Pío Baroja* (New York, Las Américas, 1971), p. 109†

One indisputable fact that we must admit is that when Pío Baroja began to write his most famous trilogies at the beginning of this century he achieved one of the most unexpected literary revolutions—not only at the Spanish level, but also at the European level. Although Baroja lived his whole life with the same *slogans,* his admiration for Balzac, Dickens, and Stendhal, not to forget Dostoevsky, and his sentimental preference for the serial writers, such as Eugène Sue, . . . when it comes to the moment of writing he seldom succeeds in verifying in its totality the childish encyclopedia of his erudition. . . .

Without Pérez Galdós, "Clarín," or Blasco Ibáñez, Pío Baroja could never have written novels. But just the same, it seems quite appropriate that he considered them his sworn enemies. It is impossible to carry out any revolution without keeping in mind the worth of one's adversary. With his unpleasant aims, his permanent bitterness, and his self-admitted sense of segregation, Baroja went into the street and adopted the position of a solitary *sans culotte*. His working tools had nothing to do with those that his predecessors had used. . . . His idea of the hedonistic entertainment of the novel had little to do with that of the great nineteenth-century masters.

Domingo Pérez-Minik. *CHA.* July–Sept., 1972, pp. 57–58†

Baroja believes poetry to be the quintessence of novelistic prose. . . . Thus it is that one finds the keys to Baroja's novels in this heterogeneous collection of *Songs of the Suburbs,* with its mocking, fickle heroes, victims of destiny, who are unable to organize their adventures, or misadventures, into actions of consequence, or a living pattern that has meaning. . . .

If *Songs of the Suburbs* is submitted to a sociological examination, its relationship to the nature of the novel, to the novelistic genre, can be confirmed. In a condensed, crystallized, quintessential form, this work presents an homologous image of the state of a society. Through it passes characters and objects that are disconnected, without a past, without a future, without usefulness, without *relevance* in the Spanish world, and to a certain extent in the European world, of the first half of the twentieth century. There appears in an incoherent juxtaposition the wasted remains of a past humanity with its productions, which no longer have any purpose, except as plaguing nuisances. It is *Weltanschauung* . . . or even *Spanienanschauung,* the vision of an anarchic community, with its poor bourgeoisie, failed and hopeless capitalism, with its intellectual or pseudo-intellectual bureaucracy, which, like a spinning-top, looks for balance in the extreme acceleration of its conceptual studies, in the schizophrenic delirium of theories. . . .

Charles V. Aubrun. *CHA.* July–Sept., 1972, pp. 378–79†

In [the series of novels called] "Memoirs of a Man of Action," Baroja captures Spanish history by means of beings who populate the pages of her history—be they historical or ficticious characters, or individuals acting on their own or in groups (hence the attention Baroja pays to crowds). But the principal ingredient of the scene is always the lives of these people. . . . It is at the same time an angle of vision and a method of composition. And it is precisely this technique of the primacy of the character, both in the historical and the novelistic sphere, that gives his novels a certain degree of artistic homogeneity, which substitutes for the conventional technique of linking through plot.

The fact that Baroja sees history in terms of human units and not abstract forces permits him to stress the moral and ethical aspects, which are so fundamental to his works. The ethical preoccupation is one aspect that really stands out, because moral censure can be applied with much more conviction to an individual than to an event. Moral condemnation, which in the case of nineteenth-century Spain is applied to both the leaders and the followers with but a few exceptions, is based on the egotistical, blind, and even animal-like conduct of the Spaniards who lived Spain's history during the first half of the nineteenth century. But who knows if in this censure of the nation that has lost its moral sense there was something of a warning. These novels, written between 1912 and 1934, appear to us, with the Spanish tragedy in perspective, an impressive omen.

Carlos Longhurst. *Las novelas históricas de Pío Baroja* (Madrid, Guadarrama, 1974), p. 265†

At the start of his third year as a medical student at Madrid University, Baroja recalled in his memoirs, he began to compose two novels: "La una se titulaba *El pesimista* o *Los pesimistas* y la otra *Las buhardillas de Madrid*" [One was called *The Pessimist* or *The Pessimists* and the other *The Attics of Madrid*]. . . . It has always been assumed that these early writings survived. Baroja himself stated earlier in his memoirs that his novels *Adventures, Inventions, and Mystifications of Silvestre Paradox* and *Road to Perfection* were born out of them. . . . It is therefore satisfying to be able to substantiate this assumption by producing the missing link, in this case unpublished manuscript fragments which, I shall argue, are the very papers Baroja thought he had disposed of. . . .

The existence of this manuscript adds to the already considerable evidence of re-use of material by Baroja. This aspect of his work has been often criticized by those inclined to cheapen Baroja's literary achievements. However, it may be argued that such repetition provides a valuable indication of the subjects and situations which Baroja found irresistible. . . . In his early years as a writer Baroja continued to pursue the interest in the psychology of pain demonstrated in his doctoral thesis *El dolor* [*Pain*] by developing his own awareness of the anxieties aroused in himself by deteriorations of the external (physiological) and internal (psychological) support systems. Pablo is described in this manuscript going through a crisis involving "una vuelta a las ideas de la infancia" ["a return to childhood ideas"]. By returning time and again to the ideas of his literary infancy, modifying and expanding them, Baroja would seem to be searching for a form of pain. There is no longer any need to speculate whether or not Baroja *desired* to externalise, through his art, his innermost feelings. It is not necessary to argue interminably whether a Baroja protagonist is or is not "autobiographical." The fact is that Baroja, towards the end of his life, pointed directly to the link between his own literary endeavours and his personal quest for self-knowledge, of which the manuscript presented here constitutes perhaps the first step. . . .

Jeremy L. Sanders. *BHS*. Jan., 1984,
pp. 14, 28–29

BENAVENTE, JACINTO (1866-1954)

Benavente represents for Spain what a[n Alfred] Capus or a [Henry] Bernstein does for France, or even better, what a Bernard Shaw does for England. And in certain ways, he is the only one who has succeeded in giving true luster and resonance to the Spanish stage.

Those who judge him with an ear attuned to Boulevard theater are poorly informed. The world in which his characters move in most of his plays is that universal world that has for a norm, of course, Parisian life, more or less applied to their respective milieus; and if not that, then pay attention to the scenes of today's Italian playwrights. That world is *le monde*. Benavente's characters, who move and act in the society of Madrid, however, do have a true classical heritage; and their sparkling and witty dialogues with which their creator endows them are nothing but the old, delightful conversations of an updated Calderón or Lope. . . .

In spite of his reputation for being bitter, put your trust in him. Amid the clumps of thistles there is very delicious honey, much human joy, much tenderness that compensates for despair.

Enter his theater of fantasy and kindness. Let yourself be taken by the hand that can push aside the unfriendly branches. He will make you a gift of poetic sweetness, of moonbeams, of the crystalline song of the nightingale; and when it is fitting, in due time, at the precise instant, he will do a pirouette for you; and you will thank him for this illusion with which he delights you.

And he will leave you standing there. Do not follow him. He goes off murmuring to himself, because he knows many things about heaven and earth. Do not follow him. You will be able to believe from the movements of his shoulders that he leaves laughing, but you cannot be sure that he is not going away crying. Has he not just given you life, life that is brutal, tragic, and painful in *The Hated Woman,* a play which he has jammed in every sort of doom and apocalyptic mystery of woman: *Misterium?*

The true power of Benavente lies in the fact that he is a poet, in that he possesses the inner vision and the all-encompassing vision of a poet, and in that he communicates the magical power of his secret to all he touches. [1916]

Rubén Darío. *Cabezas: Pensadores y artistas, políticos* (Madrid, Mundo Latino, 1919), pp. 4, 7–8†

Benavente's plays . . . acquire double significance as the summing up and the chief expression of a movement that has reached its hey-day, from which the sap has already been cut off. It is, indeed, the thing to disparage them for their very finest quality, the vividness with which they express the texture of Madrid, the animated humorous mordant conversation about café tables: that which is typically Spanish.

The first play of his I ever saw, *People of Our Acquaintance*, impressed me, I remember, at a time when I understood about one word in ten and had to content myself with following the general modulation of things, as carrying on to the stage, the moment the curtain rose, the very people, intonations, phrases, that were stirring in the seats about me. After the first act a broad-bosomed lady in black silk leaned back in the seat beside me sighing comfortably, "How typically Spanish this Benavente is," and then went into a volley of approving chirpings. The full import of her enthusiasm did not come to me until much later when I read the play in the comparative light of a surer knowledge of Castilian, and found that it was a most vitriolic dissecting of the manner of life of that very dowager's own circle, a showing up of the predatory spite of "people of consequence." Here was this society woman, who in any other country would have been indignant, enjoying the annihilation of her kind. On such willingness to play the game of wit, even of abuse, without too much rancor, which is the unction to ease of social intercourse, is founded all the popularity of Benavente's writing. Somewhere in Hugo's Spanish grammar (God save the mark!) is a proverb to the effect that the wind of Madrid is so subtle that it will kill a man without putting out a candle. The same, at their best, can be said of Benavente's satiric comedies. [1921]

John Dos Passos. *Rosinante to the Road Again*
(New York, George H. Doran, 1922), pp. 193–94

[Benavente's] theatre has been called a theatre of ideas, and it is a theatre of ideas in so far as ideas are an expression of intense intellectual activity. But Benavente is not concerned with ideas, he is concerned with thought as it formulates itself—with ideas in the making. Thus his comedy stimulates the mind to an extraordinary degree, in which it is possible for him to communicate to an audience what under more usual circumstances it would fail to perceive. This is what he means when he says that he does not make his plays for the public, but the public for his plays. He creates the mental attitude which is necessary for their appreciation, and, by a subtle psychologic or character dialectic, through which personality is revealed by sharp reversals and successive mental jolts, disclosing the innermost workings of the soul and its springs of action, he induces the auditor to become for an evening a collaborator himself, reading between the lines. His style may best be compared to a rational cubist art, in which the elements are all valid and intelligible in themselves, but which surrender their true significance only when taken in juxtaposition. . . .

The tendency of Benavente's art is away from the plastic toward the insubstantial, the transparent. A fresh adjustment became imperative. What he had accomplished with satire he next essays with plot, turning his attention to its secondary and suggestive values, transferring the emphasis from the events to the inferences which wait upon them, and the atmosphere which they create, either directly or through collocation. In the field of exposition, the method may be observed in the first act of *The Governor's Wife.* . . . In the polychromatic spectacles, *Saturday Night* and *The Fire Dragon,* belonging to the years 1903 and 1904, vast, crowded canvases which might have been painted by Tintoretto or by Rubens, teeming with an abundance too multifarious to be imprisoned within the limits of the stage, the drama is removed from the domain of structural regularity, until it depends for its effect upon the impressions derived from a panorama of incident and of situation in which the story is swallowed up and upon occasion lost from view. These dramas may be considered the romantic outburst, the ungovernable adventure of the Beneventian theatre, by very lack of restraint stimulating the imagination to a perception at once restless and inchoate, of the awe and majesty of life.

John Garret Underhill. Introduction to Jacinto
Benavente, *Plays,* Second Series (New York,
Charles Scribner's Sons, 1919), pp. viii–ix

It would be difficult to answer the very American and very natural question, which is [Benavente's] best work. The author seems to prefer *The Lady of the House,* a simple drama of passions that verge on the tragic, the scene of which is laid in the country far from urban refinements and conventions. The public and the critics have selected two other works on which to lavish their admiration. Opinions on *The Created Interests* seem unanimous; *The Hated Woman* has fervent admirers and hardly less vehement denigrators. . . . When *The Created Interests* was presented in 1907, the Spanish public could understand and savor it because it had had some thirteen years of preparation, embracing about fifty plays by the same author. *The Hated Woman* made the same easy immediate impression on the American public— probably because of its very defects—as on the Spanish. It is an unusual work for Benavente; a tragic drama on classic lines without real national bearing or spirit, although the scene is laid among Spanish peasants of today. But Benavente's peasants are neither Spanish nor of any particular nationality. His country is conventional, without real feeling. The theme itself is an old one: that of Phaedra and Hippolytus, but reversed. Here the father falls in love with his stepdaughter, and the stark, terrible tragedy which ensues is calculated to move the stoutest heart. Benavente's dramatic talent and theatrical skill reach their culmination in this work. But we stand before it perplexed, uncertain whether we have here a profound, genuine tragedy, or a cunningly contrived, calculatingly designed "thriller." . . .

The Created Interests seems to the public and to me to represent the high-water mark of Benavente's achievement, the culmination and synthesis of his entire labor. Unlike the rest of his work, it is not a portrayal of contemporary society, although the ideas and emotions, the conceptions of the world and life, are those he has been developing throughout his earlier work. Here, however, they are presented without the limitations of time and space, with a simplicity and intensity really classic. In the manner of the ancient farce, the Italian *commedia dell'arte,* the characters, seemingly exaggerated and artless puppets, reveal the threads that move men in real life, the good and evil passions that inspire human actions.

Federico de Onís. *NorthAR.* March, 1923,
pp. 362–64

From the technical point of view, [Benavente's] theater gives the impression of being an experiment, for he would have proposed trying everything in order to be called a dramatist in the fullest sense of the word. He was accused of being an elitist writer, and he wrote the impudent and naturalistic one-act farce *We Are All One,* and gave us scenes of local customs like the first act of *The Grave of Dreams,* and works with rural settings like *The Lady of the House* and *The Hated Woman.* He was accused of being cold, and he gave us the emotionalism of *Brute Force.* He was accused of not appreciating superior virtues, and he gave us *Self-Esteem, Field of Ermine, The Necklace of Stars,* and *The Honor of Men.* He was accused of a lack of theatrical dynamism, and he gave us violence, passion, and strong personalities in *The Hated Woman.* Literature for Benavente, more than a profession or calling, is a continual personal assertion, and therefore, something like the pleasure of a collector who has just acquired a new object. . . .

[Because Benavente is] in love with all of life, without prejudices, sentimental interests, or philosophical concepts, the complexity of human motivation attracts him, as well as fickle sentiments, that dark region where moral problems end in the face of the futility of defining good and evil. And thus, he gives us works without solutions, like *The Grave of Dreams,* or works with partial and unsatisfactory solutions like *Another's Nest,* or *Self-Esteem,* or instead he deals with questions from opposing points of view like the exaltation of cruel and assertive instinct in *Saturday Night* and *The Honor of Men,* which is a hymn to the spirit of sacrifice. Even in works of universal importance like *The Created Interests,* he leaves us with the impression that something has been left unresolved. *The Created Interests* can be interpreted as an apology for idealism. . . .

The art of Benavente is universal because it is a product of a disinterested study of human life in all its manifold aspects. Benavente has the good artistic instinct to free himself from devoting his art to pathological and abnormal cases, which is what many contemporary writers do.

Joaquín Ortega. *MLJ.* Oct., 1923, pp. 6, 8–10†

Benavente, the subtle humorist whose humour is the emanation of his indulgent pity for humanity, beckons to us to listen to his message. To him, conventions of society, hide-bound morality, love as it is looked on by the world, are all but bonds of interest, threads which can be pulled by the superman-showman Crispín [in *The Created Interests*], who is a Master of life. Let us not ask from this exquisite ironist whose figures have the dainty delicacy of fine porcelain, for the rude shocks of tragedy, for the kingly stature demanded by Aristotle. In his tragedies the characters make haste to throw off the cothurnus: nor can they stare rough passion in the face, but gaze at it diminished through the mist of their fantasy. Benavente in his supreme mood resembles some subtle modern musician like Debussy or Ravel, who evokes old popular melodies of his country—rugged, passionate tunes sprung from the soil, but in such a way that they float wistfully to our ears down the course of centuries. Through the ever-variable stream of modern harmony symbolizing the ceaseless ebb and flow of life, fragments of these tunes reach us, and by intuition we complete the melody, we fill in the picture. So, too, Benavente, amid his flexible dramatic harmonies, suggests faintly the outline of all those old beliefs attached to the soil of Spain. For once we see them, not in towering stature and occupying the whole stage, but dwarfed to their proportionate size in the mosaic of the modern world.

There is a touch of the sublime coldness of Shakespeare in Benavente which enables him at times to rise to the mountain peak and gaze down on humanity. His spirit has many of the qualities associated with the classic. In his best works he does not tear passion to tatters nor play on the string of a single emotion: he treats emotion as something which is aroused for an ulterior purpose, in order that all who hear it may reach a perfect human mood, wherein the various emotions of man shall properly blend. Emotion in Benavente, as in the classic artist, is always in harness. As in the classic artist, there is also in him a subtle spirit of proportion: he sees the world and human beings, not magnified through the strong lens of the romantic, but according to his own normal vision. As a critic has said—the object of the classical spirit on the stage is the creating in the mind, in proper order, the sum of all human emotions, and Benavente is forever standing at the scales.

Walter Starkie. *Jacinto Benavente* (London,
Oxford University Press, 1924), pp. 210–11

Jacinto Benavente began by going off on his own, making a special kind of theater . . . a theater that had nothing to do with the theater of any other country or with the current styles of the day or with the domestic conflicts that he encountered at the home front: a theater full of theatrical philosophizing. . . .

He was enchanted. As a child he staged his plays in a theater made of cardboard, and now he takes his mother and even the cook to

premieres. One day during the first performance of *The Wild Beasts'
Banquet,* when he came out with his little-boy look to acknowledge the
applause, his cook, upon hearing a lady next to her say, "Oh that poor
man, he looks hungry, like all writers," replied angrily: "Listen, watch
out . . . my little master gets good stews that I make for him . . .! You
should only eat as well as he eats!"

All that happened at the turn of the century, but at first it seems to
be another century altogether. It all happened in that comfortable and
pleasant milieu in which everyone was a little astounded to be so
modern, so new. Jacinto—yes, even Jacinto—was lucky in the theater;
he sounded the note of the style of the future, and he knew how to make
fun of the customs and conventions that were dying and being buried
under the falling leaves, for, after all, it was the autumn of the biases of
one century, the beginning of another. . . .

Benavente surpassed himself—of this there is no doubt—and
wrote *the* drama of his day. The poet concretized with an art that made
the sadness and entanglements of people's lives reach a synthesis,
which in turn bettered those lives and gave them a superior dialectic.
He came forth with reticence, irony, remorse, wisdom, and his theater
triumphed. His audiences were sadistic enough to attend his denounce-
ments and applaud the denouncer. Without audacious posturings, without rhetoric and poetic mannerisms, he brought to the stage for the first
time the society of his day, with its characteristic rambling and slow-
moving talk from which sometimes the drama emerged or sometimes
only the fretfulness of the play, an attempt at action of the play. . . .

Benavente, like a dedicated doctor, was attentive to the fashionable
illnesses of his times, and in the final analysis he was the healer of the
stage whom society deserved, or perhaps he was far superior to what it
deserved.

Ramón Gómez de la Serna. *Nuevos retratos
contemporáneos* (Buenos Aires, Sudamericana,
1945), pp. 93–95†

[Benavente] was a cyclops; but quantity did not impede quality. Perhaps only ten or twelve of his works will be remembered tomorrow;
however, the same thing is happening to Lope de Vega. Benavente has
been the doctor of our theater; he has purged us of Echegaray. But he
has been a wise doctor who knew that *similia similibus curantur* [like
diseases are cured by like remedies]. He did not limit himself to
opposing vociferous melodrama with his extremely fine gifts as an
astute playwright of high society, but also knew how to confront melodrama with great works for which today—and tomorrow—we will with
justice be able to call him a remarkable playwright. He constantly
followed the styles and manners of each moment by being curious and
prolific; but from that inevitable tribute emerged not only ephemeral
works but ones of lasting importance as well. He was frequently crit-

icized for showing foreign influences, and nothing better could have happened to him; we already know that many of our most authentically Spanish writers are accused of the same thing at the beginnings of their careers. He contributed, like no other Spanish writer, to popularizing quality—the most difficult and overwhelming of the problems that a writer in our country [Spain] encounters. He is a great figure for the concierge, the shoemaker, the engineer, and the writer. Can one ask for more? No. And because that is the most that can be asked for, he will not be forgotten.

Antonio Buero Vallejo. *Teatro*. July–Sept., 1954, p. 36†

Benavente's accomplishments seem a bit mild in comparison with other playwrights of his time. Indeed, considering the tradition to which he was heir, it is sometimes difficult to believe that this dramatist was really a Spanish writer. There is a striking cosmopolitan air and an ironic, almost cynical tone to many of his plays which comes across even in the tableaux-structured, semi-fantastic setting of plays such as *Witches' Sabbath* [*Saturday Night*]. In this play (as in many of his dramas, notably *The Lady of the House* and *The Passion Flower* [*The Hated Woman*]), Benavente introduced the powerfully willful character of Imperia. She is one of many of Benavente's attractive female characters. Each of them embodies noble aspirations in spite of her involvement in ignoble situations. Benavente has drawn them subtly, frequently making them cerebral like the Yerma of García Lorca and always as passionate. Finally, in Acacia the silently seething girl-bride of *The Passion Flower,* probably his best-known play, Benavente's psychological portraiture reached a finesse almost equal to Ibsen's.

Benavente's way with dialogue contributed to his influence in the Spanish theatre. His language is quick, clear, and at times even epigrammatic. But he also had strong moralizing tendencies, with the result that in practically every play Benavente has a "mouthpiece."

Robert W. Corrigan. In Robert W. Corrigan, ed., *Masterpieces of the Modern Spanish Theatre* (New York, Collier, 1967), pp. 34–35

In *Well-Known People* [*People of Our Acquaintance*], and in many other plays which he wrote in the same style and which are most typical of Benavente, plot, or dramatic conflict, is secondary. Everything is oriented toward the dramatic incident; an incident which is the implicit statement of its own essence. This new dramatic concept appears to emphasize the apparently nonessential, the mere commentary or detail. Substance has been circumscribed, and is a matter of an essence, or content, which is more conceptual than that of action. Here the action is internal, psychological; it is more a matter of conflicting attitudes than of conflict overtly expressed. Within the same or similar scenes the external action could conceivably be very different, for it is secondary; what is of most importance is the *intent* of that action.

The individual character, then, is frequently converted into an instrument which enables the author to say what he himself wishes to say. For this reason the characters often lack clear individuality. Their consistency is more conceptual than vital. They are characters constructed from without, characters which grow out of the central idea of the play and are adapted to a thesis. Their personality does not develop from a unique and untransferable individuality in the midst of a whirlwind of feelings and passions. They are, above all, characters which form a part of a milieu, of a particular social or moral climate. The significant elements are precisely this milieu and the comments expressed about it in the dialogue.

The main elements of the action, which almost always occurs offstage, are only a pretext for placing the characters in a particular dramatic situation. Action thus becomes a succession of atmosphere-creating scenes which convey the milieu; and the characters, particularly the minor ones, are more closely related to the scene of which they are a part than to the plot as a whole. What they say has a dramatic significance within that scene in the very moment they are speaking. Thus in a very subtle way the author artistically fuses milieu and dialogue.

Marcelino C. Peñuelas. *Jacinto Benavente* (New York, Twayne, 1968), pp. 87–88

Every possible setting is brought into [Benavente's] work: the rustic or urban, the plebeian, the *bourgeois,* the aristocratic, the realistic, the exotic, and the imaginary. Similarly, his characters are striking in their diversity—they are normal or eccentric, happy or sad, optimistic or pessimistic, ingenious or simple and ingenuous. Benavente's theatre is like a full-flowing river bearing characters and passions, themes and conflicts, as presented by life itself.

Benavente's theatre is devoid of ideological conceptions or philosophical observations. The dramatist's thoughts revolve on the period, on impulses, experience, circumstances. Although some of his productions contain flashes of fatality or the bitterness of pessimism, these are not the key-note of his art. In a simple and natural way, or with the use of subtle paradox (which earned for him his fame as an author of "ingenious and ironic phrases"), what he preached through the lips of many of his fictional characters—from his drawing-room comedies, provincial reflections symbolized in his imaginary "Moraleda" [the setting for many of his plays such as *The Governor's Wife* and *Pepa Doncel*], or the village folk in his "Moralines" [the setting of *The Lady in Mourning*] to his allegorical farces like *The Created Interests*—was generosity, understanding, forgiveness, love of art, truth, and beauty, the supremacy of mind over matter, the expiating value of sacrifice, and the sublime quality of maternal love, to which cult he devoted much attention. He was no inventor of metaphysical systems—for they have no place in the theatre—but he rejected the virus of anarchy and the germs of destructiveness. . . .

One of the most marked literary and theatrical preoccupations of Benavente is presenting a vehicle of shock and dispute which has strong links with the themes and enigmas of Pirandello, as pointed out by Professor Walter Starkie. This conflict originates in what the characters are and what others, the rest of humanity, the world in general, think of them. It is the conception of existence as a battle between the pure, naked truth to which human beings aspire, and distorted reality, which casts a dim and indistinct reflection of itself, for practically no one really wants to see things as they are but as he would like to see them. Too often, this caprice conceals gross presumptions and wicked or malicious suspicions. This is corroborated by plays such as *The Unbelievable, And It Was Bitter, Adoration,* and many others.

A. Marquerie. *Topic.* Spring, 1968, pp. 33–34

[*Another's Nest*], though not the best, is perhaps the most serious play Benavente ever wrote. Its basic theme, the role of married women in middle-class society, was as much a matter of topical concern in Spain towards the end of the century as it had been in northern Europe when Ibsen dealt with it. Moreover, Benavente observes with some perspicacity the specifically Spanish aspects of the problem—the way in which a senseless residue of conventions regarding matrimonial honour can trivialise, and stultify the life of an intelligent, sociable, and entirely honourable married woman. On the Madrid stage, the play was a catastrophic failure. It was taken off after three days amid a clamour of disapproval. What the critics . . . found most disgustingly offensive was a scene in which two brothers discuss the possibility that their mother had been unfaithful to their father. The critic of *El Imparcial* (7 October 1894), boiling with indignation and embarrassment, asserted that this kind of thing was not only absolutely inadmissible on the stage, but totally unrealistic.

It is easy to imagine the dilemma of the young Benavente. In a sense, public reaction has proved to the hilt how urgent was the need to penetrate the Cloud-cuckoo-land of the Spanish theatre with this kind of play. Yet what future was there likely to be in trying to reform the theatre with plays that would be booed off the stage? His second effort, *People of Our Acquaintance* of 1896, shows him feeling his way towards some kind of honourable compromise. Instead of the intense soul-searching of *Another's Nest,* the new play consisted of a series of more or less static, urbane conversation-pieces, which portray the hypocrisy, materialism, and petty malevolence of polite society. There is little action until the final act, when the young daughter of a cynical new-rich factory-owner, who has arranged her marriage to a bankrupt, morally disreputable, but impeccably noble duke, rebels in the name of personal decency against the shifty accommodations and deceits of this nasty little gathering of all the best people. *People of Our Acquaintance* ran for ten days; there were no complaints about offensive subject-matter. Evidently the critics and the public did not see any important values menaced here. The play's social criticism was sharp, but no longer "unrealistic"—that is to say, unthinkable. It stopped well short of criticising the existing social structure. Even the ruined dukes in the audience could at least approve of Benavente's treatment of factory-owners. . . .

[Benavente's] wit bites sharply, if not deeply and his attitude to the section of society that chiefly interested him is consistently critical. He was not the bourgeoisie's tame jester; indeed he may well have managed to educate them to some small degree, and to make them aware of some of their more unpleasant characteristics.

G. G. Brown. A Literary History of Spain: The
Twentieth Century (New York, Barnes & Noble,
1972), pp. 113–14, 116

Benavente, like García Lorca, was essentially an artist. Although his plays focused upon decadent morality, his primary concern was not with philosophy or ideology but with maintaining his position as the most successful dramatist of the day. Luring audiences to the theater to see plays that disparaged their morality and customs demanded the restrained, genteel satire at which Benavente excelled. With an outlook best described as "between scorn and pity," Benavente became a master of irony who presented the follies of both sides of a situation. . . .

Benavente criticized all segments of society, especially the upper classes of which he was a member. He invented an imaginary kingdom called Suavia, a name that alludes to the life of comfort enjoyed by bored aristocrats in *Saturday Night*. The fictitious town of Moraleda was the scene of middle class hypocrisy in *The Governor's Wife* and *Pepa Doncel*. In *The School of Princesses,* class consciousness and snobbery are characteristic of the nobility. . . . Like Benavente, García Lorca satirized the class to which he himself belonged—the upper class. . . .

García Lorca's portrayal of social decadence echoes Benavente's deep skepticism. [García Lorca's] *Doña Rosita* parallels *The Governor's Wife* as a play in which nearly every character is satirized. Just as Benavente ridicules both liberals and conservatives in Moraleda, García Lorca presents both the bumbling old aesthete, Rosita's uncle, and Señor X, who is obsessively on the side of progress, as comic types. While Benavente's social commentary is expressed by witty and ironic dialogue, García Lorca goes beyond the use of satiric dialogue to create preposterous caricatures. Benavente's frivolous socialites in *The Angora Cat,* who explain that a friend's engagement was broken because "at the last minute it was discovered that Aguado hadn't a cent," are prototypes of the three overdressed old-maids who, according to their mother, prefer to spend their money on reserving chairs in the park than on food. While Benavente presents both sides of Moraleda's petty politics as corrupt and self-seeking, García Lorca ridicules the exaggerated manners and the oppressive morality of an entire society in *Doña Rosita.*

Though most of Benavente's plays are in the tradition of nineteenth-century realism, he saw the innovative possibilities in ancient farce and, as García Lorca was later to do, experimented with the characters from the Italian *commedia dell'arte.* In *The Created Interests,* considered his best play, Benavente attempted to escape the confines of realism in order to give fresh dramatic expression to his view of life. He did not entirely succeed. Just as the country dialect of the peasants in *The Lady of the House* and *The Hated Woman* cannot conceal their urban middle-class morality, the names of sixteenth-century comic types from the *commedia* do not alter the characters of *The Created Interests.* Like most of Benavente's dramatis personae, the Italianate figures are members of the upper class. As in his other works, they indulge in much witty, satirical dialogue.

Virginia Higginbotham. *The Comic Spirit of Federico García Lorca* (Austin, University of Texas Press, 1976), pp. 122, 124–26

Benavente is an optimistic writer of pessimistic plays. A case in point is *Autumnal Roses,* a play in search of an ironic reading. The autumnal roses of the title are the rewards of self-sacrifice, the ties which bind forever the woman who has suffered the infidelity of her husband and the aged Don Juan who is finally too old to stray. There is no slamming of doors in this play, no prescription for social ills, no condemnation of traditional roles. The protagonist Isabel loves her husband Gonzalo. She lives in a society which rejects divorce and limits her career potential. She bears her cross in the true Christian spirit, and like Benavente she recognizes a lack of options. Her apparent happiness may derive from innate goodness, self-deception, or a wish to deceive others; it is, in any event, realistic for her to accept the inevitable, to reconcile herself to indignity and glorify her position, and to attempt to persuade other women to suffer in silence. It is realistic in this situation to win the spiritual battle and remain oblivious to the ideological war.

There is one idealistic character in *Autumnal Roses:* María Antonia, Isabel's step-daughter (and probable alter-ego), a woman who demands a system of absolute and equal values. This woman is not willing to suffer humiliation to the point when, like Isabel, she can claim an old and worn-out husband as truly hers. She dares to commit an indiscretion with a former suitor and thus reverse the roles, but no one views her act in the same terms as the follies of her husband Pepe. No one takes seriously her demand for equal rights, and when she defies convention, her father and husband are enraged because she has put their honor in jeopardy. After Isabel admonishes both men, who forgive María Antonia, she proceeds to elaborate the joys of a love made eternal by constant tests and consequent affirmation through pardon. . . .

While Isabel recognizes the unfairness of the double standard, she does not rebel against the existing social structure. Her idea of woman's honor is revealed in her counsel to María Antonia: despite the inequity and the conduct of the husband, a woman must maintain impeccable honor. . . . Isabel succumbs to Gonzalo's passionate statement of affection, which seems to counteract all past infidelity, and Isabel ends by assuring María Antonia and the audience that she is happy. . . .

Conformity, or resignation, is the evident victor in this bloodless battle, and *Autumnal Roses* is a calculated exercise in offensiveness. Benavente made every effort to satirize, but not to offend, the upper-middle-class theatrical public, and a sense of immediacy dominates the dramatic events.

Edward Friedman. *IJWS*. March–April, 1981,
pp. 168–70

BENET, JUAN (1927–   )

You Will Return to Región is the collective vision of a collective catastrophe. Just as Jorge Luis Borges felicitously remarked about Henry James that "the facts are hyperboles or exaggerations whose end is to define characters," so could the same be said of Juan Benet. In the case of Benet, it is more a question of the milieu than the characters: his economical and panting prose, his oppressive use of adjectives, the chain of dire events—dark and tragically absurd in a world of ghostlike beings who are reduced to the level of signs—constitute the starting point of disintegration to which the world has come—a world that carries within itself the inertia that will lead it to its own destruction. This book, together with *Time of Silence* [by Luis Martín-Santos] and *Marks of Identity* by Juan Goytisolo, is one of the most violently despairing and nihilistic novels that has been written in the last few years about the condition of Spain. This nihilism, this chronicle of self-destruction extends itself in Benet to the configuration of the novel itself, thus succeeding in enriching by new turns of events its self-critical dimension. As a result, the plot of the novel is practically incapable of being disentangled: each new reading belies the provisional hypothesis that was previously formulated, and the author seems to take delight in nullifying and covering his own tracks over and over again until he reduces the novel to a game of almost total chance combined with certain elements that are givens. From this proceed the symmetry and interchangeability of the events, the chronological confusion, the obscure points, the fluctuation in the names and references; it is not that the author has lost the thread of an overly intricate plot or has given up on lending some order to it; rather it is a question of an implacable and systematic process of self-destruction corresponding, within the work, to the fatal process of individual and collective self-destruction, which is its theme. On every level—and I will not insist on the philosophical and stylistic connotations—it matters little that this or something else has taken place; everything finds its unity in nothingness, in ruin, in the final silence that follows a solitary gunshot in the hills of Región.

Pedro Gimferrer. Ínsula. Jan., 1969, p. 14†

Juan Benet's fourth novel, *Mazón's Other House* (1973), offers an unforgettable dance of death, performed by already dead or dying representatives of all social classes and seemingly dedicated to the massive de-mythification of such widely ranging clichés as the common man, monarchic splendor, *machismo,* the eternally feminine, progress, and sex as a transcendent act. The microcosm of history it presents is, therefore, one of existence as a relative absurdity, possibly evolving toward a set of moral standards (alluded to in one character's laments on current wrong directions in society) which finally may lend a small measure of meaning to human muddlings. However, notwithstanding this intermittent glimmer of hope, all of Benet's characters and most of their actions resoundingly declare life to be instinctive, cyclical, and inherently senseless. We arrive at such conclusions after laughing our way through unending battles of the sexes; a smouldering master-servant dispute; blatant cheating at the "game" of life in hopes of preserving one's self-image and, with it, the entire hierarchy of created meanings; and the contemplation of bored old lovers who can't figure out what season it is, don't remember how long they've been sleeping together, and have forgotten every important conversation they've ever enjoyed.

Most fascinating among Benet's carnival of characters is a broken-down medieval king who incarnates the very worst features of anachronistic monarchy. Everything he eulogizes (torture of heretics, bubonic plague, sexual exploitation) is perceived in the novel's contemporary setting as a flagrant banality, while his objects of derision (democracy, individual rights, works of charity—all perceived Nietzscheanly as the creations of sissies) are representative of society's current externalized values. The question of course remains as to what society's values really are, and the king himself points up our inability to decide the question on the basis of testimonials, subsequently revealing to us that he is a total hypocrite and would never trade his enjoyment of today's comforts for the supposed ennobling rigors of yesteryear. In only one important sense does the king consciously make a judgment we can accept at face value: the total irrelevancy of monarchy, and both our own and the monarch's personal boredom upon observing this dead institution in our own times. With its occasional allusions to medieval history and the Spanish Civil War, one can only wonder to what degree this universal statement on archaism takes root in recent media-wide glamorization of the Spanish royal family. Benet's king, like so many sons of '98, sees no clear road to the future, preferring rather to enshrine the past through an apotheosis of his own misery: a religiously felt "Spain pains me."

Thomas R. Franz. JSSTC. Winter, 1974, p. 197

Benet utilizes a Faulknerian-like style replete with marathon sentences, labyrinthine syntax, esoteric vocabulary and an intricate system of images, the aim of which is two-fold: 1) to distinguish certain nuances of meaning or denote the complexity of actions and events; 2) to withhold meaning deliberately in order to keep the form and content of the novel fluid and unfinished. Like Faulkner, Benet offers obstacles, obtrusions and confusing digressions in his novels which discourage the passive reader but challenge the active one. However, one pronounced difference between the novels of Benet and Faulkner reveals an underlying contrast in their approach to writing. Whereas a novel of Faulkner may be extremely difficult to untangle, the intelligent reader will be able to overcome the obstacles in his path and understand the work because Faulkner furnishes (albeit indirectly) all the necessary information. Benet, on the other hand, not only imposes barriers, but by means of delaying or partially disclosing certain incidents and ideas, he in effect forecloses the possibility of total understanding of his work. . . .

His temporal conception in part determines the structure of his novels, while at the same time it constitutes one of his recurring thematic concerns. In all of his novels Benet sets at least part of the action specifically during the Spanish Civil War, and thus gives an external point of reference to the work. However, the psychological portrayal of time destroys all semblance of the chronological flow of events. Objectively, Benet believes time exists and weaves its pattern regardless of the presence or absence of any one individual. This idea is readily apparent in the symbol of the clock in *A Meditation,* the decayed mansion in *The Tomb* or the cycles of time indicated by the change of season in *A Winter Journey.* Most commonly, however, Benet focuses on subjective time in which the ticking of a clock has no meaning, and months and years lose their independent value and fuse with the psychological flow of the human mind. . . .

The ruin which forms a leitmotiv in all of Benet's novels for the individual characters must also be viewed on a national level. From the standpoint of the entire country, the mythical Región represents for Spain what Faulkner's Yoknapatawpha County symbolizes for the Southern United States: a microcosm of the social, political and existential problems which confront man in his contemporary state of being. In the novels of Benet, the Civil War provides a backdrop against which a large portion of the action is staged, and the author casts a critical eye on both sides of the political spectrum. . . . Benet portrays the nation after the war as a diseased body with the prognosis of a slow and painful death. As Dr. Sebastián insists in *You Will Return to Región,* the Civil War was fought in order to lose it, to destroy Spain in order to rebuild it.

> David K. Herzberger. *The Novelistic World of*
> *Juan Benet* (Clear Creek, Ind., The American
> Hispanist, 1976), pp. 156–58

Admittedly, *You Will Return to Región* is an extremely difficult novel to read. Most Spanish critics would perhaps agree that Benet has accomplished "a mythical transfiguration of reality" but some say that although he may use social themes combined with objectivist techniques in his efforts to create a new vision of Spanish fiction, he really has created nothing so terribly new. Several of the major difficulties in reading *You Will Return to Región* are attributed to the novel's fragmentary form, numerous changes of point of view, impersonal narrations, self-indulgent monologues, incessant repetition of motifs, pedantic use of literary quotations, imprecision of characters' names and events in which they participate, inappropriate comparisons, use of foreign words, long intellectual discourses on time, reality, conscience, and virginity, which appear hermetically sealed off from the realization or development of their character-proponents. . . . Perhaps the language of *You Will Return to Región* is the greatest single problem for readers of this novel since it is an unnatural, wild, complicated, and sophisticated language normally beyond the capacities of its audience. *You Will Return to Región* demands a thoroughly intellectual approach and a serious reading; it is demanding, dense and truculently literary. . . .

Perhaps one "new facet" of Benet's work is his revival of the conscious stylistic technique Cervantes used to fine effect in *Don Quixote*—that of "disordered order." . . . Perhaps Benet is becoming a neo-Baroque stylist and his novel an exercise in baroque behaviorism. By transcending reality and abandoning the laws of logical perception, Benet consistently substitutes illusion for disillusion, the illogical for the logical. . . . Benet's characters express their respective *idées fixes*

within the framework of reason without logic, and create such ambiguities that it is, at times, impossible to understand them, their world or
their notion of reality. At least, Don Quixote's monomania, to revive
knight-errantry, was clearly evinced by Cervantes, who also made clear
the multiple perspectives from which Don Quixote was judged. I would
not equate Benet's novel with the Cervantes masterpiece in any sense,
except to say where the latter transformed reality through a sense of
Baroque style, producing both wisdom and entertainment, the former
relies heavily upon behaviorist techniques, evincing an overwhelming
sense of confusion through a tortuous style whose total effect, because
of its fragmentary nature and multiple and illogical perspectives, produces frustration and despondency in its readers.

Ronald Schwartz. *Spain's New Wave Novelists*
(Metuchen, N.J., Scarecrow, 1976),
pp. 236, 241–42

What really binds this almost unimaginably dense novel [*A Meditation*]
together is not Benet's sense of character or of scene but his brilliant,
overarching and fascinatingly difficult style. His sentences can go on for
pages. His figures of speech are so elaborated and extended that it's
easy to forget what they are illustrating. You must struggle with the text,
rereading sentence after sentence, many of which could be called,
depending on your point of view, acts of literary defiance, slaps in the
reader's face or brilliant inquisitions.

A Meditation is told in what I can only call an absent-minded,
sometimes quasi-omniscient, sometimes uncertain first person. The "I"
that emerges is part character and part author, part wizard and part
blind seer. . . .

Benet does not write about things we can know; he writes about
what we can never comprehend, about what he calls repeatedly the
"zones of shadow" that lie beyond the ken of the rational mind. His
convolutions and circumlocutions—his symphonically arranged style—
give *A Meditation* a fidelity to the movements of consciousness unique
in the modern novel. Beyond the pale of conventional realism, Benet
has become a kind of mythic realist, guardian (like his character Numa)
of the irreducibility of the sacred grove of human consciousness.

A Meditation is a brilliant and complex novel. If you are a true
aficionado of the modern novel, if you think the novel is the ultimate
puzzle to be reconstructed by the reader, you will consider Benet a
great discovery and another rung up the Gnostic ladder begun by the
likes of Marcel Proust and William Faulkner and Malcolm Lowry. If you
have the stamina and the patience you may find that Juan Benet's
deliberately obfuscated narration creates a new bridge—or no man's
land—between the double solipsisms of reader and writer. His ironic
meditation, his universal story of time and memory and ruin, is also one

more gauntlet thrown down by Spanish-language novelists in the arena of world literature.

Allen Josephs. *NYTBR*. May 23, 1982,
pp. 13, 42

Juan Benet's fictional world is unique, complex, mysterious, demanding, enigmatic, and aesthetically rewarding. To enter the world of Región is to enter a labyrinth where everything—except ruin, death and futility—is uncertain, or a tantalizing approximation. Solutions or answers to problems or questions are never given, and perceptions are often blurred by unreliable narrators, who are sure neither of themselves nor of that which they relate, even recounting realities which never existed. Deliberately, Benet undermines the basic reliability of his narrator, as part of his ironic vision of man caught in a world where nothing is absolute and everything is relative. Olympian omniscience crumbles with the narrator caught in his own intricacies, contradictions, fears, and confusions; other spectral creatures in the narration also fall into the concealed traps of ambition, self-confidence, and passion leading them to solitude, ruin and death. And they can neither stop nor change the course of predetermined ruination because time is the confirmation of failures and not of regeneration. Their existential apothegm is, "I suffer therefore I am." Efforts are futile. The more they talk and strive to explain reality, the more elusive it becomes; like Juan Benet's marathon sentences, the more his prose runs uninterrupted the more elusive its content becomes.

This linguistic intensity is another exteriorization of the intensity of the character's inner, tragic conflict between a desire to know more about himself and the world and the inefficacy of his linguistic means or his inherent ontological limitation. Seeking the causes for their ongoing failure, his characters find not a satisfactory answer but an elusive, mysterious "truth": that the present failure is the result of a past failure whose causes cannot be explained satisfactorily. And they are inexplicable because memory cannot recall all necessary elements in order to create a satisfactory picture of past failures. Instinctively they seek "truth," but reason and memory deny them that pleasure. Irony and absurdity, again, are omnipresent in Juan Benet's fictional world: characters strive for something and end up with quite the opposite as if invisible, malignant forces of absurdity were guiding them to failure and nothingness. And neither the victim (the character), the narrator, nor the reader understands why, how, where, or when failure began to take possession of man.

Vicente Cabrera. *Juan Benet* (Boston, Twayne,
1983), pp. 137–38

There is a fundamental difference between the worlds of Macondo [Gabriel García Márquez's mythical town] and Yoknapatawpha

[William Faulkner's mythical county], on the one hand, and Región [Juan Benet's mythical town], on the other. Región is the anecdotal sum of the novel [*A Meditation*], but not its center. Región is the surrounding ambience to be defined, those who people it, the characters to be deciphered—however contradictorily—in the activity at the novel's center: the narrator's labor as meaning-giver, his existential task of self-creation. For the novel's action is mental activity—the narrator's mental activity. Creation is actually reconstruction, with memory as the recalcitrant agent that attempts to conjure up the past, not to mourn or celebrate it, but to interpret, to understand, to define that past's truth and, with it, that of the narrator within the past. The task is an impossible one. Were this not so, were the task to be fully realized, the existential nature of the novel would surely be diminished. Instead, the goals of the narrator's task are a pretext for contemplation of the process of such an undertaking, and the attempt at discovery—the narrator's action—quickly becomes more important than what is, and what cannot be, discovered. It is around this attempt that the novel's more important explicit and implicit thematic statements revolve, statements about the nature of cognition, the workings of memory and time, the impossibility of true knowing, the certainty only of failure.

The life of Región, then, becomes the material through which the narrator's action moves. Coupled with the deeper themes accompanying the concept of ruin, this life nourishes the subjective rememorative action and the implications arising from it.

> Mary S. Vásquez. In Roberto C. Manteiga,
> David K. Herzberger, and Malcolm Alan
> Compitello, eds., *Critical Approaches to the
> Writings of Juan Benet* (Hanover, N.H.,
> University Press of New England, 1984),
> pp. 65–66

BERGAMÍN, JOSÉ (1897–1983)

These aphorisms [in *Scatterbrain*] speak about religion, philosophy, politics, and music. His thought is given over in them to all temptations and curiosities; it is pure human thought to which nothing is foreign. In the first part Bergamín speaks about the aphorism itself; he considers it as a figurative dimension of thought, which cannot be called either short or long, and which is essentially immeasurable, since although words are capable of measurement, thought is not. Is the aphorism right or wrong? It makes no difference. What is important for Bergamín is that it hit its mark. The perfect aphorism is the one to which not one word need be added or subtracted; it is precisely a question of words because "words are gods, divinity, The Verb is God itself." Bergamín's thought will always appear as a sudden revelation rather than as a forced conquest of intelligence because he is not afraid of playing with words. "Beauty is expression. Expression is always a miracle." To think is to find oneself in a state of grace, and since grace [for him] is a state of play, thought in Bergamín's conception has something of a game; it is not a purely mental game, but one that also involves passion, which for Bergamín is knowledge. "It is not the idea that impassions but rather the passion that idealizes."

This first part is of great importance in order completely to understand the spiritual position of Bergamín, with all that it has of the game, in the author's meaning of the word, a playful game, a game of words in which the whole tragic human game is involved. [1934]

Pedro Salinas. *Ensayos completos de Pedro Salinas* (Madrid, Taurus, 1981), Vol. I, p. 145.†

Bergamín, a seducer seduced by words, is quite successful when he places them in a new light and obliges them, with terribly expert manipulation, to reveal without delay their most intimate and precise meanings. He knows—he learned it with the aid of Unamuno and Croce, but above all from his own instinct as a writer—that all thought is within words and only within them. . . .

Different from the other aphorisms that he studies in his book [*Book of Spanish Aphorisms*] Bergamín's aphorism is a verbal one. His magic consists of making words say not only what they keep well hidden under a carapace that has been hardened through centuries and polished by use, but also what they themselves had never suspected and that comes to them from the outside through pure structural and phonetic associations. . . . Bergamín's aphorisms have dispensed with all logic in order to leave the words free. . . .

And the transformation that he works on individual words he also performs with set expressions; perhaps it is here that his poetic magic becomes more efficient. The very title of this volume [three of the *Book of Spanish Aphorisms*] is a set expression: "One's heart in one's mouth." It is enough for him to separate it from the trivial prattle, to give it noun form, to place it there at the start of the book for it to appear to us to be a discovery of living poetry. . . .

Together with the whirlwind of verbal associations, there is also a clear critical thought and even a erudite critical content that at its peak, for example, is the evaluation of the work of Calderón de la Barca. . . . [1940]

Francisco Ayala. *Histrionismo y representación* (Buenos Aires, Sudamericana, 1944), pp. 240–42†

In his first works José Bergamín cultivated the aphorism. It was an ingenious and neobaroque type of aphorism that, like the rest of his writings, however, results from deep spiritual and religious troubles. In this zone of inner concerns, Nietzsche was a preferred refuge for Bergamín. Bergamín cites him at every turn. From the definition "Seneca, bullfighter of virtue" sprang Bergamín's essay about Spanish stoicism, *The Statue of Don Tancredo.* But whatever book of Bergamín's that we open we will find a profusion of references to Nietzsche, whom he helped to keep alive in the minds of many readers. . . .

But Bergamín's enthusiasm for the profound and aphoristic Nietzsche culminates in the book *Infernal Frontiers of Poetry,* which, introduced by an aphorism from [Nietzsche's] *Opinions and Statements* about Nietzsche's descent to hell accompanied by four pairs of his favorite men, is nothing less than a spiritual voyage of Bergamín in the company of eight other favorite guides and by Nietzsche, to whom the last chapter is dedicated. In these nine immortals—Seneca, Dante, [Fernando de] Rojas, Shakespeare, Cervantes, Quevedo, Sade, Byron, and Nietzsche—Bergamín experiences "truly an eternal life."

From his starting point—Seneca's anti-Christianity—the traveler arrives at Nietzsche's anti-Christianity, which is the end of his infernal investigation, his questions to significant men at critical moments about the poetic experience of hell. . . . Bergamín rejects the idea that the so-called "madness" of Nietzsche is evident in his books, and he also reacts against the blame that has been laid on him in the violent course of events in Europe.

Gonzalo Sobejano. *Nietzsche en España*
(Madrid, Gredos, 1967), pp. 646–47†

Bergamín's poetry . . . is not very abundant and was produced very late. The first book of his poetry, *Deferred Rhymes and Sonnets,* appeared in 1962; the second one, *Little Somethings and Songs* . . . one year later. . . . In the latter volume I see more authenticity, a profound meeting of the poet with himself, and a successful way of telling us what he is. The baroque aspect has not disappeared, not in the least, but it is somewhat hidden in order to let the traditional roots . . . of his poetry appear. These roots have been nourished on popular tradition, and they take shape almost always in ballads of a pure Andalusian type. . . .

To this popular, intensely Andalusian vein can be added the presence of . . . Miguel de Unamuno, . . . Bécquer, . . . Antonio Machado, . . . and Manuel Machado. . . . The authentic popular flavor has been attempted by many writers. But in Bergamín the difficult combination of a shrewd intelligence united with a deep capacity for the comprehension of all things takes place; this permits him to understand the most complicated metaphysical reasoning as well as the most basic feelings. . . .

Is there any influence of existentialism in Bergamín's work? Perhaps. . . . But the concept of man as a being marked for death is a basic belief of the Spanish people. The Andalusians have made this a basic theme of their popular literature. In Bergamín—a true man of Málaga, although born in Madrid—the Andalusian qualities are not limited to formal development; he fully participates . . . in the tragic Andalusian manner of feeling oneself dying. A great religious preoccupation, and a certain hope for "after death" are clearly evident in his verse, as well as in all his prose works.

Aurora de Albornoz. Índice (Madrid). July 1,
1969, pp. 33–34†

Here [in *The Burning Nail*] we discover what Bergamín, who represents Catholicism among the ranks of Spanish revolutionaries, thinks about several major areas.

This book from the start shows us, just as Unamuno's decisive essays did, what separates us from Spain, and the secular opinion that Spain has about herself. José Bergamín has written and repeats here what can most intrigue the French: for him neither Don Quixote nor Don Juan are Spanish. To us French, what book is read more in Spain than *Don Quixote*? Indeed, it is a Christian book. . . .

Bergamín affirms that everything sacred is poetry, that poetry is an indispensable expression of the faith. The bond that he establishes between poetry and the sacred seems complex, even though it is simple: poetry and the sacred convert time into eternity (which seems to me to be more evident of the sacred, because Bergamín does not clearly speak of anything but the highest order of poetry). Every life, he states, is made up of historical moments that are crossed with eternal instincts. Like the supreme poetry, the sacrament links life to eternity, it dissolves life into eternity—but thanks to that poetry. This thought goes far in our epoch of the Council [of Trent] because it makes the author state: "All *liturgical* language when subjected to Reason, and not to poetry, is condemned to death." . . .

This book is written to answer the question: "How can man understand God?" According to the theory of its author, perhaps man responds to the question less through an ideology than through an untranslatable crackling of a fire, which many Spanish writers, brothers of El Greco, have made so much of.

André Malraux. Introduction to José Bergamín,
Le clou brulant (Paris, Plon, 1972),
pp. 11–13, 16†

[Jorge] Guillén represented a kind of exemplary embodiment of the ideals that Bergamín had sketched in his theoretical writings. . . . The categoric rejection of "influences" or "similarities" in Guillén's poetry . . . should be understood not only in terms of the affirmation of the singularity of Guillén's *Cántico,* but also in terms of the critical criteria expounded in "Hermetic Thought in the Arts." Since the historical and psychological perspectives are invalid as means of just evaluation, the "situación crítica" ["critical situation"], as Bergamín calls it, of a work of poetry can only be perceived in purely rational, aesthetic terms. The critic's task, therefore, is to measure differences rather than coincidences. To isolate only personal affinities is to fall into the trap set by the "criterio vitalista" ["vitalist criticism"] and to fail to do justice to the uniqueness of the poetic artifact that each writer creates. . . .

Bergamín's supplementary comments on Guillén's poetry . . . make complete sense only when they are read in the light of his more generalized reflexions on the guiding principles of art and poetry where the value attached to particular terms and key ideas is clearly explained. This is true of the articles and reviews devoted to works by writers like Cernuda, Salinas, and Espina, for example, where it is evident that their poetry is judged in terms of its fidelity to certain aesthetic norms that he has striven to articulate. . . .

Bergamín was naturally only one of several writers who devoted attention to problems of aesthetics in the twenties, and it would be an exaggeration to consider him as the sole source of guidance to the poets of the time who, when all said and done, never rigidly adhered to any single set of poetic "rules." His importance lies rather in the way he gauged the mood of the period, formulating a series of absolute goals towards which poetry in general seemed to be striving.

Nigel Dennis. BHS. Oct., 1981, pp. 324–25

BLASCO IBÁÑEZ, VICENTE (1867–1928)

Blasco Ibáñez has, first of all, the gift of seeing the characteristic trait of a landscape or of a character, and also the gift of translating his impressions clearly. With delicate instinct he integrates the landscape into a psychological study, which together emerge convincingly and somehow complement each other. *The Mayflower, The Cabin,* and *Reeds and Mud* will suffice to show the value of the picturesque side of things; in a literature that has admirable pages of description, such works honorably hold their place. Besides, the lack of proportion between description and narration does not bother the author too much; the accumulation of minute details that act by their multiplicity alone is his preferred method. . . . Most often the descriptive tidbits that beflower and engarland the main story at the risk of suffocating it add quite a bit of appeal to the narrative, even if they reveal a slightly loose composition. We would be annoyed, I believe, at anyone who would, out of love for a more sober art, cut these parasitic ornaments with a brutal scissors.

One can almost say as much about the characters. Blasco Ibáñez excels in the art of portraiture. . . . The clarity of the fundamental trait, the realness of the dress, the appropriateness of the language, readily studded with folk sayings, in fact with Valencian expressions full of local color, the intentional insistence upon such and such characteristic detail, above all, the direct and intimate knowledge of the customs, manners, and the special color that one's thinking assumes upon traversing the consciousness of Valencia, all that explains why some of his characters, in addition to having been drawn from the people, have already become popular.

E. Mérimée. BH. July–Sept., 1903, p. 299†

The English and Russians at present seem absorbed in beating and being beaten in battle. But our sister-neutral, Spain, is doing some wonderfully good work in the fiction of Blasco Ibáñez. . . .

He seems to be an author very much known in Spain and all the countries of Europe except England, and there is now even an English version of what is the most famous if not the greatest of his novels, *Blood and Sand,* a study, mighty, dramatic, of the Spanish nature or national character as expressed in bull-fighting. The French, Italians, Germans, Russians, Portuguese, and the very Danes know some of his other ten or a dozen novels in translation. Besides, he has written travels and short stories. . . .

We confess that we satisfied our admiration of this very great novelist at less cost to our sensibilities in *The Shadow of the Cathedral* [i.e., *The Cathedral*] than in *Blood and Sand*. We are not sure that *The Shadow of the Cathedral* is not the more prodigious feat of the two; it is at least the more original and daring. The action—but there is no action till almost the latest moment—passes entirely in the cathedral and its gardens and bell-towers. Its persons are the *personnel* of the cathedral from the cardinal down to the *perrero,* the functionary whose duty is to keep the building clear of dogs; and from highest to lowest their characters are done with art which lapses into emotion only a little toward the close of the story. . . .

The master who wrote *The Shadow of the Cathedral* is able to make its pulsations felt in every part. It abounds in characters, high and low, which have their being in words and acts springing from their natures and not from any plan set for them; they create the story and are not created for it. The whole scheme, which does not seem ruled by the author, is expressive of an understanding compassion unknown to fiction until it became human through truth to life. We should say that no living novelist, now that the incomparable Tolstoy is dead, can be compared to this author, whose triumph in his art is the more sensible through its lapses at moments. But it is at moments only that his overweening pity for misery weakens into sentimentality. The humanity of the whole affair touches every sort and condition with the intelligence that is the only justice. From the cardinal to the cobbler, every character is given a fair chance with the reader, who, so far as he has the mind and heart for so much reality, lives with them in the mighty cathedral. Nothing is forced to fit those dimensions, and the illusion (illusion does not seem the word) is so perfect and so constant that you do not miss the world which you are dimly aware of going on outside, but which penetrates it only in the several types of sight-seeing tourists very sparingly intruded.

William Dean Howells. *Harper's*. Nov., 1915,
pp. 958–60

One must admit, too, that Blasco Ibáñez's universe is a bulkier, burlier universe than Mr. [H. G.] Wells's. One is strangely certain that the axle of Mr. Wells's universe is fixed in some suburb of London, say Putney, where each house has a bit of garden where waddles an asthmatic pet dog, where people drink tea weak, with milk in it, before a gas-log, where every bookcase makes a futile effort to impinge on infinity through the encyclopedia, where life is a monotonous going and coming, swathed in clothes that must above all be respectable, to business and from business. But who can say where Blasco Ibáñez's universe centers? It is in constant progression.

Starting, as Walt Whitman from fish-shaped Paumonauk, from the fierce green fertility of Valencia, city of another great Spanish conqueror, the Cid, he had marched on the world in battle array. The whole history comes out in the series of novels at this moment being translated in such feverish haste for the edification of the American public. The beginnings are stories of the peasants of the fertile plain round about Valencia, of the fishermen and sailors of El Grao, the port, a sturdy violent people living amid a snappy fury of vegetation unexampled in Europe. His method is inspired to a certain extent by Zola, taking from him a little of the newspaper-horror mode of realism, with inevitable murder and sudden death in the last chapters. Yet he expresses that life vividly, although even then more given to grand vague ideas than to a careful scrutiny of men and things. He is at home in the strong communal feeling, in the individual anarchism, in the passionate worship of the water that runs through the fields to give life and of the blades of wheat that give bread and of the wine that gives joy, which is the moral make-up of the Valencian peasant. He is sincerely indignant about the agrarian system, about social inequality, and is full of the revolutionary bravado of his race.

A typical novel of this period is *The Cabin,* a story of a peasant family that takes up land which has lain vacant for years under the curse of the community, since the eviction of the tenants, who had held it for generations, by a landlord who was murdered as a result, on a lonely road by the father of the family he had turned out. The struggle of these peasants against their neighbours is told with a good deal of feeling, and the culmination in a rifle fight in an irrigation ditch is a splendid bit of blood and thunder. There are many descriptions of local customs, such as the Tribunal of Water that sits once a week under one of the portals of Valencia cathedral to settle conflicts of irrigation rights, a little dragged in by the heels, to be sure, but still worth reading. Yet even in these early novels one feels over and over again the force of that phrase "popular vulgarization." Valencia is being vulgarized for the benefit of the universe. The proletariat is being vulgarized for the benefit of the people who buy novels.

John Dos Passos. Rosinante to the Road Again
(New York, George H. Doran, 1922), pp. 124–27

In my opinion *The Shadow of the Cathedral* [i.e., *The Cathedral*] is a much finer book than *The Four Horsemen of the Apocalypse*. It shapes better, and the theme, a devastating indictment, is logically and comprehensively worked out. But *The Shadow of the Cathedral* would never have had its present success had it not been for the "big boom" . . . in *The Four Horsemen of the Apocalypse*. Why was that work so successful? Fifty per cent of its success, perhaps more, was due to clever advertising; but *The Four Horsemen of the Apocalypse* also galloped up Fifth Avenue at the psychological moment. The war was at its height, the newspapers were crowded with bewildering details, the tongues of gossips ran ceaselessly, everybody was feverish for news, many little, jumpy men wrote long, jumpy articles, and into this hubbub of sketches rolled the big . . . crude canvas of *The Four Horsemen of the Apocalypse*. Obviously the author is a vital man, a man of parts and energy, who had seen the war, who had felt its horror and sorrow, who has a big . . . surging imagination, so riotous that while he is composing he is quite unable to pause anywhere for art's sake. "I write explosively," says Blasco Ibáñez. "I am sometimes hardly aware what I am doing. The germ of an idea comes to me; it grows and grows until there is a sort of spontaneous combustion." Just so. That is the reason why I prefer Mrs. Burnett or Edith Wharton, Barrie or Leonard Merrick.

Blasco Ibáñez begins a novel slowly, he climbs laboriously, he reaches the crest, then "once on the other side I cannot stop myself—I rush headlong, whirling, plunging, working endlessly until I reach the finale." He wrote *The Four Horsemen of the Apocalypse* in four months in Paris, in 1916, Toward the end "I worked thirty hours at a stretch." This is magnificent, but it is not art. Of course I am well aware that the readers who make up the one-hundred-thousand circulation groups do not want art: they want a story. But we must keep the flag of art flying. Perhaps I should not have penned this gentle protest had not his publishers called him "the greatest of living novelists," and had they not announced in big . . . type that he is "the dominant figure in the world of modern fiction."

But I do not want to belittle Blasco Ibáñez. He is a force; he has gusto and vitality, and he is fiercely interested in many things besides the writing of fiction—politics, history, sociology. His tirade on Ponce de León was fine, his defense of Spain was passionately eloquent. He is quick. When a heckler asked him, "Why did Spain come to Mexico to disturb the Indians?" he answered, "Why were the Indians of Manhattan disturbed?" He can make a gesture, too, as when he led the subscriptions for a memorial in the Bronx to Edgar Allan Poe. . . .

A vital, vigorous, fearless man. A sturdy man with a bull-like head; an "ag'in' the Government" man: in 1885 he was imprisoned for six months for writing a sonnet against the Spanish Government; a man of imagination and dynamic driving power. My only objection to him is that he allows himself to be called "the greatest of living novelists." But perhaps, as he doesn't read English, he is not aware that this has been said about him. So here's to you, Vicente Blasco Ibáñez.

Charles Lewis Hind. More Authors and I (New
York, Dodd, Mead and Co., 1922), pp. 166–69

In almost all the regional novels of Blasco Ibáñez, the ones that have been most accused of being low-brow, there is next to the slightly repellent portrait of coarse humanity, a lyrical and elegiac spark. This is what makes them so beautiful and poetic. As proof of this, we have the quintessential sensations of music in *Among Orange Trees,* his tender treatment of children and of adolescent love in *The Cabin,* his marvelous portrayal of provincial disenchantment in *Rice and Covered Wagon;* the spiritual solidarity of Gabriel and Rosario, the fallen ones in *The Cathedral,* the pretty words of fraternity and pardon of Salvatierra in *The Big Vintage;* his magnificent final vision in *Reeds and Mud,* when the silent lover helps Tío Toni give to the earth, the earth that he has stolen from the lake with the strength of his own arms—in supreme offering—the lifeless body of his child.

Everyone says that Blasco Ibáñez is a pessimist. We believe that he is not. It is quite true that there is too much blood in almost all his novels. In *The Cabin,* there is blood everywhere: the murder of Don Salvador, the death of Albaet, the death of the horse, the attack on Roseta, the wounding of Pimentó, and finally his death, the fire in the cabin. It is as if Blasco Ibáñez had squeezed the Huerta [fertile garden district outside of Valencia] in order to make it drip blood.

Life for Blasco Ibáñez is a hard struggle. Life is bad, but one has to try to improve it. All his work is a hymn to progress and to the noble ideas of universal brotherhood; it is fundamentally moral because it is the exaltation of human effort. Blasco Ibáñez's philosophy is not fatalism, as many claim it is. Blasco Ibáñez recognizes the existence of Destiny, but does not cross his arms and submit to it. Fatalism is a comfortable doctrine that advises trust in Destiny and not to hate or love life. Blasco Ibáñez loves life above all things. His heroes fight until they fall dead or are put out of action in battle. Blasco Ibáñez's philosophy, in any case, is one of dynamic pessimism, which at times turns into open pessimism, as in *The Dead Command,* a novel in which the dead end up commanding the living.

Joaquín Ortega. UWSLL. Nov., 1924,
pp. 232–33†

To my own mind there can be no doubt whatever that, when Blasco Ibáñez's ephemeral, ostentatious novels are wholly forgotten, as must happen very soon, the really great works of his youth and early middle age will re-emerge from the shadows and regain their rightful place in literature. In this country his reputation suffers from two disabilities: first, his best novels have not as yet all been translated; secondly, his work as a whole has never been seen in due perspective. His art was already, from a purely literary point of view, corrupted, when he wrote *The Four Horsemen of the Apocalypse,* which contributed most to his celebrity outside his own country. After offering the British public that novel, together with others of the stamp of *Blood and Sand* and *The Enemies of Women,* it was a hopeless proceeding to translate *Sónnica the Courtesan* or even *The Big Vintage* and present them as though they had been the novelist's latest writings; still less was it possible to expect the sensation-glutted public which reads its Blasco Ibáñez to savour the delicate regionalism of *The Mayflower, Among Orange Trees,* and *Rice and Covered Wagon*—all three novels which were written before he had reached his thirtieth birthday. . . .

His finest characters are a formidable gallery of genius, and outstanding among them are men of energy, determination and impulse like their creator. With women he is rarely successful, except in his earlier works, when he introduces them with great effect as minor characters mainly of emotional or pictorial appeal. For the most part his portraits are clear, sharp and incisive, engraving themselves as indelibly upon the memory as those of any contemporary Spanish writer. Let the critics say what they will, there is no young novelist in Spain today whose works are comparable, both in quality and number, with those which Blasco Ibáñez produced before the age of forty.

Nor can he be said to be far inferior, from the purely regionalistic standpoint, to that great regionalist, the Condesa de Pardo Bazán, who preceded him, or to others, such as Pérez Lugín, who have striven to create local atmosphere, and whose fame has been posterior to his own.

That his art in this respect hardly survived being transported from Valencia to Castile is perhaps not surprising; what is more surprising is that he was able later to recapture so much of it. If I am not mistaken, it is where his colours first begin to develop harshness that his voice becomes strident; and future historians of literature may well seize upon that very point as one where a regionalist of exquisite sensibility took the tide that led him to an ephemeral fortune.

E. Allison Peers. ContempR. April, 1928,
pp. 599, 604

Our time has a short memory, and there is hardly a more forgotten book than a best-seller of twenty-five years ago. By chance such a book fell into my hands recently, *The Four Horsemen of the Apocalypse* by Vicente Blasco Ibáñez. I had read this novel in 1916, when everybody was reading it, and vaguely remembered that it contained excellent descriptions of the last war. But I had forgotten completely one of the less important characters, a German professor of history, a certain Julius von Hartrott, who in this book proclaims the political ambitions of the German people—as I then thought—in a most exaggerated and even ridiculous manner. This champion of the wildest Pan-Germanism seemed to me unreal and I regarded his arrogant and arbitrary ideologies merely as malevolent exaggerations of the author.

Now as I re-read this book a quarter of a century later, I could not believe my own eyes and I had the feeling that I owed an apology to Blasco Ibáñez. For this man Hartrott, whom I had formerly regarded as a crazy caricature, now appeared to me as one of the most lifelike characters ever created by a writer, because, unfortunately, Hartrott's absurd theories have become through Hitler the official credo of seventy million Germans. The very ideas which this fictitious person proclaimed in 1914, at a time when Hitler was an unknown house-painter and his satellites, Rosenberg and Goebbels, still in school, are at this moment endangering the freedom of our earth. The fiction of a poet has become frightful reality, and there is perhaps no better proof that Hitler's conceptions of world domination are not as new as they seem than to listen to what Blasco Ibáñez' imaginary character proclaimed twenty-five years ago. . . .

One's eyes are opened by this book. All the conceptions which Hitler today seeks to impose upon the whole world are enunciated by this imaginary—and yet so real—Hartrott. And with alarm we perceive that in the subconsciousness of the German people this dream of world domination has always been present. Hitler has not invented it. He only made real by his furor what Blasco Ibáñez saw in the postulates of the Hartrotts twenty-five years ago. What formerly had been only the diabolical dream of a few isolated individuals has today become the aspiration of millions and the greatest danger for our world. Blasco

Ibáñez' fiction has shown again that it is the poet who understands his time and the future better than the professor of history.

Stefan Zweig. *Free World*. Dec., 1942, pp. 234–35

In temperament Blasco Ibáñez may be said to resemble Maupassant. He had the same animal vitality, the same earthiness and incapacity for sublimation. He possessed an extraordinary power of entering into the feelings of simple people such as peasants and fishermen—this was increased by his political activities, which taught him how they were exploited—and the sort of almost physical passion for nature that one sometimes finds in keen sportsmen. But he had a fire and a passion which Maupassant had not, and his artistic sensibility had a coarser grain, possibly because he did little to cultivate it.

As a novelist his masters were Zola and Flaubert. From Zola—the minor influence—he took the idea of portraying the life of primitive communities: from Flaubert, his general method of telling a story and also whatever a man who works at white heat can use of such an elaborately distilled style. His heavy, coloured writing—which, though often careless and journalistic in its phrasing, rises at times to passages of great beauty—perfectly suits the subjects he used it for. His method of composition was to meditate on his subject for a long time—no doubt it is for this reason that the form of his novels is so excellent—and then to write the book in furious haste in a few weeks. Although he documented himself carefully beforehand, it is only when he is writing of his native country, of which he had an intimate knowledge since childhood, that he writes well.

His first book, *Among Orange Trees,* came out in 1894. It is a regional novel about the shopkeeping classes of Valencia, among whom he had been brought up. As a picture of the life of the city it is interesting, but the middle classes were not his subject and one feels something lacking. In the following year appeared *The Mayflower,* a novel about the fishermen of El Cabañal. . . . The wonderful account of a smuggling voyage to Algiers in an unseaworthy boat is the reliving of a similar voyage he had just made himself, with the object of learning what a smuggler's life was like. Since the *Odyssey* and the *Aeneid,* I do not think that the life of the seafaring people of the Mediterranean has ever been presented so vividly.

In 1898 appeared *The Cabin,* a novel about the peasantry of the Vega, or cultivated plain of Valencia. Its subject is a vendetta between the landlords and the peasants, and the ruin which the latter brought on a family of *churros,* or Aragonese labourers, who persisted in occupying a farm which they, to pay out an oppressive landowner, had decided must remain vacant.

In every respect it is a masterpiece. Its plot has the firmness and cleanness of the plot of a Maupassant story and yet it has been able to take up and digest all the innumerable details required to convey the life of a peasant community. From the very beautiful opening, with its description of day breaking over the Vega and the work of the farms beginning, to the terrific scene of the burning homestead and the stampede of the scorched animals that closes the book, it moves with an art that is sure and faultless. And as a picture of peasant life it is unequalled, I think, in any language. [1951]

Gerald Brenan. *The Literature of the Spanish People* (Cleveland, Meridian, 1957), pp. 411–13

Like [Emilia] Pardo Bazán [Spanish writer of naturalistic novels], Blasco Ibáñez was attracted to Zola primarily by the vitality of his art and perhaps to some extent by his sensationalism. In his case, however, it was easier to adopt a naturalistic view of man's place. He was not particularly interested in philosophical ideas, but he was a lover of nature in the raw and personally inclined to co-operate with the spontaneous, natural side of his being. Moreover, he was not restrained by religious convictions from plunging wholeheartedly into the spirit of Zola's exaltation of primal natural forces. As a consequence of this affiliation between intellectual attitude and earthiness of style, he produced a more authentic version of naturalism than Pardo Bazán, at the same time achieving in his novels a stronger artistic consistency than she was able to attain under the handicap of a loyalty divided between art and her philosophical-religious outlook.

The outstanding example of Blasco Ibáñez's naturalism is *Reeds and Mud,* of which the author said: "This is my favorite novel . . . it is the one that holds for me the most pleasant memory, the one that I composed with most solidity, the one that seems to me the best rounded" (*redonda*). In this story the novelist grasps the malevolent spirit of primitive nature, holds it at close range, and achieves the sharp singleness of effect that one generally finds in a short story. His procedure is to portray a locale and to impart through his portraiture the suggestion of a sinister transcendent power. The place is the Albufera, a swampy lake region near Valencia, where the inhabitants eke out a wretched existence fishing and cultivating rice. In this setting the people harmonize with their milieu and through it appear to be oppressed by a cruelty that envelops more than their immediate situation. This blending of two levels of reality, the harsh earthiness of immediate surroundings and a fateful overtone of transcendent implications, is maintained throughout the novel. . . .

But Blasco Ibáñez not only creates the vivid portrait of a place in *Reeds and Mud,* he combines with it a theme in perfect harmony with the monistic foundations of naturalism. Man is crushed by nature, not in his separateness from it but because he is one with it. On the basis of this oneness the author builds an unusually strong singleness of narrative effect. From an artistic viewpoint, *Reeds and Mud* is a gem among modern Spanish novels.

Sherman H. Eoff. *The Modern Spanish Novel*
(New York, New York University Press, 1961),
pp. 116–17, 119

Blasco Ibáñez's ideals were high. Far from being a withdrawn Naturalist, objectively reporting on random slices of life, he violently championed many causes that are still alive today. Blasco Ibáñez enlarged his provincial vision until it became a cosmic view. His original mind and gifted imagination were employed in a titanic effort to spread widely his learning, through translating and publishing the works of European thinkers of various countries and philosophies. Like H. G. Wells, the British author whom he resembles in several ways, he embraced the task of becoming a one-man institute of adult education. His sympathy was always with the underdog, but he could portray with compassion the men and women he saw in all strata of society. He was a lover of Mediterranean culture from classical to current epochs, and this background enabled him to expand his scope and become a reliable commentator on Atlantic and American culture as well. His readers around the globe craved such an international view, and he was the most widely translated of all modern Spanish writers. . . .

Early stereotyped as a Naturalist of the Zola persuasion, he wrote some of the most impassioned and poignant passages in Spanish fiction. Disdaining "style" as a distraction from the story, Blasco Ibáñez had more than a touch of the poet, and at times his pages are redolent with perfumes and pictorial with images of almost painful beauty. He likewise became one of the masters of Spanish historical fiction, glorifying his country's past. His descriptions of places, impressionistic but precise, have drawn visitors from abroad to view landscapes and edifices he has immortalized (for many people, the province of Valencia will always be Blasco Ibáñez's Valencia). His novels of then contemporary life have become, with the passage of time, valuable sources of social history.

Blasco Ibáñez had a firm theory of the novelist's function, as he explained more than once. He was a craftsman, and his novels often were built on more firm structures than the casual reviewer could perceive. His inborn aesthetic sensibility was sharpened by the need to impress his ideas upon his chosen, broad audience. Working from live models, he created characters who could love and weep and bleed. His ability to depict women is especially notable; they are seldom pretty puppets and more often vigorous, even masculine, figures dominating their menfolk and impressing their wills on families and even nations.

Observation of Blasco Ibáñez's apparently hasty method of composition led some critics to assume that he carelessly tossed off his masterpieces and rushed into print. Usually, however, the novel composed itself in his mind over a long period, and when the time of parturition came he plunged into a feverish transcription of his pondered prose.

It is possible that, when success showered on Blasco Ibáñez after the whirlwind sales of the English translation of *The Four Horsemen of the Apocalypse,* his work declined in strength as he led the distracting life of a Riviera celebrity. It would be an error, however, to parrot the usual comment that only the Valencian novels are worthy of serious study. *The Naked Lady, Blood and Sand, The Dead Command,* or *Mare Nostrum.* The five historical novels of Spanish glorification, to which Blasco Ibáñez devoted the energies of his later years, crowned a career. . . .

Finally, Blasco Ibáñez's themes were often expressed so vigorously that they verged upon propaganda. Yet many of his ideas are still fresh today. Until our generation, or the next one, solves the problems of love, hate, war, race, poverty, art, politics, religion, the dead hand of tradition, colonization, feminism, imperialism, and national loyalties, we should open our minds to the vision of human life found in the fascinating fiction of Vicente Blasco Ibáñez.

A. Grove Day and Edgar C. Knowlton, Jr. *V. Blasco Ibáñez* (New York, Twayne, 1972), pp. 136–37

[*Reeds and Mud*] combines three levels of reality: the story of three generations (and in particular of Tonet), the constant presence and influence of the Albufera, and the "transcending," symbolic world of deterministic pressures. Just as these planes of action are brought into artistic harmony, so the major aspects of style, characterization, theme and structure function together to produce a natural and balanced whole. The near flawless causality inherent in the work's structure swerves to support the deterministic theme. The stylistic contrasts between impressionistic and savage action lead the reader to a similar awareness. The constant presence of verbs in the imperfect or conditional tenses enhances our recognition of the intemporality of nature, as well as of man's inability to mitigate a basically animalistic temperament. The costumbristic descriptions, an important element of Blasco Ibáñez's stylistic approach, serve to clarify the structure of the novel as well as to aid in the delineation of characters.

Above all, the unity of *Reeds and Mud* derives from the fact that Blasco Ibáñez wrote with the clear purpose of presenting the people, customs, and ambience of a region without recourse to moralizing. His artistry stems from the rapid, expressive, pictorial and at times poetic presentation of nature, the powerful depiction of the Valencian region and the vigorous portraiture of man's more savage instincts and desires. If Blasco Ibáñez had not strayed from the format and the setting he knew best, he might have attained a more significant place within the history of modern literature.

Jeremy T. Medina. *Hispania.* May, 1977,
pp. 282–83

BUERO VALLEJO, ANTONIO (1916–   )

[Buero Vallejo's] concept of drama is essentially tragic, for *Story of a Staircase* is a tragedy and nothing else. I am using the word "tragedy" here in the sense of the dramatization of man in his totality, since the dramatization of the partial aspects of man's life is always material for the theater. Tragedy comes about not when the author confronts the particular situation of some characters, but when he captures them all at the deepest roots of their humanity. . . . *Story of a Staircase* is a tragedy of men in their totality who are fixed in their existence. The tragic sense of life derives from the totality of our existence, not from a moment in it, which would be a mere dramatic ploy. And if the men with whom the author, in this case Antonio Buero Vallejo, plays present themselves to us with the full sense of their own existence, then tragedy flows. . . .

Story of a Staircase has been a surprise in our literary milieu because of its lack of continuity, its deviation from immediate tradition. Neither Benavente, nor Casona, nor García Lorca can be found in the work of Antonio Buero Vallejo. The surprise of all those who attended the premiere was great: it made one think of the Americans, of O'Neill, of Elmer Rice. But in my opinion, the only link with them is its contemporaneity.

Neither the language nor the complex theatrical effects—effects that are extremely complex—call to mind García Lorca. In spite of those who have glimpsed a bit of Pérez Galdós in the author of *Story of a Staircase,* this play lives by itself; it finds its exegesis in itself. Without hesitating, I dare say that *Story of a Staircase* is an original and contemporary production, a tremendous Spanish find, underwritten, bare—more than bare—open like a wound.

The beauty of the work flows neither from its language nor from its ideas, but only from its prodigious, affirmative sobriety, from its vital justification of the presence of the characters at each moment. Theatrical carpentry? And why not theatrical architecture? *Story of a Staircase* gives the impression of appearing like a vertebrate being. Bone, hard bone that hides a rich marrow. The dramatic technique of

Antonio Buero Vallejo in this work, from the moment the first characters appear, tends toward being bone-hard in order to protect its hidden marrow from harshness.

Arturo del Hoyo. *Ínsula.* Nov. 15, 1949, p. 1†

Up to the present Buero Vallejo has had a very responsive audience willing to accept fantasy as well as reality. In this respect Buero Vallejo shares the attitude [about the audience's ability to accept fantasy and reality] of García Lorca, Casona, Pemán and others. It is impossible not to think of García Lorca when reading the works of Buero Vallejo and Casona, and yet Buero Vallejo has broken away from recent literary traditions. Buero Vallejo, with proper justification, declares in his correspondence with the editor: "I wouldn't know how to perceive any analogy between my theater and García Lorca's, whom I nevertheless admire as an extraordinary dramatist." The interesting thing is that Buero Vallejo admits and agrees with his critics that his works have been influenced by O'Neill, Elmer Rice, Priestley, and Miller, among others. Ibsen, however, is his main source of inspiration. Among the Spaniards, he acknowledges his debt to Unamuno and Ortega y Gasset. Buero Vallejo, however, is extremely original in his elaborations, albeit he is the first to admit direct indebtedness whenever there has been any. The one play up to this moment which is a retelling of a classic is *The Dream Weaver,* based on Homer's *Odyssey.* The best playwrights, of course, have always freely borrowed plot material and even techniques.

Fantasy provides a considerable framework in the works of Buero Vallejo. He makes use of such fantastic elements as the blind, the dead, the disguised, the mysterious voice, fairy tales, double impersonations, witchcraft, biblical elements, superstitions, etc. to great advantage in the construction of his dramas. The most realistic play of Buero Vallejo is *Story of a Staircase,* and even here, the inner significance of the role of the stairway is the core of the story.

The sustained interest which he arouses in the audience is a significant characteristic of the theater of this author. His plots are generally compact and devoid of subordinate themes. He avoids violence on the stage. He is excellent in the creation of characters, situations and conflicts; he possesses an uncommon resourcefulness in theatrical effects, which are normally well-chosen and well-employed. His style is vigorous; his language is precise and even poetic in many instances; yet it is generally simple and easy to understand. In fact, there is a deliberate attempt to use as much popular speech as possible. His dialogue is clear, natural, brief and effective; it is an expression of the intense feeling of the characters.

Buero Vallejo is a serious dramatist; he has not written comedy or works of sheer entertainment; this is not his forte. Although there are humorous touches in some of his plays, he is not yet at home with humor. He has stayed clear of the *boulevardier* play.

José Sánchez. Introduction to Antonio Buero
Vallejo, Historia de una escalera (New York,
Charles Scribner's Sons, 1955), pp. xiv–xvi

The work of Buero Vallejo is something like a mirror in which all his humanity and morality are reflected. Buero Vallejo's work does not deceive. It is an absolute and sincere consequence of the man that cannot be separated from him. In his plays, the dramatist's social and metaphysical concerns continue to be reflected, as are his almost infinite love for all that is human, his compassion for vice, his implacable and ferocious condemnation of injustice, his repugnance for despotism, his hope, his awareness of the pathetic and limited condition of man, which is expressed by means of that obsessive blindness [in *The Concert at Saint Ovide*].

I know that Buero Vallejo is concerned about man because he is, before anything else, a man: he is uneasy about life because he lives it with a passion that is almost existential; he becomes anguished in the face of death and has a profound tragic sense. . . . It is possible that in those months of infinite anguish [it took him to write *The Concert at Saint Ovide*] lies the entire key to his theater. Could it not have been then when Buero Vallejo urgently began to come up with the question of man's blindness as something that was substantive in his own life? Perhaps. In any case, what is important to know is that in exchange for his not having discovered at that time the light that so unnerves him we now have in Spain a playwright, the best of them all, who is busied by and concerned about man and his times. The blind, the dumb, and the deaf of his dramatic work are something more than just human models outlined in compassionately moving contours. They are the embodiment of the themes that overwhelm man: his metaphysical uneasiness; the geographical and historical realities that have touched his life; injustice. His spirit, serenely rebellious, has looked for artful formulas with which he has explored new territory in spite of the awful difficulties that weigh on the soul of all of us. And he has succeeded in awakening something in that Spanish consciousness that had lain dormant in illusory self-satisfaction. He has made possible a powerful theater of testimony, and being conscious of the writer's commitment, he has not turned away from calling things by their proper name.

Carlos Muñiz. PrA. Dec., 1962, p. 9†

Rather than a dramatization of a partial aspect of life, [*Story of a Staircase*] presents a microcosm of Man's existence as a whole. The staircase itself emerges as the main protagonist of the play and as a symbol of the limitations of the characters, both those imposed from without—Time and Space—and those which are the result of their own incapacity. It is the unchanging scene which serves as a constant reminder of the immutable nature of the human situation to which the characters are anchored, in spite of their efforts to break loose. The tragic impact of *Story of a Staircase* lies in these efforts of the characters to find a way out of the impasse of their lives, in the divergence between the hopes of youth and the disillusionment of age. The general themes overshadow the individual problems of the characters, who tend to be somewhat schematic and functional, and the social context is merely the incidental landscape in which these preoccupations are set.

The themes underlying *Story of a Staircase*—the search for happiness and for a positive attitude to human limitations—are expressed in a diversity of forms in Buero Vallejò's later work: Greek myth in *The Dream Weaver* (1952), fairy tale and fantasy in *Almost a Fairy Tale* (1953) and *Irene; or, The Treasure* (1954), drama of suspense and intrigue in *Dawn* (1953). Symbolism pointing to the ideas and preoccupations behind the surface action is nearly always present, whether it be discreetly submerged as in *Story of a Staircase* or blatant and overloaded as in *The Awaited Sign* (1952). It is thus misleading to insist upon any arbitrary division of Buero Vallejo's work into "realism" and "symbolism," as this tends to obscure the underlying unity of the plays and gives the impression that in some of them (notably *Story of a Staircase* and the later *Today's a Holiday* (1956), he is principally concerned with the portrayal of naturalistic characters and social realities for their own sake. . . .

In his quest for happiness Man is his own worst enemy: Buero Vallejo insists on this element of human responsibility. The universe imposes limits, but Man aggravates his condition by his refusal to confront the reality of his situation and by the egoism which prevents sympathy and compassion for others. If the world is ever to have any significance for human beings, it must be first by a victory of the individual over himself. Man must have the will and integrity to suppress his innate egoism and see clearly what his real problems are. It is the exercise of this inviolable liberty of the individual that Buero Vallejo advocates. [1964]

J. E. Lyon. Introduction to Antonio Buero
Vallejo, *Hoy es fiesta* (Boston, D. C. Heath,
1966), pp. 18–20, 23

When he has to explain his theater, Buero Vallejo declares straight out that he considers himself a man and a writer of ideas. Insofar as he is a man and a writer, he believes life to be a totality, something that is genuine, like tragedy. Personalities and psychology do not interest him in themselves but only to the extent that they have become symbols so that he can bring forward their tragic confrontation. Put another way, the characters, just like puppets, serve the grand design of the dramatist; in no case do they get away from him in order to remain faithful to their own idiosyncrasies and temperaments. The plot, from that moment on, acquires the character of an edifying experiment. Buero Vallejo has full awareness of this: he praises tragedy more than any other dramatic genre "for the ennobling and moral qualities it has with respect to man." From this perspective, should one be surprised that his denouements correspond, above all, to his own views on man and society? They do not at all reflect life and its absurdities devoid of all morality. Since God shows Himself to be too capricious or incomprehensible, the author himself takes the fate of his characters into his own hands. But this is not at all done to reward the good and punish the bad according to his own morality. He condemns them all to an eternal purgatory; he crushes them with a scorn filled with indulgence. It is for this reason that *Story of a Staircase,* Buero Vallejo's most typical play, appears not as a tragedy but as a comedy of disillusionment. The "comedia de desengaño" [the comedy of disillusionment] of the seventeenth century, at least, opened onto a metaphysical issue: hell or eternal glory.

Charles Aubrun. In Jean Jacquot, ed., *Le théâtre moderne* (Paris, Centre National de la Recherche Scientifique, 1967), Vol. II, p. 118†

Since 1949 there has been a tremendous leap in Buero Vallejo's range and style. His more recent plays have a symbolic depth and an imaginative power which most of his Spanish contemporaries have been unable to achieve. *The Dream Weaver* is certainly the most interesting of these plays. It is a retelling of Ulysses' homecoming which has been infused with a rich fantasy and expressed in vigorous language. Much like his French contemporaries, Buero Vallejo uses the Homeric legend to comment on conditions in his own time. Penelope is symbolic of the beleaguered people of Spain who must endure the ravages of false suitors while they await the return of the true husbandman. Her efforts, which on the surface appear so futile, are revealed to be, in fact, an increasingly virulent movement of passive resistance.

The most important Spanish critics consider Buero Vallejo their nation's top-ranking playwright. This may very well be true, but the fact that he is not at all popular with audiences reflects the dilemma facing the contemporary Spanish theatre. Their best writers are rejected (if not actually harassed) by a government which pretty much controls the theatre. As a result, playwrights like Buero Vallejo are denied an opportunity for continued production, and hence the optimum conditions for artistic growth. In spite of this, he continues to work, and if and when the situation changes, Antonio Buero Vallejo is sure to be in the vanguard of the new theatre of Spain.

Robert W. Corrigan. In Robert W. Corrigan, ed., *Masterpieces of the Modern Spanish Theater* (New York, Collier, 1967), pp. 124–25

Presumably, Buero Vallejo chose to situate [*Story of a Staircase*] within the confines of a stairwell because of the visual, symbolic support which the setting could lend to the predicament of the characters. By its very form and function, the "staircase that leads nowhere" lends scenic strength to the pointless coming and going, and the cruel cycle of illusion and disillusionment, which form the substance of the characters' lives. But if Buero Vallejo's unusual setting was a stroke of theatrical genius, it was also to be the source of a serious dramatic problem. By situating his play in this tight, closed location Buero Vallejo was opening himself to the danger of melodrama. In such a location, natural encounters would be rare and dramatic movement difficult. Conflicts would have to be developed through "chance" encounters, and these might well produce an explosiveness that would work against the muted, restrained tone desirable for this drama of frustration.

Buero Vallejo copes with this problem by accepting the melodrama engendered by his setting, incorporating it into his play, and then turning the problem into an advantage by using melodrama as an ironic device. *Story of a Staircase* is essentially melodramatic, if we understand authorial arbitrariness as a prime element of melodrama. In this play situations and encounters must constantly be contrived through arbitrary, artificial means, given the implausibility of action in a stairwell. Buero Vallejo does not resist this fact. Chance encounters and surprises in the stairwell follow each other freely, and seldom does the author attempt to give them a logical justification. Rather, he simply mutes their consequences. In so doing he not only avoids an undesirable sensationalism but actually uses the event to further the play's mood of frustration. . . .

In short, *Story of a Staircase* throbs with the frustration of unrealized melodrama. The resultant mood functions in support of the play's major themes and dictates the audience's participation in the frustrations of the characters. In a similar manner, Buero Vallejo's creation and manipulation of characters suggest suffocated potentiality. One notices, for example, the great discrepancy between the large number of characters (eighteen) and the scarcity of human achievement. The drama's world is well populated—by impotent people. In addition to the specific disillusionments and disappointments that plague the characters, the humanity of this play has about it a tenuous air, produced by the brevity and infrequency of each character's presence on stage. . . .

Story of a Staircase is a metaphor of frustration, given clarity by ironic, illusory suggestions of flow, movement, and potentiality. It is a frustrated drama—a drama which makes itself faintly visible through pitiful fits and starts, but never manages to crystallize or generate momentum, and ultimately becomes a mockery of itself. Like so much of the twentieth century's dramatic art, *Story of a Staircase* tends toward "anti-theatre": theatre built on the awareness of its own impotence, built on a loss of faith in the possibility of cohesive, consequential action.

The aesthetic experience offered by this play is understandable in the terms of Kenneth Burke's definition of dramatic form as "the psychology of the audience," for Buero Vallejo has employed the dramatist's formal resources to impose on his audience an emotional trajectory parallel to the experience embodied on stage. . . . It would appear that the "optimistic" interpretation of Buero Vallejo's theatre, so frequently expounded by Buero Vallejo himself and by many of his critics, would have little validity with respect to *Story of a Staircase*: a work that projects a world in which human beings are trapped and human efforts are futile.

Farris Anderson. KRQ. 18, 2, 1971,
pp. 224, 227, 235–36

Buero Vallejo notes that his own reservations concerning what he considers the excesses of such groups as the Living Theater—the trend toward the atextual productions advocated by Artaud and toward extreme forms of participation—are shared by such widely differing directors as Jorge Lavelli and Roger Planchon in France and by director Peter Brook in England. It is for this reason he believes possible a new reconciliation between participation and distancing, between the "Dionysian" and "Apollonian," which will represent a return to true tragedy as he has so often defined it. . . . In their desperation disguised as joy, today's radical playwrights wish to erase theatrical history and return not to tragedy, but to the dithyramb, which was its origin, with its spontaneous chorus of spectator-actors as protagonist. If theater is to return to tragedy, which went beyond the dithyramb to give us man's total measure—his lucidity as well as his enigma—Buero Vallejo believes that it must result from the realization that authentic participation in the theater, like authentic action in life, must be internal as well as external.

The psychic participation which Buero Vallejo advocates is best illustrated by two of his own plays. In one of his very earliest plays, *In the Burning Darkness,* the characters are blind. Instead of having the actors approach the spectators to shout at them the horrors of blindness or forcibly to blindfold them, he extinguishes, at one point, both the stage and house lights. That this participation, although less ostensible, was effective was proved by the screams of the audience. In a very recent work, *The Sleep of Reason,* the protagonist is deaf. Rather than the actors violently covering the spectators' ears and then screaming at them, they move their lips but utter no sound whenever the protagonist is on stage, thus permitting the audience to enter into his world of deafness. Thus there is produced a more authentic participation in the reality of the tragedy—a reality which is symbolic, for the blindness portrayed represents . . . man's lack of spiritual vision and the deafness, his alienation or estrangement from his fellow human beings.

Martha T. Halsey. *Antonio Buero Vallejo* (New York, Twayne, 1973), pp. 37–38

Confinement, determined not by stage necessity but of a symbolic nature, is a strong element in several of Buero Vallejo's plays: *Story of a Staircase, The Dream Weaver, Today's a Holiday,* and especially *Adventure in Gray*. Modern dramatists have frequently displayed a taste for speaking through enclosed spaces filled with significant emptiness. [Jean-Paul] Sartre's *No Exit* has become the classic example. [Alfonso] Sastre uses the device in *The Condemned Squad* and *In the Net,* Pinter in *The Dumb Waiter*. Arrabal's *The Labyrinth* is perhaps the most frightening and despairing such case, and Ionesco fills his spaces with multiplying objects that crowd man out. The stage lends itself temptingly to this metaphor of man trapped in his surroundings. In *The Basement Window,* written by one well qualified to talk about life in a cell [Buero Vallejo spent six years in prison after the Civil War], the distancing of present time is an initial confinement: the play's temporal perspective—the present seen from centuries beyond—is a reduction of the time circumstance, the 1960's, that parallels the spatial reduction. Further, the geometric image of enclosure is here cut by a linear image: the cell is in a cellar. The cubicle and the vertical line pointing down together define the family's fate. Most importantly, of course—and we are dealing now with Mario alone—this symbol of isolation leads to the interrelated questions of who wills the isolation and what, if any, is its value. . . .

The cellar window divides symbolically the inner and outer reality (the room and the street) that exist on either side of it. But it is a passageway between two worlds at the same time as it is part of a barrier. Its nature as a window, its transparency, which differentiates it from a solid building wall that would block communication and even cross-consciousness between the two, allows the two worlds to see each other. Only through it is the drama of their co-existence possible. Particularly the members living in confinement may descry existence outside themselves and either reach out to it or remold their inner consciousness in response to what they discover. However, a cellar window is small, the angle of view is awkward, the picture is cut. The world outside is seen imperfectly. By the same token, while for those in the enclosure the window is their path to light and light's path to them—without it they would live in total darkness—its very presence indicates that light is meager, that light has been literally swallowed up. Again, vision is imperfect, full clarity is not achieved, and the distinction between outside and inside remains. Now, given the emphasized existence of outer reality combined with the reduction and blurring of its image, it is natural that those within, whether occupants or visitors, should find themselves acted upon to supply, through the imaginative projection of themselves and their experiences, elements that are not there. Accordingly, the basement window is yet another stage on which dramatic scenes are enacted. (In this sense it is a mirror of Buero Vallejo's own artistic process.) That these scenes are mental projections, based on fancy or experience like any artist's creations, is emphasized by the device of not having the window visible on stage; only the shadows of its grating can be seen when it is open. The basement window thus becomes a window onto the world of the mind. . . . Illusion and reality, event and invention, meaning and interpretation cease to have set frontiers when viewed through the basement window—or through time or through art.

John W. Kronik. HR. Spring, 1973, pp. 387–90

The dramatic catastrophe [in *In the Burning Darkness*], then, arises out of a social order which finds itself threatened with progressive disintegration due to the powerful presence in its midst of a visionary who refuses to compromise his vision, even in the interest of preserving certain traditional and stable social values. Threatened with chaos, the social order—represented here by Carlos, who . . . is egotistically motivated as well—wields its inherent power to achieve the violent elimination of the subversive visionary.

As he witnesses this conflict of opposing principles, where are the spectator's sympathies directed? In creating his tragic hero, Prometheus, Shelley was careful to show that the rebellious Olympian was without flaw, that his motives were pure, and that the order he was opposing was blatantly tyrannical and violently unjust. Shelley's tragedy, then, depicts the suffering of a totally blameless hero at the hands of an unreasonable and blind order of authority. Prometheus is the revolutionary hero of mankind, while Zeus represents the rigid order which is to be overthrown. In this case, our allegiance as spectators lies unequivocally with the cause of revolution; we are terrified at the violence with which that revolutionary impulse is punished, and we stand in awe of the hero's transcendent message of uncompromising struggle for the ideal, even as he suffers for his deed.

Buero Vallejo, of course, has set his play among ordinary people. Their physical blindness is paralleled by the blindness of their social order and its ethic; the message of light which Ignacio brings among them reveals the Promethean metaphor lying behind the drama as a whole. But the situation in *In the Burning Darkness* is far less imminently revolutionary than in Shelley's *Prometheus Unbound,* and for that reason, more complex. In spite of the catastrophe which results in the death of the rebellious figure, Ignacio, the play's conclusion forcefully suggests the possibility for reconciliation and synthesis of the two conflictive principles. The spectator's sympathies, therefore, are claimed to some degree at various moments in the drama by both sides of the conflict, and it is precisely this refusal on the part of the dramatist to yield to the categories of romance or melodrama that makes for authentic complexity of the tragic clash of character and ideals.

Nevertheless, even granting the complexity of the claims made on the spectator's moral allegiance, the play's hero is, without question, Ignacio; it is not Carlos, nor is it the social order which he represents and violently defends. And the principles which Ignacio represents are heroic by comparison; they are daring, they risk the truth which lies beyond conventional forms, and they enable Ignacio to summon the faith to carry his vision beyond the limits of formal reason as well. These are the admirable weapons with which Ignacio combats the vain practicality, the illusions upon which a society's order is founded. The spectator's sympathies are thus lured into the province of the rebellious visionary, and arrayed against the universal order that cannot accommodate his disturbing and dangerous vision of truth. From this perspective, the spectator is led to share the hero's judgment of the universal moral and social order as both shallow and artificial.

Reed Anderson. *Symposium.* Spring–Summer,
1975, pp. 7–8

The set and other visual effects [in *The Basement Window*] constitute integral parts of the work and stand as symbols of its ideological thrust. The lighting associated with the investigators, for example, is bright and in harmony with their moral enlightenment. The sparse light of the twentieth-century basement room, on the other hand, denotes obscurity in the psychological, economic, social, and philosophical sense. Fond of utilizing visual elements as projections of his theme, Buero Vallejo uses a rigid, grimy, and darkened stairway in *Story of a Staircase* to symbolize the plight of Madrid's immobile lower middle class. In *Today's a Holiday,* the roof of an apartment building suggests the characters' reaching for the sky. The dark and partially sunken quarters of the family in *The Basement Window* is a particularly apt metaphor for the situation of the vanquished in Spain's post-Civil War society: like the family exiled in its basement apartment, the losers were relegated to the lowest economic levels as well as to the collective subconscious of the victorious nation. Conversely, the victors and those who traveled with them sped headlong, like the train missed by the family, toward material success. In the postwar period, idealism became something of an anachronism. In addition to bowing before dictators, royalty, and symbols of the Church, the neo-capitalistic society illustrated its materialism through the worship of refrigerators, cars, and television sets.

The basement window and the train have multiple meanings. Since the window is situated at the front of the stage between actors and spectators, the audience assumes the position of those who pass the window and whose shadows project grotesquely on the wall. The darkened basement dwelling represents, moreover, the limitations of human understanding and perception. Like the creatures of Plato's cave (*The Republic,* Book VII), Buero Vallejo's characters grope for light, see each other imperfectly, and anguish for understanding. . . .

In addition to social and ethical implications, *The Basement Window* is a study in the human condition, portraying solitary man in a search for meaning in a hostile and absurd universe. The play suggests that man does not truly live until he has acknowledged responsibility for his destiny and emerges from passivity to conscious choice. In this sense, the train stands for the active life. Vicente chooses to ride in an aggressive fashion, while Encarna elects to be a hanger-on, and Mario refuses to board at all. In answer to Encarna's rationalization of her choices—One must live—Mario adopts a nihilistic posture: That's our misery: one must live, suggesting like Sartre before him in *No Exit* that man is condemned to live. Mario's dialogues, dialectic in nature, should be read with particular care, especially those with Vicente. Their subtle verbal confrontation at the end of the first act, one of the finest dramatic duets in contemporary Spanish theater, is particularly important.

Anthony M. Pasquariello and Patricia W.
O'Connor. Introduction to Antonio Buero
Vallejo, *El tragaluz* (New York, Charles
Scribner's Sons, 1977), pp. 12–14

[*The Foundation*], like many of Buero's works, is one of discovery, of unearthing a preexistent entity which, for one reason or another, is no longer visible. As is proper for dramas of this kind, the discovery represents a double journey: one makes us aware of the physical surroundings that shape us, the objects, the space and the pressures that define our circumstances; the other leads us to a consideration of our response to these forces and hence to the essence of our beings. The journey through which Buero takes us in *The Foundation* is a harrowing, dispiriting one. It is based on a dialectic of external reality and personal response, but it is dominated by an unyielding world which accepts only submission to its overpowering strength. What Buero proposes in order to resist all of this is the strength we derive from an awareness of what surrounds us and the consciousness of our human limitations. It is an uneven struggle, the bare, unprotected vulnerable humanity of the oppressed against the brutality of a police state that recognizes only blind acceptance. *The Foundation* is Buero's desperate cry of anguish.

Frank P. Casa. *Estreno.* Spring, 1979, p. 31

CASONA, ALEJANDRO (pseudonym of Alejandro Rodríguez Álvarez, 1903–1965)

The spiritual problems that supply the subject matter to Casona's works are those we have located within the full realization of the spirit. It is the human person, the person who lives through moments of over-powering drama and indefinable crises, who appears in the theater of Casona. It is for this reason that the work of Casona is a manifestation of the spiritual and cultural crisis agitating modern man. We are witnesses to a most profound decadence and crisis of culture. As a result, the spirit suffers a feverish journey filled with tragic situations. . . .

[Casona's] theater has arisen in the midst of a crisis produced by the historical conditions that will cause the transformation of the capitalist economy and modify the form of man's social life. It is a theater that could not be understood without alluding to this spiritual and cultural crisis. The works of Casona can be grouped into two categories: those that contain in their subtle and astute plots problems that could be called social, and those that brilliantly symbolize man's inner tendencies, the spiritual problems created by these social problems.

In the theater of Casona the person exists as a function of history. In the theater of García Lorca the person is subjectified, "de-socialized." Both are universal. But the universality of some of the works of Casona is subtly human, ineffably spiritual. The ecumenism of the theater of García Lorca is an inverted ecumenism, one that is contrary. In *Suicide Prohibited in Springtime, Once Again the Devil,* and even *Ballad of Dan and Elsa,* the subjective sense of Casona's theater is highly spiritualized. Only *Our Natacha* is a specifically social work; in it no tendency toward subjectivity exists.

In addition, the works of Casona have a sense of the importance of human life. . . . Therefore, Casona's characters always live dangerously in the critical moment of ethical reflection, moral preoccupation, and subjective internalization. The moral problematics of Casona's works, the constant self-projecting that is typical of his characters, the tendency to the tacit posing of ethical problems, communicate a subtly worthwhile meaning to the human universality of Casona's theater.

Luis E. Nieto Arteta. *Revista de las Indias.* 12, 1941, pp. 91, 95–96†

The relationship of Casona's theater to escapism is . . . complex. His best work, *The Lady of the Dawn,* belongs to a poetic order within which the idea of escapism lacks all meaning. To mention it when the subject of the drama is death even seems to indicate a lack of respect, and this assertion can be applied to some of the author's other plays, which have the same ultimate preoccupation. Nevertheless, an important part of Casona's work has to do with escapism, since he does not make out of it a theoretical place to which he dispatches the stupefied soul of the spectator, but rather the substance of the drama or the instrument of the dramatic operation itself. . . . This happens because of the pedagogic calling of Casona, which is not abandoned even when he is practicing his theatrical profession, and to which he owes the most important of his aesthetic failures, the most precipitous of his falls, *Our Natacha.* The pedagogue that Casona harbors in his soul prevents the most beautiful of all his dramatic works from reaching the peak of poetic perfection, which is the justification for the drama. Casona is always compromised by some technical truth, is always driven to philosophy, is always presenting a thesis. Hence, it is ridiculous that such a theater can sometimes seriously be classified as escapist.

The escapism is there, though, but either as an existential situation of some of the characters—*The Beached Mermaid*—or as a technical remedy used by someone—Dr. Ariel in *Suicide Prohibited in Springtime* and, even more, in *The Trees Die Standing*—a remedy for some misfortune. The characters who open the action of *The Beached Mermaid* are emigrants from reality to a world of fantasy that permits them to deceive themselves and to reach in their imaginations the being they could not have achieved in reality. If we carefully follow the development of the plot, it is not difficult to discover that Casona's idea in this play is contrary to that of escapism, since the happiness of the protagonists can be achieved only if it is situated in a hard and clear reality. This imperative of reality reappears in the other plays . . . where even if some characters find solace in the illusions set up by the disciples of Ariel, the protagonists are *always* reclaimed by the reality that underlies the illusion, and are tied to reality by some inescapable human commitment. Casona believes in the cathartic power of illusion, but not up to the point of recommending it as a solution for all misfortunes. It is possible that what there is in him of a poet (of which there is a great deal) battles with his pedagogical calling, for which illusion can not be more than a road that parabolically returns man to reality.

G. Torrente Ballester. *Teatro español contemporáneo* (Madrid, Guadarrama, 1957), pp. 352–54†

It would be interesting to compute the number of times that Casona uses words related to teaching: professor, teacher, pedagogue, lesson, to educate, to teach, etc. (Remember that on a certain occasion he even transforms the Devil into a pedagogue). But it is not only a question here of formal education such as we understand it today, or how Natacha [in *Our Natacha*] understands it, but rather a question of the education of the soul, of the necessity of teaching people to live an imaginary life that is more rewarding than everyday life. Casona has been able to see clearly that the realist-naturalist mode in art (so prevalent in all theaters, including the Spanish) did not teach man what he most needed; society in the twentieth century has not known how to resolve the problems that confront the individual, the socially, morally, or physically incapacitated person, who rarely realizes his dreams.

In order not to plunge into the despairing pessimism of the existentialists, Casona brought to his theater the conviction that the reality of our world is not only analysis but also synthesis, and by weaving a fabric of poetic truth in which everything that exists in the mind and soul of man acquires reality, he aspires to portray the "complete" man. One ought to add to this that Casona believes, as a good Christian, that man has a right to maintain an ideal, and that if society refuses him that right, the artist is then obliged to create new boundaries within which the activity of the spirit can grow. Perhaps this may explain the frequent appearance in his plays of "Sanatoriums of the Soul," "Houses of Optimism," or Institutions dedicated to cure souls and fabricate dreams—all of them refuges where those exiled from a hostile world can convalesce and be saved. The "mutilated souls" live, then, a secondary reality (an imagined one) and no longer does the primary reality (the everyday one) terrify them. . . .

What Casona proposes is to show us that the noblest qualities of man are not manifested in his submission to animal instincts nor in his giving in completely to the conventions of organized society, but that there is an intermediate point in which the individual can create for himself his own world and make himself responsible for his own salvation by using the recourses of his imagination and moral fortitude. That is to say, if man exercises his innate virtues and applies those moral values learned in school, in the family, or in church, he will become a complete man and will find within himself protection against the temptations of his animal nature or against the sufferings and disillusions that are produced in his contact with everyday reality.

Juan R. Castellano. *Hispania.* March, 1960,
pp. 26, 28†

The theater of Casona . . . is, before anything, true, authentic theater. Theater because of the successful techniques of which it can boast; because of its knowledge and command of the best stage effects, because of the appropriate and tight structuring of each of the plays. Theater because the action (external or internal) and dialogue are always the basic supports of the plays—action with a development filled with intrigue, surprise, wonder, and originality so that interest is constantly sustained with tension. A dialogue endowed with admirable artistic and poetic quality, with rich, varied, and expressive language, with suggestive and brilliant comparisons, images, and metaphors, with an agility and artistry that are difficult to surpass, and at the same time, with restraint and sobriety that make it cohesive and tightly knit, substantial and direct, perfectly theatrical. . . .

In addition to its literary and theatrical aspects, the dramatic work of Casona seems to me rich in its spiritual and generally instructive and constructive content. In each of his works he transmits to us a message that inspires us to good, to truth, a message that defends positive human values (barring some exceptional case), that resolutely attacks and repudiates negative values. Love, for example, is a theme that is often central in his plays: a love that redeems a life that is phantasmagoric and unserious, extravagant and insubstantial, on the fringe of reality (*The Beached Mermaid*); a love that saves a soul from making pacts with the devil (*Once Again the Devil*); a love that permits man to fulfill himself, to reach his full capacity (*The Third Word*); a love that brings hope for a new life and overcomes suicide (*The Trees Die Standing* or *The Lady of the Dawn*); a love that purifies a life with a dark past with sincere promises of happiness for the future (*Ballad of Dan and Elsa*).

J. Rodríguez Richart. *Vida y teatro de Alejandro Casona* (Oviedo, Spain, Instituto de Estudios Asturianos, 1963), pp. 176–179†

[Casona] asks his audiences not to expect detailed and realistic plots but imaginary situations and settings. He creates characters who are dissatisfied with the routine, dehumanized life of our time and who consequently attempt to escape in one way or another. Hence it is that illusion and fantasy occupy such a large place in his theater.

Because of their marked preoccupation with illusion some critics have erroneously detected the influence of Pirandello in Casona's works, Casona himself denies the existence of such influence. Of Pirandello he says: "I have no great love for him and therefore his influence on me can only be minimal." . . .

Casona, then, is closer to Cervantes than to Pirandello. His "perspectivism" like that of Cervantes presupposes the existence of God to whom alone is vouchsafed full vision, and of whom the author is an analogue. Consequently, like Cervantes, he grants only a certain measure of autonomy to his creatures; there are no anguished characters in search of an author in his plays. Again contrary to Pirandello's practice, Casona does not sanction illusion as an answer to the difficulties implicit in the pursuit of truth. He believes that life is a duty and regards all escapism as reprehensible. Consequently, he almost always ends his plays by subjecting illusions to the world of harsh reality: however, he leaves no doubt but there is much in that reality that could and ought to be amended. His rather eccentric protagonists (e.g., Ricardo of *The*

Beached Mermaid and Mauricio of *The Trees Die Standing*) are vanquished in their various attempts to impose a better world upon this one, a noble failure they share with Don Quijote. Nevertheless, like Cervantes' immortal knight, they remain vindicated in our eyes. . . .

Casona does not limit his criticism to the external features of our modern social structure, but proceeds to criticize the positivistic and materialistic ideology which underlies it. Because of this he has erroneously been called an existentialist. It is indeed true that with the existentialists he shares a horror of abstraction and dehumanization. It is also true that he frequently places his characters in concrete "either/ or" situations where they must exercise an "awful freedom." Still, it is also true that in making the equivalent of the "existential leap" these characters always resort to a moral standard. In this Casona is most anti-existentialist. Most of his characters accept the Christian moral code and with it moral responsibility for their acts. Those few who do not are obviously reprehensible in the eyes of their author. They are never made heroes in his theater. So it is that while he might be called an existential author because of his concern with concrete existential problems, he cannot be included among the existentialists because of his theism and his acceptance of moral and ethical standards.

Charles H. Leighton. MD. May, 1964,
pp. 29–30, 33

[Like Pirandello] Casona . . . creates for the audience a dramatic tension that is derived from his own particular ideas about the world of theater. But while the drama of Pirandello is born, as it confronts daily life, not with an attitude of certainty about what is known to be the truth but with an attitude that casts doubt on all certainty, thus creating a double plane of reality-unreality, the drama of Casona is born from the juxtaposition of these two planes, both of which are considered to be a multicolored and multifaceted reality. It is as if the theater were for both dramatists a kind of kaleidoscope through which the playwright presents reality to the audience. At each turn that Pirandello gives the kaleidoscope, reality changes form and color, and the dramatist plays with his work, the actors, and the spectators, posing the eternal questions: What are the true forms and colors within the kaleidoscope that constitute life? Is it possible to know anything with certainty? Is true reality the one we saw at the first turn of the kaleidoscope? the second? the last? or none of them?

Likewise, Casona also turns the theatrical kaleidoscope, and similarly, at each turn, reality changes form and color, but with opposite results; that is, while his dramas develop in an atmosphere or unreality, he leaves us with the certainty that each form, each color we see there, is a real and essential part for the proper functioning of life, and that the multicolored and multifaceted reality is what makes a unity worthy of admiration out of the kaleidoscope of reality. . . .

Both Pirandello and Casona present to us in their theater what happens and what can happen according to their own interpretations of reality, which are quite different. Because of these distinct concepts of reality, although both playwrights employ similar techniques, they have entirely opposite points of departure, details, and conclusions. The plays of Pirandello, on one hand, begin on a plane of some daily reality that is easily identifiable, only to end on a semianxious note of doubt, if not on a plane of unreality, or at least of uncertainty. The plays of Casona, on the other hand, generally begin in an atmosphere of fantasy, of illusion, or of unreality, only to end on a positive and optimistic note, on a plane rooted firmly in the world of reality.

For Pirandello, it is feasible to put all reality, even the most palpable, into doubt. For Casona, conversely, everything—the material world and the spiritual one beyond it—participates in reality, and as such, is material available for becoming the object of artistic transformations, since the unreal cannot be converted into art without at least having been accepted before as a possible reality.

> Esperanza Gurza. *La realidad caleidoscópica de Alejandro Casona* (Oviedo, Spain, Instituto de Estudios Asturianos, 1968), pp. 9–11†

Casona's early work—*The Beached Mermaid* and *Our Natacha*—is made out of whimsical daydreams about a world which resembles the real one in some respects, but is improved by Casona's fantasy and becomes a better place to live in. *Our Natacha* can also be interpreted as intending some mild criticism of bourgeois society. These plays were well received in the theatre. Casona, however, was a staunch supporter of the Republic, and the end of the war found himself in exile in Argentina, where he continued to write successfully for the stage. *Suicide Prohibited in Springtime, The Lady of the Dawn, The Boat without a Fisherman,* and *The Trees Die Standing,* are his best-known works. They are by no means great plays. Although they often come to the verge of probing thoughtfully into serious matters, and adopt what promises to be effective dramatic techniques, they invariably fail to fulfill the promise and veer off into whimsy. It is as if Casona did not grasp the point of the plays he was writing, and so failed to make anything worthwhile out of the Unamuno-like problems of identity and authenticity in *Suicide Prohibited in Springtime* and *The Trees Die Standing,* or the García Lorca-like symbolic and archetypal characters of *The Lady of the Dawn.*

But from the point of view of literary history, the quality of Casona's drama is less interesting than its reception in Spanish theatres. Offical postwar Spain execrated the memory of Casona, enemy of the state. A reading of *The Trees Die Standing* by students of Barcelona University in 1951 provoked furious indignation in the Spanish press. But in 1962 Casona wearied of his exile, publicly repented the error of his ways, and returned to Spain. His works at once became gems of the modern Spanish theatre. As soon as he returned, *The Lady of the Dawn* had an extremely successful run in Madrid, and Casona's personal appearance on stage at the end of each performance was greeted with prolonged and evidently sincere applause.

G. G. Brown. *A Literary History of Spain: The*
Twentieth Century (New York, Barnes & Noble,
1972), pp. 129–30

Great characterizations and great scenes are certainly vital to a successful dramatist. One other claim can be made for Casona's superiority in dramatic construction—his loving care with details—perhaps a legacy of his pedagogical background. In *Suicide Prohibited in Springtime* the idea of the play is to rehabilitate those who have contemplated suicide as an escape from their troubled or empty lives. Dr. Roda starts a Sanatorium of the Soul, inviting those who wish to commit suicide to do so where they can be taught the proper techniques and can perform the job in comfortable surroundings. His invitation is based upon two premises. The first is that those who are ready for suicide will do it without benefit of his counsel. Second, those who do come to him are people with unhappy life experiences, usually being unloved, but lack the decisiveness to kill themselves.

These people come to him thinking that they are learning how to die, and indeed they are offered the various means: poison, high places, weapons, but they are introduced to comfortable surroundings, beautiful landscapes, a lake, flowers, music. . . . They are soon weeping. . . . Death is not the problem, only a symptom of it. Their goal is reconciliation with reality whether they know it or not. Learning that death is not unkind is a step on the path.

Casona's carefulness here is not simply with the staging; it is a detailed study of the psychological sequences in the suicide therapy. Starting with good clinical techniques, he can then concentrate upon his staging problems. One such problem is to simplify; his audience came to be entertained, not instructed. But Casona, as a good teacher, is always concerned about the problems of knowing the subject matter and knowing how to transmit it. In this instance he cannot strive for memorable characterizations. He must concentrate upon making sure that the audience is with him as the characters—all minor ones—advance from stage to stage in his therapeutic program. The audience wishes to feel that the cures are plausible and effective.

Casona's stage effectiveness is not based upon clever tricks or even upon vivid imagination, so much as it is upon his broad study of history and literature, his sympathetic understanding of human nature, and his careful attention to the relationship between the stories and ideas and their adaptation to the stage.

One final question is, why does Casona use death as a theme so often? He was preoccupied with death; so was Unamuno, and the contrast is startling. Unamuno's great brain could not cope with the concept of death. He longed to understand immortality rationally. Casona approaches the subject so calmly that he leaves the impression that he has death on a leash and can exercise control over it since he has come to an understanding with it. As he presents the allegorical Peregrina, a philosophical acceptance of the inevitable, the psychology of violent death . . . he seems to have mastered death . . . and can persuade his audience that they can learn from him how to master it also.

John A. Moore. SAB. May, 1974, pp. 54–55

The principal touchstone of fantasy in three of Casona's plays is the establishment of rare institutions. In *The Beached Mermaid* an attempt is made to form a republic for persons devoid of common sense. Dr. Ariel, an individual never seen, founds what is ostensibly a suicide home in *Suicide Prohibited in Springtime,* and in *The Trees Die Standing* he organizes an institution dedicated to providing a moment of happiness for unfortunate souls. The proposed republic in *The Beached Mermaid* is organized out of rebellion against prevailing materialism. The other two institutions are founded to provide a cure for the victims of such a society. All three are established for a noble purpose, but in every case, they succumb to the very influences they are trying to avoid or remedy, for as time goes on, there is a tendency on the part of the directing authority to accord greater importance to their respective organizations than to the individual they were meant to serve. Individual problems do not readily accommodate themselves to man-made rules and regulations.

Many of Casona's characters subjectively withdraw from the society that sets human values aside. While Casona would agree with their censure of this society, he does not agree with their attempt to escape life's responsibilities. For him, life is duty. He enjoins humanity to view it with imagination and awaken its latent sympathy for "el dolor ajeno," the problems of others, thus to mitigate the tendency toward dehumanization, but he continues to sustain the innate worth of man and his inherent dignity. . . . Casona would agree with Socrates that the good, the true, and the beautiful are synonymous.

Harold K. Moon. Alejandro Casona (Boston,
Twayne, 1985), p. 129

CASTELAO, ALFONSO RODRÍGUEZ. See
RODRÍGUEZ CASTELAO, ALFONSO

CELA, CAMILO JOSÉ (1916–   )

In the last few years we have been seeing the appearance of a new and significant figure in our contemporary novel—Camilo José Cela. He could not have appeared at a more propitious moment. Some pre-civil war writers have given up; others are in complete decline; still others are repeating their same old works, all of which leads us to believe that the future of the Spanish novel is not very heartening. At the end of 1942 there appeared *The Family of Pascual Duarte*. Its public and critical acceptance was unanimous—an unquestionable success. . . .

Unlike *The Family of Pascual Duarte,* the world of *Rest Home* is much more complicated. Naturally, the inhabitants of the pavilion simplify and schematize their existence during the course of their illness. . . . This is not the first time that a tuberculosis sanitorium . . . has been chosen as an appropriate setting for a novelistic experience. . . . We all remember . . . the masterful work of Thomas Mann. . . . Neither the coincidence of the theme nor the plot being developed are prejudicial in any way whatsoever to Cela's originality in *Rest Home.* . . .

In *The Family of Pascual Duarte,* the dizziness, the speed of action, the rapidity of the events left loose threads that the author later tied together. *Rest Home* is, to the contrary, slower, more perfect, more classic. . . . Everything is measured and weighed; his invention of the morbid atmosphere is also better done. . . .

Pablo Cabañas. *Cuadernos de literatura*
(Madrid). July–Aug., 1947, pp. 87, 96–97,
102–3†

The Hive has not been published in Spain. It is not to be wondered that the Franco censorship disapproves of Cela's novels. Life in Madrid as he portrays it is brutal, hungry, and senseless. Hypocrisy, fear, and oppression are in command. Cela's political loyalties may be conservative or reactionary but his literary affiliations are of the most radical; they are with Camus and Sartre, with Moravia, with Zola and French naturalism. Only Cela has very little of the theoretician about him and has no existential, sexual or political message to deliver. It is in his directness and lack of squeamishness that he resembles Sartre and Moravia. . . .

In practice, Cela does not ramble so much as he jumps. Now we are with the powerful Dona Rosa who tyrannizes over her waiters and customers; now with a café musician; now with a mediocre non-conformist poet; then with a tender-hearted money lender; then with the bookkeeper of a black-marketeer . . . All of this is rather abruptly and sketchily represented, it is forceful and it is bald.

One sympathizes with Cela in his impatience with literature. Probably he is attacking his conformist contemporaries within Spain. But there is a great deal to be said for his attitude.

Saul Bellow. *NYTBR*. Sept. 27, 1953, p. 5

Temperamentally and spiritually there is a decided affinity between Cela and his predecessors Baroja, Valle-Inclán, [Rafael] Solana, Azorín, Unamuno, and Ortega y Gasset, who exerted their influence upon him. He is a great admirer of Faulkner, whom he approaches in the elaborate manipulation of time. An avid reader, Cela is familiar with the works of Heidegger, Sartre, Kafka, and Camus. Here and there we catch a glimpse of existentialist views in *The Hive,* but their connection with any particular school of existentialist philosophy cannot, to my knowledge, be definitely traced.

Cela's purpose is to describe, in a whirlpool of incidents, the ability or inability of his characters to cope with the vicissitudes of life. It is through his symbols and subjectivity that Cela conveys his personal philosophy. The universality of the theme is manifest in Cela's conception of Madrid society, transcending in scope its geographical confines and illuminating the banal existence of urban dwellers everywhere. The author's chief concern lies in creating a true and living atmosphere in which the characters are the predominant element, and in which plot and action are insignificant. In order to judge the merits of *The Hive,* the reader must be cognizant of the elaborate technical devices of structure, character, and style wielded by Cela in a unified and integral portrayal of the human drama of the "hive." Proliferation of sketches and characters, telescoped biographies, atmosphere, time levels, condensation of time and space, anti-heroism, personal interpolations, poetry, interior monologue, symbolism, humor, and irony are some of the aspects of Cela's technique. . . .

John J. Flasher, *WVUPP*. Nov., 1959, p. 42

In this flight along roads, in the glance ready to stare at children and fools, and in the tendency toward a simplicity of style, I find a basic attitude of primitivism [in Cela's works]. . . .

How does this primitivism occur? In two ways. First, the child and the fool are found in a primitive state owing to the underdevelopment of the working of the "socializing" apparatus. And second, Cela gives literary expression to the primitive aspects of life that surround him by means of a conscientious simplicity of his prose. Entire groups of sentences begin with the same epithet, noun, or expression, and they offer the same brevity. . . . There is also a strong anti-intellectual feeling. . . .

By using the word "primitivist," I do not intend to refer to a person who is found in a primitive state or who belongs to a primitive group, but rather to the person who seeks this state because of an intellectual decision, such as Henri Rousseau. Thus Cela is a practicing primitivist who has found the best vehicle for his end: the road. . . . The road is always there, waiting for the social fugitive to use it. It symbolizes flight; in Cela's works it takes one far away from complexity to an atmosphere in which self-consciousness—the highest degree of intellectuality—is lacking. Vagabondage is an antisocial expression because it affirms absolute liberty by means of the road, a liberty available at all times without consideration of civilization's obligations.

Paul Ilie. *Ínsula.* Jan., 1961, p. 14†

We know that the first book that Cela wrote was a volume of verse, *Treading on the Doubtful Light of Day,* which preceded *The Family of Pascual Duarte* by several years, although it was published three years later. While writing his first novels, he also wrote poems, which appeared in magazines. Yet another book of poetry accompanied the heights of his prose, *Journey to the Alcarria*—the *Songbook* of the same name. After a relatively long period, a new handful of poems attests to his Mediterranean lifestyle and his greater spiritual and physical calmness.

I want to say that writing verse is neither a pure accident for Cela nor just entertainment. No. I believe that it is a true expressive necessity, just as one cannot separate the historian and the scholar from his work. . . . Cela's poetry is closely related to his prose . . . and many of the poet's qualities are concomitant with those of the prose writer. . . .

The content of *Treading on the Doubtful Light of Day* is chaotic, an attribute that corresponds to its style. But within that chaos there is an order that is evident both externally and internally. Externally, the form is quite careful and frequently makes regular use of alexandrine and, to a lesser extent, hendecasyllabic verse. . . . Internally . . . there is an indifferent view of reality (what has been called *tremendismo*), a pessimistic conception of human society, with its consequent skepticism and its aftermath of bitterness, and a sarcastic touch that is alleviated by some tenderness.

Leopoldo de Luis. *RHM.* April–Oct., 1962,
pp. 172–73†

Jews, Moors, and Christians, the exterior title of this book, represents a new battle cry in the career of Camilo José Cela. . . . It is a creed, a new religion of passionate thought, an existential revelation. Except for some minor allusions to a Semitic heritage, Cela does not strive to essentialize his imposing title. Belief is sufficient unto itself. In the new perspective of the author, Christian Spain is another image of a land which is irreducibly composed of three distinct cultures, Christian, Jewish, and Moorish. There is, of course, a sense of ironic justice in bestowing the title of *Jews, Moors, and Christians* on "Old Castile," the spiritual heart of Spain.

Whether Cela became a standard-bearer of Américo Castro's concept of Spanish history because of conviction or because it gave him another opportunity to rebel against tradition as embodied in the regime of General Franco, is a question that may have to be answered by two yeses. There are no absolutes in the life of Cela. Obviously, Cela must have been in a state of receptiveness when Castro's interpretation of history was revealed to him. In a sense, he reacted to the "incitement" as a novelistic hero. And his proselytism encouraged his vengeance. . . .

More significant than the conjectural question of personal motivation is the matter of artistic intent—and the degree of its fulfillment. The salient achievement of Cela in *Jews, Moors, and Christians* is that without sacrificing artistic creation, without abdicating his position as the master of disproportion, he succeeds in proving himself an able and original historical scholar. In his ironical manner, Cela had made it clear in the beginning that he would strive not to appear ostentatious about his erudition because historians too had to eat while he already was making a living as a writer.

Robert Kirsner. *The Novels and Travels of
Camilo José Cela* (Chapel Hill, University of
North Carolina Press, 1963), pp. 167–68

[Theodore S.] Beardsley— . . . As you know, the zeal for academic classification has led to the invention of the literary school called *tremendismo* and has placed you among its most important exponents. It is well known that you have expressed some very interesting reactions to this label.

Camilo José Cela—To classify me as the father of *tremendismo* is to commit a dreadful error in chronology. I am certainly no child, but I am substantially younger than the Archpriest of Talavera, for example, and than most of the Spanish writers of the Middle Ages and the Golden Age. And tell me, didn't Quevedo, in half or more than half of his works, write precisely in that vein? And jumping distance and years to the Generation of 1898, the same is true of a significant portion of Valle-Inclán's work. I believe that this is a Spanish quality as old as Spanish literature itself. *Tremendismo* is a word that has become successful, but it is an expression for people like sextons or . . . I don't even think it makes sense, because *tremendismo* is nothing more than realism insofar as it tries to reflect reality faithfully. If this reality is "tremendous," well, what can we do about it? We have to come to terms with it exactly as it presents itself to us, exactly as we have found it. The world in which it has fallen to your lot and to mine to live seems to have become a little more peaceful, but it certainly doesn't give us the urge to dip our pen into a rose-colored inkwell.

B.—What would you say has been your particular contribution to the Spanish novel of today?

C.J.C.—Assuming that I have made any . . . not that it's anything new, but I think it's that I've always been honest with myself. I have tried to express my thoughts in times and in circumstances that weren't always very favorable; I have always tried . . . to avoid betraying my convictions. [1966]

Interview with Camilo José Cela. Diacritics.
Spring, 1972, p. 43

Cela's role as a novelist and his role as a man constitute a fundamental paradox that accounts for many of the technical and structural peculiarities of his novels. Cela has come to believe that the function of the novel is to give the illusion of reflecting life as it is being lived, although, of course, the final result is but one novelist's personal vision. Cela's novels stand back to record the scurrying and the scuffle, both tragic and comic, of everyday life. In doing so he has expressed his belief that man is essentially unaware of the role he plays in the vast complex of human existence. Cela has stated both in his prologues and in his novelistic asides that the majority of men and women are unconscious of life above the level of their basest needs and desires. Cela goes a step further to affirm that reflection upon mankind's plight and any sadness thereupon are forms of atavism, although I suspect that this is Cela's way of saying that the artist is an outsider to the mainstream of life. These beliefs are brought out particularly in *The Hive* and *Toboggan of the Hungry,* but they are valid also with reference to others of Cela's novels, for example, in the central irony of *The Family of Pascual Duarte*.

Cela's paradox lies, then, in the fact that, as a writer who is supposedly creating an imitation of life in his novel, he is forced to come to grips with the plight of mankind, to ponder it, and to shape his novelistic world accordingly. In so doing, Cela is practicing the very atavism against which he has spoken. Nevertheless, Cela has guarded himself against sadness while at the same time raising himself to a level of perception superior to that of the common man by means of the various devices for audience-distancing. . . . Audience-distancing refers to two external levels of the novel: the author and the reader. It is the former about which Cela is most concerned.

D. W. Foster. Forms of the Novel in the Works
of Camilo José Cela. (Columbia, University of
Missouri Press, 1967), pp. 154–55

The active fictional presence of the son [in *Mrs. Caldwell Speaks to Her Son*] fades as the work progresses; he has a measure of fictional independence only when he is directly quoted in the early portion. As Eliacim fades as an active presence speaking and reacting in his own right, rather than through the descriptions of his mother, he is correspondingly seen more and more through her fantasies, until he recedes entirely toward the end. The recession of Eliacim in the increasingly self-centered fantasies of his mother marks her progressive alienation which, as we have noted, ends in her insanity.

Setting the book as an autobiographical account of a mother's incestuous feelings for her son posed two distinct problems for Cela; psychological accuracy in depiction, and justification for Mrs. Caldwell's statements. What she feels must somehow take a shape other than the transparently Freudian, if it is to succeed as artistic prose. Assuming her incestuous love, the problem is how to transform it, disguise it as it were, to reduce its blatant sexuality, the shocking possessiveness Mrs. Caldwell feels towards Eliacim. Herein lies, for example, one reason for the tremendous emphasis Mrs. Caldwell gives to the changing shapes of things, and to the process of transformation in general; for the same reason she praises adaptability and inconstancy. Her fantasy is constantly in a state of *becoming,* conjuring the possible in the unlikely. This is a poetic symbolization of the central problem at issue: how can she *change* from Eliacim's mother into his lover?

J. S. Bernstein. Introduction to *Mrs. Caldwell
Speaks to Her Son* (Ithaca, N.Y., Cornell
University Press, 1968), pp. xx–xxi

Almost out of necessity Camilo José Cela had to turn back to the old picaresque novel, given the thematic and formal similarities between it and what he planned to tell in *The Family of Pascual Duarte;* the confession of the aberrations of a man in his social world from the point of view of the one who has arrived at the end of them and can recognize the extreme state of perdition in which he finds himself. Guzmán del Alfarache related his odyssey as a contrite galley slave; Pascual Duarte relates his—which is briefer and less intricate—as a repentant criminal who awaits in prison the moment of his execution. To a certain degree, the reflections that interrupt Pascual's narration, although very much briefer and in no way doctrinal, are in consonance with those of Guzmán in what their lamentation and the very belated recognition of their errors signify. But *The Family of Pascual Duarte* owes much more to *Lazarillo de Tormes* and, above all, to the *Buscón* [of Quevedo] than to the *Guzmán de Alfarache* of [Mateo] Alemán. . . .

Owing to the dazzling qualities of the models, *The Family of Pascual Duarte* reveals several failings that weaken somewhat the fundamental gravity of the tale. The old picaresque novel could offer adequate elements to relate the perdition of a man of the Spanish people—of the Spain that suffered through the Civil War: self-confession, linear structure of the story. . . , the implicit criticism of social evils, the solitary clarity of a person who at the point of death can contemplate his life from childhood to manhood as an aberration caused by himself and by the other people. But in the old picaresque novel there was another element: the wit, the satire, the cynical distancing, the ironic view of oneself and those closest to one; and this element, which does appear in the first chapters of *The Family of Pascual Duarte*, does not fit in with the psychology of the protagonist, who is as brutal as you might like in his actions, but basically kind and trusting.

Gonzalo Sobejano. *PSA*. Jan., 1968, pp. 42–43, 45†

Cela's love for the expressive and esthetic values of the language lead him to a preoccupation with the most insignificant details of spelling, semantics, the exact definition of each word, acceptions, and dialectal or local usages. No doubt his acceptance into the Royal Academy has intensified his love of the Word, but it is necessary to point out that even twenty years before his acceptance into the Royal Academy he sent a paper to it. Many curious and appropriate philological notes are dispersed throughout his work, but in recent times they have become quite numerous, especially in his essays, articles, and travel books, but also in his books with "established patterns," such as *Tarts, Harlots, and Prostitutes,* in which the chapter dedicated to the names for prostitutes is headed: "The Philologist Speaks." And, of course, we must remember that Cela has been busy working on his *Secret Dictionary* and thus he is compiling lots of materials. . . .

A great deal has been said about Cela's humor and its relationship with Quevedo's and Valle-Inclán's humor. . . . Cela's humor is purely verbal; it is based on absurd or trite definitions, on ridiculous uses of adjectives, on "esperpentic" names, on the parodies of popular topics, on the biting satire on all rhetorics, on the contrasting of all grandiloquences, aside from sarcasm with vile words and the most blushingly dirty expressions of the language, which humiliate with their contact the high-sounding themes, which through this humiliation are purified. It is the purification of the language's hypocrisy through laughter: this appears to be the aim of Cela's humor. . . .

Sara Suárez Solís. *El léxico de Camilo José Cela* (Madrid, Alfaguara, 1969), pp. 33, 35†

Because of the widespread European vogue of existentialism, critics have felt it necessary to touch on the possibility of such an influence on Cela's novels, although they have not weighed the matter to any degree.

The trend, of course, made itself felt in Spain: at the turn of the century, Unamuno learned Danish in order to read Kierkegaard; Heidegger's *Sein und Zeit* was translated into Spanish in 1933; Ortega spoke of "vital reason" and used the phrase "I am I and my circumstances." One critic declares that if there is a philosophy in Cela's works—a very debatable point—it has to be existentialist since no other can be detected. The parenthetical expression is most significant. Cela cites Malraux, Sartre, and Camus, and privately agrees that Sartre is pretty much a humbug . . . and affirms a high regard for Camus. . . .

Cela cannot write an anticlerical or antireligious novel, even in the traditional Spanish sense, in a country where the ecclesiastical hierarchy has just been restored in all its power; but he finds a way to express the agnosticism he shares with other European writers. . . . In the face of the absurd, Pascual is incapable of the leap to faith or of the Christian stoical pose in keeping with the guard's theocentric Spanish viewpoint. Nor can Pascual find that "freedom in death" which comes from losing all illusions as he pits himself against the nothingness of a possible impossibility of existence. . . .

Cela's sympathy for Pascual's dilemma is evidenced in his later references to Meursault of [Camus's] *The Stranger*. . . . For Cela, then, Camus's message is that happiness may be found even in the effort of seeking it in the absurd; this concept leads to charity and compassion, and that of Sartre to nausea and suicide. So, Pascual, like most people, prefers to go on living.

D. W. McPheeters. Camilo José Cela (New
York, Twayne, 1969), pp. 46–48

The title of Cela's recent novel *Saint Camilo, 1936,* is actually much longer and goes like this: *Eve, Feast Day, and Octave of Saint Camilo of the Year 1936 in Madrid.* . . . But why the Saint Camilo of the title? Cela himself clarifies the matter: because his novel begins on that very July 18, 1936, on which the Spanish Civil War broke out, and that is the day of the festival of Saint Camilo of Celis, the patron saint of hospitals—of those hospitals that would soon be invaded by the thousands wounded in the war. . . . Cela wanted to write a novel not *about* the war but *in* the war; not an epic or heroic novel, or a novel about those who made the war—hence, those who fought, who killed and fell in battle—but rather about those who endured the war and were shaken and beaten by it, as victims of its violence, its stupidity, or its cruelty. . . .

Of course, the war appears at a couple of moments, as a background, and at times as a source for the narration, and it is always seen in its misery and its baseness. The tale is neither a great story nor even a little story, but rather what Unamuno called infrahistory, but one that is limited to the daily lives of some people of the middle and lower classes of Madrid in 1936 in a very concrete and particular section of the city—

the red-light district. . . . Through this world there pass—as in Cela's previous novel *The Hive*—numerous characters—students, prostitutes, homosexuals, cabaret artists, petty politicians, innocent and perverse, foolish and amusing types, all of whom are found in Cela's novelistic vineyards. One must add that although *Saint Camilo, 1936* is, like all novels, an invention, autobiographical remembrances are not lacking. The very poor student that Camilo José Cela was in 1936, when he was twenty—and whose photograph we see on the front cover—is present in the story.

José Luis Cano. *Asomante*. Jan., 1970,
pp. 76–77†

If Cela has constructed a heavily partial picture of a society scarcely worth saving [in *Saint Camilo, 1936*] from the slaughter which begins long before the novel ends, it is a solid picture and not without evidence of positive values. Cela testifies to the decent solidarity of ordinary, harassed individuals and, above all, expresses his own sense of the waste of Spanish youth. The novel is dedicated to "the lads called up in 1937 who all lost something: life, freedom, illusion, hope, decency"; it is also dedicated against the foreigners who interfered in a Spanish affair.

Which raises the matter of the book's weird epilogue. In this the narrator is lectured by his wise, disenchanted uncle and asked to extirpate from within himself the malignity that warps every Spanish soul. The uncle's scheme for national regeneration is a good way farther out than one would have expected: love and humility, plus as much sex as you like, a programme he offers as an improvement on those of Buddha and St. Francis—the flames of the *auto-da-fé* are to be quenched finally with semen. But after the 400 icy and often sadistic pages of Cela's novel, this sermon is a bit lightweight. Is Cela being serious, or is he making a sneering obeisance to a notably humorless regime by feigning to detect patriotic virtues in promiscuity?

Whatever the answer, the publication of *Saint Camilo, 1936* is an encouraging event. It represents a definite recovery of nerve in Spain's most gifted living novelist and it suggests that Cela now believes he has a worthy public in his own country.

TLS. April 2, 1970, p. 355

The . . . stylistically revealed characteristics of the various narrators who structure this novel constitute the mode of existence on which *The Family of Pascual Duarte* is built. The editor established himself as the basic narrator by demonstrating the extent of his possible influence over the manuscript and the attached documents. The key word here is "possible" for never does he specify the exact extent of this influence. He merely implants the possibility that he has intervened anywhere and everywhere. He furthermore contradicts himself, thereby instilling doubt as to his real motives and his sincerity in presenting these alleged memoirs. In addition, he has the effrontery to advise his own readers to view the hero, Pascual Duarte, with suspicion. D. Joaquín, as a subordinate narrator, also reveals an attitude toward Pascual but in so doing likewise exposes a contradiction. Although he condemns the writings as injurious to public morality, he at the same time inserts conditions which allow for their possible preservation. The priest and the guard contribute to this overall evaluation of Pascual. As opposed to the ambiguous attitude of D. Joaquín, each of these men makes a definite statement as to his opinion. However, since their statements are diametrically opposed and since the *transcriptor* [transcriber] as the basic narrator refuses or is unable to resolve the contradiction, the conclusion as to the hero's true character is just as indefinite. Finally, Pascual as the most prominent of all the narrators merely contributes through contradiction to the overall atmosphere of doubt. [1968]

Robert C. Spires. *HR*. Summer, 1972,
pp. 300–301

Martín Marco is, without doubt, the most important and most fascinating character to appear in *The Hive*. His structural importance is twofold. First, owing to his almost constant mobility in the novel, he is—much more than any other single character—a means of linking many of the people and places presented in the narrative. Second, his recurring presence does give a measure of structural cohesion to the fragmented narrative, whilst his mobility helps create an impression of narrative progress where, in fact, there is little. Yet, despite this, it would be an error to regard Marco as indispensable to the structure of *The Hive,* or to assume that the structure has been designed around him. . . .

As a character study, Marco is unique in the novel in that he receives a significantly more profound and extensive treatment from Cela than any of his fellows. . . . Marco . . . is accorded a portrayal that constantly reveals some new facet of his character or explores in greater depth one already disclosed. . . . All in all, he is basically egotistical and inadequate. . . . His theorizing on what he sees as the prevalent social ills of his society does not, by any token, convince the reader of the unfortunate plight of many of his fellows, for although Marco does, through his thoughts and perorations, introduce the themes of hardship and inequality, his ideas are often so badly formulated as to provoke impatience or a wry smile from both reader and author. . . . Most of Marco's fellows have the insight to realize that the immediate problem of survival centres around the empty stomach or an essential medicine—in fact, money and its acquisition. Marco, on the other hand, does not seem to arrive at this conclusion until the *Final* and even at this point it is easy, in view of his previous actions and attitude, to be sceptical.

David Henn. *Camilo José Cela: La colmena*
(London, Grant and Cutler/Támesis, 1974),
pp. 51–52

In the preface [to *The Family of Pascual Duarte*] the transcriber says that he has pruned the "repugnant intimacies" from the manuscript, an attempt, surely, to expand the horrors of the book beyond what is actually narrated, without going that far. The very repugnant details of Pascual's life are thus made all the more repugnant because they are presumably already censored; and if this is what has passed the transcriber's censorship, how much worse, we are asked to consider, must the rest have been. Cela "puts in" by creating the illusion that he has taken out. Furthermore, he surrounds the book with an air of mystery and supernatural qualities: in his will, Don Joaquín had consigned the manuscript to be burned, but if it survived eighteen months, the finder could do with it as he liked. The most effective technique Cela uses to create the extreme cruelty and horror of Pascual's life, despite the framing and distancing techniques of the book, is a now famous technique called *tremendismo,* which, as its name implies, is a heightening of a described event into its extreme possibilities to achieve some devastating effect. It is a kind of sensationalism, and it focuses on the ugly, the cruel, and the violent.

For Cela violent and extreme aspects of reality become the very means of presenting what [Lionel] Trilling calls "the reality that is the perpetual quest of the novel and the field of its research."

Ulrich Wicks. *Mosaic*. Spring, 1975, pp. 36–38

Cela, at times, seems to superimpose a positive message on his negative view of man and society in *ministry of darkness 5*. This message coincides with the contemporary theme of "sexual liberation" and the materialistic conception that man's happiness depends exclusively on satisfied biological functions. Also, this sexual optimism is contradicted with a more authentic Celian position—his anti-Utopian and scatalogical view of the world. . . .

Cela attacks sexophobia in *ministry of darkness 5* (as he does in *Saint Camilo, 1936*) as a form of deviant erotomania and as a seed for cruelty in universal and, in particular, in Spanish history. But the sexophilia that he wishes to oppose it with does not appear any less perverse, nor less violent, nor less antisocial with regard to the relationship of the one individual with the next. On the contrary, Eros is totally conquered by Thanatos in *ministry of darkness 5*. The manifestations of sexuality are accompanied by the instinct of destruction, aggression, and death, to the point that instead of representing the vitality and fullness of life they reveal its poverty and decadence. From a living perspective, we can also observe that the erotic fantasies of the monologues have their roots in a certain type of nihilism, because there is such insistence upon the nonreproductive forms of sex—those that lead to the extinction of the species. . . .

Like so many other writers of our time, Cela is quite happy to be impudent and irreverent as a way of destroying the values of a false and hypocritical society. On the other hand, his interest in sex indicates a conscious desire to oppose organic values to those merely utilitarian values of our present-day technocratic society. . . .

The greatest danger that we see for the future of Cela's fiction, after this tour de force of *tremendismo,* is the possibility that Cela's disgust with human reason and intelligence will lead him to a definitive negation of all serious dimensions in literature, and finally to what would be equal to literary suicide.

Gemma Roberts. ANP. 1, 1976, pp. 78–81†

One of the primary themes that runs through both books [*Bleak House* by Dickens and *The Hive* by Cela] is precisely the widespread poverty in London and Madrid which results from this lack of interest of those who are in better circumstances. For Dickens this is just one more aspect of the inefficiency of the institution of government; for Cela the corrupt, decaying society he sees around him is due to the moral and spiritual vacuum created by the war. In both novels it is a child who is seen as the victim of the irresponsibility of others. Jo, the orphaned, illiterate crossing-sweeper of *Bleak House,* and the little gypsy boy in *The Hive* play analogous roles. Neither has a real identity. Jo lacks a surname, and the little gypsy is referred to as just that, the nameless "gitano." They both live on the margin of society, homeless, barely subsisting on the most meager amount of food. Their function in both books is to rebuke the rest of society, the state and the church who ignore their very existence yet continue to finance their foreign projects. . . .

Despite the fact that these novels were written a century apart, there are similar institutions and people under indictment. The thematic parallels are apparent in the analyses of characters such as the hypocritical and intolerant Lord Chancellor and Doña Rosa as well as the do-gooders Mrs. Jellyby and Mrs. Pardiggle in *Bleak House* and Doña Visi and Doña Montserrat in *The Hive*. The problems of the poor, whether they be English or Spanish, are partly due to the corruption around them. The chaos of these societies, enhanced by the irresponsibility of the leaders and the middle class, is illustrated by the ostensibly chaotic structures of the novels, which reflect the devastating effects of the technological and political turmoil of their respective eras.

Norma Kobzina. Hispanófila. Sept., 1984,
pp. 62, 65

CELAYA, GABRIEL (pseudonym of Rafael Múgica, 1911–   )

After sustaining a vigorous surrealism in his first three books—*Tide of Silence, Elemental Movements,* and *The Enclosed Solitude*—in this most recent work, *Poetic Objects,* Gabriel Celaya tends toward a more eclectic posture, which, in its formal appearance, fulfills his desire to give free verse, pure and unhampered, a *raison d'être* he does not think he will find in the classics. . . . Basically, this book reveals a deliberate antipantheism and a desire to construct a world commensurate with man. . . .

The volume is divided into five parts. The first includes poems in which there appear elements with double meanings—a double symbolism that makes the reader's spirit fluctuate between the concrete and the unreal. Thus, the constellations, owing to their conventional names of gods and animals, are familiar things that, only for that reason, can inhabit our hearts or that we can fit into our hands. Contradictory objects and actions are subtly balanced. . . . The second part presents actions: loving . . . being . . . breathing . . . dying. . . . The third part shows us man in relation to the cosmos and his solitude: the abysses of silence that create the echoes, the night, the twilight, the pine trees, the stars—the breathing of the dead—the sea. . . . The fourth part reveals the things that have been "pulled up from the depths." . . . The fifth part is one long poem—"Verbal Apparatus"—that attempts to express the mystery of music and the word, the very mystery of man. There is a constant juggling of things and ideas from stanza to stanza.

Concha Zardoya. *RHM*. Jan.–April, 1947, p. 56†

[*Ears of Corn*] is a typical work of Celaya, undoubtedly one of Spain's greatest poets of this day, not in his characteristic social manner—except for a few poems—but rather in his equally characteristic mood which blends philosophy and irony. It is the type of irony which crops up when man approaches the mysteries and frustrations of everyday life but it is applied to the fundamentals of the consideration of the elemental beginnings of life.

The title, *Ears of Corn,* is symbolic of the poems which are composed of words comparable to the grains of the plant. This simplicity of symbolism responds to the poet's intention to speak about realities. One could say that these special realities which we found in such "proto-poetry" are rather proto-realities. . . . Yet, we are modern men and elemental realities cannot be mythically conceived as independent of man, therefore they are in our minds and they are in close association with our daily moods. Since the moods of a poet have much to do with his verses, too, this book is also a program and a work of aesthetic analysis.

The last-named quality is perhaps the best description of this new book of Celaya's, which, from the formal viewpoint, excels in the investigation of new, syncopated rhythms and original, varied types of rhyme (including internal rhymes and rhythmical alterations of rhyme which change the prevailing sound in one stanza or between two). The verses form typographical designs.

Rafael Bosch. *BA*. Summer, 1963, pp. 318–19

The first problem that arises [with regard to Celaya's work] is a generational one. To which generation does Gabriel Celaya belong? Chronologically, to the generation of 1936. . . . Thematically and for his frame of mind, as well as for the most intense period of his production, he is a significant member of the generation of 1946, the so-called postwar generation. One must remember that in the fifteen-year period between 1945 and 1960, Gabriel Celaya published . . . seven major books of contemporary poetry. We might thus say that he is one of the members of the divided generation of 1936, who, after the civil war, incorporated themselves into the postwar generation with a thematic and ideological orientation that was quite different from the one they had during the time of the observance of the four-hundredth anniversary of the death of [the poet] Garcilaso de la Vega. . . .

Tide of Silence is a valuable book that passed almost unnoticed when it appeared in 1935. His later publications have eclipsed this volume, but its rereading is a pleasant surprise. A surprise and a problem, because Celaya, who was in his early twenties when he wrote it, does not follow the pattern of his contemporaries—revaluation of the stanza, the Garcilasian model of beauty, the return to religious themes—but rather of his elder brothers, the poets of the generation of 1925, who were then about thirty or so. There is some evidence of the influence of Juan Ramón Jiménez in his use of adjectives. . . . The 1925 poets are certainly in the background.

Leopoldo de Luis. *RO*. June, 1970, p. 320†

The theme of work has had a curious destiny. In Celaya's poem ["Letter to Andrés Basterra"] the figure of the worker begins to change into that of a bored sportsman. . . . Basically what Celaya tells us is that we do not work in order to earn a living or to maintain a family, or, judging only from this poem, with the true hope of building a more human life. We unavoidably work in order to pass the time.

In the "social" poetry of the postwar period, then, work is not social, owing to a lack of a true feeling of solidarity, of human community. Men—workers as well as bosses—live alone, isolated, and anguished. All this results, evidently, from a lack of faith in the possibility of a true revolution, of a true change in life. No matter how "social" a postwar poet might appear, no matter how much revolutionary rhetoric he might employ, his abstract vision of a better life leaves us cold. In Celaya's poetry there is not a breath of that faith, that candor, that feeling that one can speak and work with someone and for something. . . .

Thus, Celaya's Andrés Basterra loses his character of worker and of a concrete man, and he reveals himself to us as a metaphysical being. He is the Other, with whom we want to communicate but are not successful, the omnipresent character of the century's literature in all languages.

David Bary. *PSA*. March, 1971, pp. 260–61†

The use of the immediate action of dramatic scenes in the two books on Basque themes, *Basque Rhapsody* and *Basque Ballads and Sayings*, can be related to folkloric poetry, whose dramatic element has often been pointed out. The descriptions and feelings of the people take on more vitality and authenticity when Celaya places them in the light of dramatic illusion. . . . In "Night of Zungarramundi" (in *Basque Rhapsody*) the dramatic scene helps to communicate the mystery, the magical beliefs and superstitions characteristic of this ancient mountain people. . . .

At the end of each work or poem in which Celaya utilizes dramatic methods, there predominates an emotional state of happiness, which might suggest that the poet uses the dramatic structure—including characterization—not only to express the anguish-happiness conflict, but also in order to affirm his confidence in happiness as a force capable of perpetually renewing him and conquering his desperation. The progressive development has a final result; it permits him to express the complexity of his emotions, above all, the delicate interrelation that exists between happiness and anguish. He is not expressing a frivolous happiness or a superficial one, but rather one with deep roots, a happiness that is necessary for the salvation of his being, which is threatened by its fleeting and purposeless existence. Even when he does turn to immediate action it is almost always to express the intensity of a saving love that converts his anguished love into happiness and hope. These uses of dramatic means reveal the tight unity between content and expression that Celaya's poetry presents. In conflict, the basic element of the dramatic, also lies the determining force of the emotional tone of his poetry.

Sharon E. Ugalde. *PSA*. Aug.–Sept., 1975,
pp. 140–42†

Endowed with a great facility for verbalizing, yet with practically no critical judgment for selectiveness, Celaya has produced huge amounts of verse and prose texts. Not all of what he has written is socially inspired; his social poems are relatively few, since his dedication to this particular kind of literature was limited mainly to a period of a few years—from approximately 1952 to 1962—roughly coinciding with the period of concern for the social aspects of literature among critics and public. A later editorial interest for social literature accounts for some new editions of Celaya's political verse in the 1970s, while the poet experiments with the newest fads in literary production. . . .

Iberian Songs are inspired by social commitment. Taking as his main motive the theme of Spain, widely treated by postwar poets, Celaya offers a selection of twenty poems covering his basic set of social ideas. He calls for social change through armed revolution; he points to the class conflict, to the duty for action for future Spain, and mentions the new form of poetry, opposed to the aesthetically centered format of poets not concerned with the present situation. Later on, this generalized political preoccupation with Spain will be directed specifically toward Basque regionalism.

All the poems in *Iberian Songs* are based upon opposing or contrasting factors, basically between a grim present and a bright future. Out of the twenty compositions, four directly treat the subject of poetry. . . ; several others refer to it. There is no doubt that the speaker, at all moments, is the poet himself, and he is a very special orator, openly addressing other men either by using the apostrophic second person or the first-person plural, which includes himself among others. In the compositions addressed to Spain the apostrophe in second-person singular to the motherland is the common method used by most poets. The preaching attitude corresponds to that of a leader, a morally superior individual who directs his fellow men, as is apparent by the abundance of imperatives.

Santiago Daydí-Tolson. *The Post-Civil War Spanish Social Poets* (Boston, Twayne, 1983), pp. 70, 84

CERNUDA, LUIS (1902–1963)

Luis Cernuda's poetry, stripped of all external resemblances [to the work of other poets], is very original; it is as new and alive as the spring bud of a plant . . . so vivacious and inspired. It has its own new life, its ingenuous, spontaneous, uncomplicated, and coherent poetic thought. . . .

Ideally Andalusian, the poetry of *Profile of the Air* has, above all, charm—the angelic Andalusian—Sevillian—gift of charm; it has grace (authentic, not made fraudulent by any literary supernaturalism), and it has its ideal living architecture, light, erect, and clear like a Giralda [Moorish palace]. What Luis Cernuda's poetry does not have is modernity. . . . Cernuda is not modern, he is new, as are and always will be

Salinas, Guillén, Espina, Dámaso Alonso, Aleixandre, Prados—or
Federico García Lorca and Rafael Alberti. . . . [1927]

José Bergamín. In Luis Cernuda, *Perfil del aire*
(London, Támesis, 1971), p. 186†

In the process of the dematerialization of reality [in *Reality and Desire*],
the first step is remembrance, a mental form of what has been. The
second step is the forgetting of the recaptured past, in which that reality
appears to undo itself, to destroy itself. Cernuda finds a third implacable manner forgetting forgetfulness itself. But through a trajectory
similar to that which we spoke about with regard to how loneliness,
which is a negative quality of company, changes into companionship, as
well as at the end of this drama, which consists of forgetting forgetfulness, we are confronted with an analogous conversion. "We fight to
establish our desire / As if there were someone stronger than us / Who
had remembered our forgetfulness" ("Hymn to Sadness").

In other words, no matter how paradoxical it appears logically, a
memory of the forgotten can exist. The poet, upon singing from his
most personal depths about forgetfulness, perhaps creates in this way a
remembrance. The extraordinary subtlety and delicacy of Cernuda's
poetry [is] perfectly visible in this theme, in this series of spiritual
transmutations in which forms of life gradually, through poetic purification, become copies of shadows and remembrances of forgetfulness.
[1936]

Pedro Salinas. *Ensayos completos de Pedro
Salinas* (Madrid, Taurus, 1981), Vol. I, p. 184†

The eighth and, for the time being, the last part of *Reality and Desire,*
consists of the small volume that appeared in Buenos Aires with the
title *Like the One Who Awaits the Dawn;* it has thirty poems, all written
between 1941 and 1944. It is a varied book in both quality and theme;
echoes of his previous works appear. The preoccupation with formal
beauty has diminished, but the verses often have their old smooth-
ness. . . .

One could draw a parallel between Vicente Aleixandre and Luis
Cernuda. The first is protean, going through constant change and transformation. The second, after he got through his initial phase, is always
the same, as if his experimental period has ended and his only interest is
in refining his instrument to make it more precise and expressive. This
parallel would reveal some facts about the varied possibilities for
growth of the poetic talent—development through the incessant search
for new forms, or seeking to develop one approach to poetic reality to
its most powerful and densest state.

In *Like the One Who Awaits the Dawn,* Cernuda continues to be
the nostalgic man and the poet of the transparent word. . . .

In Cernuda, as Andalusian as Lorca and Alberti, the inclination toward Andalusianism—tragic, fleeting, and charming, but always deeply popular—is not evident. . . . Cernuda's Andalusian charm, like that of the author of *Rimas* [Bécquer], consists in the lightness of the forms, and in both supports a certain sentimental weight. In his generation, Cernuda represents the most nostalgic voice and perhaps the most moving. Owing to his sweetness and fragility, he wounds the reader in the most sensitive parts of his being.

Ricardo Gullón. *Asomante*. July–Sept., 1950,
pp. 61, 67†

The other paradise that Cernuda dreams about [in addition to his native Andalusia] is Greece, the ancient Greece of beautiful and free bodies, of the immortal gods. This nostalgia for the Hellenic world was a romantic sentiment expressed by many great romantic poets, such as Keats and Hölderlin. In Cernuda, as in Keats, the passion for beauty, which is one of his most frequent motives of inspiration, is generally inseparably united with his admiration for Greek myths. . . . Cernuda confesses in the poem "The Poet and the Myths," which appears in his autobiographical volume *Ocnos,* that he also felt great attraction to the beauty of the Greek world while reading a handbook of mythology as an adolescent. . . .

The concept of the Greek world as a paradise, as an Eden, about which modern man hardly knows anything . . . is also found in the great romantic poet Friedrich Hölderlin. . . . Through his reading of Hölderlin, Cernuda was able to come closer to the paradise of pagan Greece. In 1935 Cernuda, in collaboration with Hans Gebser . . . translated Hölderlin. The translation was published in the magazine *Cruz y Raya,* and it is preceded by a significant introductory note by Cernuda himself, in which this nostalgia for the Greek world is evident along with an impassioned defense of paganism—not so much in its religious sense as in its sense of freedom and adoration of the body and its beauty. In the introduction, is he not evoking his own attitude, his own personal nostalgia?

José Luis Cano. *CA.* May–June, 1953,
pp. 225–27†

What does Cernuda owe to the surrealists? The bridge between the French avant garde and poetry in our language was, as is well known, Vicente Huidobro. After this Chilean poet the contacts multiplied, and Cernuda was neither the first nor the only poet who felt the fascination of surrealism. It would not be difficult to point out in his poetry, or in his prose for that matter, the imprints of certain surrealists, such as Éluard, Rigaut, and, although we are speaking of a writer who is his polar opposite, Louis Aragon (early style). . . . For Cernuda, surrealism was something more than a lesson in style, more than a poetics or a school of associations and verbal images: it was an attempt at embodying poetry in life, a subversion that took in both language as well as institutions. A morality and a passion. Cernuda was the first, and perhaps the only one, who understood and interpreted for himself the true meaning of surrealism as a movement of liberation—not from verse but from consciousness: the ultimate great spiritual shock of the Western world. One must add André Gide's revelation to the psychic upheaval of surrealism. Thanks to the French moralist, Cernuda accepts himself; from that point on his homosexuality will no longer be an illness or a sin but rather a freely accepted and lived destiny. . . .

Surrealism is a tradition. With that critical instinct that distinguishes the great poets, Cernuda retraces the trend: Mallarmé, Baudelaire, Nerval. Although he was always faithful to those three poets, he did not stop with them. He went back to the origin of modern Western poetry: to German romanticism. One of Cernuda's themes is that of the poet facing the hostile and indifferent world of men. Although the theme was present from the earliest poems, starting with *Invocations* it unfolds with a more and more somber intensity.

Octavio Paz. *PSA.* Oct., 1964, pp. 50–51†

Mention has already been made . . . of Cernuda's use of Eden, the age of innocence, and the Fall in shaping the "myth of his existence." But these were elements in the fable of childhood, artistic constructions superimposed upon his early years from the vantage point of 1942. When Cernuda first began to write about love it is doubtful that he was aware of any particular tradition that would accommodate his "love *contra natura.*" The only vehicle at hand was, as we have seen, Greek mythology. And from this tradition, as unerringly as though he had foreseen the whole evolution of his love poetry, he selected—was perhaps drawn to—two mythological "personae"—Narcissus and Venus.

Like two stars in conjunction, both figures appear in Cernuda's first book of poems, *Profile of the Air.* Together, alternating in importance, they provide symbols for the two separate yet related facets of Cernuda's love poetry. This is exact if we make one qualification—that when the poem from *Profile of the Air* in which Venus appears was rewritten for the first edition of *Reality and Desire,* Venus the goddess became Eros the god.

Let us examine the reasons for the natural selection of these two deities. . . . First in importance was the theme of separateness that resulted from the Fall into the world—and out of Eden of childhood. . . . Secondly, . . . the attraction of the adolescent for Cernuda was primarily a function of his nostalgia for his own childhood and youth—this last one of the supreme values in the world of the poems.

Both these ideas have their common ground in the poetic truth of the Narcissus fable. Let us see what light this fable throws on the nature of Cernudian love. First there is the obvious analogy between the incompleteness—the "halfness"—of the self in Cernuda's poems and the fact that Narcissus is, in effect, two people, or so he believes on discovering his reflection in a pool. And Narcissus' desire for—and longing to become one with—his reflection has its direct counterpart in Cernuda's desire for adolescents. . . .

Philip W. Silver. *"Et in arcadia ego": A Study of the Poetry of Luis Cernuda* (London, Támesis, 1965), pp. 89–90

Satire requires a knowing "edge" on the subject; there must be a certain calculation which will divorce the poet from the poem; in the various characters created by Cernuda in his late poetry, a base polemic is always avoided—he artfully adjusts his didactic ends to an artistic ideal by choosing a representative religious or historical personage which will willfully express all that is distant, even anathema, to the poet. The prejudices within Cernuda, his own spiritual stance, are conceptualized into the character so that we indirectly divine the thought of the poet. Thus these men—Philip the Second, Caesar, Lazarus, Bernal Díaz [del Castillo] should not be seen as varying symbols for the poet, but rather allegories, for in symbol form and meaning are one, whereas an Allegory points to something other than its form—it is a mold to be filled by the poet-maker, and to be completed by the reader.

The first poem [in *The Clouds*], "Lazarus," is of special interest, for it is the least didactic of the four and consequently the most relevant to Cernuda himself. . . . The poem opens with a triple perspective on the event. Although Lazarus is speaking, he recounts the circumstantial details as they were told to him. . . . Alive again, he describes the experience of death, but with a curiously ambivalent reaction to life begun anew. It is not another life for him, but a repetition of the suffering that he thought he had left behind. . . .

This poem is particularly favored by the poet, for it represents a turning point in his constant effort throughout *The Clouds* to objectify and order his experience. If the biographical elements which form the basis of the poem are considered, the poet becomes a contemporary Lazarus: alone, having begun a new life in England, having escaped certain death in Spain. Like Lazarus, he has undergone a physical resurrection which demanded expression other than the personal, subjective evocation. . . . In the poem, the poet has vanished behind his Biblical embodiment of life begun anew. . . . Lazarus is the particular mask which the poet found most expressive of a certain state of mind.

Alexander Coleman. *Other Voices: A Study of the Late Poetry of Luis Cernuda* (Chapel Hill, University of North Carolina Press, 1969), pp. 112–13, 116

"Criticism for me is no more than a marginal product of poetic activity." Such a statement, made in 1959, seems to fit this facet of Cernuda's work into what T. S. Eliot called, in one of his last works, "workshop criticism." This is a term applicable in general to the criticism done by a poet. Cernuda, who was a member of a generation that was particularly rich in what has been called, not without a certain ironic ambiguity, "poet-professors" (Dámaso Alonso, Pedro Salinas, or Jorge Guillén, among the most notable), was perhaps the only one of the group who, in his orientation, completely adjusted himself to the critical approach—a pragmatic one—indicated by Eliot: a criticism of the poet-reader, with the singularity, the risks, and the natural limitations that it involves. His interest and his affinity were the doubly determining factors of his successes, and it is not strange that some of his best critical pages are about authors who are spiritually close to him or who had influenced him during the course of his poetic career. . . .

In sum, the most substantial contribution of Cernuda to Spanish literary criticism perhaps is to be found in his vision of what was national—a distanced vision, free from commitments. His view is not very reverential, and almost that of a foreigner, in part owing to the expressed or tacit confrontation of what is written in his native language with the literature and thought of other countries (in particular those of the Anglo-Saxon ones). Because of his sensitive projection of his own experience in evaluating the work of others, some of his judgments on occasion may be unconvincing, or even irritating, but they will rarely leave the reader indifferent.

Luis Maristany. Introduction to Luis Cernuda,
Crítica, ensayos y evocaciones (Barcelona, Seix
Barral, 1970), pp. 29, 31†

In Mexico Cernuda found a resolution for his experience of alienation, which he had sought earlier in his belief in the ancient gods, in his wish for death at the time of the Civil War, in Christianity during the first years of exile, and in the idealized vision of Spain. The discovery of his dream world in Mexico and the experience there of the love for which he had almost abandoned hope was the climactic moment of his life and the justification of the painful existence he had led until then. Mexico did offer him the quasi-mystic experience of love and the recapture of the idyllic world of his childhood, but it also provided him with an environment where he felt he could at last be himself. One of the prose poems of *Variations on a Mexican Theme* describes his discovery of Mexico as an experience of rebirth, a feeling that he had come home to a land that truly reflected his values and affirmed his identity. . . .

Cernuda's Mexican experience reveals, in fact, that his successive attempts to reach a transcendent level of existence are not concerned with evading reality, but are the symptoms of a concern with self-affirmation. The image of the hidden garden, in all its manifestations, is not in essence just a place of retreat from the world but a haven from hostile surroundings where Cernuda can preserve his identity. The hidden garden syndrome . . . is thus not an indication of an effete personality incapable of living in the real world, but a sign of Cernuda's refusal to compromise his personal truth in a world he felt would betray or destroy him.

Derek Harris. Luis Cernuda: A Study of the
Poetry (London, Támesis, 1973), p. 95

The first edition of *Ocnos* was made up of thirty-two poems. The second edition included fifteen more and deleted one, "Written on Water," which was also eliminated from the definitive edition of sixty-three poems published in Mexico by the University of Veracruz, barely two months before the poet's death.

The book was not only augmented, but the inclusion of the new texts gradually modified the initial structure until it became a work of rather distinct scope and intention.

The ambiguous and at the same time exact title remained from the beginning. . . . The name *Ocnos* never alluded to the essence of the book; thus, it could be retained for all the successive editions.

In the first edition, the collection expressed the world that arose from the mythification of the childhood paradise. . . . The second edition introduces texts like "The Piano," "Nocturnal Magic," and "The Heath," still within the reconstructing scope of the first *Ocnos*, but the rest of the volume is a response to other motivations in which meditation about nature and reflection about life itself acquire the same importance as the first poems. . . .

The definitive edition breaks with the previous ones quite clearly. Landscape moves toward meditation, and thought takes over the volume. *Ocnos* is transformed into a closed world whose three stages clearly mark the correlative states that Cernuda would reach in *Reality and Desire:* life being lived, life being meditated, life being studied. The author of the definitive edition of *Ocnos* is the same one who has decided to transform himself into an artistic entity as a means of fixing himself in time.

Jenaro Talens. El espacio y las máscaras:
Introducción a la lectura de Cernuda
(Barcelona, Anagrama, 1975), pp. 379–80†

[I should like] to point out some connections between the poem "Yankee Nocturne" and *Reality and Desire*, the complete collection of Cernuda's verse.

In this collection there are only two poems that are called "nocturnes": "Nocturne among the Little Insects," in which a "stony body, sad body," without knowing where to go or where to return to, longs in vain for the flower of desires cut at the root; and "Yankee Nocturne," which expresses an identical immanence without escape, but not at the threshold of life but rather at its decline. There is such a profusion of poems that spring from the loneliness of night, although they are not called "nocturnes," that we can consider as a constant situation in Cernuda's poetry the loneliness of a man in a room contemplating walls, a lamp, a cot, a window—surroundings that are never a home and almost always a cell. This prison of the night is more evidently present in the first three books, but it never completely disappears. With regard to the word "Yankee," I do not find it in either Cernuda's verse or prose, and perhaps the absence of this vague adjective injects it with a shade of scorn, which was already suspected. . . .

Gonzalo Sobejano. The Analysis of Hispanic
Texts: Current Trends in Methodology (New
York, Bilingual Press, 1976), pp. 101–2†

Cernuda was one of those few poets whose early and demanding poetic vision already accompanied an exceptional gift of words. The more specific aspects of that vision, however, were to define themselves more slowly than did his craft because of their profoundly existential character. Cernuda had to discover them within himself after arduous, wrenching efforts. They involved the acceptance of his homosexuality, a preference he did not fully realize until he was well into his twenties, and the rejection of traditional religious values with their customary ballast of social convention. And it is well to keep in mind these two positions as we read the poet's work, particularly from the surrealist period on, when they became firmly rooted. For Cernuda was totally engaged in the substance of his life and wanted to live it with passionate intensity.

Still, Cernuda knew himself to be a poet before he did a homosexual or a social iconoclast. In this sense it was language that first led the way for him and helped to clarify the issues.

Poetry taught Cernuda to circumscribe the problematic areas of his existence—problematic with respect to society—and to turn them into instruments of a coherent perception of the world. The first part of this enterprise was accomplished after a period of turmoil, when *Invocations* was published. By the time of his next book of verse was completed, the Civil War was over and he resided in England. Concurrent with the second aspect of his work, the achieving of an encompassing outlook on reality, Cernuda's near mystical intuitions took form.

His clarity, his total involvement, the broad spectrum of his concerns, all contribute to his importance as an early mentor of the present generation of Spanish poets. They acknowledge in him the first of the group of 1925 to express with impassioned logic the paradoxes of duration and to have made of ethical introspection the methodological cornerstone of his poetry. Poets yet to come will doubtless echo other facets of Cernuda's fertile verse whose imprint, if slow to emerge, remains indelible.

Salvador Jiménez-Fajardo. *Luis Cernuda*
(Boston, Twayne, 1978), pp. 156–57

CUNQUEIRO, ÁLVARO (1911–1981)

Cunqueiro's most definitive verses offer a total Galician perspective. They are like a subtle interpretation of a cloud of light. . . . In Cunqueiro's work the troubadours' songs are evident; the sounds of the sea, of islands, of apples, of picnics, of joyous festivals are ones that will remain as a permanent part of the annals of Galician verse.

Although certain foreign influences are evident in *Sea to the North,* the youthful and happy spirit of our earliest poetry has never been lacking in his works. . . . Cunqueiro's poetry follows a route without the slightest moral or theological complication. Cunqueiro does not have to resort to any scientific concept in order to achieve his poetic goals. . . . Poetry is consubstantial with his very being. . . . Whoever reads Cunqueiro's poems will encounter his very subtle message. It is a poetry of a friendly voice, which frees itself from the heavy yoke of metrics and music.

Manuel González-Alegre. *Poesía gallega
contemporánea* (Vigo, Huguia, 1954),
pp. 102–4†

In Cunqueiro's *Treasures New and Old* the treasures are always guarded by magical beings, principally by gnomes or by Moors and also by nereids or by fairies, or by hamadryads. These are all capable of being guards because they can exercise their evil powers over us. At times they are dark, almost black people, Moors or incognito genies. The treasures are guarded . . . by these beings who in Jungian psychology are known as "shadows," or rather as one part of our own selves . . . that we don't like to recognize. . . .

In this volume, Cunqueiro tells fables about treasure seekers, about golden mirrors, and fountains. . . . There is even a golden umbrella. The importance of dwarves is stressed as is that of fairies, gnomes, and even the horses that defend the entrance to the treasure.

J. Rof Carballo. Prologue to Álvaro Cunqueiro,
Tesouros novos e vellos (Vigo, Galaxia, 1964),
pp. 21–22†

Aside from his volumes written in Castilian, Álvaro Cunqueiro has had four prose works published in Galician. The first, *Merlin and Family,* was a resounding success. . . . In it he gave sparkling life to a group of people and fables taken from distant imagined lands and from his own fascinating imagination and brought to the palace of the old wizard in Miranda. . . .

In *The Chronicles of the Wizard* he narrates, in his very personal style, the adventures of a group of traveling ghosts in the company of the fearless and astonishing wizard. . . .

In *School of Healers* he brought together a group of stories about our land's folk healers; some scenes are real ones of daily life, embellished with several aspects of fantastic storytelling. They are told with spontaneity and unique charm, and they accurately reflect the daily life of Galician villages.

Finally, in *If Old Sinbad Were to Return to the Islands* . . . the ancient Eastern myth takes on new qualities. The old white-bearded mariner with a turban is the protagonist of new poetic episodes. . . .

Myth is also present in the drama entitled *The Uncertain Mr. Hamlet*. . . . The Hamlet of this play is a pre-Shakespearean one, almost medieval, who appears in the city and castle of Elsinore, both of which are enveloped in a wintry gloom. Nonetheless, he is a very Galician Hamlet, one of our own days. . . .

Cunqueiro discerns a world of meanings, of ultraphysical realities, and of ghosts. He is an exceptional mythographer. He creates myths about characters from literature or from his own imagination.

F. Fernández del Riego. Afterword to Álvaro
Cunqueiro, *Tesouros novos e vellos* (Vigo,
Galaxia, 1964), pp. 109–11†

To what epoch does Cunqueiro's *Ulysses* belong? To none at all—to every one. Because of his literary methods, Cunqueiro frees action, things, and characters from the restrictions of time. Any one of his pages can refer to the middle of the twentieth century as easily as it can refer to classical Greece. . . . In *Ulysses* Christianity is spoken about, of course, but pagan customs are also discussed; sun dials, goose feathers, tunics, sailing ships, lighting a fire with a flint are all mentioned, but so is the view of the foamy beaches of Ithaca one gets from an airplane.

With regard to geography, the most distant places draw near to each other, or the closest ones are separated and lost in the unaccountable distances of mystery. Time and space are entangled with themselves and with legend. . . . And thus one travels from a real city to an invented one; from a historical site to a legendary empire. The dead have a dialogue with the living, and the sirens converse with men. . . .

Although Cunqueiro's characters up to now have included the wizard Merlin, Ulysses, Sinbad the Sailor, and Galician and Breton ghosts, this does not permit us to discard the possibility that his next character might be an astronaut. . . . Cunqueiro, like Edgar Allan Poe, has faith in dreams as the only realities. . . .

Manuel García-Viñó. *Novela española actual*
(Madrid, Guadarrama, 1967), pp. 118–19†

Merlin and Family is Cunqueiro's most personal work; it does not stay within the limits of the contemporary narrative, nor does it deal with the problems that concern the contemporary narrative. He himself states that he did not write a social novel because his job is that of saving the [Galician] language. . . .

The search for a real wizard from among the populace acquires relevant form in Cunqueiro's narrative style. He defends the reality of what is dreamed with the testimony of rural imagination. Because he identifies myth with imagination, the power of the soul, which we call fantasy, has creative virtues; imagination fills the soul with emotion, images, and symbols.

Naturally, in Cunqueiro's work only Merlin's name, the fact that he is an undoer of evil deeds, his wife, and the other characters have to do with the Arthurian cycle.

But this is not even completely true, since we know that Cunqueiro wrote this work remembering his childhood and the old servant woman who used to tell him stories, even about Merlin, which he has forgotten. But the character and his mysterious figure remained engraved in Cunqueiro's memory and served as the basis for this work, which comes from his own pure imagination.

Merlin is thus a character of the Galician legends and popular tales that now only the old people remember.

Matilde Felpeto Lagoa. *Grial.* July–Sept., 1971,
pp. 358–59†

Just as occurs with Dumas's famous three musketeers, who are really four, in Cunqueiro's *The Seven Stories of Autumn* there are six tales. . . . In these fine narrative pages . . . appear several characteristics of Cunqueiro's thought, technique, and style that will become evident in his subsequent long and short narrations.

One major characteristic is the world of mystery, the "ultraworld," the otherworld, where daily routine and surprise merge, where our reality intersects with another reality that we scarcely can see, feel, or guess at. It is a world in which the tracks of the past, present, and future are blurred; they become evanescent or join together; this otherworld that the author creates is, after all, the creator of himself; it is in this otherworld that Cunqueiro's dreamlike beliefs and poetic intuition move. . . .

The thematic nucleus of *The Seven Stories of Autumn* can be summarized as "a prodigious deed." . . . Cunqueiro, who is very conscious of the mysterious ambience in which his characters move and the events these surroundings signify, often provides descriptive details that tend to minimize the distance and the mystery and provide the story with greater verisimilitude. This occurs on many occasions when the poetic and the prosaic, or imprecise fantasy and concrete reality, or the prodigious deed with the common fact coexist. Life and dream, dream and life go together.

Juan Miguel Moreiras. *Grial.* Jan.–March, 1972,
pp. 29–30, 35–36†

We find the best of Cunqueiro's works in *School of Healers.* The characters of Perión of Braña, Borrallo of the Lake, the ten healers, each one surrounded by his own world in addition to Cunqueiro's world, constitute the apogee of maturity of this wonderful writer. The book is a shining addition to the gallery of splendid types so rooted in the Galician reality. The second part of the volume—"News about the World and the Magical Fauna"—is delightful entertainment—a parade of surprising animals in a fantastic bestiary typical of Álvaro Cunqueiro.

Cunqueiro is more of a narrator than a novelist. . . . He presents stories that require a unifying thread, and then he works these stories with the patient insistence of a goldsmith. What appears to be sudden or owed to imaginative facility is nothing more than the expression of his own world—the Cunqueiran world made up of charm and fantasy, at whose service there is a truly functional prose; functional in the sense that it is adjusted . . . to the imagined reality created by Cunqueiro. At times the reader might take this delicate and startling prose as finality in itself—Cunqueiro never does.

Basilio Losada. *Grial.* Jan.–March, 1970,
pp. 115–16†

I believe that in Cunqueiro's works, as in [Jean] Cocteau's, the playful element is the essential aspect, to the extent that even tragedy, when it does appear, has the tone of a tongue-in-cheek melodrama that ends up in a semiconscious parody. What is *The Infernal Machine* if not a parody of Sophocles? What is *The Uncertain Mr. Hamlet* if not a parody of Shakespeare? The accumulation of crime and lewdness, of parricide and incest that Cunqueiro presents us in this play is far from provoking tragic dread in us because we have the impression that everything is occurring in a world of puppets and that the author is counterfeiting a tragedy, just as the comic writers of the ancient Greek theater did. . . . How else can we explain the ironical comments . . . the bursts of cold water that quite often erupt in that heated atmosphere, in the hellish temperature of the situation? Cunqueiro sees the world as a farce, but from the point of view of a satirical moralist. More precisely, tragedy is impossible in Cunqueiro's world because his universe knows no morality. Neither sin nor virtue are taken seriously. . . . Cunqueiro's world is that of the Byzantine romance, the world of traditional adventure. . . . Cunqueiro does not try to renovate myths because he basically does not believe in their vital efficacy, so he presents them in their ancient esthetic dimension, without forgetting that it is ancient. Thus lyricism and humor, which act on the still and emptied forms of culture, rather than on life itself, make up an art lacking feeling, in which the supreme value is esthetic; but always counterbalanced by the historical perspective rather than resulting from a glorifying and critical vision of mortal beauty.

Ricardo Carballo Calero. Grial. July–Sept.,
1974, pp. 276–77†

A Man Who Looked Like Orestes is an intricate account of the lives of its characters, of their innermost anxieties, and of their strongest doubts. The message implicit in the last episode—the *bola de nieve* [snowball]—supports the idea of a "revitalized" myth. The "myth of the vengeance of Orestes" as [Northrop] Frye indicates, happens only in a fiction, in a snowball. In the contemporary context, vengeance seems fruitless, as there are other, many other concerns plaguing modern man. . . .

The final result is not a myth in the traditional sense, but a modern Spanish myth with universal implications. The novel's universality lies primarily in its "existentialism," which is revealed by interiorized narrative technique: the complete uncertainty of existence; the way in which man's expectations are constantly deceived; the inability to face life's problems (past, present, and future); and anguish at the passing of time, a force which speeds us toward old age, loneliness, and death. The novel's tragicomic tone portrays Man as a prisoner of the absurdity of modern existence and a tragic pawn of the forces of time and death. . . .

Aside from its many subtle allusions to modern Spain . . . the novel offers many structural and thematic parallels with the political situation under Franco, parallels which are cleverly cloaked in the framework of the ancient myth, but unveiled by an analysis of interiorization into the minds of two human beings who are in contention with one another. . . . All of these implicit parallels hold their moral for the modern Spaniard: the crime long past, it is a time for compassion and understanding, for forgetting hatred and brutal vengeance, a time to look at both sides of the conflict, as does the novel, and for working toward a conclusive and realistic future.

Michael D. Thomas. Hispania. March, 1978,
p. 44

DELIBES, MIGUEL (1920–   )

With [*Long Is the Cypress's Shadow*] Miguel Delibes restores the narrative mode to the best tradition of the Spanish novel, placing himself, moreover, in the same line of the majority of contemporary writers who would appear to be obsessed by the psychological concerns of man. . . . When Delibes enters this contemporary literary current, he does so by maintaining a somewhat independent posture. . . . Therefore, his novel can be classified as psychological in regard to the problems it presents, but with the same concept of psychology he has always had, without those Freudian concerns of little style and that whole series of insane morbidities so in vogue today. His novel is, at the same time, however, essentially human, with characters who are beings torn from the very reality that we all live and who function and react probably as we would in identical circumstances, and whose personal problems . . . are problems that respond to a completely normal and logical genesis within the vicissitudes of their development; he does not force emotions that then would certainly appear dehumanized.

Delibes's book consists of two perfectly defined parts, which can be considered as the presentation of the problem and its development, and to a certain extent, its solution. In the first part, he relates in a rather somber tone the unprotected childhood of the protagonist, an orphan handed over by his uncle, who is his guardian, to the charge and tutelage of a teacher from Ávila who has a completely pessimistic and mediocre concept of life. . . .

The second part of the book is no more than the logical consequence of the clash of this concept of life with someone who is still young and filled with exuberant vitality. . . .

The theme of the novel is interesting and provocative and is handled by the author with loving care throughout its development; Delibes tries to have the protagonist himself be the one who explains the reactions of his mind and spirit to the various occurrences in his life.

José Manuel Vivanco. *CHA.* Jan.–Feb., 1949, pp. 223–24†

The Path is Delibes's best novel. . . . It is a novel that rather surprised many of its readers. The critics did not see the possibility in his previous novels of a third book of this dimension. And, nevertheless, [in *Long Is the Cypress's Shadow* and in *Still It Is Day*] the themes of *The*

Path are very much present. On first thought, to say that *The Path* is a continuation of the other two novels would seem to be an erroneous judgment; but in reality the atmosphere of this book gives the impression of something that we have already seen in Delibes's previous work. The secret is to be found in the author. If Miguel Delibes did not succeed, when he first started to write, in creating such an interesting, moving, and tender novel as *The Path,* it was not done out of caprice; it simply did not happen. . . .

The first impression one has upon reading *The Path* is the facility with which the author develops his narrative. He operates free of all literary formulas that lie in ambush for the author and oblige him in difficult moments to take the easy way out. In this novel, there is no external pressure; there are only freshness, agility, and renewal for the narrative form. . . .

The author's return to the world of children is a return to himself; it is the return to the beginning of the first book [*Long Is the Cypress's Shadow*], free from narrative influences and complementary themes of other novels. Delibes inaugurates in *The Path* a literary style that is fresh and personal. . . .

Theme and style are closely united. The expressions of spontaneous language have come under literary pressure, born from the artistic thrust of the author, and both elements are fused in a harmonious unity of modern expressiveness. The author is seen everywhere; we make note that we know him, but his form of writing has entirely won us over. After having read just a few pages, one is quickly convinced that *The Path* is *the* novel of Delibes.

Antonio de Hoyos. *Ocho escritores actuales*
(Murcia, Spain, Aula de Cultura, 1954),
pp. 201–3†

The Path, published in 1950, is the third novel of Delibes and shows the author's ever renewed interest in perspectives on Man's struggle to understand his own nature in relation to the lives and events around himself. In his first novel, *Long Is the Cypress's Shadow,* published in 1948, the theme is pessimistic. . . . As though to counteract this unhappy determinism, Delibes's second novel, *Still It Is Day,* published in 1949, presents a gentle character of unbounded generosity and optimism, who has no material reason for being so, since his body is twisted, his surroundings depressing, and even the woman he marries evil. Thus the first two novels show the author's early, somewhat awkward efforts to portray first the destructive power of environment, and then the victory of Man's spirit over environment. Significantly, both books indicate Delibes's interest in the early formative years of his heroes.

The Path benefits greatly by what the author learned in these previous literary explorations. . . . The novel starts and ends in those fatal hours that mark the end of the old life and the beginning of the new. It asks the reader to question which way is better. Obviously the novel is dedicated entirely to Daniel's memories of the good life of natural spontaneity in his pleasant valley. The author assumes that his reader can supply his own image of the forming and deforming forces of higher education and civilization which will characterize the new way. . . .

The novel makes no explicit judgment on the rightness or wrongness of improving oneself in order to have more status in society. It does make evident the struggle between the instincts and the demands of civilized conformity. And it does this through the real experiences and words of its characters. Expressed another way, *The Path* makes evident the struggle between forces affirming life, and others that deny it.

Ernest A. Johnson, Jr. *Hispania*. Dec., 1963,
pp. 748–49

That there exists in Delibes an entire world of religious feeling seems undeniable. That the writer flees from the complicated world of ideas of a thinker who writes novels with a specific Catholic mission is also certain. The characters of Delibes at times, as occurs in the short story ["The Nativity," in *The Shroud*], confront the idea of God directly. The novelist establishes them in uncertainty. A disconcerting moment arrives in the midst of the lives of those who perhaps make a routine out of religion. This happens frequently in other works of Delibes. The affection that he feels toward rural settings has made him create priests with the virtues and faults of peasants; this is primarily true of his early books. Later, we can observe a perceptible evolution. The religious crisis that has inspired us to live takes shape in works like *Five Hours with Mario,* where the essential elements of breaking with paralyzing tradition float about. We reiterate, perhaps tiresomely, that Delibes is not a writer of ideas, in the broadest sense of this term. Remark, then, that the religious element of his plots can be seen in the effluvium of life itself. His priests take part in earthly matters with a yearning for perfection common to all members of the population, with their weaknesses, tender moments, their prejudices and egotisms, on an equal footing with the rest of the gallery of characters whom he sets in motion. All of which does not prevent the writer, who has Catholic concerns, from rebelling against the hypocrisy, the rampant mediocrity, the lack of commitment, and the routine that work against the perfecting of the spiritual life; Delibes sums all this up, loading his paintbrush and showing, from this catalog of religious invalidities, what he understands to be authentic and true. He does all this indirectly. The margin that the novelist unselfishly concedes to supernatural sentiment remains reflected in that little swarm of painful feelings that he relates to us in the short story "Faith." A hospital on a day of Holy Week, with its attendant suffering and a certain expectation before the processional.

Does the miracle come about in an authentic manner? Or is it faith that produces relief, be it partial or total, from illness? The writer does not take sides, although it is not difficult to determine his personal belief. He has wisely mixed, in the face of this mystery, skepticism with understanding, as if he had left open for interpretation to anyone who might read it the resolution of the enigma.

Miguel Ángel Pastor. Foreword to Miguel
Delibes, *La mortaja* (Madrid, Alizanza, 1970),
pp. 24–25†

At present, Delibes's greatest importance would appear to be as the novelist of rural Castile, as an artist who has forcefully and knowledgeably presented both the beauty and the tragedy of its soil and its people, infusing with humble but intense human drama a landscape once appreciated only aesthetically. While not subscribing to most of the tenets of the movement, Delibes is a significant social novelist, with a sincere but undogmatic concern for righting injustices and promoting reforms which will enable all Spaniards to enjoy basic human rights and comforts. His contributions in this area, totally lacking in the propaganda or ideological commitments of most other social novelists, are epitomized in *The Red Leaf, The Rats,* and *Old Tales of Old Castile,* although strong echoes are heard in *Five Hours with Mario. . . .*

Delibes is a consistent writer, despite his evolution, with many constants and repetitions, and should his emphasis shift, it will almost certainly be to themes and techniques already foreshadowed in his published works. Despite his development and sustained artistic progress, there have been relatively few thematic changes. The social preoccupations, not really perceptible in his first novel (except in a negative sense) were already present in the second, and with the completion of *Still It Is Day,* the seeds of his constant themes had been sown almost totally, for they can be found in varying degrees and in different forms in the first two novels alone. There have subsequently been changes in emphasis and in the form of presentation, but Delibes's essential concerns today have long-standing literary antecedents in his work, usually reaching back to the first three or four years of his novelistic career.

In the opinion of a majority of critics, *The Path* and *The Rats* continue to be the preferred works by Delibes. While *The Path* is delightful, it does not seem to have the significance of *The Red Leaf, The Rats, Five Hours with Mario,* and *Parable of the Drowning Man,* all novels of a greater intensity and historical relevance, and of a comparable level of artistic perfection. Many critics also consider *Diary of a Hunter* a masterpiece, and it is certainly unrivalled in Spanish literature both with respect to language and mastery of the character portrayed. Thus, before reaching the age of fifty, Delibes has produced at least half a dozen novels worthy to be counted among the best of this century, several of them with excellent chances of outlasting the present era and enduring among the classics of the language. The novelist is now at the height of his creative powers, and can yet reasonably be expected to surpass these successes in the years to come.

Janet Díaz. *Miguel Delibes* (New York, Twayne, 1971), pp. 161–62

It can be said that in general terms [Delibes's] technique fits into a traditional concept of literary realism, consisting basically of well-ordered description in which the novelist intervenes, embellishing and arranging . . . in novels that are clearly structured with beginnings and well-delineated endings . . . where the author obviously allows his own personality (especially in *Long Is the Cypress's Shadow*), his opinion about the characters, his firm belief in good and evil, and in the possibility of bettering the human condition to become clear. Delibes is the typical author who is included in his own novels and represented by an omniscient narrator, diametrically opposed to Joyce's narrator, who remains invisible behind or beyond his work, and who is so refined and indifferent that he dedicates himself only to polishing his fingernails.

These attitudes explain, at least in part, Delibes's predilection for primitive and elemental beings, whose only interest comes from their common and basic humanity. These attitudes also justify the constant presence in his work of personal manias that serve to distinguish each individual from the rest. Some critics seem to believe that these manias, like the rhetorical devices and exaggerated traits of the human element in Delibes's novels, serve merely as a literary device in order to help the reader recognize and remember the characters. We do not deny this aspect, but undoubtedly it is the secondary and the more superficial one, the more important being the emphasis, which is at times symbolic but always significant, that is put on the individuality of each person and his right and tendency to manifest traits that he shares with no one else. The slang encountered throughout all his works . . . is another aspect of the same thing: slang, by definition, is a special language limited to a group or class of people numerically smaller than the society whose language is the official one or the vernacular. Slang also expresses better the personality and the concrete problems of the individuals in question than do the official languages. The same can be said about technical or specialized vocabularies that serve at times in Delibes's work not to communicate to the reader a particular semantic content, but simply to help him realize that each group, class, or profession is worthy of as much respect and as many rights as the others; we are referring to the specialized language of the weeding season in *The Rats* (Ch. 3), for example, to that of the hunt, of plants, or of birds in various of his other novels.

Leo Hickey. *Hispanófila* May, 1972, pp. 68–69†

Spanish pastoral novels would still be simply lovely and wise, like Juan Ramón Jiménez's classic *Platero and I*, were it not for the poverty, suffering, and violence that are the underlying seemingly inescapable facts of contemporary country life. Surely the loveliness is here, seen through Nini [in *Smoke on the Ground* (i.e., *The Rats*)] a waif in a remote Castilian river village who lives one year through each turn of season and weather with a preternatural sense of meaning in natural signs: sky, earth, animals, birds, vegetation, crops, water. But even his marginal existence is threatened with extinction. He and his father are to be evicted from the cave in which they live, and a stranger is poaching their rats, which they trap and sell to the villagers for their principal meat staple. Miguel Delibes paces their story as deliberately as nature's movements, and populates his tragic idyll with memorable ragtail characters whose exuberance, meanness, and distress he lets us feel with no touch of strain or sentimentality. An impelling, skillful novel, his first in translation, which makes one want to read a second soon.

AR. No. 3, 1973, pp. 496–97

The mature Miguel Delibes of *Parable of the Drowning Man* belongs to that group of recent writers who have discovered that language is duplicitous—every bit as duplicitous as the creature that invented it for his own use. The very title of this novel [*Parábola del náufragio*] communicates its multiplicity of meanings and at the same time the ambiguity fixed in language, which is one of the book's meanings. The immediately apparent duality that derives from the Latin *parabolē/parabola* in simplest terms translates into a simultaneous signal of the novel's identity—an exemplary narrative—and its metaphoric structure—a geometric figure. The latter, concretized only twice in the text, once in reference to the "liquid parabola" produced as Jacinto urinates, traces modern society's processes of formulaic reductivism. However, while it is just that, *Parable of the Drowning Man* is more than a glimpse into the likely fate of *The Path*'s protagonist after his expulsion into adulthood and into the nightmarish patterns of a technocratic society styled along Orwellian lines, more than a Kafkaesque vision of an individual's programmed dehumanization by an engulfing structure of symmetries of his own making. This parable whose moral the parabolic arch describes cannot, for its literary shape, do without language; and while language as a vehicle is essential to the communication of a social and existential vision, the form assumed by language in that communicative function causes it to mediate not only that vision, but its own nature as language. The reader of Delibes's novel must recall that although the etymology of "parábola" begins with the idea of similitude that engenders both a particular geometric figure and a particular kind of narrative comparison (proverbial tale), the notion of speech lies at its core (note Span. *palabra* [word], Eng. "palaver"). The novel's title insinuates that the word as subject is central to the concerns of *Parable of the Drowning Man,* which, at the same time as it marks the curve of the destruction wrought by carefully graphed schemes, recounts the shipwreck of language.

John W. Kronik. *TAH.* Sept., 1975, p. 7

One of the major achievements of the later novels of Delibes is the authenticity and color of the colloquial language spoken by his protagonists. This characteristic first appears in full flower in *Diary of a Hunter* (1955) and its sequel, *Diary of an Emigrant* (1958), of which their author says: "The real protagonist of my 'Diaries' is the word, the language." Delibes's discovery of characterization through language has been incorporated in all of his subsequent work. Both Carmen of *Five Hours with Mario* and Jacinto of *Parable of the Drowning Man* are convincing as characters largely through their colloquial language and equally popular modes of thought. In all four of the works just mentioned the author has conceived the novel so that each character may "speak" intimately: on the diary, age, to a dead husband, to another self in the mirror. Stream-of-consciousness in Delibes, is, therefore, always a form of silent dialogue and not the expression of pre-speech levels of consciousness attempted by some other users of the technique. Delibes has said of Lorenzo, the protagonist of the *Diaries:* "It's possible that I will offer this character the opportunity to grow old with me." Whether Lorenzo appears in person again or not, the word continues to be his creator's protagonist.

The central personage is masculine in all of Delibes's work except *Five Hours with Mario* in which the title character is dead, but nevertheless the focus of the novel and is directly addressed throughout. Language reminiscent of Lorenzo's, therefore, moves to the feminine, Carmen and Mario being equally central to the work. Carmen's language may be the link between Lorenzo's and Jacinto's, but the latter is Mario's counterpart. The two men incarnate similar themes in their respective novels, but yet they are, as men, almost opposites in relation to the problem. Mario is presented obliquely through another person. He does not appear, but he is the positive element in the novel; he is taken seriously; he struggles and achieves a certain amount of good; and, although he fails, his son does not bear his name for nothing. For Jacinto there is no hope. His sons will literally be sheep. He has been ineffectual and timid, unwilling to offend anyone, secretly in emotional need of the paternalism of the organization, and an accomplice in his own silencing. He has even been prominent in the movement called "Peace through silence" (one is reminded of those billboards in Spain reading "25 Years of Peace," "30 Years of Peace," etc., with all that they imply), and has even invented an ingenious language called *Contracto* which reduces the number of syllables in words because it is words that get people in trouble, according to Jacinto. *Contracto* is presumably meant to be the contrary of Esperanto; the *esperanza* [hope] has been removed. Indeed, Jacinto is the president of the society for peace through silence, but unfortunately the word *presidente* [president] in *Contracto* has been reduced to *preso* [prisoner].

Harold L. Boudreau. STCL. Fall, 1976, pp. 38–39

Beginning with *Five Hours with Mario,* [Delibes] concentrates his thematic thrust on the verbal experience of the character, permitting the novel to develop around that base. In the early novels, on the contrary, themes are inferred more from what characters do than from what they say, write, or keep silent about. The novelist has made clear how the urban characters of these novels returned to their origins in moments of crisis; the crisis manifested itself in a symbolic act. But from *Five Hours with Mario* on, it will not be the behavior, but language, the medium in which things take place—and it is in this that the principal aesthetic newness consists: the emphasis put on language. The particular interest of the last novels, it seems to me, rests in the meticulous construction of a language that is adapted to the circumstances and temperament of the character. Thanks to this, the themes—alienation; rebellion against the bourgeoisie or against the bureaucracy; the disillusion that accompanies initiation into adult life; the superiority of the countryside and of rural man over the city and urban man; the sacrifice of nature to industry; the lack of communication; the harmful effects of the domestic environment; the aberrations of modern medicine—seem embodied in individuals astonishingly depicted by their way of speaking. Enmeshed in the speech of the character to the same degree that Benito Pérez Galdós or Pío Baroja was, Delibes invents with great stylistic diversity and a lively turn of phrase: the linguistic structures of the character provide the guiding principle—generally dialectical—of the structure of the novel.

Agnes Gullón. La novela experimental de
Miguel Delibes (Madrid, Taurus, 1980), p. 17†

A demanding work by one of Spain's foremost novelists, *The Hedge* [*Parable of a Drowning Man*] covers a territory similar to Franz Kafka's in presenting a grotesque vision of the individual crushed by a mechanized, totalitarian society. Set in a minimal, dreamlike landscape, it follows the "progress" of Jacinto San José Niño, 44 years old, celibate, so timid people keep wondering "what kind of nest he has fallen from." He is employed as a calligrapher in a vast company ruled by Don Abdon, a Buddha-like despot with huge breasts, "the most motherly of all fathers."

One day, Jacinto, dizzy from writing zeroes, questions the difference between zero and the letter O. He is sent off by Don Abdon to Rest and Recuperation Hut No. 13 with some American hybrid seeds and the injunction to plant them around his hut. A hedge proliferates in a week and turns into an exuberant entwined wall that shuts Jacinto off from the world. Drowning in a sea of vegetation and becoming increasingly frantic, the prisoner attempts to scale the mammoth tendrils, to hack at them, burn them, explode them, to send out messenger birds. . . .

A quotation from the philosopher Max Horkheimer at the beginning of this parable . . . establishes the motif of the book—"My principal emotion is fear." . . . And along with it comes the disintegration of thought and language. . . .

The experimental technique of *The Hedge* conveys this oppressiveness. Its discontinuous narrative line is without section breaks. Jacinto's extensive interior monologues are in everyday language and italics, the rest is in repetitive, at times, onomatopoetic, bureaucratic language. . . . There is a lack of the novelist's absence of dialogue (reflecting the lack of communication and solidarity between men in that alienated world). Jacinto himself has invented a new sublanguage.

Toby Talbot. *NYTBR.* Dec. 11, 1983, p. 11

DIEGO, GERARDO (1896–   )

[*Poems on Purpose*] are external poems, ironic criss-crossings and juxtapositions of metaphors that manifest themselves through assonance in order to intertwine in a lithe dance, that look at each other, that pursue each other at a swift pace. Those marriages of the strong idea and the fragile form of the immediately preceding poetry do not appear here. The geography delineating a surrealistic poetry through images, still not extinct among us, is scarcely seen in these poems, in which the same playful imagery succumbs through unexpected movements to a higher and more poetic playfulness. . . . The unity that is achieved in clear language is a unity of the surface, made from the constantly renewed sacrifices of an inner being that ceaselessly moves toward the hypothetical and the nonexistent. Here, it is a question of essays that possess a poetic continuity, just as it was a question, in the decadence of poetry of the nineteenth century, of essays that possessed a musical continuity that resolved the poem by annihilating the poetry. Even though there is a threat of this here, the poetry does not succeed in destroying the poem.

Rodolfo Usigli. *LyP.* Jan., 1933, p. 71†

[Diego's] extraordinary talents, his extremely rooted tenderness, his acute intuition, his technique, as agile as it is bold, for which there are no obstacles, help him to express, to compress or bring forward while purifying them cloudy emotions or ideas that are still dormant or that can be born clear in the multitudinous heart of man. Here is the double function of the poet, of the bard: to sift, to purify in our hearts the dark sediment of the past; or to suggest to us the legacy of the future that we are to transmit to those who will follow us, to orient our sensibility resplendently toward the future. . . .

But in order that this poetry be produced, it is also necessary to have a double play of reactions between a focal point and a receiver: poet and audience. Let the "bard" be heard. This is why Gerardo Diego is a poet: this lark of truth shall sing joyously in the zenith of many souls. . . . To move beautifully, to ennoble, or to arouse the purest part of the heart in thousands and thousands of beings, that surely is what *Lark of Truth* is—real poetry and at the same time absolute poetry.

> Dámaso Alonso. *Poetas españoles*
> *contemporáneos* (Madrid, Gredos, 1952),
> pp. 269–70†

Gerardo Diego is the poet who listens to verses recited to swallows and hears how the rain plays the piano, how the guardian angels leave their footprints on the mountain peak, knowing full well that everything is verbally certain, but that everything is also unattainable. Diego does not fight to change the real world of houses, downpours, heat, newspaper vendors, streetcars, and taxis, for another one of cardboard houses, clowns, impossible values and violins that draw the window curtains. But he creates the possibility that everything is possible; at least he endows the word with the creative power of turning things upside down and making this new world possible. It is not the image for the image's sake; it is not the desire for dialectical juggling, but only the joy in the power of the word and of syntax. . . .

Poetry will continue to create its own universe. Things happen in poetry as in fashion: the personal touch interests us; poetry can have a social dimension only if it has first been valid for the individual. Diego begins to create a possibility; what is less important to him is arriving at a definite proof of his operations. Two and two will always add up to four, unless it adds up to something else, and then this new world of mathematics will also be new and incomprehensible.

> Antonio Gallego Morell. *Vida y poesía de*
> *Gerardo Diego* (Barcelona, Aedos, 1956),
> pp. 157–59†

A poet of quite astonishing versatility, within the space of a few years [Diego] produced collections different as the sensitive evocations of *Soria* (1923), the ultraist [vanguard poetry movement] fun and games of *Image* (1922), which took on a more specifically creationist [vanguard poetry movement] character—after he had met [Vicente] Huidobro [Chilean poet who founded the creationist school of poetry] in Paris—

in the aptly named *Manual of Foam* (1924), and the calm lyricism of *Human Verses* (1925). *Image* and *Manual of Foam* may not be his best books, but they are possibly the most important. Their exuberant espousal of total poetic (and typographical) freedom and their dedication to the autonomy of art—the poems are fragmented bundles of images which refer to nothing outside themselves—paved the way for other poets to make more interesting use of fantasy and surprise in the twenties. Diego's experiment may also represent the least flimsy memorials to the fashionable poetic -isms of the period. Many of their mental acrobatics are imaginative and amusing, though it is difficult not to grow weary under a prolonged bombardment. His later poetry is more conventional and more substantial. *Angels of Compostela* (1940) and the sonnets of *Lark of Truth* (1943) rarely rise far above the humdrum, but they are always fluent and sometimes moving, and did something to relieve the desolate state of Spanish poetry during the years immediately after the Civil War.

> G. G. Brown. *A Literary History of Spain: The Twentieth Century* (New York, Barnes & Noble, 1972), pp. 104–5

In his life and poetry Gerardo Diego attempts this most difficult of fusions, the transformation of human loves into a love both metaphysical and religious, or Christian. Diego (like Lope [de Vega]) has enjoyed, not the unique experience of the Neoplatonic poets, but a continuing vision of love centered in the various aspects of the Eternal Feminine. His first love awakened in him the awareness of the beloved "other" in the world and a desire to transform himself into something better, and he emerged from this initial "encounter" a being "all new." After many years the poet discovered his essential and enduring love in the beloved who became his wife; in *The Surprise* he consecrated this experience in delicate and chaste lyrics which became a surprise gift for the beloved. . . .

In a life of quiet dignity, Diego has managed to sustain a vision of human love both moral and licit (in contrast to Lope's) and to pursue it through the adventure of poetry to a condition of possible beatitude, an anchoring in the Catholic faith. In our time it is no mean feat.

Given his solid traditionality in theme and often in form over against flights into vanguardism mainly in form, Gerardo Diego has at times been guardedly accused of insincerity, a charge he has vehemently resisted. His quiet optimism, his assimilation of the best of all worlds, has perhaps seemed timid and tradition when contrasted with the rebelliousness of a García Lorca or the modern metaphysical system of Jiménez. Our condensed presentation of Diego's theme should not obscure the fact that he has developed this theme and related ones with remarkable versatility and originality. He is probably the most talented sonneteer since Quevedo [seventeenth-century writer of Spain]. He has provided the most unified collection of poetry of the brief movement known as ultraism or creationism. And, as an example of his versatility, it is he (not García Lorca or Alberti) who has most expansively pursued the Spanish theme of the bullfight in his *Chance or Death*. The publication of his complete works, which now includes more than twenty volumes of poetry, should put the final seal upon his reputation as a versatile, dedicated, and prolific poet, for like [Jorge] Guillén he has been blessed with the grace of expression even in his most circumstantial lyrics.

Carl W. Cobb. *Contemporary Spanish Poetry (1898–1963)* (Boston, Twayne, 1976), pp. 98–100

[Gerardo Diego] did not abandon his vanguardism. The word continues to be essential and dynamically active in his poetry. His playfulness within the poem results precisely from a perfect operation. It follows from this that for the poet Gerardo Diego poetry is a thing of "pure arithmetic." "Not algebra"—he insists and explains—"but an arithmetic" with which he seems to want us to understand that poetry is not a mechanism of substitutions but a process of combinations. In the combinatory process, the poetic word can adopt three roles: a word as an image, a word that has two meanings, and an onomatopoeic word. The word-as-image is ultraism, the word-as-double-meaning is conceptism, the word-as-onomatopoeia is music. Many things link music to the lyric of Diego, who not in vain is a great performer and distinguished lover of music. It is with good reason . . . that when he speaks of what he calls the "pains of the senses," he says that the deepest is the "pain of hearing." An admirer of and quite knowledgeable about Félix Lope de Vega [Spain's great playwright and poet of the seventeenth century], Gerardo Diego valued before all else the rhythm and accentuation in the sonnets of the Phoenix [nickname of Lope de Vega].

Leopoldo de Luis. *NE*. Feb., 1980, p. 44†

ESPINA, CONCHA (1879–1955)

As a technician [Concha Espina] seems supremely gifted. She is unusually articulate and sensitive enough to echo the subtle moods of the earth and the sky as well as the petty sufferings of her puppets. . . . Her theme [in *Mariflor* (i.e., *The Sphinx of Maragata*) and *The Red Beacon* (i.e., *Sweet Name*)] is poverty, which drives the sentimental wants of the individual to a conflict with the interests of the family and of established custom. Poverty circles over her creatures with the ever-nearing flight of a hawk, finally clawing them down to submission. It is here that she fails. Her understanding of life is too tenuous to make us feel that the failure of her victims to triumph over poverty is the tragic dénouement of what might have been a nobly successful life. Her heart's desire is vulgar. There is no difference between her idea of happiness and that of the shopkeeper. This world would be, for her, the best possible if we could manage to eliminate poverty from it. Then the beautiful girl would be able to marry the sensitive young poet, rather than sell herself to a rich elderly man who can save her family from its dire needs. Confronted with the possibility of such a Utopia we cannot help feeling grateful that human stupidity perpetuates so mean a thing as poverty, for it occasionally lends the only glimmer of meaning to human life.

It is true that Concha Espina is "the foremost novelist of Spain today," as she has been called. But it should be remembered that since the death of the Countess of Pardo Bazán there has appeared no woman writer capable of doing work of permanent human significance. The fact that she is the recipient of a prize from the Academy merely attests to her ideologic and artistic respectability.

Eliseo Vivas. *Nation*. Aug. 13,1924, p. 168

You [Concha Espina] have done me a great honor by dedicating your marvelous book, *The Nature of the Dead,* to me, and I wholeheartedly express my appreciation to you.

I have just finished your books, which you have been kind enough to give me as a gift, and I am quite astonished and delighted by the force and richness of your talent.

I am also grateful to you for all the things with which your books have familiarized me about the customs and the soul of your noble nation. You offer us a picture of a nature totally different from those in travel books.

Selma Lagerlöf. In *L'oeuvre de Concha Espina*
à l'étranger (Madrid, Renacimiento, 1925), p. 80†

Spain's greatest contemporary woman writer and one of her greatest literary artist of all times is Concepción Espina y Tagle, known to the world as Concha Espina. . . .

Most of Concha Espina's novels are realistic and are based on actual experiences of the author, on documentation that she made "on the ground," so to speak. But it is not the photographic realism of a Zola. It is, rather, the artistic realism of a Cervantes; a reality viewed with the eyes of the soul. Concha Espina seems to be the living counterpart of other great Spanish women of the past, such as Isabella I and St. Theresa, for example, whose life and works exemplified one of the most characteristic traits of Spain: that combination of idealism and realism which found such beautiful expression in the paintings of El Greco, in the novels of Cervantes and in the plays of Lope de Vega. It is this combination which in Concha Espina becomes a power to see reality projected to a higher and more beautiful plane.

In many of the works of this author, and particularly in her first novel, *The Girl from Luzmela,* and in her subsequent works, such as *The Sphinx of Maragata* . . . , *The Rose of the Winds, Sweet Name* . . . and in her latest novel, *Rear Guard,* the dominant note is Concha Espina's extraordinary understanding of the psychology of women, and particularly of their attitude in the face of failure, failure to realize what they most desire after intense suffering. In these novels, as in all her works, as far as style is concerned, Concha Espina excels in description, in description of Nature, especially. It is in these descriptions that she is at her very best, and that one fully appreciates her charming artistry. Her art is imbued with Spain's glorious traditions and is, at the same time freshly modern. Finding, as she does, deep inspiration in Spanish tradition, she transcends time and space and rises to the universal, just like the great writers of Spain's Golden Age, Cervantes, Lope de Vega, Calderón, Gracián, and so many others.

Ralph J. Michaels. *Mark Twain Journal.* Spring, 1938, pp. 5–6

The novels of Concha Espina resound in our ears like a melody played on a cello behind the curtains of a room in which jazz can be heard. It is not that one is the enemy of the other—it is a question of distinct aims—but rather it is that the excitement of what is happening now attracts us.

We have esteemed Concha Espina less than she deserves. I know for certain that she, an exceptional spirit, would pay this apparent disdain little mind. She would pay this disdain little mind—let us make it clear—as soon as she knew that the alienation of so many young people was not the fault of her work. Moreover, she realized that there were not many who were able to penetrate to the sense—the sense of form, the most problematic aspect of a work because it was the obvious one—of a classical, luminous and well-ordered creation. She would feel sorry more like a mother who sees her child keeping bad company. She knew very well that clarity ultimately becomes artistic integrity, for nothing is stronger than truth. The prodigal son whom we all have become will eventually return to the paternal home. . . .

From *The Girl from Luzmela* to *A Valley in the Sea,* passing on to *The Sphinx of Maragata, The Nature of the Dead,* and so on, you can follow the passage of a life, of a woman. This is precisely what we look for today in literature: a man or a woman. We contemplate an exemplary life, of needs and struggles, of constant activity. . . .

[Concha Espina's] work is for those of us who are accustomed to pass each other on narrow staircases in today's buildings without ever letting the other person go first, while we remember the old, wide staircases on which four people could pass at one time, and on which, nevertheless, people did allow the other person to go by first. The gesture of yesteryear seems to us totally useless. But we are in the process of learning that courtesy, like beautiful and serene forms in art, can be a thing of primary necessity. This process requires that the spirit be civilized and the sensibility purified.

When this occurs, Concha Espina will occupy the place that is fitting for her in Spanish letters.

José Hierro. *RL.* Sept., 1955, pp. 100–3†

In none of Concha Espina's creations are there dark or schismatic solutions. Spirituality is imposed with a providentialism that is inherited, perhaps, from classical taste. In any case, the plasticity—the careful, well-worked, and artistic composition—is one of the characteristics that can be appreciated as the common characteristic in all the novels of Concha Espina. Colors are kept pure; situations are not besmirched; there are no blots on anyone's honor nor any exposés; there are only delicate ranges of colors, pale shades, fugitive wisps and oblique lights of great academic craft. . . .

[In *The Girl from Luzmela,*] Concha Espina's first novel, one of [Spain's] finest and most humanistic pens is to be found in embryo, a pen with the most delightful powers of observation that are connected by moving descriptions and, also, by landscapes. They have that rare quality of being able to distance reality while at the same time embracing it as the only thing that really directs human destinies. . . .

Alicia Canales. *Concha Espina* (Madrid,
ESPESA, 1974), pp. 21, 93–94†

For many critics, Carmen [in *The Girl from Luzmela*] typifies Concha Espina's women protagonists. However, Carmen's experience of life as well as her reaction to it are markedly different. Her tragedy hinges on externally imposed conditions which lead her to temporarily embrace suffering. As the novelist comments on several occasions, her passive resignation implies a rejection of the beauty of life as incompatible with moral perfection. Like Saint Teresa of Ávila, Concha Espina stresses that spiritual and moral values cannot supersede our human condition; they must enable us to confront our reality without denying it, enhancing our appreciation of life and our ability to enjoy it. In this respect Carmen's asceticism is clearly deficient and should be distinguished from the constructive self-denial presented in other novels. Possibly because she herself has not yet fully come to terms with the need for women to transform their inevitable suffering into a positive experience of life, Concha Espina sidesteps the issue in this first novel, creating a character whose suffering depends on external obstacles eventually circumvented. Thus the optimistic ending to *The Girl from Luzmela* reflects the lack of a fully elaborated vision in the developing novelist.

Mary Lee Bretz. *Concha Espina* (Boston,
Twayne, 1980), p. 31

ESPRIU, SALVADOR (1913–1985)

Although Salvador Espriu began his literary career at the age of fifteen writing in Castilian . . . under the aegis of Gabriel Miró, his initiation into Catalan literature took place in 1931 with the novel *Doctor Rip*. The publication of *Laia* . . . represents Espriu's inevitable tribute to the rural novel. . . . The narrative art of *Laia* results from the balanced fusion of the poetic impressionism of Gabriel Miró and the tragic sarcasm of one of Valle-Inclán's *esperpentos*. Espriu's impressionist technique, which gives rise to a great diversity of scenes and a great thematic richness, neither of which is completely developed by the author, finds its definitive development in the stories of his new book *Aspects (Narrations)*. . . .

Salvador Espriu's most significant literary production in the pre-Civil War years, and his most impressive narrative work, is *Ariadne in the Grotesque Labyrinth*. . . . This excellent collection of twenty-eight prose tales . . . not only reveals Espriu to be an exceptional storyteller, comparable to Joyce and Chekhov in his biting and stinging sharpness, but also reveals him to be the most important satirical writer of Catalan literature since the death of Guerau de Liost.

Antonio Vilanova. *Destino*. Sept. 30, 1950, p. 14†

All of Salvador Espriu's works have a theme of "memorial." The invocation of death is constant in his work. He himself has defined the structure of his work through that common yet unique event. That event is both personal and collective. . . .

Death is the distinguished protagonist of all of Espriu's poetic works. The title of one is *Mrs. Death*. . . . Death has innumerable names. It is not only a lady, but also an archer, the galloping horse, the wall, *The Walker and the Wall, End of the Labyrinth,* etc. "It will never be possible to use up all the names of death," he says. His books are dictated by that personage, who is always lurking about and touches in its most icy way those the poet most loved and who were closest to him. . . .

And he deals not only with the death of men, but also with the death of memories, of the flower that is going to be picked, of words that have turned to ashes, of a land, or the death of a language. . . . That invocation of the death of a language becomes one of the essential themes of his poetry. [1964]

Joan Teixidor. *Cinc poetes* (Barcelona, Destino, 1969), pp. 131–32†

We have the impression that the basic misunderstanding that has accompanied Espriu's works is owed to the lack of importance granted to the "difficult" elements, and, in particular, to a certain rejection of the book that constitutes the crossroads of all of Espriu's poetry—*End of the Labyrinth.* In this volume the dialectic tension—that is, the force of the opposition between the subjective and the objective elements, and between the personal and the collective—are momentarily resolved. . . .

Espriu's poetry is composed of cycles, which occasionally interrupt each other only to begin once again: that is his "discontinuous" characteristic. . . . But his poetry also has a characteristic mythic structure—hence its "encyclopedic character"—which is more hidden than that of the cycles. It is more hidden, at least, in reference to the two tragic heroes who are its protagonists, but are never named: Job and Oedipus. Job, the poet himself, is the protagonist of a "tragic vision" who represents himself as a victim of the demands of a divine being, but whose salvation is in the possession of the magical and redeeming power of the word, which permits him to face God and discuss with Him his injustice, that is, at least show his intellectual freedom in the face of injustice. . . .

On the other hand, Oedipus is an absolute victim, the tragic hero *par excellance,* who is identified in Espriu's works . . . with the people. Paradoxically, King Oedipus is the incarnation of the tragic destiny of his people, subject to the evil demands of the gods. . . .

José María Castellet. *Iniciación a la poesía de Salvador Espriu* (Madrid, Taurus, 1971), pp. 237–38†

Salvador Espriu never belonged to the group of [Carles] Riba. Some of the reasons why this was so might seem external. In the first place, Espriu did not begin to cultivate poetry during his university years; he was more interested in history than in literature—thus the didactic sphere of Riba never influenced him. But upon closer examination it becomes evident that it was Espriu's own choice that he distanced himself from Riba's esthetic. Human events interest Espriu more than the laboratory of ideas—direct investigation of events rather than scholastic erudition. The two worlds that tradition gives us—the Greek universe and the Hebraic historical one—are antithetical. Riba is the paladin of the Hellenic homeland and Espriu has chosen the ethical inheritance, the religious and tragic one of the people of Israel. . . . In his choice of this and other influences for his works, it became perfectly clear even to his contemporaries that this writer would not follow the orientation of the dominant Catalan intelligentsia.

María Aurelia Capmany. Salvador Espriu
(Barcelona, Dopesa, 1971), pp. 65–66†

Holy Week brings together forty compositions—nine of which were written in 1962 and have been incorporated in this book—that can be divided into five parts. The first . . . is like an exordium in which the poet presents the theme of meditation on death. . . . The second part is a gloss or commentary on the procession of Holy Week, as contemplated by a skeptical but respectful spectator. The third part is very brief . . . ; it is like a satirical intermezzo and serves as a preamble to the fourth part, the true nucleus of the poem, in which the poet examines the myth of the Passion from a metaphysical point of view, although not a completely idealistic one. The final three compositions return to the theme of the exordium and the principal idea of the volume. . . .

From a technical point of view . . . the most important characteristic is the abundance of octosyllabic verses, which are quite common in classical Catalan poetry. . . . The other metrical modes are not repeated as often. Espriu also has occasion to use two exotic [Japanese] metrical modes—two *tankas* and two *shedokas,* which he has perfectly adapted to the metrical structure of Catalan poetry. Added to this is the predominance of masculine endings over feminine ones. We conclude that Espriu wants to express his literary fidelity to Catalan poetry by rigorously following genuinely Catalan models.

Francesc Vallverdú. Introduction to Salvador
Espriu, Setmana Santa (Barcelona, Edicions
62, 1972), pp. 8–9†

Just as the same stylistic elements reappear throughout Espriu's poetry, so do common themes. This repetitive linking provides the basic structure for *The Book of Sinera,* a representative and particularly beautiful work. . . . It reveals the characteristic meshing of abstract universal questions and concrete political concerns which makes Espriu both an intellectual and highly popular poet. The "Sinera" of the title is an anagram for Arenys, the fishing village where the poet spent his childhood summers. Symbol of a personal homeland, the community acquires a mythic force. While introducing new elements such as the rag-dealer, word of six steps and garden with five trees, the book builds on Espriu's most common materials: night, light, wind, sea. . . .

Although Espriu refers constantly to death and these "words of the void," it would be wrong to consider his poetry melancholy or morbid. . . . Although pessimistic, he is never despairing. Speaking of "the worn clothes" of hope as well as those of suffering, the poet suggests that the two may be cut from the same cloth. Though it may be a strange word to describe a poet who by definition has preserved the child's ability to marvel, Espriu is unfailingly adult. . . .

Clearly, the poet's reflection on his losses far exceeds nostalgia. The very gravity of his sorrow lifts it far beyond petty individual lament. Espriu, the Catalan, and indeed the Spanish nation have lived through defeats whose immensity can only be regarded with dry eyes. Their tragedy is of course only a variant on the human tragedy, but history has given peoples such as the Catalans—or Jews—a particularly acute appreciation of its terrible grandeur. . . .

Candace Slater. WLT. Spring, 1977, pp. 225–26

The Jewish-Catalan parallel, which has been one of Espriu's most consistent themes, is more fully explored in *The Bull's Skin* (a common expression for Spain because of its appearance on the map). This book, Espriu's most widely read and most frequently translated, is also the one most given to public themes. When it came out in the 1960's, things seemed to be loosening up a bit in Spain. The fact that such a work could be published at all was indicative of the easing of restrictions. In *The Bull's Skin,* Spain is referred to by its Hebrew name, "Sepharad." The book is a sequence of fifty-four poems, which touch on a number of themes. These themes mingle and interact, sometimes at random and sometimes for the light they can throw on each other. Espriu brings together some of his main preoccupations, including an eerie and highly personal sense of God. . . .

The motifs that tie the work together are the Jewish one . . . and the effort to draw all of Spain into a general vision of its postwar hopes and frustrations. This effort is unique in modern Catalan poetry, which has usually preferred to ignore the rest of the peninsula. *The Bull's Skin*'s pan-Iberian focus is partly responsible for its popularity in the rest of Spain. The poetic possibilities of this focus can be seen in a piece like "At Times It Is Necessary and Unavoidable . . ." Here, Espriu, whose *petita pàtria* [small homeland] had been Arenys de Mar, addresses all of Spain and Franco himself. . . . As a social program, "At Times It Is Necessary and Unavoidable" proved to be at least fifteen years ahead of its time. Nonetheless, *The Bull's Skin* did play an important role in opening new "bridges of dialogue" among the nations of Spain, with their "diverse motives and tongues."

David H. Rosenthal. ConP. 5, 1, 1982, pp. 18, 20

FELIPE, LEÓN (pseudonym of León Felipe Camino, 1884–1968)

It is time that we in the United States knew something about León Felipe. Because he is the humblest and simplest of Spain's poets, because he is a solitary who can neither hunt with the pack nor join the clique nor form part of the school nor follow the directives of the party, because he is at once mystic and equalitarian—not today a wonted combination—he is neither written about nor translated into English. For nearly a quarter century his slender volumes of poetry have been going forth, one after another, each of them heralded as a literary event throughout the Spanish-speaking world. . . .

León Felipe is the poet of Spain's tragedy. He sought to escape from it by his wanderings, but it followed him. He proclaimed in his first book that he had no fatherland, no *patria chica,* no sunlit house emblazoned with coat of arms, no ancient leather armchair nor worm-eaten table, no portrait of a grandfather with one arm on his breast and the other on his sword, who had won battles. But wherever he went, he carried Spain with him, and in whatever far corner of the earth he spent the night talking till dawn in a café with a fellow exile, there Spain was communing with itself. . . .

When Spain's darkest hour came, he felt impelled by an irresistible force to return to the land which he had said was not his. Out of the anguish of Spain's betrayal and tragedy has come the greatest of his poetry.

Bertram D. Wolfe. *ASch.* Summer, 1943,
pp. 330, 334

The evolution of León Felipe's poetry is not a question of themes or of attitudes but only one of intensity. If, in general, a poet is like a projectile that when fired into the heavens, loses velocity according to the distance it travels, then León Felipe is a stone fallen from the sky that speeds up because of gravity. . . .

He is the only poet of our time who has had the courage to confront directly . . . the "silence of the gods."

He was born a prophet. . . . He does not see, he does not hear anyone or anything except the deep hollow of the desert, in which only the voice of man alone resounds. Man, heroic man is the one who counts. . . .

The poetry of León Felipe is the poetry of a great actor, which he declaims on the stage of the grand theater of the world; a grandiloquent poetry—great in its eloquence—which he recites face to face with

173

God—his audience—in whom he does not believe. A desperate rebelliousness against the lack of meaning in the universe; an ear-splitting
scream of a man who does not know for what purpose or why he was
born. He screams, he curses, in order to see who answers him, and all
that he hears is an echo. There is no God who is worth anything. In our
times, only a Jew or a Spaniard could write this great human protest.
And León Felipe, whether he is a Jew or not—that will never be
known—is a Spaniard through and through.

Max Aub. *La poesía española contemporánea*
(Mexico City, Imprenta Universitaria, 1954),
pp. 207, 210–11†

The voice of León Felipe is and always will be one that cracks from
anguish and that, nevertheless, almost breaks with tenderness when it
often perceives a glimmer of hope. . . . His poems are covered with
heavy layers of shadow, but deep inside a live coal is hidden, which with
its small flicker of flame can announce a horizon of light.

The work of León Felipe is sprinkled with questions that, to a great
extent, lead either directly or indirectly to the investigation of the
existence of man on a planet drenched with tears. The poems concerning these questions are diffused throughout all his books, but he
devotes an entire one, with supreme despair and anguish—*The Deer*—
to the distressing reflection of human thought in the face of existence
seen as nihilism, absurdity, death.

Margarita Murillo González. *León Felipe:
Sentido religioso de su poesía* (Mexico City,
Colección Málaga, 1968), p. 106†

With his poetry, with his song . . . León Felipe has been banging on the
door of injustice and of the tyrant, in the portico of silence and
darkness. He has been pointing out with a rasping voice, with groans,
with tears, with indignant cries all the cruelties, injustices, and indig-
nities of men and nations. A messianic, inspired, agonized, tormented,
rebellious poet. . . . León Felipe has thrown to the world his prayers,
his psalms, his blasphemous speeches, his parabolic symbols. The
exodus, the tears, the axe, the dust are symbolically combined in his
poems, which are made and remade each day, with the buffoon and the
clown, the stone, the wind and the stars, so that it is Destiny that
interweaves or develops them. Suspension points abound in his poems,
because León Felipe enunciates his song—his parable—with a
breathless voice and cry, as if he were breathing in between phrases, in
between words and symbols; because everything erupts painfully in
him, from his heart, from his entrails; because each scream contains
blood; because each verse or versicle is exhaled by the breath of his
own existential breathing, of his own humanity devoured by the Promethean vulture.

Concha Zardoya. *Poesía española del 98 y del
27* (Madrid, Gredos, 1968), pp. 194–95†

León Felipe wanted to write grave and solemn poetry, and in his search for God and the meaning of life he turned to humble and simple things. He sought inspiration in the Bible, but felt that man abandoned by God was adrift in a world without meaning. During the Civil War his poetry became savage as he considered man's inhumanity to man and searched for his lost country. He passed from harangue, vituperation, and blasphemy, to sorrow and tragedy. He believed man must maintain his conscience through his tears and a sense of responsibility for his fellow man. Like Unamuno he stresses salvation, but his existential anguish emphasizes social aspects of the Christian message more than theological or religious ones.

Believing in beauty, Felipe longs to find it in daily life. Not encountering either it or God fully, he nevertheless postulates the possibility of man's love for his fellow man, admitting the absence of absolute values in an absurd and irrational world. He is best remembered as a poet of existential anguish whose themes of time, history, dreams, myth, God, and death reveal him to be a deep and original artist of profound humanity.

Kessel Schwartz. Vicente Aleixandre (New
York, Twayne, 1970), pp. 18–19

León Felipe is, in effect, a voice alone—in spite of the unmistakable stamp of Whitman and the Bible—with a unique style. . . . At times, the force of expression keeps ringing in one's ears long after the themes; his poetry would be impressive for only this—its cry—yet, nevertheless, it is also impressive for its despairing and unexpected positions in understanding and explaining the world; its multiple tones are harmoniously aligned with the themes that preoccupy him; but almost always it is imprecatory; nobody escapes it, no one can stand in its way, even if it is necessary to tear down gods, ridicule values, disavow social classes. It is a strong wind that demolishes like a blind force without regard for hierarchies, and that destroys huts and temples alike. Imprecation in León Felipe has a beginning but not an end; its limits barely accept blasphemy as a point of departure. Its anarchy, its extravagances, its contradictions are born from the poet's undirected goodness, from his timeless gospel, from his unconscious will, from his combativeness against injustice without his ever being politicized.

Mauricio de la Selva. CA. July–Aug., 1974,
p. 188†

If before the civil war [León Felipe] struggled within his poetry to link himself personally with what is essential in the Catholic religion, after it, the defeat of justice, the victory of the higher-ups of the institutionalized church, the horror of fratricidal slaughter, and the grief of exile break loose in his book *A Spaniard of Exodus and Lament* (1939). In general terms, this work is a cathartic attack against the victorious representatives of deceit. The religious focus seems similar to that of the prewar period, but the bitterness, the misery, and the repudiation of falsehood are now translated into a heart-rending profundity whose scope is quasi-mythic. In this work, the borderline between prose and poetry is erased in such a manner that the poet can sing with a voice that is more openly biographical. There are no longer any distinctions between the dominion of art and that of public life. Or to put it in more abstract terms, real space is welded to literary space. When external circumstances and internal beliefs coincide, the result is a poetic voice that genuinely reaches biblical proportions.

William Little. *JSSTC.* Fall, 1979, pp. 192–93†

FOIX, J(OSEP) V(ICENÇ) (1893–1987)

In the first stage of his poetic career, J. V. Foix's poems in prose presented us with an esthetic attitude, which he recently called magic surrealism, in order to indicate his tendency toward the poetic transmutation of reality through the reduction of the external appearance of things to images and through the transformation of the hidden meaning of things into symbols. This esthetic position was adopted by the poet in order to reveal the awful yet magical beauty of reality through a type of symbolistic surrealism, which is both hallucinatory and absurd, but also deeply attached to the concrete aspects of the real world—especially nature and landscape. This tendency enables him at the same time to concretize his subjective experiences in the form of symbolic shapes. . . .

We do not think, however, that his love of beauty and rarity, which he points to as the only and exclusive aim of his poetic creations in *From the "1918 Diary,"* has caused him to neglect other values.

Antonio Vilanova. *Destino.* Oct. 20, 1956, p. 37†

J. V. Foix, who cultivates at the same time the most perfect sonnet and the freest verse, has defined himself as an "investigator of poetry." Under this humble classification, which justifies many of his poetic experiments, there breathes one of the greatest personalities of contemporary Catalan poetry. Having been endowed with a strictly lyrical sensibility, Foix submits himself to the most rigorous mental discipline; the nucleus of his poetry rests on a previous scheme of thought, it flourishes on a prodigious verbal magic: within a profound cosmic sense of life, the dolmen and the airplane are combined in verses that, at the same time, transcribe the most archaic reminiscences of medieval poetry and the newest and most daring innovations of the avant-garde. . . .

Foix, who began as a lyrical realist, is intent on saving the negative element of naturalistic (or realistic) art . . . through the creation of an expressive apparatus in which realistic, oneiric, rationalistic, and prophetic elements intervene. But the inevitable occurs: reality, as such, disappears, and the lyrical charge it had is now transformed into a winged and magical cosmos of autochthonous value. With a different purpose and through different paths, Foix coincides with Pedro Salinas in achieving with his poetry an "adventure in quest of the absolute."

Joaquín Molas. *Cuadernos de Ágora.* May–
June, 1958, pp. 7–8†

That Foix shared [Federico García] Lorca's enthusiasm for the bold experiments of contemporary art is clear from his confession in *Alone and in Mourning* that he likes the "new world" and "the extreme paintings of today"; and his tributes in *KRTU* to Dalí and Miró singled out for sympathetic description two of its most adventurous and inventive explorers. . . . Foix displayed his knowledge of French poetry as openly as he voiced his suspicion of surrealism. . . . In conceding that the surrealists' greatest originality was "the grand adventure of setting themselves, at full throttle or lowered propellor, to navigate through the immense heavens of inspiration, without a course and with the preknowledge of emerging unharmed," Foix recognized that the imagination was liberated with particular determination by a group of writers and artists he acknowledges as "an authentically advance group." But Foix's pride in his "position of investigator in poetry" and his delight in "the risk of aesthetic investigation" allowed him to pay only grudging tribute to the achievements of the surrealists. His dislike of their "risky spiritual acrobatics" was stronger than his admission that they discovered "a few quite useful fresh and new images" and that in their writings "the images appear with an effective plasticity." . . .

In one of the "Practices" of *KRTU* Foix fused eccentric incident and what he called in 1927 "images of a living reality" to compose a short narrative of fear. . . . What makes this brief tale disturbing is the disparity between the narrator's fright and its cause: the man's apparently innocuous act of putting on a false moustache. The unexplained tension created by their entry into a stable, where the sleeping horses intensify the silence in which the episode takes place, is increased by the man's disconnected and contrasting attempts to keep the narrator quiet: the thousand rivers he points to are an unvoiced threat; the olives he puts into his hands are an unspoken bribe. The objects which encrust this and many other passages of Foix suggest that he shared the conviction Paul Éluard expressed in *L'évidence poétique* (1937) that "for the poet everything is an object for sensations and, consequently, for feelings. Everything concrete thus becomes food for his imagination." [Luis] Cernuda shared this passion for concrete objects demonstrated so consistently by Foix and elevated by the surrealists into a poetic creed.

C. B. Morris. *Surrealism and Spain: 1920–1936*
(Cambridge, England, Cambridge University
Press, 1972), pp. 52–55

The general air of Foix's vocabulary really possesses an "exotic" aspect, which is very strange in modern Catalan poetry: old and regional in contrast and opposition to the norm of the urban and modern vocabulary that the writers of the nineteenth century imposed, and which the group of the twentieth century refined. . . . For its insistence on comparisons borrowed from the plastic arts, Foix's poetry "reminds" one of the paintings of Salvador Dalí, Yves Tanguy, and René Magritte, in which *trompe-l'oeil* is used to represent images of a shocking unreality. . . .

The sonnets of *Alone and in Mourning* and many other poems—above all those in verse—correspond to themes and techniques that are traditional in symbolist circles. *Eleven Christmas Poems and One for the New Year* is the most settled moment of his work. The poet is oriented in that book by the sentimental or moral seduction of the nativity of Christ, and his verses show this with a simplicity without precedent in his work and with the most successful use of the resources of his experience. His language is correct and precise; the concision, the medieval resonance, the visionary spark, and, above all, the reminiscences of the people bring about a clear and emotional result.

> Joan Fuster. *Literatura catalana*
> *contemporánea* (Barcelona, Curial, 1972),
> pp. 235–36†

Alone and in Mourning, the first book of verse published by J. V. Foix, is a collection of seventy sonnets, divided into six sections. The linguistic aspect that first attracted attention to this work was the relative preference—dictated by the euphonic necessities of the poet—for archaic verbal forms and elision of the last vowel. . . . Basically, *Alone and in Mourning* is doctrinal and didactic poetry, a meditation on the world. In the sonnet that opens the volume—a partial paraphrase of sonnet 35 of "In the Life of Madonna Laura," of Petrarch's *Canzoniere*—the author provides the key to the sense of the work: perplexity in the face of the enigmas of the visible, questioning, introspection, and metaphysical pursuit. . . .

The fourth and fifth sections of the book, which must be considered as one unit, are a parenthesis of playful, dionysiac poetry that reveals several anecdotes about the poet's youth. The irony and the formal variety give rise to a profusion of phonetic games and internal rhymes. United by their characteristics with the history of Catalan poetry, this group of sonnets, with their joyful and frenetic rhythms, is distinguished by the great number of exotic ones it includes; these are typical of Foix, and because of the context, there is a burlesque and farcical atmosphere. . . . The last section of the book contains a series of ten splendid religious sonnets, a very infrequent theme in Foix's poetry.

> Pere Gimferrer. Introduction to J. V. Foix,
> *Obres completes* (Barcelona, Edicions 62,
> 1974), pp. 11–13†

One notable characteristic of Foix's works is that if his prose poems all form part of one work, his three volumes of verse poetry complement each other in a similar way.

Foix's poetry continues to be difficult, but it is on few occasions hermetic. At his best moments (and there are many) he presents a visionary poetry, in the best sense of the word. At the same time . . . there is a highly traditional character to the vision. That cosmic dimension, which nonetheless is deeply vivid in concrete appearance and in human pity, is without parallel in contemporary Catalan poetry. . . .

Evidently, the principal instrument in this effort (visionary poetry) is language. Through a half-century of literary activity, Foix has forged for himself a poetic language capable of expressing the most intimate convulsions of his powerful and original imagination.

Arthur Terry. Serra d'Or. March, 1968, p. 50†

Foix has always been a progressive thinker and a voracious reader in new fields. *What "The Vanguardia" Doesn't Say* gives some indication of the modern current of his thinking, especially in contrast to his middle-class Hispanic background. He enjoys playing the role of the advanced, individualistic thinker who is vindicated years later by events and scientific advancement. No doubt the experimentation of [Alexander] Calder . . . and his creation of a real—and yet very unreal—circus appealed to Foix. Calder's work, like that of [Salvador] Dalí and [Joan] Miró constituted the kind of departure from tradition and freedom of expression which we have observed so vividly in this volume, whose "news articles" would simply not be suitable for [the newspaper] *La Vanguardia.* In the same year—1970— . . . Foix published *Last Communiqué,* which he says was meant to be his last volume. The words had not ceased to flow, however, for in 1972 he published *Within Reach,* his last new prose volume. The two volumes are closely related in style; *Within Reach* is slightly more abstract. Both volumes are composed of narrative incidents and memories. Particularly in *Last Communiqué* there are corresponding poems for some of the prose selections. That volume has as its themes the solitude of the poet, his sense of "presence/absence" and a lost feeling, reminiscent of *Gertrudis* and *KRTU. Within Reach* reveals two of Foix's deep concerns: What is a writer and what is the writing process? Its title indicates that the poet has moved toward the discovery and revelation of the same mystery he has always sought, and truth is now within reach for him.

Last Communiqué contains some of Foix's finest prose selections. He uses his superb command of language to create an atmosphere ranging from the sharply specific to frighteningly real nightmares of unreality which invade his higher consciousness. The opening selection reveals a power and vehemence which Foix has restrained throughout his writing career.

Patricia J. Boehne. J. V. Foix (Boston, Twayne,
1980), pp. 96–97

GANIVET, ÁNGEL (1865–1898)

[*The Conquest of the Kingdom of the Maya*] ends by giving birth to *The Labors of the Indefatigable Creator Pío Cid*, a novel impossible to summarize, in which an undulating and capricious thread of a plot serves as a vehicle for the imponderable Pío Cid to be up to his old tricks with the greatest assurance in the world.

Pío Cid is indefinable. One must see him and hear him when he tries to instruct some student, when he pretends to govern some Amazon women, when he wishes to educate a good poet, when he undertakes the political reform of Spain, when he rushes to lift up a woman who has fallen, and when he helps a woman sick from frivolity. . . .

Ganivet's novel does not have a plot, nor is it any easier to summarize than a poem of Juan Pablo [the poet of the book] or the *Sartor Resartus* of Carlyle. It is an excuse to continue discoursing upon all that occurs. . . .

Ganivet's works have a southern clarity, a transparent and fluid form; the sense of his writing is easily understandable. Not so his mind. The person who does not penetrate into Ganivet's mind will enjoy the delightful occurrences, the highly ingenious paradoxes, the adventures full of wit; but whoever goes deeper will eventually seize the nucleus of an austere seriousness, of a heavy melancholy, and of an unbridled faith that palpitates in the viscera of this man from Granada. . . . [Oct. 23, 1898]

Miguel de Unamuno. *Obras completas,* Vol. III
(Madrid, Escelicer, 1968), pp. 1070–71†

In the second volume of *The Labors of the Indefatigable Creator Pío Cid*, Pío Cid presents a formal portrait of the man of will. The man of will is solitary, he guards the integrity of his personality, his function is to act upon other men, whom he teaches as they come to him. . . . He has no resource beyond his Self. . . . Finally, the man of will knows the transforming power of thought. . . .

In Pío Cid appears the Nietzschean superman more nearly than elsewhere in modern Spanish literature; Nietzschean too is the disdain of the individual for the institutions which clutter society and disappear before his will, the disdain for democracy. However, Ganivet met the greatest need of the society for which he wrote when he placed his emphasis upon the interpretation of will as effort towards the realisation of the individual nature, never too thoughtfullly studied, never too deeply reverenced. It is not altogether fair to judge *The Sculptor of His*

Soul, his final work, in which appear clearly signs of mental derangement, that his soul's lonely self reliance would inevitably have ended in despair, but it is certain that he was always profoundly sad.

Doris King Arjona. *RH.* Dec., 1928, pp. 603–4

Sometimes [Maurice Barrès and Unamuno] allow themselves to be won over by the old molds and they write like Shaw in *Candide,* which is an admirable drama, or like Ganivet in *The Labors of the Indefatigable Creator Pío Cid,* which is a magnificent novel. . . . Shaw melts with delight in his doctrinaire prologues to his plays, and Ganivet writes his *Spanish Idearium.* Suddenly, there bursts in them a mad desire to have an opinion; they have an opinion about everything, about major issues and minor ones. . . .

The Labors of the Indefatigable Creator Pío Cid, Spanish Idearium, and *Granada the Beautiful* are three great Spanish books. The first book seems to me to be one of the best novels that exists in our language and one in which end-of-century Madrid is best preserved. . . . *Men from the North* and *Finnish Letters* are great European books, written at a perfect time, when close contact of some countries with others still had the freshness of a discovery, and there were neither intellectual nor political "poses" on any nation's part.[1940]

José Ortega y Gasset. *Obras completas,* Vol. VI
(Madrid, Revista de Occidente, 1962),
pp. 372–73†

In his examination of the idealistic basis of Spain [in *Spanish Idearium*], Ganivet proceeds from essence to form; from the spirit to its manifestation; from peninsular Spain to the higher cultural unity of the Spanish-speaking world. He studies Spain's position in regard to Europe, and the considerations which should determine her attitude to other countries; in particular, Great Britain and Portugal. His frank discussion of the problems of his time, his examination of possible solutions of international questions, give us the impression that we are reading the notes of an observer of our own day. . . .

Neither in the man nor in the book is there anything to justify the use of the *Idearium* for partisan purposes. Intellectually Ganivet is a typical product of his time. Influenced, like many of his contemporaries, by German philosophical schools, well-read in Renan and Tolstoi, with a solid background of Spanish culture, he exemplifies in many respects the spiritual inquietude which characterises the Europe of his day, and which in Spain had its most typical results in the work of Unamuno. Hence Ganivet's defence of Catholicism has nothing in it of fanaticism or intolerance. His conception of tradition has nothing to do with "traditionalist" political parties. . . .

This book, an attempt at a philosophical interpretation of Spanish history, may in spite of inconsistencies—which are not as great as at first sight they appear to be—offer the foreign reader a background of what is permanently Spanish against which the realities of the day can be projected and in harmony with which all changes must take place.

R. M. Nadal. Introduction to Ángel Ganivet,
Spain: An Interpretation (London, Eyre &
Spottiswoode, 1946), pp. 9, 21, 24

Ganivet, like so many other educated Spaniards of his time, was a man of strong religious and even mystical inclinations, whose reason did not allow him to accept the dogmas of the Catholic Church. As a consequence he was profoundly unhappy and sought consolation in a stoic attitude. In Seneca he found the perennial philosopher of the Spanish race. The book of his, however, that most influenced his successors was not on philosophy but on politics. This was a collection of notes and aphorisms which came out in 1897 under the title of *Spanish Idearium*. It represented an attempt to define the racial character of Spaniards, the place in the world that naturally belonged to them and the steps that they ought to take to occupy it. One might call it a work of national stocktaking. If by Anglo-Saxon Liberal standards it may appear to be a somewhat reactionary and authoritarian book, coloured by a pessimistic view of the capacity of men for governing themselves, it was optimistic in that it showed how Spain could be reorientated in the modern world so as to regain, not her former power—for that had passed for ever—but her dignity, her self-esteem, her soul.

Ganivet's book helped to canalize a great deal of scattered thinking and criticism. A new, intenser stage began of that long interior dialogue and self-examination that had occupied the best Spanish brains since the eighteenth century. Spain became more than ever the patient on the psycho-analyst's couch. [1951]

Gerald Brenan. *The Literature of the Spanish
People* (Cleveland, Meridian, 1957), pp. 418–19

[Ganivet's] *Epistles* and *The Conquest of the Kingdom of the Maya* show us a violent, tough, and rebellious nature that is palliated ever so slightly by an aggressive although wavering idealism; *Finnish Letters* and *Granada the Beautiful* exude wit and sweetness; *The Labors of the Indefatigable Creator Pío Cid* seems to show us the desolation of an incredulous spirit that tries in vain to light a spark in the ashes of a lost faith; *Spanish Idearium* and *The Sculptor of His Soul* reflect, on the other hand, an ardent and enthusiastic faith in ideals and a great hope, a mystical faith in the triumph of understanding over the forces of rebellion and destruction.

We ought not to be surprised, then, that the critics offer us an image of Ganivet that emphasizes the contradictory nature of his ideas. In accordance with this image, the essence of these contradictions ought to be sought in the radical splitting of his personality: *Ganivet is a mystic without faith.* Even though he has a profoundly religious temperament, the intellectual pressures of the rationalism and positivism of his time destroyed the bases of the traditional faith in which he was raised; his deep spiritual aspirations lost their dogmatic support, and his work expresses the disenchantment and desolation of a mind that revolves around an unobtainable center and rejects it. The contradictions that flood his works spring from this religious aspiration, which is so essential in him, and from his lack of faith.

Javier Herrero. *Ángel Ganivet, un iluminado*
(Madrid, Gredos, 1966), pp. 9–10†

Both Bergson in the 'thirties and M. Eliade in the 'fifties of this century have suggested that myths, whether religious or social, have a function of meeting this sort of need in the community. They abate for the many the doubt and anxiety which individuals feel when they find themselves amid conflicting values and purposes. Myths give a pattern to life by organising knowledge and experience in such a way as to provide a security in belief which underlies the moral and philosophical pluralism of modern life. Where the myth is strong, energy is released which enables the social will to be mobilised to national tasks.

It is perhaps in this way, as an attempt at myth creation, that *Spanish Idearium* may be profitably viewed rather than as a piece of historical analysis or social theorising. Such a view could be supported by a reinterpretation of the character of Pío Cid [in *The Labors of the Indefatigable Creator Pío Cid*] which stressed the oracular and charismatic elements it exhibits. But the danger of this kind of writing should not be overlooked. It is simply that historicism has too frequently claimed to go beyond this myth-making inspirational function and to have become a form of prophecy or historical prediction. When this happens the historicist shows that his aim is to control novelty and discovery, whether scientific, social or philosophical, by asserting that even change itself is ruled by an underlying, unchanging law. Despite its interest in historical change and evolution, historicism is ultimately a conservative doctrine.

K.E. Shaw. *REH.* Nov., 1968, p. 181

An almost infinite distance separates *The Conquest of the Kingdom of the Maya* and *The Labors of the Indefatigable Pío Cid*. The former was a formula work—the condemnation of industrial society; the latter, however, does not contain any condemnation, but consists entirely of the ideas of one man—his doubts, his character—always attentive to values that the majority of us do not ponder.

Ganivet, who was lucid about the most profound things—ideas— also succeeds with words. Man's being, his perfection, is the last lesson we learn, as we are attracted by a narrative that is born spontaneously, and with which the author at the same time constructs a cosmogony by making history out of himself.

Baring himself philosophically before the reader with neither fervor nor sadness, Ganivet confesses the doubts he has about his ideas. After each labor that is undertaken and then abandoned, we guess the sorrow of a life. Upon showing us his own character, the consul [Ganivet was the Spanish consul to Finland] opens up for us evocative far-off places. Pío Cid will always be, without fail, a landmark, a memory or a companion, and his conscious bitterness—similar to, let us say, that of Meursault in [Camus's] *The Stranger*—reconciles the individual with the dark hours that surely come up in every lifetime.

When we have finished reading and we close our eyes, Pío Cid suddenly rushes into our minds. Why this continued life? What has made this character so much a part of us? Every great writer who unequivocally breathes life into his creations leaves us, if we stay with them long enough, a plentiful and lasting harvest.

Norberto Carrasco Arauz. Ángel Ganivet
(Madrid, ESPESA, 1971), pp. 70–71†

All Ganivet's thought and work is dominated by four simple postulates: that Western society's preoccupation with material progress is an error, with dehumanizing consequences; that the true law of progress for Spain in particular and for other nations in general is dictated by man's spiritual evolution; that the source of such progress is personal sacrifice and effort by individuals who are capable of formulating new guiding ideas for themselves and the collectivity; and that such individuals can be recognized by their ability to intervene positively in their own spiritual evolution and model their own souls by acts of will. However, Ganivet was never able to formulate clearly the new pattern of *ideas madres* [guiding ideas] which he regarded as the essential basis for individual and national regeneration. At the same time the evidence of his own deep spiritual disorientation and its manifestation in the ambiguity of both Pío Cid [in *The Conquest of the Kingdom of the Maya* and *The Labors of the Indefatigable Creator Pío Cid*] and Pedro Mártir [in *The Sculptor of His Soul*] necessarily cast doubt on the degree of certainty which he was able to attach to the above-mentioned postulates.

In any case their relevance to the contemporary situation is doubtful. The history of Spain and Europe has not hitherto borne out Ganivet's hopes. The renovation of ideals and ideals he hope for has not taken place; instead we have become used to plurality of attitudes inside any given society. The regeneration of Spain has not arisen for the peasant/artisan economy which Ganivet advocated, but since the 1950s has been the product of industrialization, tourism, and foreign investment. Collective, not individual, effort has been the mainspring.

Ganivet's cultural reformism was based on the missionary zeal and faith of the few leading to the individual conversion of the many. It was borrowed from a Christian model of progress, at the centre of which was a set of ultimate beliefs that Ganivet himself had rejected. It was more than an anachronism, it was a paradox.

> Donald L. Shaw. *The Generation of 1898 in*
> *Spain* (New York, Barnes & Noble, 1975),
> pp. 38–39

GARCÍA HORTELANO, JUAN (1928–   )

[*New Friends*] allows us to witness the lives of a few young people of Madrid's upper middle class—their empty lives, abundant money, drinking and easy sex. Not a single one of the intellectual or ethical preoccupations that matters to Spanish existence is present. I would like to point out that García Hortelano narrates cleanly, without introducing any crude moralistic additions; the lesson can be inferred without any necessity for the author to intervene with annoying sermons.

The novel is very well constructed; the action, which is kept to a minimum, is developed with increasing interest and gusto. The dialogues—and practically the entire novel is dialogue—are masterfully transcribed, and the characters are vigorously described. The style is fluid, it engrosses us, and the novel can be read in one sitting. In regard to the discussions, a little overdone perhaps, about new techniques in the novel . . . I believe that *New Friends* shows that one ought not fear the specter of the loss of readers if the novelist should stray from so-called traditional modes of writing novels. García Hortelano, without any concessions, has written a novel destined for the masses of readers, or at least I have the impression that this will be so, which is confirmed for me by its nature. He has planned this work with what could be called "solidity." Apparently this novel is offered to the reader with an impressive freedom in its narrative structure.

An incident, which first confronts only a few characters and then slowly the whole group with a fundamental realness . . . throws the narrative into a dangerous undertaking, filled with dynamism, skillfully wrought, that without losing any energy carries it until the very end. It does not matter that some details smack of improbability, nor that the character who little by little throws everyone into a phenomenal dissipation of energies is only nineteen years old. The thrust of the novel, with its almost aggressive sense of reality, does not allow us to stop and dwell upon these possible minute points of criticism.

> Alberto Gil Novales. *CHA*. June, 1960, p. 385†

[*Summer Storm*] is a first-rate documentary of a certain kind of society that seems to flourish nowadays. García Hortelano, the young author, is said to be working in the same vein as that explored by *La Dolce Vita*. This is hardly a new field: back of *La Dolce Vita* is Moravia and back of him a whole school of French and Italian "realists," and way back of them one can see, I think, the dim silhouettes of the frustrated troupe of *The Sun Also Rises,* of which, in truth, this tale, in manner even more than matter, is reminiscent. The setting and the history of the major figures give, to be sure, a special ironic color to the canvas. Was it for this—world weariness, hedonism, futility—that "the Reds" were beaten down and the motherland made secure for decency, faith and the eternal values? Surely this will not be the favorite reading of the Falange and possibly young Señor García Hortelano . . . may write his next novel from Paris.

Summer Storm is well done and, being both readable and serious in purpose, clearly prize-worthy [it won the international Formentor Prize]; whether the half-hearted semi-decadents it presents are really worth studying is I think an open question. Some readers will wish perhaps that they didn't talk quite so much, and many readers will have—for the first hundred pages—some difficulty in identifying who is who, since the tale is told in dialogue and the characters are, alas, very much alike. But this too is no doubt part of the writer's plan. He is in earnest, young Señor García Hortelano, and I don't doubt we shall hear more from him.

Thomas G. Bergin. NYHTB. May 6, 1962, p. 4

[*Summer Storm*] will remain as one of the greatest achievements of the documentary realism that for some time now has dominated the literary scene in Spain. The critical serenity of the author has been exerted in this work on the unimaginative *dolce vita* of the Spanish bourgeoisie, newly rich in the postwar period, with their vulgar liaisons, their immoderate desire for drinking and gossiping, and their closed-mindedness toward all that smacks of culture. . . .

Now, after seven years of silence, García Hortelano's book of short stories, *People of Madrid,* arrives on the scene; it is a book that confirms his literary talent. Five narratives make up this volume, a number that in reality could be reduced to four, since the first two can be considered as two moments of the same story.

If this new book of García Hortelano's does not represent, by our criterion, an improvement over his earlier work, that is, if it does not quite go beyond the height reached by *Summer Storm,* it serves, at least, to confirm his vigor as a narrator and the sureness of a style in which dialogue has an almost total monopoly, interrupted only a few times by brief descriptions of the situation. The characters are defined by their own words, and there is no doubt as to the skill of the author in shading the dialogue, that is, differentiating the personality of each one of them by his or her speech, which is such a difficult task for many novelists.

In this regard, the first two stories, "The Caudine Forks" and "Riánsarres and the Fascist," . . . are somewhat different from the rest of the stories in the book. The difference comes about principally because they are narrated in the first person by a child whose certain discoveries in the area of sex make us suspect that he is on the verge of puberty. If the theme of children in our civil war has been treated with undeniable skill by other novelists of his generation and if there is little new that can be added, García Hortelano effectively combines suitable portions of the violent milieu of those years with the exaggerated excitement of the emotions that any war produces on the rear-guard. . . .

In the other stories, García Hortelano continues the dissection of present-day society initiated in his previous works. This time he has chosen three different social strata: the world of office workers, of three young middle-class couples, and the subculture of Spanish servants in Paris.

José Domingo. *Ínsula*. Dec., 1967, p. 5†

In a period in which the novel scarcely pays any attention to the forging of characters, García Hortelano knows how to create [in *Mary Tribune's Great Moment*] perfectly well-defined characters, almost by means of dialogue alone, and although all are sharply outlined, some (apart from the protagonist) take on unforgettable qualities: the rather masculine woman Bert, the awkward young girl Matilde, the fawning prostitute, and the good-natured old maid Merceditas—in fact all the women in this large catalogue are well drawn. And there is, last but not least, Mary Tribune, whose efficiency and correctness, whose basic insipidness and superficial sentimentalism, justify, because she is so well observed, the privilege of her having her name form part of the title. Mary Tribune, without any diminution of her concrete self, is a translucent example of "shallowness," and she emerges as a symbol of the American penetration into Spain in the 1960s. . . . In the first part of the novel, almost day by day, the adventures of Mary Tribune in her great vital moment are revealed (shades of the film with Vivien Leigh, *The Roman Spring of Mrs. Stone,* 1962); in the second part, Mary Tribune is described at a distance, through postcards of Venice and photos of Angoulême, and through the memory of her suicide attempt and that kind charm that she learned to introduce into her coterie of friends. Mary Tribune is indistinct and vacuous, as one critic characterized her, but not insignificant: she signifies, in her concrete personal biography, the Americanized temper in Madrid during those years, which García Hortelano has been able to capture with Iberian boldness and diversified unity.

Technically, in this novel the incessant conversations of the members of Mary's gallery of friends constitute a true monument of verbal banality. García Hortelano surpasses himself as a recorder of idle chit-chat that goes nowhere, and he succeeds in portraying the conversation of the stupefied maid with her good intentions, of the prostitute with the flattering phrases, of the philanthropic and erotic Mary Tribune with her light Anglo-Saxon inflections, of the intellectuals, who are more or less Marxists, and of the haggard office-workers.

Gonzalo Sobejano. *Novela española de nuestro
tiempo* (Madrid, Prensa Española, 1975),
pp. 443–44†

There is a definite amount of experimentation in [*Mary Tribune's Great Moment*]—notably the various literary quotations—and a great deal more concentration placed on the introspection and internal characteristics of the protagonist (the various hallucinations, for instance, which at times place the action on a personal psychological level which did not exist in either of the first two novels). It seems that in this novel Juan García Hortelano is aggrandizing and intensifying the role of the narrator/protagonist in an attempt not only to portray objectively the societal problems inherent in the Spanish class system, but also the personal problems of the individual who is a product of that system. And it is perhaps the experimental element in this novel which best enhances the presentation of individual abnormality, removing the perspective from the traditional realist mold and allowing for more latitude regarding individual perception. This is the crux of Juan García Hortelano's novelistic problem. Has he succeeded in maintaining a social critique while removing his plot from a very objective social situation? The theory behind the novel seems to be that certain individual abnormalities are the result of societal pressures, but in concentrating so closely upon the individual abnormalities, basic social problems are often left undeveloped. In a sense, the main character of this novel is too strong, too charismatic. It is easy to forget, at times, that he is a result of a socio-economic situation. Perhaps this is a result of Juan García Hortelano's own identification with the problems of a bourgeois madrileño, thus "desdoblándose" [splitting himself in two] and entering the novel on a personal level much too involved to continue to allow for a prolonged objectively realistic approach.

William M. Sherzer. *REH.* Oct., 1979, pp. 378–79

GARCÍA LORCA, FEDERICO (1898–1936)

But your [García Lorca] blood is still fresh, and it will be thus for a long time. The editions of your *Gypsy Ballads* will multiply. Your name, your memory, are rooted in Spain, in the heart of all our earth. There is no one who can destroy these roots. The true earth where they placed you would not permit it. They have made the land leap with fire and gunshot and are burned with blood these ignoble hands that would do this. The Spanish Falangists—your assassins—what villainy they would have us believe of you, puncturing your glory like a sieve with bullets from their own rifles, and they made of you, falsely, the poet of the "Imperial Spain"—poor Imperial Spain of Mussolini! This was their intention. The impudence of your cruel murderers shows an ignorance of your name and of your eternally moving poetry, kept alive on the lips of our fighting people, on the lips of all Spanish anti-fascists. Each of your ballads sung, sounds as a tremendous accusation against your assassins. We have a memory. This we have. We will not forget! We recognize the faces of those who would expose your corpse. I lay them at your feet to help show the terrible farce of the most horrible and stupid crime committed in this war. But they will not win. They will go down. To you we extend clean hands. We, the poets who were your comrades—Luis Cernuda, Emilio Prados, Vicente Aleixandre, Pablo Neruda, Miguel Hernández, Manuel Altolaguirre, I . . . with these same mourning people and the magnificence of your ballads, we guard your memory, your constant presence, and we celebrate your memory with the same fervor as the poet friends of Garcilaso de la Vega [Spanish poet of the sixteenth century] celebrate his. [1937]

Rafael Alberti. *Twice a Year*. Summer, 1941, pp. 390–92

García Lorca had a right to surrealism as non-Spanish poets have not; his native literary tradition stems from Góngora. And the modern Spaniard has cut loose from the idea of a religious hell so recently that the private hell of the subconscious floats closer to the surface in both Dalí and García Lorca than, nowadays, in artists of other nationalities. These facts must be borne in mind by the reader who, like myself, distrusts surrealism's worth and pretensions and the worth of any poet who adheres too rigorously to its tenets. In the case of García Lorca, we have proof of his poetic worth in his non-surrealist work. The brilliant and popularly inspired *Gypsy Ballads* were published in 1928, and we have examples of them, translated with real sensibility. . . . His surrealist period in America and Cuba followed. Later, García Lorca published his *Lament for Ignacio Sánchez Mejías* . . . , and in that late and superb poem we can see what the poet finally did with surrealism. He used it as Baudelaire used "Gothic": he made it humane and the vehicle of emotion.

Louise Bogan. *NY.* June 1, 1940, p. 83

With each fresh addition to our knowledge of Federico García Lorca, the poet's genius becomes more impressive. That extraordinary brilliance which struck one at once, in the first few of his poems to be

translated, has turned out by no means to be an intermittent or accidental thing—it was sustained. Brilliance came as naturally to him, in fact,
as dullness or preciosity to others; it was simply his speech. Nothing
could be more remarkable, in this new collection, *Poet in New York,*
than the apparently inexhaustible fertility of García Lorca's imagination. It was everywhere at once, it was prodigal, it was fantastic—the
subjective and objective worlds rolled up and ignited in a single ball—
the quotidian married singularly to the classic, the folksong crossed
with the baroque. To call him a surrealist is a mistake, for to be a
surrealist is to be something else than a poet, something less than a
poet: surrealism is perhaps one of many names, merely, for the substratum out of which poetry is made. García Lorca devoured all the
properties of surrealism, stuffed his cheeks with them, like a conjuror,
blew them out of his mouth again as poems—but so he did with
everything else that he fed on. The papery guitars, the ingeniously
misplaced eyes, the little traplike mouths cropping out of the sides of
heads, and all the rest of that slightly sinister and somehow iodine-
tinctured phantasmagoria of the followers of Loplop and synesthesia,
these are certainly here, in the New York poems, but they have been
made into poetry.

On the whole! There are times, let us admit, when the prodigality
of image does seem to be indulged in for its own sake, and when the
virtuosity and rapidity become blinding: the Gongoresque multiplication of idea carries one too far, and on too wide a front: too many things
are required to be embraced at once, as if one tried to organize a single
wave from end to end of the Atlantic. But even so, the fault is more often
ours than García Lorca's—*he* knows perfectly well what he is doing,
and the tiniest or queerest item of the sargasso which his wave lifts will
presently yield its meaning like something heard afterward, like an
echo. Back will come the main theme, the recurring preoccupation of
this book—pain, pain and suffering, fear of death and injury, the agony
of the conscious mind in the presence of universal pain. . . .

If there is nothing in the present collection quite as good as the
Lament for the Death of a Bullfighter [i.e., *Lament for Ignacio Sánchez
Mejías*], which was perhaps the finest of all García Lorca's poems,
there is nevertheless much that is magnificent. The "Ode to Walt
Whitman" ["Oda a Walt Whitman"]—bitter, comic, wry-mouthed, dou-
ble-faced—is devastating: and so are the New York poems, "Unsleep-
ing City" ["Ciudad sin sueño"], "Blind Panorama" ["Panorama ciego
de Nueva York"], and others. There has been no more terribly acute
critic of America than this steel-conscious and death-conscious Spaniard, with his curious passion for the modernities of nickel and tinfoil
and nitre, and for the eternities of the desert and the moon. He hated us,
and rightly, for the right reasons. Intensely Spanish, he is best of course

in Spanish, which, next to English, is the best of all poetic languages; and therefore exceedingly difficult to translate. [1940]

Conrad Aiken. *A Reviewer's ABC* (New York, Meridian, 1958), pp. 276–78

The imagery of García Lorca makes its impression not because it is "pure," nor because the English reader has necessarily any knowledge of García Lorca's background, but because Spain, although very un-English in most of the aspects which concern García Lorca, is nevertheless universal. It is different only in the sense that the Spanish traditions are Spanish ways of dealing with the same human problems. The patterns of life of a community, its rituals, its traditions, are themselves a kind of lived poetry, by which the people interpret situations which are common to the whole of humanity. The Church, the bullfight, the landworker in the olive grove, the attitude of the young Spanish male to sex, these are Spanish ways of working out problems which we all recognize as real. The English pattern is different, but the situation of being alive, loving, having to die, is the same. To say that an Englishman, because he is not a Spaniard and has never been to a bullfight, cannot understand one of García Lorca's ballads about a bullfight, is like saying that one poet of love cannot understand the work of another poet writing of love, because each uses different imagery, a different ritual, to convey the same feeling. Señor [Arturo] Barea seems to imply that an English reader who has not worked in an olive field cannot understand the accuracy of the imagery García Lorca uses when he describes the olive field opening and shutting like a fan. This seems a somewhat cockeyed way of looking at poetry. The English reader can understand, because although he may never have seen an olive field, he will undoubtedly have seen a fan. The fact that a peasant witnesses to the accuracy of García Lorca's imagery is interesting and to be expected, but it does not mean that an English reader cannot understand the poem.

García Lorca *creates* just as much of the Spanish scene as he wants us to hold in our minds for his poetic purpose. If Spain ceased to exist, and if Señor Barea ceased to know about Spain, the Spain of García Lorca's poetry would still be invented, in its brilliant sunlit fragments, whenever any reader read García Lorca's poetry, just as fragments of ancient Greece come to life when a scholar reads a Greek classic.

I do not mean that a knowledge of the Spanish background will not lead to a deeper understanding of García Lorca's poetry. On the contrary, there are levels in García Lorca's writing which lead beyond the fragment he creates, which can be immediately apprehended, to the whole of Spain, and this has to be understood by supplementing the poetry itself with other reading. But it is nonesense to imply that an English reader can only understand in García Lorca an attitude to death.

However, it is justifiable to protest against the idea that García Lorca's poetry is all about nothing, which seems to be the view of some of his imitators, to judge from the results. Writing like García Lorca's is not just an idiom, an esoteric use of language which proceeds from the poet's fantasy and has no connection with anything outside. . . .

The genius of García Lorca does not consist only in crystallizing his Spanish background into images of great power and clarity. His peculiar power is to build up a fantastic world out of these images, which seems to have an inner consistency and logic, as though it was related to, yet independent of the real world. One is aware often in his poems of a double picture: the reality on which his poetry is drawing, and, superimposed above this reality, an independent, unreal picture. The effect is similar to those pictures of Picasso, in which there are two images: a portrait is painted full face and profile at the same time, the profile being superimposed on the full face. Picasso, like García Lorca, has vigorous strength of art which is firmly rooted in experience of real objects; and yet he makes something which is not only a comment on reality, but which seems to have a separate existence of its own. It is not surrealism, exactly: if I were to invent a name for it, it would be "parallelism." In Picasso and García Lorca we become aware both of the real and the unreal. Both often are seen in the same image, and they seem to derive from worlds which exist side by side, and move through time parallel with each other.

Stephen Spender. New Writing and Daylight.
Winter, 1943–44, pp. 127–28, 130

With Synge, García Lorca shares the creative mission of returning poetry to its basic dramatic function on the stage. In García Lorca's work it is impossible to speak of a consistently upheld view of life. His drama celebrates the life of instinct; which is to say, it does not come bearing a message. It comes in the ancient spirit of the magician and soothsayer—to astound; to entertain, and to mystify; it also comes in the spirit of the jongleur, to invent a world and people with whose pathetically valorous lives the audience is quick to identify itself. But it has no hidden didactic motives.

Synge's work is also notable for its artistic self–sufficiency, its renewal of the rich poetic language of the fold, and its re-creation of the primitive drama of feeling. His comedies and tragedies dealing with the folk characters of the Irish back provinces, and especially such plays as *Riders to the Sea* and *The Playboy of the Western World,* are astonishingly close in dramatic emphasis to García Lorca's *Blood Wedding* and to his folk comedies. They have alike the spontaneity of speech and poetic imagination which grows out of the heart of a fold untouched by the perversities of city life; with whom it is still possible to express pathos and tragedy in terms of the most elemental passions.

When drama reaches behind the improvised curtain of middle-class Christian morality to the lives of such people and into their wild old pagan heritage, one comes upon the springs of a new classicism in the theatre, which Synge and García Lorca exemplify. But the difference is that Synge, writing in prose, accepts the conventions of the tight coils of traditional stage techniques. García Lorca, on the other hand, a poetic dramatist reviving particular Spanish conventions on the stage and adding techniques of his own, shifts the stylistic emphasis very often from the prose speech of the characters to the verse and bright design of spectacle and musical conception.

Edwin Honig. *García Lorca* (Norwalk, Conn., New Directions, 1944), pp. 214–15

[As a child] Federico was attracted by games of theatrical nature even more than by real theatre. He liked to play at theatre and marionettes, to dress up the maids and make them go out into the street—grotesquely dressed sometimes, or dressed as ladies—wearing my mother's or my Aunt Isabel's street clothes. Priceless at these games was Dolores, my nurse, who became the model for the servants in *Blood Wedding* and in *Doña Rosita, the Spinster*. From her we heard our first folk tales—those of the unforgettable "Pot-thumper"—at the fireside while our parents passed an evening at the theatre. I can never forget one of our servants dressed as a Moor, in towel and curtains plastered with rice powder, gravely reciting and half inventing "The Alcázar of Pearls." In her wonderful simplicity the poor woman did not realize how comic her performance was, but we, with the cruelty the young sometimes have, appreciated it fully. Make-believe, disguises and masks charmed Federico the boy. They were like an unbreakable spell for even then he had begun to transform the world of fiction into a living reality and to identify all of reality with a fantastic dream. Later he was to see life as a sort of dramatic game, a "great world stage" [the title of a Calderón play] that, thought it did not lack a distant religious background, included a vaster world of mysteries and passions. . . .

The final value of Federico's theatre, and the one which most characterizes it, is [the] fundamental attitude of an author who likes to live; that is to say, to suffer and enjoy life's course as an inevitable universal drama. It seems as though in Federico, both in his life and in his writing, the man was not alive except in his moments of laughter and tears, in his extreme moments of joy and sorrow. Other times are entr'actes. . . .

Laughter and tears, tears above all, run through all his poetry. Federico is fundamentally an elegiac poet. And laughter and tears are the two poles of his theatre. This explains why all his work courses between tragedy and farce. His literary creatures, always poetic embodiments, are conceived either in a tragic sense or with the wry grimace of guignol characters. Poetry, laughter and tears are the ingredients of his dramatic invention.

Francisco García Lorca. Prologue to Federico
García Lorca, *Three Tragedies* (New York, New
Directions, 1947), pp. 1–3

García Lorca was from the beginning a pure artist, not only a poet and a dramatist but a draughtsman who drew charming and original sketches, and a musician of whom [Manuel] de Falla said that if he had chosen, he would have been as good a musician as he was a poet. Those who knew him agree that his personality turned everything about him into poetry. His remarkable vitality and creative imagination imposed themselves on others and created the atmosphere in which they lived. With him the landscape and the human beings in it took on an enchanted air and seemed different from what they had been before. His art was no mere department of his life; it filled and inspired everything that he did. His sensibility was so vivid that he was able to reveal to others much that they would otherwise not have noticed, to find undiscovered characteristics in trivial things, and to cast over all his irresistible gift of melody. He had no message to give: he followed his instincts and wrote about everything that excited his insight or his fancy. All this made him the poet for which his generation was looking. Though speculations meant nothing to him and he always denied that he had any theory of art, his practice realised many hopes and justified many beliefs. His poetry was really poetry and nothing else; his imagery was of an enthralling brilliance and originality; his vision was actual and contemporary in that it centered round his Andalusian homeland and on the varied life which he found in it.

García Lorca began by possessing two separate gifts. He was in the first place a lyrical poet who possessed a special gift for song, and in the second place a dramatist with a real love and understanding of the stage. From the start he wrote plays and he wrote songs, and the two seemed to represent quite different aspects of his genius. His songs have a peculiarly diaphanous and evanescent quality. His sensitiveness enabled him to catch those fleeting moments to which coarser temperaments are blind, and his skill translated these into airy melodious verse, in which all that exists is the impression of a single moment. García Lorca, intent on conveying the pure essence of poetry, gives only the central thrill. When his sensibility found unexpected relations between things and was able to illuminate what others had only half noticed, with deft brevity he touched on the vital relation, the point of identity or resemblance between one impression and another and produced the image which secured this. What counts is the choice of an image, or of a scene which does the work of an image in suggesting wider associations of thought. García Lorca uses his sensibility to evoke something beyond the event which provides his material. These poems are not in any limited sense descriptive, nor are they abstract. They move through varied and vivid stages, through exact and loving observation, to the evocation of an experience in its imaginative unity. García Lorca seems to possess by nature the new way of transforming inchoate states of consciousness into concrete pictures. His mind was stored with memories and what his eyes or ears noted passed into his poetry.

C. M.Bowra. *The Creative Experiment*
(London, Macmillan, 1949), pp. 192–93

The reader no sooner begins to pry into the poetic world fashioned by García Lorca in his lyric poetry, ballads and plays, than he feels himself being immersed in a strange atmosphere. It is an apparently normal setting of popular scenes and people, all perfectly recognizable. But the air is, so to speak, inhabited by forebodings and threats. Metaphors cut across it like birds of ill omen. So, for example, summer "sows rumours of tiger and flame." Day breaks in a most peculiar manner like a shadowy fish: "Great stars of white frost—come with the fish of shadow—that opens the road of dawn." The wind is an enormous man pursuing the maiden "with red-hot sword." These metaphors do not have a decorative function; they are an extension of meaning. They herald what is unusual and mysterious in this world. They proclaim that something is being prepared; they proclaim an imminence of fatality. For the poetic kingdom of García Lorca, so brilliantly illuminated and at the same time so enigmatic, is under the rule of a unique, unchallenged power: Death.

Death lurks behind the most normal of actions, and in places where it is least expected. In one poem García Lorca says, referring to a tavern: "Death comes in and goes out—and death goes out and comes in." The poet repeats the same simple idea, merely inverting the word-order, as if to point out the fatality of this act, the inevitability of Death's continually coming in and going out—over and over again—not in the concrete place of the tavern, but in the life of man and the work of the poet. The destination of nearly all the characters that García Lorca creates, whether in his ballads or in his dramas, is death. García Lorca creates them to set them on a road whose only possible end is in dying. In a poem of his youth entitled "Another Dream" ["Otro sueño"] he wrote: "How many children has death?—They are all in my breast." Yes, that is where they are, and, as his work grows, those children of death gradually swarm from his breast, transformed into poetic offspring. In the famous "Sleepwalkers' Ballad" two lovers, a horseman and the gypsy girl of the green flesh and green hat who awaits him, look forward with desire to a lovers' meeting: she is in her house. But the strange creature and her lover will never meet. For when he finally reaches the house, his breast has been torn open by a wound that will kill him: and the gypsy girl, killed by too much waiting, floats upon the water, borne up by the reflection of the moon. They have not come together in love, but they have in death. [1952]

Pedro Salinas. In Robert W. Corrigan, ed.,
Theatre in the Twentieth Century (New York,
Grove, 1963), pp. 273–74

Like Ibsen, [in *Ghosts*] García Lorca puts his central image in his title [*The House of Bernarda Alba*]. The house is the main character of the play. *Indoors* and *outdoors* are the chief spatial entities. *Doors* themselves are crucial as being at once barrier and bridge between *in* and *out*. *Windows* are equally significant, for in Spain a lady is courted at her window and it is through the window that the villagers look out upon life. The neighbors are always at their windows and are always curious to learn if you are at yours—and you are, though you hope they don't know it. In other words, all the houses are supposed to be closed; each inmate is fighting for his own privacy, his own identity. But all the houses are really open, for each inmate is fighting against the privacy of others, against letting them live their own lives. . . .

García Lorca follows Ibsen as Ibsen followed some of the ancients in adhering pretty closely to the unities to time, place, and action. Like Ibsen in *Ghosts,* García Lorca adopts the modern three-act form, but avoids finishing his play at the end of the second act only by glaring artifice. Just as the whole story of Oswald's origin is coming out, Ibsen has the sanatorium catch fire, thus postponing final discovery till after the second intermission. Just as the whole story of Pepe's affair with Adela is coming out, Lorca has a girl "lynched" in the street outside and hopes that in our excitement we shall hardly notice how the progress of the action has been postponed to the third act.

If both Ibsen and García Lorca seem driven by their forms into *forcing* the drama, it is not the director's job, as it is the critic's, to call attention to what is unconvincing in this. Rather the contrary. He must exploit the artifice for all it is worth. He must make the deceptions deceive. When he tries to do so, he finds that Ibsen and García Lorca have helped him in all sorts of ways. The very "well-madeness" that drives the playwright into excessive artifice contributes at the same time to the deception, or enthrallment, of the spectator. That is precisely what it is for: an artifice to conceal artifice. The director has only to let it work—which means to let the play unwind itself at the proper tempo and with the proper violence. He must not be lured into slowness and mildness by the banal setting and tone. Or by the comparatively slow and mild openings to the various acts. All three proceed, after a couple of cleverly contrived swings this way and that, to a big "curtain," the second more violent than the first, the third more violent than the second.

Eric Bentley. *In Search of Theater* (New York, Vintage, 1953), pp. 209–11

The poet may have failed in communicating his sense of horror and preoccupation [in *Poet in New York*], but there is no doubt that he was talking in earnest when he denounced the disorder of the world as he saw it in this ultra-modern city, representative of the most advanced stage of civilization. He was not the first to cry havoc in behalf of both a continent and the whole panorama of the occidental world, whose doom Spengler prophesied in a book today virtually forgotten but of great influence after the First World War. Other Europeans visiting the "brave new world" had expressed similar warnings. [Georges] Duhamel, in *Scenes from the Future,* Huxley and many others had reacted similarly. There was at the time a whole legion of poets of gloom. And in America, from Henry Adams through the new humanism up to Waldo Frank and the then most important novelists from Dreiser to Upton Sinclair and John Dos Passos, there was a score of writers either depicting the corruption of life or expressing similar uneasiness about the trends of the twentieth century. All this García Lorca knew; and it undoubtedly formed the background of an attitude which, as we have said in the beginning, was a result in part of the Depression that he witnessed.

Being a poet, he did not analyze or describe, he *felt*—and his feeling took the form of thematic images. There are a few which appear very soon, in the first poems, and are constantly repeated until they become leitmotifs: "things without roots," "flight and dissolution of forms," "forgetfulness of heaven," "lack of outlet," "struggle," and especially "emptiness," "vacuity," "hollowness," "void."

But perhaps more revealing than these recurrent themes and images, is the fact that all the elements of the book's style are organized in a dynamic and at the same time dialectic tension, as a result of seeing the world of reality torn by a permanent duality and conflict. This takes many forms: natural, religious, or conceptual: birth and death, heaven and earth, sin and redemption, geometry and anguish, spirit and passion, man in his constant clash with matter. All are related to a single all-embracing idea: the return to primitive, destructive instincts and passions let loose by a mechanical civilization, deprived of Grace, or, as it were, in rebellion against the spirit. The contrast is one between the primitiveness of human appetites without moral restraints, and of the perfection of technology: man, emptied of his spiritual content in a mechanized world, returns to barbarity. The result is a self-destructive confusion, as if the crumbling of this man-created chaos is necessary for the rising of a new life in which nature and the spirit will find harmony. The book is not so much an impression of New York as an indictment of modern civilization.

Ángel del Río. Introduction to Federico García
Lorca, *Poet in New York* (New York, Grove,
1955), pp. xxvii–xxviii

Federico García Lorca . . . wrote poetic drama, very much as Yeats and Eliot have taught us to understand it, yet his plays are neither cultish nor middlebrow-Ersatz; they are theatre-poetry which lives naturally on the modern stage. García Lorca did very little theorizing, but he found, at a very early age, in pre-Franco Spain, singularly direct ways to use the stage for the purposes of poetry. It is true that he is not a creature of the commercial theatre. Madrid in its time had a theatre corresponding to Broadway, but García Lorca was always in more or less hidden opposition to it. He was the director of "La Barraca," a group of University players which was subsidized by the government and toured the provincial towns and cities of Spain with a repertory of classics. . . .

García Lorca's theatre-poetry fulfills many of the prescriptions of Yeats and Eliot, but it is strongly marked by his unique genius, his rare combination of talents. And it is nourished by the Spanish tradition, which was showing new vitality just before Franco put out the light. These matters are already clear in his early play, *The Love of Don Perlimplín for Belisa in His Garden. Don Perlimplín* is a romantic farce, slighter and lighter than his most famous pieces, *Blood Wedding* and *The House of Bernarda Alba,* but it is a small masterpiece. When he wrote it he was already in control of his difficult art. . . .

García Lorca was unusually fortunate in being able to work with such fertility within his native culture; it is a commentary on our rootless state, in which all the familiar forms of life and art begin to seem vague and irrelevant, that his riches should seem somehow against the rules. It is growing harder and harder in our time for a writer to stay within one traditional culture. Yeats was hardly content with his Irish revival beyond youth. Our own Southern writers hesitate painfully between the South, where their roots are, and the national scene in which they are obliged to live, almost as ill-defined as the rest of us.

The deeply Spanish nature of García Lorca's art does not prevent it from speaking to us. His sense of history—"the masquerades which time resumes"—is very modern; in his ability to mingle the most contradictory perspectives in one composition, and to shift with sureness from the pathetic to the farcial-frightening, he is in the class of our favorite poets. And he writes poetry of the theatre as our poets would like to do. We cannot use his Spanish language, or the symbolic language of the moral and aesthetic forms of his tradition. But we can learn

to read it, and to discover thereby an authentic modern poetic drama.
[1955]

Francis Fergusson. *The Human Image in
Dramatic Form* (Garden City, N.Y., Doubleday,
1957), pp. 85–86, 96–97

Whatever problems the play [*As Soon As Five Years Pass*] may awaken,
it cannot be dismissed as inconsequential. It is a powerful theatrical
drama, the product of intense feelings on the absurd and mysterious in
human existence, and important in the catalogue of Spanish drama as
both an erudite and passionate study of psychological behavior. It is
possibly García Lorca's most important single work, and although it
has only received grudging attention in the past, the modern theatre
may soon adopt it as the earliest example of the Spanish prototype of
the "theatre of the absurd," placing it alongside the already accepted
works of Beckett, Pinter, Ionesco and Genet.

García Lorca's own "theatre of the absurd" began with the three
short sketches usually referred to as the "brief theatre"—*Buster Keaton's Promenade, Chimera,* and *The Virgin, the Sailor and the Student.*
These pieces, written in 1928, are the cornerstone upon which *The
Public* and *As Soon as Five Years Pass* are built. They established the
tradition in García Lorca's theatre of examining man's foibles in his
attempts to conquer Fate, be it implemented by natural laws or by the
artificial codes which mankind has imposed on itself. Sometimes, as in
the playlets and in the puppet farces, man's predicament is treated with
a peasant humor; their grotesque overstatement hides the sense of
impotence in the presence of Fate that these characters, as representatives of the human race, have inherited. Sometimes, as in the existing
scenes of *The Public* man is viewed with sardonic laughter and made
the object of all that is ridiculous in life. And in *As Soon as Five Years
Pass* he reaches what must be, of necessity, the climactic point—his
withdrawal into the subconscious, his negation of the values of reality
and his subsequent death. Thus, man's world is absurd because he has
become absurd, and so on in the paradoxical circling of causation.

It is this existence which García Lorca has transferred to the
theatre. Man's absurdity, based on the overwhelming complexity of life,
is crowned by his mock heroic stance. And, as in *As Soon as Five Years
Pass,* the sad moment arrives, when the realization of life's futility
strikes man the blow of despair. This is the panorama García Lorca has
deciphered with great lucidity, in spite of the fog of man's circumscrip-
tion which shrouds the process of full recognition, and which he has
chose to preserve.

Robert Lima. *The Theatre of García Lorca*
(New York, Las Américas, 1963), pp. 186–87

With García Lorca we enter an altogether different landscape in the
modern drama, the landscape of passion. His three great tragedies—

Blood Wedding, Yerma, The House of Bernarda Alba—are stripped nearly bare of the details of setting and time, that sense of locale we need for Ibsen, Wilde, Shaw, or O'Casey. Yet we do not leave the area of reality, as we do with some of Strindberg and of Pirandello. García Lorca empties his drama of nearly all forces but passion. Even his settings always seem nearly barren, simply all whites or all blacks, so that only the colors emerge that are evoked by the action and the characters. The motivation and energy for plot are in passion; the definition of character is through passion. There is no "thought," no "idea" of any significance.

García Lorca is preeminently the playwright of passion in the modern theater although we can find elements of García Lorca in Williams, Osborne, O'Neill, and Genet; but in each of these there is a significant admixture of other thematic material. García Lorca's passion is not related to a program, as in D. H. Lawrence, or in Williams, or in Genet. García Lorca's "blood consciousness" is a consciousness of what is, already; of what must be observed, acknowledged, assimilated, lived with, understood, and, finally, even forgiven. García Lorca's passion is rooted in an established social context. The tragedy in his plays comes from the tension between passion, which is necessarily always entirely individual and personal and whimsical, and the society in which the individuals move, which defines them and also gives a particular value and shading to passion and its manifestations. In García Lorca, the conflict is between passion and honor, where passion is the mark of the personal (willful and private and powerful in its needs) and honor that of the social (rigid and public and equally powerful in its rules and taboos, the denial of needs). . . .

García Lorca's tragedy, then, resides in the domain of passion: passion destroys itself and its possessors, the personal can ultimately only come in conflict with the social, the social enlarges itself into vengeance or into death-serving sterility. Life and fulfillment may reside in passion alone, but precariously, never without risk, not casually. Humans cannot truly be alive without passion, but with passion they must wage a running, alert, and subtle battle with those guerrilla forces intent on its destruction. It is the classic opposition between life and death itself; and death, of course, as Freud not least has sadly indicated, is an expression, a wish, of life itself. But to celebrate passion is to celebrate life, living, feeling, reaching, erring: vitality, vivacity, whimsicality, impulsiveness, energy of every sort. There is a final rightness about García Lorca's characters who strive toward goals that define them as they live, as there is about Oedipus, and to fail is simply—and greatly—to be human.

Morris Freedman. *The Moral Impulse: Modern Drama from Ibsen to the Present* (Carbondale, Ill., Southern Illinois University Press, 1967), pp. 89–90, 98

[*Richard*] *Burgin*: What about the plays of García Lorca?

[*Jorge Luis*] *Borges*: I don't like them. I never could enjoy García Lorca.

Burgin: Or his poetry either?

Borges: No, I saw *Yerma* and I found it so silly that I walked away. I couldn't stand it. Yet I suppose that's a blind spot because . . .

Burgin: García Lorca, for some reason, is idealized in this country [the United States].

Borges: I suppose he had the good luck to be executed, no? I had an hour's chat with him in Buenos Aires. He struck me as a kind of play actor, no? Living up to a certain role. I mean being a professional Andalusian.

Burgin: The way Cocteau was supposed to be, as I understand it.

Borges: Yes, I suppose he was. But in the case of García Lorca, it was very strange because I lived in Andalusia and the Andalusians aren't a bit like that. His were stage Andalusians. Maybe he thought that in Buenos Aires he had to live up to that character, but in Andalusia, if you are talking to a man of letters and you speak to him about bull-fights, he'll say, "Oh well, that sort of thing pleases people, I suppose, but really the torero works in no danger whatever." Because they are bored by those things, because every writer is bored by the local color in his own country, no? Well, when I met García Lorca he was being a professional Andalusian. . . .

Burgin: Well, García Lorca wasn't a thinker, but I think he had a gift for words.

Borges: But I think there is very little behind the words.

Burgin: He had a gift for hearing words.

Borges: Well, a gift for gab. For example, he makes striking metaphors, but I wonder if he makes striking metaphors for *him,* because I think that his world was mostly verbal. I think that he was fond of playing words against each other, the contrast of words, but I wonder if he knew what he was doing.

Jorge Luis Borges and Richard Burgin. In
Richard Burgin, *Conversations with Jorge Luis
Borges* (New York, Holt, Rinehart & Winston,
1969), pp. 93–95

In *Mariana Pineda* García Lorca has given a strong classical unity and tension to material that is romantic and legendary in nature. He has subordinated the characters to the central personality of Mariana Pineda, the heroine of the drama, upon whose fatal destiny the action and situations unfold. At most, the whole work—contrary to the opinions of some critics, who see in it only a mood piece of the times—is an exaltation of the heroine, an exaltation that culminates in the apotheosis and final catharsis of death, the ultimate liberty—perhaps, the only one—of humanity.

In this work García Lorca renounces—like in all of his others, excepting the farces—the mixing of the tragedy and the comedy of Seneca and Terence. Everything is momentous, serious, elevated—without any signs of comedy, levity or laughter. He does not believe that variety is entertaining. . . .

Mariana Pineda acquires great importance when one considers that it represents the starting point in the dramatic trajectory of García Lorca. Obscured by his most famous tragedies, it brought to the contemporary Spanish theater a wealth of real poetry, which flowed naturally and unceasingly not only from the characters, but which emanated from the surroundings: an emotional power that stands out as much in the tragic verses of Mariana Pineda as in the sweet and sorrowful words of the nuns as they take leave of the executed heroine.

The fundamental principle of García Lorca's theater is noted in *Mariana Pineda:* Theater cannot be anything else but emotion and poetry in word, deed and gesture. . . . Characteristics of that *total* theater to which García Lorca always aspired are noted, a synthesis of all theatrical elements: the dramatic and poetic word—reality and poetry—music and song. . . .

A long time will go by until Spain again produces another *total* playwright like Federico García Lorca, who perhaps foresaw, in his heroine Mariana Pineda, his own tragic destiny. Both of them were innocent victims of tyranny, of hatred, and of irresponsibility.

Concha Zardoya. RHM. Jan.–April, 1968,
pp. 496–97†

It is García Lorca's deft modulation of the theme of illusion-reality, in which illusion may be poetic revery or stultifying social codes of honor and family pride, and reality the norm of nature, including spontaneous instinctual, sensual life, which accounts for much of the interest of his work. The range of modulation is from virtually pure comedy, complete with happy ending, as in *The Puppets of Cachiporra: The Tragicomedy of Don Cristóbal and Doña Rosita* and *The Shoemaker's Prodigious Wife* to the stark, unrelieved tragedy of *The House of Bernarda Alba.* In virtually all cases, however, it is against the norm of nature that the divergent mode of illusion stands in contrast, the figure against the ground.

The Prologue to *The Butterfly's Evil Spell* presents in considerable detail the natural norm. The insect world, the setting of the play, was once infused with it. . . . But this life of primal, sensual joy has long since passed. Its demise has been caused by a kind of Adam-like insect, "an insect that tried to go beyond love." Such overreaching in quest of the unattainable has amounted to a breach of natural order . . . and has left spiritual confusion in place of instinctual tranquility. In this play, the natural order, violated when the cockroach falls in love with the butterfly, resembles the Elizabethan conception of the Great Chain of

Being so fundamental to many of Shakespeare's plays. Indeed, the old insect from whom the poet claims to have heard the story has "escaped from a book of the great Shakespeare." Unlike the Elizabethan conception of a natural hierachy, however, the hierachy in this play is not ontological, but simply a kind of intermediate principle of order. The audience is not to smirk or be repulsed at the sight of the insects. . . . In García Lorca, the "kingdom of God" is often nothing more or less than the norm of nature, a norm in which such dualisms as ugly-beautiful and high-low are transcended. In this sense, García Lorca's notion of the natural order, in which there is no qualitative distinction between stone and swan or man and cockroach, more closely resembles the attitude of Zen Buddhism. Just as Zen attempts to teach its students the illusoriness of the sense of ego, hence attuning them to the rhythm of all nature of which they come to see themselves an inextricable, qualitatively undifferentiable part, so the old insect advises the poet: " . . . that love exists with the same intensity on all levels of life . . ."

The principal violation of this equality is desiring beyond one's station—desire engendered by dissatisfaction with one's own position and by the illusory notion that the desired object is more spiritual, more beautiful, better in some vague way. In *The Butterfly's Evil Spell,* the violator is Curianito, a "poet and visionary, who . . . is waiting for some great mystery that will decide his life." García Lorca's mocking tone is unmistakeable. . . .

Michael C. Wells. HR. July, 1970, pp. 299–301

Whenever I compare *The House of Bernarda Alba* with *Blood Wedding* and *Yerma,* the first thing that strikes me is the radical change in García Lorca's attitude toward honor. It is like moving from the plays of Corneille to those of Racine. In *Blood Wedding,* as the moment of blood comes again, the Mother is torn by her personal desire to save her son's life and the demand to preserve the family honor. . . . We find the same thing in Yerma. She wants a child more than anything else in the world, but when the Old Woman suggests that Yerma go off with her son, Yerma replies:

> Do you imagine I could know another man? Where would that leave my honor? . . . Look at me, so you'll know me and never speak to me again. I'm not looking for anyone.

In these plays there is a conflict between principle and feeling, a struggle to fit the experience of the individual into the framework of the community life. But because honor is an attitude of virtue which is believed in, it enables man to dominate the life of instinct and accomplish actions which order the whole of his being instead of destroying it by placing him at the mercy of his conflicting desires. This does not mean there is no suffering, for the Mother and Yerma are clearly suffering, but there is a sense of meaning in painful reconciliation.

But in *The House of Bernarda Alba,* honor is the keeping up of appearances. It is not a reality, but an attitude to be maintained. It is an attitude in which the positive idea of virtue has been sacrificed; and when this happens, conduct becomes a series of postures which no longer correspond to any moral feelings. The result of this—and for more evidence we could also point to Victorian England or any other age of respectability—is the complete divorce between the public and private life of the individual. Such a divorce inevitably leads to moral anarchy and the destructive victory of unchecked passions. People become wild beasts, and the only morality is the morality of the jungle. This is what I believe to be the central action of García Lorca's last play: the conflict between the hypocritical and sterile norms of conformity and regimentation and the overpowering desire for sexual release and expression. This play, García Lorca says, is a "photographic document in three acts," but in the making of it he has used a slow motion camera which he has focused on the passions of a horrible "togetherness."

Robert W. Corrigan. *The Theatre in Search of a Fix* (New York, Delacorte, 1973), pp. 183–84

Now if there is nothing wildly improbable about this story [*Yerma*], there is nothing absolutely inevitable about it either: I don't find it a dilemma in which many women will immediately recognise their problems. García Lorca works diligently to restrict Yerma's alternatives—divorce is impossible under the laws of the church; adoption is unsatisfactory since she wants her own child; adultery is unacceptable because of her code of honour. Still, one is overly-conscious of the author's labour in closing off escape routes, as well as of considerable contrivance in his character's relentless pursuit of tragedy. Yerma is virtually alone among García Lorca's passionate heroines in resisting the call of the blood. And while it is important not to underestimate the repressive power of Spanish society and religion, Yerma seems curiously reluctant to consider the options, especially when her desire for children is consuming enough to issue in murder.

In short, I find it hard to believe in the tragic necessity of Yerma's story, though Lorca's compulsion to tell it is overwhelming enough, and this arouses in me an entirely hypothetical suspicion that the play is a pretext for expressing the agony of the male homosexual. It is the homosexual who has no alternatives to barrenness, whose body is dry, whose breasts are made of sand, for his inability to become pregnant is the major obstacle to a total identification with the woman's role (in this context, Yerma's frustrated cry, 'Oh, if I could only have them by myself' takes on an added poignancy).

García Lorca's obsession with doomed sexual love, as well as his use of water and irrigation as images of sperm and procreation, his linking of human beings and breeding animals, and his attribution to women of essentially male characteristics (for example, an irrepressible sexual appetite) are the themes in which he usually sublimated his own homosexual leanings. In *Yerma* he has in hand, for the first time, the materials for a genuine homosexual tragedy; and if the play fails to satisfy, it may be because a sublimative treatment is no longer adequate to the feelings expressed.

Robert Brustein. *Observer.* April 8, 1973, p. 34

While García Lorca's comic spirit is present in *Blood Wedding* and *Yerma,* his grim humor becomes increasingly critical in his last two more socially oriented plays. No longer engaged in purely personal conflict the heroines of *Doña Rosita, the Spinster* and *The House of Bernarda Alba* now struggle against a decadent morality that imprisons them in a tight cocoon. Doña Rosita becomes a passive member of a society of fools, while Adela [in *The House of Bernarda Alba*] and her sisters lose an emotional and pyschological combat with the ferocious bully who is their mother. The highly wrought tension between humor and anguish in these two plays is too incongruous to be described by the rather nondescript term "tragicomedy." At the same time amusing and terrifying, *Doña Rosita, the Spinster* and *The House of Bernarda Alba* recall García Lorca's puppet plays and the tragic farce *The Love of Don Perlimplín for Belisa in His Garden.* Like *Perlimplín,* these last two plays seem best described as, to borrow a phrase from Tennessee Williams, "slapstick tragedy."

García Lorca is horrified by the hypocrisy and cruelty of established morality and expresses his dismay not only by creating rigid, one-dimensional characters, but also by adapting scenes and gestures from ancient farce for the purpose of serious criticism. Although not a polemical dramatist, García Lorca never ceases to rebel against the web of social injustice, hurling satirical barbs at what he considers outmoded social attitudes that might be changed. His outlook on life, however, is darkly pessimistic. Using grim humor to depict social paralysis and decay, he joins other modern playwrights in suggesting that anguish in a morally bankrupt culture is absurd and meaningless.

Virginia Higginbotham. *The Comic Spirit of Federico García Lorca* (Austin, University of Texas Press, 1976), p. 120

One of García Lorca's critics commented that the poems of *Gypsy Ballads* were violent vignettes traced in ice by a "refined savage." Although the metaphor is slightly overwrought, it is nonetheless quite accurate in the sense that these "myths," as García Lorca called them at one point, create a feeling of emotional detachment that is remarkably unlike the mood of earlier works, such as *Songs* and *Book of Poems*. While nature and the cosmos participate in these poetic dramas and often reflect the fear or the violence of what is apparently occurring on the human level, rarely, if ever, do they afford any explicit commentary from a point of view identifiable as that of the poet with regard to the scene he is depicting. It is true that in a number of cases anonymous poetic "voices" alternate with the narrative and could be construed as authorial intrusion. Usually however, these "voices" may be easily ascribed to the conscience or mind of the protagonist or to a collective and apocryphal admonition or opinion that remains at some remove from the poet himself. In fact, it is in this "detached" participation of the cosmos and the virtual absence of the lyric *I* or poetic first person that *Gypsy Ballads* finds a great deal of its strength and uniqueness. No other work of García Lorca's is as closely and universally connected with the name of its author, and yet paradoxically it is the one in which the presence of the poet is least directly felt. While profoundly rich in descriptive detail and concrete realism on one level, these small masterpieces acquire an identity which is totally their own and which allows them to stand entirely by themselves with no apparent authorial support. No wonder García Lorca was so troubled by the immediate success of the book and his popular acclaim as a sort of regional or "gypsified" poet singing the romance and legend of his native Andalusia.

David K. Loughran. *Federico García Lorca:*
The Poetry of Limits (London, Támesis, 1978),
p. 135

We, the public of *The Public,* have seen on the stage characters in the process of self-discovery, assuming and rejecting masks in an anguished search for their own identity. They, discussing the nature of the drama, have participated in the unfolding of their own drama. Side by side with the off-stage performance of *Romeo and Juliet,* the play within the play, there has been played out for us an action which has brought alive the issues of that play, so that its characters are aspects of the figures on the stage, and these are forms of them. But for us, spectators of an action on a stage, of the action of *The Public,* its issues have simultaneously assumed a living form, its characters reflections of ourselves and we of them. It is a process in which boundaries and demarcations have dissolved and have become instead a series of mirrors. The ending of the play, presenting the Director's death, is the final image that is common to us all. The Director's room, like the rooms we all inhabit, becomes a place from which there is no escape, the Juggler's Death, the truth for which the Director has sought the final truth, the final dramatic act. Between the stage on which, alone, he encounters Death, and the stage of the great theatre of the world where we give our own performance there is no difference. We become the spectators of our own ultimate solitude, the public of our own final curtain. . . . In its intellectual and emotional power, its daring use of dramatic techniques, and the "modernity" of its vision, *The Public* is both Garcia Lorca's most experimental play and one of the most startling plays of the twentieth century.

Gwynne Edwards. *Lorca: The Theatre beneath the Sand* (London and New York, Marion Boyars, 1980), pp. 83–84

GIRONELLA, JOSÉ MARÍA (1917–   )

In Gironella, God or man, collects his energy and his traditional sense of transcendence, lost in our poetry of the last few years. When the words, "God" or "man," are heard in the work of the author of *The Tide,* the purpose is not emotional or phonetic complacency; he does not take advantage of the transcendental content of his concepts to resolve situations. In Gironella, these words sound like old coins, and man acquires a dramatic sense and human dignity in this labyrinth of pain and of misery that the last wars have created for us.

Gironella's man smiles and loves again; and he sees again with that deformed lantern, which ends up giving us a sweet and humorous image of people and things.

Gironella's man attracts us because he interests us emotionally; the happiness of his books distracts us, and his dramatism makes us meditate. The strong, healthy, and optimistic character and his clash with reality please us.

Gironella's characters, both the men and women, accept and protest about the things that life gives them, and a vein of healthy humanity and active metabolism makes his humor broad and far-reaching. It is the dark humor of the mountains, clear and powerful that cleans the way for fishermen and clowns, peasant women and women of high birth, for pretty girls with dark hair and braids gilded by the sea-air, for laughing bohemians and characters of all kinds in a broad environment, open to the roads of Europe, with landscapes and cinematic touches, in which nature, life, and people are observed without artifice. . . .

Antonio de Hoyos. *Ocho escritores actuales* (Murcia, Spain, Aula de Cultura, 1954), pp. 64–65†

[Gironella] has not written a *War and Peace,* an *Iliad,* or a *Henry IV.* His story of the Alvears [in *The Cypresses Believe in God*] has not extinguished his chronicle of what went on in all of Spain, or at any rate Gerona. The Alvears have their reality and their charm, but they never overwhelm their environment as the huge figure of Pierre, stumbling through Tolstoy's novel, blots Russia out. The explanation of this could lie in the very transparencey of Ignacio Alvear's mind and heart. Without convictions of his own, he can be and indeed is a lens through which the reader looks at the innumerable parties of opinion among whose more articulate members he strolls, listening and arguing to the end not so much that we should see or believe him as that we should see and believe them. . . .

Another explanation might be the sense Gironella gives us of having desired to make all of his person representative of something. In the greatest stories people represent only themselves, though it is true that they belong to classes and have thoughts other people can have. Gironella is often lifelike and his people have their power to touch us. The devotion of Carmen Elgazu to her husband and children is immensely moving, like the big ears of César. But we cannot escape the suspicion that Gironella has schematized his human material. The difference between the devout Carmen Elgazu and the "radical" Matías is all too neat a case of at least one difference that split Spain down the middle. So is the reflection of this difference in Ignacio and César: the first a boy whose thoughts go only to God. . . .

The temptation to make characters representative in this way must be very great for any historical novelist, particularly when he knows or believes that most of the opinions held about his subject are erroneous if only because they are oversimplified. Listen, he will say: Let me set some people before you who will demonstrate how complex the true situation was and how difficult to judge as you judge it. . . .

Gironella aims at implacable impartiality, and yet there may be no such thing. Our doubt that it exists absolutely in his case grows on us as we read. He will show the worst of every side, and creditably he does so. Yet there comes into being, implicitly if not otherwise, a relativity of worsts. Ignacio, as a part of his universal experience, at one time has two teachers who are Socialist. They remain the rational and generous persons they begin by being, but they never sound older than the children they teach. And while all of the parties have their vicious members, the Anarchist and Communist leaders outdo their rivals in a fashion suggestive of melodrama.

Not that Gironella needs to be thought of as having planned such a result. No one should accuse him of distorting what he understands to be the facts. It was a wild, insane, and cruel time for everybody. "Poor Spain!" cries Ignacio to himself as the novel nears its end; and yet that end was but the end of a beginning.

Mark Van Doren. *Reporter.* June 16, 1955,
pp. 36–37

Working in the vineyards of the Spanish literary tradition, where all growth has been above ground and proliferation takes place across giant aerial roots, Gironella has endeavored to nurture roots like those which support the giant woods of Dostoevsky, Balzac and Dickens. (And if the latter does not belong in company with the first two, Gironella himself has linked the three names—as has Stefan Zweig in his book, on Gironella's shelves in Spanish, named after the three authors—and it is Dickens that he perhaps most resembles in method, prejudice and intent.) . . .

In Gironella, Spanish writing, for the first time since the Spanish Civil War, perhaps even for the first time in this century, has a craftsman who with great deliberation has attempted to search out an organic Spain, one which obeys the laws of development and growth and is impelled in some measure by a hope beyond materialism or nihilism. Gironella has eschewed the easy caricature, the precipitate sketch of extreme types, and has assumed a Spaniard more complex, more capable of development than has any other writer. Placing his faith in the complicated, full-bodied novelistic search for truth implicit in the technique of Dostoevsky and Balzac, Gironella, has, in the first giant book [*The Cypresses Believe in God*] of his trilogy dealing with the Spanish war, assumed an uncompleted world, one which it will require his own artistry to divine. "They say of our Pío Baroja that he defines and characterizes a man with one stroke; and it's true. Dostoevsky, on the other hand, at the end of 500 pages, still has not defined his man."

The new face supplied the modern novel in Spain by Gironella might seem to be threatened with a contemplative pallor, to run the risk of being sicklied over with the pale cast of objectivity, but if *The Cypresses Believe in God* is an example of what is to come, his reasonably drawn family, his medium types, have within them, in addition to their new and hitherto un-Spanish novelistic veracity, all the resources of inspired force formerly identified with the most idealistic anarchists in the works of Pío Baroja or of the most vividly tormented and repressed intellectuals in the fiction of writers like José Suárez-Carreño.

Anthony Kerrigan. *Books on Trial*. April–May,
1956, pp. 344, 387–88

[Gironella] had courage and a sense of style, and *The Cypresses Believe in God* was a memorable performance, because it was far more than a novel. It was an act of faith, Gironella's way of putting the pieces together.

Peace after War [*Peace Has Broken Out*] is another act of faith, but it must be admitted that the faith is weakening. In telling the story of the years immediately after Franco's victory the author is at a disadvantage; he must deal with a triumphant middle class. The cause has been saved; the Reds have been put to flight; the spoils belong to the victor. Or do they? Gironella seems to be hinting that the victor is quickly corrupted by the spoils and that in fact there is no victory. . . .

Gironella has written an epic of the dispirited, guilt-ridden victors whose victory is a nightmare. There are, of course, even worse nightmares reserved for the defeated, but we rarely see them. Cosme Vila, the Communist leader, has taken refuge in Russia, where he broadcasts in Spanish, knowing full well that scarcely anyone is listening to him. Juan Antonio Dávila, the civil governor of Gerona, wages a kind of war against his restless, unhappy wife, and a health inspector with the odd name of Don Maximiliano Chaos wages another kind of war against the filth in the hospital. These are small wars; the greater battles are being fought elsewhere. The Spanish, bled white, gazing across blood-drenched Europe, feel that the whole world is being given over to senseless massacres, and are happy in the knowledge that their own massacres are temporarily over.

Peace after War finally produces a curiously static impression, in spite of its vast array of characters in perpetual movement. A provincial city going to seed, the quarrels and sudden reconciliations among the tempestuous Alvear family, a whole division of the Spanish army setting out for inevitable defeat on the battlefields of Russia—all these are perfect subjects for a novel; but we are puzzled to discover that everything seems to be taking place in a vacuum. Devout, well-meaning, respectable men are seen embracing the cause of Franco as though it were the most natural thing in the world, and we watch the life going out of them until they are like dolls spilling their sawdust. They move mechanically, jerkily, lifelessly, and they know they might as well be dead. Their appointments on this earth are very temporary, and in this they resemble Lieutenant Montero, who spent his days giving orders to the firing squads until he suffered a nervous breakdown. Then he was given a temporary appointment in the city library.

Gironella plays the game honestly, recording accurately what he knows about the provincial life of Spain. It is not his fault that a deathly silence hovers over these pages. When, a hundred years from now, historians attempt to discover what it was like to live under Franco during the early years of his rule, they will have to go to Gironella. He gives us the atmosphere and color of that medieval tyranny which survives so strangely in the modern world, and no one could do it better.

Robert Payne. *SR*. May 17, 1969, p. 49

The appeal of Gironella's work [*Peace after War,* i.e., *Peace Has Broken Out*] must partly be that of enabling the reader to watch the great men of Spain at close quarters. The reader is granted the unheard-of privilege of entering their plush offices and their minds, of eavesdropping on their conversations with the Minister of the Interior, of sharing with them the company of their delicate wives and children, of measuring with the film censor himself "how far down a neckline goes and how long Myrna Loy's kisses last." Yet not even a singularly repressed public would react so favorably if the novels were not, in their way, authentic. . . .

Peace after War ends on a note of uncertainty. The events of December 7, 1941, and after seem to shake the foundations of the brave new order. Pilar and Mateo are now married—Mateo has volunteered for the struggle against the Bolsheviks and is fighting on the Eastern Front. What, Pilar wonders, as she contemplates the blue, innocent eyes of her infant son, what sort of beastly world will he grow up into? What will happen to all this blissful domestic innocence if the Germans lose the war? Good salesman that he is, the author is principally preparing us for his next 700-page installment. The effect, however, of Pilar's candid fear that the Americans might tip the balance is frankly chilling.

It is salutory that, unlike many Spanish writers, Gironella has discovered that it is not necessary to make use of every single word in the dictionary to write a novel. Yet ultimately verbosity is replaced by a flat dourness; his prose is stripped of any intimidating distinction of style that could mar his readers' placidly facile enjoyment. Furthermore, if Gironella were a greater man, he might have risked alienating some of his readers by telling us more about those "swollen bellies oozing incredible quantities of fluid," indeed about the hundreds of thousands of undistinguished, nameless wrecks of the Civil War that he alludes to now and then only to forget them.

David Gallagher. *NYTBR*. June 1, 1969,
pp. 4–5, 21

Where the Soil Was Shallow [*A Man*] epitomizes the author's crises, vacillations, discouragements, failures. As a liberal arts student in Dublin, Miguel is frustrated by the vacuity of his studies and is dropped from the rolls. The sudden and accidental death of his mother distracts him further. He loses interest in his bookstore after deliberately seeking security in this sound enterprise as suggested by Nolan, his mother's financial adviser. When he considers marriage with Jeannette, a leading trapeze artist, he is rejected and, not quite understanding his destiny, he remains on the periphery of society, a restless, rootless and sensitive personality—a potential artist. . . .

A basic problem with the novel is that the reader knows from the outset Miguel will not triumph, for his search for ideal values is hopeless from the very beginning. Although his greatest strength is his freedom to choose his destiny, Miguel has the financial security to afford this search but lacks character and vitality to achieve his purposes. Stylistic contrast between "colorful" events and the "grayness" of Miguel's personality is clearly defined and demonstrates the lack of harmony between Miguel's spiritual life and the society in which he lives. As the novel opens, Miguel is spiritually empty. At the conclusion, he is equally vacuous. Miguel's chief problem is his inability to particularize serious goals while proceeding on his spiritual journey. . . .

Miguel's upbringing, like Gironella's, commands our interest, not because it is unusual in any sense but because the story of a young man's maturity helps us better to appreciate lives and to perceive problems. James Joyce, F. Scott Fitzgerald, and Thomas Wolfe, among others, have documented their childhood experiences at least semi-autobiographically, while writing novels of situations encountered in their particular milieus. Gironella, however, followed their example only to a point. Although skeletal autobiographical facts are partially adhered to, the chief difficulty with *Where the Soil Was Shallow* is its falsification of the worlds in which the author did *not* live. . . .

Historically, Miguel's spiritual search is the author's own quest for a new life after the shattering experiences of the Civil War. Although Gironella carefully avoids presenting this motivation as the chief impetus, he substitutes Miguel's mother's death as the principal reason for his spiritual quest. Her death symbolizes the end of a matriarchy— Spain cast into upheaval because of civil war. Just as many Spaniards were forced to cut the umbilical cord and search for a new value system, Miguel's spiritual journey is symbolic of all Spaniards' search for new directions after the chaos of war. Gironella uses Eva's death to explain symbolically what cannot be published directly because of the rigors of Franco's censorship.

Ronald Schwartz. *José María Gironella* (New
York, Twayne, 1972), pp. 39–41

Since the disjunction of history and fiction is the main structural weakness of the trilogy, especially in *One Million Dead* [the first and third novels being *The Cypresses Believe in God* and *Peace Has Broken Out* respectively], it deserves further examination. In Gironella's scheme, factual documentation serves two purposes. It provides a chronicle of information for Spanish readers, and it acts as a corrective against the allegedly misinformed works of Malraux, Hemingway, Barea, Koestler, and Bernanos. In practical terms, however, facts help to mold the historical framework without making a comparable impression on the reader. The real effect on readers is achieved in the human realm, where fact recedes before the primacy of invention. In this way, the documentary value of the novel contracts at the moment when the actual story is being told. Regardless of the "balance" in presentation, its tacit impartiality is of no historical consequence. What stands out is not factual fidelity but the author's humanitarian values, his sympathy for all participants in the war. Thus two narrative rhythms alternate their appearance: first a historical summary of events and then a fictional plot sequence, alternating currents that isolate historical anecdote from fictive plot. Separate lines of narrative exist, one where characters stand outside events and comment on the historical sphere, and the other where these same characters lead their own lives with only artificial links to names and events in history. At times facts are colorful enough to be narrated in a journalistic manner that renders their fatuality semi-novelistic. But the converse proves to be unsuccessful: purely fictional episodes rarely use facts that might make them appear veracious. The result is a surface resumé of history that fails to penetrate the shell of historical occurrence with the insight of character study. By the same token, characters' lives are rarely determined by factual details, since they are people who react to history only in a vague chronological way.

The existence of a historical perspective cannot be denied, however, and it is maintained by certain techniques. The narrator orchestrates an equilibrium in the discussion of controversial issues such as the debate over Socialism and Falàngism, and the critique of Catholicism and Church officials. Another device is narrative relativism, whereby the same event receives two interpretations, each one in accordance with the opinions of a given side. This dual perspective implies that several interpretations are possible, a healthy assumption indicating a historiographical desire to rise above partisan views. Thus we find a journalistic technique grafted upon narrative fiction as Gironella reports what has happened on one side, and then presents its counterpart on the other. Little more can be expected of a novel which is neither profound nor searching, but which successfully offers a panoramic reportage without falling into partial historicism.

Paul Ilie. *JSSTC*. Fall, 1974, pp.80–81

GÓMEZ DE LA SERNA, RAMÓN (1888–1963)

In 1926, having long studied the objects around him with impartial delight—he has something of the humour of Dickens—having recorded what he knows of Madrid streets and shops, cafés, hotels and hospitals, he shows in his novel, *The Bullfighter Caracho,* a desire of presenting suffering and its meaning, as well as synthesizing his innumerable reflections into something like a philosophic whole. . . .

Bull-fights have often been made excuses for novels, but where writers before him have given us their subject in a more or less generally descriptive way, in *The Bullfighter Caracho* we see the particular events of each bull-fight described as if we had been among the onlookers. The glitter, ferocity, and fantasy of the author's now perfected style contribute to this. . . .

In *The Bullfighter Caracho* we are far from the lightheartedness of the author's early books. He is no longer like some boyish fellow-guest at a country house—merely charming, unselfconscious, gay, overflowing with clever chatter about all that he has seen and read, thought or fancied.

In this last book we learn much, not only of bulls and bull-fighting, but of the very soul of the Spanish people. Of their love of life and extravagant adventure, their resignation before fatality, their instinctive faith warring against a sense of universal nothingness.

If in his early youth Gómez de la Serna was called a literary madman; if, as he says, doors were closed against him and he suffered insult and outrage, now at least he is respected, read and allowed to write as he likes without question.

Helen Granville-Barker. Fortnightly Review.
Jan., 1929, pp. 37–38, 42

The Dead Men and Women and Other Phantasmagorias is made up of some reflections on death, a collection of epitaphs that Ramón found in cemeteries, other reflections about funereal topics, and, at the end, a series of fantasies related to death or the dead. The most interesting part of the book, without doubt, is the one entitled "Lucubrations on Death." In it a contemporary writer studies this much-discussed and well-worn topic and gives us some new ideas about this constant specter. Ramón believes that death is a value in crisis, and which no longer exists in its old sense. It used to have a negative value, but today it has a positive one: it serves as an encouragement to life, it serves to ease and overcome it. If contemporary life is more tedious than ever before, it is because it must compensate for itself, because nowadays it lacks the concept of mortality. In the Spaniard's traditional attitude toward death Ramón sees a certain skepticism. He believes that so much thinking about death has taught the Spaniard to be nimble and unrestrained, lacking interest in everything. In this way he wants to take away ascendancy from whoever believes himself to be immortal. One must get accustomed to death, because we carry it within us. We have to take it for a walk, introduce it into our home, go all over with it, but without any sadness. "No need to kill yourself or to die, walk on with your death. It is your prescribed company." This dissertation on death contains, without doubt, some of Ramón's best pages. A large part of his literary production, of his outlook, can be explained through it—for example, one of his best books, *The Rastro*. Ramón's interest in so many things that seem dead, or are definitely dead, this game with things that no longer exist, really reveals a formidable desire for life and existence. [1935]

Pedro Salinas. Ensayos completos de Pedro
Salinas (Madrid, Taurus, March, 1983), I, pp. 142–43†

The first important book of Ramón in which "things" assume a decided importance is *The Unlikely Doctor*. This series of stories written around the amazing personality and perspicacity of a Dr. Vivar is a literal application of Ramón's theory of the influence of "things" in our lives— the idea that "things" enter into the depths of our soul and act upon us there; therefore, just as one has to go into the significance of one's childhood—one's past—in psychoanalysis, one has also to face the "things" which form part of the data of man's subconscious activity. . . .

It should be pointed out that Ramón wrote *The Unlikely Doctor* before the revelations of Freud about the subconscious mind were part of the layman's domain of knowledge. . . . But the book in which we first see Ramón's profound delight in the "things" which surround him is *The Rastro*. In this book Ramón makes a Columbian discovery of the world of "things" and takes full possession of this New World. He makes this discovery in the Rastro, the famous secondhand market in Madrid, and his book bears the name of this famous "junk-yard." With all his resources of language and poetry Gómez de la Serna returns "things" to their original confusion, not with a second logical intention, like Mallarmé, but rather with the unconsciousness of an illuminate. Each element is detached from the framework in which we are used to enclose it and acquires a personality and a soul. As Ramón penetrates more and more into this world of "things" he begins to hear the song of the wine inside the bottles, or the amorous dialogue between the Jack and the Queen in the deck of cards. . . . We no longer see the commonplace reality that we know but an entirely new universe. It is in *The Rastro* that Ramón first unfolds his poetry of the object which has caused Azorín to call him "the psychologist of things."

Rodolfo Cardona. Ramón: A Study of Gómez
de la Serna and His Works (New York, Eliseo
Torres, 1957), pp. 125–26

In *Movieland* . . . Gómez de la Serna undertakes . . . to reproduce the world of the men and women who inhabit the "city of films," citified surroundings where reality is daily masked and supplanted by the scenes that are presented there and the existences that are played out in them. In a well-harmonized succession of scenes, Ramón obliges the reader of *Movieland* to penetrate into that singular atmosphere of the city while he goes on presenting those who populate it to us. The characters and the events in the novel—both grotesque and dramatic— are subordinated to the author's aim of describing a particular and extreme form of coexistence, in which what is real and what is imaginary are intermixed to the point that it is difficult to establish a boundary between the two planes. One of the moments when this aim is best attained is the one in which he presents the madhouse of Movieland, which is inhabited by actors who one day were unable to come out of the roles they were playing and thus were separated from the others and were living out their lives in the asylum, having forgotten who they were in reality. This imagined world, which like the even more confined surroundings that served for the background of Ramón's earlier fiction, is free of all social or ethical impositions, and it appears to its creator as a preview of what the world will be one day. . . .

What Ramón possibly might have wanted to suggest is that human society might one day be made up of a great "movieland," if all men and women were to break with all the norms imposed by social existence, forgetting moral principles, customs, and prejudices. At that point, in all the world, just as in Movieland, only immediate gratification will be necessary; actions will not be inspired in any superhuman principles nor would they aspire to achieve any goal whatsoever.

Luis S. Granjel. Retrato de Ramón (Madrid,
Guadarrama, 1963), pp. 202–3†

It is not without reason that "the impersonal generation of Ramón Gómez de la Serna" has been spoken about. This is what has justified his nonconformist attitudes and the nature of his earliest works, from *Softnesses* through *The Mute Book* and *Tapestries:* a thorny and tangled jungle into which his contemporary readers would not be interested in entering. . . .

His most interesting literary characteristic is that of a liberator, who at the start has some Nietzschean and even transcendental itches toward social themes, which he later had to abandon when he oriented himself toward humor. Then he exchanges his heavy mask . . . for an ample jovial smile and his uneasy view of reality for a perspective of cosmic funambulism. The *greguería,* undoubtedly, has been his very own find, his mascot, and his compass. . . .

His poetic quality is one of the reasons we are dealing with RAMÓN. This characteristic justifies the antinomy that might exist in trying to relate a prose writer like him to an eminently lyric generation like the ultraists. Some critic has pointed out the lyric vein that runs continuously through Ramón's works, but this lyric vein is never pure; rather, it is subordinated to the presence of the picturesque—which is its favored god—and to a certain joking intention. Searching in detail through his books—especially the *Greguerías*—we can find some images that are clearly parallel to those forged by the most fevered imagemakers of ultraism.

Guillermo de Torre. Historia de la literatura de
vanguardia (Madrid, Guadarrama, 1965),
pp. 524–26†

The Spanish artistic atmosphere of the first third of this century was formed by a group of picturesque individuals who constituted a real stimulus for a writer of an ironic and playful temperament like Ramón Gómez de la Serna, or RAMÓN, plain and simple and capitalized, as he preferred to call himself. He cultivated the art of literary portraiture with great enthusiasm, sketching silhouettes of the intellectuals of the time and through them their ambience. Gómez de la Serna does not limit himself to a simple physical illustration: he creates complex psychological portraits and paints in detail the background in which the different individuals move. In *Contemporary Portraits* and *New Contemporary Portraits* we see a gallery of dynamic and colorful men, whom the author infuses with life. . . .

The most important aspect of caricature delineation is the psychological presentation of the model: the physical description is not an end in itself, but rather a means directed toward capturing the soul of the individual. . . . In his psychological caricatures of his subjects, Gómez de la Serna looks for the sentence that best reproduces the true idiosyncrasy of each of his models. . . .

Jacinto Benavente, small and delicate, was . . . a "little smiling man, like an aristocrat with his aristocracy.". . . Gabriel Miró, a serious and conscientious writer, was "a great man in mourning, . . . a literary figure with nobility and a characteristic vocabulary"; . . . Unamuno, willful and dominating, was a "Basque who became a Castilian just through wanting to be one.". . .

Aside from capturing the essential aspects of the personalities, the portraits reflect the atmosphere of the city in which they lived; the city is caricatured in details that humanize it and evidence the great love that Gómez de la Serna felt for his country and for [Madrid] . . . in particular.

María A. Salgado. *PSA*. Oct., 1969,
pp. 19, 21–22†

Since most of the innovations found in Ramón's play [*The Theater in Solitude*] can be explained by applying cubist esthetic theories, it will be necessary to show his close involvement with the artistic environment of the time. Ramón made his first trip to Paris in 1906. This was the year in which Pablo Picasso began "Les Demoiselles d'Avignon," painted in a strange new technique. . . . Much more important however, Ramón lived in Paris during 1910–1911, the most significant period for the development of analytical cubism, when Picasso and Braque completely abandoned the classical viewpoint. . . .

[Ramón] was greatly interested in the artistic innovations of the epoch. His 1931 book *Isms,* in which he studied all the artistic movements of the first part of the twentieth century, including cubism, bears witness to this. . . . In *Isms* Ramón gives us evidence of his commitment to the new attitudes. Of course twenty years had passed since he wrote *The Theater in Solitude*. However, certain evidence in the play itself . . . indicated that when he was writing it he was experiencing the same emotions that he communicated in *Isms* in a more sophisticated way. His purpose in writing this study is to explain the important epoch which was then ending. It is a very personal study—there are twenty-seven "isms," ranging from well-established ones (cubism and surrealism) to "isms" of his own invention. . . .

Ramón explains that he has always been a "vanguardist," and that he is especially a "porvenirista" ["futurist"]. . . . The chapter entitled "Picassism" is a formal study of Picasso's life and work, quite similar to those found in art history books. It has been quoted by art historians. He examines at length the theory of cubism, including the influence of Negro art, the triumph of intelligence, and collages. He thinks cubism is one of the most beautiful rebellions of men against appearances, and that it has at its disposal more means of expression than ordinary perspective gives. He also discusses the problem faced by cubists of animating flat surfaces. . . .

Since the theater has at its disposal several dimensions which were unused in traditional theater, the problem of dramatists is opposite to that of painters, but the basic concept they have in common is sincerity in showing the medium for what it is in all its dimensions and with its limitations.

Wilma Newberry. CL. Winter, 1969, pp. 54–55

Ramón's hat fixation was a symbol of profound irritation with conventional society and could be traced right back to his youth. . . . The novel <i>The Gentlemen in the Gray Bowler,</i> a farcical satire on the swindles of banking and commerce, used the bowler hat as a sign of unscrupulous seeking for power and material success to denounce the mentality of the modern age. . . . This association of hat and brains leads us on to the most important political inference of "hatlessness," and it stems from Ramón's early youthful irrationalism. Then he had wanted to take off his head to cure the intellectual pains of scepticism. . . . According to Ramón the reasoning faculty had a major shortcoming: it gave rise to abstract thought, transcendent principles, ideologies, and so to polemical argument and political conflict. Hats in this sense were the exterior labels of political thought and hatlessness therefore meant an openminded, irrational, political neutrality, freedom from grim sectarianism, in fact a revolution of non-commitment. . . .

Only the name of one politician appeared in the story—Mussolini—and then in the form of tacit criticism. On the other hand brief mention was made of three exemplary figures: Jesus, Diogenes . . ., and Gandhi. . . . They suggested the ethics behind hatlessness: an apolitical affirmation of the individual and his spiritual calm characterized by the three principles of Christian humility, cynical independence and non-violent civil disobedience. This last principle in particular underlines the point that Ramón was a cultural and psychological insurrectionary fighting on two fronts—against conventional society and against violent revolutionaries. With hatlessness Ramón wished to oppose the politics of violence from both extremes.

Alan Hoyle. Studies in Modern Spanish
Literature (London, Támesis, 1972), pp. 92–93

Ramón's self-expression through his subjects reached a high point in the two masterly biographies that followed the appearance of *Auto-deathography: Edgar Poe, the Genius of America* and *Quevedo,* both published in 1953. They were written by a man deeply wounded by the coolness that had marred the final part of his return trip to Spain in 1949, and who was still laboring under the financial strain that the trip had caused him. . . .

As a subject, Poe fits all Ramón's ideals: he lived a bohemian life, combining dedication to the literary ideal with a veritable martyrdom of poverty and hardship; he had wonderfully fantastic powers of invention and a dramatic life story. Ramón had published an earlier version of his *Poe* in 1920, but more than thirty years later, after he, too, had lived in the New World, Ramón felt that he understood Poe better and revised his biography. The revised edition revealed the extraordinary poetic level of expression Ramón had by then attained.

In *Quevedo,* it seems that the quality that most appealed to Ramón was his subject's love for expressing the unvarnished truth. Quevedo's biography is characterized by a baroque piling of metaphor upon metaphor and *greguería* upon *greguería*. In it, Ramon "becomes" Quevedo to such an extent that he even paraphrases him. He considers Quevedo's laugh essential to him, and cleverly plays upon it. In these biographical works, Ramón taught himself to laugh with the laugh of Quevedo and to dream surrealistic dreams with the fantastic imagination of Poe. He made of these two figures (as he had of other subjects from the past) living and contemporary personalities. The contemporaneity which Ramón felt with artists who had lived in the past is partly explicable by his belief that a similarity exists between the past and present experience of life.

Rita Mazzetti Gardiol. Ramón Gómez de la
Serna (Boston, Twayne, 1974), p. 116

GOYTISOLO, JUAN (1931–   )

As far as I know, *Sleight of Hand* is [Goytisolo's] first novel, and when he wrote it, he was scarcely twenty-one years old. It is a very young age for a novelist, and there is no need to repeat here what critics always repeat: the novel is a genre of vital experiences, and therefore the novelist begins to bear fruit when he has in his possession a sufficient amount of life lived, a vast and rich human experience. . . . I do not know if Juan Goytisolo has lived a lot or a little; it hardly matters at all. Whether his story is a series of lived experiences or whether it is only a product of his imagination, or—and this is the most probable—a mixture of both, the important thing is that *Sleight of Hand* possesses the necessary artistic truth so that the story interests and even excites us. Literary precedents that are easy to cite in regard to this novel—the Gide of *Les faux monnayeurs* and the Cocteau of *Les enfants terribles*—are insufficient to explain the aliveness of the work, its psychological veracity, the skill in the description of characters—young people barely twenty years old. . . .

What clearly needs to be emphasized here is that Goytisolo, barely in the first years of youth, has fully succeeded in his first novel. On reading *Sleight of Hand* we experienced the same delightful sensation as when—oh, so infrequently!—we discover the talent of a born poet in the book of an adolescent. Certainly, there is no plethora of precocious literary talents, but it is even much more difficult to find them in the novel—a genre that is more reflective than intuitive—than in poetry, where there has been more than one Rimbaud. Pay attention, then, to Juan Goytisolo. We expect a lot from him.

J. L. Cano. *Ínsula*. March, 1955, p. 7†

Fiestas is a model of harmony, sharpness, love of things and beings, originality of vision and the sense of efficacy in indirect allusion. *Fiestas* is a brilliant projection of the contrast between Spanish official and real life.

The reader need have no fear that he will find political or social, moral, or, least of all, religious preaching in this book. Nor will he find men good or bad according to their creed. There is no creed at all. Neither are there self-centered judgments. There are only the reflections through the mind of a gifted author on life in the poorest districts of Barcelona. This mind is a mirror which does not copy . . . or deform . . ., but which selects. This is our great and difficult task: to select. It is what a novelist is doing his whole life long.

Goytisolo's novel is cold and precise, with a restrained passion that makes the contrasts of light and shadow more effective in the sometimes rhapsodic, sometimes satiric treatment of the Spanish realities of today, with all their esthetic, social, moral, historical nuances, their relationships and accidents. The complexity of these values implies no confusion. In spite of its wealth of tones, the novel is limpid, with fresh colors and diaphanous perspectives.

The reader is invited by the novelist's restraint to fill in lacunae left by him in the nature of some characters, like the sailor Gorila, or the boy Pipo, or the professor Ortega, or the lyrical pre-adolescent girl. And also to complete events that are prudently sketched. One finally settles down in that zone of soft lights which separates the wretchedness of the "Murcians," who are not allowed to live in Barcelona, and the guilt and incense of a society that insists upon concealing misery instead of facing it with a spirit of justice or love.

Most of the strata of Spanish society are masterly described in this new novel by Juan Goytisolo, who is without doubt the best of the young Spanish writers. Some day perhaps he will be the best of both the young and the old.

Ramón Sender. SR. June 11, 1960, p. 35

The trick lies in the poetic skill that Goytisolo utilizes in order to give [*Trouble in Paradise*] all the human greatness, all the tenderness and cruelty that it contains. Let me explain myself: the juxtaposition of two worlds, the one of men and the one of children, both living the same external reality—war—could have produced a better or worse war novel, but in any case, one within normal literary limits. The extraordinary, the abnormal, and the poetic arise when the novelist cuts off one part from the totality of reality, the role of men, the adults, who are the causative agents and real protagonists of war. As a result, the novel's new reality is composed of the world of children, which is inserted into the external events of war as the adults are dispensed with.

The novelist, to be sure, has not dispensed with the adults gratuitously; remember the setting of the novel: the village abandoned by one group of troops before being occupied by another. Out of this special situation arises the substitution of children for adults, children who use their weapons and interpret slogans in their own way, tragically and grotesquely mimicking soldiers at war. From all of this, I repeat, arises that great poetic spirit, that unreal and fantastic aura, which is what gives this work apart from its content, its exceptional character within the contemporary Spanish novel.

. . .*Trouble in Paradise* is the authentic child's vision of the war of 1936, that is to say, the testimony of a generation who were still children at the war's end. For that reason, it explains—to those who want to listen—the unfailingly distinct views that the protagonists and the silent witnesses had of the war, even though these witnesses may still feel a vague sense of guilt, not for what they actually did, but for all that they saw and could not prevent.

For all that, it does not strike me as unwarranted to affirm that Juan Goytisolo's novel *Trouble in Paradise* opens for the author and his generation the way to an authentic Spanish literary undertaking.

José María Castellet. Torre. Jan.–March, 1961,
pp. 139–40†

Sleight of Hand portrays the moral debility of the fairly well-to-do; but Goytisolo also takes considerable pleasure in creating the rather stagy characters who enact his homily. *Sleight of Hand* gives an exciting account of how a bunch of Madrid students plan, as an *acte gratuit,* the murder of a politician, Uribe, a dipsomaniac des Esseintes [in Huysmans's *À rebours*] ("I want to steal the frost from the rooftops and make a gift of it to the blind doves"), inadvertently causes the role of executioner to fall on David, the ditherer, the good boy anxious to prove himself. The last seventy pages or so, in which climax and anti-climax force maturity, self-denial and conscience into the hermetic world of these well-heeled delinquents, are hypnotic and profound. The characterization is steady throughout and the prose is harsh and agile. Goytisolo catches the eye and dazes the mind. His beatniks have all the colour of those close to the inferno. . . . It is a novel worth dwelling on, for it supplies an intriguing antithesis to the much less violent work of John Wain and Kingsley Amis. The reader may also catch the flavour of Hitchcock, for Goytisolo's technique is essentially cinematic and flamboyant.

Goytisolo's subsequent books are in much the same vein. *Fields of Níjar* (1960) is a colourful, stylishly written travel book, as vivid in its ways as *Sleight of Hand. Trouble in Paradise* (1955) shows that Goytisolo can manage a light though apocalyptic touch. In *The Circus* (1957) he returns to harsh contrasts. . . . The novel is lush and vivid, but Goytisolo is too fond of the diabolical-Hogarthian grotesque, and the general statement he seems to be attempting disappears in a blaze of spectacular effects. Self-indulgence defeats the urge to imitate. *The Undertow,* published in Paris in 1958, is a panorama of the Barcelona suburbs. Once again, the squalid is the mainstay: not squalid personages, for the characters are very sketchy, but squalid circumstances created by a squalid regime. As a novel, *The Undertow* is hardly satisfactory; but it is a first-class social document and, depsite its blunt realism, a long way from the self-indulgent lavishness of the other novels. *The Island* (1961) has the same documentary aim, exposing the boredom of the fashionable set at Torremolinos. The odd thing is that Goytisolo seems himself bored with the technicolour boredom of his characters. . . . Goytisolo has the makings of a great novelist; but he will always, one suspects, have to damp down his natural inclination to the phoney melodramatic.

Paul West. *The Modern Novel* (London,
Hutchinson, 1963), pp. 424–25

Goytisolo claims to be nonpolitical, and politics is not directly discussed by him or his characters. Instead of explaining, he brings to life. His callous rich live by fads, hypocrisy, self-centeredness and desperation; his brutalized poor find relief in tormenting those a little worse off than themselves. He is a master of indirection at showing the gap between social reality and its official versions, and the parallel gaps between marriage and sex and love. His genius is not polemic or documentary but in his power of magical portraiture.

It is a respectable cliché of critics and teachers that novelistic genius lies in the selection of details. But an artist does not edit reality; he creates it. When he must construct on paper a personality, a human climate, he must do so with his imagination, not by winnowing down a card file of information. In fiction, the dialogue, landscape and incident

work as metaphors do in verse. Goytisolo's skill at inventing economical, suggestive details makes him a delight for other writers to read.
His prose is cool, controlled, compact. The color of the sky, a boat
being rowed, a snatch of conversation, a silence—all work like the
techniques of perspective painting, where manipulating the surface
creates a whole dimension in depth.

Goytisolo is still young, as novelists go, and still growing in the
clarity of his vision, the force of his feeling and intellectual focus, the
precision and power of his means. They are the gifts with which he
promises to become one of the major world novelists of his generation.

Arno Karlen. *Nation.* May 1, 1967, p. 569

Juan Goytisolo reaches his top form in this well-knit novel [*Marks of
Identity*] and challenges the hegemony of Camilo José Cela in the field
of contemporary Spanish narrative. The lessons he learned from the
generation of Sarraute and Robbe-Grillet have been meaningfully utilized. The variety of narrative devices results in greater breadth and
depth. The consistently short prose units quicken the pace, afford a
variety of scenes and make a long book seem shorter. The inner monologues (sometimes the pronoun is *you,* as in Butor) probe to the innermost soul. The streams of consciousness recreate moods directly
without the impeding disciplines of formal prose. The flashbacks bring
into meaningful confrontation present and past, near and far. The intercalated police or surveillance reports illustrate well Dostoevsky's dic-
tum that an author must take pains not to suffer or empathize with his
characters. The excerpts from the sound track impounded by the Civil
Guard of Yeste make up a stifled, voiceless charge against Spanish
bureaucracy's treatment of the poor classes.

It is good that Americans now have access to this important novel
in English, thanks to the splendid version of prize-winning translator
Gregory Rabassa. For *Marks of Identity* should be read by an English-
speaking public too long lulled by the political pabulum of Gironella.
Despite the many Protestants and Freemasons in our population, America, more than any other foreign country, has helped to perpetuate in
power the dictator of Spain and his oligarchs ("the voracious enemies
of life") who have driven Alvaro and many fine Spaniards into exile.
Alvaro worries about the Pentagon, about "Cardinal Spellman's
friends," and about the American Sixth Fleet lying at anchor off
Barcelona. His last recorded thought is addressed to Americans as
much as anyone else: "Perhaps someone will understand later what
order you tried to resist and what your crime was."

Robert J. Clements. *SR.* June 28, 1969, pp. 37, 40

In spite of Goytisolo's insistence on a national novel, he, more than any
contemporary Spanish novelist, has experimented with most of the
twentieth-century novelistic techniques. Goytisolo employs an unusual

amount of dialogue to increase emotional response in his readers, along with social meanings and the reactions they evoke from various individuals. He deals with life rather than language, but his word patterns, images, and stylistic devices help set off his ideas. His dialogue gives an almost dramatic intensity at times to his reproduction of reality and imbues its traditional nakedness with a new and vital passion. His short outbursts, aside from following American style, project the theme of an indifferent universe in an absurd world where intelligence avails little. In projecting his reality he may employ an almost reportorial style; at times he uses cinematographic technique by presenting deeds instead of describing them and trying to inculcate emotion through a narrative rhythm which makes use of the long view, flashbacks, close-ups, and the like. He rejects narrow formulas and tight structures.

Since life is composed of many threads and does not run in a straight line, Goytisolo structures his novels to reflect this. In his use of time flow he creates a deliberate impression, much in the manner of Faulkner, to maintain the reader immersed in his story. He uses abrupt transitions of time from past to future, but he emphasizes constantly the present in which we live, a reality which is inextricably linked to a historical past and a straight flow, as though events past and future were contemporary. The treatment of time is his dominant concern. Thus he compresses the action of *Fiestas* into five weeks, that of *The Island* into eleven days, and that of *Marks of Identity* into three days, physical limitations which, nevertheless, allow for far-reaching and unlimited mental voyages into the time stream. . . .

Goytisolo impressionistically handles small groups of people whom he joins and abandons, whose lives intersect briefly, in parallel, contrapuntal plots. Often his characters seem devoid of real humanity and appear to be automatons, but all have relevance to the total structure. Personalities impinge on one another in shifting and kaleidoscopic patterns, but the disparate characters, strands of narrative, and structural complexities are usually untangled, if not completely resolved, at the end of the novel. In early novels he employs a flagrantly bad style, grammatical infelicities, faulty sentence structure, and an apparent lack of careful structural cement. This writing may be a deliberate obfuscation on the author's part, a distortion of the supposed reality he paints. Goytisolo realizes that detailed description may not always give the essence of life; he combines atmosphere, theme, nature, language, popular transcriptions of specialized vocabularies of beggars and others, along with lyrical offsets to the destroyed lives, passion, and blood, much as he combines fantasy with realism.

Kessel Schwartz. Juan Goytisolo (New York,
Twayne, 1970), pp. 33–34

Mention must be made of a remarkable change in the writing of one of the best-known purveyors of the social realism of the fifties and sixties,

Juan Goytisolo. Since his first novel, *Sleight of Hand* (1954), Goytisolo has expressed his angry and pessimistic opinions of the state of Spain in a series of novels and essays which have got him into considerable trouble with the censor. But by the mid-sixties, like many of his contemporaries, his work was betraying signs of weariness and despair. In 1966, however, he took the important step of publishing *Marks of Identity,* an extremely thoughtful and moving view of the Twenty-Five Years of Peace, but also a highly original and imaginative literary artefact which has indisputably re-established Goytisolo as a very gifted writer who has weathered the crisis through which the Spanish novel has passed. Unfortunately, the severely critical nature of his very personal account of contemporary Spain made it necessary for the novel to be published in Mexico, and has in all probability turned the author into a permanent exile. Indeed, his latest novel, *Vindication of Count Don Julián* (1970), also published in Mexico, takes the theme of exile as its main subject. Both *Marks of Identity* and *Vindication of Count Don Julián* are very fine novels, and in their imaginative scope and stylistic inventiveness they stand comparison with the best products of contemporary Spanish American fiction. Only the fact that the author of these two impressive books must now be considered a writer in exile deters one from supposing that the Spanish novel may be about to make substantial contributions to the literature of the world.

> G. G. Brown. *A Literary History of Spain: The Twentieth Century* (New York, Barnes & Noble, 1972), pp. 150–51

Count Julian [*Vindication of Count Don Julián*] is a shout from the heart and the belly of a modern Spaniard against the triumph of all that killed the promise of freedom and love and joy in Spain. It is a fierce answer to the Spanish decadence that began in the instant of Spanish glory. It is a mockery no other writer has dared make of the hollow imperial gesture by which Spain defeated herself, fatally cut herself off from the human, cultural and economic resources that fled with the expulsion of the Jews and the defeat of the Arabs. It is, at times, the caricature of a caricature: the fruitless energies that Spain, as appointed *defensor fides,* spent fighting against the Reformation: the paralysis and quarantine Spain imposed on herself against the diseases of modernity; the cult of appearances, honor, purity and orthodoxy and the verbal masks created to uphold appearances and give them a semblance of reality; the fading away of the Habsburg and Bourbon dynasties into insanity, homophilia, syphilis, frivolity and just plain idiocy. . . .

Count Julian is the most terrible attack against the oppressive forces of a nation that I have ever read. Nothing that black has written against white, or woman against man, or poor against rich, or son against father, reaches quite the peak of intense hatred and horror that Goytisolo achieves in this novel. That he does it with magnificent beauty and perfect craftsmanship only adds to the power of his invective against his "harsh homeland." It is quite a feat, and quite a risk, for the novelist works with words, yet he is conscious that "violence is mute."

Carlos Fuentes. *NYTBR*. May 5, 1974, pp. 5–7

In *The Undertow* and *End of the Fiesta* Juan Goytisolo, in a surprisingly systematic manner, has annihilated the traditional significance of the eve of San Juan [Midsummer's Eve] and has spread the destruction through broad segments of Spanish society, ranging from thieves and prostitutes to intellectuals of the upper class. Goytisolo's version of the holiday turns the traditional fulfillment into frustration, optimism into pessimism, exhilaration into stupor. Instead of laying the groundwork for a better future, the festival becomes the antechamber of failure and death. The aura of romanticism surrounding traditional Midsummer amorous experiences is transformed into an atmosphere of sordidness and vice. City rather than country settings dominate, fertility becomes barrenness, aphrodisiacs are replaced by depressants, excitement passes into boredom. The holiday gives nothing to the protagonists, even though its empty shell is still there, and the characters from habit go through the motions of celebration, expressing the traditional "Today is the feast of San Juan; let's celebrate it." The sacrificial victim dies, but in vain, San Juan dreams do not come true, and freedom is supplanted by repression. The bonfires in Goytisolo's novels are not purificatory, but are merely vestiges of ancient ceremonies which hold no significance in post-war Spain; their lights no longer signify gaiety, freedom, fulfillment, and love but only deepen through contrast the symbolic darkness and gloom in which they now burn.

Wilma Newberry. *REH*. Jan., 1975, pp. 62–63

[Goytisolo's] primary target [in *Vindication of Count Don Julián*] is language, where all the lies, horrors, and stupidities that have oppressed him have left their mark. Against this impalpable enemy he discharges most of his ferocity. It is the fittingly literary role of this moral catharsis. Here the attack cannot be external; it would have no meaning. It is internal; it smacks of sabotage, of the crafty disintegration of that language that has atrophied from submission to the past (academicism, purism), pompous, empty, esoteric, incapable of apprehending living reality with imagination and daring, or of creating it. . . .

Something that T. S. Eliot said in a famous essay about Baudelaire's satanism still remains to be said about this book: so much evil is suspect; when God is insulted with that kind of devotion it is almost as if he were being prayed to. The narrator of *Vindication of Count Don Julián* is far from having "cured" himself of Spain as he pretends to have done. He is embittered, tormented to the point of insanity, by his country, with which, to his chagrin, he feels viscerally identified: "conscious that the labyrinth is in you. . . ." There is not the slightest doubt: his anger is genuine; the iconoclastic insolence that courses through the veins of the book is sincere. But neither is there a doubt that such a devastating indignation can be whipped up only by something to which one feels close and about which one feels deeply. The book is a crime of passion, something like an enraged shooting by a jealous lover of a woman who has deceived him. It is an attempt at purification by fire; it is atrociously loving, not totally foreign to a certain utopia whose political projection has had, precisely in Spain, a footing without equal in Europe: anarchism. The statement of Bakunin—"The desire for destruction is at the same time a creative desire"—could serve perfectly as an epigraph to *Vindication of Count Don Julián*. It is also an undertaking of historical correction. So has it been understood by at least two Spanish readers—Jorge Semprún and José María Castellet—who scarcely having finished reading this book—the most despairing and the most moving of Juan Goytisolo's—hastened to suggest that these destructive pages be declared required reading in all the high schools of Spain.

Mario Vargas Llosa. In Gonzalo Sobejano et al., eds., *Juan Goytisolo* (Madrid, Espiral Fundamentos, 1975), pp. 171, 173†

Much like the great French novelist, Marcel Proust, in his *À la recherche du temps perdu,* Juan Goytisolo [in *Marks of Identity*] has successfully re-created the worlds of Barcelona and Paris with his unique alternation of action and reflection, between what is observed and what is thought in order to present an accurate portrait of reality of the worlds in which Álvaro moves.

Álvaro, like Marcel, is in search of his conscience, his marks of identity, his self. Álvaro is particularly concerned with the past (the Civil War and the ensuing years), while Marcel concentrates on his life in Paris during the early twentieth century. Both are susceptible to concrete stimuli to evoke memory. Álvaro looks at geography books, report cards, photos, past cards and other memorabilia and is receptive to their sensory stimuli. Álvaro's *Fefiñanes* liqueur and Marcel's linden tea and *petites madeleines* (cookies) produce an evocation of the past, an enquiry into the nature of time, into the trajectory of their lives, their physical and psychological identities and their futures. If I have drawn parallels between Goytisolo's novel and Proust's, it is because they are appropriate in theme. They are certainly not so in degree. Where Proust's monumental *À la recherche* is the product of a lifetime of work and thought, Goytisolo's is the work of a few short years of meditation and writing as he indicates on the novel's very last page. "Havana-Paris-St. Tropez-Tangier. Autumn 1962–Spring 1966." But to rank Goytisolo with Proust seems fitting and entirely compatible with the writer's view of life, and his burgeoning talent. Goytisolo's world embodies a kind of tough, masculine, brutal, amoral, aggressive, alienated, even corrupt mystique—unlike the Proustian vision, which is more feminine, subtle, dilettantish (but equally sadistic and corrupt). The comparison of Goytisolo's popular novel to Proust's immortal one should not be prolonged, but the parallel as drawn is obvious and should, I hope, emphasize Goytisolo's enormous talent. . . .

Marks of Identity is, undeniably the most powerfully vibrant, lyrically poetic, experimentally artistic, politically committed novel to come from a Spanish novelist in the last twenty-five years and it may be one of the greatest, second only to Cervantes' immortal *Don Quixote.* . . .

Whatever direction Goytisolo's novels take, his influence on other writers has already augured new insights from Spain's new novelists as well as other internationally popular novelists of Latin America and elsewhere. He continues to be one of the few creative Spanish novelists working within Europe, demonstrating, disseminating and exhorting the successes (and sometimes failures) of the Spanish New Wave novelists.

Ronald Schwartz. *Spain's New Wave Novelists*
(Metuchen, N.J., Scarecrow, 1976),
pp. 198–99, 201–2

Juan the Landless reminds me of a scene from one of Kingsley Amis's novels: an English family has just arrived in Portugal and while the parents struggle to get their luggage through customs their small children are spellbound by a 20-minute exhibition of hawking and spitting, performed by a Portuguese gentleman in a homburg hat and business suit.

Juan the Landless is a 268-page exhibition of homburg-hatted, business-suited hawking and spitting. Juan Goytisolo's literary passion will not suffer itself to be diluted or interrupted by anything so conventional as characters or plot, so that I can convey his subject matter only by making a statistical computation of the recurrence of certain themes. Chief among these, in a ration of perhaps 10 to 1, is the topic of toilets and defecation. I cannot tell you what the author means by it, for these references do not tend toward any conclusion. As far as I can make out, Mr. Goytisolo simply enjoys chortling over the fact of toilets and their use, much as small children do. . . .

Social conformity, in the person of "the Couple," inspires this scathing piece of satire: "the perfumed, snow-white purity of toothpaste emphasizes their natural harmony, face creams and electric razors contribute to their wellbeing. . . ."

The last section of *Juan the Landless* might easily pass for an old "Revolution of the Word" manifesto, penned by the indomitable Eugène Jolas in the pages of *transition* magazine. "Formal, abstract writing," straight from "the genesic fountain pen," is what contemporary fiction needs. This, one gathers, will purge the novel of people and enable us to give our full attention to their waste products. Don Quixote no longer tilts at windmills, but toilets.

Anatole Broyard. NYTBR. Sept. 18, 1977,
pp. 14, 48

Juan Goytisolo continues in *Makbara* his earlier explorations on traditional bourgeois twentieth-century consumerism and traditionalism. He also adds a stronger emphasis on languages and cultures of the Third World, more specifically Arabic in Morocco. Juan Goytisolo constructs a seemingly asystematic collage of intertextual references. He is a master of equivocation, of multiple meanings, of supreme verbal pyrotechnics. His parodies include sacred texts such as the Bible or profane ones from classical literature to contemporary moguls. His defiant tone reminds one of Charles Baudelaire, of Luis Cernuda, of Voltaire; his ironies of Miguel Cervantes. . . . Pop culture is also well represented in his text, the references ranging from popular hit songs to Walt Disney movies, and all kinds of advertising extravaganzas.

As usual in Juan Goytisolo, God, Country and Tradition—especially sexual taboos—are strongly castigated. Juan Goytisolo searches for truth by inverting the order of things, by subverting traditional modes of writing, of speaking, of viewing into cognition by the sheer strength of language. Once lost in his baroque forest of multilingual, universalist Spanish there is truly no exit. That is why his novel begins with a sort of primal scream and ends with the linguistic paradox of darkness, silence, as the author, the creator, stares at the blank page. Juan Goytisolo's novel is full of rage, of negativity, but also of poetry and of love. His destructiveness carries the seeds of liberation, the possibilities of moving from a Hell upward, perhaps not as high as a Paradiso, but certainly to a Purgatorio rendered more bearable by the understanding of the suffering of the world's pariahs, and of the confrontation of the reader with his soul.

As with Juan Goytisolo's last three works, *Makbara* runs the risk of being misunderstood by focusing on the parts rather than on the whole. It is a complex text which is sure to elicit contradictory readings. Nothing would please Juan Goytisolo more.

Joseph Schraibman. WLT. Spring, 1981, p. 281

When we read *Juan the Landless* we must assume a dual posture: first as recipients of a communication from the author we infer, that is as readers of the entire text, including everything that comes to us "between the lines"—the transcendent meanings we confer upon the text; and secondly as listeners of a speaker who addresses only himself, which is to say our role is that of an eavesdropper. We must identify as closely as possible with Álvaro Mendiola, assume his attitudes, share his perceptions, and experience his mental processes and emotions.

This is an action that both delights and frustrates us, because what he is writing originates within him as conscious thought; but to us it is always new information. What makes sense to him may appear cryptic to us. Since we are cast in a role we can never fully enact, our only recourse is to make ourselves receptive to the unfolding of the text by incorporating into the totality of our personal experience a new reality imbued with Álvaro's obsessions and bearing the stamp of his turn of mind, by sharing his discourse—the free flow of images that displace one another, objects that never establish a place for themselves, setting that is in flux, beings who appear and reappear in other manifestations. Nothing is stable, no world begins to take shape, nothing accumulates.

Esther W. Nelson. Symposium. Fall, 1981,
p. 258

There are many conflicts in Juan Goytisolo's linguistic enterprise. The Spanish author's search for his own identity in writing has caused the splitting of his self into a variety of entities. As Paul De Man points out, any ironic or parodic writer divides the linguistic self from the real self. *Juan the Landless* is a testimonial to De Man's distinction, for Juan Goytisolo has not found his true identity. He has instead confused the issue of the self by transforming himself into a multitude of selves on the written page. In the whole of the trilogy from *Marks of Identity* to *Juan the Landless,* one detects a view of writing not only as self-reproduction but also as psychoanalytic therapy, as a tool to re-form the self into an integrated unit. The final words of the trilogy, the declaration that the author-narrator no longer has a need to write, are a testimonial to the therapeutic nature of Juan Goytisolo's writing, as the Spanish words metamorphose into Arabic script. The last page, written wholly in Arabic, symbolizes Goytisolo's total estrangement from his pathological mother tongue. Yet in this final page there cannot be a metamorphosis from the neurotic to the sane self. Juan Goytisolo's wish to rid himself of his hated land is doomed. His attempt at verbal suicide has failed: he will continue to write, and he will continue to do so in Spanish. The neurotic self has not been killed and will reemerge with *Makbara.*

Michael Ugarte. Trilogy of Treason: An
Intertextual Study of Juan Goytisolo
(Columbia, University of Missouri Press, 1982),
p. 145

GUILLÉN, JORGE (1893–1984)

Cántico is an anthology, or perhaps, in some way, a final book: a sum of distinct poetic unities, without lyrical fusion or confusion, complete in its poetic unity. A book of poetry is either composed poem by poem, unified by multiplication, or is decomposed, divided into poetic unities that are added to each other without ever being multiplied. *Cántico* is a fervent and poetic integrated hymn, an aggregate of exclamations—the poet would say *olés*—to the constant miracle of creation, to the poetic newness of the universe. Each poem is one of exaltation, of joys. . . . As a result, we laugh like Democritus and do not cry like Heraclitus. As a result, [*Cántico*] represents a world apart for the senses, pure construction (the poet would say a "celestial mechanism")—a spiritual arrangement and harmony. In this sense, *Cántico* is an *essential* and *unique* book, as Mallarmé wanted a book to be. [1929]

José Bergamín. In Biruté Ciplijauskaité, ed.,
Jorge Guillén (Madrid, Taurus, 1975), p. 102†

With Señor Guillén . . . there are no bandits or bullfighters, and the verses are carefully wrought and polished. The typically Spanish is absent. Instead we find a very cultivated sensibility, influenced considerably by the great French poet, M. Paul Valéry. . . . His poems are records of momentary experience, translated through a fine and intelligent sensibility. As such the author's emotion of joy, say, or wonder, is recorded along with the phenomena described. So we often find notes of exclamation, and rather telegraphic, verbless sentences in his poems. These poems are a record of the extraordinary, and not related to our ordinary everyday experiences, or in any way a part of a picture of life as a whole. . . . In Señor Guillén we find continually praises of the present moment—the moment of the poem—in its isolation. . . . It is the experience in itself that matters, not its relation to other experiences.

Edward Meryon Wilson. *Bookman*. Sept., 1931,
pp. 288–89

The root of Guillén's poetry lies precisely in his enthusiasm for the world and for life. If this has not been recognized until now in all its truth, it is because enthusiasm is generally presented under guises very different from those in Guillén's poetry. Guillén's poetry jumps about freely and unbridled; it lives in overpowering disorder; it abandons itself to caprice and to wild spontaneity; it frequently ends up in boundless orgies, so much so that at times it turns into purely embarrassing gesticulation. What is odd about Guillén's poetry is that it has achieved what we would call a poetic ordering of enthusiasm. Wherever that sentiment was expressed in confusion, Guillén has made it clear. Wherever it poured out without bounds, he has set up boundaries. So great are the luminosity with which his enthusiasm is translated and the precision of the lines with which it is delimited that many do not see anything else in Guillén's poetry, and that is enough. His poetic attitude and vital enthusiasm have a remarkable similarity to the great American poet Whitman. The poetry of Whitman has a basis identical to Guillén's; rejoicing for all aspects of life in the world, exaltation of everything that is vital. [Dec., 1935]

Pedro Salinas. *Ensayos completos de Pedro Salinas* (Madrid, Taurus, 1983), *I*, p. 150†

The art of Jorge Guillén is for only a minority of readers: it will never be largely popular, although it does not contain little-used words or recondite allusions only understandable by constant reference to the dictionary or to the encyclopedia. In order to interpret Góngora, that amazing prodigy of the seventeenth century, his contemporaries, just as we do today, found necessary all their erudition and sagacity. But the poetry of Guillén does not radiate with references to anything found outside of itself. Instead it plumbs its own depths to the springs of its poetic creation.

Guillén's lyrical expressions are hardly accessible for the reader little versed in the art of modern poetry. Sometimes the difficulty in understanding poems resides in their words or in their subject matter. But in the work of Guillén, as in all of the most exquisite contemporary lyrics, the subject matter is at a minimum; there are neither events nor external references; indeed, there is scarcely anything having reference to that world in which the reader lives. The difficulty, then, is not in the subject matter or in the words themselves but instead in the very poetic process of his poetry which exhibits itself in a marvellous nudity, only protected by itself.

Américo Castro. Introduction to Frances Avery Pleak, *The Poetry of Jorge Guillén* (Princeton, N.J., Princeton University Press, 1942), pp. xii–xiii

Certain elements of *Cántico* are deeply involved in a mathematical conception of the poetic world. Guillén is concerned with aspects more than with totalitarian feelings. And within the aspect of things, the poet observes with a sense of dimension, of volume, of density in relation to limited units of space. In this his poetry can be likened to sculpture rather than canvas, but touched with the quality of a living warmth like that which Rodin incorporates in his marble. Guillén is enthralled with the mystery of substance and mass, the actual dimensional existence of things in space. The poetic world of Guillén is not a vague diaphanous world remotely connected with actuality. It is vitally concerned with material reality. The imagination of Guillén does not wander off in an atmosphere detached from things, nor does it live in retrospect and remembrance. It does not rely upon remote associations, shifting allusions, disordered griefs, phantasms, floating fag-ends of memory. The abstraction of his poetry is not tied to abstract thought, but, on the contrary, is centered in the very substance of concrete reality in the moment of its most perfect being. The resultant abstraction is that of the poet's fancy in direct contact with the living reality and not based upon a fundamental abstraction of spirit.

Frances Avery Pleak. The Poetry of Jorge Guillén (Princeton, N.J., Princeton University Press, 1942), p. 49

It is interesting to examine the form of *Cántico* in its relation to the poet's world. Guillén, a master craftsman in the handling of words, has produced an exquisite style. . . . Not only are the content and style of *Cántico* inseparable, but the one is actually symbolic of the other. As the elements of Guillén's poetic world are familiar and concrete, with a very definite form, so the poet's words are simple and commonplace, and have the same concreteness; and his poems have the same rigorous form, often very complicated in rhyme and meter but always clear and sharp in outline. Form is being; the emergence of form from chaos is the daily process of creation; and this applies as well to the creation of a poem, which emerges from the chaos and confusion of vague thoughts as it acquires greater clarity of outline, more reality. . . .

The harmony between poet and universe is paralleled by the harmony of Guillén's verse. . . . The intense emotion felt in being is reflected in the intensity of style of all of *Cántico;* indeed we may well say that Guillén uses as his poetic method the intensification of reality. And finally, by eliminating all impure elements from his poetry, as the poet in life rejects sorrow and evil, by clinging to his intuition of beauty, by creating his own little island of peace, his poetic world, Guillén pursues his single aim: the expression of his joy in reality and life.

Ruth Whittredge. RR. April, 1948, pp. 144–45

It seldom happens that a work of twentieth century poetry is, like Jorge Guillén's, a song of praise and nothing else. Here everything is played in a major key, everything exults and rejoices in the sun. Here are no dissonances, no neuroses, no "flowers of evil." The inconceivably lofty works are glorious as on the first of days. Some readers will first have to accustom their eyes to these cataracts of light. Here is a region without tragedy, without bitterness, without accusation. . . .

Jorge Guillén's affirmation of being . . . is sole and singular in modern literature. [Charles] Maurras once decreed that "poetry is ontology." Should this statement be correct, Guillén's poetry would be a striking example of it. But fortunately it is as independent of every philosophy as it is of every passing intellectual fashion. Not even the Essentialism that is currently being brewed on the left bank of the Seine, now that Existentialism has been consumed, will be able to change that. The poetry of Guillén is self-sufficient utterance. It needs no philosophical commentary, although it might well serve the philosopher as a text for his meditations. [1951]

Ernst Robert Curtius. *Critical Essays on
European Literature* (Princeton, N.J., Princeton
University Press, 1973), pp. 430–32

Jorge Guillén knows this time of ours as St.-John Perse knows it and as [Nikos] Kazantzakis knew it. He belongs to the generation of the two wars, and—because he is a Spaniard—of that third war, too, which changed the first into the second. Like St.-John Perse, he has lived the life of exile which so many of our contemporaries lived and live. But though he is a man of this time in the historical sense—all the historical senses—he is not a man of the time so many of our critics and philosophers have described to us. He knows the dark, yes. "My certainty is founded in the dark." But the dark that Guillén knows is anything but the dark of hopelessness and despair. . . .

Guillén is a poet of this time—a great poet of this time. But he is a poet, nevertheless, who has devoted his whole life to the writing of a single book, which has grown slowly from seventy-five poems in 1928 to three hundred and thirty-four in 1950—a single book, of which the title is *Cántico* and the theme praise. And what does he praise?

Joy of joys: the soul beneath the skin.

Posterity, if it comes upon the great resounding Yes of *Cántico* among the tumbled fragments of our time, will not believe that No was all we had to answer to the world.

Archibald MacLeish. *At*. Jan., 1961, p. 128

The elevation of subject matter in *Cántico* and the purity of its style are reminiscent of [Paul] Valéry, whom Guillén knew very well in Paris. The French and the Spanish poets were united in their life-long exploration of the properties of language and the forms of poetry. The somewhat forced impertinences of Valéry in his comments on the "manufacture" of poetry are offset by Guillén's more classical view of poetry as "creation." But they are poets of a single unified work. *Charmes* and *Cántico* are among the richest legacies of 20th century world poetry. . . .

Cántico has a majesty and a candor of tone which are remarkably sustained throughout the work. Guillén's voice is as familiar with the outer aspects of reality as it is with the serious secrets of his inner life. What is communicated from this inner life is at all times clothed with chaste modesty. In the choice of his words, in the sound effects of his lines, he is a skilled craftsman, a *savant,* a technician able to produce a line of startling bareness and directness, as well as a line of lofty complex thought. There is never in his verse any break with the laws of language, never any deliberate surrealistic effects. Poetry is steadfastly a language which speaks. Poetry is a voice for Jorge Guillén.

Wallace Fowlie. *Poetry.* Jan., 1962, p. 245

Above all, *Cántico* has an overarching coherence found rarely in modern poetry. It is the kind of coherence that gives Valéry, Eliot and Wallace Stevens their stature, and the lack of which makes Pound's *Cantos* fail. It is partly a matter of assurance, partly of pertinacity. However widely the poems range, however tentatively they explore and experiment, they always seem to be circling round the same clear centre, like Donne's famous compasses. That centre is the poet's own creative consciousness, which each poem at once expands and defines. Although the subjects are rarefied—Guillén is a peculiarly philosophical poet—you are always left with a sense of the man as he is—with, in his own words, "reality, not realism."

A. Alvarez. *Observer.* April 18, 1965, p. 26

Guillén's word is not suspended above the abyss. It knows the intoxication of enthusiasm, not the vertigo of the void. The earth that sustains his word is this earth we tread every day, "prodigious, not magical"; a marvel that physics explains in a formula and the poet welcomes with an exclamation. To have his feet firmly on the ground is a reality that enraptures the poet; I will say, moreover, that flight also exhilarates him, for the same reason: the leap is no less real than gravity. He is not a realistic poet; his theme is reality. A reality that custom, lack of imagination, or fear (nothing frightens us so much as reality) prevents us from seeing; when we do see it, its abundance alternately fascinates and annihilates us. *Abundance,* Guillén underlines, not beauty. Abundance of being: things are what they are and for that reason they are exemplary. On the other hand, man is not what he is. Guillén knows that, and thus *Cántico* is not a hymn to man: it is the praise man makes to the world, praise from the being who knows he is nothing to the being filled with being. The cloud, the girl, the poplar, the automobile, the horse— all are presences that enchant him. They are the gifts of being, the gifts life gives us. Poet of presence. Guillén sings of the present. . . . The now in which all presences unfold is a point of convergence; the unity of being is dispersed in time; its dispersion is concentrated in the instant. The present is the point of view of unity, the instantaneous clarity that reveals it. *Cántico* is a sentient ontology. . . .

Guillén is a great poet because of the perfection of his creations, not because of the influence he exercised. His poems are true poems: verbal objects closed upon themselves, animated by a cordial and spiritual force. That force is called enthusiasm. Its other name: inspiration. And something more: fidelity, faith in the world and in the word. The world of the word as much as the word of the world: *Cántico.* Confronting the spectacle of the universe—not the spectacle of his-

tory—Guillén once said: *The world is well made* . . . Confronting his
work, one need only repeat those words. [1965]

Octavio Paz. *The Siren and the Seashell and
Other Essays on Poets and Poetry* (Austin,
University of Texas Press, 1976), pp. 157, 160

Few systems of poetics are more open, and at the same time more
secret, than that of Jorge Guillén. Few are more simply and directly
open to the world (though not precisely to our glance, unaccustomed to
perceiving) and nevertheless more hidden from the scrutiny of that
world. Infinitely close to things, infinitely distant. Untenable paradox
or insoluble dichotomy? And, even so, no work goes farther, continues
better; there are few works in which a profound unity appears more
dense and indivisible. To reflect on Jorge Guillén's poetic language is to
reflect through that language upon the world; and without doubt it is in
this very mediation that we find joined the apparently divergent paths
of a wholly concrete vision (I mean, centered exclusively on the concrete) and a vision which is wholly mental (that is, exclusively determined through mental re-creation). It appears from the outset that, with
Guillén, the image cannot be in any sense the banal interpreter between
reality and thought; still less is to be confused with any suggestive
description of reality. Jorge Guillén, in fact, never describes. It is not all
through allusion that he evokes or invokes reality, and he never accords
it the facility of any symbolic transference. He gives it as itself for what
it is, and his poems cite it endlessly under its most diverse and sensitive
aspects. He turns toward the external world a patient gaze, tirelessly
searching. Not to draw up a geographic map or inventory of the real,
but rather a mental atlas where reality finds itself caught in the trap of
prismatic vision, embodying and recreating what is brought to it.
Things told with an apparently perfect objectivity thus take on the
progressively living form, captured now by the poet's visual sensitivity,
of the inexpressible. We come here to the heart of the paradox: vision
does not reveal things, with whatever contained but violent delight, so
much as it reveals the missing enchantment of them, or, more often,
missing from the instant when they were deprived of their connection
with their likeness, on the one hand, and with him who perceived them,
on the other. The relations that unify them may appear fortuitous or
arbitrary under the imperative of a vision which imposes them from the
outside; it is nothing of the sort, and here we touch on what may well be
called the metaphysic of Jorge Guillén, the conviction that a dynamic
underlying the things of this world regulates their forms as much as
does the place of their arising. [Winter, 1968]

Fernand Verhesen. In Ivar Ivask and Juan
Marichal, eds., *Luminous Reality: The Poetry of
Jorge Guillén* (Norman, University of
Oklahoma Press, 1969), pp. 93–94

Guillén approaches testimonies lent by other poets, assimilates them, and obliquely incorporates them into his own work. Although these homages do not offer the reader the whole universe, they do provide for him a limitless space—open and resounding with a thousand chimes, where it is possible to fly in peaceful safety.

This is the central idea in Jorge Guillén: fly, fly, fly on wings of joy through existence, assured of being completely alive and convinced that life is for life itself and for hope. There is no Dionysiac drunkenness but, rather, a brilliant drunkenness, an exaltation produced by the realization that life is possible. In and of itself life has value; it has meaning and fulfills itself beautifully in the present, in the presents, in the continuity of existence. Several years ago Dámaso Alonso pointed out the determining, joyful nature of song, especially of Guillén's *Cántico*. It is this aspect which causes the poet to march countercurrent, in countertime. *Homage* continues in the same direction taken by *Cántico;* it is a book of completed experiences and spiritual and intellectual vigor. It negates chronological time and in the negation firmly maintains its identity; it is a work of ascendant, crowning maturity. Rising to the placid waters of love and serenity that constitute the essence of *Homage,* one discovers the nearly hundred pages so aptly entitled "The Center." Here the reader finds . . . the substantiation of Guillén's characteristic lucidity.

Ricardo Gullón. In Ivar Ivask and Juan
Marichal, eds., *Luminous Reality: The Poetry of*
Jorge Guillén (Norman, University of
Oklahoma Press, 1969), pp. 115–16

Guillén's hesitancy or caution is significant for it was to result in a first volume, *Cántico* (1928), that was relatively slim, composed entirely of short, intensely worked poems. His initial creative disposition may be described as guarded rather than precocious, but this is not to say, as some did, that he lacked inspiration; a criticism which has since been completely refuted by the pertinacious development of his life's work towards *Our Air*. What Guillén's early poems indicate, above all, is a scrupulous care on the part of the poet, an ideal of perfection that is apparent both in a thematic context and in the business of making poems. It may have been natural for a young poet to begin by trying to master short poetic forms before embarking upon supposedly major concerns, but in Guillén's case we must also remember the literary spirit of his formative years when Pound's Imagism and especially the theories of *poésie pure* [pure poetry] were in the air.

Robert G. Havard. *BHS*. April, 1971, p. 111

Silence fills the space and experience of *Our Air;* it figures as an explicit presence in more than two hundred poems. Thus, there is hardly a single aspect of Guillén's poetic vision which does not involve the action and vibrancy of concrete silence. Its diverse contexts and perspectives give it a unique artistic and human reality. Guillén has created a world in which silence has life, and in which the full range of existence feels through silence.

Conditions of silence support peak moments: in harmonious and psychic vitality silence promotes man's alliance with the world, and the experience of its sounds and texture expands awareness and sensitivity. In its most stunning resonances, silence mediates creative and intellectual insight; it bridges the distance between the real and the ideal. But just as the whole design of *Cántico, Outcry,* and *Homage* implies the polarity of plenitude and emptiness, the contexts of silence also include negative overtones. In contrast to love's shared silence, to the new life it generates, there is exposure to violence, alienation, and loss. Negative contexts of silence sharpen the pain of human conflict. Finally, the metaphysical roots of silence deepen its reality in *Our Air.* On one level, the fusion of silence with time, change, and creation gives it philosophical context; yet in another sense, the metaphorical associations with life and death humanize its paradoxical simplicity.

The lush weave of Guillén's poetry is so consistent that a single thread may carry the density of the artistic whole. And if the contexts of silence in *Cántico, Outcry,* and *Homage* reflect the poetic unity of *Our Air,* will this not offer us criteria for the discovery and evaluation of other thematic cores? The unusual symbiosis of silence and esthetics is one important constant which defines Guillén's creative achievement. Others, which may apply to different motifs in *Our Air,* are the poetic concretization of the intangible and its further projection to the metaphysical; the pervasive quality of silence in life; its role as a mediator in certain key human activities, such as creativity; and its reach to encompass polarized opposites.

Florence L. Yudin. *The Vibrant Silence in
Jorge Guillén's "Aire nuestro"* (Chapel Hill,
University of North Carolina Press, 1974),
pp. 74–75

Despite an early prejudice against an overemphasized intellectual tendency in his poetry, Jorge Guillén has gradually achieved recognition as one of the greatest poets of the twentieth century. From the beginning Guillén firmly situated his being in a reality dependent upon the persons and things of this world for fulfillment, and he has always written poetry in vital affirmation of that existence. For him, being is living in time and place in intimate contact with the world: life as its own justification. This is, in the awesome phrase of our century, "phenomenological existentialism," but Guillén's glory is that his poetry of luminous reality and radiation and affirmation creates this world in convincing unity and imperishable form. His *Cántico,* one of the half-dozen best books of poetry in Spanish literature, preserves in original form the sound, nuance, and manner of the "slender" or pure poetry of our century, along with an impressive variety of traditional forms. Even his *Homage* is unique among books of this type of poetry "on the margin." Certainly Guillén can be (and he has been) censured for not being a popular poet; but what major poet's poetry has ever been really popular? Like Jiménez in this, Guillén courted the "immense minority," that is, the diligent reader willing to educate himself in poetry. His major competitor in this generation, García Lorca himself had to confess that his poetry was grossly misunderstood. Guillén is a noble poet whose best poetry is written in time and place, yet timeless in form and theme, and surely it will preserve its freshness and vitality as long as Spanish is a living language.

Carl W. Cobb. *Contemporary Spanish Poetry (1898–1963)* (Boston, Twayne, 1976), p. 93

Reading Jorge Guillén's poetry is always a strange experience. Jorge Guillén doesn't tell—he *shows*. The poet places us in an objective world, drawn with an almost theatrical architecture, with bodily bulk, and subjects us to the painstaking observation of the lines, surfaces, and relationships of matter, including his own poetic ego as a real thing, so that we can suddenly intuit the essence of this bright, shimmering reality. The word turns into a pure verbal indicator, almost into a scientific instrument for refining and adjusting its meaning to the purpose it is made to fulfill. . . . Just as [Jorge Luis] Borges' labyrinths make up the theme and form of the story that contains them, Jorge Guillén's poems in their development show the poetic idea that gives birth to them. In a word, the poem becomes a metaphor; and all of *Cántico* turns into a myth of creation continually renewed. . . . Myth that is performed, like a playlet, before our eyes. To read is to attend a verbal ritual that makes us participate in the moment of creation itself.

Rubén Benítez. *HR*. Winter, 1981, pp. 29–30

Jorge Guillén's essential unity of vision, combined with a delicate and superbly controlled poetic style, endow the poet with a rare permanence that is increasingly appreciated by readers of his work. Ironically, the poet who was once labeled as being too "cold" and "intellectual" to be of much interest is today seen to have created works of genuinely timeless value, while many works of his contemporaries now appear as relics of a bygone period in aesthetic experimentation. Esteem for Jorge Guillén's litany to life's best and most enduring aspirations and realizations will surely increase, as readers continue to appreciate how unfettered by time, place, and circumstance his poetry really is. By his "rise to the occasion" as a universal poet, he has created an art that transcends national and temporal limitations.

Another guarantee of the enduring worth and acceptance of Jorge Guillén's work is his undaunted unfailing "yes" to the great world around us. The poet's delight with the gifts of life, love, and the grandeur of the enveloping macrocosm make his hymnal of affirmation seem forever fresh and newly charged with vitality.

G. Grant MacCurdy. *Jorge Guillén* (Boston, Twayne, 1982), p. 162

HERNÁNDEZ, MIGUEL (1910–1942)

I think about you [Miguel Hernández] often because I know you're suffering in that circle of literary pigs, and it hurts me to see your energy, so full of sunlight, fenced in and throwing itself against the walls.

But you'll learn that way. You'll learn to keep a grip on yourself in that fierce training life is putting you through. [*Knowledgeable about Moons*] stands deep in silence, like all first books, like my first, which had so much delight and strength. Write, read, study, FIGHT! Don't be vain about your work. Your book is strong, it has many interesting things, and to eyes that can see makes clear *the passion of man,* although, as you say, it doesn't have any more *cojones* than those of most of the established poets. Take it easy. Europe's most beautiful poetry is being written in Spain today. But, at the same time, people are not fair. *Knowledgeable about Moons* doesn't deserve that stupid silence. No. It deserves the attention and encouragement and love of good people. You have that and will go on having it because you have the blood of a poet and even when you protest in your letter you show, in the middle of savage things (that I like), the gentleness of your heart, that is so full of pain and light.

I wish you'd get rid of your obsession, that mood of the misunderstood poet, for another more generous, public-minded obsession. Write to me. I want to talk to some friends and see if they'll take an interest in *Knowledgeable about Moons.* [1933]

Federico García Lorca. Sixties. Spring, 1967,
p. 2

Truth against lie, honor against vengeance, the extraordinary poet of Orihuela, Miguel Hernández, published in the last number of *Revista de Occidente,* a wild elegy on the death of Ramón Sigé [his best friend] and six disconcerting sonnets. All friends of "pure poetry" must seek out and read these poems that are so alive. It is true, they have an appearance of being Quevedo-like [seventeenth-century Spanish writer and satirist], of having a pure Spanish heritage. But the harsh, tremendous beauty of his deep-rooted heart bursts open the package and overflows like elemental, naked Nature. This is exceptional in poetry— who can get excited like this with such clarity all the time! Let this voice, this accent, this young breath of Spain not be lost . . . in "Catholicism," in the marshes. [Feb. 23, 1936]

Juan Ramón Jiménez. Quoted in María de
Gracia Ifach, *Miguel Hernández, rayo que no
cesa* (Barcelona, Plaza y Janés, 1975), p. 159†

Yes, Miguel came from the earth, natural, like an immense seed that has been scooped out of the ground and placed on the soil. And his poetry never lost this feeling, the sense of a spirit and body that had come from the clay. . . .

In 1936, his first book, *The Lightning That Never Stops,* came from Manuel Altolaguirre's printing press. A genuine lightning bolt with the clear, revealing light of a natural, wise poet. Miraculous lightning, for one thought of it in reverse, leaping out of a stone towards the sky, escaping with its light from that earthy being, awkward and dark.

And July 18, 1936 [the date of the outbreak of the Spanish Civil War], also was like lightning—it uprooted, swayed, and blinded him until it opened his eyes. It was a day of challenge and reply, of attack by the dirtiest and lowest side of Spain against its noblest and most promising side. An eye-opening date. At that moment Miguel saw his roots better than ever, he understood as he never had that he was clay. . . .

And so, then, it was to the war, to his life and contact—"bleeding, in trenches and hospitals"—with those heroic people, alive and simple as wheat, that Miguel Hernández owed the whole discovery of himself, the complete illumination of his native, true self. He finally tore out of himself, in his *Wind of the People,* a crushing landslide of epic and lyric things, poems of head-on clash and follow-through, of gnashing of teeth and pleading cries, rage, weeping, tenderness, care. Everything that was trembling in him was now interwoven with his profound roots.

But now, after having made his voice heard, like a happy beanfield in the wind, after having been imprisoned, beaten, his chest punished until it hemorrhaged through concentration camps and dungeons, once more Miguel, a discouraged Miguel, returned to the earth, to the black, final hole. . . .

Meanwhile, we must let some serious boy from Miguel's own foothills mourn for him on a reed-flute with such powerful sorrow that all the scattered flocks will turn for the green ground of the day of hope sure to come. [1945]

Rafael Alberti. In Timothy Baland and Hardie
St. Martin, eds., *Miguel Hernández and Blas de
Otero: Selected Poems* (Boston, Beacon, 1972),
pp. 75–77

After the war, in the three years of his imprisonment, shut away from his beloved wife, and from their son whom he had never seen, Hernández wrote with a stoicism that had been absent from those earlier poems in which he had half-glimpsed his end. Having mastered all the traditional styles during his fêted apprenticeship, he now wrote in his solitude with a simplicity that in some poems recalls that of the old song-books, in others strikes images as telling as those of the ultraists [Spanish avant-garde poets] yet founded on an experience which was no longer literary. The last, prison years of his life yielded a group of compassionate poems that look back on the purposeless cruelties of the war, a *Song-book and Ballad Book of Absences* that dwells on his absence from his wife and son, and a handful of final poems that recapture all his old vigour and some of his old complexity. For him this time was not one of bitterness or of self-pity, but principally of this absence of all that he loved, and of all expectation of a future. . . .

A few of his sixty-three poems of absence are no more than frag-ments. Others are hideous with the news of the moment—that his child has nothing to eat but bread and onions. But the last poems of all, more sustained, graver, and more daring in their imagery than the *Songbook,* develop once more the theme of the bull predestined to slaughter, speaking now of his mortal wound not as something foreshadowed in the future but as the mouth through which his life's blood is pouring away.

Yet such is Hernández' fundamental vigour that his final note is one of hope, based it would seem on no religious belief. He lived so fully, so generously, so violently perhaps, that he could not think of death as the end. . . .

Hernández' hope, his valour, his simplicity, his feeling for common experiences, for common things, and for people in the mass—the "immense majority"—inform the whole of the poetry that has followed him. Though dead six years, it was he, and not the major living influ-ences—Alberti, Neruda, and Luis Cernuda—not even the active god-father of the new poets, Vicente Aleixandre, that led the poetic revival of 1948.

J. M. Cohen. Encounter. Feb., 1959, p. 46

Starting with *The Lightning That Never Stops,* [Miguel Hernández's] poetic world begins to mature, it organizes and elevates itself until it forms a cosmos of well-structured thought. The book opens with a broad outline of the great existential problem of Miguel Hernández in all its complex and profound contradictoriness of forces: life always tragically threatened. . . .

If we peruse the entire oeuvre of Miguel Hernández in search of the guiding idea and the central insight of his cosmovision, we will see how no thought surpasses this one in importance, in depth, and in the unifying force of his entire work. Life—the central theme of all poetry and art—is the great problem that surprises and makes our poet tremble: one's own life as an existential problem and life in general, the great mystery of life in the world. From the time Miguel Hernández met his future wife, love becomes poetry; the life of one who is in love becomes the material for art. Miguel Hernández takes his own life with all its love and pain and transforms it into poetry. That life, to which he so frenetically held on lest it slip through his hands, is the key to his art. From this emerge the shuddering and commotion, the pained passion that crisscrosses his work.

Juan Cano Ballesta. *La poesía de Miguel*
Hernández (Madrid, Gredos, 1962), pp. 63–64†

Miguel Hernández was a shepherd boy, a goatherd. The only education he got was from the priest of the village. It was wonderful because that library of the church had the classics—nobody had read the books in that library for centuries! Miguel discovered them and out of the poetry of the Golden Age he made all by himself a really beautiful language, very strong, completely classic. He is a great master of language. Hernández as a boy came to Madrid in 1934 directly to me, from Orihuela, his village. . . .

I printed his poems—not his very first—but those ones that made the revolution in himself. I must note that he had been doing a lot of reading in my *Residence on Earth,* which was published just at that time. And that reading changed his stiff composition, his classical composition, and gave him much more freedom. The fear that he had—the ice was broken and then he became freer and freer and he became a wonderful poet. Don't forget that he was only a young man when he died. [June 12, 1966]

Pablo Neruda. In Timothy Baland and Hardie
St. Martin, eds., *Miguel Hernández and Blas de*
Otero: Selected Poems (Boston, Beacon, 1972),
pp. 38–39

We all know that when poets, caught in adverse circumstances, write false and sticky poems, these poems remain outside their truly important work. Miguel Hernández, on the other hand, totally immersed in the events taking place around him, wrote his very best poems then. The timeliness of Miguel Hernández today comes not only from the esthetic qualities of his poetry—those qualities Juan Ramón Jiménez noticed and hailed when Miguel was just beginning—but also from the way in which Miguel incorporates reality into his poems, revolutionizing the concept of poetry even in his own time.

Miguel Hernández has transformed our poetry precisely because he was a poet who always spoke, as the Gospels say, "verily, verily." If today his poetry continues as the dominant influence on the new Spanish poets, it is because he knew how to take over the real. He knew how to take over into his poetry the reality of the moment, which, paradoxically, lasts longer than the "nontemporal" poetry still written by incompetents who turn their backs on the world in which they live. And if the permanence of Miguel's poetry owes itself, as the defenders of the purity and refinement of "Eternal" poetry would say, to the esthetic quality of his work, it is also true that this quality is not merely a result of but rather essential to his way of conceiving poetry, deep in the insides of what is real. [1967]

Gabriel Celaya. In Timothy Baland and Hardie
St. Martin, eds., *Miguel Hernández and Blas de
Otero: Selected Poems* (Boston, Beacon, 1972),
p. 74

Like Aleixandre, who seeks to identify with the animal and vegetable kingdoms, Hernández exclaims in a mixture of existential despair, tenderness and violence, "I am called clay, although they call me Miguel." *Wind of the People,* 1937, dedicated to Aleixandre, vital poems about the Civil War, are genuinely patriotic in their acknowledgement of poverty and pain which must clear the path for future freedom. Hernández insists that it is the little man, the representative of the people, who offers the best hope for that future freedom. Along with descriptions of the Castilian landscape and the exuberant fertility of beautiful Alicante, in his poetry the constant note is one of nobility, passion, which makes one cry and rage at man's inhumanity to man, and tenderness toward the poor of Spain and the world. *Man in Ambush,* 1939, portrays a Spain of despair and sacrificed youth. Sorrow and death prevail. In much of his other poetry he exudes the same note of personal passion, tormented and fatal love, and finally he reveals the sufferings of his imprisonment, the intimate diary of a solitary soul who feels himself close to death.

Hernández restored to Spanish poetry the eclogue, without its insipid qualities. As he talks of love, nature and shepherds, his own sweat and hard work as a youth are everywhere apparent, for the poet knows the earth and loves it. He uses a variety of meters, popular and traditional poetry, fusing the simple and the baroque with his own burning passionate voice full of tragic beauty. In his spontaneous poetry, above all, he insists always on humanity and the necessity to achieve mankind's potential. A poet of the earth, he was a creative artist of extraordinary force and originality.

Kessel Schwartz. *Vicente Aleixandre* (New
York, Twayne, 1970), p. 27

Hernández was writing poems like a whirlwind: several were printed on postcards and circulated in the army. *Wind of the People,* his first book of war poems, came out in 1937. Strong, passionate, and masculine, these poems embody the feeling of common humanity and struggle that linked all classes on the Republican side.

Between 1937 and 1939, Miguel put together *Man in Ambush*. In each poem in this book the war hits home deeper. Hernández writes about love-letters without owners, about railroad boxcars full of the wounded. He writes "thinking of freedom." Sober and brooding, the book details the grief and tragedy of Spain. Two centuries [sic] after Goya, Miguel Hernández etched once again the disasters of war in poems bordered with the dark color of blood and silenced longings. . . .

Despite everything, poems came—not in a torrent as before, but one by one, like drops of alchemized blood. The poems of *Songbook and Ballad Book of Absences* take on the willowy grace and quieter passion of a man facing death. Yet it is tenderness, not despair, that dominates the book. Out of the isolation and joylessness of prison, Hernández created pine cones of poems—compressed, resinous, fragrant: poems that haunt and are able to move. . . .

In the ten years he wrote poems, Hernández had already created a poetry of immense range. Yet even with *Songbook* he was not done. His *Last Poems* (like *Songbook* and *Man in Ambush*, never published in book form in his lifetime) are filled with something incredibly pure, a kind of light-giving darkness. As always, Hernández wrote from inside of things. He wrote love poems from inside; war poems from the trenches; prison poems when he lived off memory alone. And finally, in *Last Poems*, he gives us poems whose sources "lean more and more into darkness," poems from inside the death mask, from the inner side of the grave.

Timothy Baland. Introduction to *Miguel*
Hernández and Blas de Otero: Selected Poems
(Boston, Beacon, 1972), pp. 6–8

Hernández never quite loses his innocence and his hope. Only towards the end . . . when the poet is dying in jail . . . despair seems to engulf him. Yet he longs to escape into the happy unconsciousness of childhood, hopes also his own son will avoid becoming conscious of the cruelty and oppression surrounding him. "Don't even know what happens or what goes on": the pain had become unendurable, the poet needed a moment of respite. Yet the greatness of Hernández, and that of Auden, is based partly on the fact that each one of them tried to make his readers fully aware of what was going on.

Life continually lashes out at Hernández in cruel and rapid blows; there isn't time, no time to resist elastically, to assimilate the circumstances, to adapt and be able to smile again. There isn't time. This is, precisely, the anguished message. And time is precisely what superabounds *before* Hernández: it is in excess to the point where the poet can stop, morosely, and, reflecting—Machado, Juan Ramón Jiménez— try to grasp the essence of time: try to discover what time means. But in the decade of the Thirties everything accelerates. . . .

Love, life, death, sexuality, liberty. These are Miguel's compass points. Sex is a weapon, it must act to penetrate into history, to fashion a cleaner future for the children we dream about; sensuality has a dimension that goes far beyond concrete and subjective—always egotistical—experience; Góngora would not perhaps have been able to foresee the future of sensuality; but in any case, Miguel Hernández does so for him; it is so handled that sensations may vibrate like a chord expanding indefinitely, limitlessly: the world is written in cipher. . . . But the key which opens the secret doors is not amusement, pleasure or play; it is suffering. And suffering and poetry tend increasingly to merge for Miguel.

Manuel Durán. In Jaime Ferrán and Daniel P.
Testa, eds., *Spanish Writers of 1936: Crisis and
Commitment in the Poetry of the Thirties and
Forties* (London, Támesis, 1973), p. 79

The theater of Miguel Hernández is in principle a faithful document of a tragic period in our recent history. The schematic nature of his characters and the limitations of the operant reality in Hernández's works—above all in *Sons of Stone* and *The Shepherd of Death*—have been criticized, but it proves to be misguided to demand psychological subtleties in moments when halfway measures won't do, when the writer must opt for a commitment in a particular direction. Miguel Hernández wrote plays—and poetry—that circumstances and the historical moment demanded of him, and his works will remain completely valid as long as these circumstances repeat themselves. "When we tire," he wrote, "of war . . . you will see me perform theater that will be the very life of Spain, cleanly taken from her trenches, her streets, her fields, and her walls." Unfortunately, he never got to write that kind of theater, but he left us a sample of his purified humanity in an ideological and aesthetic trajectory that goes from an imitation of Calderón de la Barca to the profound encounter of his voice with the very soul of the people. And on the way, there was a serious and useful attempt to renovate out theater along the highly popular lines of Lope de Vega at his best.

Jaime Pérez Montaner. *RO*. Oct.–Dec., 1974, p. 105†

Love is the quintessential theme of [Hernández's last] period. In the early poems it is a physical and spiritual love for his wife, pregnant with his child; then for his first son. In the *Songbook and Ballad Book of Absences* this familiar love undergoes a transmutation corresponding to Hernández's imprisonment and separation from his loved ones: love becomes a remembered, an almost abstract, emotion. Hernández's love for his second son partakes of this abstraction, for he knows the child almost solely through pictures and Josefina's letters. In the first long hours of solitude and repose which Hernández has been able to enjoy in more than three years of war, he begins to muse about brotherhood and war and the nature of man. He reviles war because he believes it thwarts love, just as absence does. But as his vision grows more somber, he begins to doubt that other men have any natural love to be thwarted: perhaps war is the natural state, love the unnatural. In the last few poems love means charity in the Christian sense, a state of being so committed to love that all the world is a Thou.

Geraldine Cleary Nichols. *Miguel Hernández*
(Boston, Twayne, 1978), pp. 156–57

As we pass from poem to poem in *The Lightning That Never Stops,* we sense that the reiteration of antithetical imagery, irrational dualities, unexpected transformation of realities coupled with the underlying themes of anguish, disillusionment, and despair is Miguel Hernández's means of presenting us personal and deeply emotive experiences which affect us and which cause us to feel and to participate in the visions produced through these experiences. It is thus through our own participation in these poems that we transcend the anecdotal level and the concrete images in order to perceive the ideal vision of his love. By positing the negative view, Miguel Hernández conversely hints at the positive one by making us consider the larger vision. The tension as a result lies as much in us as it does in the poems themselves since by our very reactions we seek to overcome the chaotic visions by recreating through our own intuition the universal truths concerning love. And herein lies the individual quality of the love poems of *The Lightning That Never Stops.* As readers and as conscious participants we have experienced a love that is tensive and paradoxical and in having done so we have participated in a unique facet of Miguel Hernández's artistic use of poetic language.

Timothy J. Rogers. *Hispania.* Dec., 1979, p. 653

Even before the outbreak of the Spanish Civil War, Miguel Hernández envisioned a social struggle between the oppressed rural proletariat and the all-powerful bourgeois minority. Such sentiments are expressed in *Sons of Stone.* . . . Although it is the only major drama he composed in prose, Hernández' poetic consciousness pervades *Sons of Stone* in terms of language, structure, and symbol. This fact is not at all surprising, because, like two other poets of the period, Rafael Alberti and Federico García Lorca, Miguel Hernández sought a means to renovate the modern Spanish stage. He took the Classical model from the Golden Age theater tradition and reshaped it under the influence of the innovative discoveries of contemporary poetry. . . .

Miguel Hernández composed *Sons of Stone* as a poetic, dramatic confrontation between the power class and the disenfranchised. He saw the impending social revolution as the noble battle of the working class for human rights and poetically depicted it as such in this play. The realization that the masses were entitled to certain rights could only come about through several voices of conscience—poetic voices, as he declaimed in the dedication to *Wind of the People*. He actualizes the poetic nature of the struggle in *Sons of Stone* through a poetic diction not present in most prose dramas—even plays of a similar theme, like Alfonso Sastre's *Red Earth*.

Barry E. Weingarten. *Estreno*. Spring, 1981,
pp. 14, 17

JARNÉS, BENJAMÍN (1888–1949)

Benjamín Jarnés has won the title of our most important young novelist. Around 1925 our novel was at a standstill; it was living off sanctified values—the two groups of the Generation of 1898. But neither the novel of rapid action—in Baroja's style—nor the creations of Valle-Inclán, with their aesthetic richness, which dominated the early years of the century, nor the intellectual productions of Pérez de Ayala, have had a following or formed a school. . . . There is, indeed, coinciding with the universal trend, a marked antirealism in the so-called new literature. Benjamín Jarnés has sought his novelistic renovation in this spiritual area. . . .

Benjamín Jarnés . . . really likes the metaphor, which is constant in his works. We cannot state that it is the distinctive aspect of Jarnés; it is an indication of his temperament and a stylistic tool that can help us to penetrate Jarnés's peculiar attitude with regard to the novel's reality. . . . Jarnés's fictional world does not have the precision and exactitude of a reality seen face to face and transcribed on its own level—this is evident in all the novels. What we find is a vagueness, a form that never responds to the rigorously logical associations of the external world. . . . Reality always appears with certain troubling and frightening aspects of unreality. Jarnés has been faithful to the opinions and ideas that have been debated by so many contemporary artists about the problem of reality.

Anon. Archivos de literatura contemporánea:
Índice literario. Feb., 1934, p. 2†

The Useless Professor, published in 1924, is radically different from what was produced previously outside of Spain and even from any other contemporary Spanish work. If there are any Spanish connotations in Jarnés, they rather refer to the thirteenth century in Spain. It is quite clear that the last episode . . . has the slight flavor of Paul Morand; certainly at times, in the slant of a sentence, there is the suggestion, but no more than a suggestion, of [Joseph] Delteil, . . . but these are trifles that serious criticism can ignore.

What is certain is that in his first work we find a mature Jarnés, with the intensely personal view of life, the world, and the human personality—including his own, which was strongly individualistic—in relationship to the world. For him, earth is "a deficient copy of the heavens." What remedy can he offer? The remedy is myth. . . . Jarnés sees himself as a "reproducer of myths". . . . He elevates man's myths to the gods, in order to bring them back to man once again. Myth is "a little bit of humanity passed through the heavens". . . .

His allusion to the "human fever" requires us to ask ourselves to what point is Jarnés really a disciple of the school of "dehumanization." . . . Whether he learned his lesson in Ortega y Gasset or in others, he learned it well. He belongs to his epoch, which was but a brief decade, for I believe that a brusque end has come to it with a new awakening—one oriented to rehumanizing art. How Jarnés and his followers will fare is not for me to say. Nonetheless, Jarnés will always indicate the highest level—the noblest also, without doubt—that the formal "dehumanizers" were destined to achieve.

Samuel Putnam. RHM. Oct., 1935, 19–21†

Following the fall of the Spanish Republic, Mexico had the good fortune to receive a large number of great minds—Spaniards rescued from a shipwreck. One of the most beloved is Benjamín Jarnés. Mexicans have been reading him for several years, although he is somewhat difficult. . . . Jarnés's style is imaginative and subtle; it reveals an artist who is awake only to the marvelous constructions of fantasy. . . .

Nonetheless, the creator of rather refined novels such as *Theory of the Top-String* was also writing quite good short essays on the literature of our time. And what is even stranger, a good number of them were dedicated to Latin American authors. The present volume, *Ariel in Flight* . . ., is a collection of notes on the 1925–35 literary epoch in the Spanish language.

Perhaps they were ten poor years. Not one masterpiece appeared; however, Jarnés's wisdom, assisted by his kindness, finds seeds that might be fecund, buds that hold promise and reveal . . . common defects and virtues, that confirm the existence of a characteristic mental type in our region.

José Vasconcelos. Introduction to Benjamín
Jarnés, Ariel disperso (Mexico City, Stylo,
1946), pp. 7–9†

Jarnés's rationale of expression [in *Madness and Death of Nobody*] is founded upon one of the most widely indicated causes of the standardized life to be novelized: the machine. The machine symbolizes, by its uniform inhuman production, the lack of distinction which is also found in the components of the human crowd that controls it. It is quite appropriate, therefore, that Jarnés should perceive qualities in the machine which, when transmuted into a literary medium, assist in articulating his vision of modern society. . . .

The machine world is concrete, and best described by resistances of materials, while the salient properties of the substances dealt with concern textures. It is by these qualities that materials are genuinely knowable. The point is not that Jarnés has discovered a new sensibility—for my terminology is basically sculptural—but that he has endeavored to specify the elements of his novelistic setting by references typical of technological activity in order to bridge within a single novel the two realms of perception and setting.

Thus, the sense of touch takes precedence over other ways of perceiving; contact between exteriors, whether of machine and material or character and fictional environment, is deemed the most lucid method of clarifying reality. . . .

I wish to avoid the misleading suggestion that Jarnés portrays a cast of automatons. I should instead point out that his unindividualized characters are set into motion in descriptive passages marked by heavy usage of mathematical vocabulary, and that it is this terminology, rather than the persons themselves, which conveys the mechanical, dehumanized accuracy. At times the technique is suited to the subject, as in the case of the café dancer. . . . Here, geometric exactitude removes much—but not all—of the sensuality which an account of a dance might ordinarily display, but there is no question that Jarnés's choice of language is justifiable if we bear in mind that dance movements are not only rhythmical but also encompass a hypothetical center located in the dance. A glance at the words in the lexicon suffices to alert us to the many references to circles and circular effects. Geometrical concepts elsewhere also serve the double purpose of enhancing the image of the woman's voluptuousness by allusions to spheres, arcs, and curves, and of checking the emotional tenor of the description by a strictly intellectualized vocabulary.

Paul Ilie. PMLA. June, 1961, pp. 251–52

[Jarnés's] novelistic works contain a strong rejection . . . through humor and irony of the nullifying forces of being and personality that restrict human liberty. In *The Paper Guest* and *The Red and the Blue* there is harsh satire of the seminary and the military barracks, dried-up institutions—"beehives," "automaton factories"—destroyers of all individuality. In *Paula and Paulita* he mocks the shoddiness of industrialism, the utilitarian conception of life embodied in the "business" of spas of "spring waters," which is actually the Alhama spa in Aragón. In *Theory of the Top-String* he reproaches the hypocritical and pusillanimous bourgeois morality. In *Madness and Death of Nobody* he presents the situation of man in a mechanical and mass society who is reduced to a functional being. In *The Red and the Blue* he condemns the ideal of bourgeois life and the ideal of a sociopolitical revolution in the name of an ethical revolution, which was so popular in the 1930s. . . .

During the period of his maturity, the 1930s, he devoted himself particularly to biography and the ideological essay, both of which are genres in service to the themes that then, with the ethical interest being more important than the aesthetic, governed their creation: his concern for Spain and the perfection of the individual. Seconding the call for the "Group in Service to the Republic," of which he was a member, his work acquires a political sense—politics as seen from the heights of contemplation—for the defense and development of the Republican cause. Not so much for the regime, which after only a few months of existence already seemed to be a failure, a sacrificial victim of partisanship, but rather to the Republican ideal expounded by the intellectuals of the "Group": a unitary Republic, made up of all the productive classes of the nation, united in the common task of the fulfillment of Spain.

Víctor Fuentes. *CHA.* Feb., 1967, pp. 38–39†

"Voluptuosidad" is defined [by Jarnés] as the process of knowing the external intimately, and experiencing the consequent delights of such a process. . . . Voluptuosity can be experience in perceiving any object by the senses—be it a work of art, a stone, a bird or a human form. The important point is that physical sensations are the means by which man must approach his world and through which he is to fulfill his being. . . .

Ramón Gómez de la Serna provides Jarnés with the lead in a new appreciation of reality. Ramón receives his admirer's hearty praise for his part in the rebellion against the symbolists' murder of the object. . . . Jarnés rejoices at the freedom which Ramón gives to the external world in breaking the lyrical shackles. The ability to achieve a titillating presence of the object in art, with no taint of sentimentality, is the great achievement of this new esthetic.

The relationship between the person and the Ramonian, totally independent object—in Jarnés's view—must be the same as the erotic relationship between male and female. Since the real world is independent of human reason and sentiment, it can be known only by a lover—not by a would-be master. So Jarnés proposes that men reactivate their means of knowing the world—the senses—and he consistently involves the erotic, the sensual, in the nexus of perception set up between men and objects.

In his novels, even in discussing generally the act of perception, Jarnés employs the terminology of human sexual love. . . .

In *Paula and Paulita* the topic [voluptuosity] is a central consideration of the work. Jarnés interwines the protagonist's love for two specific women and his consequent relationship with the natural world.

Marion O'Neill. *MLN.* March, 1970, pp. 262–65

Saint Alexis is inspired by the legend that tells of the life of Saint Alexis, which was very popular both in Byzantium and western Europe during the Middle Ages. . . . In view of the existence of so many versions of the life of Saint Alexis, we must first consider the problem of what version or versions served as an inspiration for Jarnés? Even the most inattentive reader will see at first reading that the Spanish author is well versed in the medieval versions of the legend. Jarnés specifically cites the French version of the fourteenth century, which itself is based on an earlier Latin version, in its turn an elaboration of a still older version in the same language. . . .

In Jarnés's opinion, Alexis's parents exemplify Christianity's becoming bourgeois as a consequence of its elevation to a state religion by Constantine. This is the basis for Jarnés's extensive criticism of the Pope and the Emperor, both of whom are treated with great respect in the old versions owing to their possession of maximum authority. . . . According to Jarnés, Constantinian Christianity lacks heroism, has converted itself into bureaucracy, and it is in this way that under the mantle of Christianity paganism continues to flourish. . . .

This criticism of bourgeois Christianity—closely related to the abhorrence expressed by Nietzsche, Baudelaire, Ibsen, Wilde, and Gide toward the mediocrity of the nineteenth-century bourgeoisie, antithesis of the superman—explains Jarnés's ambivalent attitude toward Saint Alexis. On the one hand, the Spanish author approves of the contempt that the saint shows for wealth through putting into practice Christ's commands to his followers, but at the same time Jarnés is repelled by the saint's attitude of sacrificing his love for his fellow man and his contact with him to his desire to imitate Christ. . . . In Jarnés's opinion, man can only surpass the isolation and alienation in which he finds himself through love and myth.

H. Th. Oostendorp. *Neophil.* Oct., 1972,
pp. 417–18, 423†

Because of his avowed intent to fuse life and art, it is curious that the opinion persists that Jarnés and his generation produced a "dehumanized" art. It is quite common to find his generation dismissed as closed off, self-contained. . . .

Jarnés did not in fact propose a divorce between the novel and reality, but rather the transformation of the latter in the former. The antipathy felt by critics seems due more to the poetic nature of Jarnés's novels. A willingness to allow Jarnés's vision of reality to permeate one's own is necessary for the appreciation of his novels, just as this is the prime necessity for the appreciation of poetry. In this sense, also, Jarnés is distinctly modern in that he insists on more participation, perhaps more effort to comprehend, from the reader than does a Realist novelist. It would seem unfair to fault Jarnés on this score while exalting other modern novelists, among them Faulkner, Unamuno, and Joyce, who do the same thing.

Of course, the participation demanded by Jarnés of his reader is of a different sort than that demanded by Unamuno or Joyce. Jarnés's reader must enter the book to make coherent sense out of the characters' poetic perceptions, but not to complete a logical plot action, or to supply from evidence pieced together the basis for a character's motivations. Both types of participation have the aspect of problem solving, but the difference is one of magnitude.

When the reader supplies a missing link in a Joycean action, he is likely satisfying himself that he has accomplished something real. . . . In Jarnés's novels, the riddles to be solved center on a poetic link or an analogy which is missing from the page but which exists in the character's mind with sufficient force to propel him to the next action or perception.

But finding the missing links in a poetic analogy, completing a poetic perception, does not have the same sense of reality about it for the usual reader that a map of Dublin has.

> J. S. Bernstein. *Benjamín Jarnés* (New York,
> Twayne, 1972), pp. 48–49

In his book *Stefan Zweig,* [Jarnés] chooses a citation from Kierkegaard that tells us that the artist cannot be messianic, because the world is given to him as an elaborated, constructed fact, and he goes taking inventory of it, discovering laws, hidden connections. He maintains his beliefs about the function of the intellectual in spite of the extreme virulence, the sociopolitical commitment among the Spanish exiles, especially those in Mexico, during those years [1940s]. His persistence in that humanism—an open and integrating one—in spite of partisan circumstances, supposes a heroic vocation to which Jarnés clearly testified. . . .

When Jarnés wrote the biography of Zweig, he judged him a failure owing to his being a disciple of Freud and a follower of his ethical nudism, which had killed love through destroying its poetry.

Nevertheless, Jarnés, in his search for a vital art that would be more directly nourished by the very sources of life, a product of a creative interest in the balanced comprehension of the different levels of reality, incorporates both on the theoretical level and in his literary elaboration, Jung's theory of the unconscious. This occurs in his novel *Theory of the Top-String,* . . . whose introduction describes the three steps of the conscious, the personal unconscious, and the collective unconscious. The recognition of these contrary forces that struggle within the spirit is the basis for the creation of style. Let us remember that for Jarnés, style is not the man, but rather "a certain balance of forces achieved by a man." As a work of the spirit—and not as a work of chance—the sensations and experience of wakefulness, dream, and memory are integrated and harmonized.

Emilia de Zuleta. *Arte y vida en la obra de
Benjamín Jarnés* (Madrid, Gredos, 1977),
pp. 52, 55–56†

Of all of Jarnés's novels none has been so generously praised as *Madness and Death of Nobody*. Generally regarded as one of his most mature and representative works, it is also (along with Azorín's *Surrealism*) probably the best known piece of vanguard fiction, and has been the target of a number of readings. The best among these . . . have approached the novel indirectly, by way of Ortegan cultural and aesthetic theory, of which Jarnés was an exponent.

The manner of reading *Madness and Death of Nobody* is noteworthy for the emphasis it places on the novel's capacity for mirroring what are taken to be the sad and impersonal realities of life in modern industrial society, where man has been reduced to a number, a face in the crowd, a cog in a machine. Thus, the different components of the novel are searched for their mimetic resources, and the novel as a whole is judged according to how well it has impersonated certain outstanding characteristics of the real world. (Of course, strictly speaking, when one takes the novel as an illustration of Ortega's notion of *mass man* . . . one is not juxtaposing the novel and reality but the novel and Ortegan cultural theory, the latter providing a perhaps faithful, perhaps deceptive, image of the "real" world.) But these readings overlook, I think, the extent to which *Madness and Death of Nobody* is steeped in the traditions of fiction. The novel exhibits, indeed exposes, a whole set of novelistic conventions as much as it mirrors reality. One of the important scenes, for example, concerns Juan Sánchez's suspicion that he is the natural son of Count Monte Azul. To satisfy his curiosity he travels to Monte Azul's seat in the country, where it is disclosed—by an old and trusty majordomo no less—that Juan is indeed the bastard son of the Count, a Don Juan (his Christian name) who in his younger days was given to cavorting with chorus girls, one of whom (Parisian of course) brought Juan into the world. The typicality of this episode can hardly be overlooked. Like many a fictional hero, Juan turns out to be the bastard son of an aristocrat, an orphan whose biological identity remains hidden for a large part of his life. The entire scene, set in the ancient estate, with pictures of Juan's ancestors hanging from the walls, with Juan's very cradle, covered by dust and crisscrossed by cobwebs, lying abandoned with other relics in a musty room (creaking door and all), smacks of nothing so much as of parody or stylization.

Gustavo Pérez Firmat. *Idle Fictions: The
Hispanic Vanguard Novel, 1926–1934* (Durham,
N.C., Duke University Press, 1982), pp. 122–23

JIMÉNEZ, JUAN RAMÓN (1881–1958)

Juan Ramón Jiménez is not a thinker, nor is he . . . an enthusiast either; he has too much good taste to approach reality with the familiarity that is necessary to the engendering of passion; his spirit soars in a fragrant and melodious atmosphere, bathed in pleasant half-light, made of his own extra-fine sentiments, a spirit that is refined, perfected, purified in filters that are also his own thoughts. Jiménez is faithful, but he is not self-denying; his temperament . . . touches on being egotistical, a friendly and tenacious egotism, gentle in form and inflexible. . . . His poems are, like his character, obstinately personal and individual, clear, pleasant-sounding, causing tears that are both pleasurable and melancholic at the same time; they are made up of reality—a reality that is seen through a violet mist—and honorable and full of emotion for being so true. I swear to God that he feels every verse he writes. It is for that reason that he is such a delightful and dangerous poet for women. I would like to confide something about the poet's sadness to them, to the many women who will cry over *Sad Airs*. And it is that such sadness is not bitterness in Jiménez as in Heine, nor rebelliousness as in Byron, nor disillusion as in Gustavo Adolfo Bécquer [Spain's leading poet of the nineteenth century]. Jiménez's sadness is a privilege—an august, imperial privilege—and he is so at ease with this sadness and so much its friend that if he ever lost it . . . he would lose the most exquisite joy of his life.

Gregorio Martínez Sierra. Lectura. March,
1904, p. 344†

Jiménez, indeed, is a mystic of the naturalistic order of Walt Whitman. He traces the constant divine in life; he ignores the transcendental. He finds God in the sea, in the subtle sense-play of love, in the landscapes of Spain; or in the gyring thoughts of his own meditation. Yet no poet's accent could radically differ from that of the Bible, of Spinoza or of Whitman. Not the least magic of Jiménez' work is its perpetual counterpoint of meaning and substance. The meaning is cosmic, the stuff is light and casual. Often a seeming haphazard of expression fringes the ineffable; a drop of water miraculously turns into a universe. No tinge of cosmic rhetoric mars the body of his words. The universe is implicit. The ultimate gift of Jiménez is a song of life, liquid and gemmed, within whose moment silence is an inner flame. This flame is simple and constant. . . .

Jiménez' work is a sort of *comédie mystique*. Singly, the poems have variety of notes. Yet there is a cryptic quality in them, and a subtle allusiveness to something not explicit, which must repugn the shallow sense, even as it entrances the mind hungry for great vistas. His poems have prosodic value. Yet their chiefest value is that they *create aesthet-*

ically a sense of incompleteness. Aesthetically, they are whole because they contain this *lack*—this positive surge toward an apocalyptic sense which lives in them only by the imprint of its absence. Each of his poems is at once a sensory form, and a spiritual inchoation. . . . One might say that a poem of Jiménez is like an instant in a human life: full-limned, full-equipped with thought, emotion, will; and yet this fullness is but the passing function of an implicit unity which transcends and subscends it.

Waldo Frank. *Virgin Spain* (New York, Boni and Liveright, 1926), pp. 290–91

Platero and I is one of those felicitous works in which the author's most brilliant and solid qualities are responsive to the spirit of the times. Seldom has an Andalusian backdrop been shown with such poetic truth; its expressiveness is the most evocative and perfect that any author of that generation [1898] has been able to realize; the warm, solitary, and human simplicity that makes these pages tremble is the best guarantee that such a book will not diminish in the interest that was present from the very moment of its initial appearance. Its theme is nature, nature that is reflected in the eyes of the poet, and the beauty of this theme has no equal except in the crystalline transparency with which the poet's eyes reflect it, so that as soon as the vision is obscured by some veil, we do not know if it is of mist or of tears.

Luis Cernuda. *BSpS.* Oct., 1942, p. 174†

Beauty and *Poetry* (1917–1923), twins one might say, were published in 1923, and both accentuate the essential part of the poet's work, that becomes more and more subjective and intimate with light accents of intellectualism and a constant meditation on those very words: poetry and beauty. Together, the two offer the key to Jiménez's preoccupation. It is not a question of deciding in his works the relationship between poetry and truth, as in Goethe's case; between beauty and truth as in Keats or Emily Dickinson but between beauty and poetry which with love, woman and death form the abiding themes of his life. Death, for example, is constantly present in the poet of Moguer. . . . At times the *death* of Rilke is recalled by Jiménez's figure of death. This theme becomes almost an obsession, and it can be seen that this preoccupation with the death of others is nothing other than the mirror of his own imagined death, almost a dialogue with it. Now, too, we can appreciate how the total work of the poet of Moguer could be—and in fact is—a triumph, not over the D'Annunzio style of death, but over death itself; the triumph of beauty and of poetry; the ultimate triumph of the permanent over the temporal and perishable.

Eugenio Florit. Preface to Juan Ramón Jiménez, *Selected Writings* (Farrar, Straus & Cudahy, 1957), pp. xxii–xxiii

Jiménez reconciles . . . restraint and intensity: tirelessly sincere, but never given to prattling or gesticulation, he will express moments of plenitude or of rapture while preserving a muted tone, a singular poise and weightlessness. This is especially evident in his folkloric pieces, where colorful effects are shunned. Restraint is also compatible in Juan Ramón Jiménez with the boldness of the experimenter. Here his role as an innovator must be recalled once more, for he never ceased to invent, to search for that straightest line between the emotion and the reader which would be the purest form. He has been, like Gide, always a young poet, for whom every book was a beginning. Hence his considerable variety and—to mention a final wedding of opposition—the fusion of it with a remarkable singleness of intent and style. Jiménez concentrates in each poem on almost a single device, plays but one of the many strings on his instrument at a time. If one virtue or one method may be considered characteristic of his poetry, it is that of concentration above all on the single word, on the force and the magic of which language is capable.

Claudio Guillén. NR. Dec. 16, 1957, pp. 17–18

It is now generally conceded that Jiménez . . . has had the strongest influence on Spanish poetry written in the twentieth century. Unlike Rubén Darío, who first brought French Symbolism over into Spanish verse, he was not so much an imitator of this French poet or that as he was a writer of the same kind of poetry. His first poems, published when he was eighteen, were close to the heart of a native Spanish Impressionism, what has been called the "shimmering extravagances" of his native Andalusia. Jiménez later developed a style and attitude that could accommodate direct and detailed observation of the world about him; like Yeats, he worked himself free from any device that resembled applied ornament; for him, to be modern meant to be free. His rhythms became more individual as he moved away from conventional metres toward a kind of patterned vers libre. He has never lost, however, his special power over language, which has become—in his later years—increasingly transparent, shifting, and luminous.

Louise Bogan. NY. Feb. 8, 1958, p. 130

[Jiménez's] dialogue with nature, enriching the constant spinning of the creative imagination, was crystalized in that admirable work (*Platero and I,* 1914), lyrical biography, collection of etchings, Andalusian elegy . . . Yes, Andalusian and universal, as the author wanted it, striving to achieve universality by reaching into his own depth until he could touch the most particular and local, the essential human. He concentrated on the simple incidents of living, in the bare instant, to the point of not dividing his life into days, but his day into lives: "each day, each hour, an entire life." Such concentration gave his poetry density and intensity: in each line we feel him complete, gravitating above it with all the weight of his soul and of his dream—lucid dream of deep realities, penetration into the other face of reality, to the point of converting the temporal into substance of the eternal and the limited into expression of the infinite. To give himself up to poetry was to give himself up to life, to life each day different and the same, like daybreak; to life at its deepest level, with the bird and the rose, the child and the cloud.

Ricardo Gullón. Introduction to Juan Ramón Jiménez, *Three Hundred Poems: 1903–1953* (Austin, University of Texas Press, 1962), p. xxi

The reader of Juan Ramón Jiménez gradually begins to feel a certain uneasiness. This world the poet has created—a world of delicate beauty and pristine forms—is certainly not of the present time and place, the implacable here and now of the human condition.

Slowly the uneasiness becomes a sense of guilt, the cause of which is twofold. We first inquire for minimum evidence that this man had lived through two world wars, including the civil tragedy of his own country which produced half a million dead. Is there a trace of the fact that the last fifteen years of his life, he, like all of us, lived under the ominous billows of the mushroom cloud? But not only has Juan Ramón Jiménez transcended the brutality of history, he has also banished the vulgarity of routine existence from his verse. And this is the second source of our guilt feeling, for a great deal of contemporary poetry has successfully been concerned with incorporating everyday reality into verse. . . .

The fact that we are uneasy with Jiménez' poetry is a disturbing commentary on our times. We have been conditioned by the especially peremptory nature of modern history, and by critics like Sartre, to suspect literature for its own sake. We wonder if Jiménez working in his cork-lined study, shielded from the basic *contretemps* of existence by his devoted wife, ever really "lived"; and by asking the question we betray our own ignorance of living.

Howard T. Young. *The Victorious Expression: A Study of Four Contemporary Spanish Poets— Miguel de Unamuno, Antonio Machado, Juan Ramón Jiménez, Federico García Lorca* (Madison, University of Wisconsin Press, 1964), pp. 77–78

For [Jiménez] a poem has ecstasy: that is the difference between poetry and prose. Living as a poet means feeling that ecstasy every day of your life, every hour if possible. A poem flies out of the poet like a spark. Whatever the poet writes down will be touched with ecstasy—the poem will therefore be light, not light in the sense of light verse that avoids seriousness, but light as a spark or as an angel is light. With one or two fewer words the poem would leap straight up into the sky. . . .

Jiménez' poems . . . are nervous and alert, and when we come near, they see us, they are more interested in us than in themselves—they try to show us the road back to the original ecstasy. The poems are signposts pointing the reader back to the poet, that is, back toward the life from which the ecstasy came. Juan Ramón Jiménez said that he lived his life in such a way as to get the most poetry possible out of it, and he loved solitude, private gardens, cloisters, silent women with large eyes.

Jiménez' poems ask the question: what sort of life shall we live so as to feel poetry, ecstasy? His emphasis on how the poet *lived,* rather than on rhythm or technique, is precisely why so much poetry flowed from him into the young poets. In his life he embodied as Yeats did some truth about poetry that everyone, but especially poetry professors, try to ignore and do ignore.

We can understand the subject matter of Jiménez' poems if we understand that it is in solitude a man's emotions become very clear to him. Jiménez does not write of politics or religious doctrines, of the mistakes of others, not of his own troubles or even his own opinions, but only of solitude, and the strange experiences and the strange joy that come to a man in solitude. His books usually consist of emotion after emotion called out with great force and delicacy, and it must be said that his short, precise poems make our tradition of the long egotistic ode look rather absurd.

Robert Bly. Introduction to Juan Ramón
Jiménez, *Forty Poems* (Madison, Minn., Sixties
Press, 1967), pp. 5–7

The essential quality of mystical or ineffable experience is often said to be incommunicable and to defy direct expression. Juan Ramón's principal concern was with the possibilities of the poetic resources of language in being able to convey some idea, be it only a vague idea, of a state of mind which seeks after deity and tries to realise the ineffable. Expression is required in that the underlying spiritual structure, or essence, of the universe is grasped only in and through its material manifestation, that is, its external form, the spirit become word. Language used as logical exposition becomes the property of the intellect; the poet is fundamentally more concerned with the emotive power of language and its experiential consequences than with its defining values as evident in logical discourse. The nature of the ineffable becomes perceptible only in so far as it clothes itself in linguistic form, or any Art form (music, painting) for that matter. The "desired and desiring God" of *Animal of Depth* is discovered, or revealed, after a life-long struggle with symbols on the part of Juan Ramón Jiménez. God is an achievement and a finality, coming to a "poetic world" which shows itself fit for him to inhabit.

Juan Ramón's poetry, especially in the more intense moments of poetic experience, is an attempt to explicate certain mental states, or levels of consciousness, which he experienced: by means of and through the word, material form is given to those fleeting sensations felt by the poet to be of great consequence and to possess some spiritual significance. Searching into one's mental processes in an endeavor to capture a principal cause of human motivation implies not only subjectivity and idealisation in Juan Ramón Jiménez but also spiritual activity.

Leo R. Cole. *The Religious Instinct in the Poetry of Juan Ramón Jiménez* (Oxford, Dolphin, 1967), pp. 139–40

There is a striking resemblance between the hallucinogenic experience of non-ego, and the experience of Juan Ramón Jiménez, as described in his poetry; for while Juan Ramón undoubtedly attained his goal without the use of drugs, it is evident that he had recourse to no particular religious system or doctrinal guide. In this sense his mysticism, uncompromising and unremitting, is "secular" (one thinks of Thoreau), and the literature on the mind-altering drugs may well shed more light on his work than do the doctrinal guides to mysticism. Juan Ramón's life was a life full of "secular" self-discipline and preparation towards the attainment of the non-ego state as being "turned-on," and towards its expression as a symbolic reality—which is to say, poetry. . . .

The poetry of Juan Ramón is the life-long record of a man cultivating an experience. The existential reality of "turning on" to natural phenomena becomes progressively more frequent, more exhilarating, and more intense. But it is not a repetitious, static compulsion like the experience pursued (say) by the alcoholic. Juan Ramón is seeking something; he is going somewhere.

Rupert C. Allen. *RHM*. Jan.–April, 1969, pp. 308–10

In his completeness Jiménez is almost unrivaled in Spanish poetry. He began as an Adamic poet in a fresh world of inexhaustible beauty, determined to express every nuance, every emotion. He mastered all the forms of Spanish poetry: the song, the ballad, the sonorous Alexandrine, the sonnet form, free verse, and the concentrated free verse of "pure poetry." He developed extensively most of the essential symbols of Western poetry with his own emphasis: the sea, the rose, the sun, the tree, the flower, the bird, the cloud, the diamond, the glowing coal, the circle. Admittedly he failed to exploit the ugly: as a man he suffered the ugly and the confused; as a poet, discipline in the quest for beauty was paramount. Jiménez is an outstanding example of the modern poet: since the time of Poe and Baudelaire, given the disintegration of the Christian world view, the poet has been cast adrift to create his own metaphysical system of salvation. Jiménez creates such a system, grounded in a fusion of natural religion and aesthetics and employing the modern preoccupation with the extension of time through heightened consciousness. Moreover, his metaphysical system is properly created in a convincing poetic structure. Surely Jiménez, a deserving recipient of the Nobel Prize, can be meaningfully compared with major European poets such as Yeats and Rilke. Take him for all in all, Juan Ramón Jiménez may well be the greatest lyric poet in Spanish literature.

Carl W. Cobb. *Contemporary Spanish Poetry*
(1898–1963) (Boston, Twayne, 1976), pp. 63–64

The poetic vision of Juan Ramón Jiménez is one of transcendence, in which the ordinary world of dualistic existence is transformed into an integrated world of harmony. It is a vision of wholeness where the boundaries separating man from nature, from the cosmos and from his own essence are transcended, enabling the poet to participate in the essential harmony of all that exists. Paradoxically, Juan Ramón Jiménez's world of harmony is artistically created through tension, through the juxtaposition of opposites held in perfect balance, for the unity that Juan Ramón Jiménez seeks is found on the very edge of the fine line where opposites merge: in the moment of love when man and woman are united as one, in the instant when night becomes dawn or evening shades into night, where the infinite is contained within the finite, the essential within the temporal. In any vision of wholeness, opposing forces must be present in equal measure. In Juan Ramón Jiménez's world, the tension produced by the juxtaposition of opposites is resolved through the use of paradox. It is paradox, the fusion of contradictory realities, that transforms tension into harmony and enables the poet to transcend duality.

Nancy B. Mandlove. *Hispania.* Dec., 1980,
p. 666

It is true that Juan Ramón Jiménez was by no means unaware of the possible insufficiency of the Word; but what is important to observe is that no note of scepticism, as such, is discernible. Of course, as has been pointed out, this is only to be expected in conformity with his aesthetic concept of the Word. To it, as the medium whereby the poetic act is consummated, he renders up his whole self. This mysterious metamorphosis through which he is subsumed into the Word, *becomes* the Word, he describes as follows: "When I write, I disappear completely; I don't even sense myself, I am all idea or feeling, all word, name." Such loss of identity and such a perfect oneness with the "Verbum" invites parallel with the divine mystic union of the soul with God, of the kind experienced by San Juan de la Cruz [sixteenth-century Spanish mystic and poet]. It is of course a profane analogy; but although not explicit, it does appear that Juan Ramón Jiménez is deliberately calling comparison with religious concepts, and this was common Modernist practice. This clearly indicates the sacred nature of the poetic act as Juan Ramón Jiménez conceived it, and the divine holiness of the Word. The reason for Juan Ramón Jiménez's capitalization of "Palabra" (Word) is therefore apparent: it is a veritable transcript into Castilian of the Latin "Verbum" of theology. My comparison with San Juan de la Cruz is based on the loss of conscious identity mutually experienced by the two poets. Where the parallel cannot be said to be exact, however, is that in the case of the mystic rapture of San Juan de la Cruz there is exclusion of idea which, on the contrary, is ever-present in Juan Ramón Jiménez.

Mervyn Coke-Enguídanos. *Word and Work in the Poetry of Juan Ramón Jiménez* (London, Támesis, 1982), pp. 30–31

LAFORET, CARMEN (1921–   )

Constantly going from surprise to surprise, from amazement to amazement, [Laforet] looks into the abyss along with her protagonist Andrea [in *Nothingness*] until she meets, at every turn, nothingness. Never before has Spanish literature known such absolute desperation, such radical nihilism; one could say that the civil war has consumed the last hope and along with it any sense of human existence. And what makes this vision of the world more desolating is that it does not appear to be twisted or forced toward any purpose: the novel is not wrapped in a thesis, nor does it respond to an aesthetic, political, or philosophical doctrine; nor, likewise, does it reflect an influence of any particular model; in it a clean, fresh, and bold vision passes through a confused, febrile, broken, viscous milieu—it limits itself to bearing witness.

Before this lucid emptiness, before this testimony of nothingness, one must stop to tremble; for it is pure desperation in excellent souls like our protagonist's still to have the courage to bear witness. And one must also stop to tremble because the *nothingness* that the author condensed in the title of her novel coincides with the nothingness that, in many ways, the most characteristic literary outpourings of other countries continue to proclaim. Ingenuously, Carmen Laforet includes in the title the spiritual attitude of existentialism, . . . which has become a narrative device in France used by writers who wish to be completely in vogue.

What Jean-Paul Sartre, for example, achieves on a philosophic level and with a very refined artistic consciousness, can already be seen, in the same profound meaning, contained in this early work, written in a direct form and without any slips of the pen, by a girl, twenty-two years old, who was expressing her immediate experiences in life when the world war was still undecided and France was still occupied by invading forces.

Which is evidence of terrible meaning.

Francisco Ayala. *Realidad*. Jan.–Feb., 1947,
pp. 131–32†

I want to point out to you [Carmen Laforet] that what I consider most fulfilling about your novel *Nothingness* is that extraordinary Chapter IV, with its perfectly natural and revealing dialogue between the grandmother and Gloria; Chapter XV, is indeed, a sublime story, as are many of the other chapters. It seems to me that your book is not a novel in the most usual sense of the word—I say this because of the plot—nor is it in that other, more special sense that is characteristic of an "art" novel, but it is rather a series of quite lovely stories—some of them like those of Gorky, Eça de Queiroz, Unamuno, or Hemingway; and I believe this so much that for me *Nothingness* slips a bit in Chapter XIX, that is, when a continuous novelistic plot becomes noticeable. I have not read that chapter in its entirety; it was repulsive to me; and I tarried some time in finishing the rest of the book because that chapter caused me to feel a kind of knot like that of a colic attack that had the power to take away the vitality from the rest of the work. Because you really are a novelist who writes subjectless novels, as one is a poet who writes poems without subjects. And here lies the most difficult part of writing a novel or a poem. . . .

Let us see if we can interest some American editor in your book, so that it can be translated and published here [in the United States]. For this I will need two or three copies of *Nothingness*. It seems to me that it would really be appreciated, because *Nothingness,* like everything that is authentic, also has a place here; it is of today and will belong to tomorrow; it has a place in any part of the world, as it belongs to yesterday and to everyone. That is what this kind of accessible and committed writing that you do has. I was very happy to see at the front of your novel an excerpt of a ballad of mine, also a reaction against something ugly, the nothingness of life.

Well, Carmen Laforet, let us see how you are going to capture that troubled Madrid in another one of your novels without a subject. I am very sorry not to be able to speak with you, but it is clear to me that I am a friend of yours, and I will be a reader of yours if you send me whatever you happen to write.

Juan Ramón Jiménez. Ínsula. Jan. 15, 1948, p. 1†

Perhaps [Laforet's] work [*Nothingness*] should be considered merely an exercise in graphic recording, a kind of *tour de force* aimed at producing the impression of a nightmare in personal relations. Her dynamic style insures the attainment of such a goal and in large degree accounts for the novel's readability. But the treatment of character and situation, together with certain purposive remarks, confirms our belief that Carmen Laforet at least toyed with the idea of a diabolical, mechanistic universe symbolized by the small locale whose center is the house on Aribau Street. Here the cruelty of cosmic law declares itself in distorted lives, misguided energy, and uncontrollable impulses. The author knows that one immediate cause of her characters' desperation is their imprisonment in themselves. . . . But instead of treating psychologically the subject of enslavement to self and its effects in human association, the author chooses to poetize the inharmonious aspects of the latter. At the same time she links the discordance with a vague, suprahuman force. . . .

Now, Carmen Laforet joins imaginatively in the generalizations of her central character, combining a philosophical overtone with structural form and a physiological view of personality. She thus leaves a concrete demonstration of mechanistic forces fatefully operating within a specific set of relationships. She does so, however, purely as a literary diversion, allured no doubt by a materialistic vision of human experience as being appropriate subject matter in the present age. For a brief moment of concentrated literary effort, she plunges into the vision in company with Andrea and with her retires to a comfortable position after an exciting venture. The result of her venture is a vivid image of human beings tossed to and fro as though impelled by a law of mechanics. The tersely wrought structural form, which we have described as an oscillatory movement of animated objects (people), stamps the narrative with uniqueness. The novel may in time be remembered only as a curious experimentation in method and technique. But in so far as the cultivation of a decisive literary manner is concerned, Carmen Laforet has set an example which other contemporary Spanish novelists would do well to follow.

Sherman Eoff. Hispania. May, 1952, pp. 210–11

The Island and the Demons has a slow and painstaking plot full of small relevations and surprises that very soon form an entire universe of sharp and tremulous sensations. The personality of Marta and the force of her temperament are revealed by means of warm and fine descriptions of all the sensations that are present in the world of the slightly wild adolescent, who senses in herself a paternal inheritance of an uncontrollable desire for doing nothing and for living a bohemian life. Her world continues to be enriched as she goes on pruning her life of illusions; she remains alone and naked with the unencumbered truth of her existence, taking risks in life and without commitment to any kind of code or convention. José and Quino form the prison of punishment, in which Marta's surly character gains strength, and her domestic quarrels have an intense energy for fighting to keep up the physical plant of the estate. Pablo is a lively and imposing portrait, and the contrast between the sublime and ridiculous qualities of this character is marvelously realized.

The novel is written with simplicity and exactness, and with delightful elegance. No effort whatsoever is noticed in the achievement of this prose filled with clarity and precision. In *The Island and the Demons* Carmen Laforet acquires even more grace in her style than in *Nothingness,* and the forcefulness of the narrative is more skillfully accomplished. The descriptions that the author gives us of Grand

Canary Island and trips through the mountains and the nearby islands are impressionistic scenes of an intimate and poetic realism; they are powerful canvases that breathe like slices of life.

Carmen Laforet has achieved another success, her second one [the first being *Nothingness*]. She appears fully capable of telling a story and of creativity; if it is certain that everything she narrates is a product of her inner, intimate life, it is not any less to her credit that she knows how to take delight in these mental states and in all these transpositions of the most difficult complexities with a power of penetration and with an uncommon ease.

J. Castillo Puche. *CHA*. June, 1952, pp. 385–86†

After reading [*The New Woman*] one asks in what country on this earth can Carmen Laforet possibly live? The argument of her novel can have validity in many places, by conceding, which already is a lot to concede, that a woman can believe for fourteen years that she is married without being so. But that it is in Spain, which is precisely where the action takes place, makes it completely inadequate. And do not think that this woman is an ordinary one without any credentials. Paulina—that is her name—besides being facilely intelligent and pedantic, has a college degree in the sciences and knows how to take care of herself. It is that the literary models that Carmen Laforet follows count for too much in this novel, and, therefore, originality slips away through some unexpected trap door. . . .

The episodes of the narrative are always confused and digressive, without any purposeful relation to the principal subject. The Spanish that she uses is deficient, lacking nuances and flexibility. And the novel lacks "tempo" as the various biographical phases in confused repetitions are superimposed without clear discrimination and appropriate sequences. But the principal defect of the work is secondary to these small details of style and originates precisely from the exposition of the psychological conflict. The conversion of Paulina is transmitted from character to reader in such a lifeless way, so full of worn-out commonplaces and so conventional, that in the culminating moment, by breaking the mood that was set—that is to say, that was intended to be set—with the thunderous arrival of salvation, the "I" of the novelist breaks into the narrative so infelicitously . . . that the little poetic charm that she had realized comes crashing down to earth, diminishing the emotion before the writer's prosaic and analytic presence.

J. Villa Pastur. *Archivum*. May–Dec., 1955,
pp. 455–56†

The appearance of *The Island and the Demons* . . . proved that the writer had simply been developing. [Laforet's] new book contains the life of Marta, another adolescent, in Las Palmas of the Canary Islands. Marta is, one might say, Andrea [in *Nothingness*] before going to

Barcelona. However, there are scarcely any autobiographical elements in this book, or else they are so transformed as to be unrecognizable. Nevertheless, we cannot deny that the young girl goes on being, fundamentally, the same spirit full of pure inclinations that clash with brutal reality. It is noteworthy to what point the author has been true to herself. Also in *The Island and the Demons* we find a familiar group of persons who border on the psychopathic, but the story is in the third person, which indicates a change in narrative technique and a greater difficulty for the author. There is more landscape in these pages than in *Nothingness* and a more complicated plot. The style has become more conscious although keeping indelibly its personal mark. The sentiments and the characters have been analyzed more deeply. Marta could be Andrea at fifteen or sixteen, but the two books are not continuous. That is to say, *Nothingness* is not a continuation of *The Island and the Demons*. The demons of this novel "are everywhere in the world. They get into the hearts of men. They are the seven cardinal sins."

The Island and the Demons follows the author's previous line: literature of the smiling disillusioned. In spite of that reference to sins, there is no religious finality in the presentation of the emotional problems and their consequences. If the meanness and moral filth that Marta witnesses disgust her, it is only because of her good taste and ethics, just as the superficialities of stupid people bore her. She sets a high standard for herself. For that reason, those "conversations about life, people and love affairs provoke her to a rare little laugh. They were insufferable."

The best of this novel is the most objective aspect of it, the story of a servant of the house and her daughters. Carmen Laforet begins there to describe from the adult point of view the lives of others, and achieves an extraordinary and expressive vigor.

Rafael Vásquez Zamora. BA. Autumn, 1956, p. 395

Nothingness is more than a novel of contemporary Spain; it is a work that captures the anxieties, hopes, and frustrations of our time. It takes place in Barcelona two years after the end of the Civil War. There are no ruins, no bombed buildings, but the grim struggle of a postwar society is there. Even the parties, dances, and student gatherings it describes have a hollow gaiety. Everywhere memories of a bitter experience cluster to from the backdrop for the scene.

The house on Aribau Street, where the heroine Andrea arrives one rainy night, is the center of the world created by the novelist. Strange and fascinating characters inhabit it. It is a house full of dark corners, doors that slam violently, windows that are forever shut. The air is filled with human sounds, monotonous quarrels, piercing screams, a child's weeping.

The characters create infernos for one another. They are pursued by a spiritual isolation that makes each of them a haunted, tortured soul. In this world of frustration and fear, objects and things take on a new dimension. We follow the author, like a camera pausing to observe a mangy cat, catching the frozen image of a distorted face, moving in for a "close-up" of a claw-like hand.

The heroine, young and sensitive, struggles to free herself of this nightmare. She roams the streets of the city, searches for new ties and a sense of security. But always she must return to the house on Aribau Street and its inhabitants, for they fascinate her as they inevitably do the reader. This is because in the nebulous outlines of these people she finds a mystery that seems to say much of the human condition. She is moved by their yearnings and frustrations and often hypnotized by their evil. In this the work is strongly reminiscent of the Russian novelists of the nineteenth century, particularly of Dostoevski, for whom the author has often expressed admiration.

The novel moves swiftly. It has the suspense of a mystery story, the ever-changing perspective of a movie. It is written, one critic puts it, as if the author wanted to free herself of some burden. Carmen Laforet herself admits to a certain abandon in her style, to an inability to rewrite and polish. She even finds it difficult, she explains, to make corrections of detail, so concerned is she with the drama of her characters, the interior action of her plot. . . .

Carmen Laforet here gives expression to the anguished confusion of youth confronted by chaos and seeking a meaning to existence. The heroine well personifies this state of mind, its groping, its fears, and its confusion as she endeavors to comprehend the new world in which she finds herself—a world which had promised so much and seems to offer so little. . . .

Seen superficially *Nothingness* is in some ways a naïve work. Yet its breathless pace, cries, and silences, although they say little, convey much. *Nothingness* has many artistic merits, but it is truly impressive because it strikes us as real, real with passionate honesty, simplicity, and directness of youth.

Edward R. Mulvihill and Roberto G. Sánchez.
Introduction to Carmen Laforet, *Nada* (New
York, Oxford University Press, 1958), pp. xii–xv

[In *Sunstroke*] the characters are human and not very far removed from ordinary social situations. They are beings who pulsate with life. As in a faithfully reproduced miniature, the entire reality of a person with the total system of his motivations and his idea of the world, which is made transparent in each meaningful act, becomes conspicuous. Carlos and Anita help with this. These beings who share their lives in an important moment constitute the plot of the work, which achieves full structural coherence by means of these personal relationships.

Outside of the three children [Martín, being the third], the rest of the characters are simple people whose actions lack complexity. They lead relatively well-ordered lives, free of abstractions and intellectualisms, lives that are repetitive, unchanging, and predictable. . . .

Circus people constitute part of the theme of this work. Unexpectedly, it seems that there is more fantasy now in Laforet's novelizing, since she is not conveying an actual, strong, or easily imaginable existence. But then it has to be taken into account that the reality of circuses is also real, that the men and women of the tightrope act within their own lives, that behind the life that they reflect on the trapeze there is their real one that can give nourishment, like all life, to a created reality. As José Marra-López has said, "*Sunstroke* is a marvelous novel with its characters of flesh and blood. All possess a deep human reality that is alive and meaningful."

Graciela Illanes Adaro. *La novelística de
Carmen Laforet* (Madrid, Gredos, 1971),
pp. 188–89†

[*Nothingness*] contains in its very essence the lesson which Román appears best to understand. Yet Andrea, as protagonist, is allowed to take her leave of the house in Barcelona and of her readers in a way which seems to undercut this overbearing sense of time and of art's failure to save life from decay. The ending appears happy. Rather than traveling alone, rather than missing the train as she did in her trip of the year before, when the novel closes Andrea is in a moment of hopeful escape. . . .

When we consider the various hints built into the novel, it becomes clear that the author's careful structuring of the work and even its richly sensuous descriptions form part of a studied art created not out of simple recollection, but out of an effort to disengage life from time through art. The disabused author Andrea, controlling the action from the beginning, has moved away from the world view of the Andrea of the story, who only partially develops. The character Andrea is capable of illusion at the end, despite her experiences and despite her knowledge of Ena's character, just as she was at the beginning. . . .

The novel engages in bad faith on two levels. The character Andrea, who refuses the lessons Ena and Pons have taught her, and the examples of Juan and Gloria and of Román—of all of her family—continues to be as Román has said, "a child . . . good, bad, what I like, whatever I want to do . . ." She remains incapable of perceiving the underlying qualities of corruption and decay that render all such categories of existence invalid. The second level of bad faith is offered by Andrea as author. As author, she is conscious now of the overpowering truths contained in the house on Aribau Street, aware that these truths reduce to nothingness everything that is not the house on Aribau Street. She nonetheless allows the novel to end happily. The happy ending and the illusioned Andrea join to produce an effect inconsistent with the basic themes of the novel. This level of bad faith suggest that writing, like living, is always threatened with inauthenticity. Survival depends upon the maintenance of a delicate balance between hope and disillusionment. The artist tries to beguile the forces of time and death, knowing nonetheless that the effort is hopeless. Andrea, the protagonist, like Andrea, the author, participates in a more or less conscious effort at self-deception in order to hold off the desperation whose victim Román became.

Ruth El Saffar. Symposium. Summer, 1974,
pp. 126–28

It must be recognized that when seen in its entirety, the work of Carmen Laforet represents no important advance in the area of structural and linguistic experimentation; it is alarmingly removed from the novelists of this century, and in particular from those of the last decade. Nevertheless, her work brings a subtle and deep exploration of the conflict—so adolescent, so feminine, but also so symptomatic of postwar Spain—between the necessity of enthusiasm and the substantiation of disenchantment. The souls that Carmen Laforet sketches or those in which her own portrait is seen indirectly are souls hungry for authenticity, who verify their search for values in a world of reverberating violence, routine, and daily need. In this sense, Carmen Laforet's work must be put in the line of the existential realism that prevailed in Spain during the 1940s. *Nothingness* is not merely a lucky novel that owes its widespread sales to outside circumstances. If it aroused such great and lasting notice, it was, doubtlessly, because it correctly discovered aspects of the present reality that had remained outside the first novels written after the war: the hopeful attitude of the young generation, the material and psychic ravages of war suffered by the average family the imbalance between hope and daily existence, hunger, poverty, moral disorder. . . .

The fundamental theme in Carmen Laforet is disenchantment: a world that seems susceptible to being transfigured magically by a fresh vision, but which reveals itself as deficient, inferior, unworthy. This theme is developed in *Nothingness, The Island and the Demons,* and *Sunstroke* by going from more to less, or going from apparent being to latent nothingness. In *The New Woman* the process follows an altogether inverse procedure: from disenchantment about everything to a supernatural enchantment of faith, which makes Paulina Goya see all the spaces of the world in the summit of a distant instant, far from "that ardent, vulgar, petty intrigue that was life."

Gonzalo Sobejano. Novela española de nuestro
tiempo (Madrid, Prensa Española, 1975),
pp. 159–60†

The principal theme of *The Island and the Devils* [*Demons*], imagination and fantasy, the heart of artistic creation, is a natural adjunct of the island setting. The island, with its unreal ambience, brilliant seascapes, volcanic irregularities, profuse and colorful vegetation, and openness of spirit manifest in the native folklore, legends, and songs, fosters the imagination. Too, the island suggests the distance necessary to creation. The backdrop of terrible events occurring on the mainland and the physical remoteness of the Canaries (Matilde is constantly repeating the refrain, "One would hardly know a war was going on") reminds us that spatial as well as temporal distances are important to art. *Nothingness* relied upon the temporal dimension; in *The Island and the Devils* geography is more important. There is a tacit suggestion that the peninsula is reality while the island is fantasy, unreality.

The Island and the Devils contains yet another symbolic dimension in the enclosure motif. Unfulfilled aspirations are related to incarceration as Pino, and later Marta, are closed up in the country house by José, and Teresa is literally imprisoned there. . . . The island becomes a place from which to escape for Marta; she claims she will never return. Thus a dialectic of closed/open, house/sea, island/peninsula imagery is constructed to underscore hindrances to and means by which growth may take place. Fantasy, when it serves to deny reality, is a kind of personal enclosure. In the end Marta will have to leave the island, symbol of her entrapment in a life of unreality.

Roberta Johnson. Carmen Laforet (Boston,
Twayne, 1981), pp. 73–74

MACHADO, ANTONIO (1875–1939)

Antonio Machado is perhaps the most intense of [the new Spanish poets]. The music of his verse goes along with his thoughts. He has written little and thought a lot. His life is like that of a stoic philosopher. He can tell his dreams in profound sentences. He becomes involved in the existence of things in nature. Any one of his verses about the land would have enchanted Lucretius. He has an immense Neronian and Diogenic pride. He has the admiration of the intellectual aristocracy. Some critics have seen him as the continuer of the pure national lyrical tradition. To the contrary, to me he appears to be one of the most cosmopolitan, general writers, for which reason I consider him one of the most human. [1906]

Rubén Darío. Opiniones (Madrid, Mundo
Latino, 1918), p. 202†

In Antonio Machado's work—and he is beginning to be generally considered the central figure [of contemporary Spanish poetry]—there is a restraint and terseness of phrase rare in any poetry.

I do not mean to imply that Machado can be called in any real sense a pupil of either [Rubén] Darío or [Paul] Verlaine; rather one would say that in a generation occupied largely in more or less unsuccessful imitation of these poets, Machado's poetry stands out as particularly original and personal. . . .

The influence of the symbolists and the turbulent experimenting of the Nicaraguan [Darío] broke down the bombastic romantic style, current in Spain, as it was broken down everywhere else in the middle nineteenth century. In Machado's work a new method is being built up, that harks back more to the early ballads and the verse of the first moments of the Renaissance than to anything foreign, but which shows the same enthusiasm for the rhythms of ordinary speech and for the simple pictorial expression of undoctored emotion that we find in the renovators of poetry the world over. *Plains of Castile,* his first volume to be widely read, marks an epoch in Spanish poetry.

Antonio Machado's verse is taken up with places. It is obsessed with the old Spanish towns where he has lived, with the mellow sadness of tortuous streets, and of old houses that have soaked up the lives of generations upon generations of men, crumbling in the flaming silence of summer noons or in the icy blast off the mountains in winter.

John Dos Passos. Rosinante to the Road Again
(New York, George H. Doran, 1922), pp. 146–47

A new play that has made a deep appeal to the emotions of the Spanish people is *Juan de Mañara*. On its presentation . . . it was a clamorous success. The authors are the famous brothers, Antonio and Manuel Machado y Ruiz. They must not be confused with the equally celebrated playwrights, brothers also, Joaquín and Serafín Álvarez Quintero, whose works is perhaps more familiar in the United States. . . .

Whenever Juan speaks he says so many inspiring things about life, the soul, death, and what comes after, that the drama recalls a morality play, and it holds the audience in an atmosphere of mystic suspense. For the Spanish mind it teems with significance, recalling as it does the lives of so many saints whose earlier years were as turbulent as those of Juan de Mañara, and have ended as did his own. Juan's obsession at last is to help the poor, to lead sinners to the light, and he is proclaimed by all a divine messenger. . . . *Juan de Mañara* is a play destined to be widely discussed. Soon after its production, Antonio Machado was elected a member of the Spanish Academy.

Frances Douglas. NYTBR. Aug. 28, 1927, p. 2

In *Plains of Castile* Machado shows us that one can continue "to search for the soul" no matter how involved one is with a geographic reality. In addition, *Plains of Castile* signifies the poet's maximum assimilation to the mentality of the Generation of 1898. This is evident in his vision of a tormented or innocent Castile, "the noble and sad land" wrapped up in its old clothing and keeping its secret of not knowing whether it hopes, sleeps, or dreams.

In *Plains of Castile* and in the immediately subsequent poetry there is a great meditation about Spain. . . . For one moment, Antonio Machado treats the ideas . . . of pessimism and renovation, of the painful feeling about our land, and the desire for resurgence—all [the ideas] of the Generation of 1898. In this second phase of Machado's poetry, his vision of Spain is presented at times with direct clarity, with that exquisite clarity and intelligence of verbal usage that is so peculiar to Antonio Machado. Let us remember, for example, the poems about Soria ["Fields of Soria"]. However, alternating with this clear view, with this direct passage from the real reality to the poetic reality, there are other examples in which there is a conflict between the poet's eyes and the world before him. These are the ideas and concepts about Spain, about the Spanish, that were quite current among our intellectuals of the time—"tragic Spain," the Castile "through which the shadow of Cain wanders" [from "Through Spanish Lands"], the crazy types, the criminals, the deformed—all of which appear in other artistic achievements of the time: the paintings of [Ignacio] Zuloaga. [Nov. 1933]

Pedro Salinas. Ensayos completos de Pedro
Salinas (Madrid, Taurus, 1983), I, pp. 133–34†

The last and longest period of Machado's productivity—the twenty years between the end of the Great War and his death—is undoubtedly the least distinguished. Though he continued to write almost to the last . . . he can hardly be said to have produced a single poem worthy to be classed with his greatest. . . .

The *New Songs (1917–1930)* are well named, for their most attractive verses are snatches of popular song . . . some of which are interspersed with epigrammatic proverbs. Throughout his life, though never as markedly as now, we find Machado returning occasionally to the traditional poetry with which his father must have familiarized him as a child. But perhaps the principal trait of the *New Songs* is a rather surprising recrudescence of picturesqueness. Significantly he draws a larger part of this inspiration from Andalusia; and, when in imagination he returns to the Sorian country, he is inspired not so much by the "Soria fría, Soria pura," "Soria, ciudad castellana," ["Cold Soría, clear Soria," "Soria, Castilian city"] of the [poem "Fields of Soría" in] *Plains of Castile,* but by the "montes de violeta" ["mountains of violets"], which in that collection are only a detail of the background. . . .

He develops an enhanced love of color—and even plays with the mauves and violets of Juanramonian youth. He can actually import color and picturesqueness into a poem which he has entitled "Galleries." He addresses eulogistic sonnets to his contemporaries in the field of letters—Baroja, Azorín, Pérez de Ayala, Valle-Inclán, Eugenio d'Ors—but they are hardly comparable with the earlier *Praises.* . . . [1939]

E. A. Peers. Antonio Machado (Oxford,
Clarendon Press, 1940), pp. 23, 25–26

Machado's disdain for the Spanish literary baroque results from the absence of temporality, which he perceives in it. The baroque poets—Góngora, Calderón, Quevedo—try to make up their conspicuous lack of intuition by clothing their images in heavy conceptual attire. . . .

Machado is aware that his notion of the baroque differs greatly from that which contemporary German criticism has made fashionable. He rejects with particular vigor the insistence on the dynamic quality of baroque art. . . . He lashes out unmercifully at the two forms taken by the baroque in the Spanish literature of the late Golden Age. In both *culteranismo* [preciosity movement] and conceptism he sees merely a proof that the Spanish lyrical stream, until then so rich in temporal overtones, had dried up—one more aspect of the spiritual impoverishment which was gradually taking hold of Spain. It might be said that the seventeenth-century Spaniard had lost touch with the world of the senses, with the growing, changing, and rushing stream of life, with his own psychic experience, and had taken refuge in a world of concepts and definitions, of generic images which he ungracefully juggled in an attempt to attain a trivial virtuosity. Machado, however, knew too well that the literary baroque is no mere whim of a handful of seventeenth-century writers. He nowhere claims that Góngora, or Gracián, or Quevedo sought to overturn a literary tradition out of a sheer perversity. Like all artists, they were children of their time.

Juan López-Morillas. *JAAC*. Dec., 1947, p. 168†

Antonio Machado possessed the intuition [of using the language without making it either prosaic and trivial or "poetic"] to a very high degree. It is not a question of technique, although technique plays an important role. Machado's preoccupation could be summed up in this question: how can one obtain a sufficiently expressive and beautiful language to say what is important without calling the reader's attention to it? The answer can be seen in his poems, which are written with a lucid perception of the risk of common terms and preciosity. No disdain for or cult of words . . . but rather a choice of language according to the emotions to be expressed. The classical language was inadequate for his sensibility, precisely because it was classical . . . [and] the romantic vocabulary was all used up. . . . The modernist vocabulary remained, but, feeling himself too close to Rubén [Darío], understanding him and being understood by him, his message could not be stated in the scintillating, prodigious, and refined speech of the great Nicaraguan renewer of poetry.

Machado considered himself obliged to create a personal language, and he did it with such natural simplicity that it took a long time for this event to be recognized, and even today, the admirers of his poetry do not stress it as it should be stressed. This new language, rather than implying hermetic aims, tended toward common speech, giving each word in normal meaning—the one foreseeable and imaginable by the reader—searching for clarity and transparency as the basic conditions of verse. Words expressed, without veiling, the emotion in which the poem was rooted, and they were faithful to Machado's design as long as they did not come between the work and the reader; thus, they achieved the type of poetry imagined by another great contemporary poet, T. S. Eliot. . . .

Ricardo Gullón. *CHA*. Sept.–Dec., 1949,
pp. 568–69†

Machado has understood the essential themes of the poetry and philosophy of our time. No one like him has lived through the conflict of the modern poet, exiled from society and finally from his own self, lost in the labyrinth of his own consciousness. The poet cannot find himself because he has lost the others. We all have lost the common word, the human and concrete objectivity of our peers. Our poet bravely lived through this contradiction. He always refused the transcendency that the belief in a creator God offered him—for Machado, the divine is a creature of man; God is the author of the "To the Great Zero" and his own creation is nothingness. Blasphemous and reticent, passionate and skeptical, his "Popular School of Higher Knowledge" proposes an investigation of our beliefs. Machado rejects everything, except man. But his point of departure is not the consciousness of oneself, but rather the absence of the nostalgia for "you." That "you" is not the generic objectivity of the Party or Church faithful. The poet's "you" is an individual, irreducible being.

Through a loving dialectal operation, Machado's concrete man can find himself only when he delivers himself. The "you" becomes "we." In 1935, at the sight of churches on fire, the poet was able to contemplate, for the first time, the appearance of that "we" in which all contradictions are resolved. Below the purifying flames, the face of the Spanish people was no longer different from the face of love and the face of death. Liberty had taken form. Abel Martín, Juan de Mairena, Antonio Machado were not alone. They were no longer masks; they were beginning to be. The could die. They had lived.

Octavio Paz. Sur. May–June, 1952, p. 51†

The *New Songs* of 1924 have no unity of mood or form . . .; and when Machado went on to publish his *Apocryphal Songbook,* many readers thought that his fear had come true: the gold had turned to copper change and the poet had become an amateur philosopher. The philosophy was obscure; the poems were explained by the author as "complementaries," mere illustrations to a fragmentary system of thought, and themselves only fragments, showing up the ruins of the poet's mind. The golden bees making poetry out of old sorrows were supplanted by Juan de Mairena lecturing on aesthetics, or Abel Martín the black-gowned pedagogue. Much of the old Machado had gone, though the new poems were full of echoes of themes and images used before: . . . galleries of the mind, . . . rainbow and downpour, . . . the fine-ground snow, . . . wind in your face, which only seemed to show that he was exhausted, and was picking up the splinters of the magic crystal of his dreams.

A reader who tried to judge the later poems of Yeats by the standard of the lake isle of Innisfree might be disappointed. The change in aim and method is obvious—more deliberate, perhaps, than the change which came over Machado, but in certain ways not unlike it. . . . It is clear that when Machado . . . repeats an image he has used before, he is not merely repainting an old picture, as he sometimes used to do. He is alluding, like Yeats, to something which had become for him a familiar myth. The use of imagery in the *Apocryphal Songbook* is almost entirely symbolical, not pictorial.

John Brande Trend. Antonio Machado (Oxford,
Dolphin Books, 1953), pp. 28–29, 32

It is quite evident that the significance of ["The Land of Al-vargonzález"] goes beyond the simple recounting of a rural tragedy. If Machado does reaffirm the narrative tradition of the romance, we nonetheless do not hesitate to state that its best verses are those in which the lyric and dramatic tremor are continually felt. No one can deny that the poet has dignified the narration of a common event, which is sung in the lands of Berlanga by the blind men, and that he has enhanced the vitalism of the Spanish people. However, Machado does not stop here. In his eagerness to express generic qualities, to approach the elemental in human life, everything is charged with a symbolic content. Thus, the Black Lagoon becomes a central point of the whole legend. Crime and punishment. Genesis and culmination. And it is quite revealing that in the prose he clearly emphasizes this symbolic role: "The wickedness of men is like the Black Lagoon; it is bottomless."

In our view, Machado intended to create a universal symbol of eternal human evil, with echoes of the legend of Cain, basing his work on an infamous murder case. To put it another way, he intended to show the capacity for evil that is present in all men. A rural crime, which is motivated by greed and envy, appears to surpass its mere physical circumstances and elevate and project itself onto an infinitely higher plane. The real background of Castile tends to vanish, and in its place we are presented with the primordial theme of the spiritual drama of man, who is a plaything between the forces of good and evil. It is not useless to remember that the poet believed during these years "that the mission of the poet [was] to invent new poems of the eternally human." [1955]

Allen W. Phillips. *Temas de modernismo hispánico, y otros estudios* (Madrid, Gredos, 1974), pp. 325–26†

With the second edition of *Solitudes* [i.e., *Solitudes, Galleries, and Other Poems*] the volume attained its definitive development. A great new poet was born. . . . Everything in modernism that was exterior music, the sonority of clarions, brilliant colors, is absent from Machado's voice. His is an interior voice, a modest one. In place of the sonorous verses, there was now an intimate and simple feeling, a very tender one. And the words were also very simple, almost basic. The public, so used to the words of Darío, was not able to understand at first.

I was only a child at the time, and I was part of that public. While in school I heard of no other modern poetry than that of the nineteenth century. . . . In 1916 I discovered Rubén Darío: I was dazzled. What mastery of rhythm, what magnificent colors, what strange, exquisite visions! It was only in the summer of 1918 that a volume of Antonio Machado's poetry fell into my hands. I began to read it. My first impression was one of disillusion. I was already accustomed to the great music of Rubén . . ., to his easy and colorful sentimentality . . ., and in this little volume of Machado's selected poetry there were no sumptuous colors, no captivating music, no premenopausal princesses. Everything was modest and simple. . . . I didn't understand. Fortunately, I didn't throw the book away. I had it with me all summer long, and I was reading. Little by little the poetry was entering into my soul. It was, above all, a lesson in aesthetics: . . . nothing exotic or picturesque; what was close and daily was full of possibilities and could be elevated to a high aesthetic plane. His poetry was a lesson in manliness, in austerity. . . .

Dámaso Alonso. Cuatro poetas españoles
(Madrid, Gredos, 1962), pp. 140–41†

It would never have been known, but for the discovery of the [private] notebook, that Don Antonio had invented a whole school of nineteenth-century poets and another of philosophers, naming his creations, assigning them dates, and furnishing them with a little biographical background, sometimes even giving samples of their work. The imaginary Abraham Macabeo de la Torre, for instance, was a Jewish poet born in 1824 at Osuna who died at Toledo seventy years later and, according to his inventor, had been Cansinos Assens's teacher. Another poet, one Antonio Machado, born in Sevilla in 1895, had been a professor in Soria, Baeza, Segovia, and Teruel, and had died in Huesca, the exact date of that event being uncertain. "Some have confused him with the celebrated poet of the same name, author of *Solitudes, Plains of Castile,* etc."

The intention behind this pastime of creating poets, Machado wrote, was the making of a collection of nineteenth-century poetry without using the work of any authentic poet, and of doing a like sort of thing with philosophy. Among his philosophers, José Callejo y Nandín had as his subject "The Intelligence and Robinson's Island," while Eugenio March concentrated on "The Seven Forms of Objectivity." Fernando Pessoa, the Portuguese poet whose life span was a few years short of Machado's at both ends, also expressed his thoughts through imaginary poets, creating four of these who wrote in individual styles and carried on correspondence with one another.

Alice Jane McVan. Antonio Machado (New
York, Hispanic Society of America, 1959), p. 63

It is common knowledge that Antonio Machado was interested in the ideas of [Henri] Bergson. . . . Critics have also found evidence to show that his interest was by no means superficial in the prose writings published by Machado under his two professorial pseudonyms. Several of them think that Machado's preoccupation with time in his poetry owes much to Bergsonism as well, although they have tended to base their opinions on the theories of "Abel Martín" and "Juan de Mairena," and on broad impressions of the content of the poems, rather than on the text of the poems themselves in this connection. . . .

In spite of the fact that critics of Machado have linked this preoccupation with Bergson, it is obvious that many of his poems which deal with temporal themes are not in the least Bergsonian. The passage of time and man's transitory nature is a common topic of lyric poetry at all periods and in all countries, and Machado often shows his awareness of the earlier poetic treatment of it. He quotes and glosses relevant passages from Jorge Manrique's *Poems,* for instance; he confesses his liking for "the old roses of Ronsard's garden" and his dislike for Calderón's handling of the same topic in *The Constant Prince;* on occasion, when elaborating the "carpe diem" theme, he draws upon a traditional Spanish ballad. Yet only the idea of things *in* time, as opposed to subject to it, is truly Bergsonian, and there are relatively few of Machado's poems which deal with this aspect of time in plainly philosophical terms.

Nigel Glendinning. RLC. Jan.–March, 1962,
pp. 50–51

Among the doubles of Machado, Juan de Mairena is the most important and representative—so much so, indeed, that without an adequate understanding of this identity, the poetry of Machado would lose much of its resonance and depth. It is Mairena's function, along with Abel Martín, his teacher and fellow contrary, to act as theoretical exegete to the lyrical Machado, unfolding those preoccupations with the Spanish temper so essential to a search for basic social criteria. Personages like Mairena and Martín achieve a singular kind of relief; they are in effect a repertory of living and problematical beings who act as interlocutors of emotive and intellectual predicaments that the poet, for complex and occult reasons of his own, has decided not to engage at first hand. What the intimate being of Machado might have been is difficult to determine in fact, in spite of our proximity to him in time. . . .

We might well intuit that the apocryphal Mairena and Martín function in this instance as screens or masks, at once concealing and provocative, for the personality of their creator. They furnish clues to his temperament and character, given Machado's characteristic introversion and mournful timidity; and they assist in the dialectical unfolding of a mind riddled by insecurity—by ontological and methodological doubts regarding the validity of doubt. . . .

In all probability Juan de Mairena is hewn from the pedagogical block of that very Institución Libre de Enseñanza [Free Academy] which showered Machado with so many fruitful illuminations; he is perhaps an amalgam of human types and character traits of his teachers and associates. . . . Another seminal figure present in that earlier fiction [*The Complementaries*] is Abel Martín, the apocryphal teacher of Mairena. . . . Abel Martín, in his earlier epoch, reflects philosophical preoccupations present in the mind of the poet Machado, and functions as his ontological mentor, expounding his thoughts much as Machado might have done it—had he but dared—ex-cathedra.

Ben Belitt. Introduction to Antonio Machado,
Juan de Mairena . . . (Berkeley, University of
California Press, 1963), pp. xii–xiii

The image of the centaur is a minor one in Antonio Machado's poetry. . . . Its first appearance occurs in the well known poem "Through Spanish Lands," in which Machado describes the Hispanic soul of Cain. . . . The symbol of the centaur appears again in the great poem "A Crazy Man." The crazy man is the hero of the Generation of 1898— the idealist reduced to madness by brutality, sterility, and common-sense foolishness of a cursed country. . . .

It seems . . . that the astrological background of Machado's metaphor is quite clear: the shadow of the Archer, the centaur-warrior which dominates Castile, is no other than the power of the zodiac monster whose influence (the decree of a tragic, divine destiny, of a fatal necessity) marks the Spanish character with a tendency towards violence, envy, and civil strife. His cross-bow leaves an imprint on Spanish men and soil; . . . it is another image of the "mark of Cain" which Machado, a typical man of the Generation of '98, saw as the expression and cause of Spain's decadence, the emotional heritage of the Spanish people. . . .

A secondary side to this image seems worth mentioning. . . . The image of the centaur for the modernists expresses the divine character of the sensual part of man, tends to suppress the sense of tragedy and to flatter, through aesthetic justification, the animal in us. Machado has taken a purely aesthetic metaphor and charged it with philosophical depth and rational and personal meaning: men are divided in themselves because they do not master the monster which inhabits them, and Spaniards specially suffer this domination with characteristic intensity.

Javier Herrero. *BHS.* Jan. 1968, pp. 38–41

The excessive complication of the plot should not obscure the fact that *Bitter Oleander* is a modern psychological drama of definite value. In an early passage of the dialogue we learn that the authors (and especially Antonio) are aware of the new Freudian psychology and the characters proceed to reveal both the good and the evil in themselves. . . . The Machados were to say later in their manifesto that the contemporary dramatist now has to be aware of two kinds of dialogue, the Socratic and the Freudian. . . .

In 1929, the Machados achieved their most enduring dramatic

success in Madrid working with a traditional theme of Andalusian *cante jondo* (the deep song) in *La Lola Goes Off to Sea,* which premiered at the Fontalba Theater with the actress Lola Membrives. In fact, Lola, who had starred in one of the Machados' adaptations, was largely responsible for their composition of the play. Of course neither brother set out to rework a traditional situation: the older Andalusian landowner of noble background competes with his own son for the affections of a lass, often of the lower class, but who possesses beauty and charm. . . .

In this drama, whose substance is mostly Antonio's, the theme is not the usual Andalusian (and universal) one in which the artist discovers life through love; here the artist (La Lola), who shows the way of life to others, must by her destiny lose herself in sublimation, becoming a symbol of her art, the song of the *cante jondo.* . . .

The Machados achieved an example of competent poetic theater in *La Lola.* The success of the play depends largely upon the depth of the two main characters, La Lola and the guitarist Heredia, whose voice is often that of the poet and philosopher Antonio Machado himself. . . .

After the success of *La Lola* in 1929, the Machados found themselves with a reputation to sustain, but apparently their inspiration began to fade.

Carl W. Cobb. *Antonio Machado* (New York,
Twayne, 1972), pp. 155–58

Apiarian elements (the honey-bee, honey, honeycomb, the swarm and the hive) are pregnant with representational and symbolic possibilities. It is therefore understandable that Machado, heir to a rich literary tradition, should have utilized several symbolic values traditionally associated with his selected image: sweetness from corruption; the poet as bee; the bee's mystical connotations; the bee as herald of Spring; the biblical (milk and honey) identification of a Golden Age; bees and their activities as the staple of folk-cultures.

The sweetness-from-corruption variation is only found in Machado's poetry in conjunction with the poet = bee/poetry = honey tradition. But what the Spanish poet does is quite innovative. The traditional formula (poet = bee; poetry = honey/wax) is extended by Machado into the following: poet/bee distils poetry/honey-wax from sorrow-anguish/flowers.

Although the sweetness-from-corruption theme is always tied by Machado to the metaphorical poet = bee image, he does also employ the latter as an isolated distinct entity. . . . The direct symbolic relation between apiarian imagery and poetic creativity explains the almost invariable presence of the former in Machado's feelingly expressed self-appraisals. As a humorously inverted lament, on one occasion, over his creative limits. . . . As an expression of doubt concerning the continuation of his poetic capacity. . . . As a regretful concern, on another occasion, over the philosophical direction of his art, a nostalgia for the simple poet he had been. . . . And later, as a proclamation of joy when he thought he'd found himself again. . . .

Whether leaving his personal imprint upon the literary tradition that he follows, or innovating beyond its parameters, Machado, despite his repeated use, is neither redundant nor superficial. It seems equally clear that apiarian imagery—its full range of bee, beehive, honey and beeswax—is at the very heart of Machado's metaphorical perception of poetic creativity.

Ernest A. Mares and Alfred Rodríguez. *MLS.*
Spring, 1982, pp. 13, 14, 15, 19

MACHADO, MANUEL (1874–1947)

In the pleiad of poets who have brought change to our poetry, Manuel Machado stands out for his subtle inspiration, his aristocratic lexicon, and his unsurpassed elegance of form. Manuel Machado is a poet of grace. . . . Whether he sings in the morning or at night, an airy charm is evident in the verses of this extraordinary poet who makes tiny, child-like poems out of the most serious and gloomy matters. The blackest and most tormented anguish becomes, when it passes through his soul, an elegant melancholy, a melancholy that suits a blithe spirit well. The sadness of an Andalusian ballad—that is the sadness of Manuel Machado. . . . Manuel Machado is a Sevillian poet in whom are incarnated all the beautiful and fine things that are contained in the name of Seville: blue skies, golden wine, light and fragrant air. [1900]

Rafael Cansinos Assens. *La nueva literatura,*
Vol. I: Los Hermes (Madrid, Paez, 1925),
pp. 185–86†

Don Manuel Machado is more accomplished than his younger brother [Antonio], though his earlier work suffers a little from once having been very modern and very *chic.* "To the purity of Greece (he says in the "portrait" of himself), I prefer the *chic* and the bull-fighter. . . . Yet rather than be an ordinary poet, my one desire would have been to become a good *banderillero."* This shows that the root of the matter is in him. Nothing more graceful or more beautiful can be imagined than the movements of a good *banderillero,* or nothing more certain to achieve exactly the effect intended. The younger brother can go rather wide of the mark, and yet accomplish what he set out to do; the elder must hit or miss—but the hits are palpable. . . .

Like his brother, Manuel Machado has written much in the form of the characteristic *coplas* and *cantares* [ballads and folk songs], they contain some of his happiest inspirations, and are indeed the soul of Spanish poetry. . . .

Yet his most memorable piece of work, it may be thought, is the sonnet on the *Conquistadores,* in which he returns to the earlier manner of *Museum* (1907) and *Apollo* (1911), poems which are "pictures from an exhibition." It shows the explorers in an ideal light, "Dream-captains of Dream-ships"; but it is a noble poem, for they were not only idealists, but leaders as well.

John B. Trend. *Alfonso the Wise, and Other Spanish Essays* (Boston, Houghton Mifflin, 1926), pp. 142–45

Ars moriendi [The Art of Dying] is like a swan that sings before dying. This is what the book tries to symbolize. . . .

Nevertheless, Manuel Machado does not have the taste of death in his mouth; he does not have a preoccupation with death, nor is he tormented by any uneasiness about the beyond. He has, and this is enough for him, a profound disdain for life, for the things that life customarily offers as a spectacle. His curiosity made of him a twenty-four-hour-a-day observer, and he knows that there arrives a moment on the world's stage in which the innumerable plays that are performed end up as melodramas: the lover who does not love, the gambler who does not dare bet, the rich man surrounded by brass instead of gold, the braggart without courage, the lord without dominion, the philanthropist without generosity, the artist without spirit. And he has discovered all that in the indecisive and confused instant of the early morning when the harsh light gives back to everyone his or her truths. The characters are left naked and unmasked.

Miguel Pérez Ferrero. *Vida de Antonio Machado y Manuel* (Madrid, Rialp, 1947), pp. 235–36†

As a Modernist, Manuel Machado found elements of primitive poetry pleasing, and successfully integrated them into his poetry. At its best his Andalusian poetry was original and prepared the way for the poets who came after him. But he exaggerated a tendency when he posed as a spontaneous, "popular" poet, and on occasion gave himself away with his exotic refrains. Much of the attention paid to him as a "popular" poet has been despicably motivated. It is to his credit that Antonio [his brother] should have realized the small importance Manuel's *coplas* had in his work as whole. . . . If Manuel Machado has suffered as a superficial Andalusian, in the view of those who have never read or wish to ignore his best poetry, it is his own fault. He knew what he was doing.

He shares the responsibility for the perversion of the originally generous faith of the Romantics in the idea of a "popular" poet.

Gordon Brotherston. *Manuel Machado: A
Revaluation* (Cambridge, England, Cambridge
University Press, 1968), p. 138

The principal injustice of this idea of Manuel Machado [that he is a
minor poet] is that it ignores the impressive, if unequal, range of his
poetic output and talents. His first and best book of poems, *Soul* (1902),
reveals a wide variety of skills. . . . Some of the poems of *Soul* explore,
often with striking symbols, the theme suggested by the book's title, an
inner world of deep longings, hopes, and fears, delving deeply into the
same corridors of the mind which his brother Antonio was roaming at
this period. [*Soul's*] profound existential pessimism is quite as serious
as that of Antonio's better known *Solitudes*. *Soul* also includes the first
and most famous of Machado's attempts to convey in a poem the
impression given by a painting, "Felipe IV." The experiment had been
made by a number of French poets before him, but he was the first
Spanish exponent of this kind of evocative verse portraiture, of which
he produced many fine examples. A different kind of evocation of a past
age, also in *Soul,* is "Castile," a vivid version of an incident in the *Poem
of the Cid*. The contrast between the robust descriptive force of this
poem and the languid subtlety of "Felipe IV" gives a good idea of the
versatility of Machado's poetic capacities at this time.

G. G. Brown. *A Literary History of Spain: The
Twentieth Century* (New York, Barnes & Noble,
1972), pp. 68–69

It was apparent from the very first folk songs of Manuel Machado . . .
that this new minstrel was different. Afresh, he had truly come upon the
buried treasure of popular wit, which is also the wit of high culture, that
unique and spiritual cleverness that does not make us laugh, but smile
at our good fortune, as if the invisible wing of an angel had tickled us.
Cleverness, angels, exquisite wit are found in the verses of *Soul* and of
Folk Songs, The Evil Poem, Ars moriendi, and *Cadences of Cadences.*
The wit of the Andalusian people, of the Spanish people, an easy and
very difficult wit of a fresh childhood, alive at every age of life. An
exemplary wit from the best verses of Manuel Machado, a model and
stimulus for his Antonio, his first and greatest disciple. . . .

Manuel . . . seems to play, to draw on water, to sketch on air. But
that water is of such limpidity on its surface that the purest sand can be
seen on the deep bottom, and that air is of such translucence that the
sleeping stars show through it in the daytime. Nothing deeper or purer

has been uttered in Spanish poetry than the delicate poems of Manuel Machado.

Gerardo Diego. Manuel Machado (Madrid,
Nacional, 1974), pp. 17–19†

Machado was an exquisite poet, refined in the expression of sensations and nuances as was the master Paul Verlaine. Other facets of his poetry are also singularly important and bear brief mention here: the constant use of masques and situations taken from the *commedia dell'arte,* surely following again the practice of Paul Verlaine and Jules Laforgue; a strong tendency to self-portraiture. . . . He was not . . . indifferent to national concerns and the contemporary socio-political plight of his country. This fact, sometimes forgotten, again confirms the artificiality of trying to separate the writers of the period into two clearly defined and exclusive groups (modernists and the Generation of '98). . . .

Both in his life style and his literature prior to 1910, the year when he married and settled down to a much less bohemian existence, Manuel Machado gives clear-cut evidence of being a decadent writer, although he never exclusively limited his art to its cult. I use the term decadentism here in its broadest sense, considering it both as a style and an attitude. Manuel Machado's poetry almost always gives off an aura which is both sensual and voluptuous, elegant and aristocratic. He was a conscious writer who—under the spell particularly of Paul Verlaine, in whom he saw the paradoxical but typical fusion of mysticism and sensuality—cultivated, as we have seen, exquisite themes normally associated with *fin-de-siècle* motifs and modernism: the courtly scenes of Versailles, the playful or tragicomical themes taken from the *commedia dell'arte,* and above all, the pleasures of erotic love and his amorous triumphs. Then there is also a studied pose of nonchalance and indolence in Manuel Machado, which reaches a degree of apparent indifference or frank disdain of life on the whole.

Allen W. Phillips. In Roland Grass and William
R. Risley, eds., Waiting for Pegasus: Studies of
the Presence of Symbolism and Decadence in
Hispanic Letters (Macomb, Western Illinois
University Press, 1979), pp. 66, 68

MARTÍN GAITE, CARMEN (1925–   )

When we finish reading a first book . . . we are always left looking toward the future, trying to make conjectures. And when the book [*The*

Spa] is so well written, so beautifully written with such truth and urgency as is Carmen Martín Gaite's, we are compensated and have something to be joyful about. Carmen Martín Gaite is a perfectly formed writer, in spite of "The Spa" [the title story]. . . . For me, "The Spa" is not the best of the four stories that make up this first book, precisely because, without leaving its narrative qualities aside, she has attempted a more abstracted and intellectualized undertaking that is more in the line of Kafka than in the line of her own nature. . . . "The Spa" seems to me to be somewhat confused, whereas the style of the other stories ["The Information," "A Day of Freedom," "The Girl Below"] is crystal clear, very intimate, with a delightful and highly cultivated feminine insight, with very specific features. The complexity of the subconscious does not seem to be the dominant feature in Carmen Martín Gaite, who is outstandingly endowed with the qualities of sobriety and economy of language, tenderness and transparency. . . .

The young writer [of these stories] possesses an uncommon descriptive elegance of a writer who is well adjusted and alert, without affectation and irregularities of composition. It is, therefore, logical that her stories—principally, the last three—turn out to be stimulating. Her concise, sober prose attains a lean and well-modulated emotional level.

R. de G [arciasol]. *Ínsula.* Sept. 15, 1955, p. 9†

We have [in *Threads of Discourse*] a form of interior duplication: a written narration which consists of an oral narration in which speaking, writing, and reading are frequent topics of conversation. The relationship between the two interlocutors is analogous to that of the writer and the reader. Carmen Martín Gaite hopes to find in the reader her own ideal listener and to enlist his or her collaboration as a silent participant in a dialogue, just as Eulalia and Germán are, alternately, listeners rather than speakers. At one point Eulalia reflects upon the joy of reading which she describes as a dialogue with an absent person, adding that when a reader responds to a book it is as if he had actually seen the author's face and heard his voice. Ideally, the sharing of experiences which occurs on one level between Eulalia and Germán will be paralleled by the communication on a second level between author and reader. . . .

The key image in the novel is that of the thread, the *hilo* of a conversation, of interpersonal relationships, of one's own identity, and of life. It gives or can give continuity to an otherwise fragmented existence by connecting one's actions so that they cease to be isolated happenings. . . . "We have a thread that is lost" is the refrain of one of Germán's friends who sees this loss as the basic cause of contemporary alienation. The solution lies in communication. Participants in a conversation are depicted as grasping the two ends of a thread which they pass back and forth, weaving a fabric, embroidering a design.

Kathleen M. Glenn. *RomN*. Spring, 1979,
pp. 281–82

Between Curtains's most notable structuring feature is its proliferation of points of view and even of narrators. It shares with the modern novel its loss of confidence in a single, authoritative narrative voice, and for a peremptory, reportorial embrace of reality it substitutes an assemblage of private perceptions (*Inner Fragments* is the apt title of Martín Gaite's 1976 novel), much like the beveled mirror in which Pablo sees multiple, cubistic images in motion. The traditional third-person narrator is not absent, and Martín Gaite's experiment is not nearly so radical as others of her day, but her self-conscious text is enslaved by no laws of mimetic composition and accomplishes its design as much through the playful invention of expressive modes as with the dutiful representation of reality.

Lest the reader-critic take umbrage at the notion of a serious social-realist novel vested with playfulness in its execution, it is only fair to point out that Martín Gaite openly associates herself with that bevy of modern artists who suffer no sense of shame or erosion of purpose when they view art as a game.

John W. Kronik. In Mirella Servodidio and
Marcia L. Welles, eds., *From Fiction to
Metafiction: Essays in Honor of Carmen
Martín Gaite* (Lincoln, Neb., Society of
Spanish and Spanish-American Studies, 1983),
p. 52

By letting [an] image of the past come alive and leap out of the fixed limits of the mirror onto the flowing space of her consciousness, Martín Gaite embarks on that inward odyssey that Adrienne Rich [American feminist poet] has so eloquently called the journey of the woman artist through "the cratered night of female memory to revitalize the darkness, to retrieve what has been lost, to regenerate, reconceive and give birth" ["Re-Forming the Crystal," in *Poems: Selected and New, 1950–1974* (New York: W. W. Norton, 1975), p. 228]. Thus, in countless pages of the novel, we see her peeling away layer after layer of the past, savoring its taste and touching its contours. And it is precisely through this process of retrieving not the photographic image of the past, but its flavor, nuance and subjective reality, that Martín Gaite has further multiplied the many readings one can find in her text [of *The Back Room*] . . . . Martín Gaite's singular ability to capture the pulsations of the period and her great facility for converting the mundane into the interesting, transform *The Back Room* into not just a hybrid of the fantastic, sentimental, historical and autobiographical, but rather, a unique *Bildungsroman* for a whole generation of Spanish women who will undoubtedly see themselves reflected in the minute descriptions that the author provides of her own upbringing.

Linda Gould Levine. In Mirella Servodidio and
Marcia L. Welles, eds., *From Fiction to
Metafiction: Essays in Honor of Carmen
Martín Gaite* (Lincoln, Neb., Society of
Spanish and Spanish-American Studies, 1983),
pp. 167–68

One reading suggested by [*The Back Room*] is that the reality of the Franco years cannot be apprehended by a static presentation of dates, statistics, and events; it cannot be reduced to univocal statements. The dynamic interplay of texts in *The Back Room*, on the other hand, does allow us to apprehend that the literary text is integrally woven into the sociohistorical text of the country. Above all, it points toward the plurality of meanings inherent in the very concept "text." . . .

A plurality of meanings is the effect created by nearly all the textual strategies employed in the novel. When the protagonist begins to read the manuscript she earlier created, for example, her action bestows upon the original text a whole new plurality of meanings. Even the title of the novel itself points toward this liberating plurality. "El cuarto de atrás," or back room, was the place where the protagonist as a child enjoyed the freedom to develop her creative imagination. As the mature narrator attempting to come to grips with post-Franco Spain, she now sees that the present context imposes a new plurality of connotations on this text from the past.

Robert C. Spires. *Beyond the Metafictional
Mode: Directions in the Modern Spanish Novel*
(Lexington, University Press of Kentucky,
1984), p. 123

MARTÍN-SANTOS, LUIS (1924–1964)

A great deal of monotony can be seen in novelistic forms. In my opinion, the younger novelists must find original forms that respond to a reality they must reflect. . . .

The monotony I am speaking about—monotony of characters, situations, action—explains part of the attention that Martín-Santos's *Time of Silence* has been receiving. This novel has nothing to do with the patterns already in use. Its sources are Joyce, Kafka, Proust, and Sartre. Even when there is in *Time of Silence* an apparent multiplicity of styles—which are nothing more than the author's game, his exercise of skill—the whole novel seems astonishingly unified. And different, absolutely different from all the other novels of the younger generation.

Another reason that *Time of Silence* has fared so well is the evident lack of intellectual depth among other young writers. . . . That is to say, among [other important contemporary novels], a novel of profound intellectual depth was lacking. That novel is *Time of Silence*. . . .

The action of *Time of Silence* takes place in Madrid in fall 1949. The action is presented as if with rapid and forceful strokes of a brush. Reality is very acute; every accessory element is automatically eliminated. The author is basically concerned with presenting the scene of a situation: the existential and historical situation in which a series of characters, representative types of different social strata, and, in particular, the central character, the young doctor Don Pedro, who is a symbol of human frustration, are all developed.

The elimination of the accessory elements—which is one of the most serious demands that a novelist can make of himself—at times produces wonderful results. . . .

Ricardo Doménech. *Ínsula*. June, 1962, p. 4†

There are many criticisms of a historical nature in *Time of Silence*. The topic of Spanish reactionariness . . . , the historical stagnation of the nation, the lack of projects to be achieved . . . and ironically, . . . the apathy of the Spaniard whose inertia finds a riverbed in religious pseudoactivity are alluded to. . . .

In his criticism of intellectual life, he censures the lack of facilities for research . . . ; the upper class's pseudo-interest in culture is satirized, . . . [and] the literary social gatherings are also assailed. He makes quite clear [his opinion] about the inanity of the younger artist's ideas and theories. . . .

In his study of the national pastime—a theme that greatly attracted Martín-Santos, as is evident from the large number of bullfight images, as well as his best short story, "Bullfighting"—the novelist investigates the Spanish idiosyncrasy. He analyzes the fondness for bullfighting from a historical-social point of view and states that the hatred that the bloody tribulations of the Spanish Civil War left has been officially institutionalized and directed against the bullfighter in order to avoid the eruption of this hatred through other more dangerous paths.

The author also breaks the silence or semisilence that postwar Spanish novelists have maintained for diverse reasons and he denounces without any softening the whole situation of contemporary Spanish life.

Martín-Santos belongs to that "wounded generation" that is made up of writers who were children during the civil war and knew the horrors of peace [in the postwar years].

José Ortega. *Symposium*. Fall, 1968, pp. 258–59†

After having read Martín-Santos's novel [*Time of Silence*] one has the impression of having been faced with a collage of conscious echoes of Spanish writers of many diverse periods—[Camilo José] Cela, Mateo Alemán, [Francisco de] Quevedo, and even [Luis de] Góngora. And let us not forget that the same thing occurs with Spanish painting, especially in the continuous use of Goya throughout the work. Nonetheless, in spite of the amalgam of diverse sources of inspiration—possibly a deliberate attempt to capture the historical context of a spirit of protest quite peculiarly Spanish—Martín-Santos has produced an original and complex novel in which he presents the absurd as a profound psychological experience in a character and in a people. In a way, the most original feature of his narrative technique is the manner in which he appears to speak objectively from within the mind of the protagonist, who at times is completely identified with him, and who at other times is almost imperceptibly converted into an objective commentator whose role is to evaluate what is happening in the deepest layers of the protagonist's consciousness. In this overlapping of the author with his character there is a very exact suggestion of how existential psychoanalysis functions, since its objective is not only to understand the "deformed" world of the patient, but also to bring him to a desirable reintegration with society through self-analysis. The central part of this cure is the process of transference, through which the patient brings to the surface his repressed emotions and attributes them to the analyst instead of to himself. Of course, the analyst must remain impassive, on the border of the dislocated world of the patient. Martín-Santos, a psychiatrist and author of a lucid treatise on existential psychoanalysis, writes with clear objectivity when he exercises his profession in this novel.

Sherman Eoff and José Schraibman. *PSA*.
March, 1970, pp. 228–30†

The object of the satire [in *Time of Silence*] is Spain, but not a phantasmagoric eternal Spain . . . . In this Spain a young man directed toward the study of a truth useful to all sees his work made impossible and his vocation undone owing to a series of misfortunes that demonstrate the inexorable aspects of social conditioning more than the absurdity of existence. If his laboratory had had the necessary equipment to carry out his experiments, he would not have had to become involved in the rat-supply industry of Muecas. The need for rats brings Pedro to Muecas's shack and the need to conceal a case of incest and an abortion leads Muecas to Pedro's boardinghouse. Thus, owing to poverty, a shack-boardinghouse (or middle class-poverty class) clash is produced with fatal results for both sides, as the victims Florita and Dorita illustrate. But, in addition, it is outside of this sad boardinghouse where Pedro eats his fish that he succumbs not only to the crime that the shack confronts him with, but also to the mediocrity that little by little the atmosphere of the boardinghouse has spread through his soul (matchmakers, passive classes, conventionalism, and general senility). The most cultured circles do not provide stimulus or support for him; in the artists' café there reigns neo-Garcilasean tranquillity, "low realism," and clownnish incompetency . . . .

The humanity that passes through these dense pages of *Time of Silence* is an alienated humanity, but Martín-Santos's theme is not properly alienation, as in Cela, but rather failure: failure as seen from indignation.

Gonzalo Sobejano. *Novela española de nuestro*
tiempo (Madrid, Prensa Española, 1970),
pp. 360–61†

When *Time of Silence* appeared in 1962, it was hailed as a new stylistic experiment and a possible break in the impasse of neorealistic objectivism then in vogue in the Spanish novel. Critics were unanimous in welcoming a new and promising writer in Hispanic Letters. Two years later, Martín-Santos died tragically in an automobile accident. He left behind a new novel, *Time of Destruction* . . . and a series of short narrative sketches and essays which are collected in the present volume under the general title of *Apologues* [*and Other Unpublished Prose*].

The editor of this collection emphasizes the fact that Martín-Santos left his manuscripts unordered, and that in compiling this work he guided himself only by certain affinities in theme, or, at times, vaguely similar titles. . . . The material is very uneven and at times quite trivial; nevertheless, the editor felt that all of it provided useful insights into the personality and main preoccupations of the author.

The apologue is a curious genre to choose. These stories include short parables ranging in size from half a page to seven pages. . . . There is a definite Kafkaesque quality in their ambiguity and in the composition of some of the stories. . . . The tone also recalls the detached irony of some of J[orge] L[uis] Borges' fantasies. Stylistically, they bear no trace of the baroque neologisms and circumvolutions so abundant in *Time of Silence*. Some recurrent themes, insofar as they can be determined with certainty, are: the fiction of appearances, satire of the modern world—without sin and without virtue, the lack of human communication, and the problem of artistic creation.

One of the essays, "Ramuncho's Complex," provides insight into the psychology of the Basque people. Two others are highly technical psychoanalytical treatises which really have no place in the volume. . . .

John Crispin. *BA.* Spring, 1971, pp. 287–88

In *Time of Silence* time as a component of external structure does not have great importance; the novel's action takes place over an apparent period of five days whose fragmented segments are clearly linked through an obvious night-day sequence through references to an event which is to occur, for example, the following day. The importance of time in the novel is rhythmic and existential. Spatial units, however, are significant. There are four spatial centers: the research institute where the protagonist Pedro engages in genetic investigation with the limited help of Amador; the rooming house which initially is the only center of concern in Pedro's life; the *chabolas* [shacks], inhabited by a society apart; and the house of prostitution to which Pedro is linked through his wealthy, ornamentally intellectual friend Matías.

Through these four centers a series of character oppositions focused on and through Pedro is joined. The initial opposition is that established between Pedro—intellectual, seemingly passive—and the vital Amador. . . . Through Amador, a broader opposition is created between Pedro and Muecas—the shrewd, illiterate master of survival—which sets the basis for the compositioning of two coexistent spheres. Amador, who partakes of both, joins the intellectual, sterile, acceptable world with that of "la miseria que no mata" ["the misery that does not kill"], a world much more vital than the other but whose vitality is distorted and made negative in the constant process of dehumanizing animal survival.

In *Time of Silence,* the internal structure is equivalent to the means by which these two worlds are brought together in Pedro. Martín-Santos utilizes vital, connotative links. Thus the animal sensuality of the atmosphere in Muecas's *chabola* is not essentially different from that existing in the house of prostitution and the rooming house, both of which, like Amador, constitute intermediary realities partaking of both worlds.

Mary L. Seale. *Hispanófila.* Jan., 1972, pp. 45–46

In *Time of Silence,* a modern work in both theme and form, several narrative techniques corresponding to the several angles from which the main character and some of the secondary ones are focused upon for individualization are found. These techniques are narration in the first, second, and third persons.

Narration in the first person, is interior monologue, is used very often in order to reach Don Pedro's consciousness as well as that of the hero's widow and that of Cartucho. The form of the interior monologue has several nuances. Sometimes it is logical in its idea and syntactical in expression; at times this logical meaning makes us seriously think that it is not an interior monologue at all, properly speaking. One example of this doubtful interior monologue is the first monologue of the widow. At other times the monologue does not follow any set form, with regard either to ideas or to expression. This is the case with some of the monologues of Don Pedro and those of Cartucho.

The second-person point of view occurs in the interior monologue of Don Pedro. The *tú* [familiar *you*] is the doubling of the *I* person of the same character. The *I* of Don Pedro of the present is defending and accusing the Don Pedro of the past. . . . This schism of I into I*a* and I*b* (both at the same time critical and criticized) is the factor that defines the internal conflict of the protagonist. This schism is the cause of the protagonist's tragedy, a tragedy from which he will no longer be able to escape.

The third-person point of view is that of the narrator, who knows his characters as much in their psychology as in their external actions.

Vicente Cabrera. *Sin nombre*. Jan.–March,
1973, pp. 68–69†

It is evident . . . that *Time of Destruction*—or at least its plan as we know it—is more complex than *Time of Silence*. If the latter was, for the most part, a novel of implicitly understood things—the gray postwar world, the sharp class distinctions, and including, as we have seen, an implicit socioliterary typology of the petite bourgeoisie—*Time of Destruction,* on the other hand, presents *ab ovo* the development of a double and suggestive process: in the first place, the influence of Spanish life, its prejudices, and its frustrations, on the development of an individual; in the second place, the response that same individual has to his own life. Pedro of *Time of Silence* was, definitively, a common being, more representative than individualized, but Agustín of *Time of Destruction* is formed with the qualities most opposite to commonness: a brilliant speaker . . . , a man inclined to theorize about experience . . . , but above all a man conscious of fulfilling a destiny that will bring him, first, to recognize the fact of his sexual impotence, and second, to plunge into the investigation of an insoluble crime. . . .

When Agustín experiments with his stupid cousin, when he understands the fundamental importance of the attainment of the judgeship, when he decides to undertake his own deflowering . . . , when he decides to overrule the mayor's authority, Agustín adds a high percentage of self-will to his existence, as a bet against the aimless and habitual, which—as the author himself points out—make him into a symbol.

A symbol of what? the feigned author of the prologue will ask with some sincere perplexity. Of liberation? Of the destruction of the myths that imprison our freedom? Of the annihilation he expects for his precursors? It is evident that each one of these meanings is to be found in Agustín's personality and destiny . . . . [1973]

José Carlos Mainer. Foreword to *Tiempo de destrucción* (Barcelona, Seix Barral, 1975), pp. 25–26†

With the novels of Martín-Santos and [Carmen] Martín Gaite, the genre [of the social novel] reaches a higher level: now social criticism is wedded to complex, non-linear portraits of unique individuals in conflictive situations. The protagonists of *Time of Silence* and [Martín Gaite's] *Ritmo lento* [*Slow Rhythm*] function in two ways to communicate a social analysis. On one level, the main characters verbalize social criticisms directly. On a second plane, the nonconformists illustrate society's shortcomings through their encounters with representatives of the social order. Points of conflict between the nonconformist and his society indicate society's deficiencies, for one crucial reason: in each instance, the character who refuses to conform is superior to his environment. It is he who invariably is right, and society who is wrong. . . .

In *Time of Silence* as well as in *Slow Rhythm,* the authors move beyond the objective realism which prevailed in Spain in 1962. Martín-Santos uses linguistic innovations to involve the reader in formulating (or deciphering) information. Martín Gaite presents a non-chronological portrait for the reader to put together in constructing (or, again, deciphering) the process of a unique personality. The nonconformist protagonist in each novel advances social criticism directly, through personal observations. But he also plays a representative role, as a device for focusing on contradictions between revered absolutes—truth, rigorous thought, moral consistency—and the reality of *franquista* Spain. The reader sympathetically interprets the protagonists' dilemmas from the character's point of view, because each nonconformist is a young idealist of great potential. Society's destruction of such admirable young men is a harsh indictment of postwar Spain. This condemnation is conveyed all the more strongly by its method of presentation, whereby the reader participates in assigning meaning to the experiences of the nonconformist protagonist.

Joan Lipman Brown. *HR*. Winter, 1982, pp. 65, 71–72

MARTÍNEZ SIERRA, GREGORIO (1881–1947) and MARÍA (1874–1974)

Devotion to art has made of Gregorio Martínez Sierra one of the distinguished literary figures of Europe. Although gifted with undeniable genius, his rise has been due to years of painstaking effort. It is a frequent boast of modern authors that they send their copy uncorrected to the publisher, making no attempt to eliminate crudities of style, and to this, no doubt, is due the ephemeral character and the unsatisfying effect of so much of the literature of the hour.

Martínez Sierra, however, acknowledges that he is unsparing in self-criticism of his work. He goes over it many times to give it elegance of style and polish. He composes slowly, keeping in view his desire to express his emotions in the most pleasing manner. By this method the greatest works of literature have been produced. Martínez Sierra lays special stress upon the sincerity of his productions. His writings are true to nature and true to art. They deal only with the simple, everyday events of life; he finds his inspiration in the play of sunshine and shadow on the grass; in the music of the wind . . . . With light, seeming trivial matters of this nature, he has said, his works are concerned, and yet, although so simple, the events represent life's complex. They bring both smiles and tears. His books should not be read hastily while making a dashing round of a city in the street car; they may better be appreciated in a softly lighted library during a long, rainy evening. They must be read in the original in order that the beauty and lyric charm of the diction may not be lost. . . .

The Cradle Song is generally conceded to be Martínez Sierra's magnum opus. While all of his works are intensely Spanish, *The Cradle Song* could have been written nowhere except in Spain, and by no other author. Here his tender, sympathetic understanding of women, children, and all helpless creatures is revealed. As Professor [Federico] de Onís suggests, the subject matter is somewhat difficult and it is rather far removed from the comprehension of the protestant American; yet with his charm of expression, and his grace of diction, the author arouses a sentiment of extreme cordiality between the reader (differences of religion and nationality notwithstanding) and the gentle nuns who exist behind convent walls . . . .

Frances Douglas. Hispania. Nov., 1922,
pp. 257–58, 266

The law [Martínez Sierra] esteems very little in face of the gentle wisdom whose increment is sure with the years. Social progress is individual progress and individual progress is spiritual progress whose conquests are recorded first in the heart. This, of course, is no new doctrine, but it is the core of Martínez Sierra's philosophy and the main-spring of his art. In so far as the Church is a liberating and humanizing force he is a Christian, but he is a dissenter from all creeds and doctrines which restrict and inhibit the upward march of man.

Curiously enough, as a playwright, Martínez Sierra, for all his tenderness, has little concern with the individual. This is the source of his calm. One of the most sensitive of men, he is also one of the most detached. His drama is expository, chiefly for the reason that the inception of his plays is invariably generic and abstract. They are illustrative each of some general axiom or principle, whether human or social. He is no apostle of personal causes. Every man must be suffered, none the less, to shape his own career—*Live Your Own Life*. The old virtues are destined to make way before the advance of the new—*The Shepherds*. Sometimes, again, he has paused to probe some universal passion or emotion, devotion as in *The Lover,* or, as in *The Cradle Song,* to echo the cry of the eternal mother instinct which has been stifled and denied. Sometimes, as in *Fragile Rosina,* in a sportive mood, he is content to parade mere temperament or an idle trait. Plays like *The Cradle Song* and *The Kingdom of God* are eloquent too, above the plane of feeling, of a social scheme, a new, a better life. The course of the story is the setting forth of the idea, the impelling emotion in all its significant phases, now by direct statement, now through contrast, but, in whatever way it may be effected, the content is plainly implicit in the theme from the beginning to become evident in detail as the action proceeds. For this reason the volitional element, in so far as it passes beyond mere childish caprice, is almost wholly lacking. Martínez Sierra draws no villains, creates no supermen, heroically imposing their wills, inherits no complexes, and cherishes small love for the tricks of display. His taste is unfailingly nice. Mystery, however veiled, he abhors, complication of plot, all thrill of situation. He even flees those internal crises of character which are so absorbing to the great dramatists, through whose struggles personality is built up and self-mastery won. These savor always of violence and conflict, no matter how subjective or subtle they may be. They are dramas of action, and Martínez Sierra's drama is static drama. He is content to sacrifice movement to visual quality, excitement to charm.

> John Garret Underhill. Introduction to *The Plays of Gregorio Martínez Sierra,* Vol. I (New York, E. P. Dutton, 1923), pp. xiv–xvi

The plays are admirably constructed. To this aspect of Martínez Sierra's art, Benavente and the Álvarez Quinteros have contributed, but there is no other point of similarity between his works and theirs. Jacinto Benavente is a pessimist, cold and intellectual; Martínez Sierra is an optimist, warm and human; and while this might be said of the Álvarez

Quinteros also, the optimism of these Andalusian writers is really quite different. It is rather like a burst of gay laughter, compared with Martínez Sierra's quiet smile of contentment. He sings the joy of simple souls, full of ingenuous faith—and of hope. Faith, hope and love, these are the three essentials of the theater of Martínez Sierra. He does not preach, for he is a poet. The characters and atmosphere are everything, and all his art goes into their creation. His taste is exquisite; delicacy is never lacking, even in the most realistic scenes (*A Lily among Thorns, The Kingdom of God,* etc.). The language is always simple and natural.

Mama has for its theme the awakening of a frivolous, pleasure-loving woman to her real role of motherhood when confronted with a crisis in the life of her daughter. Inspired by Ibsen's *A Doll's House* . . . , *Mama* is similar in theme and treatment. The difference between the Spanish and Scandinavian plays lies in the solution of the wife's problem. *A Doll's House* had been coldly received by Spanish audiences, principally because of the third act in which Nora decides to leave husband, home and children. Martínez Sierra, although an ardent admirer of Ibsen . . . , nevertheless rejected Ibsen's emancipation of the heroine. Instead he gives a typically Spanish solution to the problem. The Spanish heroine cannot be happy in a freedom that takes her away from her home. Rather than break ties, she binds them more firmly about herself. She demands equal rights with her husband, but she does so in order to acquit herself better of her responsibilities toward home and children.

Margaret S. Husson. Introduction to Gregorio
Martínez Sierra, *Mamá: Comedia en tres actos*
(New York, W. W. Norton, 1937), pp. 14–15

Martínez Sierra is, by his upbringing and sensibility, a Europeanized writer . . . . Generally speaking, his theater is not moralistic or full of ideas about reform. The debt that he owes Benavente lies more in the area of narrative technique and dialogue than in that of theme or purpose. In some ways under the influence of Ibsen, nevertheless Martínez Sierra does not omit ideology and thesis in reference to the social and emotional situation of women; but this is not the dominant note of his theater. What does characterize his theater, though in a general way, is his preference for female characters, his capacity for understanding their emotions and problems from a point of view that is hardly masculine. When one talks of Martínez Sierra it is necessary to refer to a possible collaboration on the part of his wife in his dramatic work. It does not appear to us to be an important issue. In any case, the author and his wife form a unit, a literary unit that we know by the name of Martínez Sierra, and on that we must rely. This *feminine* vision goes further than the female characters, and upon confronting the theme of

Don Juan (*Don Juan of Spain*), he pushes the hero toward a behavior that is shot through with femininity.

The judgment of the Martínez Sierra entity had a propensity toward overvaluing typically feminine sentiments. *The Cradle Song,* in two acts, exalts the maternal reaction of nuns in a village convent toward a foundling baby girl. The atmosphere suffers from softness and cheapness: Martínez Sierra is not ignorant of the ultimate fact that in the most vulgar Spanish theater, maternal feeling becomes the only loving sentiment that is respectable.

The theater of Martínez Sierra lacks dramatic energy, sensitivity to the highest values of society; it lacks, in a word, virility. Out of all his works, we prefer the plays of sheer entertainment, endowed with agile and witty dialogue, skillful in the presentation of comical situations and in their resolution. In this respect, *An August Night's Dream,* although unoriginal, but with characters, especially the female ones, who are well observed and studied, seems to us most representative. [1956]

> Gonzalo Torrente Ballester. *Panorama de la*
> *literatura española contemporánea* (Madrid,
> Guadarrama, 1961), p. 221†

[Martínez Sierra] learned much from Benavente, but he introduced into his dramas a poetic note of idealism and love. He, too, abandoned his university studies to write poetry and novels on themes which later appeared in his dramatic work. Like the Álvarez Quintero brothers, he portrays mainly the pleasant aspects of life in his search for beauty, and he demonstrates a faith in human nature and the human soul. Although he undertook many types of drama, his best are comedies of manners. His plays are steeped in an idealism based on simple emotions, and in his world virtue always triumphs over the weaknesses of humanity, as good works achieve their reward. His plays do not end tragically, and his themes are usually those of family living. Like Benavente, Martínez Sierra finds women to be representatives of the nobler aspects of life. . . .

Martínez Sierra shows the necessity of faith even among evil persons, the power of religion, the goodness of women through whose virtue even weak and selfish men may be redeemed, and the blessings of old age. His wife, María de la O Lejárraga, an ardent feminist, collaborated with him in many of his dramas, and it has been said that his penetrating feminine psychology may be due in part to her help. Martínez Sierra is tolerant and sincere, with a sincerity which is at times almost naive, but which in its stress on the sanctity of life, nobility of soul, and maternal love charms the reader into forgetting the baser aspects of human nature.

> Richard E. Chandler and Kessel Schwartz. *A*
> *New History of Spanish Literature* (Baton
> Rouge, Louisiana State University Press, 1961),
> pp. 153–54

[Martínez Sierra's] irony . . . is not Jacinto Benavente's indifferent or cold irony of purely intellectual origins, whose characteristics have been compared to pricking pins . . . . The irony of Gregorio Martínez Sierra is somewhat more cordial and effusive, similar to the good joke of the mystics, and also comparable to a kindly maternal smile that makes a naughty child blush. It is an irony not of the salon or of an eighteenth-century literary gathering, but of a school and of a reformatory; it is an irony that has a definite and benevolent objective, and whose prickings are comparable to those that certain fruits are given in order to speed up ripening. It is, in short, a sentimental irony, totally different from the intellectual irony of Jacinto Benavente. In the same way, Martínez Sierra's optimism and joyfulness, that thrilling joyfulness of his theater, are not the optimism or the joyfulness of the Quintero brothers . . . . The joyfulness in Martínez Sierra's theater is a more profound and intimate spiritual contentment, attained by the will aided by grace, as in the ecstasies of the mystics or by pure innocence, as in childhood dreams; it is a joyfulness of simple souls full of ingenuous faith . . . .

> Andrés Goldsborough Serrat. *Imagen humana*
> *y literaria de Gregorio Martínez Sierra* (Madrid,
> Gráficas Condor, 1965), p. 118†

Critics of contemporary Spanish theater have long speculated about María Martínez Sierra's important contribution to her husband's success in the theater. Prior to the publication of this book, however, no evidence had been offered in support of María's collaboration either as writer or as consultant. Material discovered after her death in 1974 firmly establishes her as author—far more than merely inspirer or editorial assistant—of much of what was published under the name of her husband. . . .

The early works, set rather consistently in rural Spain (particularly Asturias and León), demonstrate strong admiration for the simple, natural life. In a fashion reminiscent of Rousseau, man is portrayed as naturally good, but capable of corruption in a false environment. As long as the characters remain close to nature, they are happy; when they abandon the village, they generally become disoriented and depressed. A unifying theme of the early period is an optimistic, idealistic pantheism. The universe for Martínez Sierra is a unity with outward manifestations being expressed through phenomena. Although not a religious writer consumed with the idea of God and the goals and causes of life, Martínez Sierra is more than willing to believe that there is purpose in human existence. Although he does not mention God directly, a positive force is evident in the beauty of all growing things and the elements that nurture them. Man is portrayed as naturally good but capable of corruption in an unnatural environment. . . .

In addition to shifts in style, setting, and character, the Martínez Sierras adopt an increasingly optimistic, even playful, attitude toward life (e.g., . . . *All Is One and the Same*). After *The Cradle Song* (1911), they do not return to the pessimism of *Frost Flowers,* nor will they close their works abruptly amidst fear, moans of frustration, or cries of terror as they frequently did in the early works. While the admirable women of the early novels and stories are portrayed as consolers, content only when submerging their frustrations in the problems of others, the female characters of the plays gradually become positive about overcoming their limitations and emerge as the most successful ingredient of Martínez Sierra's literary creations. After some experimentation, the authors found their characters, style, and message in *Mistress of the House* (1910). . . .

Although not an iconoclast, Martínez Sierra seems not to favor the cloistered life. The nuns of *The Cradle Song, Lily among Thorns,* and *The Kingdom of God* are happiest when working to find an outlet for their social and maternal impulses. Not mysterious, ethereal, or even particularly spiritual, these nuns enjoy participating actively in the world of people rather than of ideas or abstractions. Consistently moderate in their approach to almost everything, the Martínez Sierras favor a balance of physical, emotional, and spiritual expression, blending in their writings idealism with realism. Their practical goal is the healthy mind in the healthy body through simple health rules, work, love, and charity.

Patricia W. O'Connor. *Gregorio and María
Martínez Sierra* (Boston, Twayne, 1977),
pp. 133–35

MATUTE, ANA MARÍA (1926–   )

The name of Ana María Matute was completely unknown to us before it was heard in the voting proceedings of the Nadal Prize of 1947 . . . . Her novel, which played a big part in those proceedings, has just been published, and followers of this prize—so unjustly and stupidly attacked these days by a legion of resentful people—can judge for themselves the merits of *The Abel Family,* whose young author is no more than twenty-two years old. I mention this fact about her age not because I believe that it is enough information for us to agree about a novel that is of decent quality—and *The Abel Family* is much more than that—but because one cannot demand from a novelist in her twenties what can be expected in one who is sixty. Let us say right away that the first half of *The Abel Family,* the whole section that takes place in a mining town, strongly attracted our attention from the first pages, and revealed a novelist to us. The sober description of the environment, the slightly acidic portrayal of the characters, the modern sense of narrative and dialogue, and above all, the bold and contradictory strength of certain characters—like Valba and her brothers and sisters—succeed in capturing our interest. The author achieves naturalness in the narration and knows how to avoid overly elaborate literary effects. The harsh and bare world of the Abels—the father and the six children—is captured in its exact and mysterious waves of light and shadow, of goodness and evil. . . . The author soon decides that they should abandon the village and escape to the city. One after another they flee their land and themselves. The reader laments this disbanding and thinks that it is a pity that the author has not maintained up until the end of the novel the dry and harsh, although harmonious, atmosphere of the piece of unyielding land that the Abels inhabited in the village. If the author had not given in to the easy recourse of moving her characters to the city to search for new contrasts and accidental happenings, and if she had granted more space to passion in her work, we would probably have been able to say of Ana María Matute that she was the Spanish Emily Brontë. But the Abels' reaction in the city disconcerts us, and the arid harmony of the violent world of the village loses its freshness and ends up disappearing. Everything falls apart, not only the house in the village, but the intense world, the beautiful flame of the Abels. In the city they soon seem like rag dolls, wretched puppets who do not convince us. We stop loving them and close the book thinking that a great novel has been stymied. But the name of Ana María Matute will not be forgotten by us. In her is the mark of a true novelist.

J. L. Cano. Ínsula. Feb. 15, 1949, p. 5†

We have before us a short, exemplary little book [*The Stupid Children*], a minuscule wisp of a book, a violent and very tender book, a deep and venomous book that by itself would be enough to give a stamp of uniqueness to its author. Ana María Matute, in a most potent and honest voice, forces her bitter and naked soul to cry out amid a panorama, that is, a literary panorama, in which women writers, for the sake of appearing pious and proper, sweeten—or weaken—the voice that God gave them and dress up in—or hide behind—the vain clothing of empty whited sepulchers.

Joyously, openly . . . we proclaim our admiration for these stupid children who have sprung from the head of Ana María Matute, a woman who has learned how to prolong, to unforeseen limits, the cruelty, the ingenuity, and the astonishing amazement of children. Up until the age of ten we are all geniuses, according to Huxley. Ana María Matute, with the knowledge of her thirty years on her shoulders, has had the good sense—and the good fortune (everything is not preplanned)—to leave her heart in girlish braids. And from this attitude has been born the most important book, in any genre, that a woman has published in

Spain since Doña Emilia Pardo Bazán [nineteenth-century novelist]. . . . *The Stupid Children* will leave an indelible mark on Spanish letters. . . . And as we do with Federico García Lorca with his *Gypsy Ballads,* we will be able to do with Ana María Matute—to blame her for the mindless sterility of her followers, who will not be few in number. Kant said that genius is the means through which nature gives rules to art. And the art of Ana María Matute, in this brief, exemplary little book, comes ruled by her memory of childhood, which constitutes for our author all its authentic and fresh nature.

Camilo José Cela. *PSA.* July, 1957, pp. 107–8†

[Matute] is a writer who gives a feeling of grandeur rather than one of novelty. *Fiesta in the Northwest* and above all *First Memory* vividly recall to us the work of Truman Capote, in particular his *Other Voices, Other Rooms.* Both the Spaniard and the American recount difficult adolescences, childhoods that stick to adults like mud to the souls of boots, paradises that are green and black at the same time, incorruptible destiny. Even more, the loneliness of people, those tragic lands: Castile and Louisiana. In Matute and also in Capote, children create the myth of the all-powerful father, a myth that one day collapses and pushes Joel Knox to pederasty (*Other Voices, Other Rooms*), Juan Medinao to the weak and systematic forgiving of offenses (*Fiesta in the Northwest*). . . .

First Memory tells about how one becomes an adult; *Fiesta in the Northwest,* why and how one does not become one. Juan Medinao will never leave his childhood, which has branded him, and in some manner, stopped him. But what childhood? In fact, from the age of five, with his twisted legs and big head, he is an old man. . . . In *Fiesta in the Northwest,* escapist dreams play the same role that the myths of Borja and the imagined cities of Matia do in *First Memory:* one must conceal the world of men and things in order to tolerate them.

And it is true that the world here below is cruel to Juan, whose father is a usurer. Over the wretched and resigned laborers, who are passively hostile, in that corner of Castile, Juan senior exercises unlimited power and behaves forcefully, brutally, with frenzy, like those landowners in Bolivia or Ecuador for whom the peasants are not quite men. Juan junior is traumatized because of this. . . .

Harsher, tougher, and more violent than *First Memory, Fiesta in the Northwest* is a book of brutality, of cruelty, of man's misery. Of their hunger and of their death. It is also a more ambitious and complex novel than the first. Here Castile is present, and out of that province Ana María Matute wanted to create a backdrop for her characters. Like Juan, Castile never changes, and like him, it is miserable and tragic. For Juan, for Dingo, nothing is ever new; everything is always beginning again and everything is repeated; after thirty years, after time immemorial, there are these broken-down roads, the mud after the rain, children who die of hunger. Nothing alters the landscape or changes the destiny of the people. Ana María Matute has written a novel about time that does not pass.

Yves Berger. NRF. May, 1961, pp. 896, 899–901†

[Matute's] mode—her choice—is what in the axiological language of form we call the trivial. Her method [in <i>The Lost Children,</i> i.e., <i>The Dead Children</i>] is to combine the stammering, mind-refusing world of childhood with the almost idiot, brute world of the senses. Hence we get a queer "poetic" prose which even in the most conventional narrative is stiffened by a complex degree of imagery and refrain, all to account for a very simple state of mind. . . .

In <i>School of the Sun</i> [i.e., <i>First Memory</i>], Miss Matute's heroine reads in [J. M.] Barrie's [<i>Peter Pan</i>] that Peter " 'did spring cleaning at the time of the gathering of the leaves in the forest of Lost Children.' And the same Lost Children were all too grown up, suddenly, for playing, and too childlike, suddenly, to start life in a world we didn't want to know." The shift in personal pronoun here is indicative of the author's commitment, and in her new book we have the same stubborn, stuttering, mindless refusal to know the world beyond the senses, beyond the preoccupation with immediate, unreflected experience that makes this 500-page book no more—and no less, for it is remarkably written—than a lyric cry, a long cortical spasm.

Miss Matute's retreat from history—from the notion that not only do things happen, but that their happening has a meaning, that a set of values can be assigned to them—her preference for unmediated Experience, reminds us of a famous moment when Dorian Gray, appalled by the "truth" of Lord Henry Wotton's shocking words, stares at a spray of lilac he has just dropped on the gravel path. . . .

The young Spanish novelists, and Miss Matute chief among them in her long, terrified lament, have fallen into Dorian's trance. The lobotomy-by-childhood, the anesthesia-by-intensity which <i>The Lost Children</i> so insistently evokes gives us, as no ideological intervention could do, the measure of the "high import," the terror and the surrender to which the Spanish writers have been, and are still, subject.

Richard Howard. NL. July 5, 1965, pp. 19–20

[Matute] has a very personal style, rich in imagery, often poetic, that does not lend itself as readily to translation as do less imaginative works. In Matute there is always the hint that behind the surface realities of the everyday world hovers another existence, strange and secret. Her fiction rests on a solid substratum of realistic and concrete detail, but Matute's special talent lies in extracting the invisible interior reality from the visible reality of the external world. These qualities, at times iridescent and at times somber, appear in all of her writings, but they reach their maximum expression in her imaginative creations like *The Stupid Children* and *Three and a Dream*. In both of these the author is dealing with children, or grownups with childlike minds, having sensitive feelings but forced by the harsh realities of life to live in a world of fantasy. These studies, at times touched with surrealism, reflect one of the author's preoccupations: the shock which adult hypocrisy gives to youthful minds. . . .

[Matute] is more concerned with the recurring season, the anguished eroticism and frustrations of adolescence, the disappointments of age, relations between the rich and the poor, the tensions between the past and the present, than she is [with] current events and fashions. . . .

The Matutean concept of life is not a rosy one. Despite the long golden hours dreamed away in the lost paradise of youth, we are caught in a trap and destined to a tragic end. Her attitude is in many respects similar to that of the late Pío Baroja, who saw no solution for man's major problems.

George Wythe. *BA*. Winter, 1966, pp. 19–20

Ana María Matute's personal vision of life dictates the norms for her literary world, and nowhere is she so subjective as in her treatment of childhood. Her interest in children, her disregard of objective analysis, the tenderness and pity evident in her treatment of them, are a far cry from the objective approach to literature so popular today. Such subjectivity may stem from personal experience: Ana María Matute has always stressed the importance of her own childhood. She has doubtlessly transferred much of her own childhood to her literature, for a suggestively autobiographical note permeates her writing. Her picture of childhood reflects a personal and unique conception of life. The children follow a specific pattern: they are solitary, misunderstood creatures lost in a hostile world. The author's obviously pessimistic outlook, however, does not permit the child to remain in this state: the inevitable intrusion of reality destroys his world. Childhood must end, with death or with maturity. The loss of childhood is irrevocable; the character must begin life anew, completely cut off from his former state. Thus the ending of childhood forms the foundation of a fatalistic outlook. The loss of the child "who did not die nor is not anywhere" will be mourned by the older characters, whose wretched existence is made more wretched still by nostalgic remembrances of their own childhood, for the slow process of disillusionment has erased from their souls the imagination and innocence of a lost paradise.

Margaret E. W. Jones. *The Literary World of
Ana María Matute* (Lexington, University Press
of Kentucky, 1970), pp. 55–56

Matute's work is multifaceted, but its two extremes and most frequently represented variants are the stories of fantasies and the works whose theme or background involves either the Civil War or the Castilian peasant. Her interest in this is constant, lifelong, as shown by the study of her work from the earliest preserved juvenilia and her writings of pre-adolescence, up to the latest publications. Despite certain changes or modifications in her evolution as a writer, Matute's style has always been extremely personal and subjective, dominated by a primarily lyric vision of reality, or a deceptively childlike conception. Beginning with a fairly traditional structure, Matute has gradually tended to ever greater experimentation with the novelistic architecture, point of view, and treatment of time. The importance of formal plot, never a major element in her novels, has decreased, while the novelist's interest in psychology (a constant in her work) has grown ever stronger, with special emphasis on the problems of motivation, and an almost obsessive interest in the key formative factors and experiences which make people "what they are" such as the half-buried childhood trauma which may suddenly erupt in an apparently inexplicable act of adult violence. . . .

Matute's treatment of the child and adolescent is certainly the outstanding achievement of her characterization, with most adult figures paling by comparison. Adult and children's worlds are entirely separate and for the most part impenetrable or mutually incomprehensible. The typical Matute character is the solitary, isolated child or adolescent, often handicapped either physically, socially, or mentally (orphans, sick and abnormal children abound). Closely seconding this type is the rebellious youngster, who for any number or variety of reasons, usually feels closer to—and more accepted by—the lower strata of society, or the society of outcasts.

Matute continues to be intrigued with time, both as a theme and as a narrative possibility, being apparently particularly fascinated with the "threshold" moment or experience (of passage from childhood to adolescence, or adolescence to adulthood). At the same time, there is some experimentation with the contrary possibility, the unreality of time, and the possibilities of annihilation. Likewise, (and more frequently of late), the reader encounters factors which render meaningless the passage of hours, days, and years. A key motif, Cain and Abel, is obviously related to two of the previously mentioned obsessive concerns, social conflict and the Civil War (often symbolized by the violence between brothers). It may well be significant that in the early works, this conflict is almost inseparable from the soil; later it becomes (by implication) more closely related to other means of production. Matute is far from being either an ideologist or thesis novelist; in fact, it would be difficult to find anything resembling doctrine or dogma in any of her works, aside from such thoroughly Christian formulas as "Love one another." Her idea of charity . . . is much broader than simple alms-giving, and extends to many areas of human relationships, but especially to the concept of equal rights of all to the necessities of life, and to be treated with dignity and justice. Matute is sufficiently fair in her treatment of the Civil War that, even though by family, background, upbringing, and class contacts she should belong to the Nationalist (or Franco) faction, her implicit sympathies are with the vanquished, with the poor and suffering of all creeds, and with all whose rights and liberties are curtailed. Her concept of true Christianity, as expressed in "Love thy brother," implies acceptance, understanding, and sharing.

Janet Díaz. *Ana María Matute* (New York,
Twayne, 1971), pp. 145–47

The world of *The Trap* (1969)—the last novel in the trilogy *The Merchants* [the first two being *First Memory* and *The Soldiers Cry at Night,* respectively] by Ana María Matute—is characterized by an isolation between the self and others; between the self and itself; pervasive solitude; separation caused by death, divorce and faulty communication. The universal separation symptomatic of alienation is communicated and reinforced in this work of fiction by a form and structure which corresponds to and discovers the thematic content. . . .

The theme of alienation emerges in the novel through each character's delving into the storehouse of memory, as well as acting in the present. However, external action for its own sake is underplayed, the novel concentrating instead upon static internal action as a means of portraying fragmented, alienated characters. . . .

The principal challenge of the writer who sets out to portray this modern predicament is how to create a form which not only corresponds to the existential situation but also enhances it. The technique of presentation employed in *The Trap* could be termed an aesthetics of alienation. It would be difficult to conceive of a form more suited to the portrayal of the problems of alienated consciousness. This is consonant with one of the strengths of Matute's art, according to Enrique Sordo: "Ana María Matute's art has among other essential qualities, that of sticking closely to the theme that is being narrated . . . ." The novel is divided into chapters corresponding to the four principal characters' perspectives. . . . Most importantly, each character seems to be isolated within his own private world. Any of the rather sparse dialogue which does occur is encased within the recollections of each character. . . .

Matute has been criticized by Joaquín Marco for her use of nonfunctional language in *The Trap*. At times, though, linguistic nonfunctionality seems to be both medium and metaphor for the breakdown in communication plaguing modern society. Matia's diary is indecipherable to her, seemingly written in an unknown language. We are witnesses to a modern despair and distrust of the powers and faculties of languages and its ability to effect communication. Isa's aunts employ a private "semi-language" of unintelligible monosyllables and gutteral sounds. Repeatedly language, like the culture in which it exists, is dehumanized. It is transformed into hollow sounds which have ceased to signal meaning and serve only as constant reminders of the impossibility of authentic communication. So the very use of a specific kind of language or non-language underscores the fatal isolation and separation of the characters from one another.

Although the principal plot of *The Trap* is rather simple, it is contained within a complex labyrinthine structure of flashbacks and musings which at once parallels and reconfirms the characters' alienation from their world and from each other. The use of a baroque-like, involuted style and structure, probably inspired by the works of Faulkner, is able to portray and to be strongly analogous to a disturbingly alienated outside world. This world view is expressed through imagery and action, as well as conceptualized through structure in *The Trap*. Dialectical analysis reveals the indissoluble interrelationship between an alienated literary and nonliterary culture, between this world of fiction and the real or external world outside it.

Elizabeth Ordóñez. *JSSTC*. Winter, 1976,
pp. 180–81, 187–89

First Memory (1960) represents a new direction for the Spanish novel and the New Wave because, unlike its predecessors, it is the first to encourage a new variant of style I shall call "subjective Realism." A work of astonishing beauty, *First Memory* is deceptively simple. . . .

Critics may warn readers of a writer's stylistic excesses, but for me Matute is the only writer up until 1960 who has developed an original style and unique facility to transform her experiences and feelings into an *artistic* and subjectively Realistic fictional world. When asked about any writers that influenced her career, at first she said she did not know of anyone and then volunteered these names—Sartre, Camus, Malraux, Hesse and Knut Hamsun. She also felt certain Spanish publishers such as Lumen, Seix Barral and Destino have furthered her career since these publishers are particularly against government censorship. Also, thanks to the many literary prizes she has won, she finds there is greater interest in her life and work, and consequently, she has become prolific as a writer. Matute's consummate skill at avoiding direct questions about her work in no way parallels her unique artistry as a writer. Careful not to discuss the war, she feels *First Memory* is ultimately not a "war novel" but one about a young girl's adolescence. . . .

Whatever the verdict may be about her attaining literary greatness in the future, and Matute is probably only just now entering her most significant period, she surely now represents the epitome of the true artist, the seeker of truth, the master story teller, humanity's lover, the nobility of the soul.

Ronald Schwartz. *Spain's New Wave Novelists*
(Metuchen, N.J., Scarecrow, 1976),
pp. 115–16, 127, 130

Matute suggests that the causes for most of the current loneliness and frustration of her characters may be found in the past. She indicates that many of them are extremely concerned with the strong influence of the past in their lives when she permits their stories to be told, in first and third persons, by means of retrospective narration. Some of her characters . . . are attracted to the past because their earlier lives, in spite of holding the origins of their current low status, are much less problematic than is the present. The past, though frequently unpleasant, represents a security which these people no longer can know.

Her novels also show a close relationship between the extent of her characters' involvement in historical events and their limitation by the past. Pablo Barral [in *In This Land*] and Daniel Corvo [in *The Dead Children*], . . . fought to reduce the inequalities that they suffered and observed. At the war's end they believe that further efforts are useless, and they refuse to participate in the life of postwar Spain. Other characters who have made lesser commitments apparently feel less limited by their earlier failures. From the foregoing it is possible to conclude that in the fictional world of Ana María Matute those who have participated actively in the past are often doomed to be destroyed by it.

J. Townsend Shelby. *REH.* May, 1980, pp. 91–92

MIRÓ, GABRIEL (1879–1930)

One of the most unusual of books to come off press, not only in recent years, but at any time, is *Figures of the Passion of Our Lord* by the Spanish writer Gabriel Miró. It is a book especially difficult to judge against the background of America; its correct setting is Miró's native land of Spain, with its religious fervor and its religious tradition. In this country the appeal of the book will be a group appeal: powerful, one would say, in many quarters, less powerful in others. For those strong in what Edmund Burke called "the dissidence of dissent," it will be necessary to reconstruct for the *Figures* such a medieval setting as one constructs imaginatively to bring into perspective the religious painting of the older masters. This done, then Miró's portraits stand out upon the canvas in all their splendor of coloring, and with all their profound significance.

To say that a book is unusual is something of a generality, and it is essential that one become specific at once. And the book is not unusual in its selection of theme. "The Passion" of the Lord—His progress to judgment and death—has been a favorite theme of religious writers down through the centuries . . . . The uniqueness of Señor Miró's contribution lies in its peculiar method of approach, and the effect resulting therefrom. The Spanish author has not written a historical novel—although the book is narrative; and he has not built up a drama—although the effect is that of drama. Miró has taken each one of the principal characters of the Passion, has reconstructed that character's past, and has drawn him in the light of that past, playing his part in the final tragedy—has projected him out of that past into the tragedy. Thus the whole becomes a continuous narrative, moving to the tragic end; at the same time the book is drama—of an amorphous sort—with its characters continually coming on and going off the stage. Also, and at the same time, *Figures of the Passion* is such a series of paintings as, it would seem, only a medievalist could have conceived and executed.

NYTBR. March 15, 1925, p. 6

Several times I have picked up a book by Miró. I have taken in a few lines, perhaps a page, and I have always been surprised at how good it was. Nevertheless, I have not continued reading. . . . Now I have read one complete book by Miró: *The Leprous Bishop*. I read it from start to finish in quite a rush. . . .

It greatly irritates me to say resolutely that the novel is not to be included among good books. But I repeat that my opinion has no value. Both you readers and the author must remember that some years ago I offered a definition of the novel genre. The general opinion was that I was more or less wrong. Thus, if I erred in defining the novel in general, it is probable that it is dangerous for me to appraise a single novel. Let the reader judge for himself; whether it is a good or bad novel, Miró's work is a splendid book, one that reverberates, shining with so many lights and images to the point that it must be read with one's hands shading one's eyes to protect them. . . .

In spite of [Don Magín's] being one of the main figures of the book, he is, like all the others, faultily drawn: we can scarcely make him out, and what we discover is a character made up of the necessary "topics." One notices that the author has tried to make this character more "original"; but in the end he has succumbed to his general manner for building characters, which is most frequent among novelists. The bishop is not a man-individual, who happens to be a bishop, but a bishop in kind; the various Jesuits who appear in the novel are not diverse, but only one sort, which indicates that they are not individuals but the Jesuit "type." [1926(?)]

José Ortega y Gasset. *Obras completas,* Vol. III
(Madrid, Revista de Occidente, 1957), pp. 544–46†

There exists [in Miró's literary world] a double process that goes from the spiritualization of the incorporeal to the materialization of the immaterial. For Miró, an odor or a tactile sensation can be a step toward infinity or spirituality. But at the same time, something so incorporeal as that very odor can acquire the contours of a solid and tangible thing. Eyes can be born to the fingers, ones that can touch far horizons, skies, or clouds. And what the fingers—the real ones or the visual ones—cannot grasp seems capable of being conquered by the sense of smell. . . .

Miró is not content with the visual or tactile caress that the shape or the temperature of things give him, but he also hopes to fill himself with their particular smell, embodying it in himself, making it his own flesh. One could not imagine a more intense process of corporeity, if there were not still one other important aspect to this . . . : what we might call the corporeity of language. . . .

All [the examples of this] reveal Miró's knowledge as a profound stylist, his concern with language, which for him, more than a common means of expression, is something like a pliant, flexible material with which one can obtain extraordinary and very beautiful effects of light and color. . . .

The images of the incarnated, materialized voice abound in all of Miró's prose, starting with his first tales . . . . Miró gradually makes this image of the materialized voice more complex, shading it and giving it more sensual substance. At the same time, he begins to use one of his favorite descriptive processes—getting us acquainted with a character through how he says things, through the sound, the body, the mellowness of his speech, rather than through what he says.

Mariano Baquero Goyanes. *Prosistas españoles
contemporáneos* (Madrid, Rialp, 1956),
pp. 223–25†

Our Father San Daniel . . . deals with Don Álvaro's seeking the hand of Paulina, daughter of Don Daniel, in marriage, with their marriage, and with the subsequent death of Don Daniel. Everything takes place in Oleza (geographically, Orihuela). The conflict among societal forces, politics, and religion, which forms the center of the action, results from Don Daniel's being a property owner in Oleza and Don Álvaro's being a Carlist captain. This background is hardly passive or simply one of local color. On the contrary, it develops with the plot and often determines the plot's direction. The mechanics of the plot are so complex and so precise in their details that if I were to try to describe them here, it would be like rewriting, and very clumsily, the whole novel. . . .

Broadly speaking, all the characters are divided—owing to their actions and to the imagery system that Miró applies to them—into two groups: those of life and those of anti-life. Expressed in this way, the distinction is very simplified; you would have to read the novel to understand it completely. Those who are of the life group affirm the value of all life: that of the senses, the spirit, and the soul. The anti-life people, while recognizing that there are spiritual and moral values, seem to us not only as lacking these values, but also as determined to destroy them in others. The book is not purely anticlerical; there are priests in both camps. Nor is the contrast always one of black and white. Álvaro, who is the leader of the group of "antis," is depicted sympathetically.

L. J. Woodward. *BH*. Jan.–June, 1954,
pp. 111–12†

The theme of the artist is not very common in Spanish literature of the nineteenth century. . . . Miró, in *The Novel of My Friend* . . . , tells us the life of the painter Federico Urios. It is a life of misery. . . . If the title might make us think of positivist naturalism—the novel as a synonym for life—this very autobiographical material misery, and above all, the moral and spiritual misery, leads us to impressionism. Clearly, Miró has no contact with naturalism, the naturalism that in part still governed Blasco Ibáñez's fiction, which has a value not to be despised. It is surprising that Blasco was still able to have a naturalist vision of the world and to use the already moldy methods of that epoch, when at the time in Spain we were well into spiritualism and, more so, into impressionism. But the fact is that in Miró there is nothing impressionistic, either. . . .

Federico Urios tells us his life . . . ; his narration does not create an artistic atmosphere. In recollecting, he divests himself of all lyric value; in exchange, he organizes the past in relationship to the present, showing them to be clearly limited and mutually dependent.

The first thing that Miró impresses us with in the composition of his narrative is that he brings out the mystery, the transcendent meaning of life, the complexity of the human soul, the indivisibility of the body-soul in its external essence.

Joaquín Casalduero. *La torre*. April–June, 1957,
pp. 81–82, 84†

Gabriel Miró, wishing to avoid the boredom of a prolonged monologue, created several characters in his own image. These pseudonyms are not masks; they are barely labels. In *Little Boy and Big* the author revives memories of his youth through the voice of Antonio Hernando; in *The Sleeping Smoke* Don Jesús often serves as his mouthpiece; nevertheless, his predilection will always be for the licentiate Sigüenza, his most vivid character and the one through which he expresses himself completely.

What had led the writer to choose the pseudonym Sigüenza? Sigüenza is not a very common family name in Spain, and never a first name. It is also the name of a village in the province of Guadalajara, on the road from Madrid to Saragossa, made famous by Ortega y Gasset's description of it in *El Espectador*. Could it be that Miró has borrowed the name for his literary double from Father José de Sigüenza (1544–1606)? Certainly, there is no similarity whatsoever between the figure of the monk Sigüenza and Miró's hero, but perhaps it could have been the musical assonance of the name that attracted the writer? One can only put forward hypotheses on this subject.

Sigüenza reflects all the interior life of the author; he embodies his most secret desires, his aspirations, his youthful lusts . . . . How is this literary hero, this "alter ego" named Sigüenza presented? He is a young intellectual, from the old bourgeoisie of the Mediterranean shores of Spain, a refined, cultivated, idealistic man with a melancholic nature. Being timid and reserved, he avoids noisy meetings; he prefers, owing to his temperament and his taste, to withdraw from worldly problems in order to become better acquainted with his most vibrant emotions through the contemplation of nature and in meditation.

An enemy of violence and injustice, his life is an anxious search for truth, a harmonious ascent toward beauty. This stranger, this Sigüenza, resembles Miró like a brother.

Jacqueline van Praag-Chantraine. *Gabriel Miró; ou, Le visage du levant . . . Terre d'Espagne: Essai biographique et critique* (Paris, Nizet, 1959), pp. 65–66†

All the passages in Miró's works have the character of free-hand sketches . . . . *About Living* is a succession of sketches in which the lives of the lepers are presented. *Corpus, and Other Stories,* as the title indicates, is a collection of short stories, without any relationship and without any one having a real plot. Miró presents scenes and characters as if they had been photographed at a specific moment of their existence. *Enriqueta's Feet and Shoes,* although the title character shows up from time to time, is nothing more than a series of scenes in which the grandmother, the Hungarians, the lady of the village, the sacristan, etc. appear. In *Little Boy and Big* and *The Sleeping Smoke* Miró retrieves from his memory, like "sleeping smoke," recollections of his childhood, fragmentary moments of his life in the village, with his parents, in school, on trips, as well as of those people who surrounded him and whom he cannot now recall clearly. In *The Angel, the Mill, the Lighthouse Snail* he gives the name "engravings" to the various passages that make up the book . . . .

Miró's achievement is in his prose, his language. All these free-hand sketches of which we have spoken are presented by Miró with an impressionistic technique of free brush strokes that gives us the exact sensation of what the author sees and feels. It is a technique of suggestion, one that says things through intimation, with an almost magical power in the use of the exact word, which contains a synthesis of sensations, concepts, and shades of meaning.

Carlos Sánchez-Gimeno. Gabriel Miró y su obra (Valencia, Castalia, 1960), pp. 99–101†

It was natural that Miró should choose the novel as the form best suited to his multiple endowments. In the novel there is room for everything. And Miró, so well aware of his lyrical gifts, poured all his ambition into narrative writing. The effort was successful. His capacity for describing landscapes is so exceptional that it seems to overshadow his vigor as a novelist. It pained Miró that his tales should be read as if they were not more than a collection of descriptive and lyric pieces. Let us not commit this error. There is an abundance of lives and of passions in the Levante created by Miró on the basis of his real Levante. *The Novel of My Friend* is the best of his youthful efforts. *Our Father San Daniel* and *The Leprous Bishop* mark the summit of his maturity. Pity, cruelty, sensuality, devoutness, love, hatred—motivate and agitate, raise up and destroy this multitude of gentlemen, churchmen, and villagers under a universal sun and moon—especially under the sun. Miró is a solar poet. His style, terse, compact, pithy, becomes an admirable screen reflecting everything, although for some readers it may constitute an obstruction that does not let the content show through. Even for some supposedly cultured readers, a well-written page is merely a decorative page, and all form to them smacks of formalism. In point of fact, there is no creation without its adequate expression, and Miró's world could not exist apart from the overflowing mass of vocabulary.

Even so, it is just possible that the shorter narratives are superior to the longer ones. They are closer to the author's personal experience, memories of his childhood or recollections of a less distant past; they are a treasure-house of the most intimate and direct experience of Miró.

Jorge Guillén. Language and Poetry
(Cambridge, Mass., Harvard University Press,
1961), pp. 194–95

Sigüenza always coexisted with Miró. The books in which he appears as the protagonist stand out significantly among Miró's works. Although *About Living* is not Miró's first work, it appears as such in his *Complete Works* because he repudiated two earlier works for artistic reasons. *Book of Sigüenza* coincides with the middle point of Miró's novelistic production; a great part of his work had already been published. And *Years and Leagues,* the last book about Sigüenza, turns out to be the very last book by Gabriel Miró published during his lifetime. . . .

As Sigüenza ages, he withdraws more and more from men. In *About Living* he pities the lepers in a compassionate fellowship; in *Book of Sigüenza* he walks through the streets of the city surrounded by people but separate from them, and in *Years and Leagues,* having left the tumult of city life, he takes refuge in the solitude of the countryside. . . . The hero is not *per se* a misanthrope, since he does not choose to be isolated from his fellow men; he has not elected this solitude, but he is condemned to it. The problem of Sigüenza is that of the modern hero whose life is also a road that leads nowhere, with arbitrary beginning and end; the destiny of each person— the destiny of *homo viator*—is the uncertainty of an end that is both awaited and feared at the same time. Nevertheless, the Sigüenza "case" is different in the sense that in the search for or the nostalgia for the absolute-eternal his identity and existence are not attached to the history of the moment; he is distanced from all contingencies. He exists in the biblical bad time of the lepers, and, nonetheless, he lives in the twentieth century. His irrational desire to persevere indefinitely, as well as his alienation from society, he shares with all humans, from Adam from the time "he knew himself to be mortal" to his own self.

Richard López Landeira. *Gabriel Miró: Trilogía de Sigüenza* (Chapel Hill, N.C., Estudios de Hispanófila, 1972), pp. 141, 149†

Miró's earliest references to Christian scholars appear in the article entitled "The Power of a Judge," in which he defends himself against the accusation of blasphemy brought against him by the judge who, in 1917, had imprisoned the editor of *El Noroeste* of Gijón for publishing an extract of *Figures of the Passion of Our Lord.* One of these scholars is M.-J.-H. Ollivier, author of *The Passion* (Paris, 1902), a book Miró had bound in Barcelona and which he quotes—accurately—in this article. In his own defence Miró also referred to "Doctor [Johann] Sepp, a German theologian—he is German and everything that goes with it." As the quotation shows he was not only appropriate because of the reputation of Germanic learning, but also in the context of the conflict within Spain between Germanophiles on the right, such as would support the incarceration of the editor of *El Noroeste,* and supporters of the allies, including Miró, on the liberal side. A little later Miró used Sepp again, this time quoting in *The Sleeping Smoke* a passage, translated into Spanish, from a French version of Sepp's life of Christ . . . . This is the same work Miró used in "The Power of a Judge," where he gives its title in a footnote. . . . This is the only nineteenth-century scholar Miró mentions who does not appear in the library, but clearly Miró read this life of Christ, a reply to the Straussian school, and it must be added to the list of works that might be sources for the *Figures.*

Another writer who appears in *The Sleeping Smoke,* and an important one, is Renan. . . . Unfortunately neither Miró's library nor his solitary allusion to Renan help one very much to understand their relationship.

Ian R. MacDonald. *Gabriel Miró: His Private Library and His Literary Background* (London, Támesis, 1975), pp. 174–75

The analysis of *Our Father San Daniel* and *The Leprous Bishop* has shown that Miró uses an elliptical technique in various aspects of his narrative art. Nevertheless, a technique without a purpose would have little sense, and thus we have attempted to show that Miró uses his technique to develop his original conception of the novel—as he puts it, "to say things through suggestion." The principal objective of a work of fiction is to create the illusion of reality, and logically Miró's intention is to evoke such an illusion. . . . We conclude . . . that the elliptical technique has been used successfully to create the illusion of reality. This technique applies first to point of view in its distinct uses, as the author endeavors to register the events as they occur in life, and then to elliptical syntax, as the idea is to express reality through a cumulative form that takes in everything. The same method is effectively repeated in the elliptical presentation of the chronology of the events, which indicates that the author's interest is not in chronological time but rather in psychological time and duration, reproducing the process as it occurs in reality. . . .

Nevertheless, Miró's novels are not simply an intent to register and reproduce reality; they have a message that is also transmitted in an elliptical form, principally through the irony that pervades the novels. Further, the implicit social criticism of a backward nineteenth-century society transcends the theme and represents a philosophy of values. It is this underlying message that permits Miró to awaken compassion for his characters, although he sees many of them with indifference and as objects of caricature.

Yvette E. Miller. *La novelística de Gabriel Miró* (Madrid, Códice, 1975), pp. 147–48†

In [Miró's] novels, description of the landscape quite habitually intrudes on the action—not, again, as mere background, but as an active force in itself (compare Hardy's Egdon Heath) or as some separate mute drama constantly being enacted whose secret humanity ignores or seeks vainly to fathom. . . .

In anticipation of the later *tremendista* trends, Miró's landscape serves now and then as a backdrop of horrendous contrast, as the incongruous scenario of tragic occurrences, of sacrilege, or of the crassness and vileness of human behavior, the more lamentable in such a setting. . . .

While saddened by the decadence of the landscape fallen victim to the inevitable advances of human materialism and its desecration to utilitarian ends, he has learned to accept, even welcome, certain intrusions (the railway, the telegraph) as not esthetically or spiritually offensive. But he does resent the rending obtrusion of the highway and adulteration of the countryside by urban encroachments. (Compare present-day Benidorm with its evocation in Miró!) This consideration of the decadence of the countryside as a "modern" phenomenon is related to a romantic resentment of the bourgeois vulgarity and efficiency of present-day living, in contrast to the graceful dignity and simple traditionalism of the past, for which his nostalgia is ever explicit. . . .

Notwithstanding this nostalgia for modes of living of the past and more particularly of his own past, he reveals an evident sympathy with persons of a liberal and progressive turn of mind, even though the material outcome of their way of thinking may wound his esthetic susceptibilities. Despite his censure of the motorcar and other modern appurtenances that blemish the landscape in his eyes, he was not altogether one to rough it in the country, sharing more than a little Rousseau's bourgeois penchant for comfort and good living.

Henry C. Schwartz. In Ricardo Landeira, ed.,
Critical Essays on Gabriel Miró (Lincoln, Neb.,
Society of Spanish and Spanish-American
Studies, 1979), pp. 17, 39–40

ORTEGA Y GASSET, JOSÉ (1883–1955)

[In *Meditations on Quixote*] Ortega y Gasset returns to Cervantes's book. But Ortega y Gasset does not come from the field of scholarship but from that of philosophy. For this reason, Cervantes's book must take on for him a meaning very different from the one it has for its annotators and explicators. For Ortega y Gasset, Cervantes's work is material that demands our attention; there we will find the ideological elements that permit us to attempt a formation of the immortal character. . . .

The spirit of Cervantes finds its maximum and most noble expression in his work, not in the comings and goings and the ups and downs of his private life, in the thousand contingencies that chance kept putting in his way; in his work we will look for the Cervantes who conceived Don Quixote, not the one from whom they collected taxes or the one who endured imprisonment in Algiers and hunger in many places. In this Cervantes that Ortega y Gasset's work and style are able to reveal to us, in this essential and creative Cervantes, is found, in turn, the quixotic substance that communicates with us across centuries in the form of a nobleman of La Mancha whom books of chivalry have made mad.

It is this that, in my opinion, Ortega y Gasset sets out to do. It is evident that Don Quixote lives in our hearts and takes nourishment from them. There is room for diverse concepts about *Don Quixote,* depending on the spirits who consider it. The Quixote of a Heine, of a Turgenev, or of a Miguel de Unamuno are very lovely Quixotes, but they are not the same; they are, without doubt, more real than the Quixotes of the scholarly commentators; but let us not forget the original source, Cervantes's *Don Quixote,* the quixotism of Cervantes. This is the Don Quixote that Ortega y Gasset tries to explore in these his *Meditations on Quixote*.

Antonio Machado. Lectura. Jan., 1915, pp. 63–64†

Ortega y Gasset impresses me as a traveller who has journeyed through the world of culture. He moves upon a higher level, which it is difficult to reach, and upon which it is still more difficult to maintain oneself.

It may be that Ortega y Gasset has no great sympathy for my manner of living, which is insubordinate; it may be that I look with unfriendly eyes upon his ambitious and aristocratic sympathies; nevertheless, he is a master who brings glad news of the unknown—that is, of the unknown to us. . . .

As far as I am concerned, every man who knows more than I do is my master.

I know very well that philosophy and metaphysics are nothing to the great mass of physicians who pick up their science out of foreign reviews, adding nothing themselves to what they read; nor, for that matter, are they to most Spanish engineers, who are skilled in doing sufficiently badly today what was done in England and Germany very well thirty years ago; and the same thing is true of the apothecaries. The practical is all that these people concede to exist, but how do they know what is practical? Considering the matter from the practical point of view, there can be no doubt but that civilization has attained a high development wherever there have been great metaphysicians, and then with the philosophers have come the inventors, who between them are the glory of mankind. Unamuno despises inventors, but in this case it is his misfortune. It is far easier for a nation which is destitute of a tradition of culture to improvise an histologist or a physicist, than a philosopher or a real thinker.

Ortega y Gasset, the only approach to a philosopher whom I have ever known, is one of the few Spaniards whom it is interesting to hear talk. [1917]

Pío Baroja. *Youth and Egolatry* (New York,
Alfred A. Knopf, 1920), pp. 189–90

With Ortega y Gasset philosophy does not function as irony and Humanism, but rather as a striving for order, a way to the hierarchy of values, constructivism.

Another trait of Ortega's originality is the manner in which he assimilates and brings together German and French culture. I do not know any critic in Europe capable of writing with the same sympathy and the same understanding on Madame de Noailles and Simmel, Marcel Proust and Max Scheler. Ortega can and does. And in language sparkingly pointed, nervously clear, sensitive, and unrhetorical. He is acquainted with and ranges over the entire impressive development of the German humanistic disciplines (*Geisteswissenschaften*). . . . There cannot be many foreigners who are so thoroughly conversant with the researches of German historians and philosophers and follow their work so carefully as Ortega y Gasset. But this is augmented by the aesthetic-literary culture of nineteenth century French and the France of the present. So in Ortega the France of the *Nouvelle Revue Française* (to put it briefly) intersects with the Germany not of the poets (the contemporary poets) but of the thinkers. And the one amends, expands, and complements the other. . . .

I cannot think of a better introduction to the problems of the Spanish mind than Ortega's little book *Invertebrate Spain* . . .—that is to say: the Spanish disintegration.

The brochure came out in 1922. It is an attempt to diagnose Spain's illness. Ortega defends himself against the reproach of pessimism. Spain's greatest need is clarity of insight. In Spain there are incessant debates about domestic conditions, but they lack a total perspective that would assign details to their proper places. The Spaniard's view is clouded by the fact that he has an exaggerated notion of Spain's past importance. He consoles himself for the unhappy events of the present with the thought that we did, after all, have a Cid. But this is the true pessimism: the idea that Spain was for a time the most perfect of nations and has been on the decline ever since. [1924]

> Ernst Robert Curtius. *Essays on European*
> *Literature* (Princeton, N.J., Princeton
> University Press, 1973), pp. 282–83

What Professor Ortega y Gasset denounces most violently in his book [*The Revolt of the Masses*] is precisely the idea upon which the whole science and art of republicanism has always been based, to wit, the idea that there is some mystical virtue, and what is more, some mystical wisdom, in men in the mass—that what everyone believes is somehow likely to be true. Upon this doctrine he flings himself with great enthusiasm, and, save at moments when he loses the thread of his discourse and argues against himself, with considerable effect.

The liberation of the masses, he believes, has done Europe a lot of harm. It has upset the old scale of values, especially in the field of government, and substituted a kind of moony indifferentism, grounded upon simple and even childish desires. The mob is impatient of all ideas, and hence refuses to consider and discuss them. The one thing it esteems is a comfortable conformity, and that conformity is naturally pitched upon a low level. Moreover, it is quite irrational, for there is no coherent concept behind it, but only a yearning to be "undifferentiated from other men," to pass unmarked and unmolested in a vague crowd. Thus mere quantity is substituted for quality, and all the high aspirations and emprises [sic] of superior men sink into desuetude.

Señor Ortega's thesis is here clear enough, but it cannot be said that he maintains it with unfailing consistency. . . . Nor is it easy to agree, on the one hand, that the stupidities of the mob now engulf and smother *homo sapiens,* and on the other hand that his "vital tone," which "consists in his feeling himself possessed of greater potentiality than ever before," is now at its historic maximum.

But such confusions, of course, are apt to occur in a book which covers so wide a field, especially if it comes from the studio of a metaphysician. When Señor Ortega turns into bypaths he often writes with great clarity, and is pleasantly persuasive. In one of his later chapters, for example, he has an excellent treatise on the nature of the state, along with a hearty denunciation of the current tendency to regard it as a stupendous Peruna bottle, with a cure in it for every ill. And he pleads with fine eloquence for some of the standards that democracy has tended to destroy. From his main contention few will dissent—that it is bad government which particularly afflicts the world, and especially Europe, today.

H. L. Mencken. *Nation*. Sept. 21, 1932, pp. 260–61

Though a trifle too popular in style—for [*The Revolt of the Masses*] is basically a book for the few—and occasionally a trifle rhetorical, this remarkable volume is the work of one of the few men who have real knowledge of the nature of mankind, the nature of history, and therefore the state of mankind today. I am in unreserved agreement with the presentation and analysis of the mass man as Ortega gives it; it has never before been put forth so consistently and clearly. No less do I agree, and agree actively, with his conception of the state, and therefore with his conception of the only possibility for Europe's future—Europe must become a single nation. Among a series of clearly formulated and originally selected examples from history there are many individual passages of striking, witty comment, as, for example, this about historians: "One sees of the past about as much as one guesses about the future." All in all, it is a rousing, demanding, thought-provoking work that is important to Europe. The majority of German youth, instead of wrangling over their teen-age problems that will have disappeared by tomorrow, should read such books, not in order to be witty and clever about them in conversation, but to learn from them. [1932]

Hermann Hesse. *My Belief* (New York, Farrar,
Straus & Giroux, 1974), pp. 371–72

No less an authority than the *Wall Street Journal* hailed . . . *The Revolt of the Masses* as "of first importance in aiding the reader to an understanding of the fundamental causes of the world's distress" . . . .

Coming on the wave of popularity that accompanies these days almost anything with an economic tinge, his book was reviewed with laudatory marvelings by the most influential literary supplements in the country, and in a few months it achieved the status of a best seller.

Yet there were drawbacks to this sudden fame. If *The Revolt of the Masses* reached an audience that did not in the long run properly belong to its author, it also alienated part of the audience to which his real genius entitled him. Its very facility, the erudition obvious on every page, the ease with which it juggled difficult problems made it suspect among the thoughtful. As the first work of an unknown it said too much and too little.

This was a phenomenon not unfamiliar to readers of translations, but in this instance it was rendered particularly distressing by the nature of the book and of the man who wrote it. José Ortega y Gasset is neither a dispenser of economic nostrums nor a one-book man. His work over the course of the last twenty years is an organic achievement whose parts are closely knit, and whose whole has many facets. . . .

The relentless and passionate logic of *Invertebrate Spain,* the beautiful precision of *The Dehumanization of Art, and Notes on the Novel,* all the charm, the fire, the poetry of his seven volumes of *Spectator* papers are imprisoned in a language which comparatively few Americans read. His ideas on the novel, the things he thinks about the citizen's service to the state, politics, the lost Atlantis, women, economics, the Escorial, music, the Spanish provinces, life, history, mathematics, and the Catalan problem are all hidden except for those to whom Cervantes is possible in the original.

And this is most unfortunate, for in the very fertility and the abundance of the man's thought lies part of his value. Philosopher he is, but he has never seen men and events from an ivory tower.

Mildred Adams. Forum. Dec., 1933, pp. 373, 378

These essays [in *Toward a Philosophy of History,* i.e., *History as System*] represent a gleaning from some of Señor Ortega's more recent writings. Though composed against the tragic background of recent Spanish history, and in spite of exile and serious illness, they bear no trace of self-pity and self-righteousness (which are often forms of the same thing). Though concerned with the fate of our civilization, they have nothing in common with the yammering prophecies of doom, the neurotic jeremiads so many of our incurable illusionists are tossing off to quiet the nerves they call their consciences. It would be unfair to Señor Ortega to accuse him of so Eleatic—an un-Spanish—a virtue as serenity: but balance, moderation, controlled imagination, all qualities rare among contemporary philosophers of history, he displays throughout these essays.

In content, at first sight the volume looks like a collection of incidental writings. . . . As a matter of fact, these essays are more closely integrated than they seem to be in a brief report. To their varied factual stuff Señor Ortega brings a firm and well-formed mind, made up but not closed, and already familiar to us from his *The Revolt of the Masses.* It is to be hoped that in his South American haven [Buenos Aires] he will be able to carry to completion the more systematic works he has already begun. In the meantime, *Toward a Philosophy of History* is a first fruit worth having. The metaphor is, however, misleading: there is a great deal of highly concentrated nourishment and very little water in this fruit.

Señor Ortega's philosophy is too subtle and many-sided to be fairly analyzed in a concluding paragraph. Briefly, he would seem to share with Whitehead, Bergson, and many other moderns a distrust of the intellectualist traditions of Western philosophy, which he here traces back to the Eleatics. He also distrusts natural science, but only when it goes beyond what he thinks its necessary limits, that is, study of "nature." For what science has done and can do he has the highest respect, and he never voices romantic dislike for science and scientists.

Crane Brinton. SR. April 5, 1941, p. 5

Ortega's personality is enigmatic and widely criticized. Yet he manages to attract us by the transparent elegance of his style, at once stimulating and subtle in its shadings, sharp in its irony, rich in allusions and evasions. He is circumspect and aristocratic, given neither to sudden rage nor sublime enthusiasms. Encased in bright images, his ideas dazzle rather than convince us. Gently they slip into the soul as a sweet and brilliant theory which calms the feelings and delights the intellect. Only after freeing ourselves from the strange influence are we aware of having been victims of a fraud. Ortega's prose, impeccable in its classical serenity, always raises in the soul a turmoil of anxiety. Like the tranquil sea it hides its depths.

His style has betrayed Ortega. It might be said that behind the unapproachable gentleman, on whose lips skepticism has painted a thin sneer of irony, lies the scoffing features of the Nietzschean Zarathustra carrying an incendiary message to the world. An irrepressible suspicion arises that the whole work of the Sage of the Escorial is no more than the tragic projection of that eternal battle which Dionysus and Apollo carry on in his own spirit—reason versus life.

If he praises order, mental clarity, hierarchy of values and norms, he also exalts sport and the luxury of living to the highest philosophical level. In his opinion art and morality are superfluous sports, though of a value equal to that of philosophy. Society and the state had their origin in a group of young warriors who were as likely to go hunting as to steal young maidens from distant nations. . . .

Ortega's olympic serenity is a myth. Between the lines we can glimpse the drama of an agitated spirit, victim of a secret anxiety which in spite of his lofty intelligence and enormous culture has not yet achieved the essential equilibrium which harmonizes thinking with living. [1943]

José Sánchez Villaseñor, S. J. Ortega y Gasset:
Existentialist (Chicago, Henry Regnery, 1949),
pp. 136–37

José Ortega y Gasset was born to the intellectual purple. He never had to fight for his birthright: his father was the owner of one of the most influential newspapers and a prominent member of the ruling "aristocracy of letters." Young Ortega was in touch with the most enlightened teachers and thinkers, the most advanced writers, without having to gatecrash, as Unamuno was forced to do in heart-breaking years of struggle. He was not driven. No wonder, then, that Ortega developed a theory of "excellent men" and "mass-men" as though those qualities were inbred and unquestionable. To be sure it irked him that the best brains were not at the same time the rulers and leaders of the Spanish body politic. But he was not driven to negative criticism, because he had no need to clear his starting ground. The backwardness of the Spanish universities, which drove the most progressive pedagogues and scholars to work with a private institution, Giner de los Ríos' Institución Libre de Enseñanza [Free Academy], must have appeared to him as a crime against the spirit, but it did not drive him to despair; he saw wider and freer horizons opening. It is his great merit that he wanted those horizons to be open to all Spanish intellectuals, and tried to do something about it. From the beginning of his public career, he urged a communion between Spain and Europe—that is, the liberal spirit of Europe. But he found that liberal, humanist spirit above all in German philosophy and German cultural standards. He studied at Marburg under the Neo-Kantian philosopher Cohen and in the orbit of Wilhelm Dilthey. Ortega's theories bear obvious traces of those German thinkers who interpret the life of nations in terms of biological cycles and assess them by the role of an elite in society.

Arturo Barea. UObs. Winter, 1947, p. 31

Señor Ortega's observations are as keen as ever [in *The Dehumanization of Art, and Notes on the Novel*], while the polemics and manifestations of that decade [the 1920s] make dull rereading, because he was "moved exclusively by the delight of trying to understand and neither by ire nor by enthusiasm." The meditative habit, the spectatorial role of his earlier writing well befit the critic; though they have their political limitations, as he was subsequently to show. A generation whose rallying cry is engagement will not apply to him for its philosophy of history. Yet the intellectuality that chills, whenever he condescends to discuss the masses, illuminates his vivid interpretations of the cerebral life. His German training blends with his Latin temperament to produce a zest for ideas which is never dogmatic, a flair for epigrams which is seldom verbalistic. And since Anglo-American criticism tends toward evaluation rather than formulation, we stand in particular need of the clear-cut distinctions that continental writers and thinkers have sharpened. . . .

And Ortega y Gasset is willing to face, with the mixed emotions of irony, the implications of art for art's sake: its narrowing horizons, its tongue-in-cheek attitudes. Poetry, for Eliot "a superior amusement," is for him "a higher algebra of metaphors." No one has more sharply or paradoxically formulated the alternative to the propagandistic and humanitarian position of Tolstoy's *What Is Art?*"

Harry Levin. NYTBR. June 6, 1948, p. 4

Ortega continued the work begun by Unamuno, which was to enrich, deepen, and broaden the Spanish dialogue. . . . Unamuno and Ortega brought with them new themes and a new language. They looked with a sincere curiosity at yesterday and today and the eternal problems or perplexities of philosophy. How not to be grateful for this beneficent and useful work for Spain and for all of us who share her language?

Throughout the years, I have frequented the books of Unamuno and with them I have ended up by establishing, in spite of the "imperfect affinities" about which Charles Lamb has spoken, a relationship similar to friendship. I have not earned that relationship with the books of Ortega y Gasset. Something always kept me from reading his work, something prevented me from going beyond the indexes and initial paragraphs. I suspect that the obstacle was his style. Ortega, a man of abstract reading and dialectical discipline, allowed himself to be enchanted by the most trivial artifices of literature about which he evidently knew little, and he lavishly used them in his work. There are minds that proceed by images (Chesterton, Hugo) and others by syllogistic and logical means (Spinoza, Bradley). Ortega did not resign himself to staying in this second category, and something—modesty or vanity or an eagerness for adventure—moved him to embellish his manner of reasoning with unconvincing and superficial metaphors. In Unamuno bad taste does not bother you because it is justified and gets carried away by passion; Ortega's bad taste . . . is less tolerable, because it has been fabricated from scratch.

The stoics declared that the universe is one single organism; it is fully possible that I, through the working of the secret affinity that unites all its parts, owe something or a lot to Ortega y Gasset, whose volumes I have scarcely leafed through.

Forty years of experience have taught me that, in general, *the others* are right. Once I deemed it inexplicable that generations of men would venerate Cervantes and not Quevedo; today I see nothing mysterious in such a preference. Perhaps some day the great reputation of Ortega y Gasset will not seem mysterious.

Jorge Luis Borges. Ciclón. Jan., 1956, p. 28†

The first memory [of Ortega y Gasset] goes back to August 1951. We met in the German city of Darmstadt, where each year, in attractive surroundings, a lecture series is held on a given subject. That year the subject was "Man and Space." Among the various men of science and the architects who had been asked to speak were Ortega and myself. After my lecture, entitled "To Build, to Inhabit, to Think," a speaker began to attack violently what I had just said and asserted that my lecture had not resolved the essential questions, but rather had "unthought" them, that is, dissolved them into nothing by means of thought. At that moment, Ortega y Gasset asked for the floor; he seized the microphone from the speaker, who was standing at his side, and said the following to the audience: "The Good Lord needs his 'un-

thinkers' so that the rest of the animals do not fall asleep." His ingenious riposte made the situation change at once. But it was not only an
ingenious riposte, it was above all a gentlemanly one. I have greatly
esteemed and admired Ortega's gentlemanly behavior, which he had
also shown on other occasions toward my writing and lectures, since it
is clear to me that Ortega has denied his approval to many and has felt a
certain uneasiness with some part of my thought that seemed to
threaten his originality. . . .

When I think of Ortega, his image returns to my mind . . . speaking, being quiet, his gestures, his nobility, his solitariness, his candor,
his sadness, in his multifaceted knowledge and in his captivating irony.

Martin Heidegger. Clavileño. May–June, 1956,
pp. 1–2†

Ortega's comments on love [in *Studies on Love*] are sharpened by many
a shrewd remark about men and women and their relations with one
another. For me these suggestive insights are interesting less as commentary upon human nature than as reflections of the Spanish soul.
When Ortega says that every woman presents to the public a conventional impersonal mask but lives her true life in the recesses of her
privacy, I see ladies on a trellised balcony, their mysterious faces
obscured by mantillas and silken fans. When he says that every man
lives for the sake of public appearances and theatrical demonstrations,
I see the matador baring his breast to the bull and offering his heart to
the ladies. Ortega suggests that women are by nature irrational and this
is what endears them to man, the rational being; that women are a
retrogressive force in human selection, preferring to mate with medi-
ocrities rather than the superior individuals that men generally wish to
emulate; that for women, living instinctively means surrender of
oneself, for men, the possession of others—particularly the possession
of women; that men are restless because of super-abundant imagination, whereas women have superior understanding of realities but are
generally deficient in imagination. . . .

Man is the only animal that loves, just as he is the only animal that
hates. Why is it, then, that since the age of rationalism—when (ironically) philosophers thought that man was to be defined in terms of
reason, not feeling—there has been no really thorough philosophy of
the sentiments? Ortega, too, is astounded by this failure in modern
thinking. If it is ever overcome, much of the credit will go to his
pioneering work. In this age of analysis, this age of techniques, this age
of instrumental refinements, fuzzy subjects are left to fuzzy minds.
There is no fuzzier subject than love; there are few minds less inclined
to fuzziness than Ortega's. Here as in his other writing, his example
could have a salutary effect on the barrenness of so much contemporary English and American philosophy. "Why write," he asks, "if this

too easy activity of pushing a pen across paper is not given a certain bullfighting risk and we do not approach dangerous, agile, and two-horned topics?" That's the spirit! ¡Olé!

Irving Singer. *HudR*. Spring, 1958, pp. 153–54

The passages [in *The Modern Theme (The Theme of Our Time)*] in which Ortega keeps insisting upon the fact that reality and life are both valuable and perishable—or rather valuable because perishable—are too numerous to be quoted here. Let us simply sum up his views on the subject by stating that he tries again and again to lay stress on muta-bility as opposed to fixity, on playful behavior as opposed to utilitarian action, on richness of appetites against puritan restraint, and last but not least, on acceptance of reality as opposed to reverence for utopia. The pleasures of life are ephemeral. So much the better; they are thus authentic. Spontaneity ruins conventions. No matter; it will give rise to new and better ones. Play seems to lack dignity. It is because we forget that pure science, art and philosophy are products of purely disin-terested behaviour. The philosopher must therefore foster all that is living and real, namely all that is authentic.

José Ferrater Mora. *Ortega y Gasset: An Outline of His Philosophy,* new rev. ed. (New Haven, Conn., Yale University Press, 1963), pp. 34–35

Ortega suggested in *The Dehumanization of Art* that modern art would always be unpopular because it is extreme: it is essentially unpopular, he said, moreover, it is antipopular. The more recent proliferation of popular publications on modern art, the immense crowds that have been attracted to certain exhibitions of modern art in the larger cities throughout the world, and the appearance of a late phase of modern art that is actually called popular ("pop-art"), might seem to throw some doubt on Ortega's assertion, but I am willing to concede his point for, crowds or no crowds, the masses do not *understand* modern art. It is an art for the minority, an esoteric art, and remains most esoteric when it would be most popular. On account of that fact Ortega proceeds to his main deduction, which is, that not being accessible to every man, the impulses of this art are not of "a generically human kind"—which, incidentally, is the charge that Tolstoy brought against modern art. . . .

Ortega was far too intelligent a philosopher to dismiss the ex-tremism of modern art as an aberration of the mind, a twilight of the intellect. He realized that it is an historical phenomenon that has grown from a multitude of entangled roots, but he thought that an explanatory investigation of the kind required was too serious a task for him to attempt. He concluded his polemic with a final all-embracing charge: the modern movement is a disguised attack on art itself—"a mask which conceals surfeit with art and hatred of it"; and he hinted that this was but one aspect of a wider phenomenon, the rankling grudge which modern Western man bears against his own historical essence. . . .

Freud eclipses the high noon of the intellect with his theory of the libido, but contrary to the opinion of some of his interpreters, he does offer us some hope, and it is precisely through art. His interpretation of art as an overcoming of neurosis or mental sickness is too narrow, but at least it does explain the significance of that type of art which Ortega despises—or at least fails to understand: the art that corresponds to the dark night of the soul rather than to the high noon of the intellect.

It is with a sense of betrayal that I take leave of Ortega on this critical note. Ortega was not a reactionary philosopher; on the contrary, he welcomed the fact that modern man orients himself in the future, and not—like the man of the Middle Ages and indeed the man of the Ancient World—in the past.

Sir Herbert Read. The Origins of Form in Art
(New York, Horizon, 1965), pp. 169, 171–73

I am not certain that anyone has pointed out the similarities between the French philosopher [Sartre] and the Spanish philosopher. Ortega y Gasset's name is seldom mentioned these days, whereas Sartre is famous the world over. This may be because Ortega was a conservative, while Sartre is a revolutionary. Although the views of both have their origin in German phenomenology, this common source is not the only reason for the similarities between them. What makes these two philosophers resemble each other is not so much the ideas they share as their style of attacking them, making them their own, and sharing them with the reader. Though the two of them struck out in opposite directions, each of them in his own way turned modern thought into a moral and historical meditation. Despite the fact that neither of them cultivates a spoken style, we *hear* them thinking: the tone of their writings is at once passionate and peremptory—a magisterial tone, in both the good and the bad senses of the word. They excite us and irritate us, and thus force us to participate in their demonstrations. Ortega once said that he was only a journalist, and Heidegger has said the same of Sartre. This is quite true: they are not the philosophers of our time, but philosophy in our time. [1967]

Octavio Paz. Alternating Current (New York,
Viking, 1973), pp. 164–65

If [Ortega's] style is coruscating, it is because this characteristic of it is the condition for the reflection of reality. The uncovering function which belongs to truth as *alétheia*—and which Ortega was to formulate in an early version in 1914, at a time when European philosophy knew hardly anything about this concept and had no intention of reviving it and using it—was already in play through the agency of his literary style. Each label used by Ortega, each figure of speech, each transposition, reveals an aspect of reality either named or alluded to; it makes reality new, presents it reborn before our eyes, *ready to have thought act upon it in a creative way,* not to have thought fall back on it in an inertial way.

But we must take seriously the figure of speech in which Ortega defines his style, the justification for his innumerable images: it is a question of *the sun's* making reflections upon things; its shining and its heat are essential; the dead indication of things with a school pointer will not do. The unveiling of reality, its patentization, cannot be attained except from a certain adequate temper, and in the end it turns out that this has to be a *literary* temper. The unexpected result is that the "sober," "cold," "objective" attitude, which seems proper to science, is less scientific. The truth is uncovered, made manifest, only by making things glow and perhaps even burn. In an essay in which he reflected upon his own life, Ortega said something which seems to me to be one of the profoundest and most important truths that he has shown us: "the set of teeth with which one devours a culture is called enthusiasm." This is why I said something before that might have seemed to lack justification and truth: that only by means of literature can a certain kind of higher precision be attained, and that to cultivate true precision there is no solution but to cultivate literature.

Julián Marías. *José Ortega y Gasset:*
Circumstance and Vocation (Norman,
University of Oklahoma Press, 1970), pp. 263–64

In his earliest pronouncements Ortega was already critical of "cloying liberalism," and it appears certain that in the 1920s he became ever more receptive to conservative ideas. He never shared Friedrich Hegel's idolization of the state. In full agreement with the poet Juan Ramón Jiménez, his friend, Ortega demanded intellectual and moral freedom for the elite, the eminent minority (*inmensa minoría*). Just as Hermann Hesse had scorned his era for the degeneration that he epitomized in his label "the age of the *feuilleton,*" so Ortega attacked the "culture of verbiage" and the "reign of the shop window." These, along with other hidden persuaders, are still holding sway today. It was hardly unalloyed praise of the culture of that time for Ortega to say that "its fruits . . . are world citizenship, philanthropy, humaneness, and parliamentarianism" while mentioning in the same breath "the barbarism of the specialist" and characterizing the modern scientist as "the archetypal mass man." In *The Revolt of the Masses,* Ortega betrays certain secret yearnings for the world of the eighteenth century and reveals that he failed to understand his era and its younger generation. This can be seen, for example, when Ortega asks: "What will these football-playing Europeans do when they are forty?" The Charleston and jazz music worried him; Ortega has all too frequently succumbed to the temptation of writing music criticism.

Franz Niedermayer. *José Ortega y Gasset* (New York, Frederick Ungar, 1973), pp. 52–53

The literary criticism practiced by Ortega y Gasset is one more operation of his philosophic activity, perfectly meshed with his way of understanding this activity, that is, with what constitutes his system of thought. The objects of said literary criticism belong to his circumstance, and by means of the treatment to which he subjects them, he carries them to the fullness of their meaning. . . . He compares the work and personality of Pío Baroja, typical representative of the negative attitude of the generation of ninety-eight, in order to scrutinize, from his own perspective as spectator, the Spain and the historical world of his time, that world which he was given to inhabit and interpret ("the theme of our time" is a very indicative epigraph about vital or historical reason conceived by Ortega as system and key to his thought). Literary analysis has allowed him to probe deep into the area of his own personal reality, that is, of his circumstance: but along the way he has permitted us, his readers, a profound comprehension of artistic creations toward whose aesthetic value the critic perhaps felt more intellectual curiosity than emotional participation. I would say that the philosopher's natural propensity after he has recognized the intranscendental nature of the work of art prevents his enjoying a lingering dalliance in its pure immanence.

Francisco Ayala. *CritI.* Dec., 1974, pp. 413–14

In spite of masterly texts in which not one of our ills goes undiagnosed, and despite books which are remarkable too for the quality of their prose, José Ortega y Gasset remains a great unknown. When he is not being trivialised, as the academic world does when it embalms him in phrases such as "ratio-vitalism," he is blamed for not having paid heed to social factors—they say that he "undervalues economic conditions" and reduce him to a latterday exponent of 19th-century liberalism.

    The truth is that Ortega is unequalled as a debunker of dogmatisms, and this still bothers people. The truth is that he was the first to dissect "the mass-man," and to denounce the danger he constitutes. But it would not be correct to equate this man with the proletariat. For Ortega, the mass-man flourishes as profusely among the upper as in the lower classes. Not that this man of the world will always look like a philistine. He has read Nietzsche; he has read everything; he knows that philosophy is play, that it is ludic. And play he does, observing that no truth binds him other than Life, which is a riddle. But of course, this game is serious: the whole vital drama of life is expressed in it, when it is Schopenhauer or Ortega who plays.

Where is the life in the systematising, structuralising minds that despise Ortega? Dogma makes them only into well-oiled pieces of machinery. Ortega is a *source,* a spring. He is so unpedantic, so unbombastic, that he is only barely a traditional philosopher at all: he seems so transparent that he is nothing but light. On any theme he ponders (Bullfighting, Sport, Communism), he sheds a noonday brightness, in which prejudices, idols of the tribe, entelechies, all dissolve. Ortega has been classified as *un grand Européen,* and so he was, but his Europeanism should not conceal the fact that he is a very Spanish philosopher, very down to earth, closer to the peasant, through his realism, or to the torero, through his precision and elegance, than to the "progressive intellectual."

David Mata. *Encounter.* Feb., 1982, p. 52

[Ortega's] standing among the great philosophers of the West remains to be determined by another age. His ideas are rarely difficult and the clarity of his style, when it does not merely dazzle, serves to facilitate the reader's task. Yet, in his concern to be original, he was often guilty of neglecting to be thorough. Few serious thinkers can have been so consistent in their refusal to see their intuitions and insights through to their logical conclusions. This fact in Ortega made it possible for so many conflicting critical approaches to exist side by side, with equal claims upon our allegiance. It is not enough even to rely on the primary texts, for the fact remains that Ortega did not say enough about almost any important subject. He allowed himself to be intellectually alluring, and all too often moved on, failing to complete even the project at hand, into which he had seduced the reader with unfulfilled promises. Yet his thought is evocative, and that is no small gift. Even in his most pessimistic works, he saw life as aesthetic and intellectual enjoyment; the scope of his enthusiasm was universal, but the ceaseless creation of introductory studies of themes left the door open for succeeding writers to presume conclusions that cannot be easily discarded, although common sense dictates that they are erroneous and ill-intentioned. And yet, he was never dull, never repetitive, never false, and never intellectually careless. He is one of the pillars of a new Spanish intellectual tradition. As Antonio Machado declared, he is "a new gesture."

Victor Ouimette. *José Ortega y Gasset* (Boston,
Twayne, 1982), pp. 152–53

What are the characteristics of Ortega's mass man? He is unable to distinguish between the natural and the artificial. Technology, which surrounds him with cheap and abundant goods and services, with packaged bread, subways, blue-jeans, with running water and electrical fixtures that light up at the touch of a finger, has as it were worked itself into his mind as an extension of the natural world. He expects that there will be air to breathe, sunlight. He also expects elevators to go up, buses to arrive. His ability to distinguish between artifact and organism withers away. Blind to the miraculous character of nature, as well as to the genius of technology, he takes both for granted. So in Ortega's mass society the plebeians have conquered, and they do not concern themselves with civilization as such but only with the wealth and conveniences provided by mechanization. The spirit of a mass society bids it to abandon itself freely to itself and to embrace itself; practically nothing is impossible, nothing is dangerous and, in principle, no one is superior to anyone else—this, Ortega submits, is the mass man's creed. The "select man" by contrast, insofar as he serves a transcendental purpose, understands that he must accept a kind of servitude. "To live at ease," said Goethe, "is plebeian; the noble mind aspires to ordinance and law." It follows from this that the mass man lacks seriousness. With him nothing is for real, all parts are interchangeable. For him everything is provisional. He may occasionally play at tragedy, but the prevailing mood is one of farce. The mass man loves gags. He is a spoilt child, demanding amusement, given to tantrums, lacking the form, the indispensable tension which only imperatives can give. His only commandment is Thou shalt expect convenience. "The only real effort is expended in fleeing from one's own destiny."

Saul Bellow. Foreword to José Ortega y Gasset,
The Revolt of the Masses (Notre Dame, Ind.,
University of Notre Dame Press, 1985), pp. x–xi

OTERO, BLAS DE (1916–   )

Blas de Otero's work until now is small in quantity; I know of two books: *Fiercely Human Angel* . . . and *Doubling of Consciousness* . . . , which was awarded the Boscán Prize in 1950.

Blas de Otero's poetry is perhaps the poetry that has most moved me in the last two years. . . . Otero has expressed with more clarity than anyone else I know—at the beginning of *Fiercely Human Angel*—the essential facts about the problem of uprootedness. . . .

The first theme that the reader becomes aware of and one that as he continues reading will establish itself as the obsession of the poetry is nihilism: desolation, emptiness, dizziness . . . .

This vision of an enormous, limitless night of sorrow, a night of desolate emptiness, is spread like an essential sadness that penetrates all the corners of Otero's poetry. It is a growing and invading hollowness, which absorbs us and brings us to our singular problem through the poet's effectiveness and power of understanding. Otero has a capacity to condense language and to consolidate material that is perhaps superior to that of any of his contemporaries, and comparable, with regard to its strength and clarity—taking into account, of course, the great difference—to those of a García Lorca and other poets of my generation, who brought so many expressive inventions to our language; at times, he is comparable to the most anguished and intense Quevedo. . . .

What is also quite evident in his poetry is how the theme of emptiness is linked to the religious theme. Definitively, man's emptiness is only a desire for God. . . . Thus, all of Otero's poetry is a desperate path toward God, a search in solitude, a search that is also a struggle with God, a struggle to find him, so that he will reveal himself. . . . [1952]

> Dámaso Alonso. *Poetas españoles*
> *contemporáneos,* 3rd ed. (Madrid, Gredos,
> 1969), pp. 350–53†

We meet [Blas de Otero] in the post-civil war poetry following a very personal and separate path, although three tendencies do appear in his work: the religious, "uprootedness," and the social . . . . In none of these is he the mere follower of a poetic style; . . . all his poetry is extremely unified.

In this regard—unity in variation—Otero reminds us of his great compatriot Don Miguel de Unamuno. . . . With regard to both verse and language . . . both adopt an analogous position and appear to be fighting tooth and nail with language, as if language were not really part of them but rather a hard material that, like sculptors, they chisel to bring out the necessary elements. Both appear to consider words as something solid, with tactile qualities and not only rhythmic beats. Music and the musical value of the verse are secondary to them— although in Otero through a renunciation and not through a lack of ability; the melody is internal, one of thoughts that are felt or feelings that are thought, rather than pleasing to the ear; it is a rather plastic poetry, made more for pleasure and feeling than for the ear. The relationship is also visible on the plane of life experiences that feed their creations . . . . In both the agonizing attitude toward the metaphysical problem—death—is basic, although the two do not coincide in the degree of anguish.

Unamuno has been one of the prime teachers of Otero, in spite of the latter's protests to the contrary that in face of Unamuno's "absorption in thought" he has been led to a progressive "alienation." [1955]

> Emilio Alarcos Llorach. *La poesía de Blas de*
> *Otero* (Madrid, Anaya, 1966), pp. 23–24†

Many things happen to words in Otero's poetry. One senses a strange transformation in language. The poet has control in an opposition between him and his material. Dislocations, enjambements and sudden breaks at the end of a line are used to make images and feelings work on more than one level at the same time, as in "Letters and Poems to Nazim Hikmet" where he speaks ". . . about things that don't exist: God/is eavesdropping behind the door . . ." What an amazing God is this that does not exist yet eavesdrops behind prison-cell doors! The irony grows by suspending the word "God" at the end of one line and dropping it suddenly on the next line. It also drops like a mask behind which the enemy is hiding.

He can surprise with a sudden twist of phrase. For instance, the expected "cogidos de la mano" (holding hands, hand in hand) is made over into the pathetic "cogidos de la muerte" (holding deaths, death in death). An ordinary piece of furniture, "armario de luna" (simply a wardrobe with mirrors on the outside of its doors), is changed by the attachment of another phrase, "y de manteles" (and for tablecloths), into a new kind of wardrobe or closet where moonlight as well as linens are kept. The poet sees something with the sharp insight of a child and the thing is familiar and brand new at once. Otero also makes us look in a fresh way at phrases or lines he borrows from other poets ([Francisco de] Quevedo, [Antonio] Machado, [César] Vallejo). In his work each sound looks for the companion that will follow it and once found they cannot exist without each other.

Hardie St. Martin. Introduction to Blas de
Otero, *Twenty Poems* (Madison, Minn., Sixties
Press, 1964), pp. 9–10

One of Otero's favorite themes, I would say the predominant one of his second poetic phase, which goes from *I Ask for Peace and a Chance to Speak,* which appeared in 1955, to *Speaking about Spain,* published in 1964 . . . is that of Spain, an almost obsessive theme that has two principal sources: on one hand, the concern for Spain—its being, its destiny, and its drama; on the other, its landscape, the varied and beautiful physical appearance of the homeland, of all the "Spains" that the poet has lived in and contemplated slowly and with relish. . . . Starting with *I Ask for Peace and a Chance to Speak* . . . Otero's poetry is concerned with the Spaniard in his collective destiny, and linked to this concern is the theme of the homeland, Spain. This is not a new theme . . . but in Otero's works it reaches its maximum intensity and beauty.

As with Unamuno and [Antonio] Machado, Spain bitterly grieves Otero; the thorn of an unjust and cruel homeland pricks him painfully, the bitter cup of the civil war. . . .

The theme of the civil war . . . reappears over and over again, like an obsession, in this phase of Otero's poetry. Every once in a while he calls out to Spain to give everyone a breathable peace.

José Luis Cano. Introduction to Blas de Otero,
País: Antología 1955–1970 (Barcelona, Plaza y
Janés, 1971), pp. 9–11†

Otero often lifts phrases from other poets and, subjecting them to slight joltings and distortions as he grafts them into his own structures, confers on them a new power but at the same time bonds himself in a verbal relationship to voice the echoes or the image he picks up in his mirror. The procedure is so common with Otero, as a matter of fact, that his poetry gives the impression of a tissue of quotations. . . .

Verbal echoes, however, are easy to pick up. The more cultured the ear, the more it will hear. . . . But more important than the recollection of prefabricated phrases and images for new expressive purposes is the technique that might be called deliberate *pentimento* or palimpsest (I claim no originality for the metaphor), that is, the rewriting of someone else's entire poem, which is thus affirmed, amplified, revised or contradicted, in such a way that the original inspiration or provocation seems intentionally to have been poorly erased from the parchment and to be constantly legible underneath the new ink.

Edmund L. King. In Jaime Ferrán and Daniel P.
Testa, eds., *Spanish Writers of 1936: Crisis and
Commitment in the Poetry of the Thirties and
Forties* (London, Támesis, 1970), pp. 128–29

"And I Will Go Away" [in *Meanwhile*] presents the ancient topic of the abandonment of the city by the satirist with the aim of engaging the listener's compassion and persuading him that something must be done. . . . The intrinsic antagonism between honest man and corrupt city, the despair of city life, the pride of absolute moral judgement devoid of compassion for his victim or doubts about his own moral standing are all conventional features of the satiric mask. Yet rather than piously fleeing the satirist stays on, horrified at the vice he sees but ever eager to seek it out and to thoroughly enjoy exercising his skills in exposing it. This tension between the paraded disgust of the honorable man and his salacious cataloging of human vice is an artful invention that engages the reader's emotions and adds color to a fairly continuous mood of outrage.

Even though unable to retire from the busy world, the speaker presents himself as a simple, honest man and draws attention to his plain, humble origins. He prides himself on his Basque roots, praising rustic virtues in "Orozco" where he summons up his youth in the idyllic innocence of a Basque valley, nourished by nature's bounty, healthy exercise on the frontón court, and the homely staples of his grandmother's orchard. . . .

The claim to humble, honest origins is reinforced by rejecting the world of books and calling attention to a blunt, simple style, the use of current speech idiom, a conversational manner, and a Romantic faith in the natural art of the folk. This pretended scorn for controlled artistic effects coincides with Otero's decision to find his muse in the daily life of the broad masses. The fifties evidence a change of style marked by the movement away from sonnet and quatrain, increasing recourse to plain style and the diminished importance of hyperbolic images. The declining influence of Golden Age poets and the growing admiration for Machado coincide with this development. In short, the insistence on his plain no-nonsense style, while fanning distrust of literature as the mother of lies, is a conventional device: it allows the satirist to tilt at pretentious and pompous effects while suggesting that he is a down-to-earth truthteller. The speaker skillfully and repeatedly insists on his lack of skill in speaking, his contempt for bookish verse . . . .

Geoffrey R. Barrow, HR. Spring, 1980, pp. 222, 223

PASO, ALFONSO (1926–   )

"Which shall it be tonight?" the husband in the [widely circulated Spanish newspaper] *ABC* cartoon asked his wife. The movies or Alfonso Paso?" . . .

Because he is so prolific critics have compared him to his father-in-law Jardiel Poncela, to Pedro Muñoz Seca, to Lope de Vega; and they profess to see in his work resemblances to half a dozen Spanish and foreign authors. Paso acknowledges legitimate debts to Priestley, to Anouilh, even one to his father-in-law; but he would prefer not to be placed in any dramatic line. He would like to leap from one type of play to another in an effort to be very much of his own day and to treat the problems of today. The Spanish author, he believes, must be on guard lest he lose contact with his public, and Paso wants to communicate across the footlights. What he does not want to be, he says emphatically, is "fodder for posterity."

His theater has, indeed, a broad range within the delimitations of comedy, and he is unexcelled today in evoking laughter based on character, wit, and situation. He is highly competent in such potboilers as the currently popular detective farce *Careful with Serious People!* (1960), for example, has no other pretension than to make the audience laugh. The *ABC* critic Alfredo Marqueríe called it a "comic absurdity," and no one—least of all the characters themselves—takes seriously a dead body that is carted on and off stage.

Alfonso Paso is at his best in that mixture of laughter and tears which gets closest to the Spanish outlook on life. *The Poor Little People,* which won the Carlos Arniches Prize in 1956, takes its title from a quotation by Quevedo. These people, in Quevedo's words, "will make you laugh at their hunger and misery. But also they will make you cry. They are poor little people." . . .

Alfonso Paso is also confronting an interesting problem in form: the trend toward the two-act play. In Spain, where two daily performances take place at seven and eleven p.m., the theater is subject to the pressure of time; for between nine-fifteen or nine-thirty and the eleven o'clock show the actors and technicians must also have their supper. . . . Both audience and actors are content with a single intermission; and more and more, playwrights, including Paso, attempt the two-act play. Whether it is in two or three acts the overall limitation of time puts the Spanish dramatist on his mettle. He cannot treat themes extensively. His work must be both intensive and schematic. Compared with the more leisurely development of foreign plays, the Spanish play must, in the metaphor of Alfonso Paso, be like a telegram.

John C. Dowling. MLJ. May, 1961, pp. 195–97

We have two new writers [William Layton and Augustin Penon] adapting a play [Song of the Grasshopper] for three new producers [Gene Dingenary, Miranda d'Ancona, and Nancy Levering]. The author of the original play, of course, was that incredibly successful figure, the author of 112 produced plays by the age of forty, the famous Alfonso Paso.

Who?

Now the feel is starting to come. If Paso is so famous, why hasn't anyone heard of him? Obviously because his plays haven't been done here. But if he's so successful, why haven't his plays been done here? Whatever the reasons, valid or not, it must be admitted that there hasn't exactly been a bull market for Spanish plays on Broadway lately. The last Spanish smash was _____(fill in your own blank). There may never have been a Spanish blockbuster, which doesn't mean there couldn't be one, and if Song of the Grasshopper was going to make it, the director was going to be crucial. For director: Charles Bowden.

Who?

Charles Bowden, the producer. He produced Williams's Night of the Iguana and Camus's Caligula and he worked for 14 years with the Lunts. But in the sixties, he had not been credited with the staging of a single Broadway production. So Song of the Grasshopper was going into production with three untried producers, two untried adapters and one at least recently untried director. For star: Alfred Drake.

No "Who?" here. Alfred Drake is famous, gifted, dynamic, intelligent, and he is a terrific musical-comedy performer, the only man active in the theatre who has starred in three blockbuster musicals: Oklahoma!, Kiss Me, Kate and Kismet. But Song of the Grasshopper wasn't a musical; it was a play. . . .

What was this play, and why did it die?

The main character, Aris (Alfred Drake), lives, separated from his wife, in a terrible pit of a house on the outskirts of Madrid. He has a lovely marriageable daughter, assorted younger children from assorted women, plus a crocodile in the bathroom. The latter, a recent addition, was found wandering on the property. He also has no money, the electricity is about to be turned off, the furniture taken away, and his last ten pesetas are invested in a raffle ticket.

He is also absolutely unperturbed about his situation. He knows that somehow everything is going to turn out all right. And the course of the play proves him right: he wins the raffle, returns the crocodile for a reward, etc. He is also reunited with his wife, who comes to see that his world view is the only one that really matters. So what if a grasshopper dies? You can never take away the singing it has done.

Clearly, this is a delicate play and must come across as such if it is to succeed. Said the authors: "The subject of the play was ignored in direction and interpretation; what we got was situation comedy, and the jokes aren't meant to carry it. Imagine *Harvey,* for example, being played as a situation comedy." . . .

And remember, too, that this was a simple play, as author Penon put it, "about a man who believes in Providence." He's got no money, he's deep in debt, there are mouths to feed, yet somehow it's all going to turn out. . . . Bowden put it this way: "I feel he writes poems or takes in students. Occasionally, I don't think he does it for any set fee, but I think he does it." . . .

I think I'll always remember *Song of the Grasshopper* . . . caught with its curtain up, its numbed star staring around, the audience staring around, everybody staring around, all of us confused, a piece of Pirandello in the night.

William Goldman. *The Season: A Candid Look
at Broadway* (New York, Harcourt Brace &
World, 1969), pp. 33–39

Alfonso Paso has not stopped raising important problems even in his apparently most superficial works. Plays that are almost exclusively humorous have hidden beneath their superficial appearance of light theater a satiric and parodic sense of high quality. . . . The author is on top of it all. He possesses that "sixth sense" . . . so necessary for writing theater. . . .

Alfonso Paso, from his very first works, learned how to link literary quality—purpose, poetry, tenderness, humor, satire—with dramatic technique, that "sixth sense" that has come to be called the "craft" of the author. In some works, *Heaven in the House, There Is Someone Behind the Door, The Song of the Grasshopper, Call for Julius Caesar, Aurelia and Her Men, Dear Teacher,* etc.—literary quality predominates without the author's forgetting other basics of dramatic production; in others: *Careful with Serious People!, Let's Tell Lies, Occupation: Suspect, The Hunt of the Foreigner,* technique predominates over any other element, and the plays are constructed with the know-how of a skilled playwright, producing in the spectator the desired result: to make the audience laugh without noticing if the means employed are legitimate or not, literary or not, of high dramatic quality or not. . . .

Another characteristic of Alfonso Paso is that his theater has been considered by many to be apolitical, which has put some of them off. Paso has not been interested in bringing to the theater the game of politics as such; but he has certainly shown interest in rebellion, through specific themes, plots, theses, or characters, and with behavior, styles, and political activities with which he was not in agreement. In many of his plays he has shown himself to be against the impulses of the right, in others against those of the left. And he has done this—and is still doing it, I suppose—precisely because it gives him pleasure to pillory the evils of both extremes, just as he is fond of praising and defending what is salutary on the right and on the left.

Julio Mathías. Alfonso Paso (Madrid, EPESA, 1971), pp. 68–69†

Paso has proved to be the most productive theatrical writer of the postwar Spanish theater. Dramatic fecundity is hardly new in Spain, but any dramatist who completes more than a hundred and twenty-five works in a period of two decades is a rare individual regardless of the degree of literary importance of his efforts. Prolificness does not necessarily indicate routine or mediocre results, and Paso's contribution to the Spanish stage is such that it cannot be ignored. He is an eclectic writer at best, admitting influences ranging from his late father-in-law Jardiel Poncela to Tennessee Williams. Like several other Spanish dramatists, active during the past twenty years, he has varied his product—offering comedies (serious, light, poetical, satirical), mysteries (both straight suspense and those with elements of parody), works of dark humor, serious dramas, and historical plays which demonstrate a personal view and interpretation of major figures of the past. Although he has not followed the single-minded course of the controversial Sastre, Paso has frequently demonstrated his awareness of the staleness of writing and production that prevailed during his early career. As a man of the theater, he also noted the antiquated staging facilities as well as the conservatism of the theatergoing public. He has spoken frankly about the inhibiting censorial prohibitions and of the sometimes amusing ways in which he has circumvented them. But for the most part he has devoted himself to providing a steady theatrical fare of a traditional type that more often than not must be treated as ephemeral entertainment. Nevertheless, an examination of almost any Paso play selected at random would provide some evidence of the theatrical know-how of the playwright and even of his undeniably subtle intelligence.

Paso's careful application of his talent in the creation of popular comedy can be illustrated by *Old-Fashioned Notions* [i.e., *Papa's and Mama's Things*] (1960), which enjoyed a run of some six hundred performances (far more than those achieved by any of his more serious efforts). By reversing the traditional situation of parental opposition to the marriage of their children and placing a son and a daughter in the position of opposing the autumnal union of their respective parents, the playwright creates a dramatic conflict for *Old-Fashioned Notions* that is calculated to appeal to an older (and more loyal) theater public. . . .

Although *Old-Fashioned Notions* is the type of play certain to trigger the ire of the spokesmen for committed theater, an attack on such a comedy because of its lack of transcendental content would be a waste of ammunition. At the time of its premiere, the leading critics Adolfo Prego and Alfredo Marquerie both accepted the play for what it is: brisk, farcial entertainment. Marqueríe noted numerous influences that could be detected in the work (Thornton Wilder, Gómez de la Serna, the Quintero brothers, Félicien Marceau, and others) but recommended that it not be considered a piece of second-hand theater since the stamp of Paso himself was unmistakable throughout the comedy. . . .

Paso takes his writing seriously and stands on his own judgments of the relative merits of his plays rather than accepting instances where he considers his achievement to be solid. Among the serious dramas of the playwright, *The Poor Sad People* [*The Poor Little People*] (1957) is one of the most highly regarded. . . .

The Poor Sad People is undeniably an engaging and sometimes affecting piece of dramatic writing. It is not, however, one of the major works of its time nor is it profoundly involved in the social injustices that have created the desperation and frustration that darken the lives of the characters.

Marion P. Holt. *The Contemporary Spanish
Theater (1949–1972)* (Boston, Twayne, 1975), pp. 136–39

Alfonso Paso remains a remarkable craftsman, a playwright whose grievously conventional comedies represent an authentic source to reveal the grievously conventional social scene of today's Spain. While his detractors continue to label him an incurable manufacturer of plays, attacking his theater for its dearth of literary pretensions and mocking his public for its conditioned response to frivolity, distortion, and expansive mediocrity, the fact is that Alfonso Paso's successful career in alternating froth and trivia with some truly exciting accomplishments now deserves a serious critical hearing. Nevertheless, it will take an enormous dose of seasoned objectivity to weigh Alfonso Paso's superb attributes in balance with his many flaws. The few outstanding plays in his vast repertory of rubbish have all too often been consigned to a speedy oblivion, the result, perhaps, of Alfonso Paso's overlarge reputation for writing so many comedies to please a public of fairly low cultural standards. . . .

Federico C. Sainz de Robles [a leading critic of Spain] may insist that *You Can Be a Murderer* is "a masterpiece of the contemporary Spanish theater," but if such a statement is true, one cannot say very much in favor of the contemporary Spanish theater scene. The play's plot and humor are derived from the mechanical manipulation of the element of surprise, a common characteristic of many of Alfonso Paso's entertaining, funny, and clever well-made plays. . . .

Nero-Paso, . . . is an arresting psychological drama of considerable literary and historical interest. Combining Brechtian distancing techniques with carefully documented historical data, *Nero-Paso* depicts a bewildered anti-hero victimized by the evil of his own social milieu. The play's outstanding merit lies in its vindication of Alfonso Paso as a consummate craftsman of good drama.

Douglas R. McKay. MLJ. Feb., 1975, p. 142

PEDROLO, MANUEL DE (1918–   )

De Pedrolo's one-act play *Cruma* . . . is a study in human isolation. "Cruma" is the name of an Etruscan measure or measuring instrument, and the play shows an attempt to measure the human situation by standards that have become inoperative and meaningless. In an empty and bare-walled corridor that seems part of a larger apartment, a man who is at home there—and is therefore called "the resident"—is about to measure the dimensions of the walls. He is joined by a visitor who helps him in this work—which is in vain, because they discover that the measuring tapes they are using are blank, without markings or figures.

The situation of the resident in the corridor of his apartment is as mysterious as those of the two tramps on their road in [Beckett's] *Waiting for Godot*. The resident is unaware of an outside world. He does not know how the objects he uses have reached him. . . .

This strange short play poses the problem of the reality of the "others" and the possibility of establishing contact with them. Each character represents a different level of being. The resident occupies one end of the scale—he is an authentic being exploring his own world, hence unable to relate himself to others, unable even to distinguish his friend from a stranger. On the other end of the scale is the young girl—she exists only insofar as others want her. The other three characters represent intermediary steps on this scale. The greater the *inner* reality or authenticity of a human being, the less able he is to establish contact with the outside world, in its crudity and deceptiveness. And yet this interior solitude is bound to be disturbed; at the end of the play, the whole cycle of invasions from the inauthentic, everyday world is about to begin anew. . . .

Men and No is indeed an investigation—an investigation into the problem of liberty. Man is imprisoned in an infinitely receding series of enclosures. Whenever he thinks that he has broken through one of these barriers (the barrier of superstition, the barrier of myth or tyranny, or the inability to master nature), he finds himself face to face with a new barrier (the metaphysical anguish of the human condition, death, the relativity of all knowledge, and so on). But the struggle to overcome the new row of iron bars continues; it must go on, even if we know in advance that it will reveal only a further barrier beyond. [1961]

Martin Esslin. The Theatre of the Absurd,
revised updated version (Woodstock, N.Y.,
Overlook Press, 1973), pp. 214–16

Pedrolo['s plays] are obviously allied to, if not influenced by, the theater of the absurd. Pedrolo's vision is of a world in which men fight desperately, stubbornly, instinctively to push back the knowledge of the indefinable menace that they feel surrounding them. His favorite image is that of an enclosed space, usually a room. . . . The action of these plays never consists of what we might call social movement: the recognizable everyday actions, that is, of human beings. In many dramatic works, of course, these "social" actions are merely the outward indication of an inner essence that they represent or symbolize. In Pedrolo's plays we see the skeletal inner essence: reality laid bare, without the "clothing" of social movement, unobscured by the web of conventional gesture that covers reality and ameliorates our apprehension of it in everyday life and in ordinary drama. His plays are not set in a specified time or place but in an extraterrestrial ultimate reality where the Platonic essences of being exist. They show us the reality for which the reality we know is the name. Samuel Beckett is the only other playwright to have accomplished this transposition effectively. . . .

In *The Room* [i.e., *Technique of the Room*] . . . there is no escape: the room *is* the world, *is* life. The scene is a dormitory room in a hostel. Miscellaneous objects are scattered about. One by one, seven young people are introduced into the room by an invisible landlady whose voice can be heard fulsomely praising the room's comforts. The seven people are different types of humanity—domineering, submissive, selfish, and so on. They are not caricatures in any sense, however. As they come in, each carries an empty suitcase, preempts a space in the room and some objects from the shelves, and settles down. But this room is the world, and there are neither enough beds nor enough objects to go round. What Pedrolo shows us here with consummate dramatic skill is a microcosm of life and its conflicts played out in the compass of this ordinary room. At the end the characters are called out of the room by the voice of the landlady, one by one, just as they were introduced. They leave—for they have no choice—some reluctantly, some resignedly, discarding their earthly dross as they go. At the end the room is again empty, but the eternal cycle of life begins afresh as we hear the voice of the landlady lauding the room to a new tenant. *The Room* is a bold experiment, for the representation of life as a whole in everyday terms runs the danger of becoming trite; but Pedrolo succeeds in making the dramatic image into which he has compressed his view of life a valid and workable one.

Full Circle is a more socially oriented play [than *Cruma* and *Technique of the Room*]. The leaders of the rebellion against an apparently senseless imposed social order themselves become the representatives of that order and suppress those whom they incited to rebel with the same mindless ferocity exercised by the previous rulers. The play is essentially a powerful political parable, in which Pedrolo speaks of the corruptive effect of power and of the faithlessness of political victors to the ideals for which they fought. Political revolutionaries are like Cronus, swallowing their children lest they in turn be deposed. Their rebellion founders on the reef of their own insecurity and the insincerity, both malleable raw materials in the process of conversion from pristine idealism to the moral putrefaction that the possession of power brings. As the disappointed rebel leader in Genet's *The Balcony* remarks after it is all over, "No truth was possible."

> George E. Wellwarth. Introduction to *3 Catalan*
> *Dramatists* (Montreal, Engendra Press, 1976),
> pp. 3, 6

Manuel de Pedrolo, the most prolific Catalan writer of the moment, with *Anonymous II; or, On the Permanent Dimensions of the Triarchy* (1970) continues one of his main interests, that of exposing the repressive procedures and shortcomings of the totalitarian state. Chronologically, the work is the forty-seventh of his sixty-plus novels to date and number two of his Anonymous trilogy. . . .

Anonymous II, suggestive of a real situation, that of Franco's Spain, is narrated in the third person with a style befitting the chronicle. There a tetrarchic regime established by brute force is composed of the triarchs, symbolizing the three armed forces, and by the moral dignitaries, priestlike characters who put the interests of the state before religious considerations. The book incisively blasts the double standard in relation to sex and points out how sexual deviations are considered normal and straight sex improper. It also portrays the complete alienation of the common people, given to bizarre practices.

The novel is a "secret" guide to direct the reader through the intricate maze of a self-perpetuating political system which thrives in the chaos provoked by its order. The panorama of utter confusion unfolds with the subdued humor, irony and sarcasm characteristic of Pedrolo. . . .

There are basic similarities with Pedrolo's play *Full Circle,* a curious forecast of Adolfo Suárez's moderate government under King Juan Carlos I, too rightist for the Left and too leftist for the Right. . . . *Anonymous II* is another resourceful novel by Pedrolo, resolving with great literary skill the thorny difficulties of an extraliterary topic, that of the ills of a totalitarian system and the problem of its eradication.

> Albert M. Forcadas. *WLT.* Winter, 1982, p. 98

The evil that a tyrant does redounds to the mass tragedy of countless wrecked lives. As the prime mover of a perverse order of things, Jutge Domina (literally "Justice Dominates") lurks ubiquitously in the background. From the ruthless dictator radiates the atmosphere of doom that permeates the distinct situations vividly depicted by Pedrolo in twenty-one chapters and effectively integrated into a primordial "act of violence" [in *Act of Violence*]. . . .

Nothing short of epic is the formidable movement which Pedrolo intuits in society at large reacting against Domina's pernicious machinations. After enduring with uncommon resilience and stoic resignation some fifteen years of oppression and virtual bondage, writers and shopkeepers, actors and railroad employees, bureaucrats and factory workers, the bourgeoisie and the pariahs of the civic realm—members all of the silent and not-so-silent majority—have learned to exchange the slogans of strident militarism for a motto of peaceful defiance: "It's very simple: just stay home." Particularly dramatic is Pedrolo's sizing up of the momentum of the final nemesis, brought to realization within a framework of contrasts. . . .

Dated May–June 1961, *Act of Violence* is a belated Catalan exemplar of the so-called objective or documentary novel, well represented in its salient characteristics of the collective protagonist and multiple viewpoint by Camilo José Cela's *The Beehive* (1951), and Rafael Sánchez Ferlosio's *The Jarama* (1956). Given its sensitive subject matter—Pedrolo is much more outspoken than his counterparts in Castilian literature—Pedrolo's book, understandably, could not reach the printing press before 1975. . . . Attesting to a political crisis much too common throughout Spanish history and conjuring up the classical resolution memorably dramatized by Lope de Vega in *Fuenteovejuna*, Pedrolo's latter-day version of government by Big Brother marks a lasting contribution to Hispanic letters of the twentieth century.

Peter Cocozzella. WLT. Summer, 1984, pp. 402–3

PÉREZ DE AYALA, RAMÓN (1880–1962)

Ramón Pérez de Ayala has just sent me a book he wrote. It is titled *A. M. D. G.: Life in Jesuit Schools*. The author was a student of these reverend fathers, and so was I. . . .

In what way do the Jesuits influence the life of Bertuco [the main character]? . . . Like those who go to Saint Patrick's Purgatory, Bertuco will never again be able to laugh: laughter is the expression of a healthy and elastic soul, a unified and integrated one. If this is so, in order for the soul to be able to laugh it must believe with deep faith in three things: that there is a science worthy of the name, that there is a morality that is not ridiculous, and that art exists. Fine: the Jesuits will lead Bertuco to make fun of all the classical humanist thinkers: of Democritus, Plato, Descartes, Galileo, Spinoza, Kant, Darwin, etc.; they will accustom him to call morality a bunch of stupid and superstitious rules and exercises; nothing will be said about art. . . .

Bertuco will see humanity divided into two groups: the Jesuits and the others. And he will hear that the *others* are false, vicious, ignorant people, lacking ideals, ready to sell themselves for a little money, and without any appreciable merit. To the contrary, the Jesuits are of such a specific character that not one has yet been condemned. . . .

Bertuco will leave the school with hope shattered; no matter what efforts of mind he might make to overcome his original distrust of the others, he will never overcome that original disdain for them. . . .

This book transcends literature and is a valuable document for the reform of Spanish educational system. . . . [1910]

José Ortega y Gasset. Obras completas, Vol. I
(Madrid, Revista de Occidente, 1946), 532–35†

Prometheus is not the central figure of the story to which his name is given; his father, Ulysses, the Wanderer, alias Marco de Setiñano, is its theme. In him Ayala has created another type, after the fashion of Alberto Díaz de Guzmán [of *A.D.M.G.*]; his pilgrimage through life is whimsically based upon the *Odyssey;* his ultimate disillusionment and failure are typical of the modern style. Marco is a theorist and a dreamer; experience with grim irony shatters his house of dreams. . . .

The other two stories of the collection [*Poetic Novels of Spanish Life*], *Sunday Sunlight* and *The Fall of the House of Limón,* are of a different type, perilously close to the novel of propaganda. Their purpose is plainly to scourge the evils of *caciquismo,* the Spanish form of political "bossism," as it flourishes in the rural districts and provincial captials. It is not necessary to read between the lines to hear a call to revolt.

Each chapter in these tales opens with a brief poem, in which the author foreshadows the psychological nature of the chapter, a device which inevitably suggests the musings and forebodings of the chorus of Attic tragedy; they form an organic part of the whole. . . . Pérez de Ayala's poetic gift has nowhere found more perfect expression than in the crystallizations of a fleeting mood. And the same perfection is evident in his prose.

Hayward Keniston. Introduction to Pérez de
Ayala, Prometheus, The Fall of the House of
Limón, Sunday Sunlight: Poetic Novels of
Spanish Life (New York, E. P. Dutton, 1920),
pp. xiv–xv

It is perhaps in his poetry that Ayala gives the clearest exposition of his philosophy and his creed. This poetry is so far represented by three volumes . . . bearing names which suggest a certain sequence: *The Peace of the Path, The Path of Infinite Variations, The Flowing Path.* The uniformity of the titles does not, however, correspond to any continuity in treatment or in outer subject, though the recurrence of the word *sendero,* path, does convey the idea of self-development along the road of experience which is the real inner subject of all. The first volume, *The Peace of the Path,* appeared in 1903 . . . and was ushered in by no less a prefacewriter than Rubén Darío. Despite its display of almost peasant-like simplicity, this work betrays the intellectual reader of home and foreign poetry. Thus, the opening poem, that which gives its title to the book, is an admirable adaptation to modern use of the mediaeval stanza known in Spanish literature as *cuaderna vía.* We note here a merely formal reminiscence of Juan Ruiz, the Archpriest of Hita, in more ways than one. . . . Together with the revival of this national vein, Ayala's early poems show a strong subservience to the poetical manner of Francis Jammes. This is clear in Ayala's attitude towards old houses, animals, and nature. . . . As an imitator of Jammes Ayala naturally proved inferior to his model, the youthful Asturias poet already revealed in some compositions of his early work an earnestness which was to prove his salvation—an earnestness in which it was possible to detect two wholly different moods; one dominated by a philosophical, almost religious preoccupation with the idea of destiny, the other marked by an aesthetic instinct towards truth and restrained expression.

Salvador de Madariaga. *The Genius of Spain,*
and Other Essays on Contemporary Literature
(London, Oxford University Press, 1923), pp. 75–77

If Ramón del Valle-Inclán makes us live the life of the Galician peasant and noble, Ramón Pérez de Ayala is the true representative of the mountain region of the Asturias. He is one of the most brilliant of the younger generation, and his novel *Mummers and Dancers* is without doubt one of the masterpieces of contemporary literature, and true to the traditions of the country that produced the *Celestina* and *Lazarillo de Tormes*—knights-errant of the picaresque. What Emerson says of Goethe is true of Ayala: "He sees at every pore"; by his eye he understands the world, and by means of his fastidiously beautiful style he is able to transmit his sensitive impressions to his readers. . . .

He is always at his best when describing vague and queer individuals who forever tilt at windmills, and his epicurean sincerity recalls at times George Gissing. But Ayala writes like a redeemed Gissing, one who could rise untarnished from the contemplation of New Grub Street, and there is not the uniform sadness. There is still left in the brothel scenes of his other powerful novel, *Darkness at the Heights*, a touch of Rabelaisian vigor inherited from Lazarillo that makes it a contrast to the typical modern novel of vice, always sad in its disillusion. And Ayala always closes his work with a spiritual moral that acts as a balm.

Walter Starkie. The Living Age. Nov. 7, 1925, p. 282

Succinctly stated, *Tiger Juan* is the love story of a bitter soul who in youth had almost killed his wife for suspected infidelity. She soon dies from neglect. Tiger Juan blames the whole sex. . . . The plot, like most plots means practically nothing when retailed and boiled down like this. Action is at all times slight, there is far more thinking and talking than doing. . . .

Stylistically, Pérez de Ayala is a delightful innovator. In *Tiger Juan* he has broken several of the usual literary canons. For instance, the novel is set up quite naturally with one broad column across the page while Tiger Juan and Herminia are together; when Herminia runs away, there are two parallel columns down the page. The life of the Tiger is related in one, that of Herminia in the other. While this is obviously artistic charlatanry, it somehow gives no offense when first noticed.

Again he departs from the tradition—though perhaps not so far from the practice—of the professional novelist when he offers two endings to the story. He announces at a certain chapter-end that the tale of Tiger Juan is now completed, and then he writes fifty more pages to prove it. . . . In *Tiger Juan* Pérez de Ayala has created a character impossible and yet natural, obviously exaggerated but in the end restrained. Tiger Juan is an obstinate fool. At the end of the narrative, the author has introduced several hundred lines of verse, as a sort of spiritual nirvana for Tiger Juan.

W. A. Beardsley. SR. May 15, 1926, p. 790

A word must be said about Ayala's erotic philosophy. If he exposes and castigates the hypocritical treatment of the problem of the sexes with prophetic wrath, no one is further removed than he from a hedonistic or loose conception of the love life, or from one contaminated with the artificial values of romantic effusion. In close conjunction with the treatises on sexual education by the great Spanish physician Gregorio Marañón, Ayala pleads for a reestablishment of the ideal natural form of erotic relationship. With a vigorous, heroic, and severe ethos he proposes a theory of love and marriage which might be designated the normality of genius were the notion of the normal, especially in this area, not discredited by feeble banalities. Ayala's protagonists must suffer many setbacks, must take many a wrong road before they grasp the norms eternally prescribed in nature and the soul and embody them with renewed innocence. But they always aspire to the ideal type of the wholly feminine woman and the wholly virile man, to ideal fulfillment in one lifelong amorous association, to authentic marriage and paternity exempt from everything problematical. . . .

Inasmuch as he struggles for the new man, the new ethos, Ayala joins the ranks of those minds who have a message to bring to the entire world of our culture. He belongs with the very few novelists whose view of the whole has not been cramped by the ordinary exercise of their craft. . . . He remarks on occasion that art can serve the goal of a Spanish renaissance more effectively than philosophy and sociology because art provides the Spaniard with the refinement and development of his emotional and spiritual sensibilities. [1931]

Ernst Robert Curtius. *Essays on European Literature* (Princeton, N.J., Princeton University Press, 1973), pp. 324–26

Ayala's *Belarmino and Apolonio,* since its publication in 1921, has perplexed the many critics who received this novel as an outstanding creation of contemporary Spanish fiction. There have been statements of its philosophy, never clearly defined or substantiated—for the reason, obviously, that no such philosophy exists. The novel is a humorous *reductio ad absurdum* of a reigning literary mode to which Ayala is unconditionally opposed. The critics . . . have mistaken the ironic subtleties of the parody for what they differently have called the novel's philosophical merit. . . .

It is evident that the principal, and, strictly speaking, sole speculative preoccupation of the book, Belarmino's theory of language, based on the intellectualizing of analogies, is a poetic rather than a philosophical matter. The recreation of the word "camel," for example, which Ayala offers as an exemplary instance of the cobbler's efforts, has a close parallel in one of Rubén Darío's poems, "The White Page" . . . .

The popularity of these esthetico-linguistic theories in contemporary literature is now world-wide. Pioneer among them are Mallarmé's doctrines . . . .

Proceeding to write a novel in his usual manner about an abortive love affair, Ayala sought a subject of quarrel between the respective fathers of his young lovers. Preoccupied, on the one hand, by the vain grandiloquence of the drama, and, on the other, by the recondite inanities of the poetry of some of his contemporaries, he pitted his cobblers against each other as travestied symbols of his literary abominations. Not that he abandoned his customary acuteness of psychological observation or his realistically exquisite descriptions. The parody, however, soon began to occupy him more than his initial purpose. This explains the uniqueness of the novel in Ayala's fiction.

Bernard Levy. *SpanR.* Nov. 1936, pp. 74, 77, 81

In *Belarmino and Apolonio* is presented also the question of the Don-juanesque lover, a theme which is treated more intensively in *Tiger Juan* and *The Doctor of His Honor*. Ayala's theory of Donjuanism derives directly from the thesis of the paradox, for Don Juan is presented in these novels not as the man who communicates his love to women, but as one who merely provokes love in them, and this inevitably involves once again the internal frigidity of the dramatist. . . . It is no mere coincidence that Apolonio, the dramatist, whose prime characteristic is the aptitude for simulation, should also be a Don Juan who cannot resist making love on the slightest provocation, or without any. The fact that this faculty is accompanied by a facile eloquence demonstrates again the concomitance of theatrical simulation and readiness of speech.

Diderot himself foresaw the connection between the actor and the glib lover when he wrote of the former that "He cries like an unbelieving priest who preaches the Passion; like a seducer at the knees of a woman whom he does not love, but he wants to conquer." The description aptly fits Vespasiano, Ayala's interpretation of Don Juan, who appears in the role of a sensuous, somewhat effeminate travelling salesman in the *Tiger Juan* series. Ayala avails himself of the theses of the paradox to develop his presentation of the Don Juan type not as a real lover, but as a consummate simulator of love, in short, an actor, incapable of love. . . . But the real lover, as Ayala views him, is not Vespasiano, the incessant pursuer of countless women, but Tiger Juan, the lover who completely, even fanatically devotes himself to one woman, for such devotion is the mark of virility.

Leon Livingstone. HR. July, 1954, pp. 218–19

The basis of Ayala's [optimistic] system [of vital concepts and values in total contrast to the nihilism of '98] rests on his recognition, simultaneously with his rejection of death as a negative influence, of the dual imperative of universal tolerance and vital utility: *el espíritu liberal* [the liberal spirit] and *seriedad* [seriousness]. Definitions of both are to be found in *The Masks,* particularly in the essays on Galdós, which hold the key to Ayala's later ideological position. Characteristically, Ayala's point of departure is that of the tragic struggle between the vital instinct and intellectual insight, . . . which is at the root of the dilemma of '98. In contrast to the anguished assertion of Unamuno . . . and the bitter insistence of Baroja that the conflict is to be solved only by the conscious acceptance of a *mentira vital* [living lie], Ayala reaffirms the existence of an *"agente superior y armónico"* [a superior and harmonious agent] capable of bringing about the desired synthesis. . . . This superior agent is universal tolerance. . . . In turn it rests on the firm conviction that there exists beneath the conflicts of earthly existence an inner harmony in which, with the aid of a liberal outlook, we may perceive the working of *"el sentido común cósmico"* [the cosmic common sense] toward *"la gran armonía universal"* [the great universal harmony]. Returning to the second imperative [seriousness], we are led to observe that the universal harmony and equilibrium thus postulated are, above all, the result of the conformity of the individual to his role with a preordained pattern of universal archetypes. . . .

D. L. Shaw. *MLQ.* June, 1961, p. 162

Honeymoon, Bittermoon and *The Trials of Urbano and Simona* are the most didactic of Pérez de Ayala's novels, but also at the same time the most extravagant. Ayala is inspired by the idyllic circumstances of *Daphnis and Chloe* by [the Greek writer] Longus, and around the theme of sexual education he creates a grotesque tragedy in which, in the manner of a fairy tale, truth and fantasy are mixed. . . .

The idyll of Urbano and Simona and the problem of sex education which it involves are grotesquely presented to us by Ayala with buffoonish situations and characters. It starts from the old classical education which does not prepare the individual for life's battles because it enforces the ideal and noble to the disregard of the natural, and takes it to its consequences. Childlike Urbano, in spite of the fact that he is twenty years old and a lawyer, does not have any idea whatsoever about the facts of life, owing to the insistence of his crazed mother on making him a "perfect man." When her dream is achieved and he, "pure as snow," marries Simona—an equally innocent girl—Urbano is so childlike that his ideal of marital happiness is to hunt butterflies with his wife. When the "angelic" couple get ready for their "marvelous and incredible" honeymoon, Urbano clings "fiercely to his father's neck and stammers into his ear: 'For God's sake, don't leave me. I'm scared!' " The tragedy springs from this, since "a married angel is a monster." Under these conditions the honeymoon must turn into a bittermoon. Then a series of fantastic-buffo episodes takes place, the "angels" going through the trials that Simona's grandmother had warned them about, until "they themselves become enlightened," a theme that allows Pérez de Ayala to develop his vast ideology about the theme of sex education.

Mary Ann Beck. *Hispania.* Sept., 1963, pp. 485–86

The fiction of Ramón Pérez de Ayala is notably intellectual; his stories and novels develop or illustrate various speculative problems. A topic central to his work and the underlying theme of his best novel, *Belarmino and Apolonio,* is the relativity of reality, its fragmentation into many different points of view. Pérez de Ayala, like his contemporary Ortega y Gasset, is a perspectivist. He believes that since each man apprehends only a small portion of the world, all theories, whether complementary or contradictory, are equally worthy and equally unverifiable; every one of them is in some way true because the truth is infinite and diverse. Thus, although knowledge is always relative, it can be expanded by bringing together the most contrary aspect of things. In his novels and stories, Pérez de Ayala attempts to present the numberless faces of any subject by multiplying his approaches to it: he varies the angle of vision and the emotional distance between narrator and action; he shows the action now as fiction, now as reality; he uses puns, private language and fanciful terminologies to point up the unreliability of a world built on words. Breaking the progression of events into the opposing views and responses of his characters, he makes fun of attempts to interpret experience by any single system of thought. . . .

Belarmino and Apolonio is Pérez de Ayala's most thorough fictional treatment of perspectivism. At the close of the novel, commenting on the contradictory opinions of two characters, he affirms his belief in the relativity of truth.

Frances Weber. PhilQ. April, 1964, pp. 253–54

Ever since Aristotle declared that the tragic character is good, yet marred by a misfortune-producing frailty, the question of ethical responsibility has lain near the heart of the problem of defining tragedy. . . .

In 1913 Ayala published a novel entitled *Mummers and Dancers* that contains an exposition of his theory of tragedy. Alberto, the protagonist, reads *Othello* to the untutored but appreciative Verónica. As each character acts or explains his acts, she comprehends him and sympathizes with him, despite the fact that the characters are often in conflict with each other. Little by little she begins to feel the weight of that conflict, and this oppression, according to the narrator—whom Ayala in a later article quotes approvingly—is the appreciation of tragedy. Verónica has at first felt what he calls the "lyric spirit." . . . This "lyric spirit" is then supplemented in Verónica by the "dramatic spirit" as she witnesses conflict among the characters. Having sympathized with each in turn, she can only feel the conflict among them as one of good against good that must result in the defeat of good. Lyric emotion and dramatic emotion fuse in her to produce tragic emotion. . . . For Ayala, tragedy results from the characters' inability to escape the dictates of determinism . . . .

Ayala's fictional characters frequently disclaim all responsibility for being the way they are, and the narrator backs them up. The clear comprehension of man's situation leads to a moral attitude of sympathy, tolerance and love. Ayala recommends this attitude not only as an ethical approach to life, but as an indispensable prerequiste to successful literary creation. . . . With this frequently expressed

Weltanschauung in mind, it is not difficult to understand Ayala's founding his theory of tragedy on man's inability to escape his fate.

Brenton Campbell. *HR*. July, 1969, pp. 375–78

The author's love for his *patria chica* is evident in his beautiful portrayals of his native Asturias . . . . But they are not mere paintings of scenes and customs. His characters have universal problems, which they work out in this background. . . .

Ayala's love of his country is evident in his preoccupations for Spain. He seeks vital ethical values such as justice, which he finds too often unfair, due to dishonesty and bribery. He seeks honor which is integrity, honesty to one's self, which has little to do with the time-worn code of honor. He believes in freedom, but freedom with responsibility, and tolerance is important to him.

Intelectual and philosophical speculations are prominent in [his major] novels as in most of Ayala's writings. He continues to seek man's relationship to God and to the Universe, and in these more mature products of his art, he appears to solve the problem more satisfactorily than in his early poetry . . . .

Ayala deplores the thought that the Church has become a political power, thus lessening its spiritual power. He is less anticlerical as he portrays many good priests in these [later] novels. He has not forgotten, however, that there are too many priests who enter the clergy without vocation, as a way of life, . . . and too often a priest's advancement depends on the influence of his wealthy and powerful friends. . . .

Ayala seeks beauty and finds it, sometimes in the most unlikely places. We may recall the dual description of the Rúa Ruera, which gives the reader an artistic vision of the street. The author has an excellent sense of proportion, and there is balance and rhythm in his prose. He likes to portray scenes and characters, often in contrast. . . . These perspectives add greatly to the effectiveness of the novels which have frequently amusing and ironic complexities.

Marguerite C. Rand. *Ramón Pérez de Ayala*
(New York, Twayne, 1971), pp. 126–27

[Alberto Díaz de] Guzmán [in *The Fox's Paw*] is a negative figure whom Ayala tried to polish until he changed him into a character less personally disagreeable for the reader, and whose metaphysical concerns and frequent failures might be clarified in all their complexity by means of the author's corrections.

From the first to the last edition of *The Fox's Paw* three distinct types of changes by the author can be noted. The most frequent and least obvious are the small stylistic refinements of vocabulary and syntax, such as the substitution of synonyms or the repositioning of a pronoun. The greatest changes in the novel are in the long explanations or clarifications of Guzmán's activities or motivations, which Ayala throws in at crucial moments. Also, as a reflection of the implicit intention of these additions to the text—that of increasing the possibility of Guzmán's becoming agreeable to the reader, who in turn will feel compassion for him—Ayala has eliminated some of the less attractive aspects of the protagonist's personality and actions. . . .

In spite of Ayala's constant eagerness to correct, refine, and modify his novel, in order to make Guzmán a positive model, an "alter ego" of Ayala whom we must admire and imitate, a violent compositional change, a very different view of the circumstances, the action, the atmosphere, and the novel's characters would have been necessary. The protagonist of *The Fox's Paw* does nothing more than escape from difficult situations. . . . The ironies of the rapid changes in the narration of time and place, the long period of years that go unnarrated, the distance from the reader established through poems, letters, long reflections or meditations, and other indirect means of narration, inhibit the reader's feeling compassion for Guzmán. Guzmán always fails in his plans for action, he never finds his identity, and is still, in novelistic terms, a negative figure in the final edition of *The Fox's Paw*.

Constance Sullivan. *Hispanófila*. May, 1972,
pp. 75–76, 80–81†

Valle-Inclán wrote *esperpentos* because Spanish life is a tragic deformation, in relation to that of other European nations. Pérez de Ayala [in *Mummers and Dancers*] offer us a tragicomic novel, because Spanish life is tragicomic. . . . The true problem, according to the novel, is to make authentic men; for Spanish national consciousness, the means by which Spaniards become completely, integrally men—nothing less than men—must be found.

What are these means? Raniero Mazorral (Ramiro de Maeztu) speaks about kindness and the desire to work. Through the mouth of the skeptic Don Sabas, the narrator laughs at the innocence of the 1898 figure: What is necessary is to find and to propose to the people collective practicable [*hacederos*] ideals. (This last word [*hacederos*] is very typical of Ayala's "mental style.") And to achieve this, what is lacking above all is imagination. . . .

For Pérez de Ayala—faithful to the spirit of the Institución Libre de Enseñanza [the Free Academy] the Spanish problem is a question, above all, of education. This is the major justification for his essays and his scandalous work *A.M.D.G.* . . . Pérez de Ayala does not concern himself . . . with the good or bad taste of the Spanish, but rather with something more profound and radical: their inability to "see" reality. The Spanish are a race of mystics and a people given over to crazy ideals, but they lack that authentic imagination that begins with reality. The Spanish need sensibility and sensuality (for Ayala the two things are intimately united) in order to achieve their full development as human beings. . . .

Andrés Amorós. *Vida y literatura en "Troteras y danzaderas"* (Madrid, Castalia, 1973), pp. 262–63†

The story of Beauty and the Beast, with the exception of the role of the Father, can be seen in clear outline in *Tiger Juan*. The beast-like Juan causes only fear and horror, at first, in the beautiful and virginal Herminia. Married against her will, Herminia leaves Tigre Juan for a brief period, but returns after her recognition of the depth of her love for him. Upon her return, she finds him dying, and cares for him, promising to love him if he will not die . . . .

Doña Iluminada has the function of developing the myth in explicit terms in the novel, for it is the frustrated old beauty who persuades the youthful Herminia to marry Tigre Juan. The widow knows that one must not judge a man by his external appearance, that within Tigre Juan's rough exterior a prince is hidden. Furthermore, not being able to marry him herself, she chooses Herminia as a surrogate. The unfortunate widow will thus find happiness in the vicarious joy of their marriage. Doña Iluminada relates the story of Beauty and the Beast to Herminia, while explaining that it is the wife's task to transform her and her husband's lives into a happy dream . . . .

Herminia is the virgin menaced by man's sexual force. Beauty fears sex, which to her equals ugliness and brute force; eventually, she must overcome her fear to succeed in a normal love relationship. Beast is the symbol of the virgin's fears, the external appearance, the ugliness of sex. . . . The image of Juan gradually changes during Herminia's abortive "escapade" with Vespasiano; and when she returns, at last, to her husband's house, she herself has been transformed into a mature woman, and Tigre Juan's metamorphosis is complete . . . .

Maruxa Salgués Cargill and Julian Palley. *REH.* Oct., 1973, pp. 412–13, 415

The crisis depicted in *Darkness at the Heights* is the crisis of fiction itself. The novel is born out of the multifarious cross-currents of the early twentieth-century literary and cultural scene, in which Ayala was an intelligent and critical participant. In the novel, the excesses of *modernista* aestheticism and existential despair are shown to emanate from and respond to a shared spiritual situation. They, and the climate which produced them, are the primary stimulus for Ayala's probing of certain assumptions about the writing and reading of literature and about the nature of literary fictions. Ayala stresses the fictional character of narrative, reveals the artificial and conventionalized nature of the structures that underlie it, and maintains that literature draws its inspiration, not from reality, but from other literature. He emphasizes that all books relate to previous books by incorporating into this work a plethora of pastiche, parody, citation, allusion, and implies that all novels are created within a tradition that imparts value to certain kinds of experience and to certain modes of representing it. He interprets true originality, not as novelty, but as an acknowledgement of sources, of origins, and highlights the persistence of tradition in an overtly self-conscious way by imitating directly or obliquely classical antecedents. At the same time, the juxtaposition of classical and popular forms, the ironical use of footnotes, the blend of erudition with the crudest naturalism, all point to the death of a high literary culture. For one thing, the referential richness of literary texts is lost on those who lack the humanist education necessary to their full appreciation. In fact, the whole humanist value-system is shown to have been undermined. Notions such as the immortality of great works, and of their creators, are no longer regarded as unassailable.

J. J. Macklin. *ALEC.* Vol. 8, 1983, pp. 28–29

PÉREZ GALDÓS, BENITO (1843–1920)

Doña Perfecta is, first of all, a story, and a great story, but it is certainly also a story that must appear at times potently, and even bitterly, anti-Catholic. Yet it would be a pity and an error to read it with the preoccupation that it was an anti-Catholic tract, for really it is not that. If the persons were changed in name and place, and modified in passion to fit a cooler air, it might equally seem an anti-Presbyterian or anti-Baptist tract; for what it shows in the light of their own hatefulness and cruelty are the perversions of any religion, any creed. It is not, however, a tract at all; it deals in artistic largeness with the passion of bigotry, as it deals with the passion of love, the passion of ambition, the passion of revenge. But Galdós is Spanish and Catholic, and for him bigotry wears a Spanish and Catholic face. That is all. . . .

Yet it is a great novel . . . ; and perhaps because it is transitional it will please the greater number who never really arrive anywhere, and who like to find themselves in good company *en route.* . . .

What seems to be so very admirable in the management of the story is the author's success in keeping his own counsel. This may seem a very easy thing; but, if the reader will think over the novelists of his acquaintance, he will find that it is at least very uncommon. They mostly give themselves away almost from the beginning, either by their anxiety to hide what is coming, or their vanity in hinting what great things they have in store for the reader. Galdós does neither the one nor the other. He makes it his business to tell the story as it grows; to let the characters unfold themselves in speech and action; to permit the events to happen unheralded. He does not prophesy their course; he does not forecast the weather even for twenty-four hours; the atmosphere becomes slowly, slowly, but with occasional lifts and reliefs, of such a brooding breathlessness, of such a deepening density, that you feel the wild passion-storm nearer and nearer at hand, till it bursts at last; and then you are astonished that you had not foreseen it yourself from the first moment. [Nov. 2, 1895]

William Dean Howells. *Criticism and Fiction,*
and Other Essays (New York, New York
University Press, 1959), pp. 134–36

Galdós was a man of letters, pure and simple, and more strictly a novelist, and in his last phase a dramatist. Or even better, a novelist of the theater. He was not a teacher, although he taught, without meaning to, more than most teachers; he was not a journalist, although he wrote articles for newspapers on occasion; he was not a historian, in spite of his *National Episodes,* in which history, the specific and technical mode, is reduced to almost nothing—his Contemporary Spanish Novels are more historical; he was not an orator, although some of his characters may speak at times as if they were; he was not a politician, although he served more than once as a deputy to the Cortes. He was a very hard-working man of letters, pure and simple. . . .

And within the literary scene Galdós was a novelist who became, in his last years, a playwright. The man who was bent on capturing the attention of each of his readers individually now tried to capture their attention *en masse.* And the day arrived on which he was acclaimed publicly, on which the cry of "Long live Galdós!" loudly proclaimed . . . seemed like a password for rebellion, if not for civil war. But the man who with the eyes of a novelist saw at age twenty-five the September revolution of 1868—and remained always faithful to his liberal ideology—and then saw the second round of Carlist Wars, did not succeed in seeing, at the exorcism that his play *Electra* represented, anything of what he had seen when he was young. [Jan. 8, 1920]

Miguel de Unamuno. *Obras completas,* Vol. III
(Madrid, Escelicer, 1968), p. 1205†

[Pérez Galdós's] *National Episodes* are indeed an imposing work. All this romantic material of the nineteenth century is turned to account, from Trafalgar (the title of the first episode) to the beginnings of the present reign. In these forty-six volumes, many of which are admirable, and none of which can be passed over, Galdós gave us the history of Spain as seen from the drawing-room of contemporaries, not from the study of the historian. It is a living history, not the historical novel in the somewhat grandfatherly manner of Erckmann-Chatrian, nor again in the romantic and even romanesque manner of Walter Scott, but a vivid and dramatic interpretation of the life of the people through the events of the century, their hopes, feelings, thoughts, and disappointments.

Apart from their literary merit, the *National Episodes* have been one of the most important elements in the formation of a Spanish national consciousness. Galdós was and is the most widely read of Spanish writers. His influence as an educator of the Spanish mind is incalculable. [April, 1920]

> Salvador de Madariaga. *The Genius of Spain,*
> *and Other Essays on Contemporary Literature*
> (Oxford, Clarendon Press, 1923), pp. 49–50

To demonstrate was Galdós' aim, not to entertain or to reproduce life. Hence, in the studies of unusual or mystical types, in which he grew steadily more interested, one always feels the presence of a *cerebral* element; that is, one feels that these persons are not so much plastic, living beings as creations of a superior imagination. In this respect also Galdós resembles Balzac. The plays having the largest proportion of realism are the most convincing. That is why *Reality,* with its immortal three, *The Madwoman of the House,* with the splendidly conceived Pepet, *Bárbara,* which contains extraordinarily successful studies of complex characters, and especially *The Grandfather,* with the lion of Albrit and the fine group of cleanly visualized secondary characters, are the ones which seem destined to live upon the stage.

We should like to emphasize the cerebral or intellectual quality of Galdós' work, because it has been often overlooked. . . . Nothing shows this characteristic of Galdós more clearly than his weakness in rendering the passion of love. . . . The Galdós of middle age seemed to have lost the freshness of his youthful passions, and *Doña Perfecta,* precisely because its story dated from his youth, is the only play which contains a really affecting love interest.

> S. Griswold Morley. Introduction to Benito
> Pérez Galdós, *Mariucha* (Boston, D. C. Heath,
> 1921), pp. xvi–xvii

The world of Galdós is one of life and hope amid a possible social, historical, and human harmony, a world conceived out of the noble dream of the nineteenth century . . . . Unamuno's world is an agonic one that belongs to our times . . . . In Galdós there breathes the optimistic idealism of his century, in Unamuno the cold metaphysical passion of the pessimistic intellectualism of our century . . . . Together, Galdós and Unamuno are the greatest witnesses of Spanish literature at two singularly intense moments in the historical and spiritual drama of modern mankind. Both fulfill a necessary function because in order that there be reborn in us the hopeful optimism that brought Galdós to write *The Madwoman of the House* and other works showing the same faith in the possibility of spiritual, social, and human coexistence, it was necessary to pass through the deep aesthetic and philosophic individualism that inspires Unamuno's work and discover the great depths of the personality that renounces itself, without anything external to maintain it, ending by annihilating itself. Galdós and Unamuno, Spaniards of the world, thus represent in Spain and for Spain the two greatest experiences in the world of art and spirit through which man has passed in the last hundred years: the experience of the ideal of communion with other men that comes to give an ultrapersonal feeling to his life; and the desperation of intellectualist individualism, of the man in solitude, thirsting for the absolute. [March, 1945]

Ángel del Río. *Estudios galdosianos* (Zaragoza, Librería General, 1953), pp. 80–81†

In view of Galdós' nartistic integrity it must be assumed that the critical drone which followed the appearance of his works must eventually have palled on him. He discounted almost everything that the literary arbiters uttered by way of approval or advice, though he appreciated their contribution to the promotion of his works. He had his own esthetic, but he was none too confident that he had realized his purposes. Often he felt that he was groping in the dark toward a goal whose validity could be determined only by the reaction of the readers. The professional critics he was inclined to include in the category of the neoclassic rhetoricians whom he had abhorred in his younger days. He reacted ironically to the pseudo-scientific pretensions of modern literary criticism, and he took its authority lightly. His own experience as a critic had inoculated him against the species. The humility with which he apparently accepted critical dicta was only a screen for his personal criteria, which admitted no challenge. Without impugning the authority or the influence of professional critics in the abstract, he set more store by the spontaneous reaction and the honest comment of the intelligent readers of the rank and file. Like a genuine Spaniard, Galdós had slight respect for laws that were neither natural nor divine.

H. Chonon Berkowitz. *Benito Pérez Galdós, Spanish Liberal Crusader* (Madison, University of Wisconsin Press, 1948), pp. 148–49

The Spendthrifts [i.e., *The Bringas Case*] is a brilliant, well-constructed comic story, blooming absurdly out of the political realities of its time. . . .

There is a mildness in Galdós, in spite of the vigour of his mind. . . . The historian broadens the note of the novelist who lacks the intellectual edge of the French novelists of the time or the English sense of theatre. There is a certain idleness in the Cervantesque irony, as if we were listening to the shrewd brain of a lazy mind. But to feel his full effect, it is necessary to see this novel in relation to others, to see it as a corner of his large, sad speculation of the Spanish predicament. There is no "Spanish soul" to compare with the "Russian soul," in the same kind of novel, nor does Galdós feel that he is making a natural history of human nature. Galdós is deep in Spanish egoism. But he was sufficiently a European to explore that; he wrote at the time of intellectual revival; he is free from that "typical" regionalism which travels so poorly in literature. He has the certainty, sharpness and power of the novelist who is saturated in his subject. If, as they say, everything in Spain is personal, then Galdós is the novelist of this kind of society which destroys every idea and issue by the thickly involved personal concern. In Galdós one is deeply involved in 19th-century Spain, yet *The Spendthrifts* itself is one of his novels which seems to be about the present day. [Dec. 15, 1951]

V. S. Pritchett. *Books in General* (London,
Chatto & Windus, 1952), pp. 32, 35–36

Like *The Spendthrifts* [i.e., *The Bringas Case*] . . . *Torment* reveals the qualities of the best Galdós: intensity in describing the physical world, harmony of composition, and an interpretative gift more kind than sharp, which should not be taken as a slur on Galdós' sharpness but as praise of his goodness. In his interpretation of persons and things he displays once again the generosity of a Cervantine spirit. There is nothing in his work recalling Zola's fatalistic pessimism. . . .

The anti-heroes of Galdós have renounced many things. They are often vanquished by money, conventional morality, or simply adversity. Yet behind the bitterness of each experience a new faith is being born. They will be tricked again but they will not accept deceit as the final answer. Galdós' people seem to be saying to each other: "Life is mean and hard. Sometimes unbearable. But we know better."

The characters of Pérez Galdós know that to live is a constant struggle for life. The fight is heroic or grotesque, or both. If life did not frequently offer us a wise confusion of ideal with necessity, the people's good faith would be inexplainable. In a more or less conscious way, the human beings of Galdós direct their energies toward that ideal. All the catastrophes will be futile. For they are like the humble and tenacious ants that begin all over again when their ant hill has been trampled underfoot.

Ramón Sender. *NYTBR*. Aug. 2, 1953, pp. 4, 11

Although very much a product of his age, Galdós was an independent and poised thinker who occupied a firm middle ground in which he evinced neither a worship of science nor a worship of religion and yet respected both. Like Zola, he was interested in man as a product of nature and of society, but his attention was directed more to the upper reaches of the evolutionary slope and hence showed a greater interest in psychology than in physiology. Moreover, in his conception of man as a social being, however deeply entangled in relations with others, he saw always an individual character rather than a fragment of group consciousness at the mercy of a mysterious vital force of "will." Much more of an intellectual than Zola, he persistently tried to harmonize all knowledge, exact and speculative, in an interpretation of human nature within a comprehensive view of total Nature. At times, especially in his early works, his antagonism to certain excesses of static society, such as religious and social prejudices, led him into the emotionalism of an evangelistic progressive. In his mature and most characteristic posture, however, he contemplates studiously and often with quizzical amusement the relationship between individual personality and its social environment. He thus constructs a novel of character, which typically is a psychological story of struggle, adjustment, and growth.

Sherman H. Eoff. *The Modern Spanish Novel*
(New York, New York University Press, 1961),
pp. 120–21

Where Balzac is always theorizing, Galdós lets an ethos speak for itself: his method is that of exposure, with himself well out of sight. . . . Galdós does well to reconcile his serious moral concern with his gift for unlaborious comedy. He writes with a light touch that belies the exploratory part of his mind. That part, fascinated and appalled by the spectacle of human turpitude and back-sliding, gets to work in *Fortunata and Jacinta* on a young, indecisive man vacillating between Fortunata, his tumultuous and plebeian mistress by whom he has had a son, and Jacinta, his childless bourgeois wife. Two worlds are rammed side by side: that of the wife's family, prosperous through the manufacture of silk, and that of Fortunata—squalid, unpretentious and animally vital. It is a novel of the city; stone and asphalt challenge the characters as they go about their daily business and their regular illicit errands. It is also a novel of nerves, and this is where the Dostoevskian element shows. . . .

[Galdós] tends to let the *comédie de mœurs* slip away a little while he probes into the souls of the near-demented, of monomaniacs and cranks. It is as if he suspects that truth is no longer to be found on the social surface but in man's suppressed lusts, dreams and sensitivity. The later novels concentrate on odd men out: Torquemada the miser [in the *Torquemada* series], Nazarín [in *Nazarín*], the oddly Dostoevskian cleric, and all manner of layabouts. From Galdós's concentration on such types we get something like the upsetting reversions that [E. M.] Forster achieves when he unleashes Pan or Hindu awareness among the quiet, dull conformists of his middle class. But, notice, the direction is inwards, away from the conscious, sophisticated art of social comedy. It is the direction of the Spanish novel as a whole; *mores* have not inspired many modern Spanish novelist. But (to borrow two of Galdós's titles) *Reality* (1889) and *Compassion* (1897) have.

Paul West. *The Modern Novel*, Vol. II (London,
Hutchinson, 1965), pp. 410–11

In his view of tragedy, Galdós begins by accepting the common premise that tragedy confronts man with the mystery of human suffering and tries to explain it. It would seem that tragedy, however, despite its unifying effect in *Fortunata and Jacinta,* lacks ability to provide an answer to this mystery. Galdós knows that; his answer would be that tragedy is no more capable of providing such an answer than the other solutions. But tragedy seeks for answers relentlessly, and its function as a cognitive instrument gives to it a centrality in the novel. Galdós' use of tragedy as a unifying factor of diverse themes forces upon us the mystery of human life in its clash between the "inner" and "outer" forces. As tragedian, he views the universe as something incomprehensible which cannot be morally, socially or religiously governed. If Galdós fails to provide philosophic answers concerning the essential rationale of evil and suffering, he does, through tragedy, offer telling insights of the human condition. No man can possibly understand the totality of human experience and, consequently, it is not for anyone to judge, condemn or even punish. It is for him to try to understand and to tolerate if possible, because man can never be reduced to one formula of behavior. The best man can do is have self-integrity, that is, be able to understand and act within the realizations and limits of his inner world. Then, like the novelist, he might realize that what often appears to be a question of judgment, as between morality and immorality or right and wrong, is not even a valid question.

Anthony Zahareas. *Symposium.* Spring, 1965,
pp. 46–47

Galdós's warmth of sentiment is due to his understanding of the instincts and passions that rule the human animal and his willingness to forgive any transgression against the moral code of society caused by these instincts and passions. Galdós saw flesh as its own redeemer and passion as its own justification. In *Fortunata and Jacinta,* his most ambitious and representative novel, he invests the noble passion (Fortunata) with the attributes of the noble soul (Jacinta). Fortunata's bequest of her child to Jacinta is the gift of flesh to spirit. This belief in nature as a bounty and a blessing, so clearly expressed in *Fortunata and Jacinta,* makes the Contemporary Novels unique. The harrowing picture of man in naturalistic fiction is replaced here by a faith in the natural order of things. The author's sympathetic response to the most vulgar and trivial lives stems from his idea that nature, the source of life, is also a source of good. This response—indulgent, quizzical, often paternal—is the sum and substance of Galdós' humor.

Michael Nimetz. *Humor in Galdós* (New
Haven, Conn., Yald University Press, 1968), p. 210

The Unknown is presented as a mystery story in which an amateur detective (Manolo Infante) tries to find out if Federico Viera has been murdered or committed suicide. As implied in the title, the novel ends without solution, even though Infante collects all the external evidence possible. What is lacking is the internal evidence—the forces which motivated Federico and the people closely associated with him.

Hence the story can be retold stressing the spiritual drives that must be known to solve the mystery. The second version is aptly named *Reality*. It marks the novelist's renunciation of one of the prime tenets of naturalism, the belief that all human activity results from the physical stimuli of heredity and environment, in a word, determinism. Infante had investigated the possible materialistic causes of Viera's death without reaching a conclusion. It is only when the characters reveal their aspirations, emotions, and dreams that the truth comes out.

In order to have them express their innermost selves Galdós chooses the dramatic form, writing his novel in five acts, using only dialogue, soliloquies, and stage directions. Perhaps we should say at once that the dramatic form brings with it difficulties. Pérez Galdós abuses the soliloquy in order to penetrate the subsurface motives of his personages. He also employs numerous asides so that a character in the physical presence of others speaks without being heard by them. Since the novel is meant to be read, not acted, we can think of these asides as the individual's silent thoughts. They become a real problem later, however, when Galdós converts *Reality* into a stage production. The same difficulty obtains for the apparitions or dream figures of the novel, a device which enables the author to have a solitary personage talk in a most revealing way with hallucinatory projections of other characters.

Walter T. Pattison. *Benito Pérez Galdós*
(Boston, Twayne, 1975), pp. 111–12

Throughout Galdós's novels point of view undergoes a process of interiorization. In that process language itself undergoes a great change. Because the reality it conveys (the level of mental activity) becomes increasingly less conceptual, abstract, rational and more emotional and irrational, language itself begins to disintegrate. Ordinary language, which reflects (in syntax, for example) the ordered patterns of the conscious mind, is increasingly incapable of revealing the state of mind of the character as it approaches the subconscious. This breakdown of language is first apparent in interior monologues and periods of insomnia, which represent states of mind somewhere between the conscious and the subconscious mind. . . . As the narrative enters the character's subconscious mind, the language of ordinary discourse becomes incapable of expressing the realities found there. So the language used to describe that region of the mind is not the verbal language of the conscious mind, but the language of image and symbol. . . . So we would not expect the language of dreams to be expressive of the character. As [Ricardo] Gullón says, to understand the dreams of

Galdós's novels and the images used in them, "we will have to accept them as a translation into a different language of ordinary phenomena."

Kay Engler. *The Structure of Realism: The "Novelas Contemporáneas" of Benito Pérez Galdós* (Chapel Hill, University of North Carolina Press, 1977), p. 91

In the *Nazarín, Halma, Compassion* trilogy there is a different dynamic [from that in *Fortunata and Jacinta*]. Rather than seeking integration into society and proposing that this synthesis lead to a renovated society, here the protagonists strive to establish an alternative to society or to transcend it. Thus in *Nazarín* and *Halma,* the impossibility of regenerating society from within is a given, and the protagonists seek to provide an individual or collective example which would serve as an inspiration to the rest of society. And although Benina [in *Compassion*] does not consciously try to transcend society, she in fact does realize such a transcendence; she is separated and clearly distinguished from the social norm.

Whereas the novels before *Ángel Guerra* were profoundly historical, in this trilogy there is an effort to transcend history. In works like *The Bringas Case, Fortunata and Jacinta,* and *Miau* the historical reasons for the decaying of Spanish society are examined, and the alternatives are posed in historical terms. The clearest case is *Fortunata and Jacinta,* where the social structure is examined in specifically class terms, and the alternative Fortunata offers is based on the role the lower classes should play in a process of social transformation. In this trilogy, on the other hand, there is little concern with the historical development of society, and the proposed alternative is ahistorical. Each of the protagonists is in some way a Christ figure, and their problematic stems from their efforts to fulfill the Gospel message within bourgeois society. This problematic entails a temporal problem which stems from the fact that the message had been articulated in a world far different from that of late-nineteenth-century Spain.

John H. Sinnigen. *MLN*. March, 1978, pp. 234–35

[Benito Pérez Galdós's] ambition wasn't going to sleep as he approached his fifties. It was something to have regenerated the Spanish novel. Now it was his job to regenerate the Spanish drama. He felt that he had written the best Spanish novels, and he had better try to write the best plays.

So he wrote plays, twenty-one between the early nineties and 1918, when he finished the last at the age of seventy-five. He had some enormous successes (that is, by Spanish standards, where runs were not long), and a few total flops. He became the best-known playwright on the Spanish stage. To one of his temperament, first nights meant acute suffering, acute even compared with those of other playwrights anywhere. He sat in the wings, inarticulate, smoking packs of cigarettes, unable to comprehend. To much of the public, in Spain and Spanish America, he was soon more famous as a playwright than as a novelist. Here an Anglo-Saxon commentator is at a disadvantage. The Galdós plays didn't reach our stage, and it isn't possible to guess how they would have struck us at the time, or how they would strike us if they were put on now.

Passages of his novels are intensely dramatic, in the best sense. We know for certain that he was a master of dramatic dialogue—which is quite different from naturalistic dialogue. Adaptations of those novels should have worked on the stage, and we are told that some of his own did so through the efforts of professional playwrights.

From what we know at secondhand of his own original plays, it does appear that they are not of the same quality as his best novels. Like other realistic novelists turning to the stage, like Henry James, he may, despite his strong literary conscience, have taken the form too lightly. That is, he may have become too mechanical or abstract, where his novels are rooted in the twists of motive which no one could foresee; he may have been too linear in the narrative sense, and probably too propagandist. That is the impression one receives from accounts of his great success, *Electra,* which became a kind of national anthem for liberal Spain. In cool blood, and in a different culture, it sounds like a crude piece of anticlerical melodrama—villainous priest, innocent girl sequestered in a convent. People in Spain said that here is our Ibsen. One has to make a confession of ignorance, but from this distance that is hard to believe.

C. P. Snow. *The Realists: Eight Portraits*
(London, Macmillan, 1978), pp. 189–90

The objection frequently raised that *Doña Perfecta* is a pertrified novel, a narrative tragedy, which conceals far more of its action than it reveals, would be hard to refute. Yet that very reticence is also the condition of its efficacy. After reading it and coming to know its denizens in their society, we realize that we have been led to comprehend certain fundamental characteristics of Spanish interpersonal relations far more profoundly than in the *National Episodes.* Presented without superimposed intrigue, resistance to history has been held up for our close inspection long enough for the meditation it deserves.

Aside from deceleration, the representational superiority of *Doña Perfecta* as compared to *The Golden Fountain* [Pérez Galdós's first novel] emerges from its characterization. If Coletilla [in *The Golden Fountain*] was expertly drawn as the personification of a political stance or force (the notion of party is, of course, alien to him), Doña Perfecta is the perfected exemplar of a thousand and one of her kind living throughout provincial Spain. Rather than a decrepit yet frightening verbal cartoon, she is an archetype, and archetype all the more vigorous and dangerous because it feeds on the lives it represents.

Stephen Gilman. *Galdós and the Art of the European Novel: 1867–1887* (Princeton, N.J., Princeton University Press, 1981), pp. 71–72

The theme of contemporary history in the *Contemporary Series* [a category that Pérez Galdós himself devised for his oeuvre], though one of many, is vitally important for a correct interpretation of Galdós's intentions and achievements in these novels. Because that theme is consistently treated in a meaningful way, all of the novels of the series can be regarded as special types of historical novel, as historical allegories or novels of the historical imagination. History is never bluntly slapped down on the page in blotches; rather fine details are sketched in here and there to suggest wider horizons for the alert reader. Though a separate division in Pérez Galdós's fictional writing, the *Contemporary Series* provides an important link, not hitherto recognized, between the first two and the last three series of *National Episodes*. There is a continuum in Pérez Galdós's writing on Spanish nineteenth-century history, an interest he could never forsake although he was clear-sighted about its depressing negativity. His shorthand, suggestive style in the *Contemporary Series* allowed him to maintain that interest while developing others. The consequence is that the novels of the series are enriched in a manner unequalled by anything written by his immediate predecessors or contemporaries in Spain.

Peter A. Bly. *Galdós's Novel of the Historical Imagination: A Study of the Contemporary Novels* (Liverpool, Liverpool Monographs in Hispanic Studies, Francis Cairns Publications, 1983), p. 186

QUIROGA, ELENA (1919–   )

I have in my hands a rich and beautiful book [*North Wind*], which won the Nadal Prize in 1950.

You can spend a long time with this book in your hands because although its reading holds your attention throughout the narration and the perfectly achieved dramatic atmosphere reaches a high point at the end of the novel, there are in this book passages and calm spots and beautiful sections that ought to be savored slowly, as one savors the colors of the earth and fragrances and the sparkling of water during a slow walk through the country. As in a walk in the countryside of Galicia—described so magnificently—when one reads this book the senses are drenched with the clean and delicate surrounding moisture, with the softness of mud, with the greenness of groves, and with old legends. A great restfulness, a serenity, a sweetness of life with a sense of continuity, of quietude, of peace, comes upon you. I, the reader, feel profoundly moved and thank the author of this novel for the presence of eternal roots deeply implanted into the soul of the land.

This book is without time. In the anguish of time that surrounds us, the anguish of the hours that pursue us, of the intense and burning problems, which although we may not wish them to, grab us by their claws, I do not know if this lack of obsession about time is a defect or perhaps the most accomplished mark of intuition that the great writer has had and has revealed to us in *North Wind*.

The characters from the patriarchal life of the Galician estates do not live in our age. Respected and beloved masters, servants content with their lot, united by a mysterious respect and love in the obedience to a kind but firm gesture of their master. They are not from our anguish-filled times—these people for whom life flows slowly and ponderously. Elena Quiroga has not wished them to be, but by leaving the period to which they belong open, perhaps, secretly, she has wished that they were our contemporaries. Upon reading her novel, we wish they were too. . . . Elena Quiroga, youthful, full of creative energy, impulsiveness and love for her craft enters the front ranks of contemporary Spanish novelists with *North Wind*.

Carmen Laforet. Destino. May 12, 1951, p. 7†

Among the many young novelists writing in Spain today, Elena Quiroga is unquestionably one of the most able and interesting. . . .

Notably manifest in the novels of Elena Quiroga are the qualities most essential in a writer of fiction: imagination, creative ability, and command of subject matter. Perhaps the highest compliment that can be offered this author is to say that interest in her stories rarely ever flags. Her novels possess that power of sustained attraction, which Ortega y Gasset calls "imperviousness," whereby the reader is held engrossed in a novelistic world from which he has little desire to withdraw. Part of Elena Quiroga's success in this regard can be attributed to her faculty for producing and maintaining a captivating mood or compelling atmosphere into which the reader is readily drawn. Interest in her fiction, however, derives chiefly from character portrayal, for which she has a superb capacity. Although her primary concern is the depiction of the inner lives of her character, she knows how to effect a proper balance between the purely psychological and external reality. Her novels, free of transcendental intent except as the reader may choose to infer, are penetrating studies of human nature in which the problems and conflicts presented are of a kind to give the reader a deepened understanding of human experience and a sense of personal enrichment.

Albert Brent. Hispania. May, 1959, pp. 210, 213

We believe that [The Mask] is a fine and perfect example of harmony between novelistic technique and the level of consciousness that is communicated to the reader. Elena Quiroga's The Mask has not had all the critical fortune it deserves. For some critics it is no more than a tour de force of technique, difficult to read, and therefore, something less than satisfactory as a novelistic creation. In accordance with what is already a tradition in stream-of-consciousness novels, when the key or structuring motif is grasped, the problem of comprehension is eliminated, and all the elements that make up this strange world are justified—a world that forms itself according to how the protagonist is stimulated by memories that come bubbling up from his past. . . .

A great number of contemporary Spanish novels are touched by the theme of the civil war and its social and personal consequences. Moisés is, in a certain way, a product of that Spanish experience. The Mask is part and parcel of this tradition, not on a sociological level but on a psychological one. Moisés is a social failure, an alcoholic and without hope. As a human being he is complex, apathetic, and totally frustrated. Elena Quiroga does not focus on her character as a social entity. Consequently, she does not censure him. She creates an individual for us who is naked on the inside and whose raw and painful truth evokes contradictory feelings in the reader. He is annoying because he lacks vital energy in order to emerge from his psychological morass. Compassion for the child Moisés! The novel transports us to his world, and seeing him flee into cowardice and into an inability to overcome his personal mode of being, angers us. His egotism is terrifying. Nevertheless, he is a man who has suffered since childhood and is now in need of salvation. The possibility of his enjoying life without bitterness, without disgust, escapes him when he leaves Augustín wounded or dead (we do not know exactly). The blood that he spills and that stains his hands anew does not redeem him from the nauseating smell of blood that has been with him since his childhood.

Juan Villegas. *CHA.* Aug.–Sept., 1968,
pp. 638–39, 648†

Something's Happening in the Street is a good, well-modulated novel, poetic, simple in its structure and plot but complex in its psychological implications. It describes fairly well the society of Madrid of the 1950's. Although it is decidedly *not* a mystery novel, we still have no clear answer as to whether Ventura fell accidentally or committed suicide. Of major concern to us is Ventura's revelations through the thoughts of his family about the society in which he lives and the people he dealt with on a daily basis. . . .

One . . . notes Quiroga's tendency towards poetic lyricism, which diffuses the action of the novel, as well as the lack of psychological analysis of the motivations, conduct and beliefs despite the heavy reliance upon interior monologue to reveal the realities of her protagonists. We never have a *clear* idea of how the characters look or what they do. Nevertheless, *Something's Happening in the Street* is definitely a New Wave novel and Quiroga is firmly entrenched in this group precisely because of her efforts to renew the novel genre, inject it with poetic lyricism, deal with contemporary problems and probe her protagonists' psyches through the use of interior monologue. In this way, Quiroga definitely departs from nineteenth-century Realism. . . .

Quiroga's character creations do speak frankly . . . . She is concerned with Spanish society as it is, implicit with its moral and social implications. Although some of her characters do not reach a level of reality for me because they seem more imaginary than real and because at times she refuses to concretize their feelings, heavily insisting upon poetic lyricism, Quiroga is still one of the few novelists, in keeping with the New Wave, who has tried to give new directions to the Spanish novel. Although we may consider her use of interior monologue, flashback, dichotomies between what is thought and said rather stylistically archaic now, we must have thought Eugene O'Neill mad in the 1920's when *Strange Interlude* was first presented on Broadway and his characters stepped out of their roles to talk to the audience and directly reveal their thoughts to us. In similar fashion, Quiroga does this in her novels of the early 1950's, but her insistence on writing about contemporary themes combined with an easy facility with words and a marvelous creative sense make her one of the leading novelists of modern Spain today.

Ronald Schwartz. *Spain's New Wave Novelists*
(Metuchen, N.J., Scarecrow, 1976), pp. 70–72

Throughout her novelistic development Quiroga has articulated themes of freedom and solitude, concepts that relate both to her growing disillusionment with institutionalized religion and to her increasing emphasis on existential philosophy. Her characters are often solitary, even alienated individuals who know that they must seek the meaning of their lives within themselves; like Tadea [in *Sadness*] they insist upon the liberty to do so. Such a viewpoint is closely related to that of existentialism. . . . The individual has the freedom to shape his or her own identity, but with that freedom goes responsibility. Quiroga goes beyond merely symbolizing freedom through such images as the sea *(Blood)*, bulls *(The Last Bullfight)*, and wild horses *(Sadness)* to insist upon responsibility in a Sartrean sense. Felisa in *The Mask* accuses the older generation of using the "senseless circumstances" of the Civil War as an excuse for failing to take positive action. For her even Moisés is to blame for his own destiny. The progressive priest in *I Write Your Name* thus rejects Ortega's formula "I am I and my circumstance" because the individual should transcend and indeed mold that circumstance as part of himself. Among Quiroga's characters there are at least two who behave as existential heroines, willing not only to accept their freedom and act but also to assume full responsibility for those acts. Presencia in *Something's Happening in the Street* has been faithful to her own conscience and is able to withstand society's ostracism for the choices that she has made. Carola in *I Write Your Name* expresses what she believes and with dignity accepts her punishment—expulsion from the convent school—assuming responsibility for the group even though her classmates are too cowardly to stand with her.

Phyllis Zatlin Boring. *Elena Quiroga* (Boston, Twayne, 1977), pp. 127–28

RIBA, CARLES (1893-1959)

Of Carles Riba one could state simply and axiomatically that he is the greatest contemporary Catalan poet and the most classic of all our literary history.

Within that very categorical statement, the word classic must be understood in the sense of a poetry that contains an abundance of nuances that can transcend the limitations of time; a poetry that furnishes a stimulus and offers nourishment to many generations. . . . It is very clear that man's different spiritual values are found in Riba's poetry in perfect equilibrium. Any one of them can predominate, any one can annul or weaken the other. Any form of the spirit may be hidden in the shade. All joyously realize themselves. The moral and intellectual preachings have an equal voice. . . . Introspection is balanced and mixed with the most precise objectivity. Life is mixed with abstraction, dream with reality. A richness that seems inexhaustible is revealed throughout. . . . One sees a poetry in which every temperament will be able to grasp a decisive word and every epoch a valuable message.

Jaume Bofill i Ferro. Introduction to *Carles Riba* (Barcelona, Oreig, 1938), p. 7–10†

In the two volumes of *Stanzas* (1919, 1930), the poetry of Carles Riba shows the line of an interesting evolution. There are echoes of that medieval court poetry, of the melancholic delicacy and reverie that derive from the troubadours and the *dolce stilo nuovo;* there are definite affinities with the English "metaphysical poets" of the seventeenth century; and there are the subtle melodies of the symbolist manner. . . . Carles Riba's poetry appears to be the product of a much more normally matured culture than our own. His language achieves a certain degree of refinement, a capacity to express the most delicate aspects of complex thought, and an ardent and deep passion. . . .

Like Mallarmé in France, Riba has created in Catalonia the idea of difficult poetry. In a culture that tended excessively toward superficiality and facility, he offered from his very first works a poetry constructed with solid and demanding art, and the spectacle of a truly meditative passion. With regard to that poetry there are the usual reservations—obscurantism, preciosity. . . .

Two themes, repeated throughout *Stanzas,* appear to have a special significance in Carles Riba's poetic evolution. One is the theme of the poetic professional—the mystery of lyrical creation. . . . This pre-

occupation with the intimate secret of the poet in his special function . . . is not a form of narcissism, but rather reveals a reverent love
for the mysteries of language. . . . Along with that limited, personal
theme, . . . there also appears repeatedly in *Stanzas* a preoccupation
with collective emotions.

> Marià Manent. Introduction to Carles Riba,
> *Estances* (Barcelona, Biblioteca Selecta, 1947).
> pp. 11–12, 15–16†

At their most obvious (but not most superficial) level, *Elegies of Bierville* are poems about exile—an account of personal suffering reduced
to its basic elements so that it may stand for the collective experience.
Riba himself has explained how the entire sequence was composed in
exile after the [Spanish] Civil War. The first seven poems correspond to
the actual period of exile; the remaining ones were written in what Riba
calls an *esprit de retour,* after he had made the decision to return to
Catalonia. This double movement—exile and return—recurs in various
forms. On the spiritual level it stands for privation and restoration, the
death and the rebirth of the soul, a sense of being temporarily withdrawn from the collective life in order to participate in it with greater
knowledge. Cutting across this is a different movement, in a sense the
exact inverse of the first. In exile the soul is driven back on itself;
stripped of its illusion so that it is compelled to seek the real. Riba's key-
phrase echoes Novalis: "To return to one's soul as to the home of one's
ancestors"—so that exile becomes the return journey, the backward
search for the preconscious impulse which must be regained, and the
return becomes a fresh setting-out.

   Also running through the poems are several other general notions:
the association of the preconscious impulse with grace and salvation;
the idea of charity, of enriching one's spirit through devotion to others;
the idea that the final aim of the conscious soul is to see its individual
life as something existing outside time.

> A. H. Terry. *Atlante* (London). Oct., 1954,
> pp. 179–80

Carles Riba's poetry is exceptional in twentieth-century Spain. It is
exceptional because it is the work of the only scholar-poet that we
possess. It is true that there are other professor-poets, for example
Jorge Guillén and Dámaso Alonso. About Guillén one might say that his
professorship is indirectly evident in the rigorous, formal, and deliberately "cold" structure of his poetry. . . . In Dámaso Alonso, an extreme
case, poetry *wants* to be violently disassociated from study and knowledge. . . .

   Carles Riba's poetry, which is the expression of his profound
oneness with the person who wrote it, is the poetry of a studious and
reflective man. This does not mean that his poetry is merely *illustrative*

of an already formed philosophical or religious idea. No. Carles Riba, like a true poet, thinks poetically. But also, and this is the most important aspect to stress here, he makes his knowledge work poetically. . . .

One might think that we find ourselves before a sample of humanistic poetry, like that of those scholars who, from time to time, wrote poetry imitating the Latins (e.g., Menéndez Pelayo), or those that have created a poetry composed in the classical-vernacular, such as [Gabriela] Mistral. Carles Riba writes with a human and poetic sensibility that is completely of our day, in a living language that is his own, and not in an archeological language he wants to resuscitate, looking back to olden days. It is true that Riba at times gives a philologically erudite note to his poems. This agrees with what we have said previously: he writes poetry with his whole personality. . . .

José Luis Aranguren. *PSA.* Nov., 1961, pp. 133–34†

Riba never fell into the temptations of experimental poetry in the interwar years, as did many of his contemporaries; rather he remained faithful to the symbolist tradition.

Riba's classical foundations prevented him from following these paths of experimentation, which he considered frivolous. However, this very fidelity to the orthodox symbolist tradition prevented him from developing in the way that many of his contemporaries did—during and after the Spanish Civil War and World War II—toward realism, toward a descriptive and narrative poetry in everyday language. Perhaps one may say that Riba attempted this in his last volume, *Sketch of Three Oratories,* and this is true. But the desired realism of the three poems was overshadowed, uprooted by the mythical character of the work. It was not our reality that Riba was attempting to narrate, but rather a certain Christian, ahistorical mythology.

The growth, the enrichment of Riba's works was thus essentially achieved from the same immoveable base, that of the symbolist tradition of his first writings, and not through following, dynamically and progressively, the steps of the historical evolution of his time.

J. M. Castellet. *PSA.* Nov., 1961, pp. 149–50†

Each volume of Carles Riba's poetry is a surprise; in stylistic techniques, in symbols, in his attitude toward life, there is always something new. Thus, *Savage Heart* (1952) is not a purely intellectual work of classical symbolism, as are, in great part, *Stanzas* and *Three Suites.* Based on a long and intense experience, *Savage Heart* has the same roots as *Elegies of Bierville* because it also represents that "return to the profound reality of myself." An "existential" value that gives life to these sonnets, which are often labyrinthine or abrupt like those of [Gerard Manley] Hopkins, is evident and makes them more powerful. It is a question, as the author himself recognizes in the prologue, of "some human verses, perhaps too human." With a violent heart more than with pure intelligence, he delves into the most transcendental or elemental themes, and the book almost always leads toward a religious asceticism. . . .

Sketch of Three Oratories (1957) freely re-creates some episodes from the Gospels. . . . The book is made up of three poems: "The Three Kings of the Orient," which is a lyrical and plastic representation of the trip of the Magi; "The Prodigal Son"; and "Lazarus Resurrected," which is the best of the three and which reproduces completely an imaginary dialogue between Lazarus and a fisherman. There are moments of a living archeology, and their themes are those that most preoccupy the poet: death, faith, basic life. . . .

. . . *And the Poems* (1957) brings together "notes on poets and poetry." Not all the texts are critical. . . . There are moments when the author "confesses" and the moralist or theorizer predominates over the pure critic.

Albert Manent. Tres escritores catalanes
(Madrid, Gredos, 1973), pp. 289–91†

RODRÍGUEZ CASTELAO, ALFONSO (1882–1950)

There is still one aspect of Castelao's multifaceted work that is important to be noted because it is probably the one most relevant to a Portuguese magazine: this Spaniard, or "Hespaniard" as he deliberately wrote, had a great affection for Portugal, since he quite correctly saw it as the larger part of one whole that man's caprices and errors had divided. In his last book, *Always in Galicia,* he speaks about his youthful interest in becoming acquainted with Portugal and its culture. . . .

His affection for our country is evidenced in the album *We* . . . . The scene shows the porch of a rural home, which looks out over the Minho River. A small child asks his grandfather if those on the other side (the Portuguese) are more foreign than the people of Madrid. The old man scratches his head, embarrassed. The legend at the bottom is quite charming . . . : "The old man's answer was unknown."

Castelao's great aspiration was for the union of Portugal and Galicia, the correction of that great mistake, the great injustice that divided the two brother peoples, true brothers even in their language.

Manuel Rodrigues Lapa. SeN. Feb., 1951,
pp. 435–36†

The most orthodox definition of humor seems to be that which recognizes that its smiling exterior is a shell or even a mask for a severe and deep inner pain. With this "orthodox" definition Castelao's words and works agree. In words, because, otherwise, he would not have looked for a motto for his *A Glass Eye* that is so similar to one of Mark Twain's: "Beneath humor there is always a great pain." And with regard to his works, because the literary version of Castelao's archetypes are bitter, torn, and even sad characters, such as a skeleton, a mother who keeps her five miscarried children in bottles of alcohol, a pair of oxen who promise to "see" each other again at the tanned-hide market. . . .

The great paradox of Castelao's humor is based on horrific or scatological elements. And this makes the works of this great figure of Galician letters almost completely autochthonous, and perfectly representative of the most central and undeniable preoccupations of the Galician spirit. . . .

At some point in *Banterings,* it is said that "the dead are lazy." The use of the adjective "lazy" to describe dead people is proof of the singular and strange marriage of humor and death in Castelao's works. . . .

M. Rabanal Álvarez. *Ínsula.* July–Aug., 1959, p. 7†

Morally and sentimentally Castelao identifies himself with his people, as they suffer, as they sin. . . . With a penetrating critical eye he investigates things and men. And if he is ironic and satirizes and ridicules, it is in order to expose errors, prejudices, fears, and vices. . . . But he never condemns, because he knows that behind the drama there is salvation.

In his drawings and in his prose there breathes a deep ethical feeling. He does not deform the images he presents. . . . Castelao's humor is found in the tragic seriousness of man's inherent nature. . . .

Castelao's diction is always popular and lively. For this reason his language hits its target; without circumlocutions or foreign emotional stimuli, he achieves great expressivity and great communicative power. He offers, at the same time, a clear example of the relationship between literature as fiction and language as a cultural creation of a people with a singular psyche and spirit.

The style of Castelao's works is clear, distinctive, and natural. It is oriented toward the simple, the primitive, and the basic.

Marino Dónega. Introduction to Alfonso
Rodríguez Castelao, *Escolma posible* (Vigo,
Galaxia, 1964), pp. 14–15†

Castelao began his career as an artist. At the bottom of many of his drawings he wrote admirable epigrams. But it was not until 1926 that he published this aspect of his work in *Things,* where he attempted to balance drawing and literature. Eight years later, he had improved his ability to produce tales and stories, which were of value in themselves—not as glosses for drawings, but rather as tales with illustrations. . . .

In all his works, Castelao is present with the integrity of a complete man. . . . In *Things* he portrays the bleak, small existences of people tormented by everyday problems and humiliations—concentrating on the sufferings of the Galician people in an ill-fated society. But in spite of this realism, at times quite biting in its truthfulness . . . the organization of his tales is quite evidently poetic.

Things is one of the best volumes published in our literature. The writer possesses that precious gift of sentence structure, in which the secret of rhythm resides. The way he fits all aspects of his thoughts into the paragraph structure is admirable.

Salvador Lorenzana. Grial. April–June, 1966, pp. 221–22†

In the book *Things,* there is a text near the end called "He Was a Little Butter Boy." The illustration is of a boy in pajamas, with his hands in his pockets, holding onto a toy—a wooden horse. The boy has lots of curly hair and eyes that indicate tenderness and complete innocence. The drawing reflects a state of innocence. . . . The short story that Castelao tells is sad. The values are made evident through contrast: the kindness of the mother reflected in the kindness of the child suffering through the brutalities of war; the youth which ends so brutally and which was not prepared for a life so different from the one he dreamed about. Did Castelao write this text in 1926, 1927, 1928, or 1929? It was surely one of these years.

This story reminded me of the poem "Mama's Boy" by Fernando Pessoa. The theme explored is the same: the contrast between the youth, a beloved and spoiled child, a "mama's boy" made of butter and kindness and that of the brutal war that takes over with a shocking senselessness.

Pessoa did not always date his poems. "The Mama's Boy" is not dated, but it first appeared in 1926. Both Pessoa and Castelao are not too far apart in dealing with the same theme. In addition, they were contemporaries. . . . The same emotions and the same shock. The same absurd and terrible world. The same metaphysical stance in the face of death.

Joaquim Montezuma de Carvalho. Grial. July–
Sept., 1969, pp. 371–73†

The . . . problem of frustrated maternity is presented by Castelao in "I'm Going to Tell You a Story" in *Things.* Here, Micaela also wants to be a mother; when the fruits of her love affairs are miscarried, she keeps them as if they were real children. . . . When she is an old woman, one of the maids accidently upsets one of the bottles in which she has kept her children, and Micaela dies.

Between truth and jest, Castelao shows us the tragedy of this poor woman, and at the same time makes us feel compassion for her problem and makes us laugh at the solution that she finds. . . .

In the pages of *Things,* we see a great sympathy for the working rural woman, for her problems and her pains, and also for her way of loving. The greatest interest is shown for the older village woman, dried up by time.

Isabel Miramontes Nieto. *Grial.* April–June,
1971, pp. 225–26†

The technical innovations Castelao began in 1922 with *A Glass Eye* and continued in *Things* culminate in *The Usual Two.* This is the first really innovative Galician novel on several levels: in substance, in manner of expression, and in content.

Castelao enriched the language through his selective choices and through his skilled structuring; he eliminates the scenes of local color that were so frequent in earlier works; above all, he breaks that constantly repeated pattern of the traditional narrative: his novel lacks that pattern of the good and the bad who meet and bring the action to a happy conclusion.

Nor is the action centered exclusively on a love story. The traditional idyll disappears. Pedriño's marriage, which is arranged by his future mother-in-law, occurs suddenly, without any amorous dialogues. But this is an unhappy event for him; love is destroyed by the family tyrant; the character lives harassed, submerged in a "cold hell." The constant confrontations with his mother-in-law, the "glutton's" eating needs, the fine, the involuntary emigration, his constant frustration do not leave room for romantic fiction.

Neither do Pedro's adulterous activities follow the traditional scheme. His nighttime meeting with the dressmaker is nothing more than a ridiculous situation.

Benito Varela Jácome. *Estructuras de la
narrativa de Castelao* (La Coruña, Librigal,
1973), pp. 52–53†

The motivation for *Old People Should Not Fall in Love* is very simple: the old person who falls in love does ridiculous and low things, aside from being a victim of greed and deception. There is nothing sad or serious in this play; rather, it has a farcical tone. . . .

The play has three acts, but each one is independent and can be presented as a separate play. . . . It is known that the third one, *Pimpinela,* was written in about 1935, and only years later were the other two added to precede it.

The characters, judgments, prejudices, values, and ideas are of rural Galicia, and are not very far from those of Valle-Inclán's *Barbarous Dramas.* In more than one situation, the author, who has a powerful style, roundly rejects a photographic realism. Some scenes, such as the one in the garden of the Saturio sisters, are prodigious literary constructions. . . .

The problems of love in old age, suggested in a general way in the title, are more specifically delineated in each of the plays of the farce. These old men, when they fall in love, behave the way they do because they are rich, because this wealth arouses in them certain desires in this precarious world, and because the desired women, one way or another, see them as the only possibility to free themselves from their hated poverty.

Jesús Alonso Montero. Introduction to Alfonso Rodríguez Castelao, *Cuatro obras* (Madrid, Cátedra, 1974), pp. 26–28†

RUIBAL, JOSÉ (1925–   )

Long, rambling, frequently inchoate, *The Begging Machine* has so many philosophical ramifications that is almost impossible to enumerate all of them. The two principal objects of the author's satire are the hypocrisy of charity and the mechanization of life. Ruibal portrays charity as an easy tranquilizer of the consciences of the rich, for whom the eternal division between their economic state and that of the rest of the world is an indispensable condition of existence. Just as good cannot exist without evil, as generations of theologians have never tired of informing us in their eager apologia, so the rich cannot exist without the necessary (to them) contrast of the poor. The analogy does not hold, as Ruibal shows us in his play, however, for while good and evil are necessary opposites, rich and poor are artificial differences.

Ruibal depicts the mechanization of life with his brilliant device of showing the ruling powers of the world as hybrid machine-men, their heads in the form of miniature computers if they are civilians and in the form of weapons if they are military. An American is irresistibly reminded of the uniformed robots in the Pentagon and the businessmen in the Cabinet, chosen less for their human qualities than for their success as calculating machines. Ruibal also continues his mastery of animal symbolism here. The yellow octopus who gives birth to oil tankers is the robber-baron businessman who cuts through all rules, operating unscrupulously in the single-minded pursuit of money. His success makes him an object of awe and respect to those whom he is swindling by manipulating the rules that they themselves have set to control his ilk. Like the bankers in Dürrenmatt's *Frank V*, the octopus is an atavistic animal who will inevitably be replaced by the dehumanized electronic man.

It is hard to predict at this point in what direction Ruibal will go. He has the talent and the versatility to accomplish almost anything in the theater, and the maturity and insight to treat any subject. The only conceivable obstacle in his path is the discouragement that might develop as a result of his inability to have his plays produced in his own country.

George E. Wellwarth. *Spanish Underground Drama* (University Park, Pennsylvania State University Press, 1972), pp. 35–36

The Man and the Fly is a dramatic allegory of political power and an exploration of the psychology of power by means of the relationship of Man to his Double. The play reflects the experience of the Spanish Civil War, the long postwar years of an endless dictatorship that still grips Spain, and the playwright's reaction to the world in the 1960s, particularly to the traumatic war in Vietnam.

The Man is any dictator, any custodian of power, whether of the right or the left, although many details remind the reader of Francisco Franco. Aside from dictators, we may also observe in The Man's traits and rhetoric characteristics of certain heads of democratic states. . . .

Ruibal has reacted strongly against the drama produced in Spain in the 1950s and 1960s. This drama is largely of a realistic nature and tends to use facile, conventional symbols. Ruibal's allegorical method presupposes the utilization of numerous devices such as the splitting of characters into doubles, the use of lyrics, proverbs and epigrams, phantasmagoria, and so on, in order to achieve a representation of what he deems to be a hidden truth that the viewer often does not want to see or hear. For Ruibal there are two kinds of playwrights—those who write for the public and those who write against the public. He sees himself as a playwright who writes against the public, particularly the Spanish public, which he has judged to be rather narrowminded. This obsession against a particular public leads Ruibal at times to strongly negative attitudes. This is nothing unique, for the spirit of *épater le bourgeois* (shock the bourgeois) has been in vogue since the beginnings of the romantic movement, when the artist emancipated himself from his monied patron and established himself as an independent, usually bohemian, spokesman for society. . . .

[*The Man and the Fly*] can be understood not only as a political allegory but as a religious one as well, inasmuch as it involves Man's longing for immortality. Ironically, we see a cynical and corrupted creature, physically decrepit, who also seeks eternity. The playwright presents to the viewer a consciousness that attempts to achieve self-sufficiency and total dominion over others, but that encounters a limit, an external world, an otherness that it wants to negate. . . .

The play is written with a meticulous eye for stage effects. . . . Laughter and tears follow each other, fear and courage, tenderness and sadism, nostalgia and hardheaded pragmatism. The very versatility of The Man is undercut by the frozen mechanical imitation of the Double;

as one emotion unmasks its opposite, the viewer perceives one common emotional substratum animating the will to power—irremediable total fear. Thus Ruibal creates a truly pathological character without the usual aids of psychological drama; there is no traditional psychological development of character, but rather the disintegration of The Man into a variety of hollow roles, the ultimate one being his ephemeral successor, the Double. Ruibal presents a view of man that has the ability to traumatize the public: what stands for heroism in the contemporary world is the utter brutality of unredeemed cynicism.

Antonio Regalado, Gary D. Keller, and Susan
Kerr. In Antonio Regalado, Gary D. Keller, and
Susan Kerr, eds., España en el siglo XX (New
York, Harcourt Brace Jovanovich, 1974),
pp. 360–63

Of all the many aspects that define and give unity to the works of José Ruibal, it is without doubt his ability to work with concepts that is the most outstanding. According to the author's own words, his theater is "tremendously conceptual." The concepts or ideas that regulate his creative process are closely linked to the important themes of the twentieth century: technology, the abuses of political power, individual freedom, hunger and poverty, and injustice. A mental mechanism that structures the themes into symbolic forms with great evocative power exists in each work to a greater or lesser degree of complexity. This mechanism operates through the integration of dialogue, action, and setting. The expressive totality resulting from such integration produces in the spectator an instantaneous grasp of what is being communicated without the necessity of detailed analyses.

In order to achieve his purpose, Ruibal assumes a perspective of aesthetic distancing, as if he were an objective witness, devoid of any emotionalism in regard to what is going on. He does what Ortega y Gasset has called "to dehumanize" and what he has explained as the objectivization of subjective schema. Ruibal abstracts from reality those schemata—which are nothing more than ideas or concepts—and he molds onto them symbols that have some aspects of reality itself. It is not a question, to be sure, of mimesis in the manner of the realists, but rather one of a creation of autonomous forms that, while aesthetically new, are at the same time familiar because of their concrete references. . . .

When we say that Ruibal's theater is conceptual we do not mean that there is a philosophical, political, or economic purpose to elevate humankind or save it from its vices and foolishness. The conceptuality is found in the use he makes of the mental schemata as instruments of his aesthetic creation. By following the thesis of Ortega it is easy to explain Ruibal's aesthetics as a systematic effort to "purify" ideas just as they are. We can interpret his purification or objectivization as the process of emptying the content of its concepts and filling it with new ones, in accordance with data chosen from reality. In the selection, Ruibal utilizes concrete and familiar elements that are linked to contemporary life. The result of the double process of abstraction and objectivization is translated by the presence of figures or symbols of great suggestive power.

Magda Castelví de Moor. JSSTC. Spring, 1975,
pp. 45, 51†

It cannot be doubted that José Ruibal is a unique dramatist. Even within what we would be able to consider his generation, he embraces heterodoxy. The fact that he has lived so long outside of Spain and the reception that his work has had in the United States probably have produced different criteria by which to judge him and, above all, have created the distinct language that he employs. While the other dramatists [Antonio Martínez Ballesteros, José María Bellido, etc.] who are mentioned as representatives of this new theater manipulate codes and a language that we could consider ordinary and quotidian (even in its deformations or somewhat familiar corruptions), Ruibal has given his theater his own very personal stamp. Be that as it may, scarcely do we start reading his work when we begin to discover the same limitations as in the other dramatists of the new generation. . . .

The reading of José Ruibal's plays leads us to two conclusions that, to a certain extent, are valid for all the new theater in Spain, if we conceive of it as an expression of our most vital dramatic literature. . . . On one hand, there exists the danger that such a theater can become hermetic and can become a theater in which the community from which it is born and for which it is destined is not recognizable. On the other hand, there exists an equally dangerous simplification that tends toward Manicheism, and consequently tends to close off what ought to be an open-ended critique. . . . Personally I believe that a sincere examination of conscience would have beneficial results for the new Spanish theater that is beginning to lose the initial vigor with which it seemed to come into being.

Rodríguez Padrón. Ínsula. Sept., 1976, p. 15†

Imagine Hitler training Chaplin to be The Great Dictator, and you will have some of the flavor of José Ruibal's The Man and the Fly, a bitter but playful black comedy. . . .

The comparison with Hitler is not entirely valid: . . . the aging ruler of an unidentified country is meant to be a comic figure. His chosen replacement, his double . . . , is an altered ego, a shorter, slighter and clumsy version of himself. When he puts on [the ruler's] uniform, it is so large that it looks like an overcoat.

In his high-vaulted glass palace—an eye-catching evocation of a see-through spider's web . . . [the ruler] is showing his successor how to replace him after his death. Not only does he teach this former bank clerk the rules of autocracy, but in order to make his scheme complete, he is duplicating on the double the scars of his own lifetime. He flogs him with his swagger stick and even simulates a cavalry charge over his body, announcing with relish, "The blows I give you make my flesh tremble."

[The ruler] is reliving his past excesses and injuries, and [the double] is his eager victim, a man who lives to grovel—and who grovels in order to live. As master abuses servant who will eventually become master, the scene is somewhat reminiscent of Fernando Arrabal's *The Architect and the Emperor of Assyria.* In common with his fellow Spaniard, José Ruibal has written a political parable that makes its points through apocalyptic humor. . . .

Having introduced his two characters and issued his indictment of miscreant regimes, Mr. Ruibal seems indecisive. The dialogue begins to dawdle, but then picks up in the darker second act and takes an imaginative leap into surrealism. The two musicians . . . become puppeteers manipulating life-size figures of an angel and a devil. The two puppets battle over the dictator's corpse, represented by a soft, stuffed dummy. They send body parts flying in several directions, until their contest becomes an absurd celestial equivalent of a pillow fight.

The double calmly assumes the throne where, of course, he will be pinioned by the badge of his office. Among other things, *The Man and the Fly* is a provocative comedy about role-playing, as the dictator handpicks an heir and "slips the fraud into history." It takes one to know one.

Mel Gussow. NYT. Feb. 5, 1982, p. C3

SALINAS, PEDRO (1891–1951)

The title of Pedro Salinas's recent book *Eve of Joy* exactly expresses the state of sensual receptivity in which the poet places himself—at the center of the universe ready to face whatever chance might bring. . . . It is a modest title . . . and one that indicates the author's intention of seeing the world only through the trembling smile of illusion. We never possess things; only a reflection of the fragilities and fears of our existence comes to us and more or less represents the desires of our sensuality and imagination. This is the theme that is developed in the course of this exquisite little book. In it life seems a tissue of insignificant events, while at the same time an neverending and desperate tragedy. . . .

This book is one of the most beautiful in Spanish literature in a long time. . . . In the tone and accent of the sentences, in its nature, in the chosen details and images there is a unique and ineffable quality . . . that makes Pedro Salinas a European spirit while at the same time a profoundly Spanish one—one of the most worthy that the last Spanish literary generation has produced.

Jean Cassou. *Mercure de France*. Oct. 1, 1926,
pp. 438–39†

In his previous books Salinas was excessively distracted by certain stimuli and attractions—themes, visions of a mechanical civilization, and modern society—that, in spite of what critics said, did not make a substantial contribution to his poetry, which is an intellectual, intimate poetry, made up of a few pure and essential concepts. In *The Voice Because of You* he ignores the majority of these exterior stimuli in order to express, . . . around a specific theme, his own true poetic world, "where love invents its own infinity." This specific theme is that of love, into which all of Salinas's poetic world fits. The result is a concentrated and beautiful poem, full of changing shades, and monotonous, which is a virtue, not a defect. . . .

If the word were not dangerous, we would say that Salinas here comes closer than in his previous books to mystical poetry. The starting point and the goal are perhaps different; the intensity of the pleasure, of the confusion, of the anxiety, and the search are the same. . . . It is not an easy book; only the good searchers, those who know how to exclude what is accidental, will be able to enjoy it. It does not change anything of the author's previous work; it is rather an achievement and an improvement of what was most valuable in it.

Ángel del Río. *RHM*. Oct. 1934, pp. 39–40†

The Voice Because of You has been generally accepted among Spanish critics as one of the greatest contemporary love-sequences, and few, if any, living poets in any language have dared anything to equal it in ambition. In it Salinas seeks behind any beyond for the real meaning of the duality of the universe, and the grave simplicity of his language serves to heighten his mystical and metaphysical implications. At times his conceits, taken from our modern materialistic civilization, remind one of Góngora; they range all the way from the quaint to the vitally fresh and original. He writes of love as an experience entirely transcending physical sensation, and, like the true Spaniard that he is, slips often with ease into a fourth dimension of his own.

There is an undeniable monotony in all these variations on a single theme, which is emphasized by the simplicity of form. . . . But read carefully enough and it will be discovered that the poet is not so much repetitious as he is anxious to explore all phases of human love.

Señor Salinas is another of the dozens of leading European writers brought to this country by war in Europe, the Spanish civil conflict forcing him into exile in 1936. He is at present a member of the faculty at Johns Hopkins University.

Herschel Brickell. *NYT.* Dec. 22, 1940, section 6,

p. 2

"To Live in Pronouns" is nothing more than a verbal paradox for Salinas, but it is also an attitude toward life made up of disenchantment and desperation, in which man, having lost faith in *substances,* keeps himself *on the edge* of reality, holding on, before the precipice, to an intellectual aspect that is formulatable in exact terms, but which, nonetheless, is colored by an atmosphere of playfulness; what is left to him is the human language, his language, an expression of his intellect, a creator of new relationships of thought. Living in pronouns is a fact observed by the poet in himself, and at the same time a possibility for life suggested by the language. The living paradox is translated into a verbal paradox: the correspondence is not arbitrary, it is exact. We have noted the simplicity, the clarity, and the moderation, the pathos of nakedness, the necessity of exactness and precision in the notation of interior facts: Salinas searches for the rigorously *necessary* expression, the consciously *sincere* one, in short, the classical one—not the surprising or overcharged one. There probably exists in our generation a consciousness of human misery that would not fit in with the "glitter of Tasso." Salinas replaces *culteranismo* [preciosity] with scientific and technical terms. The humanism of the Golden Age was able to take pride in its philological aristocraticness, in its decorative refinements of style; today we are in the era of *Realwissenschaften,* and technique belongs to everyone.

Leo Spitzer. *RHM.* Jan.–April, 1941, p. 65†

Among the poets of the Generation of 1925 is Salinas, one of those whose work seems the most difficult to judge fairly; the somewhat conventional admiration of some does not outweigh the indifference of others, and perhaps more time must pass before we decide about Salinas's contribution to our contemporary poetry. Nevertheless, with the inevitable misgiving one has in venturing such an opinion, I should like to state that *Presages* seems to me to be the most important of his works; he reveals there the spontaneous poetic qualities of his temperament, which are qualities that his subsequent books leave aside, without doubt because of the author's belief that they are inferior to the other artificial ones he later acquired and cultivated. The fact that I read *Presages* when I was quite young and perhaps less accustomed to the objective examination of my readings does not, I believe, play a part in my liking for this book; a recent rereading has confirmed my belief that this is the most valuable of Salinas's books. And also that it is one of the best of the Generation of 1925. [1955]

Luis Cernuda. *Estudios sobre poesía española*
contemporánea (Madrid, Guadarrama, 1970), p. 164†

We have already noted how Salinas, in the poetry he wrote in Europe, played around with technical things. This playing resulted in the assimilation of these things into the poetry through the wit of the poet. In a poem in *Fable and Sign* (1931) called "The Telephone," we see the ironic use of this apparatus so familiar in poetry, of course, but with a balanced tone that shows the dominance of the mind over the machine. . . . In this poem man's invention is still at his service. But once in the United States, especially in New York, with mechanical modernity an end in itself, Salinas perceived the lack of an intimate relationships between man and his inventions. He was astonished and horrified at the same time. He went into the big stores and reacted like a child in front of so many things, but deep down he feared what he called the "thingness of the world."

The result in his poetry becomes evident in *Everything Clearer*. We can study this through one poem, which evidently originates in a walk through Times Square in New York and which is called "Nocturne of the Advertisements." The senses are overwhelmed before the demands the lights of the advertisements make. His reaction is in defense of humanity. Salinas sees this world in terms of what it is not. We could call his technique Ruskin's pathetic fallacy in reverse. He takes something made by man and describes it as if it were a product of nature. His metaphor tries to give life to something inert. . . .

Salinas struggles to maintain his human personality in face of all this pressure. The fact that he goes into battle through a poem is in itself a partial victory. But in the storm of metaphors that do not succeed in taking shape with his old skill and in the loss of his fluency of style, a partial defeat is also to be found. And nothing better proves this than the fact that in America he began to develop other genres: drama and the novel, and principally criticism . . . .

Howard T. Young. *CHA*. Jan., 1962, pp. 11–12†

Always in the foreground, confronting the observer, the appreciator, the critic, there was the literature that [Salinas] loved. There was always a deciphering, analyzing intelligence accompanied by a sensibility ever active in delight. For the critic pays attention only to great texts, and criticism functions as an act of admiration. But the poem, the novel, the play are there, facing the reader, in space and time. Without a sense of history one does not see the work, not even in an immediate sense. . . . The criticism of our teacher-poet [Salinas] was always as living as it was historical. An excellent example of this is his book of [Jorge] Manrique, the subtitle of which sums up the whole matter: *Jorge Manrique; or, Tradition and Originality.* How can one be aware of the originality of Manrique's poetry without exploring the deep tradition implicit within it? . . . Salinas develops his analysis making use of previous criticism. Since his Manrique study is written in the style of a literary essay, his erudition is absorbed into the body of the text, not scattered in foot-notes. Any other approach would have conflicted with the critic's standards and the writer's good taste, which are of course different from those of the philologian. Who has ever reproached Eliot's critical essays for not being "scholarly"? In Salinas too the critic is inseparable from the poet, for knowing is inseparable from making.

Jorge Guillén. Introduction to Pedro Salinas,
Reality and the Poet in Spanish Poetry
(Baltimore, Johns Hopkins University Press,
1966), pp. xvii–xix

The Contemplated One represents . . . a dramatic sketch of the search for eternity in poetry. As we read part after part, the dialogue of the poet and the sea, we can follow and feel the diverse moments and aspects of Salinas's complex struggle to find perennial values through art and to transcend his own limitations. The trajectory culminates when the poetic vision is embodied in the sea, which is the compendium of what is artistic and what is eternally natural.

It is important to stress that the dramatic progression of the book not only links us with the protagonist's search; at the same time an objective organization imposes itself on this search and gives it more exactness. This organization, although it is dynamic, is no less precise for being so. The contrasts between the various types of sections . . . clearly reproduce the conflict between two key aspects of reality—the temporal and the eternal. . . .

Comparing *The Contemplated One* with the poems of *Confidence* shows that the latter offers a more successful vision. This is due to the great skill in the use of form and the dramatic development. In this way, Salinas simultaneously is able to link us with the poet's trajectory and make this trajectory both exact and progressive. Consequently, he vividly embodies the desperate struggle of the creative artist, his very human and difficult effort to transcend the limits of reality, in which he—as we are—is immersed.

> Andrew Debicki. *Estudios sobre poesía española contemporánea* (Madrid, Gredos, 1968), pp. 104–5†

[In *Complete Poems*] the chronology of poems has gone by the wayside . . . because today we know that today is only today, *hic et nunc,* or, if you prefer, . . . what point is there in respectfully beginning with the stages of work in which the poet is searching for himself?—for the reader to arrive exhausted at the great encounters? We are not reading the complete works . . . ; rather we go to the essential, without the progression from youth to maturity that is the poet's personal problem and not useful, moreover, in the study of Salinas. The proof is in the eighth poem of *Presages,* his first book, which already has the unmistakable tone that will later create *The Voice Because of You.* In the same way, if many of the late poems are missing it is because instead of what is called the evolution of a body of work I prefer an atemporal vision of poetry—putting poems together because of affinities, rhythms, and contacts. . . .

I have evaluated once again what I knew thirty years ago in Argentina—that Salinas and Cernuda were the greatest poets of love in their time and in their language. [1970]

> Julio Cortázar. *Ínsula.* Nov.–Dec. 1971, p. 3†

Salinas's work before 1936 shows . . . a constant basic theme: the paradoxical way in which the apparent clarity and solidity of external reality changes, in subjective experience of it, into a mysterious complex of fleeting, tenuous impressions and intuitions which it is very difficult to name or express exactly. The aim of his poetry is therefore to explore the relation between outer and inner reality, and to exploit the hints and premonitions provided by inner experience that there is more to the outer world than meets the eye. Some readers have seen this exploration as a quest of something like Platonic Ideas, and it has to be admitted that Salinas himself has given vague encouragement to such a view by defining poetry . . . as "an adventure toward the absolute," which makes him sound like another Jiménez. . . .

But his long inquiry into the relationship between inner and outer reality belies these Platonic intimations, and turns out to be very unlike Jiménez's. He remains fascinated by the external world, its perfect explicability and existence-in-itself. . . . All through *Sure Risk* and *Fable and Sign* he moves restlessly between the two worlds suggested by the paradoxical titles, endlessly comparing them and puzzling over their incompatibility, fascinated especially by the "geometry without anguish" of things that can be counted and measured exactly, or things that stand still and solid in time and space, like the Escorial, to which two of his most suggestive poems are addressed.

Fortunately, he did not remain for ever in a state of impotent perplexity. Already in *Fable and Sign* the juxtaposition of the two worlds produces subtle insights into the nature of both of them . . . .

G. G. Brown. *A Literary History of Spain: The
Twentieth Century* (New York, Barnes & Noble,
1972), pp. 90–91

Most of Salinas's plays dealing with the love theme end on this happy dream of romantic escape, without exploring the eventual consequences. But in a few works, such as *The Head of Medusa,* and more conclusively in the three-act allegory entitled *The Director,* the inevitable journey from illusion back to reality occurs as the protagonist succumbs to an overwhelming desire to test her dreamed adventure in real life, meeting thereby with disillusionment and despair. The antithetical attraction of dream and reality is seen as a fatal cyclic struggle from which there is no escape, at least within the confines of Salinas's theater.

One more play deserves more than a passing mention, since it reveals something of the author's feelings towards the emotionally charged subject of the Spanish Civil War. This play, *The Saints,* was not included in the volume of *Complete Theater* because, due to its subject matter, it could never have passed the Spanish regime's official censure. . . . Yet, the play is in no way polemical. Although the author's Republican sympathies are obvious, he rises above political considerations to condemn the fratricidal hatred on both sides of the conflict. . . .

The Saints is undoubtedly Salinas's most compelling play. The subject matter itself brings it close to our sensibilities. Moreover, its characters strike one as completely authentic Spanish types, whose personality and language Salinas has so faithfully reproduced. But the play is also well constructed; its fantastic ending does not seem gratuitous because the saints' metamorphosis has been prepared in the previous scenes.

John Crispin. *Pedro Salinas* (New York,
Twayne, 1974), pp. 153, 155

If Salinas's view of love, the *amada* [beloved] and external reality is changeable and difficult to pin down categorically, so too is his concept of poetry and of the function of the words in poetry. Reference to Guillén's comments . . . provides a good yardstick for appreciating this, both because of the latter's unerring consistency and because of the likelihood of mutual influence, the product of many years of intimate friendship. Not surprisingly, Salinas's ideas about poetic creation and his taste for poetry often run adjacent to Guillén's. As is well known, their thorough knowledge of the French symbolist tradition, their personal acquaintance with Paul Valéry and others, and their periods of residence in France channelled their ideas very strongly. Yet the influence of *poésie pure* was muted by their delight in the less cerebral purity of Spain: San Juan de la Cruz, Bécquer and Jiménez. To some large extent the poetry of Salinas and Guillén is a simplification, even humanization, of the French theory. . . .

For both poets . . . poetry is related to a concept of verbal purity created within a primordial atmosphere; a concept which is partly explained by Gerhard Hauptmann's definition of poetry . . . "Poetry evokes out of words the resonance of the primordial word." It may be said that both Salinas and Guillén are aware of the word's primordial force. Initially, for Salinas, it appears that the poet's duty to create is based simply upon the act of *naming*. . . .

Salinas was not always content with the ritual of naming. Indeed, between his early poetry, which often indicates a strong influence of Mallarmé, and the poetry of his last period, complacent in its attitude of homage, there is found Salinas's great poetry, which is remarkable for the way it sustains a deeply inquisitive and even quarrelsome attitude towards words.

Robert G. Havard. *BHS.* Jan., 1974, pp. 30–32

The point of departure for the poem "Zero" was Pedro Salinas's daily anguish about the new disasters of the ongoing war; of course, one must cast aside any motivation critical of the United States. Technology had taken possession of man and, according to the poet, had made him its blind slave. The aerial bombings were the most patent example of the power of technology over man. . . .

We wish to point out that these prophetic verses . . . were published a year before the first use in war of the atomic bomb—a historic event that would later give rise to his "fable" *The Incredible Bomb*. For Salinas—who greatly admired the American mechanical genius—the great tragedy of contemporary man was the moral blindness produced by technology. The bomb (the "zero") falls "blindly" ("from an altitude of six thousand meters"), but the pilot cannot be held responsible for its terrible effects. . . .

With the "zero" of the title Pedro Salinas wanted to accentuate the type of warlike destruction that made man's technical power a blind, destructive nihilism, a nihilism that when finished with man's deeds kills history itself. . . . Pedro Salinas, like his admired Jorge Manrique, does not stop with death: "Zero" is also a song to life, to the wonder of human history.

Juan Marichal. *Tres voces de Pedro Salinas*
(Madrid, Taller, 1976), pp. 77–79†

SÁNCHEZ FERLOSIO, RAFAEL (1927–   )

In Joyce's novel [*Ulysses*], that spans one day, what is attempted is the digging into the deepest recesses of the human soul; Sánchez Ferlosio works in an opposite manner, [in *The Jarama*], in an absolutely different way: he projects himself outward to an extreme degree . . . . Sánchez Ferlosio has chosen some ordinary types (therefore, hardly complicated), whose vital reason for being consists of enjoying Sunday and taking pleasure from it, as the only day of the week on which enjoyment is possible for them. For those of their social class, the eagerness for the day at hand is much more acute. Therefore, everything moves them toward the exterior: the landscape, the surroundings, and they themselves; the human props of the novel and their development indicate the realist intention. Realism is a word that can be dangerous. Here it is perfectly suitable. The characters of Sánchez Ferlosio act out their diversion, and principally they speak it. That is, the novelist does not play with their inner beings, nor with their memories, nor with their monologues. We observe how they are because they speak to each other. Dialogue is the most important innovation in *The Jarama*. Just as in life, the word is what explains us. But the word in *The Jarama* has a discursive function; the lack of a plot causes the novel to turn into, a series of words that zigzag with no determined reason, like the river that flows nearby. The characters speak to each other about what is happening, and thus they go on forming psychological characterizations. On the edge of the river there exists a small, dynamic world; in the country inn there exists another small world that is static, tired, old, and Sánchez Ferlosio plays, almost until the end of the novel, with this scene-changing by contrasting river and inn.

The pause in the dialogue is the landscape. There is silence because descriptions are interpolated with detail and poetry. *The Jarama* is entirely removed from the impressionist technique, since it manifests an enormous effort to do away with improvisation. The picture is finished; the prose is solid. There is no fusion of characters and landscape; it is a question of two distinct levels, well separated in the composition. The Jarama River appears like a Renaissance painting—rigorous in its details—and gives off at times a similar vitality, transformed especially for our times.

Sánchez Ferlosio has given the landscape a symbolic value, more or less on purpose. It is a field of battle, of death, and in this same place, we can observe some young people who did not live through the Spanish tragedy [of the civil war] but who have only heard about it: "Yeah, my uncle—they killed him here."

Luis Jiménez Martos. CHA. Sept., 1956, p. 188†

Rafael Sánchez Ferlosio is an innocent and restless young boy who wishes to be a novelist but is passing himself off as a soldier in the regular army. He has the look of an awkward young prince . . . he is the friend of a boy named Alfanhuí [in *The Projects and Wanderings of Alfanhuí*], which is the sound with which the bitterns, birds that also have gold-colored eyes, shriek at each other. . . .

Rafael Sánchez Ferlosio is a noble lad who knows the taste of wine, the flame of oil, and the color of bread. Rafael Sánchez Ferlosio knows the occult arts because of all the years he has been with Alfanhuí. Rafael Sánchez Ferlosio, in order to amuse himself, wrote a geography book that is especially personal to us: a geography of the best roads, the worst, the most dusty, of a road that winds along the plateaus of our mountains, which are inhabited by wolves, and where the quail sings, where the wild boar attacks, where the "peddler" rages and drinks the blood of children; he knows the art of tuning bells and he knows how to decipher the remote and guarded heliograph of the stars.

Rafael Sánchez Ferlosio has just published a strange book, a unique book, a timeless book. Rafael Sánchez Ferlosio smokes black tobacco and drinks white wine. Rafael Sánchez Ferlosio, a student in Madrid, a soldier in Africa, and always, no matter where, a gentleman with a sad smile, crowns his Alfanhuí with myrtle, like a pagan hero, while his Alfanhuí—that fantastic rogue!—laughs under his breath with a laugh that in the end becomes contagious like measles.

Rafael Sánchez Ferlosio has in these days a gesture more astonishing than ever. He likes to pull out a dove from his sleeve or three black cats from his top hat.

But still he much prefers to discover a friend who may be named Alfanhuí, which is the sound with which bitterns shriek at each other.

Camilo José Cela. La rueda de los ocios
(Barcelona, Mateu, 1957), pp. 294, 297–98†

Every re-reading of *The Jarama* is a different experience from the first impression . . . . When, suddenly, one of the picnickers from Madrid—Lucita, the shy one—drowns, there is a change. The action continues in the same manner, with the same rhythm and the same inexorable recording of details; but once we know that Lucita has died, the first part of the novel takes on a different aspect. Thus, just as when we finish a good detective story and find out "whodunit" we are in the habit of turning back in search of the unnoticed clues in order to verify how all the pieces fit together, when we pick up the thread of *The Jarama* again we discover incidents that were insignificant at the beginning but now seem loaded with presages, pathos, irony. The reader will have noticed, without doubt, the specific prophetic moments in the course of the day that are recounted in this novel, particularly toward nightfall; but there are elements in the first three quarters of the novel that cannot be meaningful for those who are ignorant of Lucita's death, unless it were evident to them. With extraordinary skill, Sánchez Ferlosio insinuates into his novel signs of the presence of a kind of fatalism that is only revealed *in toto* retrospectively and even then remains ambiguous.

This suggestion of a tragic destiny in action increases the intensity with which the emotions of the reader are aroused, contrary to what could be expected from a work where the characters are presented with such austere objectivity. And although we do not know Lucita as we do other literary characters into whose hearts and minds we are permitted to penetrate, when she drowns any reader of ordinary sensitivity ought to feel an emotion similar to that of a witness who, on the river's edge, would have observed the girl and ten other young people during the entire day. The implicit compassion of the first observer, Sánchez Ferlosio, is transmitted to the reader without the slightest sentimentality. . . .

[The ambiguous signs] constitute, in their very mystery, a vast part of the poetry that Sánchez Ferlosio integrates with artificiality in the prophetic realism of the novel. This realism and this poetry represent respectively the worlds of physical reality and of super-reality in whose obscure conjunction the logical incompatibilities can exist: such paradoxes like the fact that the hour of death is not determined until it has come, and once it has come, it had already been predetermined. Only in a few great works of literature has the eternal problem of universal determinism and the fortuitous nature of events been presented with such a piercing human quality.

Edward C. Riley. *Filología*. 9, 1963, pp. 202–3, 221†

In fighting against [an] outdated manner of writing the most conscientious of writers have been seeking, since the beginning of the century, a more coherent narrative syntax, one characterized by the elimination of the discursive intervention of the author from the body of the narrative in accordance with the model abstract literary category that Benveniste [a French structuralist] later called "histoire," i.e., "the presentation of things happening at a given moment without any intervention from the narrator in the relation." Benveniste tells us that in this type of narration there is not any narrator, nobody speaks within the narrative, the events are reported exactly as they are generated, as they appear over the horizon of the "histoire"; the events seem to tell themselves. An in-depth, cross-sectional examination of this trend in the novel during the first half of the twentieth century calls to mind work which, like *The Bold Ones* (1954) [of Jesús Fernández Santos] and *The Jarama* (1956), pass, and properly so, as the greatest achievements of our so-called "social novel." *The Jarama* doubtlessly signals the high point of this trend in the narrative; and it serves to reveal why later works of the same type seem to be simply redundant, shoots which neither strengthen nor debilitate the trunk or branches of the "tree of the novel"—as insignificant in the majority of cases as ubiquitous naturalist still-lifes which we see in the galleries of every city of the world.

Now, while *The Jarama* brilliantly brought to completion a full cycle in the history of our novel and excluded, due to its very perfection, the possibility of a whole new family of such works, there was beginning in Europe, chiefly in France, the development of a narrative form of an opposite type, which, fleeing the dryness and limitations of the literary category Benveniste called "histoire," was an attempt to renew the genre in the sense that, still using Benveniste's terminology, there resulted a vindication of "discours": expression through subjective language, or, if you prefer, "utterance that assumes a speaker and a listener, and in the former the intention to influence the latter."

Juan Goytisolo. *BUJ*. Spring, 1971, pp. 29–30

[*The Jarama*] closes as it began, with a few lines of textbook description of the river Jarama, thus hinting, like *The Projects and Wanderings of Alfanhuí,* at a completed cycle. Like a *da capo* in music we are invited to consider a sequence which would exactly repeat what had gone before. This is a formal solution to end a novel which would have no ending. The quotation by Leonardo da Vinci in the title page of *The Jarama* is, I think, intended to emphasize the monotony of life, the lack of a separate identity to each day. "The water that we touch in the rivers is the last of what has flowed by and the first of what will come." The passage of time is not visible in their lives, the water is always the same and an effort of imagination is needed to become aware of any divisions in it. I see in the characters' reference to the time of day a similar concern, the concern to impose a pattern of time where none is visible.

This avoidance of times allows Sánchez Ferlosio to make the absence of plot much more credible. What is suggested in this way is the absence of pattern, of meaning, of purpose in life. Like *The Projects and Wanderings of Alfanhuí, The Jarama* leads nowhere because Sánchez Ferlosio doesn't want it to lead anywhere. In *Alfanhuí,* it is, I think, the quality of the fantasy which sustains the reader's interest. In *The Jarama,* this is accomplished by giving the novel something which *looks like* a plot structure without being one; two groups of people in different places are described. There is the inn near the spot by the river where they spend most of the day, and there is the spot itself. The characters come and go from one place to the other. The author spends, say, five or six pages on each, breaking off abruptly at the end of each section. These breaks are indicated in the printed version by asterisks. In this way, a crude, primitive sort of plot, with pregnant doses of mild suspense, is created. Our involvement with the characters grows every time their presence is temporarily denied to us.

I suspect that half consciously we expect the two separate sets of events, or rather the two sets of simple conversations taking place in the inn and by the river, to meet at some significant point in the novel. As it is, they never do. The events in one place contribute nothing to the elucidation of the events in the other. Any suggestion of counterpoint, of parallelism or contrast is as deliberately avoided as causality was avoided in *Alfanhuí*. If life is meaningless, art must be meaningless too. Art could not afford to say that life was meaningless without, by the same token, becoming meaningful.

Salvador Bacarisse. FMLS. Sept., 1971, pp. 57–58

It seems to me the similarity between [Wallace] Stevens and Sánchez Ferlosio extends beyond the original and unique imagery. There is, to a point, a similarity of thought, perhaps better expressed as "feeling," between these two contemporary poetic writers. I find a strong relationship between Stevens' conception of his task to make of man himself the instrument of knowledge and the medium of universal value and Alfanhuí's [in *The Projects and Wanderings of Alfanhuí*] own self-appointed apprenticeship to the master and to the herbalist. In the course of these apprenticeships Alfanhuí is seen, first, as discovering the knowledge of how to create new forms of life. In addition to merely participating in the experiments under the guidance of a master, it is Alfanhuí himself who must descend to the cave and reveal to the master what he finds there. The master is unable to make the descent into the well, which symbolically may be taken to mean hidden secrets of nature. In the workshop of the herbalist, Alfanhuí penetrates the secrets of the nature of green things and of how these secrets must be learned. He learns how to know things in both life and death. Alfanhuí learns from his master that death is merely going to the kingdom where all colors—human attributes, emotions, memories?—unite to become white. This fact of importance to all mankind Alfanhuí reveals for our consolation, just as in "Sunday Morning" Stevens writes, "Death is the mother of beauty." The master's death quickly recalls this similarity to the mind of the reader familiar with Stevens' poetry.

Ruth M. Danald. Introduction to Rafael
Sánchez Ferlosio, The Projects and Wanderings
of Alfanhuí (West Lafayette, Ind., Purdue
University Press, 1975), pp. 22–23

The Projects and Wanderings of Alfanhuí reveals an unsuspected logic and internal consistency when one interprets it in relation to certain ideas drawn from the domains of anthropology and psychology. Seen in this way, it encloses a moral: that of the continuity of human existence. Modern man, in the period of "unconscious childhood," is the living archive of the spiritual experience of our species. The child's manner of perceiving the world and of relating himself to it displays a great number of archaic traits which coincide strikingly with what we know of primitive superstition, myth, ritual, taboo, religious and mystical experience. More than this, at a certain point in his development, at the moment of conscious awareness of his interaction with the world—the awakening of adolescence—he is forced into a new and painful state of consciousness; he becomes disorientated, separated from his tradition. Aware of his "self" as a separate object floating in a confused sea of external forces over which he no longer seems to have control, his problem is now that of discovering, or "retrieving the memory" of previous models of perception and thought which will enable him to continue his existence. The model lies in childhood, or so it seems to me that Sánchez Ferlosio is saying. This does not mean we must regress, but rather renew our tradition, in a spiritual sense. Wisdom (and the serenity it brings) is the discovery of a new innocence, the recreation in adult life of child-like, but not childish, perceptions of the world.

The moral I attribute to *Alfanhuí*—and I fully recognize that this may only be one of a number of completely different interpretations which the work is capable of sustaining—is not in itself new. The idea of the child-like spirit of the Wise has many precedents, from the Biblical "unless you become as a little child you shall not enter the Kingdom of Heaven," to Wordsworth's "Ode on Intimations of Immortality from Recollections of Early Childhood." What is significant, however, is that Sánchez Ferlosio's understanding of this theme seems to have come to him through a deep familiarity with the ideas of what are now called the classical psychologists and anthropologists—Jung, Frazer and so on. What is even more significant is that by giving literary form to these ideas, he has created an outstanding example of a type of fiction which I believe, so far as modern Spanish literature is concerned, has gone unidentified or at least has been little commented on. I qualify the statement because the phenomenon of "archetypal perception" has been identified elsewhere. The first reference to it, under the name of "the mythical method," must surely be that quoted by [Robert] Langbaum, of T. S. Eliot when the latter was reviewing James Joyce's *Ulysses*. I quote it again for its aptness: "Psychology (such as it is, and whether our reaction to it be comic or serious), ethnology and *The Golden Bough* have concurred to make possible what was impossible even a few years ago. Instead of the narrative method, we may now use the mythical method. It is, I seriously believe, a step forward towards making the modern world possible for art." I would place *Alfanhuí* firmly within this same, expressly modern tradition.

Harold Reynolds. *BHS*. July, 1976, pp. 223–24

It is indeed unfortunate that [*The Jarama*'s] *real* significance does not appear between its covers. *The Jarama* consequently comes off as a work without much art, profundity, insight or guts, simply because the author's preoccupation with an objectivist style and the problems of censorship in Spain precluded his direct revelation of the social criticism of the Spain he knows too well and in which he continues to live. Other writers of his generation, like Matute and Goytisolo, have proven themselves more courageous and artistically ebullient. Thus, *The Jarama,* if anything, represents for me a work of great frustration. I see it as a paradox since it pretends to reveal objectively the problems of a cross-section of Spain's lower middle class yet in actuality it reveals little directly about its characters or the society in which they move. We can consider *The Jarama* a successful experiment in writing if we take the author's word that he has completely realized his novel according to the limits he himself set for it—the parameters of action, time and place. *The Jarama* is quizzical, episodic, prolix, fascinating at times, but totally frustrating. Its style results from the dimension of an aesthetic that is not purely eclectic if we agree by conjecture on its huge French influence by the purveyors of the *nouveau roman.*

Sánchez Ferlosio himself is a question, a perpetual promise; Spanish letters must still await his evaluation. Although *The Jarama* as a novel would not augur well for psychological insights, it does succeed in establishing a new direction, a new style for other New Wave novelists to emulate. However, if we consider that "style is art" and what Ortega calls "dehumanization," then it is possible to stretch our convictions and judge *The Jarama* to be a true art work since the novel contains the elements of distance, artificiality and style. From my own view, *The Jarama* is more of a document, a trendsetter, an experiment, a startling new effort (in 1955) to renovate the decaying novel genre in Spain, a transitional work exemplary of "something rendered as a certain handling of the ineffable," perhaps a work of "art" more potent for its silence than for what it expresses.

Ronald Schwartz. *Spain's New Wave Novelists*
(Metuchen, N.J., Scarecrow, 1976), pp. 97–98

SASTRE, ALFONSO (1926–   )

There are many worthwhile things to praise in Sastre: his sense of the dramatic, his instinct for economy in staging, his effective dialogue—appropriate, sober, profound, and meaningful—his admirable ability for characterization, his desire to construct the drama from within, giving to it just what its internal development requires, and that courage to confront the most risky scenes. . . . All these qualities make him an important literary reality, not a promise to whatever offers him an opportunity. It does not matter, or it matters little, that at times one can recognize touches of other writers—*Desire Under the Elms* [of Eugene O'Neill] and certain plays of the French theater. . . .

If now, after this enumeration, I would ask myself why *The Gag* leaves me really unsatisfied deep down, and were I obliged to answer myself, I would have to say only the following: *The Gag* lacks beauty, not the beauty that is a result of an accumulation of purely formal values, but that other kind that we can call poetry. A "something" that permits us to be traitors along with Iago, cowards with Hamlet, arrogant men with Coriolanus, prevents us, on the other hand, to identify with Isaac Krappo, the protagonist of the drama. What is the virtue that establishes a profound interaction between the being of a character and that of the spectator? I know, of course, that it is indescribable. Alfonso Sastre has meticulously avoided it because of an excess of moral sense. Perhaps, in the last analysis, he has not wished to play the joke on us of making us feel as one with a few sordid types by means of poetry. It is not a defect of Alfonso Sastre. There are many writers today who avoid poetry. I am almost tempted to consider it a characteristic of the generation. [1957]

G. Torrente Ballester. *Teatro español contemporáneo,* 2nd ed. (Madrid, Guadarrama, 1968), p. 598†

The theatre of Alfonso Sastre is revolutionary in more than one sense. When we consider that the majority of the plays produced in Spain are intended to amuse a public of middle-class spectators without disturbing them too deeply, Sastre's originality is at once apparent. His plays are aimed at a much wider group than that represented by any single segment of the population, and every one of them betrays a profound preoccupation with man's problems and the meaning of his existence. They represent a revolt against the provincialism of the Spanish theatre, and an infusion of the most vital currents in world drama of the twentieth century. Don Alfonso's masters are not the Spanish dramatists of the late nineteenth century and early years of the twentieth, but the great renovators of western drama: Pirandello, O'Neill, and "the great master," Ibsen. Toller, Galsworthy, and Kaiser have all influenced him to some extent, and among living dramatists he feels affinities particularly with Sartre and Arthur Miller.

Such affinities and influences are based upon style as well as ideas. The mainstream of artistic and literary work in our epoch has been described by Sastre under the name "social-realism." It is logical then that he should be writing in that manner called "realistic," and trace his roots to the theatrical movement fostered by Antoine and the Théâtre Libre. . . .

Realism in Sastre's plays does not mean enslavement to photographic detail, but faithful reproduction of the language, emotions, and thinking of human beings. His style is nonrhetorical, with nothing of what is usually considered "poetic," the characters using an extremely lively and colloquial speech. Sastre excels in depicting scenes of everyday life among the working classes. Each of the characters in *Death in the Neighborhood* for example, is an individual, in spite of the fact that the major character in the drama is the neighborhood as a whole, the group which one evening in a bar kills a doctor because his irresponsibility caused the death of a child.

Scenes which show high pitches of feeling, extreme tension, and even extraordinary emotions are not eschewed. Indeed, there would be no tragedy without them, and the mystical frenzy of Professor Parthon in *The Blood of God* is as convincing as the quiet anguish of the mother in *Every Man's Bread,* condemned to death by her intransigent son's fidelity to the Party. For the most part, however, highly emotional scenes are rare and contrast dramatically with the very contained, almost silent tension which underlies many scenes.

Sastre's characters are alive not only because they speak a real language, but because they are free, and may react as they wish. The author does not hold their strings or force them to conform to a particular ideology—they are not the puppets of a thesis. This is one reason that it is often difficult to determine the dramatist's position. He sees not only his own point of view, but that of his antagonists, and therefore conserves a certain objectivity. It is sometimes with surprise or pain, Sastre tells us, that the dramatist hears certain words coming from his characters, but they are the character's words, and not the author's, and it would be dishonest to ignore them. Sastre has been astounded at the interpretations placed upon some of his plays. *Condemned Squad* has been called anti-militaristic, *Every Man's Bread* anti-communistic, *The Gag* pro-collaborationist, and *The Blood of God* pro-mystical. He has rewritten the ending of the latter play to make it clear that no divine intervention has occurred in the case of Jacob Parthon, as it did with Abraham and Isaac, whose story this play retells in modern terms.

Leonard C. Pronko. TDR. Dec., 1960, pp. 111–13

Sastre is a writer of the cities, and in most of his plays he is concerned with dramatizing the difficulty of maintaining one's sense of self within the context of demoralizing social forces. Like so many of his contemporaries, he is a child of the Spanish Civil War and his plays are aflame with his burning indignation over social and political injustice and corruption. For this reason, Spanish censorship practices being what they are, Sastre is what might be called an "underground playwright." His work is known, respected, and practically never produced in Spain. Furthermore, unlike so many of his fellow writers, Sastre is not so much a Spanish writer as he is European. All of his work is tinged with the despair and negation which characterize the main current of the modern theatre. The influences of Pirandello, Shaw, Ibsen, and Strindberg are clearly present. But so, too, strangely enough, is the social optimism of Arthur Miller, the playwright Sastre seems to respect and admire above all others.

Anna Kleiber was written as an experiment and is not typical of Sastre's other work. But the very absence of social stridency in this play may very well make it the best one he has written thus far. In it he attempts to come to grips with some of the most difficult problems confronting us all, and he refuses the too-easy solution of social reform that oftentimes weakens his other plays. Broadly, the theme of *Anna Kleiber* is the futility of life and the impossibility of love in the post World War II world. But like all generalizations, this is too easy and finally not descriptive of what he has achieved. . . . This play is really a drama of selfhood and it is concerned with the possibility of integrity in human relationships. The love affair between Anna and Alfredo is poignant and doomed. Their meetings are joyous, but because the lovers haven't the capacity to sustain their relationship their bliss is always short-lived. They separate and then their sense of loss is inconsolable. The old saw about not being able to live with each other or without each other is certainly applicable here. Throughout the play Sastre is conscious of the fact that while falling in love is an act of discovery, the relationship between lovers is a process of maintaining, and when the lovers are incapable of transforming the excitement and exhilaration of discovery into the strength of maintenance, their relationship flounders. The action of *Anna Kleiber,* then, concerns itself with man's bedevilled quest to find love. We need it and we seek it, but because of our divided and irreconcilable nature we are doomed in all of our attempts to achieve it. This hardly qualifies the play as a drama of selfhood, but Anna's death at the end of the play changes matters. She, after many failures, can finally accept the fact that her relationship with Alfredo can never be. Rather than destroy him, she chooses to end her own life. This may be a negative action, but it is not without heroism. Anna, even in her realization that man must always fail in his attempt to achieve an enduring love, is nevertheless still capable of a freely chosen act of love. In her death, failure is somehow vindicated. Sastre seems to be asserting his belief that, flawed though man may be, he is capable of an act of integrity; and from this sense of wholeness we impose meaning on the void.

Robert W. Corrigan. In Robert W. Corrigan, ed.,
The New Theatre of Europe (New York, Dell,
1962), pp. 21–22

Some critics have said that *Condemned Squad* is an anti-military play, a cry against war and extreme discipline. Others see in it just the op-

posite: a call for discipline and military authority. Both of these interpretations miss the mark. Sastre's play is not a war play in the ordinary
sense despite the fact that it deals with the fate of five privates and a
corporal awaiting an offensive in an isolated forester's cabin during an
imaginary third world war. The setting may be timely but the theme is
timeless: the story of six men in a dramatic crucible. The only significant object in an unfurnished void is the human figure, more or less ugly
and infirm. These men are haunted by the expectation of something
(symbolized by the offensive) that is continually delayed—the same
"something" for which we live or die. Like most people, they are
capable of feeling that existence is at once both unsupportable and
indispensable. The brutal assassination of the Corporal is a grotesque
blow for freedom; whether their freedom will become liberation or
bondage is the suspended note on which the action of Part I comes to
an end.

The death of Goban permits the action to enter a phase of anti-
action. Anguish replaces rebellion as the tale takes on an almost myth-
like march in a rapidly descending denouement. When Javier says,
"Goban was here to punish us and allowed himself to be killed," he
suggests that the weaving together of their lives was fated, unwilled, as
in classical Greek tragedy. From the very beginning, they had no power
to change the void. . . . The real theme of *Condemned Squad*, therefore, is what Eugene O'Neill called "not the relation of man to man but
the relation of man to God." It is the dilemma of living and dying found
in plays like O'Neill's *The Iceman Cometh,* Sartre's *No Exit,* Beckett's
Waiting for Godot, A Sleep of Prisoners by Christopher Fry, and *Tiny
Alice* by Edward Albee. . . .

One senses that Sastre is writing about real problems, about
human problems. He does not infringe on the mystery and confusion
that is part of every human soul. He does not intend to clear things up,
clean them up, straighten them up, oversimplify, or indulge in any kind
of dramatic trickery. With unrelenting honesty, he goes straight to the
heart of the people he creates and, by his honesty and compassion,
makes worth while a searching examination of their characters and
fates.

Anthony M. Pasquariello. Introduction to
Alfonso Sastre, *Escuadra hacia la muerte* (New
York, Appleton-Century-Crofts, 1967), pp. 5–6, 8

From [*Sad Are the Eyes of William Tell*] and [*Red Earth*] and other
Sastre plays—*Every Man's Bread, Death in the Neighborhood, In the
Net, The Gag*—one can see that rebellion is Sastre's recurrent theme.
The rebels are idealistic people who wish to be free but have no lust for
power, no deep-seated feelings of vengeance. The avengers never rejoice in death. They may feel an exhilaration for having acted, but they
turn immediately to realistic thoughts about the consequences and to

the planning of the next phase. On a few occasions—*Anna Kleiber, Death Thrust, The Blood of God*—a protagonist exhibits psychopathic weaknesses, but they are in general simple men whose conscious minds are in control of their emotions. The regular low-key approach makes the men seem plausibly delineated despite their idealism.

We may now arrive at some tentative conclusions. The primary emotion that Sastre feels is anger, which is often directed toward the tyranny of those in authority. In *The Gag* it is one man's tyranny over his family. In *Death Thrust* it is the promoter's tyranny over the bullfighter. The force which oppresses the protagonist is not cosmic. The spectator is allowed to assume that at least in theory this force can be overcome. Sastre leaves open the question as to whether the offending authority can be replaced by a more enlightened one. *Red Earth* at least suggests that tyranny is likely to endure despite all efforts against it.

Sastre has an excessive preoccupation with violent death. In theory he wishes to avoid melodrama since it is ineffective in mobilizing for lasting social reform. His Dostoyevskian interest in the psychology of murder is quite interesting in itself, but fails to achieve either the development of the classic tragic hero or the realistic social action that Sastre so earnestly seeks.

Sastre does not always have a hero. Too often the victim of tyranny is weak, ineffectual, drawing more derision than pity from the author. Where there is a hero, he is still likely to be ineffectual because of being surrounded by weak people, but he upholds the dignity of man and refuses to compromise this dignity to preserve his life. Therefore, despite the latent strength of Sastre's protest, the hero does not have the breadth and depth of character for the spectator to feel the strong compassion that tragedy demands.

Sad Are the Eyes of William Tell provides an interesting straw in the wind and a possible key to an understanding of Sastre's nature. Tell repudiates the whole idea of the traditional tragic hero. Overcome with grief, he sees no reason why he should be honored in the sacrifice of his son. He is disdainful of those who would idolize him. We who admire the great heroes of classic tragedy must include ourselves in Tell's condemnation. We purge our emotions vicariously in the exploits and downfall of the tragic hero when we should become as angry as Sastre toward the forces of tyranny which are ever with us. If we follow him we would marshal our nervous energy to successful overthrow of all those who would mock the dignity of man. To accept this premise we must sacrifice our idea of the titanic hero. Sastre's hero is no larger than life.

Granting Sastre's knowledge of the history and nature of the theater and his emotional interest in striking a blow for man's freedom and dignity, we may yet see him pen a work which can qualify as great tragedy. We may hope so; Spain needs him. Meanwhile we can at least admire the efforts he has made in drama to stir us into action against our omnipresent evils.

John A. Moore. *SAB*. May, 1970, pp. 27–28

Ultimately one sees in Alfonso Sastre's vision, and in its literary formulation, a desire to reintegrate modern man, alienated from himself, his fellow men, and the forces that control his life. A fundamental suggestion of Sastre's best work is that modern humanity is the fragmented, neurotic result of social systems that turn people into objects, foment a split between the individual's personal and social lives, and render the complete personality impossible. Recovery of this personal completeness is implicit in Sastre's call for a realism that reflects both extremes of the fragmented human being, with the hope of achieving synthesis, or reintegration. However, this recovery can be realized at the personal level only through implantation of a humanistic social context for the individual's activities.

In his works for the theater and his prose writing Sastre uses the phenomenon of alienation as a dramatic element. It is the ultimate source of the loneliness and anguish that torment his characters. The acts through which his heroes find their authenticity are painful precisely because one can become a real human being (recover his humanity) only by establishing a burning friction between himself and the forces that undermine his integrity. The polarized forces that produce dramatic conflict in much of Sastre's work are precisely the individual and the vaguely perceived determinants of his destiny. The condemned squad suffers because its enemy is inscrutable, as do the characters of *The Raven*. Luis Ophuls [in *The Blood of God*] defines God as "absolutely different." The tyrant of William Tell's country is nicknamed "The Other" because he lives and thinks apart from the men whose lives he controls. Miguel Servet [in *Blood and Ashes*] is consumed by a passion that drives him to seek unity in the universe. *Lugubrious Nights* presents imaginary human beings being tormented by their inability to define the forces that pursue them. Until men become absolute ends, rather than objects, and until the individual knows, and becomes, the force that controls his life, unity will not be realized, and anguish will continue to be the prime characteristic of human existence.

Like the thinkers who have influenced him, Sastre realizes that man's existence can be meaningful only when he is free, and that freedom exists only as the correlative of fluidity, change, and ultimate reunification of the human being. The rational enunciation and aesthetic embodiment of these truths are the tasks to which Sastre has passionately dedicated himself.

Farris Anderson. *Alfonso Sastre* (New York, Twayne, 1971), pp. 144–45

[Sastre] has . . . made an attempt to fashion a work of his own in the matrix of Complex Tragedy [Sastre's term for the dialectical interaction of the avant-garde and the New Objectivism]. It is *Blood and Ashes: Dialogues of Miguel Servet,* a play refused publication in Spain. . . .

In it, Sastre, dramatizing the tragic plight of a sixteenth-century Spanish physician and theologian who was burned at the stake in Geneva, employs some comic relief and a plentiful display of modern stage effects such as lighting, ballads, projections, and tapes, all designed to "complex" his tragic work.

Servet, in a series of dialogues, makes a sharp attack on the Trinity, and expresses his concern for freedom of the press, his ideas on the circulation of the blood, and his sympathy for those afflicted by the plague. Yet what shines through most clearly is a parallel between the times of the Inquisition and those of Hitler. In accordance with the principle of the delayed "recognition effect," the Spanish audience would be expected to react, belatedly ("boomerang"), against a current counterpart of Inquisition-Hitlerian oppression, which is, for Sastre, the Franco dictatorship. Such a reaction would constitute the cathartic commitment of Complex Tragedy.

With this first attempt at Complex Tragedy Sastre was attempting to educate the public to the "new theater." He expects to add other works in a similar vein, following out his theory of Dialectical Realism as applied to the writing of Complex Tragedy today, and he hopes other dramatists will follow his lead.

In essence, then, Sastre is applying his dramatic theory (Dialectical Realism), inspired by Marxist doctrines, to the writing of revolutionary theater. This theater, the dialectical outgrowth of earlier types of drama, is expected to foster a growing awareness of the true dialectical evolution of history. And that evolution, which, for Sastre, is at a prerevolutionary stage in a decadent Spain, is expected ultimately to produce a radical change in Spanish national life.

In this way is it possible for art—Complex Tragedy today—to intervene meaningfully in the social process, illuminating the need for commitment by audiences to sociopolitical activism, thereby helping to pave the way for the socialist revolution.

Francis Donahue. ArQ. Autumn, 1973, pp. 212–13

An assessment of Sastre's theatre as it has developed over a period of more than twenty years reveals both constancy and change, variety and consistency. From the early plays and their portrayal of man's anguish in an incomprehensible and hostile world, Sastre has continued to dramatize the tragedy of injustice in increasingly specific terms. Specific problems have come to be a point of departure, a manifestation of the ills of a society not attuned to alleviate human problems but rather to further the interests of those in power. The focus on the individual in a dual role has remained constant. Sastre's protagonists have not changed in their determination to take definitive heroic action for the sake of human dignity against the powers which threaten it. Their portrayal as vulnerable dependents on love and belonging has become increasingly skillful as Sastre's theatre has developed. As an innovator and philosophical thinker Sastre has taken for himself the difficult task of bringing together the contradictions inherent in an inclusive vision of life which avoids preconceived notions of good and evil and pat formulas for change. Early in his career he identified realism as the appropriate medium for a committed dramatist, and he has remained innovative in an expanding concept of the meaning of realism and tragedy. From an adherence to Aristotelian principles, his plays have become increasingly Brechtian. Yet elements of epic theatre were present in his early plays; and his first important play, *Condemned Squad,* relied on situation and characters rather than on plot.

The most important contradiction to be faced by Sastre from his present vantage point is that of remaining outside the charmed circle of success and acceptance while being no longer young and avant garde. Even now, living in exile, he looks to a near future in which there will be a new freedom in Spanish theatre. How Sastre's theatre might have developed in another time or place, free from a hostile and rigorous censorship, cannot be determined. What new climate for his work may be created in Spain remains to be seen.

Lynette Seator. *PLL.* Spring, 1979, pp. 222–23

SENDER, RAMÓN J. (1901–1982)

No novel of contemporary Spain, and certainly no novel about the revolutionary forces in contemporary Spain, can be discussed at the present moment in terms of its literary value alone. Were *Seven Red Sundays* even less of a novel than it is, it would retain signal importance as a comment and a revelation; it offers one of the clearest and fullest accounts available, I think, of the ideas and type of men now embroiled in Spain. What gives the book its depth as a novel, however, is the very nature of that information, for *Seven Red Sundays* has the conception, if not the richness of texture, of some of the finest novels that have been concerned with twentieth-century man in his role of political animal.

Sender has written, as André Malraux did before him, a study of revolutionary portent and failure, and has cleverly evoked thereby all the atmosphere of crisis. In this extremely acute novel about the revolutionary instinct, he has conveyed the same sensation of futility that faces the philosophical revolutionary. Most of the characters in this novel do not know that futility: they are immersed in their plans for action, carried away by compulsions. They are the men without good will—the anarchists who hate "culture" because it is the property of their landlords, their political rivals, their church: the young hopefuls of the revolution who have never had a life of their own, the underdogs who have been bludgeoned into submission, and will bludgeon others to gain their freedom or the appearance of it. . . .

By reflecting in the pattern of his narrative the actual confusion and excitement of their minds, Sender has given the masses a single character and the novel a collective drama. "My method is logical," he explains in his preface, "because chaos has its own logic." Occasionally, it must be said, the logic is concealed within the chaos. In an effort to convey the psychology of the group, he has divided some of its principal emotions among individuals who are not characterized adequately: as a result, the emotions of some are not intelligible and the turmoil supposed to be indicative of the group, or of its environment, becomes external to it—the looseness of the narrative reveals nothing, in these passages, but the looseness of the narrative.

As a whole, however, Sender's intention is fulfilled. Thus, though the ostensible scene is Madrid, the larger issues at stake, and with them the future of Spain, hang over the scene like an imperceptibly falling curtain. The real crisis has not been broken when the novel ends: the strike has failed, the Communists still quarrel with the anarchists, and the latter still deride the Socialists. Is Plato bourgeois or not? What shall they do with Marx? But it is only a moment, one knows, remembering what is happening today as one reads, until they will all be bombed from the air by the men who flogged them so familiarly in police stations. What Sender makes you feel is that they know it too.

Alfred Kazin. NYHTB. Oct. 11, 1936, p. 11

In *Dark Wedding* [i.e., *The Wedding Song of Dark Trinidad*] Ramón Sender does not succeed in solving the problem of how to deal with misery and the brutalization that results from it, but at least he makes a considerable and admirable effort. He has chosen the method of fantasy and symbolism. His story begins in sober and rather brilliant realism and tells of the director of a Latin American penal island who returns to the colony with his new young bride and, after a more than usually brutal display of authority, is murdered on his wedding night. From there, by gradual stages, the story moves into fantasy as the convicts, insane to a man, struggle for the political control of the island and the possession of the virgin widow. The fantasy is wild and sometimes obscure, but the ideational intention of the book is always kept clear—it is that the horrible past crimes of the convicts and their present lust for the girl are, despite all appearances, actually perversions of love and twisted manifestations of the ideal; and this idea is of sufficient scope to require that the mind keep pace with the emotions as we read; and it effectually keeps us from *condescending* to the almost inhuman creatures we are reading about.

Perhaps the comparison will seem extravagant and certainly it is bitterly unfair to an admirable if not wholly successful book, but there are many elements in *Dark Wedding* which brought *King Lear* to my mind. Both works are concerned to show man as naked as possible; both have a plethora of madness, by which they achieve their largest effects; both are pervaded by the themes of justice and both involve justice with sexuality; in both there is a dominant sense of the horror of nature (of creeping, crawling, and decaying things) as well as of the terror of nature, and both constantly question whether nature is good or bad; in both love in its perfection (Cordelia; the virgin widow) is true salvation, in its perversion (Goneril, Regan; the mad convicts) the source of evil. . . .

But eventually Sender does not succeed. The pressure turns out to be insufficient. The symbols cease to work, the language becomes false . . . because eventually Sender's moral sensibility does not support them. His moral sensibility is modern: like all of us, he wants to hope, and since hope is hard to come by these days, he descends to facile optimism. Throughout the book I had the uncomfortable awareness that even a gifted modern man cannot discourse about "love" without making it seem disconcertingly squashy. When the young hero, the schoolteacher Darío, begins to think of himself as "Lord of the Dawn," the débacle of sensibility begins; and when the hitherto sinister convicts begin showering the young lovers with the thousand-peso bills of the stolen fortune, the fantasy begins to deflate to the dimensions of a René Clair picture. . . . This collapse is dispiriting but it does not negate the energy and the rightness of the book's intention.

Lionel Trilling. *Nation.* April 24, 1943, pp. 603–4

The world of Sender's most recent novel [*The Affable Hangman*] is one assembled, stumbled upon—as a man will stumble—again of necessity. We cannot call Ramiro "the affable hangman" until we have also stumbled, willynilly, into or upon, that thread of *occasional* purpose by which a man directs himself, given eyes and mouth, hands and legs, and a mind, and also a heart. . . .

An account of Love is, loosely enough, what later commentators have called the "picaresque novel," i.e., a story of a man who travels much, who becomes involved in untoward events for singular reasons, and who "distills" (as the book-jacket in the case of Sender's novel puts it) an "idiosyncratic" philosophy.

Yet Ramiro is a hangman: "he felt real gratitude toward me (the story's narrator) because I had offered him my hand, knowing that he was a hangman . . ."; and Love would do no less.

But why does a man become a hangman—these days? Or, better, how is it that a man—in whom love moves, or else he is not—arrives at that "authority" which allows, as Ramiro's instructor does: "It is not that one is ashamed of one's work. Someone has to do it, and nowadays they don't mistreat the *pobreto*—poor wretch—as before, but dispatch him neatly and rapidly . . ." And is not this, also, a rather *familiar* "man's world"?

Faced with a loyalty to this or that idea, he finds himself on either "side," in this case on the one hand witness of the killing of men and women with whom he has sided, and, later, on the side, of those who have killed them, at another like incident, where men are forced to jump into a well and then sticks of dynamite are thrown in after them.

Sender's method, in this book, is a constantly shifting character of "reality," i.e., of fable, of naturalistic detail—of the supposed "real" put against the hyper- or also-real. And in the narrative occur other "stories," for example of Lucia, who is in love with her sister's husband, whom she denounces, whereupon he is killed. . . .

When Ramiro was a little boy, his mother "told tales that made (him) cry with pain, and then she would tell everybody how tender-hearted (he) was . . ." What is the man who will witness, and thereby "do" what all others imply, but will not do—as, for example, we all know that this or that has to be done, yet wait for someone to do it. Is that why we have armies, etc.? At the close of the book Ramiro and the narrator are sitting in a cafe, talking. Noise is heard outside. A fiesta of some kind seems to be starting. . . . People are all around the cafe, the building: the two men are "prisoners," and then going out Ramiro asks "questions to the right and left of him, but no one seemed to give a satisfactory answer."

Robert Creeley. BMtR. Summer, 1955, pp. 20–24

Ramón Sender, beyond any doubt the greatest Spanish novelist of this century, with his first book of poems [*The Migratory Images*] obliges us to consider once again, and more radically than ever, the problem of the essence of Spain. For there can be few books as tremendously Spanish as this one, where the soul of writer and man is revealed in a new light. Only Spanish literature is exclusively oriented to man *per se* in all its periods. Even Spanish transcendentalism, treated by Vossler and others, is an invention of absolute values merely to justify vital immanency. In Spain the mystic himself went no further than the study of the states of consciousness: the creation of objective worlds describing other superior realities of the beyond did not interest the Spaniard. Hence the most authentic Spanish literature has two dimensions, revolving around a kind of proud modesty: the metaphysical and the social atmosphere.

Sender's novelistic work has been the best evidence in our time of the metaphysical and social intensity of true Spanish literary creation.

His primordial concern, and perhaps we could say that this is unique with him, has been bitter and impassioned insight, filled with love of life and existential anguish. Both related to immediate destiny as well as the final value of living. Sender's originality is due in part to his purity and intensity, but above all to certain exclusive qualities derived from his intuition of the world.

These personal traits so evident in Sender's novelistic creation now appear in the field of poetry. Sender is a radical existentialist in both his poetry and novels, while at the same time he is closer to us as well as beyond existentialism. The trait of cutting sobriety in this tendency of twentieth century Spanish poetry (not all of it—there is also a basically essentialist position in the Spanish poetry of this century, as exemplified in Juan Ramón Jiménez and Federico García Lorca) consists in getting along without recurring to absolutes. . . . Life is not only our creation, our responsibility, the result of our choice, in the manner popularized by Sartre, but an elemental force making us become what we are. And this reality more powerful than our determination is not only life in a biological sense, but the meaning of spiritual vitality.

Sender loves the immediate realities intensely and enjoys natural pleasures despite the constant presence of transcendental anguish. In *The Migratory Images* Sender appears not only impassioned but virilely sensual. Virility does not depend on show or ostentation and is fundamentally in direct opposition to it. Virility depends on the frankness and strength of expression of man's attitude toward women, society, and the surrounding world. In this sense Sender appears naturally and passionately involved in the joys of life and love, and even profoundly impassioned. Nothing could be further from him than the purely spiritual attitude of most of the Generation of '98 and the 1914 group (Machado, Juan Ramón Jiménez). Here as elsewhere Sender is closer to the mode of feeling of his admired Valle-Inclán, though lacking the latter's superficial sense of perversion, knowing as he does that we are born with the inherent seed of sin even before we commit our first innocent offense by soiling the sheets on our cradles.

Rafael Bosch. BA. Spring, 1963, pp. 132–33

[Sender's] progress, obviously, has been from the social protest to the metaphysical quest. His method has become increasingly surrealistic but at the same time more abstract and theoretical. Since 1938, when he settled in the United States, he has written nostalgically about his youth and childhood in the *roman-fleuve* which begins with *Chronicle of Dawn* (1942): Pepe Garcés drifts gradually from place to place, hemmed in at first by an excitable father, a jeering older sister and a weeping younger one; then escapes to a steadfast sweetheart called Valentina, with whom he hunts grasshoppers, sacrifices a pigeon and eventually practises free love. The second section of the trilogy deals with schooldays in the monastery at Reus, where the fiery boy and a humble lay brother achieve a profound friendship that Sender has the sense to present without philosophizing, but studs with little items from the boyhood caper—communal yawns during the Good Friday sermon, jaundice induced by taking saffron, and gulling the devout young Catalonians. Such a return to the source, a movement backwards and then forwards into our own times again, is a natural enough action: Sender, in exile, is retracing his steps, becoming more and more mystical as he goes. The struggle upwards (of man in general) and the individual effort to attain self-definition (sometimes through a Cause, a revolt or a passionate defence) are Sender's themes. Arturo Barea's estimation of him as "the only important novelist of the young pre-Civil War generation" is just. But Sender, like Malraux, reaches a vision of plenitude and peace only through increased inattention to the immediate contemporary scene. The compassionate, deep, brave, active man of the world is still there, but he has to be inferred from beneath the veils of mystagogy. Previously, we had to take care to credit the man of action (Malraux too) with his mystical inwardness, which it was easy to overlook.

Paul West. *The Modern Novel,* Vol. II (London,
Hutchinson, 1963), p. 416

For Sender the historical novel is always a *pretext* for speaking about "Spanishness," which he always contrasts with other racial or national values. Nothing is linear in Sender. In *Mr. Witt in the Canton* an Englishman is the protagonist; in *Byzantium* the real protagonist is the Greco-Bulgarian Princess María; in *Carolus Rex* we see a contrasting character in Queen María Luisa of Orléans; in *The Tontos of Conception Mission,* we have as background the Indians and as foreground the Indian Ginesillo; in *The Equinoctial Adventure of Lope de Aguirre* we also have as background the world of Indians; in *Three Novels of Teresa* a contrast hardly exists because it is the least historical of all the novels, although foreign elements, like the oriental tone of the *auto,* the execution of the Flemish Baron Montigny, etc., are not lacking. And in *Saturnian Creatures,* "Spanishness" is mixed in with "Russianness," "Frenchness," "Italianness," "Moorishness," and "Persianness," even "Australianness."

Sender does not forget about this *pretext,* literarily speaking. I mean that he does not mistreat or disparage the historical elements. More than once we have seen him dust off archives, copy down old documents, and even offer us discovered dossiers and interpretations of questionable points of history, for their own sake. But he is not a slave to this historical pretext for that reason alone; it is that he chooses to deal with history because of his own sovereign creative will.

Francisco Carrasquer. *Imán y la novela
histórica de Sender* (London, Támesis, 1970), p. 253†

If *Requiem for a Spanish Peasant* is a narrative noted for its stark realism and expressive austerity, within a tight unity of classical length, *The Affable Hangman* is a good example of a more complex structure, of a baroque framework, which Sender has also given to other works. . . . Besides *The Affable Hangman,* the works that fit into this group are *The Wedding Song of Dark Trinidad, The King and the Queen, The Five Books of Ariadne, Chronicle of Dawn* (the totality of the nine books that compose the series and in particular the next to the last one, "The Shore Where Madmen Smile"), *Saturnian Creatures,* and various short stories.

In his baroque narrations Sender does not use amorphous verbal accumulations that often do not necessarily result in a greater depth of expression, as Joyce does. In this type of narrative technique, which frequently produces an effect that is similar to that of a slow-moving camera, details (stasis) and chaos (ambiguity) are often confused with profundity. Nor is Sender inclined toward violent distortions or dislocations of time, of place, or of narrative point of view, techniques which on occasion end up being pure gimmickry. Such formal devices, which appear combined in many outstanding contemporary novels, are usually directed toward an expression of the vital chaos in which the action develops, as well as pointing, in displays of experimental virtuosity, to questions about the possibilities and limits of narrative art. In Sender, the baroque complexities—which in part pursue analogous objectives—focus around less drastic methods and more subtle structural combinations. Instead of violent and complicated dislocations in the action, or torrential accumulations of words, he uses an equally complicated interweaving of multiple and less perceptible thematic focuses, in an organic whole that displays several spinoffs of the central theme. From different vital and narrative levels, such an interweaving, which is essentially dynamic, continues to produce a framework of strong contrasts and subtle shadings that creates multiple perspectives for the most important concerns of the author: the exploration of the nature of "reality"; the desire to get to the bottom of the ultimate meaning of good and evil on the border of conventional attitudes; and the determination to delve into the dark corners of man's soul.

Marcelino C. Peñuelas. *La obra narrativa de Ramón J. Sender* (Madrid, Gredos, 1971), pp. 157–58†

Sender's *A Man's Place* is set in a rural province in Spain; the narrative time is the mid-twenties and the story reaches back through more than sixteen years into the first decade of this century; the action turns on a miscarriage of justice, and both oppressors and oppressed are vividly characterized; the narrator is a liberal. (Sender himself fought on the loyalist side during the Spanish Civil War; Malraux had already shown in *Man's Hope* how to sacrifice that experience to the greater glory of Z [Zeitgeist].) Now Zeitgeist sternly adjures his votaries west of the iron curtain, and maybe east of it, too, but I know little about that: Government is bad; the State is the enemy of the individual; all inequality is unjust; the rulers and institutions of our society must be changed; dissent, reform, rebel. (Marx, that Hegelian, seems to have in Mao his extremest descendant: Mao, I conjecture, is so zealous for Zeitgeist, believes so fanatically in the spiritually enriching benefits of rebellion, that in the mid-60s he stimulated the young of China to rebel against his own regime. Surely this is a new thing under the sun?) Sender's story obviously contains ingredients useful for fulfilling Z's solemn adjurations. The second of the book's three sections centers on the trial, breaking, and long imprisonment of two innocent people; this is clearly one of the set occasions for high Zeitgeistery, as Koestler demonstrated in *Darkness at Noon* for the 30s, Orwell in *1984* for the 40s, and Malamud in *The Fixer* for the 60s. Sender turned down every such opportunity, doing something quite other instead. But though (perhaps because?) he did what he did very well, this novel of his has been punished by obscurity.

To begin with, the story does not force or encourage or even permit you to identify with the victims (for some reason Z seems to be keen that readers should "identify with" characters and especially with victims). Sender is impartial: he keeps you at the same distance, emotionally and morally, from both rulers and ruled. He shows both—with sympathy, true, but also with a nearly comic detachment—as part of the same social system, yet without insisting that you see The System, The Establishment, The State, as the supervillain of which even the victimizers are victims. The crimes in the novel are all impure, even the cruel ones committed by agents of the State, and so are all the characters, even the most unfortunate and victimized. So too are the reader's emotions impure; my own got so complex that I threw up my hands, not knowing whose side to take. I took everybody's side. And this is the sin against the Holy-Spirit-of-the-Age for which there is no forgiveness. What the god likes is good guys against bad guys, or, at the very least, us against them.

George P. Elliott. *Conversions* (New York, E. P. Dutton, 1971), pp. 32–33

The Sphere has a philosophical-metaphysical dimension: the self and its differentiation, the concept of the "sphere" as a symbol of wholeness and recurrence, the influences of Aben Tofail, Schopenhauer, Otto and modern physics. It can be viewed merely from the point of view of plot: a familiar story of love and murder, crime, discovery and retribution. There is also a basic and ancient myth that underlies these other perspectives, a myth which provides a unifying poetic vision. *The Sphere* can be seen also as an existential novel, sharing certain characteristics with novels of Sartre and Camus, and attempting a total ethical and existential world-view that does not exclude the problem of God's presence or lack of presence in the life of contemporary Western man. These diverse perspectives and the wide-ranging speculation have perplexed some critics, but for others, including the present writer, the difficulties and ambiguities—and the clarities—of *The Sphere* have served to heighten interest and admiration.

Though Sender's early novels (*Magnet*, 1930; *Public Order*, 1931; *Night of the Hundred Heads*, 1934; *Seven Red Sundays*, 1932) have tended toward an overt and unequivocal social criticism, symbolic and poetic elements, though subdued, have never been absent from his style. The war and its suffering appear to have radically transformed his approach to the novel, a fact which some critics, who should know better, never seem to have recognized. Novels such as *The King and the Queen* (1949), *A Man's Place* (1939), *The Wedding Song of Dark Trinidad* (1942), and *The Sphere* are essentially philosophical, poetic, and symbolic, and the social criticism, which is not totally obscured, is relegated to the background.

The Sphere, is, in one of its facets, an autobiographical novel, a "confession" according to the categories of Northrop Frye. Its hero's name is Saila, which is "alias" written backwards, that is, Sender himself, or his alter ego. The incidents, and Saila's adventures, of course, need not be autobiographical. But, like his creator, Saila, a Spaniard, is sailing toward America after the Spanish holocaust that was a prelude to World War II. Saila's prejudices and inclinations are Sender's own. It is difficult to separate Saila the creation from Sender the author: and Sender's repeated affirmation that *The Sphere* is his most ambitious and definitive work suggests that this novel is the most complete expression of the whole or "spherical" man and artist, a man of flesh and blood.

Julian Palley. Symposium. Summer, 1971,
pp. 171–72

Ramón Sender is an original voice in the Spanish fiction of this century, and an established figure in world literature. Though primarily a novelist, he has written substantially in other genres—short story, drama, poetry, essay, and journalistic articles. In fundamental substance and vision his prolific literary work over more than four decades reveals a remarkable unity and consistency. Exploring a few fundamental concepts, Sender has written about them from widely different angles and under a surprising variety of conditions, times, and places. Disdainful of excessive attention to style, he has written much and polished little; consequently, the totality of his production is highly uneven in quality but includes numerous passages which can surely rank with the best Spanish literature of all times.

Since his earliest works Sender has exhibited pronounced philosophical and metaphysical preoccupations, and his writing has served him as a vehicle for ceaseless probing of certain immutable problems of existence, especially for the question of death or man's mortality, but also of the enigma of evil in the individual and in the world at large, the struggle of the individual for self-realization and a sense of worth (because he is human), man's desperate need for a transcendent ideal, the search for an ultimate basis for moral judgments, and the function of the mysterious and the nonrational in life (seen as originating in the unconscious). Sender has made a constant effort to comprehend and reflect total or "essential" reality in his work; in such a view, he ever seeks to accommodate both life and death, reason and intuition, "good" and "evil," the "real" and the "unreal," etc. His deep sense of human worth is rooted in his private view of the ultimate nature of reality, a view which has given him a feeling of essential unity with all mankind and has motivated his vital interest in the social and political issues of today; his work has never lost its dimension of quixotic protest against social injustice.

The most distinctive contribution Sender's fiction makes to Spanish and world literature of this century is its peculiar fusion of ordinary or "photographic" realism with fantastic and lyrical metaphysical dimensions. Ordinary reality is only the necessary supporting base allowing the author to launch incursions (sometimes successful, sometimes unsuccessful) into the realm of the mysterious, the marvelous, and the lyrical-metaphysical. Successful merging of the two "worlds" creates a new twilight "world," pregnant with poetic truth and capable of opening the "eyes" of the reader to new ways of perceiving that mysterious reality we call life. Don Ramón's "realism" is in accord with the generally antirealistic tendency of European literature in recent decades. In originality and depth of thought and vision, poetic sense, human understanding, breadth of interest, and sheer volume of production, I know of no living Spanish writer who can equal Ramón Sender.

Charles L. King. Ramón J. Sender (New York,
Twayne, 1974), pp. 166–67

The intertextual richness of *The Golden Fish* is two-pronged; that is, the novel . . . can be read against historical treatises and recorded documents of the day. However, more interesting is the notion that it can be read against Sender's other novels. It is as if Sender were discoursing on the problems of the historical novel by having written *The Golden Fish*. What part fact? What part fiction? Or should the reader just give up and be contented with reading "faction"?

Faithful readers of Sender are rewarded by seeing here certain themes further developed and techniques re-employed in a slightly different manner. For instance, the Platonist discussions about the separation of men and women into two distinct entities have been spoken before in *The Five Books of Ariadne;* the deaf and dumb virgin Dodoette is a combinatory character who has her roots in the bionic woman Tánit of the novel of the same name, and the off-beat Lizaveta of *Saturnian Creatures,* which happens to take place in part in Russia also; the allegorical play with biblical resonances that Sender interpolates in the middle of the novel recalls other such interpolations, as in *In the Life of Ignacio Morel* and *The King and the Queen. . . .*

It may, therefore, not be too presumptuous to suggest that part of the discursive indulgence, especially the conversations between the truth-seeking Alexander I and his part-time mistress, the mystical but fiercely intelligent Mme. de Krüdener, conversations that border on apocalyptic gossip or just plain post-pubescent intellectualisms, are attempts to wink at the growing coterie of Sender followers, by testing their knowledge, if not their patience, about the rest of his literary production. Unfortunately, it is these long discursive passages that weaken the novel, making it an uneven work. But then again, Sender is an uneven novelist. Who can expect or dare demand sixty or so perfect books from one author?

The intertextual encounter of *The Golden Fish* has another dimension that is related to the supra-structure of the novel. Basically the novel details a peregrination; Alexander is a sort of pilgrim en route to Russia from France somewhere between 1814 and 1815 after an enormously successful campaign against Napoleon, which has brought him innumerable encomiums throughout all of Europe. His trip to Russia brings him full circle.

Coincidentally, *Magnet,* Sender's first novel, unavailable in Spain for over forty years, has recently been republished; it is also historical in nature, but paints an immediate history of the Moroccan War of the '20's. *Magnet* leads us back to the idea of peregrination as a model for novelistic structure, for its protagonist Viance also goes on a pilgrimage through a war-torn landscape and finally returns to Spain, himself torn and unable to surmount history. Therefore, it can be seen that 1976 is an important year for Sender; his own work has come full circle—itself a type of pilgrimage in which the parentheses of his historical works, *Magnet* and *The Golden Fish,* are structured in an echoic fashion around the idea of pilgrimage. . . .

Alexander's return to Russia, though, is not altogether similar to Viance's return to Spain, although the consequences may be homologous. It is not that Alexander cannot surmount history, it is rather that he *chooses* not to, and pursues his mystical bent. . . .

Just like his creator who has built a strong, although imperfect novelistic structure fortified with playful temporal strategies, literary realia, important historical figures, interpolated plays, incursions into both the pageantry of royalty and the deeper one of psyche, Alexander too has fled history and discovered poetry. Perhaps, this is ultimately what *The Golden Fish* is about: the celebration of poetry, of all art— (after all, history is only a literary pretext for Sender)—the earnest marshalling of all energies to expand the consciousness and limits of the genre of the novel, the broadening of its epistemology.

Marshall J. Schneider. *ANP.* 2, 1977, pp. 123–25

Requiem for a Spanish Peasant is surely more than the condemnation of the Spanish Church for its part in the Civil War. Although the weight of Sender's case is tipped against that institution—mainly because he chooses to narrate his story from the perspective of its representative in the village—his picture of confusion unequivocally includes both sides in the conflict. Sender has succeeded in representing in literature the extreme disorder of this period in Spanish history whilst at the same time intimating that this tragedy was essentially due to the innate eternal tendency of the Spaniard to confuse his neighbor with mystifying actions and words until mutual comprehension and social intercourse break down into the absurdity of violence. Yet by means of his artistic re-creation of the historical reality, Sender is able to convey the impression that his picture refers to any society at any time, to Mankind in general. As he remarks in his *Preface of the Author:* "Man is the same everywhere if we go by the subtle registers of moral sensibility and human essentialness." The great success of this novel is that such a once-politically-committed author as Sender was able through the catharsis afforded by the processes of art to see and express the reality of the Spanish Civil War for participants and observers, and furthermore to extract the universal elements from this particular tragedy.

Peter A. Bly. *IFR.* July, 1978, p. 102

TORRENTE BALLESTER, GONZALO (1910–   )

In *The Voyage of Young Tobias* Torrente Ballester wants to bring about a union of all the dramatic epochs; thus, he takes from each one of them the elements he considers most important. . . . He has joined the latest stage techniques with theatrical and emotive values that call to mind the Greek theater or our own theater of the Golden Age.

The Voyage of Young Tobias . . . is like a new theatrical experiment, which was begun by Pirandello and which has had great representatives in Spain. . . .

In the play, the ending is given away too quickly, in the first two dialogues. The Spanish public should not be presented with plays where the end is told at the beginning—they have too much imagination. They need complicated events to maintain the tension. Nonetheless, despite the resolution of the theme, the fine development of the situations throughout the work and the fine irony make the reader pay attention until the very end. . . .

The poetic force of the third and fifth dialogues and the end of the sixth one would be extraordinarily difficult to understand in a recited form. The chant at the union of the soul with Tobias's body is also quite good.

Revista Haz. Nov., 1938, p. 64†

It is his occupation as a professional reader [i.e., teacher and critic] that provided Torrente with the theme of *Lope de Aguirre*. The history of the conquest of America and Shakespearean theater—the former quite evident, the latter partially evident—serve as the springboard for this theatrical resurrection of the great, supreme rebel. . . .

Torrente wants to dramatize the exemplary history of this ambitious man who had no limits or scruples. His theatrical construction seems to have been faithful to the content of the chronicles. But this is not the most important thing for the reader. . . . What is important is that with his *Lope de Aguirre* Torrente has tried to bring to the stage the human problem of the thirst for unlimited and absolute power. . . .

The action occurs during the characters' journey through the Amazon. . . . When reading *Lope de Aguirre* the reader realizes that from the first to the last scene time has passed, but he does not understand that a journey has been made. Torrente's tendency toward rationalization has changed the journey into a series of historical scenes. . . .

In *The Voyage of Young Tobias* the irony belongs to the author; in

Lope de Aguirre it belongs to the action itself. . . . Lope de Aguirre is constantly viewing himself, and thanks to his self-awareness he can cynically rationalize himself and his passion for power. . . . Lope de Aguirre, a spectator of himself, invents ironies around his very existence.

Pedro Laín Entralgo. *Vestigios* (Madrid,
ESPESA, 1948), pp. 108–10, 114†

Don Juan is an example of a very free creation, situated not only at the edge of styles, but also at the edge of traditions.

As the author himself confesses in the prologue, Don Juan was conceived after an "indigestion from realism," and it was meant principally to be a pure work of art—which does not mean, of course, a work of pure art. And it is for this reason, it seems to me, that even in spite of the coherent world of ideas on love, sex, freedom, life, death, religion, and God, which he has inserted throughout the novel, he is careful to do away immediately with the possibility of the reader's believing that he has intended to present a thesis, let alone an interpretation, of the universal myth of Donjuanism. Exactly on the page where the reader hopes for the revelation of the reason for Don Juan's immortality, the reason for the Devil's presence in his existence, the reason for the irresistible fascination that the "seducer" has exercised over Sonja, as well as over other women, the anonymous narrator "discovers" that Don Juan, just like Leporello and Sonja, are nothing more than actors. These lines—the last two pages of the novel—convert what was expected to end as a tragedy into a farce. And you do not know whether to be happy about it or to regret it.

Manuel García-Viñó. *Novela española actual*
(Madrid, Guadarrama, 1967), pp. 135–36†

Off-side is constructed on three planes: the static, the dynamic, and the superreal. Torrente Ballester's theatrical background, his dramatic talent, and his knowledge of the development of the theater make him conceive the narration from a dramatic point of view: exposition, plot, and resolution. *Off-side* has twenty main characters. Thirteen of them appear in the first 89 pages of the 544 pages that make up the novel. Of the seventeen secondary characters, twelve appear in the first one hundred pages of the narration. The author, as a good dramatist, increases his cast only at the beginning of new acts of his tragicomedy. The first act goes from the sale of the fake Goya until its presentation to the critics as an authentic work (three chapters); the second act goes from the visit of Landrove and the Countess Waldowska to the millionaire Fernando Anglada until the latter appears to have won the heart of the noble lady (four chapters); the third act begins with the sly attempt of Verónika to obtain a higher price for the fake Goya and concludes with the end of the novel (two chapters). The story of the counterfeit and the attempt to pass it off as the original work of the painter from Aragón is the dramatic thread that motivates the action and characters. . . .

Each of these acts is divided into various scenes. The author's theatrical passion makes him see his novel as a comic spectacle. All we have do is look carefully, and we will see that each scene begins with a description of the setting and the movement of the characters. . . . No director could ask for more.

Antonio Iglesias Laguna. *Treinta años de novela española,* Vol. I, 2nd ed. (Madrid, Prensa Española, 1970), pp. 353–54†

The Torrente Ballester of *The Saga/Fugue of J. B.* is—with more knowledge and experience—the same one who wrote *The Voyage of Young Tobias* in 1936. Torrente is what is generally called a writer of ideas. In 1936 Torrente was still at the stage of believer and learner. Now he is at the stage of skeptic and artist. . . . This development has not been easy, and because of the general lack of attention given to his work . . . he has been obliged to accomplish it in a zigzag fashion, testing all the genres and hoping that "finally" someone would find out about him. In his first period (theatrical), he goes from *Young Tobias,* as a man of ideas, to *The Return of Ulysses* (the ironic debunking of a myth), while passing through the tragic objectivity of his *Lope de Aguirre.* In his novelistic period, *Javier Mariño* represents his didactic interest and moment of thesis. . . .

Next comes saturated realism—although with great humor—in his trilogy *The Pleasures and the Shadows.* He writes "experimentally" yet another work of ideas: *Don Juan.* And then he returns to the novelistic satire with *Off-side.* And now in *Saga* he brings together all his experiences; technically it is his super-*Don Juan.* Satirically it is grounded in *Off-side.* In the symbolic-interpretative-ironic aspects he leaves his *Tobias* and his *Ulysses* far behind . . . and he does not fail to integrate the most essential psychological analyses, which appear somewhat less natural than those of the trilogy.

Dionisio Ridruejo. *Destino.* Aug., 1972, p. 12†

All of Torrente's work is a continuous desire to construct a literature that is at the same time unique and complex, one that is capable of suggesting a continuous reading and expandable relationships between the different ways of examining the text; its [points of] reference, at the same time, are clearly recurrent and can be followed throughout his whole work. . . .

The extraordinarily lively and flowing language is the fundamental characteristic of *Fragments of Apocalypse.* . . . It is a language that comes from the classical writers as a logical consequence of a narrative form that begins with Cervantes and often crosses [the path] of Torres

Villarroel [1693–1770]. Torrente's language is as active a component of his work as is his imagination, his memory, or the novelist's peculiar irony. . . . The reading of *Fragments of Apocalypse,* the immersion in the world of Villasanta de la Estrella and basically into the imagination of its anonymous author (although he is not so anonymous because he does not smoke much and he is, just like Torrente himself, very myopic) constitutes a supreme example of the pleasure of literature. . . .

The experience of *The Saga/Fugue of J. B.* is amplified in *Fragments of Apocalypse*—with the limitations that the great ambitions of the former can project on the lesser difficulty of the latter—and confirms the presence of Gonzalo Torrente Ballester as an exceptional novelist.

Luis Suñén. *Ínsula.* March, 1978, p. 5†

Today, Torrente is unquestionably the most highly lauded novelist in Spain, but nothing essential in his stance has changed: it is the public which has changed. Vanguardism and experimentalism are now in fashion, and intellectualism is no longer regarded as suspicious; readers and critics are better educated and more liberal than those of the 1940s, 1950s, and 1960s, while the country as a whole has moved to a less extreme political posture. Abolition of the censorship at the end of 1977, while symptomatic of the democratization and liberalizing currents, did not essentially alter Torrente's mode of writing. He has continued to be the subtle satirist, studying the formation of historical myths and humorously parodying the cultural, religious, intellectual, and social foibles of his contemporaries. Torrente continues to be indirect, for that is his style, but also because that is the style of his most significant model, Cervantes, and because the absence of directness, sermonizing, or moralizing is one of the hallmarks distinguishing the novel from propaganda, pamphleteering, or other sociopolitical documents. . . .

Over the course of more than four decades as a novelist, Torrente's technique has evolved and his emphasis has changed, but the essentials have not: intellectuality, humor, satire, a critical stance, a fascination for myth and history, the alternation of fantasy and parody with an underlying realism, self-conscious experimentalism, and the interest in novelistic theory. All are present to varying degrees in all his narratives, although in some the mythic predominates, while in others it is simply a minor element of a generally realistic panorama; in some, humor and satire overwhelm other elements, while others are more sober. If a continuing trend can be distinguished in Torrente's work, it is the sustained increase in humor, parody, and self-conscious theorizing, accompanied by an ever-growing intellectual complexity.

Janet Pérez. *Gonzalo Torrente Ballester*
(Boston, Twayne, 1984), pp. 158–60

UNAMUNO, MIGUEL DE (1864–1936)

When Unamuno's volume of poetry [*Poems*] appeared there were some expressions of admiration and infinite protests. How is it that this man who writes such strange paradoxes, this man who is called wise, this man who knows Greek, who knows half a dozen languages, who taught himself Swedish and knows how to make incomparable little paper birds, wants to be a poet too? The hangmen who love to pigeonhole, those who see a man as being good for only one thing, are furious.

And when I declared in front of some of them that in my opinion Miguel de Unamuno is, above all, a poet, and perhaps only that, they looked at me strangely and thought they had found an irony in this opinion.

Certainly Unamuno is fond of paradoxes—I myself have been a victim of some—but he is one of the most notable movers of ideas that there is today, and as I have said, in my opinion, a poet. Yes, to be a poet is to look through the doors of the mysterious and to return from there with a glimmer of the unknown in one's eyes. And few men like that Basque put their soul into the deepest core of life and death. [May 2, 1909]

Rubén Darío. Obras completas, Vol. II (Madrid,
Afrodisio Aguado, 1950), pp. 787–88†

One need not be interested in immortality to appreciate [*The Tragic Sense of Life*], but one should be interested in windmills; one should be able to like a losing fight. Unamuno fights because he knows there is not a chance in the world to win. He has tasted the glory of absurdity. He has decided to hope what he cannot believe. He has discovered grounds for faith in the very fact that there are no grounds. . . .

There is comedy in the fact that we who made God can doubt Him; there is tragedy in the fact that we must doubt Him. The tragic sense of life is nothing more or less than a sense of the disparity between what we know we can be and what we can think of being, between the limitations Nature has imposed upon us and the limits of our imagination; or as Unamuno puts it, between the necessities of reason and the necessities of life. Both reason and life are necessary, but they slay each other, and the spectacle of the double death is tragic. . . . We begin to live, says Unamuno, as soon as we have become aware of our limitations. Men live in different ways; Unamuno lives in faith. Let it be said again that one need not be interested in faith to follow him in his flight, which is not, of course, orthodox. Sancho Panza was never deceived about Don Quixote's madness, but Don Quixote was never dull. He was exhilarating in his madness, and so is Unamuno. He leaps from metaphor to metaphor; he writes like fire. Above all, there is none of the nonsense in him of "reconciliation" between knowledge and belief. Supremely intelligent, he never believes; religiously alive, he hopes. His book is very absurd, but it is tremendous work and fun for the mind.

Mark Van Doren. *Nation*. May 17, 1922, p. 600

Instead of rationalists and humanists of the North, Unamuno's idols are the mystics and saints and sensualists of Castile, hard stalwart men who walked with God, Loyola, Torquemada, Pizarro, Narváez, who governed with whips and thumbscrews and drank death down greedily like heady wine. He is excited by the amorous madness of the mysticism of Santa Teresa and San Juan de la Cruz. His religion is paradoxical, unreasonable, of faith alone, full of furious yearning other-worldliness. His style, it follows perforce, is headlong, gruff, redundant, full of tremendous pounding phrases. There is a vigorous angry insistence about his dogmas that makes his essays unforgettable, even if one objects as violently as I do to his asceticism and death-worship. There is an anarchic fury about his crying in the wilderness that will win many a man from the fleshpots and chain gangs.

John Dos Passos. *Rosinante to the Road Again*
(New York, George H. Doran, 1922), pp. 224–25

[Unamuno's] *Life of Don Quixote and Sancho* has a religious background. It is supposed to pave the way for a holy crusade to deliver the tomb of Don Quixote from its captivity at the hands of the bachelors of arts, priests, barbers, dukes, and canon lawyers who are familiar to us from Cervantes' novel. It proclaims the holy crusade for the folly of belief and against reason.

Unamuno follows the order of Cervantes' narrative. He will dwell on some chapters at length; others, which do not suit his purpose, he will pass over in a sentence. He assumes the privilege of selection, and he does not interpret the meaning but constructs a new one. Unamuno rediscovers all his favorite ideas in the novel—because he inserted them beforehand.

Cervantes' profundity is a gay pensiveness, and his wisdom is the ripe fruit of a life rich in pain and travail, of a loving, smiling humor. Unamuno complains, to be sure, that the atmosphere of modern Spain is filled with an oppressive seriousness, and that no nation today is so incapable of understanding and feeling humor as the Spanish. But he himself has expelled the humor from Cervantes' novel down to the last trace. And how could it be otherwise? He wants to breathe none but tragic air. The anxious struggles of the mind, the painful and passionate torments of the soul—this is the mood that he depicts with magnificent one-sidedness and the only one whose validity he is prepared to acknowledge. But great humor—the humor of a Shakespeare, a Jean Paul, a Cervantes—is precisely the heavenly and serene release, born of tears and laughter, from all tensions and rigidities. For that reason Unamuno's book is a splendid violation of the authentic Don Quixote. This can and must be said without disregarding the loftiness and amplitude of spirit that Unamuno has breathed into his legend. [1926]

Ernst Robert Curtius. *Essays on European*
Literature (Princeton, N.J., Princeton
University Press, 1973), pp. 234–35

Unamuno transfigures the despised and comic person of Don Quixote. This symbol of his land's wrong-headed action becomes for Unamuno the god of a new Order, the prophet of a new national revelation. Don Miguel de Unamuno of the Basques identifies his cause of pure and personal effort with the crusade of the old hidalgo of La Mancha. Like that knight, he will construct his world platonically from the ideals of his inheritance and go forth *really* that it may prevail. As Quixote fought common sense, Unamuno fights "business." The old windmills are now factories, the old inns are industrial cities, the old King's police are the votaries of Demos. Where all that is glorious has become so sterile, all that is serious so low, let Don Quixote be savior. The final jest of the bitter, broken Cervantes becomes our Man of Sorrows. . . .

So with inimitable verve and wit, Unamuno identifies his will with the old body of Spain: and hobbles forth, like Quixote, to enact justice. He wants it for himself. But since Spain is in him, since Spain is his Rocinante, Spain must go along. Spain must wake, if only for his sake.

Waldo Frank. *Virgin Spain* (New York, Boni
and Liveright, 1926), pp. 284–85

Unamuno sees in man not the creature who must live merely through a fulfillment of the body. He sees the man who cannot fully live in body or mind until, discarding the objections of Reason, he discovers faith in his personal immortality. The cult of death has often been noted in the sombre Spanish nature. Like a Spanish Tolstoy, Unamuno is asking in all his books, "What does Truth matter if a man dies?" It is the characteristic and gnawing problem for the out and out individualist. . . . Against western European rationalism, and its great culture, particularly as it is expressed in France, Unamuno puts the mysticism of Spain. . . . Against a religion of happiness, is placed the stoical argument that a true philosophy teaches men the value of suffering, how to live by preparing them for death.

V. S. Pritchett, *Spectator*, Feb. 28, 1936, p. 350

[Unamuno] is forever talking of plans for human benefit, while seeming to prize nothing so greatly as the thought of human suffering. His pages at times are a kind of bullfight, a gory spirituality concerned with the need to incur risk, to inflict and suffer misery, coexisting with an almost morbidly intense yearning to see mankind housed in a very pigeonry of ease. Thus, in his *Essays and Soliloquies* [i.e., *Soliloquies and Conversations*], he speaks of a groaning, heard at night from an adjoining room: "It produced upon me the illusion of coming out of the night itself, as if it were the silence of the night that lamented; and there was even a moment when I dreamt that the gentle lament rose to the surface from the depths of my own soul." Is not this the "connoisseur" speaking? And in the social sphere, he sees in Don Quixote the tragic symbol under the guise of the ridiculous—for it is ridicule which puts us most cruelly apart from others, hence one may poetically commend his wares by the symbol of ridicule. Martyrdom creates the creed—though out of the creed in turn may come a "rationally compensatory" codicile to the effect that martyrdom will be rewarded. [1941]

Kenneth Burke. *The Philosophy of Literary Form* (New York, Vintage, 1957), pp. 217–18

Unamuno's novel puts us in contact with that true reality which is man. This is its principal role. Other modes of thought—for we are dealing with thought—have their point of departure in previous and abstract diagrams. For example, they consider human life from a biological point of view, based on the perhaps unconscious supposition of the fundamental unity of everything we call life, and therefore they cast human reality into modes of apprehension which are alien to it and which cannot contain it without deforming it. Or again, they move from the outset within the compass of what we could call "culture," leading us to an extremely deficient and nonessential view of man. Unamuno, on the other hand, tries to obtain the highest possible degree of nakedness and authenticity in the object to which he is trying to find access. He attempts to reach the very core of the human drama, and simply to recount it, letting it be just what it is. The purpose of the existential or personal novel is to make plain to us a person's history, letting his intimate movements develop before our eyes, in broad daylight, and thus uncovering his ultimate nucleus. The purpose is, simply, to show human existence in all its truth. [1942]

Julián Marías. *Miguel de Unamuno* (Cambridge, Mass., Harvard University Press, 1966), pp. 60–61

For all his affinities with European thought, it is no accident that Unamuno constantly points to Spanish prototypes who embody his own attitudes. He does not claim to be the first Spaniard to suffer from the metaphysical malady. The grotesque character blundering through a world he does not understand, a world less real than his own imaginings, is a favorite among Spaniards. The great mystics, St. John of the Cross and St. Theresa, had no patience with any obstacles between themselves and God. And Unamuno likewise brushes aside the courtly ceremonies of Catholicism in favor of an invisible temple where he may worship in his own profane way. Common sense and good taste are blind; Unamuno prefers the exalted bungling of Don Quixote. Calderón's Segismundo, of *Life Is a Dream,* was also one of those who wandered along the edge of his dream, not knowing whether his plunge into the social world was less of a dream than his private one. For Unamuno, such semi-madness is the only attitude to be championed, since it is the only one which corresponds to a true confrontation of man's plight.

Once man realizes that death is real, then the constant consciousness of death must reduce all things in life to unreality. Though he is still in life, he cannot participate in it with conviction because death seems more real. But though the fact of death is more real, the aftermath of death is even less real than its present awareness. Reality, then, loses its constancy, shifting from the awareness of death to the awareness that one is at least alive; and yet it does not wholly settle upon aliveness since that cannot last forever in each man.

Rachel Frank. Accent. Winter, 1949, pp. 82–83

Unamuno had an ardent wish to be recognised as a great poet in verse and prose. He insisted on an assessment of his writings which his greatest admirers were unable to endorse; for instance, he gave pride of place to his first novel, *Peace in War,* and he maintained that he would be best remembered by his poetry. His rough-tongued poems with their blend of fervour and contemplation brought indeed a new note into Spanish lyrical poetry at the turn of the century, but their poetic form was never strong enough to absorb the sentiments and thoughts that inspired them. It was not Unamuno himself who found the right lyrical shape for his visions, but his much younger friend Antonio Machado. And yet Unamuno was not wrong when he called himself a poet: he was a poet who had to create a world in his image so as to assure himself of his self. Taken in this sense, Unamuno's true poetic creation was the personality he projected into all his work; his "agony," his ceaseless struggle with himself and the universe, was the core of every one of his novels and stories, poems and essays.

If he sometimes failed as an artist, it was because he handled his tools clumsily; he often insisted on the rights of his thesis against the intrinsic demands of the tale which was to clothe it. What he wanted to write was not something that made "good reading," but something that penetrated below the surface of the truth.

Arturo Barea. Unamuno (New Haven, Conn.,
Yale University Press, 1952), p. 37

In the majority of his works Unamuno confines himself to asking questions that he does not answer and to offering things that he never manages to give. Almost all his works are a pleasant and heated digression, and his most ambitious essays have universal appeal because of the manner in which they allude to the great problems and not in the way they confront them. . . .

His poetry . . . is marked by a lyric and tenuous quality. The energy, when there is any, lies in the concept and in the idea, which is often not a poetic one. On the other hand, his essays are saved by a certain lyric quality that makes up for the dialectical thread weakened by its obviousness. His novels go wrong because they are too conceptual and excessively speculative; and with the exception of *Nothing Less Than a Whole Man,* all the rest are diffuse and uneven. As far as his theater is concerned, Unamuno, who knew so many things, never succeeded in understanding what it was to stand a character on his feet and make him speak. However, at any rate, no Spaniard can fail to admire Unamuno, who had an impressive eloquence in his successes as well as in his failures. What impresses us is the force of his dedication. Spaniards, who are generally accused of having no understanding of literature, have demonstrated their generosity by accepting Unamuno for what he himself thought he was worth, independently of the weight and specific value of his work. Which is, incidentally, the lowest of the Generation of '98. [1955]

> Ramón J. Sender. *Examen de ingenios: Los noventayochos* (New York, Las Américas, 1961), pp. 13–14†

With the unclassical, Christian passion for sorrow and immortality burning in one's soul, it is an easy step (as Arturo Barea suggests in his book on Unamuno) to greed and envy; greed for immortality, envy for immortality and fame of another. And thus we have the study made in *Abel Sanchez,* where Joaquín (or Jo-Cain) feverishly envies the favored Abel his easy fame and the possible immortality inherent in his painting, envies him from a driving desire to supersede and to himself live in. Even the Lord God is engaged in this struggle for eternal glory and survival: for did He not create the world for His own greater glory? Not to struggle for immortality is not to be alive. . . .

It may be objected that the monomaniacal Joaquín of our story is scarcely a real personage; he is, then, a quintessential personage, for there *are* people who live a love, or a hate, and whose whole life is their passion; and more often than not, the great dreamers and actors are monomaniacs. And if, suggests the commentator José Ferrater Mora on this head, Unamuno's characters are not realistic to a critic, they appear quite real to a poet.

Saint Emmanuel the Good, Martyr is the story of an unbelieving priest, or a priest who thought he did not believe, or who said he thought this (he said so to only one person, and this person was an unbeliever). The theme has always been a powerful and intriguing one.

Raphael painted it in the Vatican fresco *The Mass of Bolsena,* where an unbelieving priest, eye to eye with a kneeling Pope, watches in fascination as the Host begins to bleed in his hand. The terrible tragedy of the earnest man who can no longer believe is familiar to all religious. On the face of it, the doubts assailing a spiritual guide for whom the words of his own guidance begin to ring false is a double tragedy. But Don Emmanuel is not clearly an unbeliever; in the eyes of the pious country girl [Angela] who is the story's narrator he is much more clearly a saint, for his martyrdom has been to be racked with doubt. . . . Unamuno for the first and only time situates his characters in the world; but it is *their* world, and not the world of things, not the "real" world. And in this existential world, the tragic sense (all three of the main characters are united by their concern over the immortal life of their village) turns them back toward themselves, and immunizes them against the trivial.

Anthony Kerrigan. Introduction to Miguel de
Unamuno, *Abel Sanchez, and Other Stories*
(Chicago, Henry Regnery, 1956), pp. xii–xiv

To leave everything unfinished, whether a literary work or life itself, was one of Unamuno's constant aims. Small wonder that his works impress us as being a kind of continuous creation, a sort of "interminable poem." . . .

In the essentially unfinished character of Unamuno's works we encounter . . . that impulse to overturn, to pour out, to overflow, . . . and which so faithfully represents Unamuno's temperament, his aims. Such an impulse is present even when, as in poetic forms fixed by tradition—like the sonnet—all would seem to end with the final verse. But if the last line of any of Unamuno's sonnets is a formal conclusion, it is also a new beginning; the poet has ceased to move his pen, but he keeps his spirit—and the spirit of his readers—mobile. Thus in the majority of cases—as in *Teresa,* in *The Christ of Velázquez,* in considerable portions of the *Book of Songs*—Unamuno unequivocally adopts those poetic forms that are least encumbered by formal exigencies and abound with "loose ends" that can be resumed at any time—and developed indefinitely. Not that Unamuno avoids rhythm; on the contrary, he finds it everywhere, even in Kant's *Critiques*! But this rhythm is the rhythm of life. It is not difficult to find hendecasyllables in *The Tragic Sense of Life.* But they are not intended as poetic ornament; they are meant to be songs. Perhaps, after all, Unamuno's writings are songs of a sort, sung by a soul made of living words. [1957]

José Ferrater Mora. *Unamuno: A Philosophy of
Tragedy* (Berkeley, University of California
Press, 1962), pp. 95–96

A work like [Unamuno's] *Mist* simply could not exist without the multiple narrative ambiguities on which it is based. The reader is deliberately kept in a state of confusion about the borderline between fiction and reality. . . .

This humorous undermining of ordinary reality in favor of the world of ideas could never succeed unless the reader were left in doubt—at least through most of the work—about which character, if any, speaks for reality. If reality is in fact not what it appears to be, if an imagined character is in fact more real than its author's "real" life outside his imaginings, then the reader must be led through a series of false inferences to an imaginative apprehension of the true reality. No reliable narrator can give him the truth, since the truth is itself beyond literal, non-imaginative formulation. The narrator, "Unamuno," presumably could never state the truth, except in the form of a dialogue among his various heroes and narrators, no one of whom can speak entirely for him.

Wayne C. Booth. *The Rhetoric of Fiction*
(Chicago, University of Chicago Press, 1961),
pp. 289–90

Since [Juan, in *Brother Juan; or, The World Is a Stage*] is a reincarnation of a theatrical figure, Juan's consistency can be only theatrical: he is really only a fiction, and in fiction he seeks truth. He discovers the devil, Satan, and discovers him to be a character playing a role. And God, can he also be a character in the play? Is that His substance? If so, the only truth is performed truth, and it lasts only as long as the performance. Appearance, as Unamuno said over and over, is the foundation, the inner core, all there is.

"A stage of ghosts" is the term Unamuno used to define both life and the theater. In a play he planned to write but never did (*Maese Pedro* was to be its title), the protagonist was to engage in a dialogue with the marionettes of his show just as Juan, or Unamuno, does with the linear figures in the present play. At the end of *Aunt Tula,* the protagonist Tula murmured the confession implicit in *Brother Juan:* "Marionettes all!" And in her desolate conclusion, in the depths of despair—for that "all" includes Tula as well as you, my reader, and me—I believe I detect the expression of a secret, abysmal, irrational belief; for if we are puppets or marionettes, it means that there is someone moving the strings, and that the someone, the creator of the farce and the puppets, could convoke them—and convoke us—later on for a new and lasting performance.

Ricardo Gullón. In José Rubia Barcia and
M. A. Zeitlin, eds., *Unamuno: Creator and
Creation* (Berkeley, University of California
Press, 1967), pp. 154–55

The central themes which implicitly pervade Unamuno's complete works are reducible to the human biped, God, and Spain and the world, perhaps in that order of importance. His essays, as well as his complete works on the whole, inevitably thread their way along a baroque course destined to crystallize in the form of these few considerations; lesser themes all owe their genesis and sustenance to omnipresent essentials. If the path toward these basics is often oblique, tortuous, and intentionally blurred, and if during our itinerary, we are sometimes treated to histrionics, harangues, effrontery, and other indelicacies, we eventually come to realize that these apparent defects are simply part of the ingredients of Unamuno's method whereby the obdurate provocateur seeks in every way conceivable to strain the attention of his readers to a point where each and every one of them is forced into a dialogic give and take; an exchange, sometimes a confrontation, between reader, author, and/or work. Unamuno's attempts, as one of its goals, to involve the reader-participant in an elaborate dialectic which would facilitate his role as a "co-laborator." Beneath the fractured, incoherent surface of his art, there lurks an exemplary lucidity, a coherent challenge which is the product of an apparently asystematic method. Ephemeral man versus immortal man, an abstract God versus an anthropomorphic God, Spain versus the universe, all embroiled in a vital tug of war, are thrust against a massive, dislocated canvas created to startle, seduce, and then transfix the reader to a few universal essentials.

Demetrios Basdekis. *Miguel de Unamuno* (New York, Columbia University Press, 1969), p. 5

[*Richard*] *Burgin:* Now Unamuno you never met.

Borges: But he sent me a very nice letter.

Burgin: Yes. I think you mentioned it. It was about infinity.

Borges: Yes. Unamuno's a very great writer. I admire Unamuno greatly.

Burgin: Which works of his do you admire?

Borges: Well, his book on Don Quixote [*Life of Don Quixote and Sancho*] and his essays.

Burgin: So you think he's a good thinker, I mean, apart from his writing?

Borges: Oh, he is definitely, yes, a great mind. What I said against Unamuno is that he was interested in things that I am not interested in. He is very worried about his personal immortality. He says, "I want to go on being Miguel de Unamuno." Well, I don't want to go on being Jorge Luis Borges. . . . But that, of course, those are merely personal differences. You might as well say that I like coffee and he likes tea, or that I like plains and he prefers the mountains, no?

Jorge Luis Borges and Richard Burgin. In Richard Burgin, ed., *Conversations with Jorge Luis Borges* (New York, Holt, Rinehart & Winston, 1969), pp. 96–97

To re-read Unamuno—especially when one is reading to find where one stands at last with him—is itself to be in a contest. One emerges a little shaken and winded, for here is an author that insists upon coming at you head on. Yet the man himself is so simple, direct, beguiling—a true friend, but a troubling friend. He troubles us above all when we try to follow too straight a line in trying to pin him down. . . .

All philosophy, Socrates said, is a meditation upon death; yet the subject had received scant attention from his contemporary philosophers before Unamuno wrote *The Tragic Sense of Life*. Since that time, the movement of Existentialism arose and is still flourishing; and in its light (or darkness) Unamuno's own reputation as a man of vision has been considerably enhanced. Existentialism seems to mean many different things to different people; but at least one thing about it is clear: it has tried, and sometimes succeeded, in bringing questions of life and death back into philosophy. . . .

The Tragic Sense of Life is to be read as a great philosophical lyric. It expresses how one man—and an exemplary man—felt about death and immortality at a certain stage in his life. Those feelings, Unamuno repeatedly insists, cannot be justified logically; but neither can logic, and least of all logic, dismiss them. The reader will respond to Unamuno's passion with his own capacity for passion. But one thing that seems to me inarguable about this book is that it is also a *noble* lyric, the voice of a man, an *hombre,* speaking to his fellow men in the midst of our disheartened century. Nobody can come away from it without being quickened once again for that ceaseless contest with death—and particularly death of the spirit—that goes on day by day, and sometimes even hour by hour, in the lives of all of us.

> William Barrett. Afterword to *Selected Works of*
> *Miguel de Unamuno, Vol. 4: The Tragic Sense*
> *of Life in Men and Nations* (Princeton, N.J.,
> Princeton University Press, 1972),
> pp. 361, 368, 373–74

Unamuno escapes intellectual appreciation but exercises a powerful fascination, for it is in the affective response to existence and in his emotional involvement with kindred spirits that he lived out the plenitude of his metaphysical struggle. He combines the imperious, warrior-like vitality of a Nietzsche with the intellectual paralysis of a Pirandello, the stirring pride of an Ibsen with the frustration of a Kafka, oscillating between his frenzied exaltation of the "man of flesh and blood" and the diaphanous concepts of dreams and shadows. The heroic adventurer plunged into the tragedy of impotence, Unamuno relived the irreducible opposition of the real and the ideal, the all and the nothing that Don Quixote lived before him. He sought the quixotic in all things, whether in creative writing or in contemplation of other writers, and assumed with his patron saint Don Quixote the tragic contradiction of all the great "feelers" of Europe. He tussled incessantly with the attitudes and feelings of many literary giants, transforming them, by a strange osmosis, into an intimate experience. Like Nietzsche, he was romantically inclined but infinitely surpassed the Romanticism of the nineteenth century, wrestling with the spirit of yearning in order to forge for himself the ideal of the heroic existence. Again, like Nietzsche, he wrote with his blood for he saw language as the blood of the spirit, resolving the struggle for life in recreation through identification with others and personal confession, seeking salvation not in art but in the act of self-expression.

R. E. Batchelor. Unamuno Novelist (Oxford,
Dolphin, 1972), pp. 11–12

[In *Mist*] the reader is caught in a curious play of mirrors as Augusto begins to stride uncontrollably off the pages. Unamuno does, of course, eventually manage to kill him in a God-like way, but it is inescapable that he does so because he is afraid Augusto will overpower him. Unamuno leads himself into a situation similar to that of Cervantes; but he protects himself by inserting himself directly into the novel so that he is guaranteed to have no less reality for the reader than Augusto, who achieves no small victory when he succeeds in coming back to haunt his creator in his dreams. He then exemplifies the independence an idea or concept can have after the creator is through with it, and also shows the precise relationship that exists between any "real" character and the reader. A character may be able to exist without his creator, but he cannot exist without a reader.

Unamuno defeats Augusto with life, or history, by imposing his phenomenological personality upon Augusto's fictive one. It is a Pyrrhic victory at best, since he had to become fictional himself in order to do it, but he does succeed in keeping Augusto largely within the bounds of the printed page. All distinctions become arbitrary at this point, since Unamuno has moved us entirely into a spiritual mist in which no dividing lines are clear. . . . In *Mist* it becomes impossible to make any significant assertions regarding who is totally fictional or who is completely historical, since both Unamuno and Augusto cross those limits.

Victor Ouimette. Reason Aflame: Unamuno
and the Heroic Will (New Haven, Conn., Yale
University Press, 1974), pp. 181–82

In the domain of cases and causes, of comic and tragicomic situations, Unamuno's imagination never runs dry. His is the imagination of the logician, the demiurgos who strips down to the equation, the schema, the barest outline. Down to dialogue. But to pure dialogue, without any hint of décor or stage directions, tone of voice or facial expression, dialogue, reduced to pure dialogue, dry, stripped and bare, brutal, primitive, striking. It is a dialogue in retaliation for a monologue. But in this dialogue form each of the adversaries reaches the zenith of individual self-affirmation.

Under this sign the characters lose nothing in pathos; on the contrary, they gain from this ease of representation, quick figures on a blackboard. They are presented in a situation from which varying consequences can ensue. And the author takes them out of this situation to push them into still another equally uncomfortable one. On a subsidiary plane, he invents other characters to live other cases, analogous or opposed, but just as likely to end up in ridiculous shambles, in some sorry fiasco. Is there cruelty in all this? Certainly there is, but it is cruelty combined with a strange tenderness of a frightfully lucid father who never laughs outright, but contains this laughter in a spasm which makes him all the fiercer. A fierce tenderness, therefore, but tenderness all the same. And it is not in the interests of love, out of love of love, which is action, work, and life, that Unamuno makes use of a farcial ferocity? This love is all the more admirable because it does not fulfill itself in effective procreation, but rather, as with the beloved, sublime *Aunt Tula,* must confine itself to patterns of substitution or sublimation, and therefore, evolves into a passion, a boiling point for love, and this passion reveals itself as pure will, pure spirituality. It is not possible to love on a higher plane than this, nor more intensely.

Jean Cassou. Foreword to Miguel de Unamuno,
Selected Works of Miguel de Unamuno, Vol. 6:
Novela/Nivola (Princeton, N.J., Princeton
University Press, 1976), pp. xxiv–xxv

It was necessary for Unamuno to immerse himself daily in routine, tradition, and kindly looks in order to achieve some peace amid his tempestuous searches for eternal life and social justice. Projected upon his characters is a great deal of figurative language whose apparent purpose is to universalize and exemplify this conviction that the family, as a womb-like refuge, constitutes man's natural way to transcendental integration with all life. In a similar fashion, it would appear that Unamuno's novelistic family, his "spiritual children," are also relied upon to accompany and comfort the author and author-character. Embodying differing facets of the writer's personality, they lend him the solace and illusion of being among those who understand his own predicaments. Moreover, since they reflect the quirks and manias of their own author, they stand in a position to convince him that his own behavior falls within the human norm. We should remember that on countless occasions Unamuno wondered whether he was losing his mind, particularly when everyone that society held in respect seemed united against *his* positions, though visibly unable to agree on anything else. In a manner possibly described as a quixotic variant on the term "looking-glass self," Miguel de Unamuno appears to project onto his characters precisely those characteristics which might allow him continued self-esteem.

Thomas R. Franz. *Hispania.* Dec., 1980, p. 652

What *Peace in War* finally comes down to, I strongly suspect (and what rescues it from being merely one more historical novel from the nineteenth century about events that somehow hardly seem to matter any longer), is that it is a novel about *jabber,* in which it is abundantly rich: idle political discussions among friends in the nightly *tertulias* or intimate conversational gatherings; children taunting one another in the streets; soldiers shouting friendly obscenities at one another in the trenches dividing enemy armies, during a lull in combat; pompous, meaningless sermons in village churches, and open-air Masses said by armies who repeat the liturgy mechanically and know that God approves their cause—all these things combining to form a chorus of demonic jabber. There is no clearly defined hero in this novel—Ignacio is a tedious dullard, and Pachico Zabalbide is an intrusively autobiographical spokesman for Unamuno himself—but there is a villain: the slogan.

Allen Lacy. Introduction to Miguel de
Unamuno, *Peace in War,* Vol. I of *Selected
Works of Miguel de Unamuno* (Princeton, N.J.,
Princeton University Press, 1983), pp. xxxi–xxxii

VALLE-INCLÁN, RAMÓN DEL (1866–1936)

By the phenomenon of spiritual alchemy, the author of *Sonata of Summer,* a soul of the *quattrocento,* becomes a dilettante of the Renaissance, and those ideals [the ardent desire for a free and instinctual life and the worship of chivalrous times and heroes] appear to be exacerbated in a mannered and dissolute cult. It is the sad lot of men who are out of step. Zarathustra, as a state of mind, has been nothing else than a dilettante of individualism in these meager times of democracy.

But there are even more characteristics that Valle-Inclán has that make a rare artist out of him, a product of other historical latitudes.

Today we are all sad: some carry their sadness adorned with a healthy smile, others are full of complaints and gloom until they twist our hearts into knots, but it is a fact that pessimism plays with us like a macabre buffoon. French naturalistic literature has been a prolonged complaint, a mournful psalm for the disinherited. Dickens weeps for the poor in spirit. Russian novelists present us only with rags, hunger, and ignominy. . . .

The literature of Valle-Inclán, on the other hand, is agile, without transcendence, pretty like useless things, even joyous in its pallid and dying women, witty like a conversation in Versailles, full of amorous and chivalrous power. . . . The characters in *Sonata of Summer* do not have to contend with the little inconveniences that the rigid and worn advice of contemporary morality sees as necessary prerequisites for enjoying life to its fullest. Therefore, to read *Sonata of Summer* is pleasant and gives solace and refreshment to the soul. In these fortuitously found stories, our nerves can relax from the surrounding sadness.

Such a joyous disposition of spirit is much to be admired nowadays. Not to see anything but strong and daring protectors, magnificent love affairs in this country of sadness, is something rare and infrequent. . . .

Yes, the author of *Sonatas: Memoirs of the Marquis of Bradomín* is a man from another century, a rock from another geological period that has remained forgotten upon the face of the earth, solitary and useless for the purposes of industry. [1904]

José Ortega y Gasset. *Obras completas,* Vol. I, (Madrid, Revista de Occidente, 1946), pp. 20–21†

Whenever the work of an artist appears to suffer from one dominant defect, it is wise to search for the root of this defect in the very region where the root of his main quality lies. The main quality of Valle-Inclán, that which gives formal excellence and emotional music to his art, is the purity of his aesthetic attitude. He turns his soul on nature like a mirror, the limpidity of which is untarnished by any moral or philosophical preoccupation. He sees, feels, and reflects in perfect peace. Now, this is as it should be. A work of art should be—indeed, can only be— conceived in a purely aesthetic attitude, which neither the eagerness to learn nor the desire to teach should disturb. Neither proving nor improving have anything to do with art.

But when we have said that the mood in which the artist looks at life should be free from ethical or philosophical influences, we do not mean that the artist himself should be altogether free from the ethical and philosophic preoccupations. Here lies the kernel of that most vexing question, art for art's sake. Yes, of course, art must be for art's sake. But provided the artist has a philosophic mind and an ethical heart. Let his mood, while creating, be wholly aesthetic, but not the soul which goes into that mood. Ethics and philosophy are not the music of art, but they are the sounding-box which gives depth and sonority to it. Let the artist look at Life with purely aesthetic eyes, but unless his mind breathe the high summits of thought and his soul move true to his divine origin, his art will never rise above that of the embroiderer—and it will never grow.

It is here, to my mind, that the flaw in the art of Don Ramón María del Valle-Inclán is to be found. His aesthetic attitude is not merely the natural one of an artist intent on creation. It arises also from a real indifference towards the higher philosophic and moral issues. His emotion is purely aesthetic, and evokes no resonances in the recesses of his soul. The vacuum which surrounds the strings of his sensibility reflects back its inaneness on the sound that they yield. The aesthetic emotion itself, lacking the necessary resonance, becomes thin and false. Hence that jarring note of insincerity throughout his work. There is in it a literary preoccupation which savours too much of the *métier*. . . .

It explains the indifference with which man's most sacred passions are handled without leaving the slightest tremor in the hands of the artist, a circumstance which leads him to commit strange breaches of taste. It stimulates the search for the merely weird and picturesque, for the horrible and the morbid. It is, in fine, the manifestation of an aesthetic sensibility without philosophical guidance nor ethical ballast.

Nor is this meant to imply that Valle-Inclán is lacking in mental powers and curiosity. Far from it. His work is full of most ingenious symbols, images, and ideas which reveal a penetrating mind. It is not from lack of ideas that his work suffers, nor do we here suggest that it is worthless because of its unmoral philosophy. This philosophy, which is that of the freedom of passion as opposed to the philosophy of repression and discipline, is perfectly defensible, and the deliberate choice of it implies in Valle-Inclán a power for discernment and a capacity for high thought which no one thinks of denying him.

Salvador de Madariaga. *The Genius of Spain,*
and Other Essays on Spanish Contemporary
Literature (Oxford, Clarendon Press, 1923), pp. 145–47

The mysticism of *Saintly Flower,* the chiseled beauty of the *Sonatas,* the power and tragic pathos of the *Barbaric Comedies,* the stately detachment of *The Carlist War,* the graceful fantasy of *The Dragon's Head,* the raw brutality of *Divine Words,* the delightfully cynical irony of [*Farce and License of*] *the Native Queen,* on these and other valid qualities was built the solid reputation of Valle-Inclán, the impressive figure that one knew before 1924. His gallery of full-length portraits was small but very choice. At least two of the figures are certain to live— Don Juan Manuel Montenegro and the more celebrated but somewhat meretricious Marquis of Brasdomín. Valle-Inclán's singular ability to catch and reproduce the spirit of the Middle Ages without recourse to its stage properties, to project into modern times a living embodiment of feudal lord and vassal by a psychological analysis of the mental and emotional reactions of Don Juan Manuel, was, next to the extraordinary beauty of his prose, his most notable achievement. He remained always an artist pure and simple, in the sense in which our generation understands the term, free of preoccupation with propaganda or "moral lessons." His studies of the more or less wicked poor, e.g. in *Divine Words,* did not contain either censure or suggestions for the amelioration of their condition, which he evidently considered divinely ordered. His analyses of psychopathological types . . . were done without the semi-technical jargon which clutters up the pages of our modern psychological novelists. He wrote always as an aristocrat, contemplating with perfect detachment the struggles and tragedies of an inferior race, for whom he was not without the sympathy which is implicit in perfect justice of treatment, but in whose lives he had no other immediate personal concern than that of the painter in his models.

With *Lights of Bohemia* one notices a subtle change of attitude. Max Estrella, a radical and a man of genius, who by his talents is the first poet of Spain, has lost his sight and fallen into great poverty. Dissipated, sick and destitute, he is ignored by critics, press and the respectable public, by reason of his rebellion against conventional authority, although he is still adored by the little group of wretched bohemians among whom he lives. We see him in the last day or two of his life, drunk, arrested and barbarously beaten in jail, finally released to die. The play is a mordant satire directed against a smug, bourgeois society and its venal government, as well as against those feigned liberals who prate of humanitarianism but are concerned only with their own advantage. The tone is cynical and discouraged, both with Spain and with humanity. The salient difference between this and the earlier works lies in the fact that the author is here genuinely concerned with the matter for its own sake. It is true that he has not a remedy to propose, but it is clearly on his mind and conscience that genius is of less consequence in Spain than conventional morality.

Arthur L. Owen. BA. Oct., 1927, pp. 9–10

Our good friend Don Ramón del Valle-Inclán—may posterity be kind to him—will continue, for a long time to come, to fill books of anecdotes rather than anthologies. . . . People will speak of him more than they will study his work. Was not his chief work his very own self—the actor more so than the writer? He lived—that is, he made himself—on a stage. His life, more than a dream, was a show-business routine. . . . His prodigious memory—he was a wonder—permitted him to collect many roles. And he mixed them all up and confused them, just as he did with times and places. The history that he fantasized was neither chronological nor topographical. The principal model that he forged, the Marquis of Bradomín—from the quarry of Barbey d'Aurevilly—was noble, ugly, and Catholic. A literary Catholic, as in Chateaubriand, of course. . . . Like a good actor, he behaved at home as if he were on stage. In a very serious vein, he made everything into a big farce. He achieved a certain degree of greatness because of his selflessness. He fused tragedy with the *esperpento*. And he adored beauty, the joy of his life.

But now I want to talk about his language. Language is the best expression for the poetic—artistic—work of one who was more than a writer, more than an orator—a conversationalist and an admirable declaimer. . . .

Because he was a man of the theater, Valle-Inclán's speech—his dialectal idiom or idiomatic dialect—was theatrical. Not lyrical, not epic, but dramatic and in some instances tragicomic, devoid of lyrical intimacy and epic grandiloquence. Language of the theater and not infrequently of street theater. How it burst forth in his *esperpentos!*

One must not look for precision in his language. Words sounded right to him or they did not. And according to the sound, he gave them a meaning, oftentimes one that was completely arbitrary. And it was a real treat to hear his philological and grammatical theories. He was not capable of getting inside the expressions that he used because for him— actor before and above all—the insides were in what I have previously called "the outsides"; the content was in the form. And perhaps he was not misguided, if one understands by form something more substantial than mere surfaces, for the formal is hardly superficial. Didn't the scholastics say years ago that the soul is a substantial form? [Jan. 29, 1936]

Miguel de Unamuno. Visiones y comentarios
(Buenos Aires, Espasa-Calpe, 1949), pp. 83–85†

Valle-Inclán found unity only in his extremes. Led astray by the initial phase of his work, critics thought he was only a delicate artist, a painter of miniatures. But the real Valle-Inclán is rather the writer who treats barbarous themes with refinement, who stylizes violence. Crude human nature is violence, barbarity. And words are the divine power which elevates it to the quality of art. The art-process in Valle-Inclán, who always scoffed at the reality of the realist, lies in passing through stylization of the real, concerned above all with the aesthetic, such as in the *Sonatas,* to another kind of stylization—mystic and profound— which we might call a stylization of psychological origin. At first he proceeded inwardly and dressed his characters in artistically designed costumes taken from literature and painting. But in his last period the characters emit from within themselves their own elements of stylization as they become their own caricature; and what accounts for the tragic element in the *esperpento* is precisely man's encounter with his own acts, with his own farce and grimace. He converts himself into a tragicomic motif as he encounters his own true character. At the beginning of his career Valle-Inclán may have indeed been a sensual contemplator and sceptic, but in the end he is a man in anguish, and in his works, what he gives us is a plastic transcription—for Valle-Inclán could never be anything if not plastic—of man's conflict with his conscience. [1936]

Pedro Salinas. Quoted in Ricardo Gullón, ed.,
Valle-Inclán: Centennial Studies (Austin,
University of Texas Press, 1968), p. 101

Ramón del Valle-Inclán, the great and unfortunate Valle-Inclán, had been, was, and is a Galician, an authentic Celt. For his equal one must look in Ireland more than in Galicia. Like his contemporary peers, the best Celtic writers of Ireland, George Moore, "AE," Synge, Yeats (Bernard Shaw is another matter, although he is also relevant to Valle-Inclán), he began by being influenced by the ubiquitous French symbolism, the yellow era of symbolism. Almost all the great poets of the world who were starting out or purifying themselves in that period, the magical poets and the notable rhetoricians, D'Annunzio, Claudel, Stefan George, Edward Arlington Robinson, Rilke, Yeats, Valéry, Hofmannsthal . . . used as their point of departure symbolism. In England, Valle-Inclán has been compared to George Moore, but he really is not very much like him; in fact, he is very much superior to him. In truth the writers whom he does resemble are . . . Synge and Yeats, Yeats in poetry and Synge in prose. The conceptual theme of the rose, for example, is treated by Valle-Inclán in the same liturgical and rhetorical manner as in Yeats, although Yeats may at times soar higher, may be more metaphysical, more exquisite, and at times supreme; the profound vision of his theater and the movement of his dialogue (compare, for example, *The Well of the Saints* with *Divine Words*) are, in their best moments, like Synge. This similarity is seen in everything, body and soul. Galicia and Ireland continue being twins, and as Ireland did for Yeats and above all for Synge, Galicia freed Valle-Inclán from the exoticism of modernism, which passed quickly in him, luckily for everyone, and from "Spanishness," which had such lamentable and lasting results in some.

Valle-Inclán was not a man of ideas or of cultivated sentiments; he did not want to be one; he wished to satisfy himself, to go forward or not on his own accord. Profound criticism did not have any effect on his high-flying spirit. Hence, his "marvelous lamp," which had no oil, gave off so much empty smoke. But when he was doing what he did best, the ironic and emotional removal of shocking beings and things, in what he called *esperpento,* a brutal romanticism, he had no equal, and those who imitated him, García Lorca, for example, did not come up to him. He was a vivid aesthete of unextinguishable popular daring. His style, his vocabulary did not come out of any dictionary, which he did not use, not even to correct his spelling errors, but from the street, the café, the road, from his own inner being, his heart, his viscera.

Juan Ramón Jiménez. UMHAS. Jan., 1941,
pp. 112–13†

[Valle-Inclán's plays are] more contemporary and more theatrical than when first written. To reread *The Captain's Daughter,* for example, and other titles of his, fills us with amazement: they almost seem as if they were written today by some lucid dramatic commentator about our worst sore spots. What is paradoxical is that Valle-Inclán's theater did not even pretend, when it was written, to be total "theater." Don Ramón himself presented his plays as often as possible, since he did not have to or want to have them performed out of context or at the wrong moment; but coming up against an atmosphere overwhelmingly deaf to his best instincts, and possessing, on the other hand, very brilliant qualities of a narrative writer, he himself frequently opted for a uniquely "literary" theater so adorned with stage directions that were as valid—and almost as extensive—as the dialogue, that it did not even occur to him to offer his plays to producers; instead he sent them to be published as books. In spite of this, time has given us proof that Valle-Inclán, a marginal author in his own time, was and is a great dramatic writer. And his formulas, which perhaps he himself did not at time believe to be sufficiently theatrical, and in fact, at times are not, now appear to us to be alive and full of impact in not a few of his plays. And not only in those that saw the stage, but also in those that he preferred to commit directly to print. Here is one of those extremely rare cases of an author who does not succeed in commanding respect in his lifetime, but whose failure is only one of appearance. For the moment, he nurtured the greatest playwright who succeeded him: García Lorca. And today Valle-Inclán is looked upon as a writer of unique and unparalleled talent, a formidable analyst of his country and of the sullen or ludicrous face of the truth of men: that truth, among others, of a man-puppet who is at the mercy of his conditioned reflexes. . . .

The demythification, the critical distance of the author—and therefore of the audience—in respect to his creations announces what Brecht later promulgated. His popularism, his rough and harsh laugh, grow into other tragicomic finds of our day. The *esperpento* is not the only formula that is adequate for today's theater . . . but it is a felicitous Spanish formula that will not lack new cultivators, who, we certainly ought to hope, find their personal manner of understanding it without imitating more or less in a servile manner the one who baptized it.

Antonio Buero Vallejo. *Ínsula.* July–Aug., 1961, p. 4†

Today when I reread *Divine Words* I was afraid that I was going to be disappointed. I was wrong; the play has lost none of its impact for me. That idiot-dwarf with whom I was so taken, and whom I feared I would find quite "picturesque," is not an accessory who is employed gratuitously to provoke "terror and pity": he is an article of commerce. Alive, he is an exhibit at a fair and in great demand because he brings in money; dead, he is "palmed off," since he obliges his friends to beg in order to pay for his burial. Is all this cruel? Certainly, but it is a very simple cruelty that centers around the law of supply and demand. Somebody will probably say to me—more accurately, somebody will say to Valle-Inclán—that a monster is superfluous and that a normal person, an agricultural worker, for example, in so far as he is a commodity, would have filled the bill. It's true; and it is also true that the wretched population, in Spain as elsewhere, does not consist only of sextons and members of traveling circuses, and that along with the world of fairs and that of faith, there is quite simply the world of work. But in a country where misery has given birth to so many monsters, and where a *monstrously* active Church has disguised the sordid reality with so much tinsel, it is altogether normal that a poet first tries to describe what he sees in the foreground. And the situation, such as Valle-Inclán sees and reveals it, has no other outlet than a miracle. A retrogressive play, then? A religious play? I do not think so. Valle-Inclán knows well that this "gilded and religious marvel, which in the world of unschooled souls who believe in miracles, causes the unknown Latin of the divine words to be understood," is a precarious refuge. The wonder, in effect, does not impede the unfortunate people from knowing that a definite danger exists: the intervention of the forces of order. Is it not significant that the last retort is some prudent advice vis-à-vis the civil guards? The miracle, in short, will not have any other real effect than putting an end to the orgy, a possible generator of troubles in that rotten society—literally rotten—which the clergy and police, together, feel obliged to maintain as is.

Arthur Adamov. *CRB*. March, 1963, pp. 56–57†

To what audience is the work that we are discussing addressed? It is a question that must be asked if we wish to understand this extraordinary "theater." . . . In [Valle-Inclán] there is the same hatred for the bourgeoisie as in Rimbaud . . . , and this hatred is a terrible handicap for a dramatic author at the beginning of the twentieth century. Valle-Inclán does not wish to write for a bourgeois audience. Neither his poems nor his novels are addressed to them; but this is not as pronounced as in his dramatic works. A novel that is in print, a poem that almost no one reads, remain a novel and a poem. The theater of Valle-Inclán was destined, from its inception, not to be performed, or almost never. From the earliest work it is seen that the author is completely conscious of this phenomenon: not only does he make no concessions to the select audience capable of filling the theater, but he does not even try to make his works technically capable of being performed. The scenery is always reduced to only the most significant elements; the characters perform a role as a function of a would-be audience who observes and listens to them; there is an action that continues to be compelling throughout the scenes, that creates a constant tension, that leads to a powerful dénouement. The participation of the observer is constantly solicited at the same time it undergoes violent shocks, a fact that clearly shows that the author takes the audience into account: he is writing for the theater, and not anything else.

But the passion for what is impossible that animates Valle-Inclán is so violent that his theater frequently seems unproduceable, unplayable, because of the practical difficulties. Frequently, each scene calls for a different setting.

Jean-Paul Borel. *Théâtre de l'impossible*
(Neuchâtel, Switzerland, Éditions de la
Baconnière, 1963), pp. 121–22†

A profound sense of absurdity is not easily explained away by strict aesthetic criteria; one must account for the harsh criticism and engagement of the absurd, or the historical orientation of the *esperpentos,* as something more than just another example of skilled contrivance. Otherwise we would read some of the most immediate, painful, most brutal, most unsettling pages of modern literature, we would be confronted with unheard-of pain and incredible mockery, without really being moved. It is true that Valle-Inclán was a craftsman through and through but the *esperpento* has also much to do with impact, that is, it is not simply an aesthetic doctrine but above all a sense of life. It plays with the distorted, the absurd, the tragicomic; as with the grotesque, the malformed and the capricious intrude and cause an estrangement from the normal world and a horrific but also amusing loss of familiar footing. The grotesque implications of the Spanish circumstance or the human condition are no less distressing and no less engaged for being integrated into a highly stylized perspective.

No single *esperpento* raises in a more accurate form than *Lights of Bohemia* the problem of reconciling the grotesque as literature with the grotesque as reality. Valle-Inclán's first *esperpento* is a modern, nocturnal Odyssey about the frustration, death and burial of a blind poet, Max Estrella. The setting is "an absurd, sparkling, and hungry Madrid," the characters are puppet-like figures putting on an inconsolable yet comic exhibition of misery, and the background is an artistic elaboration of political events that include the famous 1919 strikes and disturbances. A striking, and hitherto overlooked, feature of the first *esperpento* is the fact that Max forges the deforming technique of concave mirrors by analyzing contemporary events. The vivid experiences of the violent strikes, the rampant chaos, the disturbances, or the economic and political collapse are rooted, even in the context of Valle-Inclán's most inventive situations, in a solid bedrock of remembered or observed fact. He plucks the most distressing and ludicrous elements of the 1919 strikes and successfully grafts them into the narrative of the blind poet's last day. There are important implications, of course, if Valle-Inclán's stylistic grotesque is rooted in actual historical calamities: the *esperpento* is not simply a grotesque quality but a grotesque situation; the gesticulating puppets are also real Spaniards; the ludicrous, painful action is not only a shadow play but also a map of Spanish life, the epitome of grotesque experience; and finally, Valle-Inclán's stylistic virtuosity is not only a case of aesthetic gymnastics but also aesthetics of commitment.

Anthony N. Zahareas. *MLN*. March, 1966,
pp. 160–62

Valle-Inclán's personages [in *The Tyrant Banderas*] resemble T. S. Eliot's hollow and stuffed men, lacking the vital substance or spirit that once linked them to the world of meaning. But they are different, too, in that they have been moved off-center through no fault of their own. It is as if their gears have slipped and their lives no longer mesh with the real world around them. And here is Valle-Inclán's diabolical irony. He is saying that the world also moves mechanically, but that as long as one keeps his wheels meshed, everyone is satisfied and no one is the wiser. But as soon as the inner spring is pulled out of shape, one's entire mechanism is exposed for the cheap trickery that it is. In this discovery there is an element of sadness, and on occasion the author permits himself a moment of compassion. He can, for example, mitigate his technique of animalization by giving a downcast man the expression of a whipped dog; or he will find a "baroque and statuary pathos" in a sinewy figure. But for the most part Valle-Inclán lets little stand in the way of his ruthlessness in stripping men of their prerogatives as human beings. This is justifiable in isolated cases, like that of the degenerate Spanish minister, whose facial cosmetics, egg-like eyes, and smile of "inverisimilar elasticity" lend themselves easily to the idea of masks and dolls. But the novel's widespread deformed dehumanization can only be explained by Valle-Inclán's personal theory of the concave mirror.

Here, then, is where cultural and political concepts gain stronger impetus in the *esperpento* than in the surrealist mode as we have seen it thus far. Social ideology is not necessarily a part of the surrealist's repertoire, although there is often a close connection. But *esperpentismo* is both an outgrowth of an ideological position, and also the aesthetic medium for expressing it. And conversely, the raison d'être of the *esperpento* aesthetic is a cultural or political theory. Thus, the compassionate moments just referred to are not missions of his intellectual role vis-à-vis the aesthetics of his novel. For example, he sketches in the "ambiguous expression of compassion and disdain in the funereal face" of a dying old man, a description that fits the author's attitude perfectly. But the statement seems insufficient for contemporary art, and incompatible with the notion of Spain as a grotesque deformation of Europe. And so Valle-Inclán twists the ambiguity into a definitive deformation, without withdrawing his personal position: "The waning of that buffoon in misfortune had a certain grotesque solemnity like the mummers' dance burials that conclude the pre-Lent carnival."

What is of interest here is not the incongruity of misfortune and buffoonery, for this juxtaposition is a standard technique for creating the grotesque. The point is that the author has endowed grotesqueness with solemnity because he himself regards Spain's condition with gravity, even though her destiny may be ridiculed by Europe. There is little amusement in the *esperpento*. Its comedy never occurs in pure form, and laughter is never light-hearted. Humor is always sarcastic, black, and slightly demented, its bitterness being derived from the sad thoughts concerning Spanish life, and its madness stemming from the reckless dehumanization of the characters.

Paul Ilie. *The Surrealist Mode in Spanish Literature* (Ann Arbor, University of Michigan Press, 1968), pp. 146–48

In regard to personages, *Lights of Bohemia* brings into focus a gallery of alienated human beings—as alienated as the author himself—, most, if not all, of them known as real persons in the "outside world" (the physical world) by the author, the author's friends, and even some of his readers. The situation is repeated in the "inside world" of the book itself, where they all intermingle to illustrate a side of human society not recognized as valuable by "normal" people, or by those occupied in normal and respectable activities. The author appears in the work *hidden* as the third-person narrator, apparently responsible only for the equivalent of stage directions; and he appears also *in the open* but in a marginal capacity, disguised as an idealized *alter ego*. *The Horns of Don Friolera* placed together, in a much more structurally complex pattern, another disguised *alter ego* of the real author, accompanied by a transfiguration of one of his closest friends in real life [Ricardo Baroja, the painter, brother of Pío Baroja], and both of them appear in the same alienated or marginal capacity, while the author takes care also of his narrator role. The three of them—the narrator and the two marginal characters—view from the fictitious outside a presentation of a single problem—the sempiternal Spanish case of *honor* on three different levels. Underlying all three, there is also an actual happening in the outside contemporary world, with identifiable disguised persons, and others mentioned by their real names. *The Captain's Daughter* lacks the marginal appearance of any direct or disguised *alter ego* of the author. All fictional pretenses are put aside and the author plays, in a demiurgic manner, his role as the *hidden* but identifiable narrator. In this case, he seems to prefer not to get close to his characters, to keep his distance, motivated perhaps by a mixed feeling of pride and disgust in regard to the type of puppets he is manipulating. This *esperpento* coincides, nevertheless, with the other two in also being an artistic re-elaboration of a recent actual happening, in this particular case a big historical event; the *pronunciamento* of General Primo de Rivera (1923), in connivance with King Alfonso XIII, both of whom appear in the book, along with other recognizable and historical figures, as a Glorious General and the Monarch, respectively.

José Rubia Barcia. In Ricardo Gullón, ed.,
Valle-Inclán: Centennial Studies (Austin,
University of Texas Press, 1968), pp. 82–84

The dramatic tension of Valle-Inclán's plays does not lie in the linear structure of events; it rather *permeates* the total situation, from the counterpoint of scenes and incidents to the very texture of the language. The dialogue constantly stimulates with conflicting suggestions and impressions. It is alive with a rich blend of incongruities reminiscent of the plays of J. M. Synge. In the plays of *Altarpiece of Avarice, Lust, and Death,* especially *The Paper Rose,* much of the dramatic effect stems from the deliberate disparity of style and subject matter, between the almost burlesque rhetoric of the speeches and the horrific nature of the situations. The duality of burlesque melodrama and horror in this "melodrama for marionettes" is finely sustained, creating a subtle and compelling tension. Valle-Inclán does not provide a synthesis of these antagonistic elements; they are left as an unresolved tension in the mind of the spectator. In Valle-Inclán's intuition of reality no rational synthesis is possible. Like Ionesco, he presents in stylized form the objective contradictions of the world.

Dramatic tension, then, derives more from the texture of the plays than from the structure. To transcend the purely individual and anecdotic Valle-Inclán reduces the importance of the narrative line. It is interesting to note that he dealt with the narrative structure as he did with the grammatical structure of the sentence—by suppressing the logical links and relying exclusively on juxtaposition and sensation. . . . He chops the narrative into a succession of graphically immediate images, each isolated in a present devoid of logical connexion with past or future. He submerges the causal links and allows the juxtaposition of the images to operate on the spectator's imagination. Our memory is not involved completely as in naturalistic drama since we are not required to see what is happening in any given scenes as the logical consequence of the foregoing ones. Our intellect is not solicited to speculate on how certain events may influence the future action or on what the significance of certain ones might be once the total structure is revealed to us. We are held in the present, stimulated by the image before us. Now while the texture of each of these "present" images may be dramatic *in essence,* the plays would be useless for the theatre unless they also possessed some form of dramatic or dynamic continuity. . . .

To be theatrical a play must sustain a *pattern* of interest. Valle-Inclán's problem was to determine how far that pattern of interest was to depend on the narrative line. Too much emphasis on the temporal narrative development would jeopardize the collective and timeless spirit of the work. Too little would result in obscurity and lack of dramatic continuity. Obviously, he could not disarticulate the narrative sequence in his plays to the same extent as he did in *The Tyrant Banderas* and the novels of *The Iberian Ring,* with their frequent and abrupt switches of environment and characters. In *Lights of Bohemia* and *The Horns of Don Friolera* he develops a single narrative line and in *Divine Words, Marquise Rosalinda* and *The Farce of the Maid Who Loved a King* he combines two simultaneously. In all these plays there is an underlying narrative structure without which dramatic continuity could not exist. As we have seen, however, there is not a plot in the generally accepted sense, since the element of causality is suppressed. The narrative structure is not the substance of the play as it would be in naturalistic—and symbolic—drama, but the functional framework which supports the flesh and the blood of the play or the central melodic line around which Valle-Inclán orchestrates the harmonies of collective feeling. . . . The principal agents of continuity should therefore be sought not in the logic of the action or the development of a chronological sequence, but in the rhythmic pattern evoked by variation of light, tempo and key in the scenes.

J. E. Lyon. *BHS.* Jan., 1969, pp. 148–49

Although the most successful of his writings were novels, Valle-Inclán's best work was done for the theater. He may have stated periodically that his works were not intended for the stage, but those denials stemmed from moments of ire in his confrontation with the theater's commercialism. Too often were his plays refused production or given limited engagements for him not to feel bitter toward the theatrical establishment. And yet, throughout his career, he always sought out the theater, be it as actor, playwright, translator, or director . . . .

For Valle-Inclán the theater was a setting for freedom: of the playwright to articulate his ideas with artistic integrity, of the public to accept or reject these ideas audibly according to the measure in which it was or was not entertained, of the critic to comment candidly on the play's merits or faults. In vitalizing the first freedom, Valle-Inclán often encountered indifferent audiences who preferred the euphuistic melodramas of Echegaray and the confectionary comedies of the Quinteros. Audience and management alike failed to recognize that Valle-Inclán's plays were important steps for a dramaturgy moribund since the Golden Age, except for the brief life of Romanticism. In exercising his right as a critic, Valle-Inclán found that his vocality in the theater was not appreciated and that at times he had to succumb to the greater authority of a magistrate. Nonetheless, despite its shortcomings, it was the theater which held the promise of best fulfilling the aesthetic he espoused, and Valle-Inclán wrote for it with expectation.

As a playwright he believed that the audience must be moved intellectually as well as emotionally. To achieve this dual end, he made his characters inferior to their creator and chose to oversee their activities in the style of the puppeteer; the audience, too, he thought, should stand above and beyond the play's characters. Only through this alienatory tactic could there be objectivity. The theater could aspire then to be both a museum and a laboratory, a place in which experience and experimentation would function jointly. To implement the museum concept, Valle-Inclán looked to the great theater of Spain's past and found in it an atmosphere which suited his needs. He savored the history and themes, traditions and superstitions, archaic names and language which its plots featured. These aspects served as a springboard for his own experimentation. . . .

Rather than encourage empathetic response in his audiences, as did classic tragedy, Valle-Inclán opted for their objective exploration of the enigma of human existence. This approach was more appropriate to the times, he believed. The *esperpento* concerns itself with sociopolitical injustice, the instability of personal relationship, the oppressive reliance on tradition, the subservience of the populace to superstitions (including religion), the implausibility of selflessness in contemporary life. Because it attains its goals so admirably, the *esperpento* is the apogee of the playwright's efforts and helps establish him as a major figure in Spanish drama; because it views life in an absurdist mode, the *esperpento* marks Valle-Inclán as the precursor of Beckett and Ionesco.

Robert Lima. *Ramón del Valle-Inclán* (New York, Columbia University Press, 1972), pp. 23–24, 45

Valle-Inclán's evident interest in the structure of the novel is a reflection of a very general preoccupation among authors of the period under consideration, which continues to the present day. Like his contemporaries, Valle-Inclán was seeking to render the novel infinitely more flexible than its nineteenth-century predecessor. The rejection of chronological time is a further aspect of his later novels which reflects a very general preoccupation with the subject from the early years of the century. Its philosophic basis lay in an altered attitude to time, which was viewed cyclically and not chronologically as had been the case from the Renaissance onwards. Its most obvious manifestations are to be found in the works of the Simultanists—Apollinaire, Joyce, Virginia Woolf—who sought to grasp the moment in its total significance, or to manufacture a moment that contained eternity through sheer intensification of the present. Thus if Valle-Inclán's later novels are considered in a wider context, it will be seen that he is not adopting an eccentric attitude towards the structure of the novel; rather, he was but one of a number of writers who were rebelling against the narrow confines of the well-made novel, to which pattern a majority of novelists had adhered in the previous century. . . .

Valle-Inclán and Joyce agree on the need for dramatic form in the novel: the novelist may be omniscient in the fictional world of his own creation, but he must not be omnipresent. Where the writers differ is in the methods they employ to turn theory into practice. Joyce, like Virginia Woolf, favors the interior monologue, while Valle-Inclán exteriorizes his characters by employing a maximum of dialogue with short, impressionistic descriptions to introduce and round off individual scenes. It is only infrequently that Valle-Inclán resorts to a stream-of-consciousness technique to achieve particular effects.

The desire Valle-Inclán expressed in an interview to avoid the use of a central character in the *Iberian Ring* novels is something else that links him with a number of contemporary writers. Dos Passos' *Manhattan Transfer* (1925), Joyce's *Ulysses* (1922), and Virginia Woolf's *Mrs. Dalloway* (1925) are the products of other novelists of the period who, like Valle-Inclán, sought to break away from the limitations of the well-constructed novel. No longer does the author restrict himself to describing the fortunes of a few individuals through a series of situations presented in chronological fashion; instead he chooses to explore the wider reaches of society, availing himself of a large number of characters to achieve his purpose. . . .

It is unnecessary to elaborate further on the effects which the newly developed arts of juxtaposition exercised on the structure of Valle-Inclán's novels and on those of many contemporary writers. The emphasis shifted from a strict sequence of events giving meaning to the whole, to a series of "images," described by Ezra Pound as "that which presents an intellectual and emotional complex in an instant of time." This stress on diversity of events, together with the technique of the film which uses juxtaposed details in a montage construction, account to a considerable extent for the structure of Valle-Inclán's later novels. He has often been criticized for the supposed formlessness of his novels, but critics mistake a lack of orthodox form for a lack of any form whatsoever. The structure of the *Iberian Ring* novels and *The Tyrant Banderas* is, rather, very formal indeed, as is also the case with another apparently disjointed and haphazard work, Joyce's *Ulysses.*

Verity Smith. *Ramón del Valle-Inclán* (New York, Twayne, 1973), pp. 64–67

The Iberian Ring comes as close as is possible to challenging the validity of the historical novel as a genre. The problems provoked by this hybrid or bastard offspring of two disciplines, or of a creative activity which has had a passing flirtation with a discipline now made attractive by its clothing in anecdotal rather than formal fact, have partly been avoided, partly solved, partly re-posed with dogged insistence. . . .

The solution adopted by *The Iberian Ring,* to take history as both content and medium, and the novel as both content and medium, is perhaps the most elegant, but also the most problematic. We may blush at the obvious way in which Pérez Galdós will stage a discussion of contemporary or past events, showing a historical awareness which undermines the credibility of many characters as simple folk who are the natural salt of the earth, but we are at least provided with a solid corpus of facts to guide us through the novel. Valle-Inclán, by contrast, plays a game of intellectual one-upmanship with the reader. The novels of *The Iberian Ring* demand not only that the reader should be well acquainted with nineteenth-century Spanish history, but that he should be prepared to pick his way through an obstacle-course of nicknames, rumours, and informal references, hindered additionally by the occasional chronological disjunction, and the over-riding determination of the author that he should not be allowed to read the novels comfortably.

The result of this tantalising and uncompromising attitude of Valle-Inclán is that either the reader gives up, or he reconciles himself to reading *The Iberian Ring* as a series of unconnected and frequently enigmatic sketches. Perhaps only a fully annotated critical edition of *The Iberian Ring* will finally give the reader the tool he requires, and presumably if such an edition existed, it would frustrate the author's intentions of teasing and bewildering his readers so that they are in the same state of ill-comprehension as were the contemporary spectators of the 1868 revolution. If, however, the alternative to this frustration is to have a reduced and irritated body of readers, there seems to some case for at least giving the average reader orientation in the Iberian arena.

Alison Sinclair. *Valle-Inclán's "Ruedo Ibérico":*
A Popular View of Revolution (London,
Támesis, 1977), pp. 1–2

Valle-Inclán conceived the *esperpento* as a tragicomic representation of contemporary Spanish life; a representation in which he is totally removed. In this way he becomes an omniscient and omnipotent author who manipulates his fictional entities as if they were puppets and he a puppeteer. The tragic aspect was the result of a historical reality: the disaster of 1898, in addition to the socio-political inability to cope with twentieth-century values on the part of the restored Bourbon monarchs, this being a reality long before Primo de Rivera's takeover. The comic element of this vision arose from the absurdity of the maintenance of a traditional value system in a changing society. The clash of these two value systems produced the perfect conditions for an esperpentesque view of life. This vision could not effectively be represented by Realism or Naturalism, and so the time was ripe for a new style, for a literary renovation which would make literature of the twenties and thirties one of the most avant-garde in Europe.

The comic element of the *esperpento* is realized by means of a grotesque stylization of the fictional characters who are often reduced to sub-human status, while the tragic element is achieved by the critical nature of the themes and Valle-Inclán's intention in presenting them. The author mockingly creates personages who seem quite incredible to the reader-spectator, yet their resemblance to real-life personages is always evident. Sometimes they are merely grotesque re-creations of historical figures. Regardless of the process used for character-drawing, the purpose of the *esperpento* is always to "demythify" the glorious past of Spain of the Restoration period or contemporary Spain under the dictatorship of Primo de Rivera. In this sense, Valle-Inclán is a true member of the Generation of '98, charged with the task of dispelling the illusion of the grandeur of Spain (in which many of his contemporaries wanted to believe) and bringing to light the sad situation in which he viewed his country. This ethical change in an author, who in his earlier period delighted in describing an idealized version of the world by employing the Modernist recourse of *preciosismo* to one who portrays a debased and grotesque world in the *esperpentos* was necessarily accompanied by a change in his aesthetics.

Barry Weingarten. *Hispanófila.* Sept., 1981,
pp. 30–31

ZUNZUNEGUI, JUAN ANTONIO DE (1901–   )

[Zunzunegui's] novels offer us a considerable newness in our literary habits, because in Spain the short novel has been widely cultivated, that is, narratives of an hour's reading that could be finished at an easy and leisurely pace; the medium-length novel of two or three hundred pages, to which our authors have adapted their standards, has also become well established. Zunzunegui now returns to the type of novel in the grand style, the long novel that demands of the author a sustained effort and of the readers a prolonged commitment. *Chiripi, The Ship Chandler,* and *Oh . . . These Children!,* although each was published in a single volume, are novels that in a normal format would supply enough material for two or three volumes. We find ourselves, as result, before a great novelistic oeuvre that, in its panoramic magnitude and technical meticulousness, has required an ample format, analogous to that of the great creations of the genre in the nineteenth century, like a *Fortunata and Jacinta* [by Pérez Galdós] and *The Regentess* [by Clarín]. It is interesting, then, to note this return in Spain to the long novel in the grand style, which is also taking place in the English-speaking countries. The experiment could not be more interesting.

Zunzunegui has read widely the great novelists: Cervantes, Dickens, Balzac, Stendhal, Flaubert, Tolstoy, Eça de Queiroz, Pérez Galdós, Clarín, Baroja. Notice that all of them are authors of extensive works, of great novelistic constructions. Yet although thoroughly familiar with the works of all of them, he takes none of them as his teacher or guide. His technique is very different. We know his predilection for the great masters of naturalism—Flaubert, Pérez Galdós, Zola—but his style could not be further from naturalism. . . . Put on the spot to look for antecendents of Zunzunegui in the old masters, we would link him with Dickens, because of his having two aspects in common with him, tenderness and humor, or to Eça de Queiroz, because of his irony.

J. A. Tamayo. Foreword to Juan Antonio de Zunzunegui, *Dos hombres y dos mujeres en medio* (Madrid, Summa, 1944), pp. 33–34†

Zunzunegui is brusque, outspoken, but friendly. His enthusiasms are on the grand scale, and they make him prone to exaggerate. His praise is great for Madrid, its water, its weather, its clear blue sky, its spirit; for Spain, its people, its history, its food.

Today Zunzunegui is one of the few Spanish writers able to support himself from his writing, and he does not achieve this completely, for he depends also on a small private income, much reduced in value by the rising cost of living in Spain and the fall of the *peseta*. But he does try to avoid doing newspaper articles, which rob many Spanish writers of time that might be more profitably spent. He is frankly interested in money, a concern often reflected in his novels and stories, and which has led him to consider writing for the theater, which offers better returns. His literary production has shown a remarkable increase recently. In his formative years, when he was not concerned with monetary returns, he could publish a book every five years. Now things have changed. "One must write novels to survive," he says. But many of the greatest novelists have written under financial pressure. At fifty, Zunzunegui is filled with new ideas for stories and novels. With a solid literary reputation already achieved, he still possesses a promising creative vein.

John Dowling. *Hispania.* Nov., 1952, p. 427

Without any doubt whatsoever, the most important of the novelists now writing in Spain is Juan Antonio de Zunzunegui. . . .

The aspects of Zunzunegui's novels are multiple. His importance in the history of Spanish letters comes from his capacity to re-create Spanish society of the twentieth century as he goes about portraying it in his work. Although his novels abound in interesting types who leave an impression on the reader, what truly interests him is not so much the individual psychology of the characters as their relationship to the social milieu. In other words, what concerns Zunzunegui are human values and how the attempt at realizing them generates a specific moral environment within society.

As a result, the author has constructed an extraordinary complex artistic world in which the characters appear to be in possession of specific values or in the process of forming them. Simultaneously, the intertwining of these diverse activities creates in society a norm of moral practice that for the majority is invariable. For centuries the norm in Spain has been Catholicism. In general, the values were idealistic, and traditional Christian morality adhered to them. But in our century a change has become noticeable; a reappraisal and a new morality began to spread through the Spain of Zunzunegui. . . .

The criticism that Zunzunegui's characters have about Catholicism affect various areas of prime importance. The first is the dogma and the religious ritual: while intellectuals like Alfonso in *The Greatest Good* can attack a principle like the prohibition of contraception, ignorant characters like Pranchiso in *Oh . . . These Children!* protest against the pomp of the papal ceremonies that contrast with their own privations. The latter of the two novels questions the dogma of transsubstantiation of the sacramental wine, at the same time that in *This Dark Flight* León's humble submission to his faith becomes problematic. The second criticism concerns personal destiny and conformity, exemplified by

Jacinto, the new moral man of *The Ship's Rats*—Jacinto advocates a religion made up of self-serving conveniences, established on the basis of experiences of extreme hardships.

Paul Ilie. CA. Jan.–Feb., 1957, pp. 221–22†

And what is it, according to the novels of Zunzunegui, that gives meaning to life? Work, vocation, art . . . only those things. . . .

For Zunzunegui the great enemies of existence are money and death, and the only possibility of redeeming oneself consists in disinterested work done with love. But his characters are, in the majority of cases, incapable of working for the pure love of work without the greed for money destroying them completely. Only the female characters are capable of exercising this disinterested love and of leading more authentic lives than the men. Without doubt, the women created by this writer are infinitely superior to the male characters who abound in his works. True enough, the women are interested in money, but not as an end, but rather as a way of passing the time, of living, and never as a goal of life. The best example we have of this is in Beatriz, in *Bankruptcy,* whose true motivation in life is love, not money, proving this when she runs off with the jai-alai player, who offers the love that Ramón [a banker's son] is incapable of offering. Zunzunegui's women "are passionate, deeply emotional, with a great calling for motherhood (a calling that is always frustrated) and with religious anguish, which does not prevent them from crossing the boundaries marked by that very Church." Thus, we have, for example, Carmen *(The Ship's Rats),* who is capable of living and dying faithful to her first love, Ismael. And we have Sole [in *The Happy Road*], who after trampling over all the teachings of the Church seeks the Church's pardon with a strong will.

Zunzunegui's men are almost always weak-willed and cowardly, while his women are strong, decisive, and idealistic.

Delfín Carbonell Bassett. La novelística de
Juan Antonio de Zunzunegui (Madrid, Dos
Continentes, 1965), pp. 124–25†

The short novel cultivated by Zunzunegui and many Spanish authors in post-Civil War Spain is actually a kind of compromise between the novel and the short story. It retains the small cast of characters and the thematic unity of the short story, but with the advantage of length, the novelette offers more opportunity for digressions and for a more gradual development of the series of decisive incidents of human experience that form the plot. Zunzunegui chooses to call some of his short narratives *patrañas,* and because of their farcial nature, they are indeed "tall tales," filled with humor and lively imagination.

Zunzunegui's technique of composition is highly objective and imaginative. In a series of brief but extremely powerful vignettes, he often bends reality to caricature in interesting candid-camera shots. Characteristic devices of his prose are very short sentences with their feeling of arrested speed, repetitive phrases for dramatic impact, and the use of inanimate objects with their accompanying power of suggestion to create moods. He uses an abundance of striking images, metaphors, paradoxes, classical allusions, and words fallen into disuse. A consciousness of style and language is always present, and his rich vocabulary frequently involves complex syntax and the tendency to make adjectives and nouns from verbs or vice versa. His style is singularly virile, sometimes eloquent, at times simple and unadorned. The dialogue often moves abruptly with sensuous detail between normal communication and inward speech. He speaks deftly, and with wry interest and humor often gentle, subtle, or ironic he sketches the lives of real-life characters in an effective nonchronological arrangement.

> Rex Edward Ballinger. Preface to Juan Antonio
> de Zunzunegui, *Cuentos y patrañas* (New York,
> Appleton-Century-Crofts, 1966), p. vi

[In] *This Dark Flight* (1952) Zunzunegui succeeded in painting an exact and repulsive picture of the moral corruption of the middle class of Madrid that resulted from the financial hardships of the postwar period and blackmarket activities. The protagonist of the story, a sickly heir, ends up giving in to the shame of renting part of his lodgings to some spongers, and even has to endure a greater disgrace: seeing the breakup of his marriage when his wife decides to run away with the highest bidder. The case, treated with the cruel exaggeration with which Zunzunegui is accustomed to punish his protagonists (all so moderately sinister!), recalls other fictional cases treated with more compassion by Galdós. However, it is not the narration of the story but the revelation of the environment that gives to *This Dark Flight* its documentary value, which is so expressively summarized in the title. On the other hand, the title of another one of the most praised novels of Zunzunegui, *Life as It Is* (1954), turns out, in the final analysis, to be misleading, since what is offered in this fat volume is nothing more than the exploits of some underworld characters in pre-civil war Madrid. Similarity of the ambience is oblique not only because of the temporal distance, but, moreover, because of the similarities to the *sainetes* [short genre plays] and the costumbristic literature, which are more visible than the picaresque echoes in spite of the fact that the author subtitled his work "a picaresque novel written in a very popular Spanish language," dedicating it to the memory of Mateo Alemán [seventeenth-century Spanish author of an important picaresque novel].

The realism of Zunzunegui transmits the impression of anguish and of existential absurdity indicative of the urban and material contemporary world, which it attempts to reflect. But this writer without doubt has not learned or wanted to rid himself of the naturalistic perspective or costumbristic trappings, so that the impression proceeds almost solely from this limited material and not from the attitude of the author or from his style of writing. Zunzunegui's novels recall those of Zola and the Blasco Ibáñez of *The Mob* rather than those of Galdós, whom the Basque writer so admired.

Gonzalo Sobejano. *Novela española de nuestro
tiempo* (Madrid, Prensa Española, 1975),
pp. 222–23†

Zunzunegui is justified in his somewhat arrogant attitude towards his critics, for he must be reckoned as one of the most important contemporary novelists in Spain. Criticism of his prolixity and the external style of realism reflects more about contemporary tastes than it does about the literary quality of his work. Numerous critics are careful to point out that Zunzunegui is no imitator of Galdós nor of any other nineteenth-century novelists. Although Zunzunegui turns out good quality novels which appeal to a large audience, his readers must be limited to a very narrow political spectrum to tolerate his social views. . . .

[In *This Dark Flight*] the author presents a view of the miserable life of two people in Madrid. No one can fault him his excellent powers of observation, description, and construction of dialogue, but the thesis is buried in the heap of detail. The author is not in control of his medium. He may well have meant the novel to be taken with the moral that Roberto and Dolores could have added a little beauty and dignity to their dreadful situation through mutual self-denial and understanding of each other, but most critics simply do not view the novel this way. What comes through strongly is the author's inability to deal with the basic human situation. The author cannot force the reader to draw morals from the novel which he himself intended, nor can the author keep the reader from drawing conclusions which he considers to be unwarranted. Merely because Zunzunegui tells us what the thesis is supposed to be, does not mean that it is developed consistently. Even if the thesis is consistently presented, it is inappropriate and completely out of touch with the reality of the social and moral problems which afflict his characters. Zunzunegui fills the novel with descriptions of the struggle of Roberto and Dolores to make ends meet, and at the same time takes an almost cynical pleasure in describing the crimes of the black marketeers and other assorted cheats and thieves. Not only is his thesis inappropriate, it is directed cruelly at the victims of society. In this lies the coldness and arrogance of the novel. We would not agree more with the critics who suspect that Zunzunegui himself has never known what it is like to be hungry.

Randal C. Fulk. *REH*. Oct., 1979, pp. 324, 330

PORTUGAL

Em memória do Professor Hermilo Branco Ramalhete

Dai-me ũa furia grande e sonorosa;
E não de agreste avena ou frauta ruda,
Mas de tuba canora e belicosa,
Que o peito acende e a cor ao gesto muda;
Dai-me igual canto aos feitos da famosa
Gente vossa, que a Marte tanto ajuda. . . .

Luís de Camões, *Os Lusíadas* (I, 5)

I.S.

ALVES REDOL, ANTÓNIO. *See* **REDOL, ANTÓNIO ALVES**

* * *

BRANDÃO, RAUL (1867–1930)

Raul Brandão is an eminent caricaturist. Few know how to give life to a character, to a historical scene or novel as he does. . . . The march of the French troops from the frontier to Lisbon [in *King Junot*], the embarkation of D. João VI, for example, are extraordinary scenes of tragedy, in the first case, and tragicomedy, in the second case, but both [are] in the nature of caricature. . . .

Raul Brandão has yet another great quality as a historian: he takes in, with one sweeping view, the whole perspective of an epoch, the men in body and dream and shadow, and the surroundings that dominate them.

His pages about Spain are equally admirable. It is the Portuguese contemplating the Castilian, without hate, but from his spiritual distance; the pantheistic soul, overwhelmed with tears and sun, staring at the ghost of Torquemada in the fires. . . .

His characters live tied to a ghost that commands and directs them. They love, cry, laugh, hate under the terrible impulse of a shadow . . . the Dream, the Fatality of the tragic Greeks, reappearing, taking on Lusitanian flesh and blood. . . .

And all this dizzying pain that is life is condensed in a literary form crazy with movement. The works are jumpingly alive, the sentences follow each other like lightning bolts, whispers of water and tears. . . .

It is sad that such an intense and profoundly dramatic work, so revealing about our nation, cannot be understood, for the time being, in Portugal, where literary taste does not go further than a liking for a certain exterior and musical lyricism. . . .

Teixeira de Pascoaes. *A águia.* July, 1914,
pp. 30–31†

Raul Brandão's work, owing to many various constraints, is not vast, but it is complex, and it can be placed at the spiritual crest of our literature in spite of certain visible blemishes. Perhaps verbosity and swollenness are its most marked faults. . . . But two or three books are enough to perpetuate his name, placing him in the first rank of national writers. These books would be *The Fishermen, King Junot,* some pages of his *Memoirs.* . . .

In *King Junot* there are stupendous pages of sarcasm; in *The Fishermen,* the watercolorist could withstand a confrontation with the palettes of [Félix] Ziem, [Joseph] Turner, or [João] Vaz. In *The Farce,* he diffuses in low-relief . . . the canine and tender angelic humility of Joana. . . .

The stylistic structure suffers from an analogous flaw. Half a dozen pages are finely expressed, sparkling in the psychological observation of the human being; they are followed by others, without any sense, superfluous. . . . In the impressionistic painting of nature, he exceeds his own subjective discourse, in which he is often a master. He sets himself apart from all others in Portuguese literature in attempting to portray the human being in his moments of crisis through a halluci- natory chord, in his unbearable and even absurd desperation . . . in attempting to interpret the enigma of existence, the *quid* of certain fatalities. . . . In fact, no one has been able to interpret the nightmare of souls weighed down with the chains of the past as he has; the anguish that possesses us as travelers without a destination; ghostly thoughts like the one of feeling the dead, crowded in the eternal blackness behind the living, pushing the living toward the fatal cliff, as the water of a waterfall pushes itself. . . .

Raul Brandão was a generally timid and taciturn being. . . . Under- standably he had to be a revolutionary, fluctuating between Kropotkin, the organized doctrine, and Jesus, the Word in the hunger and thirst for justice. In this duality, practiced with the mirror now of Dostoevsky, now of Michelet, is perhaps the secret of his so singular and at the same time so human art.

Aquilino Ribeiro. *Camões, Camilo, Eçae alguns mais* (Lisbon, Bertrand, 1949), pp. 267–70†

It is in the presence of the social conditions of life on the Azores island of Corvo [in *The Unknown Islands*] that Raul Brandão gives us the key to his literary work. An anxious search had taken him there, and in the midst of a hostile nature, he is surprised at the village that provides an example of happiness. A soil of lava, hillsides battered by storms, the sea roaring all around . . . and, with all this, there has never been a robbery or a murder. The doors do not have locks. . . .

Owing to the invariably negative physiological balance that emi- gration and mortality maintain, social life there has stagnated . . . . Did the humanization of the earth lead to the dehumanization of man?— that is the question to which Raul Brandão's works incessantly respond yes. The indispensable dream through which man made himself, lifting himself up from animal primitivism and dominating the forces of nature, that indispensable dream . . . if indeed it facilitated progress, degraded the human into being his own wolf.

Mário Sacramento. *Vértice*. Feb., 1958, pp. 69–70†

In fact, there is in [Raul Brandão's] cult of trees and stones a type of exalted pantheism that ends up in a very emotional mysticism. But in

the dark regions of the thinking man doubts and rejections are generated: a fatalistic resignation that considers good and evil as products of
the earth's chemistry is preferred over a tenuous rationalism, which
leads him to extreme individualism, a relative of that anarchism that he
had defended in his *nefelibata* [group of eccentric writers of late-
nineteenth-century Portugal] phase; and then there appears a religious
tendency that elevates pain to the moving force of life and defines it as a
type of tribute to an undefinable God, who feeds himself on it.

The drama of poverty is the starting point of all this rambling
philosophy, in which emotion, ingenuousness, lyricism, and some moments of almost cynical disbelief alternate. The stories of the Gebo
[shabby person], of Luísa, of the prostitutes [in *The Poor*] illustrate it.

The story of the Gebo is the one that has the most continuity, the
most coherence. It develops on an apparently realistic level, in which
the concrete facts are rapidly stated . . . . Outside of this, the novel is
developed monotonously and is stopped in only one situation: the
Gebo, deprived of resources, scoffed at and rejected, tries to maintain
in his home a vital illusion, but at every moment there escape from him
confessions of defeat. One might say that the writer does not narrate: he
evokes, disdaining plot, alternating the levels of time, in what approaches certain novelistic conceptions of our own day. He places Sofia
among the prostitutes in the first chapters, he next describes her, with
some brilliant touches, as an unemancipated minor . . . . An unskillful
novelist, on purpose or owing to a laziness of composition, the writer
anticipates the direct narration of the events. But isn't there in this
chronological rambling a "divination" at a distance of modern [novel-
istic] techniques?

João Pedro Andrade. *Raul Brandão* (Lisbon,
Arcádia, 1963), pp. 98–99†

Humus [is] Raul Brandão's masterpiece and perhaps the work in which
his modernity stands out best. It consists of fragments of two monologues—that of the author and that of a visionary philosopher who is
his double, and who has the grotesque name "the Gabiru." These
fragments are dated, and they extend for one year; they are grouped in
chapters whose titles disclose the nature of the work, which is at the
same time mediative and poetic. . . . But one also finds there figurative
and novelistic elements: from a subjective atmosphere, in which space
and time seem distorted, from the beings and the things, emerge a
provincial village and its inhabitants with their feelings, their manias,
their dramas, some morsels of action that the author does not fully
develop. There are thus some beings and scenes that have become
frozen, some images of a magic lantern that from time to time erupt in
Raul Brandão's obsessed spirit. Indeed, reiteration is here, one of the
dominant principles, both of the composition and the style.

We penetrate into the limbo of a fiction in which the author asks himself if he himself has not created the time, the space, the characters about whom he is speaking. His most important subject is the terrifying dichotomy of man and life. . . . In each character there inhabits another rejected "I." And the principal action of *Humus* consists, if I am not mistaken, in the clash between the apparent world and the authentic world, or perhaps that troubling discovery, often like a flash of lightning . . .—a revelation which is produced in the author's spirit and which he projects into all the inhabitants of the village. In Brandão's works, the exterior reality, let's say, presents an oneiric and symbolic character. Thus the village of *Humus* is at the beginning a deserted village, like a tomb. . . .

Social and metaphysical problems are intertwined in Raul Brandão's works. He is a faithful reader of Dostoevsky and a contemporary of Freud, and he describes man in all the cruelty of his instincts, multiplying the scenes of misery and degradation; he is at the same time revolted and fascinated by the spectacle of human pain.

In attacking an unjust and shabby society that lends itself to satire, Brandão had made *Humus* an act of accusation. In its first edition, the work ended in a kind of epic nightmare, the universal revolt of the miserable people, their defeat, and the installation of an even more despotic dictatorship for which the ruling doctrine is that of the superman. Later those pages were suppressed as, in a general way, were the most evident pamphleteering traits. . . .

Jacinto do Prado Coelho. "Entre le symbolisme et l'existentialisme: *Humus* (1917) de Raoul Brandão," *Actes du Ve Congrès de l'Association Internationale de Littérature Comparée,* Belgrade, 1967 (Belgrade, University of Belgrade/Amsterdam, Swets and Zeittengen, 1969), pp. 357–59†

To what extent is the plot of *The Farce* connected to the personal problems of Raul Brandão? or; to what point do the conception and development of its "story" reflect and document some of the author's dominant preoccupations? Throughout his whole work an abstract entity—a principal idea, let us say—constantly reappears and dominates: the dream.

In *The Farce* it is also a question of a dream.

Beginning with his first significant work, *Story of a Clown* (1896), Raul Brandão had proclaimed the use of the dream as the only solution to or the only way of overcoming the absurdity of existence. Although he has not left us any clarifications that might permit us to attach to it any specific moral or psychological content aside from that implicit in the literal and literary meaning of the word, it is nonetheless possible to point out two qualities of dreams that are more or less clarified in that book: the romanticism-related dream, which "pulls us up"—the dream of the ultraromantic K. Maurício—and the dream that "pulls us down"—which is the disenchanted dream of Pita, a cynic and pessimist.

If the first is ascetic, the sublimation of the spirit through the elevation to a plane of moral beauty, the second is the flight from reality through the freeing of the evil forces repressed by the many barriers that divine and human laws have established so that the "creatures" can keep themselves within the indispensable limits of social existence. . . .

The creation of [the] character [Candidinha, in *The Farce*] and the situations her actions unleash are not as strange for her creator as one might suppose. . . . In the dream of that woman who is defeated in her goal of freeing repressed instincts, Raul Brandão sees the defeat of *his own* dream.

Guilherme de Castilho. *Colóquio/Letras*. Sept.,
1972, pp. 31, 34†

CARDOSO PIRES, JOSÉ. See PIRES, JOSÉ CARDOSO

CASTRO, JOSÉ MARIA FERREIRA DE (1898–1973)

To the young, somewhat dainty aristocrat [Alberto of *The Jungle*] the new life [in the jungle] is one of intensifying horror. In the beginning he shrinks from contact with his fellow workers, men of mixed strain with African blood predominating. And he is fearful of the jungle, the sporadic depredations of the untamed Amazonian Indian tribes, the fevers and the reptiles, the hordes of insects, the brutality of the management, the darkness of jungle.

He describes at great length the way in which rubber-tappers are exploited. . . . Long passages of the book are given over to rhythmic descriptions of the jungle in winter and summer, when flooded and when parched: to descriptions of the fauna and flora of the Amazonian wilderness; to incidents which illustrated the strange, greedy, generative spirit of this growing mass of vegetation. . . .

But the fiery young, dandified, ambitious Portuguese aristocrat has gained much under the ordeal. He has come to know what men are like. He has come to love his mulatto fellow worker, Forminino. . . . He has lost his immature enthusiasm. . . .

One feels that the translation is an excellent one.

The book's somewhat too elaborate, too self-consciously stylistic descriptions belong, no doubt, to the original, although in the original they may sing in a way not to be captured in any translation.

Fred T. Marsh. *NYTBR.* Feb. 3, 1935, p. 4

In my opinion, what has principally accounted for the immense success of *The Jungle,* to date translated into fourteen languages. . . , is its profound humanism, its truth, the lived details that [Ferreira de Castro] remembers, his sharp and thorough observations and notes about the lives of the poor rubber-tappers, a complete absence of commentary which permits the deed to act directly on the reader, and a very scrupulous faithfulness of vocabulary in the discourses, so that the most minor dialogue between these primitive and simply presented people lost in the farthest depths of the riotous jungle touches the heart.

The Jungle is one of the most difficult books I have ever been given to translate, and, if I myself had not often voyaged to Brazil, if I did not know that land and the people of that land . . . I would never have finished my translation. And I am not only alluding to the difficulties in vocabulary that crop up on every page.

That is to say, I wanted to avoid the hold of the Portuguese sentence, the seduction of Ferreira de Castro's style—Portuguese is the most voluptuous language, the most melodic of Europe, and as it is a tradition in his country, Ferreira de Castro is a brilliant, an ardent stylist. [1938]

> Blaise Cendrars. Introduction to José Maria
> Ferreira de Castro, *Forêt vierge* (Paris, Bernard
> Grasset, 1957), pp. vi–vii†

This novel [*The Wool and the Snow*] is divided into three parts: "The Flocks," "Wool and Snow," and "The House": but it is bound above all by the very human adventures of Horácio's fight for life. The protagonist is a shepherd from Manteigas, on the outskirts of the Estrela mountain range, who, tired of a monotony without a future, exchanges the bucolic life of the annual *snows* in which the flocks live and suffer for painful activity, first as an apprentice, later as a weaver, in a spinning factory in Covilhã. The psychological contradiction between the wool and the snow, which is documented by the protagonist, animates this splendid novel, with dialectical and ideological postulates, of Ferreira de Castro. . . .

Horácio loves Idalina; they live in a place that the author dissects to the bone in the most insignificant human and folkloric details in order to establish Horácio's dullness and his moral and social coldness. His humble parents, like his future in-laws, are also poor people, and represent the force of age-old prejudices: Ferreira de Castro beautifully describes the pastoral life and delineates the themes of rural and simple-minded scandal-mongering. . . .

Horácio ends up marrying Idalina and becoming a weaver. His biography, however, in spite of its insignificance (or perhaps because of it) is an attempt to represent, in his successes and failures, the effort of the Portuguese factory worker in his continuous battle, now against the owner, now against his comrades—but also the pain of his defeats, the happiness of his small triumphs, and his normal tendency toward revolt. [1947]

> Manuel Anselmo. *Meridianos críticos*, Vol. II
> (Lisbon, Portugália, 1950), pp. 239–41†

From the beginning Ferreira de Castro belonged to no newspaper or magazine. He placed occasional articles or short stories with one or another. Literature in Portugal seldom provides a livelihood, and in his case it provided even less. Needless to say, the young writer suffered great privation and even many days of hunger.

Finally, in 1921, his first work published in Portugal, *But. . . ,* appeared. A certain boldness of style and even of punctuation in this book revealed his desire to create something new, to break away from accepted formulas, to flee from the beaten path. But he was groping his way though territory still unfamiliar testing his wings.

In the following year, Ferreira de Castro published in Portugal, in a short-story collection, his first fictional work, *Famished Flesh*. In it he evoked the anguish of sex-hunger in the loneliness of the Amazon jungle, a torment that was resolved in incest. The audacity of the theme provoked indignation. This could have contributed, in a way, to his fame as a writer, but he did not exploit it. He even wrote the novel *The Easy Success,* an expression of the writer's refusal to satisfy the public tastes. This novel and another, *Black Blood,* were published in 1923, also in collections of short novels. . . .

Between this date and 1928, Ferreira de Castro published several volumes of short stories. But it was in the novel that he was to reveal his exceptional talents as a fiction writer. Thanks to his novels, later translated into all the languages of culture, Portuguese literature acquired an international audience.

Jaime Brasil. BA. Spring, 1957, p. 119

Superficially, at least, the emphasis [in *Emigrants*] is sociological. The author protests against an environment that traps men like his protagonist and condemns them to poverty. The most memorable element in the book, however, is the paradox of Manuel's character. He is a hard-working son of the soil, a family man, an apparently solid citizen. He is also gullible, vain and willful, eager to run after the will-o'-the-wisp of quick riches and ready to blame his consequent disaster on bad luck. He desires wealth not merely for the purchase of comfort but also (and perhaps even more) for ostentation. . . .

Manuel is not just a victim of society: it is his own fatuity that changes a hard but decent life into one of utter defeat and humiliation. His misery is the joint product of environmental resistance and personal inadequacy, and the candor with which the author presents this inadequacy gives the book its stamp of honesty and truth. At the same time, his non-hero's smallness of spirit makes his defeat sad rather than tragic. . . .

Everywhere the author's compassion and indignation come through, despite the restraint that keeps them fairly free of excess and sentimentality. What gives his novel a claim to a place in world literature is less its social protest than its revelation of how a poor man's own folly may destroy him when poverty itself cannot.

William L. Grossman. NYTBR. Nov. 18, 1962,
pp. 4, 64

Already in *The Bend in the Road* the novelist had attempted, effectively, to portray a succession of human problems whose essential drama is enacted within the mind. Ferreira de Castro, in his portrayal of the old socialist leader, corrupted by his thirst for power, by disillusion and by the simple physiology of inexorably advancing age, paints a penetrating picture of political psychology. To pragmatic observation was added, in this work, subtle evidence of a profound understanding of human frailties. The striking dramatic atmosphere in which the narrative occurs, although always set in an accurately descriptive realism, impels the reader to an impulsive dialogue, not only with the persons created there, but also with the author himself, in that vital, underlying reality of his moral and intellectual character. And both in the most particularly edifying description of the socialist's political adventure, and in the admirable dialogues of exceptional intensity, Ferreira de Castro sustains throughout the note of indecision, the powerful sequence of events and balance in the structure of the novel, which form the distinguishing mark of the fully developed novelist.

In *The Jungle* the subject matter still dominates the writer; in *The Bend in the Road,* as in *The Mission,* it is now the writer who dominates, who selects, who guides and shapes his creation. There is also, apparent throughout his work, a perfection and controlled flexibility of style, capable of expressing the most difficult nuances of the analytic novel.

The Mission was clearly born from this newly acquired, inventive command of themes and their form. This fundamental naturalism, enriched, when used in the novel, by the penetrating portrayal of the contrast, the uncertainties and fluctuations of characters, of inner realities present in the more complex souls, reached a point where wider horizons might be discovered. Both the social exterior and the inner states of restless, divided, sharply differing souls, which ran through the novella, are firmly based in a perfect awareness of the human condition. And the atmosphere, together with the men subject to it, are reflected in the narrative with the exemplary art of the novel as defined by Stendhal. . . .

Álvaro Salema. Introduction to José Maria
Ferreira de Castro, *The Mission* (London,
Hamish Hamilton, 1963), pp. 20–22

The Supreme Instinct, notwithstanding its generous motivation, is not the book that we would like at this point in the career of the author of *The Jungle.* The theme needs no discussion; we applaud it. In form, however, the book appears excessively "elaborated," too well "woven," as if Ferreira de Castro wanted to find less pleasure in the "nerve" and the implacable rigor that his story demanded (in our opinion) than in the opportunities it provided for "aliterary" use and for local color. It is there that Ferreira de Castro probably has betrayed himself. This expedition of men who go to pacify and try to civilize a tribe of Parintintins Indians is described and explained at great length through a thousand and one roads that, in main, turn away from the central flux. Paradoxically, if we think that Ferreira de Castro lived, fought, and suffered in those surroundings, the work seems "imagined," when it was the flavor of forest life and the life of its inhabitants that we were awaiting. And in this way it is only from time to time that we feel the excitement of the profound adventure that was being lived here.

José Saramago. *SeN*. Aug., 1968, p. 281†

In [the] snow storm scene of *The Wool and the Snow*, Ferreira de Castro demonstrates his ability in the art of descriptive technique. The reader becomes a part of the storm itself and shares the coldness, the fears and anxieties of the two men as they fight the terrible forces of nature. The reader also feels lost and frost-bitten, as he travels through the dark, ghost-like woods and sees the trees execute before his eyes the dance of death, as it were, and hears the forlorn cries of the wind as it beats the snow against his face and causes him to stiffen.

The second example of extraordinary artistic use of sensationism in Ferreira de Castro's works is also taken from *The Wool and The Snow*. In this passage a thunderstorm is described. . . .

As in the snow storm, nature here also penetrates man. Visual impacts are produced by the use of the words "thunder bolt," "raging flash," "darkness," "blow of light," "ray," and "live coal." Auditory impressions abound, as words suggesting various types of sounds aptly appear in the paragraph, causing a gamut of amorphous vibrational energies to pierce the reader's ears. . . .

The qualities of sensory textures and atonalities incorporating all of the five senses . . . typify Ferreira de Castro's use of sensationism in descriptive passages throughout his novels, especially in the later ones.

William Megenny. *RomN*. Autumn, 1971, pp. 64–65

The author of *The Wool and the Snow* and *The Jungle* dealt with Portuguese and Brazilian themes, and with the vast audience of readers that he reached, he brought the Brazilians into closer contact with Portuguese reality and the Portuguese with Brazilian reality: in addition to his works on Portuguese themes, *Emigrants, The Jungle,* and *The Supreme Instinct* have Brazil as a backdrop and are part of Brazilian thematics. . . .

We believe that one could go even further in the analysis of the meaning of this presence in the two literatures, seeing in it not only the treatment of different themes but diverse perspectives on the same [themes], depending on whether they are made part of the cultural system of Portuguese literature or that of Brazilian literature. Thus, there are two complementary readings for each work, since in each literature each one occupies a different place and has a different value. . . .

The Jungle and The Supreme Instinct occupy a special place in Brazil's literature of the Amazon, specifically in the area of its most important literary interest, which is the one that manages to overcome the dominant tendency toward easy and picturesque regionalism in praise of the land, its life and mores, [and] establishes itself as authentic literature through artistically transforming the reality of the ambience into a human drama of universal proportions.

Looking at the collection of these literary productions [Amazonian literature] as a whole, we see, in fact, Nature defined from four complementary angles: the genesiac Amazon, as Euclides da Cunha, Alberto Rangel, or Raul Bopp saw it; that of the historical and scientific fiction of Gastão Cruls; that of the "accounts," "tales," and voyages of José Veríssimo, Peregrino Júnior, or Braga Montenegro; and that of man conditioned by natural determinism or exploited by other men, of [Herculano] Inglês de Sousa and other novelists of the extreme north [of Brazil].

It is precisely in this last current that The Jungle and The Supreme Instinct fit. Their author did not let himself be astonished by the exoticism of the forest, but he discovered how to take advantage of it, not only functionally as an element of the plot but also as a means of aesthetic embellishment. Ferreira de Castro . . . established the basis for the authentic Amazonian novel of human coordinates.

Fernando Cristóvão. Colóquio/Letras. Sept., 1974, pp. 20–21†

CASTRO SOROMENHO, FERNANDO MONTEIRO. See SOROMENHO, FERNANDO MONTEIRO DE CASTRO

FERREIRA, JOSÉ GOMES (1900–1985)

Called a *divertimento* by the poet, this first long prose narrative [*Marvelous Adventures of Fearless John*] presents a series of dream adventures in the lands of mischievous fairies, odd creatures, and ghoulish monsters. At times, the allegory amuses, e.g., when Fearless John visits the people who have phonograph records instead of heads. At other times, it becomes sinister, as when John is caught in a cave where he cannot avoid breathing air poisoned by fear "that all of us have been breathing for a long time." Author and hero alike grow weary of the magic world, which is more monstrous than real life, for it lacks friendship and love while containing its share of prohibitions, policemen, parasites, stupidity, hunger, thirst, and sleeplessness. Inspired by traditional tales and perhaps also by Lewis Carroll's fantasies, Gomes Ferreira has written a Portuguese *Alice in Wonderland* with a pinch of Swiftian ferocity. Such satire in allegorical form is a welcome novelty in Portuguese literature.

Gerald Moser. BA. Winter, 1963, p. 103

Certain words constantly recur [in *Imitation of the Days*]—moon, stars, dream, clouds, death, trees, rain, shadow, etc.—almost all associated with nighttime, and in every case related to nature. Many of these words refer to a reality that projects upward (and for this reason and even for others—for example, flying fireman, the violins he describes, the scene of him dancing in the room all alone, etc.—I have the desire to classify him, perhaps erroneously as the Chagall of Portuguese literature).

Humor also can assume somber tonalities, from the disillusionment that comes from the realization of how materialism is a pervasive force in life . . . to the descriptions that we might call black humor. . . . At the same time, however, humor appears to color the end of a section, in a final unexpected twist that the author gives to the narrative. . . .

Much more than humor itself, irony is present. Irony appears in the very titles of some of the selections . . . ; irony about himself . . . ; and bitter irony . . . .

Irony . . . works with particular efficiency in the function of nullifying or counterbalancing a previous effect, such as diminishing the grandiloquence of certain statements or softening some trite idea . . . .
[1967]

José Palla e Carmo. Do livro à leitura (Lisbon,
Europa-América, 1971), pp. 282–83†

José Gomes Ferreira decries the fact that in Portugal there are no institutions or structures concerned with the organized teaching of art and literature, that is, culture. What occurs is that he deeply feels the "distance" [between himself and rural people], but [in *The Daily Unreality*] he does not place his finger on it as precisely as he does in *The World of the Others,* where he openly attacks the mechanism of national education, which is a failure. . . .

From a doctrinaire point of view, the pages of *The Daily Unreality* reveal a complacent tone in the ideological statements and the positions he takes; the author has [elsewhere] been much more incisive, or hard, or polemical, or implacable, or intransigent—whatever adjective you want to use. *The Daily Unreality* is less open to external polemic, much less liable to indulge in direct statements, which at times, in an almost pamphleteering way, are found in *The World of the Others.* What concerns the author in this new volume . . . is still, as in the body of his poetry, the problem of feeling himself a spectator in a world he cannot change. He feels this so sharply that at times his perspective about the "human flood" disintegrates. As an artist he feels himself quite at a distance from the common people. . . . This truth produces a shock of a social nature. It is, once again, his conscience as a bourgeois accusing himself of being an aristocrat. After all, he "is not a member of the proletariat."

Alexandre Pinheiro Torres. *Vida e obra de José Gomes Ferreira* (Lisbon, Bertrand, 1975), pp. 256–57†

Gomes Ferreira does not propose to give a chronological overview of his life [in *Poetry VI*], but rather a picture of his life as his memory intermittently reflects on it over the last fifteen years of his poetic inspiration; it is a type of poetic diary of his most recent intimate existence.

This impression of an "intimate diary" is further stressed through the frequent allusions to contemporary events, which have been symbolically grouped around several essential dates: 1919–20, 1926–31, 1968, and finally the April 25 [,1974,] revolution and what followed. . . .

Whoever thinks . . . that this is a partisan poetry, a poetry at the service of a cause, would be quite mistaken, no matter how much it might appear so, first, because the freedom the poet defends is simultaneously social justice and the freedom of the spirit, . . . and second, and above all, because the necessity of "telling the truth," of denouncing oppression, or of cultivating regained happiness does not relegate a concern for "poetic diction" to a secondary level. . . .

We can say that Gomes Ferreira's poetry is excellent proof of the futility of literary-school labels. We can consider him a "neorealist" because of the content or the themes of his poetry; nonetheless, Gomes

Ferreira is a careful "formalist" in many ways . . . . He is an extraordinary poet, a poet of a vigorous and original personality.

Pierre Hourcade. *Colóquio/Letras*. March,
1977, pp. 74–75†

It is interesting to notice the subtitle the poet has given to the three volumes of *Militant Poet:* "Twentieth-Century Journey Inside Myself," which is quite different, as his interest in the big events of this century might lead us to think, from "My Journey Inside the Twentieth Century." The subtitle chosen points to a personal experience, a lyrical attitude—that is, to subjectivity, on which a poet bases his response to History. Similarly, the epigraphs which precede most of his poems and refer either to the major convulsions of our century or to the struggle of the Portuguese people for freedom and dignity during the forty-eight years of fascist rule are just a starting point. Only seldom do the poems become illustrations of the events which in principle acted as their immediate inspiration. . . .

The author takes up the posture of the bard; he tries to awaken his readers' minds, to disturb them. According to the theory of the Militant Poet as explained in the memoirs [*The Memory of Words*], Gomes Ferreira sees himself as a mixture of "knight-errant, prophet, minstrel, bard, journalist." But irony is an important ingredient in Ferreira's poetical praxis as well. The existence of a persona in his texts is something the reader, although fascinated by the virtuosity of the *metteur-en-scène,* never forgets. At the same time that he follows the persona's indignation (and sense of bewilderment in the face of the terrible mystery of being in this world with all its contradictions) he is fully aware of the undeniable verbal reality that a poem is.

In some measure, in spite of the author's attraction for the committed poetics of neorealism and the visionary quality on the verge of surrealism in many of his poems, he still pays tribute to *saudosismo* [the nostalgia movement], whose main objective was to materialize the spiritual. This dialectics of reality and unreality expands to another theme which pervades Ferreira's poetry: the conflict within the persona between his individualistic tendencies and the need to share his fellow man's drama and suffering. Gomes Ferreira puts his individual voice at the service of man's redemption in a new society, but he never forgets that he is at the service of Poetry too. In order to be a militant of Utopia, a poet must be first and foremost a militant of Poetry. And that is what Gomes Ferreira's work so well illustrates.

Fernando J. B. Martinho. *WLT*. Spring, 1979, p. 270

FERREIRA, VERGÍLIO (1916–   )

Vergílio Ferreira's first published novel, *Where Everything Was Dying*, is a typical work of neorealism in its structure and style. . . . The principal characteristics of this first literary effort are psychologically well-described and well-constructed characters; a sense of chronology in the story's development; and the interweaving and linking of episodes so as to form a unified novel.

This work was followed by *The Road Is Long.* . . . This novel is about Coimbra University students, . . . but . . . it is not the best modern novel on the theme. In *Coach J* we have plain neorealism, with its worst characteristics: verbose, empty, and pamphleteering lyricism. However, from another point of view, *Coach J* is an interesting effort. I refer to the style. For the first time in Portuguese literature and in a very accomplished manner, the author achieves an impressionistic style through the use of direct speech, in which he writes as if the characters were speaking, with their rapid jumps and illogical thought processes. The communication of details, of exclamations, of psychological or physical observations, which are apparently unconnected, end up forming an impressive and imposing whole. . . . In this way Vergílio Ferreira was able to extract effectively new aesthetic and expressive values from the language.

> Franco Nogueira. *Jornal de crítica literária*
> (Lisbon, Portugália, 1954), pp. 126–27†

Brief Happiness is another step in the novelistic evolution of Vergilío Ferreira.

We note, before anything else, that there is no emotional integration of the narrator-character into the narrative level of the past; rather, one verifies the flood of present events by the past events. In fact, neither in *Apparition* nor in *Pole Star* did the present have such a defined existence as it does in *Brief Happiness*. Here, the present stops being a simple reference point for the spirit totally involved in earlier situations, and is a level that exists in its own right; it is level of actual existence just as it is felt, without ignoring day-to-day details and events. . . .

Thus, while past events were stressed in *Apparition* in order to provoke a denunciation of human problems, and while that past in *Pole Star* presented the conflict provoked by that denunciation, one that repeatedly occurs to the ever-renewed narrator, *Brief Happiness* presents us with a narrator who is well fixed in the present, although his attention is directed toward the past . . . .

> Maria Alzira (Seixo) Baranhona. *Para um
> estudo da expressão do tempo no romance
> português contemporâneo* (Lisbon, Instituto de
> Alta Cultura, 1968), p. 148†

Two decisive presences are easily detected in *Apparition* and *Brief Happiness:* the tutelary shadow of Kafka . . . and the giddiness of Beckett. They are diluted, however, in the *morality of literary language,* which we can find glowing examples of in Vergílio Ferreira's earlier novels. All we have to do is browse through the passage on pages 188–90 of the original edition of *Coach J* in order to verify that already in 1944 [when it was completed] Vergílio Ferreira was beginning to dominate the processes of perspective, which were completely foreign to the characteristic mode of neorealist prose. In any case, either under the influence of the Kafka's unreality, or having been impressed by Beckett's saturation with the absurd, Vergílio Ferreira used literary language freed from the subservience that tradition imposed, and it attains a superior unruliness and disorder. . . .

With *Clear Void* . . . the processes of montage are bound up in a much more labyrinthine structure than is normal in the literary product. The narrator is so involved with himself that it is almost impossible to point out his participation in the construction of the cathedral of symbols, of allusions, of metaphors . . . , of recapitulations of the past, of memories of the future that make up the foundation of the whole structure.

João Palma-Ferreira. *Vergílio Ferreira* (Lisbon,
Arcádia, 1972), pp. 28, 31–32†

Rapidly, the Shadow, as a "novel-problem," speaks to us as the human beings we are; it is a constant appeal to our subjectivity, and hence the closeness of the narrator to the reader will be all the more authentic the more integrated the image of one with the other.

But, of course, there must always be a relationship of dependence of the first on the second, since the narrator knows much more than the reader. This kind of dependence reveals itself at the end, when the narrator takes off his "mask" and tells us that everything was nothing more than a "fantasy." . . .

The dominant themes of *Rapidly, the Shadow* are old age, death, pain and suffering, illness, anger, lechery, jealousy and mistrust . . . as if Pandora had once again opened her box and all evils had escaped. . . .

Rapidly, the Shadow is a unique and isolated novel in our literature, and it questions, among many important elements, the role of the writer and art in our day; the belief in the book as a message of faith and hope for future generations; the role of nonconformity in face of man's smallness in the universe and before death . . . .

Leonilda Aparecida Tonin. *Colóquio/Letras.*
Sept., 1976, pp. 85–86†

FERREIRA DE CASTRO, JOSÉ MARIA. See CASTRO, JOSÉ MARIA FERREIRA DE

GOMES FERREIRA, JOSÉ. *See* **FERREIRA, JOSÉ GOMES**

* * *

MIGUÉIS, JOSÉ RODRIGUES (1901–1980)

It is not possible to isolate the enthusiasm that resulted from the publication of *Happy Easter* . . . from an ideology in which the relatively recent discovery of Dostoevsky, the prestige of Raul Brandão, and the tendency toward the "psychological," vaguely psychoanalytical, novel (poetry or diary) were all integrated. . . .

The philosophy of *Happy Easter* clearly follows the realistic type of the nineteenth century. . . . Nonetheless, the novel is a product of its time, if not for the author's position in the narrative, at least for the problem the narrator presents. This problem had been formulated quite specifically in Dostoevsky's *Notes from Underground* (1864), and it can be considered typical of our most important literature of the 1930s. . . .

The situation of the narrator-protagonist of *Happy Easter,* Renato Lima, "Mr. Clumsy," can be pointed to as an illustration of Dostoevsky's pretentious idea of free will.

Renato is an unfortunate man who had been educated since childhood with all the dependencies, enslavements, and confusions of his humble condition, and for whom, he believes, "life has forced him to live on a solitary island of dreams." "Mr. Clumsy" creates for himself a daydreaming double, who goes through the daily routine without any pleasure, ambition, or great interest. Then an opportunity to be the business partner of a wealthy capitalist arises. It is then that his dream double leads him on to the very first adventure of his life; owing to simple, irrational will, he risks everything—his own future and that of his wife and son—in embezzlement, in drunken stupors, and, as the final link in the chain, in crime. He ends up in an insane asylum, and there, at the insistence of a psychiatrist who wishes to establish a concept of personal responsibility in him, he reconstitutes his life. Renato feels *free,* happy, unrelated to anything that he had been in the past. . . . He sees himself as the man who obeyed . . . in two ways: first, while he was unable to choose, he obeyed the mechanical orders of personal advantage and the rules of the society in which he lived; later he obeyed a force different from his own conscious desire, which is nothing less than the "most advantageous advantage" conceived by the anarchist of *Notes from Underground.*

Óscar Lopes. *Cinco personalidades literárias*
(Oporto, Divulgação, 1961), pp. 55–56, 58–59†

All of Miguéis's works force us to reflect on man and human destiny. An antimetaphysical writer *par excellence,* the author of *The School of Paradise* refuses to give us the image of man's movements in the daily world as the underlying substance of history. To reflect on man, to define him through the game of his social relationships is one of Miguéis's dominant preoccupations. . . .

When Miguéis takes a critical position with regard to the world of experience, it frequently acquires the form of satire. Pages like those of "A Trip through Our Homeland" offer us a very striking example of this metamorphosis of social criticism. *It's Forbidden to Point,* a recently published volume, is also of this type, as the author himself points out in the preface. But what was only a secondary intention in "A Trip through Our Homeland" here becomes a clearly explicit design by the author.

The Brechtian maxim that beneath the daily things the author must find the unusual and that he must shed light on an abuse finds complete observance in this volume [*It's Forbidden to Point*]. With biting criticism Miguéis presents the dossier of certain set ideas or forms of characteristically bourgeois life, with its accompaniment of little cowardices and faults, small or great cruelties, ridiculous weaknesses, gigantic contradictions, and also some virtues. In this book Miguéis examines the cloth of daily experiences thread by thread, the real problems of men of our society and our time.

Rogério Fernandes. *SeN.* Sept., 1964, p. 285†

I think that everyone who reads *Nikalai! Nikalai!* will do so with a certain amount of astonishment. Anyone who knows Miguéis's works— "Léah" or *Third-Class People*—cannot help but constantly ask himself while reading this novel, who are these Russians? Who exactly is the narrator? Answers will be found throughout the novel and above all at the end. White Russians, exiled after the Russian Revolution, who now are living miserably in the West, longing for Russia and the Czar, are the heroes of the work. With regard to the very much more complex narrator, who will appear almost to the end of the work as a character-narrator (basically a third person transformed into a first person), who is an agent for the S.I.S. [Secret Service], but really a double agent, and who changes his allegiance at the end of the work, he will be *an* author (not *the* author) of what had been written earlier and is a "fantasy" at the end.

This reader noted during *Nikalai! Nikalai!* the game of the narrator who appears and disappears, who is both character and creator, who explains himself, explains himself again, and "unexplains" himself; that we are in Léah's country and that Venusiinen is a new Léah; that the narrator has both identity and language problems.

This reader also understood that the general theme of *Nikalai! Nikalai!* is not political; this reader understood that the work constitutes another variation on a theme of human experience, and she began to make the inevitable identification between characters and author: Miguéis far from his homeland.

Eduarda Dionísio. SeN. Aug., 1971, p. 40†

With the second volume of *Reflections of a Bourgeois,* Rodrigues Miguéis appears to have wanted to undertake for contemporary Portugal what Paulo Prado had done for Brazil of the 1920s with his *Portrait of Brazil,* and what Octavio Paz had attempted for Mexico of the 1940s with *Labyrinth of Solitude*—what [Hermann] Keyserling called a "spectral analysis" of their respective countries: an analytical description of the psychological components of their people, from which they make a judgement about the past and an evaluation of the present state.

Rodrigues Miguéis has not failed in this; I would be inclined to say that he has gone overboard. He has a tendency to give his symbolic character Arthur, "the common Lusitanian," all the ridiculous features, all the defects, all the sins of heart and spirit. Nothing and almost no one is safe from the avenging satire, neither the mores, nor the institutions, not urban life, nor the past, nor the present. The author, through his caricaturelike Arthur, denounces almost all the traits common to all the beneficiaries—or the victims?—of the so-called "consumer society." . . .

If the ideological side of Rodrigues Miguéis might seem debatable, the writer himself is without question tasty, juicy, dextrous in his use of words, following in the great tradition of Camilo [Castelo Branco] and Aquilino Ribeiro; and I am almost tempted to say "doing a better job," owing to his spontaneity and lack of verbal obscurity. Rodrigues Miguéis is one of the contemporary masters of prose; and that is not a small achievement.

Pierre Hourcade. Colóquio/Letras. March,
1975. pp. 74–75†

As might be expected from Miguéis's earlier works, "Léah" is replete with social problems. Many of them are familiar. There is, for example, the problem of the modest means of the protagonist. Carlos's genteel poverty has its effect in many ways, but with relation to the plot it is particularly important to note that it is his lack of money that first brings him to Mme. Lambertin's *pensão* [pension], where he takes a room which is far from being luxurious and is only passably clean. It is at the pension, of course, that he meets and falls in love with Léah. Then, as Carlos and Léah's love affair progresses, it is primarily his impecuniousness that stops him from accompanying Léah to her native France, where she hopes they can marry and settle down. Thus poverty, or at least a certain lack of affluence, not only leads to Carlos's meeting his lover but also militates against the couple's regularizing their relationship. . . .

There is, however, a group of psychological problems which is both central to the development of the plot of "Léah" and is observable in many other works by the same author; that is, the problems a foreigner has in adjusting to his new surroundings, which are manifested in Carlos by his disillusionment with his Belgian surroundings, a recurring sadness and loneliness and a longing for home. He is dissatisfied with life and even with his own compatriots. . . .

The most striking of the various complementary aspects of "Léah" which come to the fore is the author's depiction of the worker as an essentially noble being. . . . The theme of the nobility of work itself is incorporated into that of the nobility of love between man and woman as well. . . . It was perhaps one of the reasons why . . . Adolfo Casais Monteiro could place on Miguéis's brow the perhaps unwanted laurel of being the true, if unacknowledged, mentor of the Portuguese neo-realist movement.

John A. Kerr, Jr. WLT. Spring, 1977, pp. 222–23

A few years before his death in New York, Miguéis had published the last of his novels, different in concept and theme from all the rest. [*Bread Does Not Fall from the Heavens*] appeared as a newspaper serial aimed at a broad reading public, its plot abounding in surprising turns. In it Miguéis . . . used the theme of the tribulations of farm laborers in the Alentejo. In the final note to his novel he points out that he had written an anti-fascist play on an Alentejan smuggler and his vengeance against the gentry in 1937, for the Portuguese textile workers of New Bedford. He then combined the smuggler's story ingeniously with the more common theme of the landless, starving peasantry: the daring, very masculine *contrabandista,* worshiped by the poor folk, men and women alike, as a heroic rebel, becomes a loner contrasted to the rural proletariat that is gradually being organized by a third and new element in the cast of characters. . . .

In the novel Miguéis abandoned the psychological subtleties that were his hallmark. Instead, he composed a superior kind of thriller, whose characters are clearly identified as either villains—the big land holders, the Government and its armed hirelings—or as noble heroes: the common people, the young student of peasant background, his poor childhood sweetheart preferred by him to the rich heiresses he could have married, the idealistic engineer, the Robin Hood-like smuggler, a paralyzed old veteran who wants to build a school, and other individuals. Although Miguéis was not a native of the Alentejo . . . his keen, sympathetic observation of manners and speech and his careful, methodical way of writing enabled him to create an epic around memorable characters, superior to the fiction on the plight of the Alentejan farmers and laborers by others . . . . It is a relief to read a well-written, old-fashioned novel for a change, where nothing has to be laboriously puzzled out.

Gerald M. Moser. *WLT.* Autumn, 1981, pp. 650–51

NAMORA, FERNANDO (1919–   )

In this new novel, *Fire in the Dark Night,* Fernando Namora uses the same process he did in his first novel [*The Seven Regions of the World*]. . . . Namora has an endless number of characters whom the reader cannot get fixed in his mind, since they are presented in quick scenes of little significance. . . . The characters that pass through the novel do not make a mark on our imagination. They speak, they gesticulate, and they pass by like shadows. . . .

One strange thing: although seemingly objective, this novel is really extremely subjective. Identifying with his protagonists, Namora never separates himself from them. Perhaps one could say that he takes them too seriously. The novelist must give the impression that he is superior to his characters. He must convince us that he knows more than his characters and that he knows about their lives. This does not occur in the novel. The novelist here seems to want to force the reader to accept his characters. . . .

The consequences of this attitude are evident. Fernando Namora rarely manages to seem spontaneous to us. The effects of this can be felt in his style. . . . For this reason he uses rhetorical devices when he does not invoke some banality. The common characters are confused with one another. We cannot follow them. We are not interested in them. It is only in their love affairs that they manage to show some life. [1943]

João Gaspar Simões. *Crítica,* Vol. III (Lisbon, Delfos, 1969), pp. 99, 101†

[In *The Night and the Dawn*] . . . the author discovered how to tell us a story and was able, with verisimilitude, to imagine and to give life to a plot. Namora does not spread himself thin, he does not deviate from the fulcrum of the narration. There are secondary incidents, of course. But they contribute to the novel. They are well drawn and linked, they give structure to the whole. They serve as a foundation and make the principal events possible. . . .

The *types* that Fernando Namora presents to us do not appear isolated. They fit into the atmosphere and into the problem. Nonetheless, it must be said that *The Night and the Dawn* has a limited story. The action is weak, and its chronology is not sufficiently fixed. To summarize, the novel describes the anxiety of some farmers in the defense of the land that they cultivate and which provides their livelihood. Old man Para and, afterward, his son, personify this anxiety. A small village, hidden in the rural mountains near the border, fights against impositions that make life unbearable. This battle is not transmitted through action. We feel it in an indirect way. It is through the characters or the descriptive part that Namora translates it into reality. . . . Thus, one can assert that Namora has not directly confronted the social aspects of his theme. They are, without doubt, present, and the reader understands them. But this understanding is developed through implication. More than the problems of the social aggregate, of a complete village, the human problems and the temperaments of the various characters stand out.

Franco Nogueira. Jornal de crítica literária
(Lisbon, Portugália, 1954), pp. 131–33†

Like almost all the young Portuguese writers, Namora began his literary career with a book of poems. The Portuguese lyrical tradition is very rich and is supported by some well-defined constants. Namora brought a well-defined personality to these constants and with only three works of poetry (*Reliefs, Sea of Sargassos,* and *Earth*) he gained attention and appeared in several anthologies of Portuguese poetry.

Afterward, Namora's literary creation tended toward the narrative genre, the novel or short story, which will be, it now appears, his definitive means of expression. His original inclination toward lyric poetry at times appears in an evident and impetuous way in certain passages of his novels, but never at the expense of the purely narrative. . . .

Mines of São Francisco deals with the tungsten rush in certain regions of Portugal, the human flood that came to exploit the mines in search of economic salvation. Many of those men abandoned their villages where they had been defeated by hunger and poverty; they brought with them the obstinate hope of returning with enough money to buy a piece of land for themselves, a piece of the countryside that would repay the sweat of their brow and the body's fatigue. But tungsten carried in it the poison of adventure, the poison of easy money that burns holes in the most sober hands and stains men's hearts. Those crazed ones who run after the river of gold of tungsten burn their last hopes in artificial fires.

Ildefonso Manuel Gil. CHA. Sept., 1958, pp. 325, 327†

Many new things appear in this newly published series of narratives [*Sketches of a Doctor's Life,* 2nd series]. We can summarize them in a few words: the contact with the urban atmosphere of a "solitary city." And also the gentle and discreet way in which the illness penetrates the tranquil streets we walk daily. Nonetheless, this objective (which I believe to be the most important for Fernando Namora) is diluted a little in the course of the 350 pages, in which the tone of the *Scenes* [1st series] (1949) is not always harmoniously combined with the new realities of the *Scenes* [2nd series] (1963). And, if this tone, this style, that incisive and profoundly human manner of being witness, awakened our admiration in the first series, perhaps they are now insufficient for us, having been readers of *Solitary City* or *Sunday Afternoon.* . . .

But let us speak of the illness, the thread that links the eleven narratives, which are different and of unequal merit. . . . The illness is this: a slow destruction not just of the body, but rather of everything in us that gives the possibility of life, of happiness, of an open and firm voice, of hope. . . . Some of Namora's best pages are those in which the illness and misery are described as something that dehumanizes, that makes us strange, unrecognizable to our own selves, as it gradually reduces all flesh, which had been an instrument of tenderness, of comprehension, to the most repugnant state. . . .

"A Crime" . . . is the best narrative of the volume for me, in spite of its somewhat disorganized structure. In it the city is the most vigorously presented in its attendant hypocrisy, which slowly poisons the doctor's words and thoughts and those of his colleagues. . . . The city is, for Namora, a place of discord. . . .

Eduardo Prado Coelho. *SeN.* Feb., 1964, p. 53†

Like Knut Hamsun and Sigrid Undset, Fernando Namora is close to the soil; he digs it as they did; he knows its warmth, its smell, its energy and its quality of everlasting unto everlasting. But there is a difference. In place of the Nordic temperament, Fernando Namora's characters possess a haphazard, whimsical character with Moorish additives. . . .

A mouse, a donkey and, for villain, a pet raven play leading roles [in *Fields of Fate,* i.e. *The Wheat and the Chaff*] as links between humans and revivifying land, as if man were Antaeus and required physical contact with mother earth—not just to survive, but to become full statured. . . . Compact and neat, designed within narrow bounds, this book does not spread out to cover an entire people: it is an incident rather than an entire saga. And yet, in its way, it points up lessons we would be better off heeding. Namora's mouse and donkey delight and shock you. Though you are used to big gambles and a large-scale, outsize existence, you will find yourself as concerned as Loas about the piddling sum of approximately $14; does it go for a donkey or for a pair of floozies?

Barbaças the *naif,* the innocent, is a scamp, but never a sinner. Without benefit of church, school or family discipline, he learns the enduring values, as if we could not, however we behave, shuck them off: honesty, fairness, mercy, gentleness, repentance, and unselfish love. Though no human dies, though there is occasional high comedy, *Fields of Fate,* in a deeper sense, is a near-tragedy.

W. G. Rogers. *NYTBR.* March 22, 1970, p. 38

It is not as a philosophical idea, evidently, nor as a speculative theory of human nature or individual behavior, that Namora reflects, principally and dominantly, the sense of inevitable solitude of every human being and the anguish, the battles, the expectations, the hopes and disillusions that are generated in solitude. . . . The feeling or state of solitude in Fernando Namora's characters are forms that are implicit and intrinsic to life and, in the situations that turn out to be fundamental in the sequence of his works, are consubstantial determinations of the behavior of those characters. . . .

The novelistic work of Namora continued; it opened itself up with its readiness to react to experiences from new angles of vision about life and about men, from the rural people of the Beiras and the Alentejo to the city folk of Lisbon and the cosmopolitan people of international society. The theme of essential and irremediable solitude endures; taking on greater diversity and complexity of expression, it comes upon new dramas. In the cycle of rural novels, the bitter, at times almost desperate, roguishness of certain characters stands out as an exterior representation and a behavior of the always unsatisfied anxiety of communication, of communion with life—and the inexorable rejection that life opposes to this anxiety. Clemente of *The Night and the Dawn,* Candolas of *Solitary City,* who appear to be characters of secondary importance in the narratives but who reveal themselves to me to be essential in the novelist's human typology, are degraded and demoralized men owing to the collision of their ways of being and living with the real world and the miseries and baseness that survival imposes on them. But they are, at the same time, carriers of an ideal that transcends them, carriers of exalting and heroic hopes that the vileness of daily life is not able to destroy. . . .

The flight from solitude, . . . the feeling, almost an instinct that "everything is preferable to isolation," the necessity of creating myths to cover the evidence of implacable and inevitable human distances, all appear as themes in Fernando Namora's literary fiction, each time more insistently and more dramatized.

Álvaro Salema. *SeN.* Feb., 1971, pp. 29–31†

A Bell in the Mountain (1968) and *The Sun Worshippers* (1971), the first volumes of a series that Namora calls "a writer's notebooks," are compilations of columns, notes, and articles published in the daily press. . . .

If in *A Bell in the Mountain* Namora moved in a vast and varied atmosphere of cities and diverse countries—Berlin, Paris, Saragossa, Portugal, Finland—and evoked writers and even wrote literary criticism, in *The Sun Worshippers* . . . he has collected a series of columns based on a trip to Sweden and Denmark, in addition to a short trip to Leningrad. . . .

Namora does not only aim at seeing, he is intent on understanding, in getting to the bottom of what is happening. After informative pages on which the coldness of statistics abounds, there follow warm pages, detailed commentaries and observations, pulsing with life, in a balanced prose, always revealing the great writer that Namora is, and from which, if I do not err, the novelist peeks out.

José Ares Montes. *Ínsula.* May, 1972, p. 14†

Namora's neorealism is . . . not one of accommodation to a determined set of ideas with regard to the society in which we live; [rather] it is in the tenor of his humanism, which is one of exalting all types of oppressed peoples, the exploited ones, the outcasts, and one of condemning in turn a social system that denies these humanist values. . . .

More than an uninterrupted polemical flow, there is in Namora, diffusely or clearly expressed, a desire for perfection, in the sense of overcoming a mistake through the desperate search for purity and coherence, which many of his characters evidence, and which permits him to be cruel in his condemnations but solid in his judgements, biting in his criticism but complete in his fraternity, owing to the judgements to which he submits everything and everyone. . . . As the only writer . . . whose works follow the evolution of Portuguese life of the last decades, since the difficult times of neorealism, he discovered a way of correctly predicting the path that the history of man would take; for this reason he never failed to give depth to his extensive gallery of protagonists, after their most apparent defects and virtues had been analyzed, always keeping in view, however, the deep and authentic ballast of their human condition, in the existential terms adopted by literature beginning in the 1950s.

Whether it is a virtue or a novelistic strategy, the fact is that Namora frequently confronts the reader with characters in whom he will disclose a coating of mistrust and greed, courage and fear, pride and humility, from which he little by little later frees them, exposing their true inner existence.

Taborda de Vasconcelos. *Fernando Namora*
(Lisbon, Arcádia, 1972), pp. 15–17†

The Clandestine Ones constitutes—as thirty years earlier the author's second novel *Fire in the Dark Night* (1943) did—a novel about an entire generation at the earlier time about students on the eve of their battles for the future, and now about a mature group of intellectuals who must take account of several dozen years with regard to their public activities and personal relations. The beginning of this novel, which is the author's most recent, has a banal story of adultery, [but] it unexpectedly develops into a profound analysis of a destiny and, at the same time, of a social class. The key word of the title—clandestine—is characteristic of the meaning of the life of the protagonist's generation. The sculptor

Vasco Rocha, previously an active participant in the political opposition in Portugal and today a tired man, hiding his weakness, his remorse about his abdications, and his revolt against his own degradation behind an apparent aggressiveness, goes to a clandestine meeting with his lover, and it seems to him that the whole city is watching him. From a childhood full of inhibitions, through years of illegal activities in Spain and Portugal, always alert and untrusting, right down to this clandestine love affair, which is hidden from the tyrannical view of his wife, Vasco Rocha is still living in that same atmosphere of clandestineness, even worse off because of his exhaustion, degradation, and disgust.

The narration is developed through the sculptor's memories. . . . Brief glimpses of streets, cafés, and apartment, complete the view of daily life in the Portuguese capital. At times, some of the images are of an unexpected freedom and spontaneity, as for example the description of the bus strike. . . .

Fernando Namora's latest novel is something unique in contemporary Portuguese literature, since it is a work that deals with contemporary social and political problems from the point of view of a progressive intellectual, with an admirable maturity of expression. . . .

Pavla Lidmilová. *PP.* No. 3, 1974,
pp. 144–45, 146†

Fernando Namora definitely attempted to link his novels with the Peninsular tradition . . . but when he attempts to do it, the characters escape from him and the picaresque qualities fail. In addition, the landscape as seen by the poet and by the painter, which the author also is, gradually gains more consistency and, although the narrator follows his characters step by step, he nonetheless stops to introduce new esthetic elements and dimensions that are completely foreign to the narrative's heroes. We come across the same affirmation of plastic beauty in the works of Camilo José Cela, who has also been attracted to the picaresque.

This plastic beauty and its transcription could have remained marginal to the work. . . . But rather what we see through the evolution of Fernando Namora's art from the publication of *The Migrant Workers' House* through *The Wheat and the Chaff* is that background and nature are one and the same, and that there gradually develops a more lyrical union between the Land and the Background, between the author and his characters. Thus the author is able to show, through his vision of Portugal, the harmony that is established between man and the land. What the author finally reveals is a visceral love [of the land] that does not exclude eroticism, any more than misery, injustice, and rancor; his vision is not simply rural, but Vergilian.

Yvonne David-Peyre. *Colóquio/Letras.* Jan.,
1978, pp. 52–53†

PASCOAES, TEIXEIRA DE. See TEIXEIRA DE PASCOAES

PESSOA, FERNANDO (1888–1935)

Mr. Pessoa's command of English is less remarkable than his knowledge of Elizabethan English. He appears to be steeped in Shakespeare: and, if he is not acquainted with [Samuel] Daniel, John Davies of Hereford, and other Tudor philosophical poets, this affinity with them is even more remarkable than it appears. *Antinous* is not a poem that will appeal to the general reader in England; although the reflections of Hadrian over the dead body of his minion are interesting for what we should now call the Renaissance style and atmosphere, and the poetry is often striking. The sonnets [in *35 Sonnets*], on the other hand, probing into mysteries of life and death, of reality and appearance, will interest many by reason of their ultra-Shakespearian Shakespearianisms and their Tudor tricks of repetition, involution and antithesis, no less than by the worth of what they have to say. . . .

TLS. Sept. 19, 1918, p. 443

The most worthy of universality of the Portuguese poets of today, [Pessoa] gravitates toward the edge of all literary spheres, a solitary planet and an ironic witness to the customs of the clan. Of the considerable literary work he has produced over some twenty years, only a few little bits have appeared in various short-lived magazines. Will his first collections appear this year? He himself is not sure. This explains, although it does not completely justify, the almost complete indifference of his compatriots, with the exception of a minority who, after a long time, have seen fit to grant him his just place. . . .

Sprung from a symbolism still charged with theoretical and verbal preoccupations, according to his own admission, Pessoa has not stopped trying to fulfill himself poetically through all sorts of personas, starting with an original persona he discovered around 1914: Alberto Caeiro. Alberto Caeiro is, to be exact, anti-symbolism; he is man against anthropomorphism. All his clarity of knowledge is used to strip the universe and the living of the prestige of poetic metaphor. No abstract pantheism whatsoever, no preconceived philosophy enters into this attitude. A man no longer tries to consider himself *man,* but rather to feel himself a *being.* He does not succeed in this until the end of a long labor of destruction, in which the most stubborn rhetoric, consciously absurd and mercilessly logical at the same time, exasperates itself to the point of redundancy, to the point of hatred of men and their fake caresses, to the point of a type of solitary and obsessed mania. Such is the bitter brew that the "shepherd without a flock" distills. Considered on an aesthetic level, this attempt is in short a definite and significant dismissal, not without rudeness, of all the graciousness of the symbolic and magical art. A considerable attempt, but purely a negative one. Alberto Caeiro barely lasts and Fernando Pessoa who often savored evoking the memory of and commenting on the lesson of the one whom he calls "his master," tells us that he is dead, and long gone.

From [Caeiro's] ashes Álvaro de Campos was immediately born. . . .

Pierre Hourcade. *CS.* Jan., 1933, pp. 66–67†

Did [Pessoa], and his critics and commentators as well, attribute too much importance to this invention [the heteronyms]? Rather than a poetic invention, are they not the revelation of an unexpressed vocation as a novelist or a dramatist? In any case, is this invention not responsible for a certain artificiality and monotony in his poetry, within each of the pseudonyms? The truth, which must be told, since the authentic glory of Fernando Pessoa requires no patronizing, is that many of the free verses of Álvaro de Campos or Alberto Caeiro are not really verses; that is, they do not become poetry; and always being very interesting literary documents by the extraordinarily talented author, some of the little poems would pass as nothing more than perhaps *exercises,* although of a superior kind, if their psychological base in the poet's attitude of weariness, bitterness, and sarcasm had not given them, perhaps improperly poetic coloration.

Thus, the understandable unity among all the works of the heteronyms of Pessoa appears to us, at least, as interesting as the diversity that the existence of the heteronyms implies; as interesting, and possibly more real. We repeat that this unity seems to result from meditation, through intelligence, from inspiration, and from sensibility. . . . The truth is that Fernando Pessoa seems to place the resources of his verbal genius, of his metrical science, of his imagination, of his own emotion at the service of a theme, pretext, or some motive, which makes him an admirable translator (as his translation of Poe's "The Raven" would be enough to prove) and a disconcerting faker. But perhaps the deepest roots of his poetry lay in an understanding of the *occult sense* of everything, of the *mystery* that prolongs everything; and perhaps it is there that is born that magic which we cannot help but recognize in poetry, which, on the other hand, we feel has several limitations and shackles.

José Régio. Pequena história da moderna
poesia portuguesa (Lisbon, Inquérito, 1941), pp. 99–101†

Thanks to astrology, a science that Fernando Pessoa cultivated so proficiently that in 1916 he thought about establishing himself as a professional astrologer in Lisbon—a profession, by the way, in which he would have earned more money than he did as a "commercial correspondent"—the poet came to know a rather strange man, a true Cagliostro of modern times, in whose complexity and development the typical characteristics of a mixture of charlatan and someone inspired, which our timid mystifier vainly tried to be, are evident. In fact, one day, upon reading the autobiography of the famous English magician and astrologer Aleister Crowley, [Pessoa] noted that his horoscope had been incorrectly cast. Putting everything else aside, Pessoa wrote a letter to Crowley telling him about his objections. Sometime later, not without surprise, he received a letter from Crowley in London, in which the famous magician agreed with his Portuguese colleague. The two men established a correspondence; Pessoa sent Crowley his *English Poems,* and one fine day Crowley announced to his rival lost on the western edge of Europe that he would come to Portugal especially to meet in the flesh the prodigious astrologer that he was.

That is how one of the most curious phases of Fernando Pessoa's occultist adventures began. The announcement of this unexpected visit caused him great apprehension. For Pessoa, Crowley was a demoniacal and satanic magician. Everything that the poet himself never dared or would ever dare—not for lack of imagination but owing to timidity, a lack of initiative, a lack of decisiveness—was personified in [Crowley]. It is certain that he conceived Álvaro de Campos a little in the image of Crowley, but he had confined his audacity to literature. And now he was suddenly going to find himself face to face with the true incarnation of that type of demiurge that he himself had dreamed of bringing to life. . . .

In August 1930 Fernando Pessoa received a telegram from the magician informing him that he had embarked on the *Alcântara* bound for Lisbon. Fernando Pessoa, full of anguish, translated his desires that the magician not arrive into astral emanations. But on September 2 "Master Therion" landed on Portuguese soil, after the ship had been delayed for twenty-four hours in the port of Vigo because of a thick fog that had suddenly rolled in over the coast of Portugal. On the dock, Fernando Pessoa greeted the tall, broad-shouldered man, wrapped in a black cape, whose evil and satanic eyes stared at [Pessoa] accusingly.

And, in fact, the first words he said were a censure: he accused Pessoa
of having specifically sent the fog that detained the *Alcântara*. . . .

João Gaspar Simões. *Fernando Pessoa* (Lisbon,
Inquérito, 1955?), pp. 71–73†

Pessoa's bilingualism may indeed be the cause of his extraordinary and
almost psychopathic diversity as a Portuguese poet too. Not content
with writing in two different languages and literary traditions, those of
late-nineteenth-century English poetry and of post-romantic Portuguese poetry, Pessoa wrote and published his Portuguese works
under six different names, in six poetic idioms, each one of which
constitutes a separate identity among what Pessoa and his Portuguese
critics have called his heteronyms.

Denied any Wordsworthian spontaneity of expression because always forced to choose whether to express himself in English or Portuguese, Pessoa thus made a virtue of the self-alienation imposed upon
him by his having to hesitate between either of the two languages that
remained, through this very choice, both equally familiar and foreign to
him. In either language, Pessoa had to pretend, at all times, to ignore
the poetic traditions and conventions of the other, and in Portuguese to
ignore also the idioms that were particular to the five other personalities whom he repressed each time that he allowed the sixth one to
write.

Even Pessoa's name seems to imply this particular fate. Derived
from the Latin word that means a character in a play or a mask, it now
means, in spoken Portuguese, a mere person, in the vaguest sense of
the word. . . . To this very theme of the mask or person, Pessoa
devoted one of the *Thirty-five Sonnets* that he published privately in
English in 1918. . . .

When he expressed himself in English, Fernando Pessoa generally
closed his metaphysical considerations and erotic fantasies in somewhat learned diction, creating for himself an idiom as personal as those
of Edward Benlowes, William Blake, Hopkins or even Laura Riding. He
was one of the hermits of our language, a kind of Trappist of English
poetry who wrote an idiom that he often read or imagined but rarely
spoke or heard. . . .

Edouard Roditi. *Poetry.* Oct., 1955, pp. 40–41

As its ironical pseudo-scientific Greek title indicates, this poem
["Autopsychography"] expresses Pessoa's idea of the relationship of
the poetic experience to truth. The writer attempts, by means of an
imaginative "graph" of his own psyche, to present the essence of the
creative process. His starting point is the Nietzschean idea that "only
the poet who is capable of lying, consciously and voluntarily, is capable

of telling the truth." But what is the "poetic life" ultimately? This is what Pessoa hopes to answer.

His criterion of poetic, as contrasted with ordinary, truth seems to be "feigning"—that is, giving a mental existence to something neither actual nor real in objective existence. But this is not simply an imposture which the poet creates and to which he himself may fall victim in self-deception. For Pessoa, the only truth in poetry is that which the poet may arrive at after eliminating all sentimental accessories, all accretions of emotional and sentient experiences in everyday life. And this much the poet can accomplish during the gestation period, through voluntary self-control and through conscious exclusion of such "objective" truth, until he reaches the point at which he is able to simulate that other truth which is a genuine act of knowledge and a true vision of the world. The resulting poet then, to use the word of [Archibald] MacLeish, does not "mean" any more, but simply "is"; if achieved, the poem is "equal to: not true. . . ."

"Autopsychography," like all of Pessoa's poetry, moves in the realm of interior life and aims at nonrational intuition. A kind of abstract emotion infuses the writer's lucid intellectuality until it becomes as moving and intense as the immediate emotions of the heart; it becomes almost like the toy train itself, perpetually running around reason.

Ernesto Guerra DaCal. In Stanley Burnshaw,
ed., *The Poem Itself* (New York, Holt, Rinehart
& Winston, 1960), pp. 198–99

Fernando Pessoa was in an unusual position [because of his personality] to create styles, the styles of his heteronyms. But did he achieve in this area a complete depersonalization? In an affirmative case, criticism would recognize, like Álvaro de Campos in "Ultimatum," the inanity of the "dogma of personality," since rather more individualizing than the frequency of certain themes, or even the preoccupation with certain problems, is a stylistic atmosphere that is expressive of a temperament, of a culture, of a particular point of view. Without doubt, in linguistic communication there is always a more or less conscious choice of the means of expression, and the more conscious the choice, the more refined and intentionally literate the language. Style, and principally written style, is in part voluntary. Fernando Pessoa was able, to a certain point, *to make* the styles of the heteronyms while he looked into himself, dividing himself in order better to understand himself, exploring the possibilities of [Ricardo] Reis, of Campos, of Caeiro who cohabited within him. But—I repeat my question—is there not evident a nucleus of a unified personality, a stylistic common denominator invulnerable to sophistical arguments or reasoning beyond these diverse styles? In confirming [Karl] Vossler's assertion that each man has his own style, would not Pessoa have engraved the singular signals of his soul and his mind on the languages of his heteronyms? . . .

Even though the styles of the heteronyms translate different temperamental attitudes and ways of conceiving life, it is possible to respond to the above questions affirmatively, that is, it is possible to reduce the affinities of the style of the heteronyms to one basic psychic unity. [1963]

Jacinto do Prado Coelho. *Diversidade e unidade
em Fernando Pessoa,* 4th ed. (Lisbon, Verbo,
1973), pp. 135–36†

Why does Pessoa have such an evident interest in Whitman. . . ? The question requires two answers, one of a historical-literary nature, the other of a psychological nature. . . .

Pessoa probably became acquainted with Whitman through futurism. Such a statement can be confirmed if we take into account the divergences between Pessoa/Campos and Whitman, on one hand, and the affinities of Pessoa/Campos with futurism, on the other. With regard to Whitman, Pessoa/Campos's behavior is no less conformist than that of the other futurists. As they do, he salutes Whitman—not without some criticism and irony—as a futurist, completely omitting the clearly different aims and purposes, or rather forcefully altering what has been designated as the spirit of Whitman's works. Thus, in a historical-literary sense, "Salute to Walt Whitman," although not satisfactory to the "honored one," does not fail to reveal the typical characteristics of futurism.

The futurist phase of Pessoa/Campos, both transitional and short, coincides with a constant psychological phenomenom in him: I refer to the factors of psychic torment and intellectual clairvoyance that accompanied Pessoa throughout the futurist period. . . . This psychic torment, in turn, awakes in him a special interest in Whitman: the historical meeting occasioned by futurism gives him the chance—always from a psychological point of view—to take individual and momentary profit from Whitman. He sees Whitman's most outstanding quality as the power of multiple identification, an identification that promises impassive calm and the freedom of the soul. Thus, he aspires to the same state through the imitative identification with Whitman, invoking him as the guide for his soul.

Rainer Hess. In *Aufsätze zur portugiesischen
Kulturgeschichte* (Münster, West Germany,
Sociedade Científica de Goerres, 1966), pp. 210–11†

The "Maritime Ode," the most ambitious and most characteristic of the poems attributed to Álvaro de Campos, derives its power from an extreme tension between a sense of dynamic movement and an opposing sense of stasis. . . . The "Maritime Ode" vacillates between a vitalist, often brutalist, affirmation of the savagery not only of the sea itself, but of sailors, and a weary, gentle and tender return to an "inner ocean" for ever at rest beneath the surface commotion. There is something morbidly masochistic about this intellectual's apostrophes to the sailors and his invocations of a "horrible and satanic God of a blood-pantheism." . . .

In the spirit of the Futurists—rather than of Hart Crane, with his historical and mythical preoccupations—machines and the machine age are also celebrated in the "Maritime Ode," though unlike Marinetti, Álvaro de Campos ascribed the cult of machines to the waking and rational mind, not to daydream fantasies of a "blood pantheism," so that a crucial distinction is made between animal and mechanical energy. . . . The barbarous fantasies—threaded with erotic, passively homosexual overtones—are connected not with these modern phenomena but with an obsolete schooner; and this schooner, in turn, is associated with idyllic childhood reminiscences in stark contrast with the same violent fantasies. In its drastic modulations, therefore, the "Maritime Ode" spans differences and distances as great as those between the productions of the four poets whose works are written by Pessoa. . . .

Michael Hamburger. Agenda. Autumn–Winter, 1968, pp. 108–9

Owing to their common interests, Yeats and Pessoa employed common hermetic images in their art: Mount Abiegnos, the Rose and the Cross, the Initiation, the illusory nature of death, and the Mask. Of these images perhaps the most exotic and the least familiar is Mount Abiegnos. . . . Mount Abiegnos became the mount of mystic ascension through purification of the soul, the mountain of infinite knowledge. In Pessoa's poem "In the Shadow of Mount Abiegnos," the poet attempts to reach the castle atop the mountain, but cannot find the path. Perhaps the "Castle" is the "inner castle" of the great Spanish mystic Santa Teresa de Ávila, the goal of her ardent quest toward unification with God. In Pessoa's poem, the poet, having freed himself of all longing and desires and having renounced all the pleasures of the world, rests in the shadow of the mountain. . . .

Yeats and Pessoa have a remarkably similar outlook on death. Both consider death as a mere illusion, a false idea of the mind. To Pessoa, death regenerates man in the Unity from which he has separated on birth. Writing under the name "Fernando Pessoa," he considers death as a mere curve in the road, after which we are not seen, but exist just the same. . . .

What links Pessoa most directly to Yeats is the idea of the Mask. A mask has several functions. It may be the face one wears for society. It may be a shard of one's fragmented personality. It may be the personality one strives to become—one's opposite or counter self. Yeats, in "The Mask," suggests the mask is more fascinating, more important than the face behind it. . . . Pessoa, through the heteronym Álvaro de Campos, expresses the anguish with which he seeks his own identity— putting on masks and dominos to find out who he really is. . . . In Sonnet VIII, from *35 Sonnets* . . . he affirms that the mask is so inherent to man's nature that his soul does not know its real face.

Sol Biderman. LBR. June, 1968, pp. 62, 69–71

From around 1913 to the end of his life, Pessoa showed a marked preference for the type of poetry in which the subject matter is vague and indefinite, yet lucidly expressed and viewed positively. He cultivates vague, musical qualities in verse, hazy analogues, ambiguous images, deliberately blurring the outlines of things and avoiding clear-cut distinctions. His intense and painful awareness of antithesis, of opposites, of the Either-Or, leads him to make frequent use of oxymorons such as "a silent cry," "dark brightness," "sees blindly," "the still movement of flowers" and "far-off anguish . . . near by." Some of the early poetry, written to demonstrate a theory and to make propaganda points, is extremely obscure and involved, though it contains brilliant flashes, but already in 1914 he was writing some of his best poems, such as "Oh Church Bell in My Village" and "It's Night"; and with the exception of a small number of items of occultist inspiration, his later poetry can hardly be described as obscure, and still less as hermetic. He could be admirably lucid, even when expressing the ineffable and the esoteric. His strength lies in his ability to create mood, to start a train of thought by suggesting an affinity, a *correspondance* between the material and the nonmaterial world. . . .

If there is one fundamental belief which is a presupposition and *sine qua non* of his poetry, it is his belief in the positive value of idealism, in the sense of "tendency towards the highest conceivable perfection" or "love for or search after the best and highest," even if some would regard such a quest as madness. He is also the poet of absence, of silence, of negation, for the cause of his sorrow is frequently presented, not as something positive, but as something which is absent, lacking, negated: dreams undreamt, music not heard, things which vanish when you turn to look at them. Even happiness has a negative definition for the poet: it is "not thinking." His poetry could be described as confidential, in that it is inspired by real emotions and sensations of his personality, but these emotions are expressed objectively, with reservations as to their validity, or are transmuted and intellectualized. His use of images, metaphors and other figures is anything but conventional: it rests on a fundamental principle of occultism, the idea of *correspondances,* and the links are subtle.

What does Pessoa stand for in the poetic tradition? He stands for the denial, not only of sentimentality, but even of sentiment itself as a matter of poetic content. He stands instead for the primacy of thought, intuition, vision and prophecy over sensibility and feeling. His literary ideas, as expressed in a large number of provocative articles, stand in the main for a questioning, a reappraisal, a deepening and heightening of the content of poetry, and for a search for new forms of expression. In his own practice, he introduced into Portuguese a new poetic syntax of the kind already achieved in French symbolist poetry, and he renovated the poetic vocabulary, carefully avoiding, except in parody, anything resembling the stock poetic diction of the accepted Portuguese literary tradition. For many of his contemporaries, this, indeed, and not the content of his verse, was his most remarkable achievement.

Peter Rickard. Introduction to Fernando
Pessoa, *Selected Poems* (Austin, University of
Texas Press, 1971), pp. 52–54

Pessoa conceived of *Message* as a ritual; or, say, as an esoteric book. If one is looking for external perfection, it's his most complete book. But it's a contrived book, by which I don't mean that it's insincere but that it's born of the poet's speculations and not his intuitions. At first glance, it is a hymn of glory to Portugal and a prophecy of a new Empire (the Fifth) that will be not a matter of substance but of the spirit; its dominions will extend beyond historical space and time (any Mexican reader at once recalls Vasconcelos' "cosmic race"). The book is a gallery of historical and legendary characters, displaced by traditional reality and transformed into allegories of another tradition and of another reality. Without fully knowing what he was doing, perhaps, Pessoa violated the history of Portugal and, in its stead, presented another, purely spiritual, which is its negation. The esoteric character of *Message* keeps us from reading it as a simple patriotic poem, as some official critics would like to do. One must add that its symbolism does not redeem it. For symbols to work effectively they must stop symbolizing and become palpable, live creatures, not be emblems out of a museum. As in all work where the will intervenes more than inspiration, few poems in *Message* reach the state of grace that distinguishes poetry from *belles lettres.* But those few live in the very magical space of the better poems in *Songbook,* side by side with some of the hermetic sonnets. . . .

The *Songbook,* a work containing few creatures and many shadows. No women, the central sun. Without women the sensuous universe vanishes, there is no terra firma, no water, no incarnation of the impalpable. The terrible pleasures are missing, and also the prohibited ones. Also missing is passion, that love which is desire for a unique being, whoever it may be. There is a vague sentiment of fraternity with nature: trees, clouds, stones, everything fleeting, everything suspended in a temporal vacuum. The unreality of things, reflecting our unreality. There is negation, weariness and disconsolateness.

Octavio Paz. Introduction to *Selected Poems by Fernando Pessoa* (Chicago, Swallow, 1971), pp. 18–19

The thematic unity that prevails in both the heteronymic and orthonymic poetry is an intriguing revelation in the writing of poetry. Rather than search for what psychologists might call an integrated personality, Pessoa gives free rein to the divergent forces within his own psyche. Integration to him is a façade foisted upon the individual by external "reality." Rather than channel his varying ideas and impressions into a unifying course, he has opted for capillary expression, preserving the shape of the under-feeling by creating or giving birth to poets *(personae)* who are within him. Be it schizophrenia, divinity, or dramaturgy, it is admirably successful. Included as hidden heteronyms might also be Pessoa the poet in his own name, Pessoa the efficient organizer and Pessoa the quiet drinker. We must wonder which one is real and which one is the *paredros,* to use the ancient Egyptian concept that Julio Cortázar introduces in his novel *62: A Model Kit.*

Under his own name, Pessoa goes back into the Portuguese past, touching upon moments of it in his book *Message.* The simplicity of the narrative has the tight depth of a medieval *cantiga* [song], but along with it there is the drive of Camões, the *saudade* [nostalgia] of the Portuguese explorers which became the negative obverse with the death of King Sebastian at Alcázar Kebir in Morocco and the resultant yearning for his return and the redemption of Portugal. Here he states what may have been left unsaid but felt in the poetry of [Pessoa's heteronym] Ricardo Reis. Perhaps the whole idea was too vulgarly popular for the classical skeptic. The touch of a search for national definition is another link to the Brazilian Modernists, who also mingled the new and cosmopolitan with a search for "true" national identity. And still, this search seems more superficial, less intense, than the poking around that Pessoa does within himself.

Gregory Rabassa. *Parnassus.* Spring–Summer, 1973, pp. 136–37

The dual nature of art, the collaboration of thought and feeling, was of great importance to Fernando Pessoa because he considered it an essential criterion of art as indicated in his aesthetic theory and because he had difficulty in effecting that collaboration in his own work and life. For Fernando Pessoa, the Self and the Other represented thought and feeling. Although they are both part of the same man, they are somehow estranged in a schizoid relationship that can hold no hope for reunification.

As a poet, the orthonymic Pessoa experienced the schizoid relationship within himself. He bears his creator's name and expresses the most basic preoccupation. Alberto Caeiro found at least a temporary release from his self-doubts in the bucolic existence where just being was enough. Ricardo Reis found solace in the classical imitations he forged, while Álvaro de Campos's noisy poetry evidences his lashing out at doubt in an attempt, albeit futile, to eradicate it. The orthonym, however, is without recourse. The epigrammatic poetry of *Songbook* probes deeply within the empirical self and finds none of the solutions which the Pessoa augmented by heteronyms achieves.

The orthonym may be viewed as the most important member of the coterie. It is he who poses the problem basic to all four poets and their creator, and it is he who surrenders to the futility of finding a solution. The heteronyms explore potential solutions and in a sense each satisfies himself at least in the trying. None of the three, however, satisfies "F.P. himself," and so the orthonym Fernando Pessoa's poetic voice encompasses the heteronym's voices and expresses what neither they nor their creator dared.

Marilyn Scarantino Jones. *LBR*. Winter, 1977, p. 261

Pessoa is a fascinating figure. Being both complex and simple, he is always hovering over some piece of mysterious ground, like moonscapes with mile-deep craters—terribly attractive but also very forbidding. Reading his best poems, you never know if you're plumbing the depths or if you're dangling there above without even touching ground. There's always that paradox in his secret, something unanswerable. Though he invites you to share it, he resists your advance the moment you accept the invitation.

To get to the universal in Pessoa you have to distinguish his Portuguese, national side from his bilingual, international side. There's lots yet to discover about the effects of his bilingualism. Complicating the process is the fact that what's Portuguese in him is often a frame of mind which makes the work impossible to translate into another language.

Let's see if I can explain that. Something in his nature is totally isolated, even hermetic, but also genial. Wide open, and apparently guileless. At the same time there's his aggressive pride in being Portuguese—you might say, at times, in being absurdly Portuguese. Like T. S. Eliot, with whom he's often compared, his intellectual sympathies are international while his sources of feeling and identification are essentially national, even parochially so, as in "Maritime Ode." Maybe it's because he grew up in South Africa, where he attended English schools; and later deciding to become a Portuguese writer had to be a deliberate choice. . . .

It's hard to cast the Portuguese Pessoa in the long-established international context of Pound, Eliot, Rilke, Lorca, and the rest, whose reputations were fixed back in the twenties. Pessoa was all but unknown, even in Portugal, till the fifties. When he expresses so perfectly, as he often does, what's special about the Portuguese temperament, it's something one expects only the Portuguese themselves to appreciate. He's different from an Apollinaire or an Éluard, say, who consciously addressed readers not specifically French but European, even American. The resistance I felt on first reading Pessoa had to do with something else—with his conscientious modernity, his philosophical jongleurism. Other non-Portuguese readers report feeling the same uneasiness, and many fall away from him at this point. Still others think his work largely prosaic.

Edwin Honig. In George Monteiro, ed., *The Man Who Never Was: Essays on Fernando Pessoa* (Providence, R.I., Gávea-Brown, 1982), pp. 157–59

PIRES, JOSÉ CARDOSO (1925–   )

Let us examine . . . the role of irony. Cardoso Pires does not seem to use it in the accepted classic sense of saying one thing and meaning another, but rather as a means of preparation, to place the value of a character's attitude or the opinion into question early on. In "Ritual of the Little Vampires" Heliodoro, Oliveira, and the Deaf One enter into Simas Anjo's room "at a respectful pace." This "respect" would permit one to suppose that its object merited it; but it is not true, since the atmosphere is sordid, awkward, and repugnant, and both the recipient and the givers of this respect are dissolute. . . .

Images of the animal world abound [in Pires's works]. . . . At times the animals even have a symbolic value: the crows in the preface to *Games of Chance;* the old women who resemble crows—an omen— and the Rosinante "werewolf" . . . in "Dom Quixote"; the "fabulous fish" and the cormorant in *The Anchored Angel.* In this novel, the animals appear pretty often, as in the stories. Their function is, normally, that of representing the animalistic subhumanity of the state of some of the characters. In other situations, as often occurs in the case of birds, they are elements contrasting with man's situation. . . . Birds exercise a very strong metaphoric fascination for Cardoso Pires; the angels themselves are winged creatures, although the only two referred to, Esmeralda and Guida, are a "black angel" and an "anchored angel"—not to mention the black Simas Anjo, who is not an angel, but a vampire.

The recurrent physical deficiencies of the characters have a symbolic function, with a common characteristic of accentuating the marginality of their existences. Old people as a rule are deaf, lacking teeth, or blind. Independent of age, blindness, or difficulty in seeing, attributable to illness or environment, is pathetically stressed. . . . The commentator on the action in *The Surrender of the Heroes* is a blind man—although a fake blind man. [1963]

> José Palla e Carmo. *Do livro à leitura* (Lisbon,
> Publicações Europa-América, 1971), pp. 107–9†

Cardoso Pires can be related to, in part, the neorealist tendency . . . which has already gone beyond its purely documentary stance. Pires rejects any purely documentary concerns that one might try to see in *Job's Guest*. His position is natural and acceptable, since *Job's Guest* is a work of art, but in spite of the author's protests, I believe that the novel is a documentary in that the characters' problems and their geographic and other circumstances, which do not escape any careful reader, serve to confirm a reality which urgently needs to be corrected.

Following the intersectionist theory of narrative technique, Pires uses two situations throughout the novel, which serve to contrast and complement each other in his critical intention: the problem of the farmer in Alentejo province and life in a military outpost in that region. . . .

There are many intense, tender, and ironic pages that could be pointed out in *Job's Guest,* such as Chapter V, which reveals in a tense and anxious climate the levels of light and shade in the tavern, and the presence of police in the town's plaza; the delightful scene in Chapter VII, in which a young farm girl gives the guard watching her a simple geography lesson; or the dramatic escape of Anibal and his cellmate through the burned-out flatlands of the south; or the military maneuvers with the Americans, accompanied by "Yankee Go Home" written on the walls.

> José Ares Montes. *Ínsula.* July–Aug., 1964, p. 16†

What are the characteristics that would describe José Cardoso Pires's style? Schematically, we would say, the dialectical nature of its structure expressing the author's strict dialectical view of the world; a notable capacity for detection and definition of the internal contradictions of our contemporary world; an exceptional capacity for a very rapid sociopsychological portrayal of characters from the most varied social strata; . . . a successful laying-out of the demogogic aspects and of everything that might appear as polemical; a novelistic universe with an understanding of "example" and "fable"; a language that is reduced to the essential "telling" of the story or the "values" through the most direct means, but without disregarding the most penetrating esthetic subtleties; the predominance of the plastic over the descriptive and the contemplative, and the immediately visual aspects over the conceptual ones. . . .

Let the reader discover for himself in Cardoso Pires's works the rich originality of a language that is in appearance lean, bare, and poor. The secret of the author of *The Anchored Angel* is in a pseudosimplicity and not in a simplicity lacking in dexterity.

Alexandre Pinheiro Torres. *Romance: o mundo em equação* (Lisbon, Portugália, 1967), p. 313†

"If one had to define the state of the Portuguese mentality in one word, that word would be provincialism," wrote Fernando Pessoa. The quotation served José Cardoso Pires as the text for one of the chapters of his *Primer for the Marialva,* a treatise on the *macho* and the libertine, and he takes it up again as a theme of his most recent novel *The Dauphin.* The *marialva* (the Portuguese equivalent of the *macho*) was seen by Mr. Cardoso Pires as essentially a provincial type, whose anachronistic and defensive attitudes had their roots in a feudal society and in the supposed biological inferiority of women. He was thus completely different from the urban and urbane libertine who was essentially a metropolitan type, anti-establishment and progressive rather than reactionary in his attitudes.

In *The Dauphin,* an engineer, Thomás Manuel Palma Bravos, embodies the characteristics of the *marialva.* He is the dauphin (or the dolphin) of the title, the inheritor, like the dauphin, of a kingdom, but also, like the dolphin, neither fish nor fowl. His mind is ridden by the clichés of the past and his anachronistic attitude precipitates a Portuguese tragedy. . . . This is not to say that the survival of primitive attitudes in a technological age is only a Portuguese problem, but it is certainly a central problem of a nation which is living, according to Mr. Cardoso Pires, in the "ruins of its history."

However, the author is not only concerned with presenting a problem but also with achieving "density of specification." If the abstract and polarized protagonists recall the *nouveau roman,* the narrator through whose consciousness the events are filtered bestows on the novel a Conrad-like opaqueness. . . . The novel is thus a dynamic process in which memory, conversation, perception, things read and seen, relationships present themselves haphazardly, but are gradually shaped into new states of understanding. Reconstruction of the past and understanding of the present are interconnected.

TLS. Jan. 29, 1970, p. 115

After having read *The Dauphin* . . . many readers of José Cardoso Pires's works are naturally astonished at the excessively jocose tone of his *Most Excellent Dinosaur.* Instead of the impressive economy of words his fiction has accustomed us to, we find a style that is often playful and lazy. . . . Cardoso Pires's works take on a deliberately accusatory tone because, since his first published work, he has been more interested in uncovering the roots of Portuguese existence and the reasons for flagrant inequality instead of stirring up either his or the reader's emotions. Upon changing his theme, apparently, and moving to a kingdom located near the sea, which one could imagine as symbolic, José Cardoso Pires does not deviate from the path that has oriented his works, as far as I am concerned. Indeed, I believe that this biography of a dinosaur is an unsuspected example of . . . the strength and power of his writing.

It is an authentic fable, and thus without any possibility of having been real; it is so far from our day-to-day life, it appears so archaic and incredible, that we do not want to believe its truth. Indeed, is it possible that such an emperor as this could have existed, having come from nothing and managing to dominate and to silence a whole kingdom?

People say that for great evils great remedies are required. José Cardoso Pires must have thought that for great evils great laughs are needed. Thus, the most effective manner of punishing the emperor, of denying his existence, and of halting his passage through the twentieth century was the use of a comic, clear and almost vulgar style.

Liberto Cruz. *Colóquio/Letras*. Nov., 1972, p. 75†

What Next, José? is a collection of suppressed essays, opinions and unpublished conferences which further testifies to the strangulation of cultural life in Portugal during the Salazar/Caetano years, as well as to the confusion of the first three years of the post-revolutionary period (through June 1977).

What we discover once again is that politics and culture do not blend when they are at the opposite extremes. We learn a great deal about Cardoso Pires's professional development . . . and his attraction to the plastic and visual arts both in Portugal and abroad. There is a moving account of his literal "fight for culture" during the bleakest years of the dictatorship, as well as intensely emotional tributes to cultural victims of the regime—Alves Redol, Castro Soromenho, et al. One section deals with the writing of his *The Dauphin,* one of the most successful Portuguese novels of the last ten years. Further, there is an interesting overview of the significance of the contemporary Angolan writer Luandino Vieira. . . .

What the 1974 Revolution has wrought strikes Cardoso Pires as a case of "the past in the present." The abuse of the media, the attempt at redressing past injustices through a philosophy of letting bygones be bygones particularly infuriates, confuses, and embitters him. Indeed, uncontrolled bitterness is a major tone of these writings. Like the character in [the Brazilian writer] Carlos Drummond de Andrade's well-known poem which serves as the title for this volume, the generic (and specific) Portuguese José has reached a critical point in his Portuguese existence and now must decide "what next?"

Irwin Stern. *WLT*. Autumn, 1978, pp. 611–12

Cardoso Pires's fiction has searched for the key to the Portuguese soul; this concern pervades his previous novels and essays. In *The Ballad of Dogs Beach,* a fictional account of a real 1960 plot to overthrow the Salazar dictatorship, he once again deftly examines a characteristic of Portuguese existence—fear.

Cardoso Pires's characters are syntheses of aspects of Portuguese life during the late 1950s and 1960s. His protagonist is an astute, sensitive detective assigned to discover what actually happened at Dog Beach. As he takes testimony from the accused and their accomplices and as he fills in the elements of the supposed conspiracy, we discover the climate of Portuguese life and the detective's own bourgeois existence. The professional class, the youth and the peasants who supported this and other attempts against the dictatorship are poignantly drawn. Their belief in the "mission" is undaunted, regardless of the social or personal consequences faced. The events are presented in cinematographic flashes or through monologues, dialogues and dreams. The intensity of the narration is enhanced by the real people and events which make up the background: Humberto Delgado, Henrique Galvão and the beginning of the colonial wars.

What Cardoso Pires reveals to us is a society paralyzed in a siege of fear: fear of a neighbor or a friend, who may be a secret police agent; fear of thinking; fear of speaking and acting. The underground opposition forces also live in this atmosphere of fear and distrust of one another individually and collectively, which is, ultimately, the answer to the events of *The Ballad of Dogs Beach.* This powerful novel was awarded the prestigious Portuguese Writers Association Prize for Fiction for 1982.

Irwin Stern. WLT. Winter, 1984, p. 78

REDOL, ANTÓNIO ALVES (1911–1969)

Alves Redol sought, in my opinion, to write more of a poem than a novel [in *Tides*]. He did not intend to do it with his characters' lives, but, in a sense, by giving them the quality of representing various social types in the most general way possible, draining their blood in order to make them symbolic. This is the only way to explain the ashen tone that permeates the whole novel, in whose three hundred pages there does not appear one character who, when the novel ends, leaves any vibration of sympathy—or antipathy—in us; this is like saying that there is not one living character in *Tides,* and that the author wanted it that way. . . . Giving up the characteristics of a novel in order to try to be an epic poem, let us say, *Tides* finally comes to fall into a schematism that has no poetry; at the same time nothing stands out that may have symbolic value. . . .

Action has a very small part in Alves Redol's novel. . . . There is reportage and there is bad literature. Or pages and pages in which the life of the shop-boy and the grocery are minutely described, in a reedition of last century's realism . . . or in an endless number of phrases and sentences that adorn the whole novel, and whose use is certainly far from achieving what the author must have looked for. . . .

And it is only because of these unclear ambitions that many passages of *Tides* turn out obscure, and at time completely incomprehensible. The novel loses in clarity without gaining in profundity or beauty. In addition, with his preoccupation with being elliptical, with expressing himself in a poetic language, and, probably with "making art," Alves Redol begins and ends scenes abruptly and breaks up the novel to no clear advantage. . . . [1941]

Adolfo Casais Monteiro. *O romance (teoria e crítica* (Rio de Janeiro, José Olympio, 1964), pp. 313–15†

And now we come to the recent trilogy of novels that Alves Redol has called the "port-wine cycle." *Clouded Horizon, Men and Shadows,* and *Vintage of Blood* try to give us an extended picture of the port wine business in the Douro River region. The permanent sacrifice and struggle of generations of countryfolk who received small reward for their hard work are contrasted with the fabulous profits made by the Portuguese merchants and, particularly, by the British wholesalers in London. The topic is broad and has novelistic interest. . . . Technically, the three novels are full of defects: sudden cuts in narration, a lack of skill in interweaving scenes and making them reflect on others that we are presented with. . . . The three volumes cannot hold our attention, and we have no interest in knowing the destinies of the characters. . . . One feels that the novel about life on the Douro River is a foreign theme to the author, and that he imposes himself on it from outside; he did not live through it nor did he experience it before thinking about it.

Franco Nogueira. Jornal de crítica literária
(Lisbon, Portugália, 1954), pp. 124–25†

Alves Redol is at the height of his powers as a writer, which is well proven by *The Boat with Seven Rudders* . . . and *Gully of the Blind* . . . and even in some of the stories of his new book [*Eloquent Stories*]. . . . In some stories it is the very material or the very structure that is at stake. Let us choose three different aspects at random: In "Why Am I Not Supposed to Believe in Felicidade?" the contradiction between the protagonist's condition and the account in the first person, which keeps to a middle road between the naturalistic solution and a literary transposition, exemplarily used by Graciliano Ramos in *São Bernardo,* and even by Redol in *Grain Fields,* and the play on words, in questionable taste, of the two "felicidades" (the person's name and the common noun [meaning happiness]); the progressive conventionalism of "The Tranquil Night"; the confusion in "The Forgotten Night" between the delirium of one of the characters and the bipartite narration by the author and by the other character, which does not succeed in creating a nightmarish atmosphere. . . .

Redol ought to avoid poetic and symbolic expressions, which are not part of his talent, in order to get closer to the direct, bare narration of facts and situations, in which nonetheless the lyricism and symbols can be inherent.

João José Cochofel. SeN. March, 1964, p. 87†

With this translation of one of his recent works [*The Man with Seven Names,* i.e., *The Boat with Seven Rudders*], Alves Redol, . . . the founder of "neo-realism" in Portuguese fiction and a popular writer in this tradition, makes his American debut. Although there is controversy about the true nature of their movement, the Portuguese neo-realists appear, in general, to be concerned with the lives and problems of poor people, to imply an adverse criticism of the Establishment, and to prefer plain narrative statement to literary adornment.

These characteristics apply to Redol in *The Man with Seven Names.* The major part of the book is the biography of Alcides, a bit of human flotsam whom circumstances turn into a vicious killer. . . .

The structure of the work is perfectly suited to its substance. At the beginning we meet Alcides in the prison, where he tells his life story to another prisoner, an intellectual who happens to come from Alcides's home town. Most of the book is ostensibly written by this man, who reads each chapter to Alcides as soon as it is finished. About two-thirds of the way through the book, however, Alcides becomes angrily dissatisfied with his fellow prisoner's way of telling the story and thereupon undertakes the narration directly in the first person, with consequent intensification of its dramatic quality, a change strikingly appropriate to the developments in his life from that point on.

By interrupting the story line from time to time and reverting to Alcides in prison, Redol forces us to see all the aspects of his protagonist's life, even the picaresque, the comic, and the idyllic, in tragic long-term perspective.

William L. Grossman. *SR*. Sept. 26, 1964, p. 46

Although *The Man with Seven Names* [i.e., The *Boat with Seven Rudders*] is a novel of several stories, it is also primarily the story of just one man, Alcides Bago de Milho, called Cidro. If we can speak, with sufficient warnings against oversimplification, of "facets" of characters, or "levels" of characterization, then we can say that Cidro suggests, on one "level," the condition of modern Portugal, at least before and during the Second World War. One objects, of course, to such "nationalizing" of characters, but Cidro is vaguely anti-semitic, vaguely pro-Nazi although insisting on his neutrality, insisting that his crime was a crime of passion rather than of politics. Yet the nameless Narrator is also Portuguese, is repulsed by Cidro's treatment of the Jews, and is imprisoned on political grounds. But although Redol guards against simplistic allegory, a reader's knowledge of Portuguese history need not be extensive for him to notice certain correspondences: both Cidro and the Narrator are outside their native land, wanderers in the great tradition of Prince Henry the Navigator, Da Gama, Cabral and Albuquerque. Both men have fought for France (Cidro in the Legion, the Narrator in the Resistance), since apparently it is impossible to fight for modern Portugal. Cidro's abuse of the Jews in the Nazi prison recalls the expulsion of the Jews from Portugal during the reign of Manuel I and John III. His neutrality in politics and his admiration of parties in power (partly a naive respect for power itself—that respect for power which becomes a *source* of power, whether for dictators or deans—and partly a peasant's awe that makes possible the power of even incompetent despots and ignorant priests) recall the vaguely pro-Nazi neutrality of Portugal during the Second World War, and at least some of Salazar's still current power. This respect for power leads Cidro to respect and vaguely fear the narrative power of the Narrator, the man who had it in his power to create Cidro's life story.

James Korges. *Crit*. Fall, 1965, pp. 15–16

It seems quite correct to state that Alves Redol's novel *Gaibéus* [field workers of Ribatejo province] was constructed with the inspiration of a fundamental dialectical category: that of the struggle and the unity of contraries. To a certain extent, and amplifying the self-destructive sense of neo-realism. . . . the art that puts itself by the side of the victims promotes the critical examination of the social structure that supports it. . . . To be by the victims' side is equivalent to penetrating the process of reality, to attempting a dialectical interpretation of the relations between man as producer and his society. As has already been stated, the working class penetrated into literature for the first time, free of folklore, of its picturesque aspect, of its simplicity, in the novel whose twenty-fifth anniversary we are commemorating. [It was] the people as a social class. Perhaps the focus was still insufficient, but it was a question of a *new* focus in the analysis of human relations and in their transposition to the artistic domain. The struggle of the contraries was also present there in that Redol, who became the echo of a new critical and philosophical point of view, presented something new, in polemical contradiction to past and contemporary literature. . . .

On a literary level, Redol's book marks the possibility of the writer's representing a critical class consciousness, embodying esthetically all that until then had been unilaterally placed in the world of work. The birth of a new realistic, critical, documentary art corresponded to a certain level of development in the productive forces. *Gaibéus* is for this reason an index of Portuguese social history. . . .

The stylistic deficiencies of *Gaibéus* result, obviously, from the fact that the author had at that time not yet found his own style. The author's own drama begins here; as he tries to write for the people, he knows that he must simultaneously progress toward the difficult unification of form and background, between his conception of the real world and the way it is conceived and imagined. . . . *Gaibéus* was the book of the moment, and historically it is a work that belongs on the vectorial lines of a *committed* art.

Alberto Ferreira. *SeN.* July, 1970, pp. 226–27†

With *Waterspouts* (1954), a "short novel about a village without a history," as the author calls it, Alves Redol returns to his Ribatejo province in order to give us the loving view of a people of the Ribatejo through a series of impressions about types and customs, short dramatic and comic narrations that make up a fragmented yet at the same time coherent picture of the village. Owing to its structure and its ironic and tender tone, *Waterspouts,* which is also the name of the village, reminds me of that admirable *Winesburg, Ohio* [by] Sherwood Anderson. . . .

Alves Redol, savaged perhaps by criticism that was always demanding new novelistic forms from him, entered a stage of investigation, of attempts at renovating his narrative technique. . . . His next novel, *A Crack in the Wall* (1959), represents a return to the documentary novel, in the style of the first stage, that of the [port-wine novel] cycle of the Douro [River]. Alves Redol now went to find his setting on the beach and sea of Nazaré, the typical little fishermen's village of Portugal's Estremadura, with its economic and labor problems, to which the author adds a sentimental conflict. In spite of the harsh and wild atmosphere in which the existence of those people is developed, Redol, who is intent on objective realism, falls into long lyrical images. Aside from this, the narration, which unfolds in twenty-four hours and is divided into three parts, is constructed almost like a drama.

A new experiment is represented by *The Frightened Horse* (1960), the most intellectual of the author's novels because he here attempted a narrative with an international setting and with psychological depth. Alves Redol's latest novel is *The White Wall*, published in 1966, twenty-six years after *Gaibéus*. . . . Without forgetting the people—without ever betraying them—Alves Redol has been . . . abandoning . . . the collective hero in order to center on the problems of the invididual who can or cannot embody the virtues and the weaknesses of the people. . . .

[Redol is] tied to the native soil, a regionalist in a more ample sense than is customarily used for other novelists of this or the last century; his novels will probably remain as a document of an epoch characterized by social injustice and political persecution.

José Ares Montes. *Ínsula*. July–Aug., 1971,
p. 11†

In *Gully of the Blind* Redol expressed the subterranean decomposition and the transformation of a historical process through the incessant eating away by the dry rot—the chorus of fatal decadence that took over and corroded the agrarian society that the old farmer, Relvas, represents, but whose symbolism is much broader, since the writer takes aim at the archaic fascist society overflowing with contradictions and that is personified in that human reject [the dictator António de Oliveira Salazar]. . . . The stuffing of Relvas's corpse, a way of prolonging the myth and preserving the tyranny, is a grotesque farce, which was attempted a few years later by Salazar's lackies, following the latter's cerebral hemorrhage, which was his death sentence; they tried to delay the post-hemorrhage phase of fascism, Caetano's reign, by maintaining the legend of the active role of Salazar, while he was barely biologically alive. . . . Owing to the depth of its insertion in reality . . . Redol's novel jumps out from its pages and dialectically continues to write itself, to the rhythm of life's pulsations. Understanding the incurable, *clandestine* rotting of the terrorist dictatorship with sharp perspicacity, Redol foresaw and stressed its approaching death sentence.

Augusto da Costa Dias. *Literatura e luta de
classes: Soeiro Pereira Gomes* (Lisbon,
Estampa, 1975), pp. 108–9†

Although *The Reinegros Family* is a posthumous work, published in 1972, three years after Redol's death, the truth is that the first version was ready in 1945. Its publication was prohibited by the fascist censorship. We should remember, in this regard, that Alves Redol was the *only* Portuguese writer who had to present his originals for the *imprimatur* of [António] Salazar's colonels [the censors]. Over three decades, Redol made several attempts to publish it, but was never lucky. . . .

The Reinegros Family . . . is the most transparent and significant volume of ideological and political substance of all of Alves Redol's works. In spite of its being a fresco of Lisbon popular life, *The Reinegros Family* is essentially a novel about the masses.

The case of Luís Polidor [of *The Reinegros Family*] is extremely interesting. An enlightened man, he stands out from the mass of illiterate people with whom he involves himself in order to obtain the popular support he needs. He plays politics, not to genuinely aid the people, but to use them, because he has what is known in bourgeois and capitalist countries as "political ambitions." . . .

Through Luís Polidor, Alves Redol intends to communicate to us that no matter how much these privileged classes seem to possess the spirit of revolution and no matter how much they may hate a certain image of the bourgeois state—the monarchy—the bourgeois state is in itself sacred, the bourgeoisie is not undone by the Republic.

Thus, in *The Reinegros Family,* we see that the honeymoon between the Republican bourgeoisie and the working masses was quite stormy. . . . For the people, the monarchy and Republic assume gigantic forms of conspiracy against it—the capitalist conspiracy of the minority against the majority. It is this that makes the masses of *The Reinegros Family* replace the cry "Long live the Republic" with "Long live the proletariat."

> Alexandre Pinheiro Torres. *Os romances de*
> *Alves Redol* (Lisbon, Moraes, 1979),
> pp. 113, 133–34†

RÉGIO, JOSÉ (pseudonym of José Maria dos Reis Pereira, 1901–1969)

Whoever reads *Blindman's Bluff* hoping to find a novel in the current meaning of the word will be in for disillusionment. The author does not tell a story: the plot, what the characters do, is not the most important thing to him. . . . Don't think, however, that there is nothing novelistic in this novel. The characters of *Blindman's Bluff* not unreal, neither abstractions nor incarnations of ideas. Some, like Dona Felícia, are creations of a great novelist of manners. But this does not prevent the book from diverging totally from those works that have as an essential objective the description of a series of *types,* integrated in a specific action. There is "dramatic action" in *Blindman's Bluff:* but that action and this dramaticism are in the first place spiritual: the gestures, the words, the characters' actions are not important for their quotidian aspect, but they are important for their spiritual weight, for their meaning on a plane of values. . . .

Scandalizing the "puritans," Régio insists, with significant frequency, upon revealing the personality of his main characters when under the domination of sex. These are precisely . . . the most beautiful, the most praiseworthy . . . and, at times, the most tragic passages of his work. Even in José Régio's poetry one notes—let us remember, for example, "Poem of the Flesh-Spirit"—the significance that the domination of sex has for him. The characters of *Blindman's Bluff* express, on a plane of lived reality, what had already been revealed to us on the plane of lyrical-metaphysical expression. [1934]

Adolfo Casais Monteiro, *O romance (teoria e
crítica)* (Rio de Janeiro, José Olympio, 1964),
pp. 330–31, 332†

To a certain point, we can rejoice at the change in course that has taken place in the narrative style of José Régio. The second volume of the series *The Old House,* which is called *The Roots of the Future,* represents, in fact, a revolution in the fettered and didactic methods that the author used almost exclusively in the first volume of the series, the novel *A Drop of Blood,* published in 1945. . . . In truth, the *cicerone,* the *gate-keeper,* moves away from the reader in this new novel, and the *life* of the characters becomes more independent, freer, although we must recognize that the bill of manumission that José Régio granted his characters has brought about the disturbance of the regular pace of the novelistic action of his novel.

It was with surprise that we opened *The Roots of the Future* and confirmed that Lelito is not on the scene when the curtain rises. The novel's action begins with the expectation of his godmother Libânia, who for many years has been awaiting the return of João, Lelito's oldest brother, whose personality was almost completely unknown to us. With a jump back to the past, José Régio uncovers for us the tangles of the existence of the family of Martinho Trigueiros, Lelito's father, João, Maria Clara, and Angelina, whose home—"the old house"—breathed in the shadow of the austere godmother Libânia. And the narrative's movement, which in *A Drop of Blood* was *present* and *active,* becomes *past* and *retrospective.*

José Régio, having abandoned the exclusively introspective method of the first volume, which was centered on the personality of Lelito, plunges into the thickets of the novel of observation and manners, but without the precaution of making the reader stick to a central action around which all the narrative digressions revolve, with the lack of that fixed point, they end up absorbing all the novelistic material of the work. This is what really happens in *The Roots of the Future*. The action runs aground: what remains is the sterile sand-pit of a story in which the details assume immoderate proportions, the psychological study of the characters attains excessive prominence, and the local, insignificant customs overflow the dramatic banks of what could be of the most importance in a narration that is as detailed as it is insignificant. [1948]

João Gaspar Simões. José Régio, *Crítica III* (Lisbon, Delfos, 1969), pp. 303–4†

My Case, which the author calls a farce—and it is one in the immediate sense of the word—comments on, in the form of successive monologues that suddenly interrupt each other, another of Régio's favorite themes: the lack of communication between men, each one a prisoner of his own situation, and because of it, alien, blind, and deaf to others' situations. And the curtain will fall without "the unknown one" presenting his "case" to the public, promoting the message of redemption for humanity, which it is not interested in hearing. . . .

The last moments of the life of Mário de Sá-Carneiro inspired the "tragicomic episode" [*Mário or I Myself*] by José Régio. . . . Even without previous knowledge of the life and work of the genial poet of *Traces of Gold,* one can appreciate and understand this episode in all its sharp dramatic flavor. Through a dialogue between "he himself and the other" . . . we see explode the tragic contradiction that tore the poet to pieces during his short lifetime, his terrible inability to adapt to the real world and the impossibility of his transcending it. "Why does beauty appear to me in my dreams if I cannot pass into its body?" he asks himself, a prisoner of matter aspiring to an impossible escape (and for this reason, he would attempt it through death), is in itself highly dramatic; and Régio, using the poet's own verses as support, was able to extract from [the dialogue] all the fundamental human resonances that are implicit in [Sá-Carneiro's poetry]. *Mário or I Myself* ends with a "circus scene," which is the theatricalization of Sá-Carneiro's poem "End."

Luís Francisco Rebello. *Vértice*. Feb., 1958, p. 121†

In "Foundations of Reality," José Régio gives us another short story with the greatest psychological and philosophical interest. Starting from the loss of the sense of reality, Régio presents us with a character for whom the perceptional constructs and his own personality are progressively losing consistency, to the point that not only do the external objects that are inferred from these constructs begin to appear unreal to him, but also his belief in the existence of beings with whom he lives is considerably shaken. "Life is a dream," murmurs the character, updating the old idea that the world is a theater in which the social comedy unfolds. This idealism gains a singularly disintegrating force: men are actors who try to imitate what they would want to be. Finally, Silvestre has no other choice than to admit that he is a great dreamer of everything, even of life, an entity to which he, paradoxically, attributed a real existence. . . .

It seems to us that through this story [in *There Are Other Worlds*], the author wanted [to reveal] the disintegrating and anarchic forces of extreme idealism when it is dictated by the deepest being of man and lived out on an authentic plane. It is in behalf of the demand for human authenticity, against the simplistic, deforming mutilations of our view of man that José Régio raises his voice. For the author of *The Prince with Donkey Ears,* freedom is equivalent to the unlimited possibility of the perfection of the spiritual being of creatures, which in today's world, from Régio's point of view, is often confused with "monstrosity," which men begin by rejecting, only later—too late—to recognize its beauty ("Christmas Story"). It is in behalf of this very demand that Régio rejects, as too simplistic, the distinction between normal and abnormal and the attribution of an aberrant (antisocial) character to certain psychological situations ("The Depths of the Mirror"). Even in his very own name, he gave us in the story "The Paradoxes of Good" (in which he combines biography, dialogue, a didactic style, and the fantastic short story) a very penetrating sounding of the psychology of a writer, and he gives us, in my opinion, the first outline of his personal theology.

Rogério Fernandes. *SeN*. Aug., 1963, p. 221†

The poet explains the title *Poems of God and the Devil* right in the first work, entitled "Picture." The anguished existence of the nocturnal apparition of two contradictory elements in human consciousness, the tendency toward Good and the tendency toward Evil, is susceptible to a psychological interpretation. José Régio, however, descends to reach the subjective elements of consciousness in an objective representation tends to evoke Manichean dualism. . . .

From the book's title, the ingenuous reader might get the notion of being in the presence of religious thematics, that is, the human problems referring to birth and death, eating and loving, growing and multiplying. José Régio's thematics, however, are more varied and perfected by the reflective talent or by the speculative genius of such a noble and esteemed poet. In this way we can explain that all his poetry is intrinsically philosophical.

The volume has only twenty poems; all, or almost all, focus on adventures and experiences of the rebel poet, who thus symbolizes the dramatic vicissitudes of mankind. Before the duality of Good and Evil . . . there appears in classic form the problem of freedom, which has so tormented human philosophy. José Régio enunciates it in the relationship of the will with the sentiment, in the very terms of adolescence, which knows already what it does not want, but does not yet know what it is supposed to want. . . .

One of the principal works of this book of poetry is the very famous "Black Hymn," in which the poet proclaims his rejection of the passivity of the sensible world and the social world. . . . The same attitude is reflected in the poem "The Diary," in which the poet, after reflecting on his life experiences is ready to tear up the papers of his adolescence, in which he had written immature secrets and imprudent confessions. This purifying fire, or purgatory, of the elements of subjectivity, which does not interest mankind, exemplifies the superactive state of false individualism. Soon the poet will repress this adolescent indecision, attempting to give his life the direction and the meaning it should have.

Álvaro Ribeiro. *A literatura de José Régio*
(Lisbon, Sociedade de Expansão Cultural,
1969), pp. 164–66†

Régio conceives each human individual as a bundle of incompatible tendencies, some social (or moral), others unsocial (or immoral, or demoniacal). One of the aspects of the moral human drama would be the inability of truly synthesizing the intimate inclinations, an inability that Régio attributes to himself in the sonnet "Universality." Another aspect would be that each inclination would demand an unattainable absolute. . . . Among the demoniacal tendencies, Régio distinguishes those that both Freudian and Adlerian psychoanalysis point out: the sexual libido, particularly in its socially condemned fixations, and the *vis dominandi*. . . .

As had already occurred with Teixeira de Pascoaes, for Régio the demoniacal is an aspect of the divine. . . . Régio breathes the air of psychoanalysis, but particularly in dealing with the topic of the Desired King [King Sebastian] and unfortunate fates, he is evidently the heir of those who converted the national failures, the love tragedies of our legends, principally *that of the one who after death was queen* [Inês de Castro], into a metaphysical *saudade* [nostalgia], like a representation or hypostasis of the divine present to the national sensibility. The chapter "Incomplete Pseudomemoirs of Jaime Franco" of *Blindman's Bluff* is, in a certain way, *saudosismo* [the nostalgia movement] translated into terms of literary psychoanalysis.

Óscar Lopes. *Modos de ler: crítica e
interpretação literária/2* (Oporto, Inova, 1969),
pp. 370–72†

Suspended Hymn (1968), the eighth volume of José Régio's poetry, begins with a poem "There Was in the City," in which the poet once again follows one of his recently preferred directions: satire. . . .

Choosing this opening poem as representative of the new collection, one sees that it is yet another poem by Régio about the artificiality of urban life, yet the poet does not contrast urban life to his ideal of rural life, according to the standards that reached their highest expression in Portuguese literature of the sixteenth century. . . .

This poet exhaustively details the places, people, and style of the life that typify corruption. And the satire that he writes is simultaneously a utopia, in which what is imagined as ideal is the destruction of the city, perhaps according to the patterns of the biblical events of Sodom and Gomorrah. . . .

What I would like to suggest is that the satire of José Régio simply does not work, perhaps because he has an outmoded view of reality. . . .

The other poems of the book, satiric or not, are of equal or even lower quality. We are viewing (and I have no doubt about this) the fourth successive failure of Régio. The fourth failure in twenty-seven years, counting the very insipid *But God Is Great* (1945), the work that marks the end of the truly great creative poetry of Régio.

Alexandre Pinheiro Torres. *SeN.* June, 1969, p. 214†

Thematically, technically, and stylistically, Régio's works form an integrated whole and do not lend themselves to a genre-by-genre study. "Everyone else had a father and a mother," he says in "Black Hymn," "but I was born of the love that exists between God and the Devil." His *fado* (fate), or what he calls pre-experience, made Régio highly sensitive to this moral duality. His protagonists constantly struggle between madness and sanity, good and evil, perversity and purity. This duality forms part of their vital existence, and when one side triumphs over the other they cease to exist. In the novel *The Prince with Donkey Ears* (1942), for example, Leonel conquers evil, becomes perfect and purified—a purification symbolized by the loss of the floppy ears—and then becomes nonexistent. A similar process takes place in the play *Benilde; or, The Virgin Mother* (1947) . . . . Too innocent and pure, the protagonist cannot live in the real world.

Régio implements these moral conflicts and heightens their dramatic intensity by playing free with chance and reality. Both the Prince's ears and Benilde's pregnancy, the symbols of their conflicts, stem from some sort of contract with the devil, or with God, or both.

Time in Régio's works moves at a leisurely, day-by-day pace; people grow up, fall in love, get married, have children, and die. The simplicity of the established patterns enables Régio effortlessly to capture the timelessness behind a specific moment in the big house, the little village, and the small, half-forgotten country called Portugal. . . .

Many aspects of Régio's style—his long, flowing sentences in the style of Cervantes, his images, his use of language—belong to past centuries. His didacticism, his preoccupation with moral questions, and his concern over the real values and virtues of Portuguese literature also tend to place his works in an older literary tradition.

Régio's contribution to literature rests on his study of man—quite often grotesque in his abnormality—and his relation to himself. Although he focuses on the young man or woman from a small village, like so many other writers of our century he achieves universality by capturing the essence of his native land and its people. [1971]

Leo L. Barrow. In Encyclopedia of World
Literature in the Twentieth Century, Vol. IV
(New York, Frederick Ungar, 1984), pp. 20–21

RIBEIRO, AQUILINO (1885–1963)

The most revealing work of Aquilino Ribeiro . . . [is] *The Winding Path,* in which all the mental anarchy of contemporary Portugal is embodied in several impressive characters who are skillfully drawn from the most direct reality; these characters take on an even more impressive existence as they evolve against a background closely linked to their souls. . . .

Even in the central character of Libório Barradas, a failed priest, a book collecter, an occasional revolutionary and libertine, a troubled man who always hesitates and is more lazy than mystical, but sincerely full of generous sentiments, the novelist embodies today's Portugal, a man eager to create, but who suffers from a lack of principles to which he can give himself over with complete honesty. The anguishing drama that develops in Libório's soul is that of a people: it is the drama of hesitation. Libório's soul is full of provincial atavisms. . . . It is this that augments the meaning of the synthesis attempted by Aquilino Ribeiro, who better than any writer before him excels in the painting of the picturesque details of Portuguese regional life.

Aquilino Ribeiro possesses the supreme quality: he knows how to see; from this comes the gift of an admirable style. His most recent novel, *Lands of the Devil,* shows us that the best aspect of his talent consists of the love with which he treats his characters. . . . Never have peasants or the mountain folk of Portugal, who lead a hard life among the furze and the firs, been painted with such truth.

Philéas Lebesgue. A águia. July, 1919, p. 87†

This book of short stories [*Santiago Road*] is a new affirmation of [Aquilino Ribeiro's] exceptional qualities as a prose writer and novelist. It consists of two regionalistic short stories, . . . a short story evoking the history of the French invasions, . . . and two fantastic short stories . . . with a symbolic intent, the last one presenting Aquilino's skepticism about life.

Aquilino has neither wings for spiritual flights nor a talent for psychological investigations. Compare his novels on topics similar to those of Pina de Morais or Raul Brandão and you will see the distance that separates him from the lyric flight of the first and the profundity of the second writer, and you will also note how Aquilino prefers to let the common life bloom in an epicurean manner. . . .

The metaphysical thrill is always fleeting and rare in Aquilino's works. . . . But this is not a censure. It is rather a verification of the attitudes that document what has been said about the writer's *sensualistic structure*. The writers of this category have a purpose. Exactly because he wants neither to investigate the abysses nor to conquer heights, Aquilino can see clearly and can faithfully reproduce the exterior aspect of life, the epidermis of reality.

Hernani Cidade. *A águia*. Dec., 1922, p. 210†

All the action in [*The Winding Path*], which revolves around Libório, is a realistic study within a provincial format (based on the social milieu of the last years of the monarchy) during the period when a false belief in an idealistic renewal appeared among the youth. . . . Aquilino's novelistic process is almost unprecedented, aside from the suggestion of a certain realism and the too solid and excessive form of his descriptions of human affairs. The author reveals himself, he lives and he subjectifies himself in Libório Barradas, and thus the book has human existence, because they are two characters of the same soul. Aside from the latent conflict, which is the picturesque and moral dressing, he presents Beira province in all its beautiful landscape, full of color and religious soul. . . .

The principal character of *The Winding Path* has a high national awareness; he is a moral product of his environment and of the conditions of his psychological revolt. Educated in the shadow of the Church, finding in it a refuge, he later negates this educational orientation, giving birth to the revolutionary. Libório's childhood, the details of his youth, the description of Lamego and the provincial atmosphere of that small Portuguese city, the battles with his own mother, all explain the principle of his rebellion. After his sexual contacts, after his involvement with Bento Chinoca in a well described political scene, Libório understands himself better, he creates more reasonable ambitions for himself, and his trips to Uncle Fome Negra's home give Aquilino Ribeiro the room to achieve some of the most beautiful and polished pages. . . .

Joaquim Correia da Costa. *Eça, Fialho e Aquilino*. . . . (Lisbon, Livraria Clássica, 1923), pp. 163–65†

Since *Garden of Torments,* which appeared over forty years ago, Aquilino Ribeiro has pursued a literary career without interruption. During
this period he published dozens of volumes. . . . Of course, his work is
uneven; not all his volumes hit their mark; and some constitute more of
a repetition than a new work. . . . This first work [*Garden of Torments*]
of his youth, in fact, constitutes the key to and basis for later developments. Without doubt, the writer perfected his style and attained control over technique. But the style, the topics, and the *manner* of
Aquilino were already almost totally revealed in *Garden of Torments.*
The pictorial power of his descriptions, the satire, sometimes the sarcasm, the wild sensuality, the land and the village, the provincialism
that overflows even in the urban setting—are all characteristics that fill
that volume and that are developed and take hold later. . . .

[There are] works that clearly fail as novelistic constructions, as
with *Mónica* and *Maria Benigna.* Neither the power nor the exuberance of the style saves them. Aquilino here shows a complete inability
for the urban novel, for the novel of manners, for the novel of psychological analysis. . . . He shows himself incapable of in-depth psychological analysis, of a subterranean investigation of the human
being. . . . Mónica is an aware bourgeoise who cannot express herself:
the author tells us about her social awareness; but in the eyes of the
reader she remains a ghost, who *on the outside* does not distinguish
herself from others and whose *insides* we do not know. In this fundamental detail there resides the abyss between a novel like *Malhadinhas,* in which the author is integrated into the atmosphere and
the land, and a novel like *Mónica,* in which the author is a mere
spectator of characters who speak a language full of secrets for him.
Fortunately, the novels in the style of *Mónica* are rarities in Aquilino
Ribeiro's works.

Franco Nogueira. *Jornal de crítica literária.*
(Lisbon, Portugália, 1954), pp. 93–94, 96, 97–98†

In many of [Ribeiro's] books, perhaps the most substantial part of his
works, he has shown his predilection for the short story or narrative, as,
for example, . . . *The Skin of the Bass Drum* and *Malhadinhas* . . . or in
the short sketches and descriptions that abound in *Village, Sentimental
Geography,* or *The Man of the Nave.* In the more complex forms of the
novella and the novel he presents surprisingly grand scenes of nature
and the dramatic behavior of man, who is daring in his struggle for his
own interests and passions, in his greed for land, and in his feelings of
freedom.

The Winding Path, with its evident tendency toward a regional
literature, is his first novel in which the literary taste of the French
masters of the time, particularly Anatole France, is abundantly felt. . . .

But then we see the writer involved in the most authentic and perhaps densest of his early works, *Lands of the Devil,* [in which] he vigorously describes the obscure and conflict-filled life of that lost world of the hill country, the world of the village of his birth, which seethes in desperation, in the obstinate and blind furor of its gloomy, deafly larval existence. In this volume, the writer is seen in the plenitude of his original novelistic inventiveness and his very personal style, full of the reforming intentions that brought him to the literary scene. Afterward, works of a similar novelistic type would follow, such as *Battle without End, The Man Who Killed the Devil, Maria Benigna, Tungsten,* or *When the Wolves Howl,* but he would return from time to time to his delightful short stories, culminating . . . in the superb literary composition *The Big House of Romarigães.* . . .

Manuel Mendes. *Aquilino Ribeiro* (Lisbon, Arcádia, 1960), pp. 21–22†

One of the outstanding characteristics in Aquilino's works is the enhancement of the instinct that impels a man toward a woman, against all preconceptions of a moral, religious, or social order. Perhaps no other Portuguese writer has created such lovable feminine figures as Celidónia or Mónica and many others. The erotic tradition of the troubadours, of [Luís de] Camões, [Almeida] Garrett, Camilo [Castelo Branco], appear in his works to be reduced to a simple game between the human situation and the amorous instinct, without platonic evasions to the pure dialectics of feelings and the flesh, without Petrarchan logomachies, without the romantic process of measuring love through the simple contrast with the biblical sense of sin, which even today is rather strong. . . .

The second dominant trait in his work is found in the struggle of the roguish cunning of the forces of life against the stratagems, the interested parties, the tyrannies, the socially enthroned stupidity, the feudal or bourgeois inhumanities. From *The Tale of the Fox,* in the realm of children's fables, to *Malhadinhas,* from his Viriato, chief of the bandits, *dux latronum,* to his Luís de Camões, from his rural characters, from his Portuguese bunglers from Sete Partidas to his more or less adventurous protagonists, Aquilino Ribeiro finally brings the *pícaro,* which Castilian prose fiction has known for centuries, to Portuguese fiction, before [Miguel] Torga and [Fernando] Namora discovered him.

Nonetheless, this *pícaro* presents, in general, a pathetic face. . . . His artfulness, even when it manages to triumph over an imbecilic force or an unctuous hypocrisy, affirming the happiness of the vital instincts and battle, has all the air of the *hubris* of Greek tragedy—of the vain challenge to an implacable destiny. The glory of living in the fullness of the intelligent struggle is sketched, in a way that might be called heroic in the manner of Nietzsche, against a background of all the inevitable human failures, of all the degradations of the flesh, of death, of old age, of illness *(Saint Bonaboião, Marvelous Adventure [of D. Sebastião], Black Archangel),* of the boredom of success *(The Man Who Killed the Devil),* of oppression, of brutal and unpunished violence.

Óscar Lopes. *Cinco personalidades literárias*
(Oporto, Divulgação, 1961), pp. 44–46†

When the Wolves Howl . . . is the work of Aquilino Ribeiro, a Portuguese author who is seventy-five years of age and who was put on trial by his foolish and obscurantist government for the offense of having written it. This is not because it is to the smallest degree erotic but because it was thought to hold Dr. Salazar's judiciary and bureaucracy up to ridicule and contempt. No doubt this places Senhor Ribeiro on the side of the angels, but it must be said that although he writes with remarkable vigor and clarity for a man his age, and although his story keeps moving readily along, he makes the Portuguese government's hostility to his work seem well-nigh incomprehensible by the time he has done. Senhor Ribeiro's victims of bureaucratic tyranny are peasants whose lack of charm is exceptional. Mountaineers living in squalid poverty among the uplands whose forests were destroyed by their remote ancestors and whose soil they have impoverished by centuries of bad farming, they regard every visitor from the outside world, whatever his purposes may be, with morbid suspicion. Senhor Ribeiro's bureaucratic villains come into the district with a scheme for closing off the scrub-covered wastes on the heights above these people's farmlands and replanting them with trees. He does his best to make the proposal seem inhumane and unreasonable, but it is quite clear that it has been designed as part of an altogether sensible attack on the district's problems of poverty and human degradation. Are the angels really in favor of prejudice, ignorance, slyness, primitive land hunger, slut farming, rural slums, and destructive malice? Senhor Ribeiro's peasants lose their fight to keep their upland wastes barren, and the government at length gets its trees planted. . . .

Senhor Ribeiro describes [the peasant's] night-long ride as he goes from point to point setting fires with holy glee. . . . Senhor Ribeiro's burning forest, like the mounds of dead in Katyn, Auschwitz, Dresden, and Hiroshima, is an all too effective reminder that there is always an ultimate enemy beyond the enemy who can be named and attacked— the mindless savage called instinct. . . .

Anthony West. *N.Y.* Dec. 28, 1963, pp. 73, 76

The stories [in Aquilino Ribeiro's last published volume, *House of the Scorpion*] that I liked the most are, first "You Have a Good Body . . . So Work!" and then, "The Ass-Driver and His Ass." In the latter, Aquilino presents those creatures whose existence is reduced to a delayed satisfaction of the fundamental necessities: the necessity of eating, sleeping, resting, loving, even though it is with an animalistic and crazed fury, the necessity of being free and even of communicating with others, in a subtle and agile way, through their behavior in different situations. It is a necessity that ends up placing Lúcio, the ass-driver, and Fagulha, the ass, on the same plane, in which Fagulha thus becomes human and Lúcio shows some lack of humanness. It is curious to note that in characters without interior existence, characters who falter with every movement, with every word, with every decision, there is nonetheless a visceral desire, be it through silence, through violence, or through sensuality, to reach other beings. . . .

The best-constructed narrative of the volume is perhaps "You Have a Good Body . . . So Work!" It tells us the story of the just Mathias, who identifies all his dreams of happiness and tranquillity with the destiny of a calf, Formosa; the animal ends up representing his life, his hope, his human dignity.

Eduardo Prado Coelho. *SeN.* Jan., 1964, p. 24†

Aquilino Ribeiro, who was so close to [Henri] Bergson—he attended his classes—was not to become the herald of Bergson's doctrine in Portugal. Such a position was to be assumed by some of the intellectuals of the magazine *Presença,* and thus it is not surprising . . . that Aquilino sustained so many attacks and unjust criticisms from the [*Presença*] literary generation of 1927.

In an epoch in which Bergsonism was judged to be the watchword, it is natural that the non-Bergsonian Aquilino might seem anachronistic. It is natural that those spirits who grew up on the creed that outside of Bergson or Proust there can be no modern literature condemn Aquilino for his literary manifestation of his rebellion, which is typical of those who do not join a literary vanguard simply because it is a literary vanguard. Well, the literary vanguard of 1927 follows the line of the French decadents. Aquilino Ribeiro had rebelled against this decadentism, expression his rebellion in many different ways in his literature. . . .

This means that Aquilino's position, when *Presença* appeared, was not one of backwardness owing to a lack of information. Perhaps [he was] more aware of modern currents of thought than some of the principal members of the *Presença* group. . . . In the midst of the principal members of the *Presença* group. . . . In the midst of the assault against reason . . . by the first Modernist generation—1915—and the second Modernist generation—1927—Aquilino Ribeiro was fated to remain an isolated personality, at the edge of literary movements, and misunderstood by almost all—even by those who admired him—[and] to be relegated in a spiteful way by competitors for a place to the comfortable position of a *regionalistic* writer, or a *prose* chronicler of the annals of the lower classes of the Beira province.

The literary vanguard decreed that a certain thing was then the novel. It was evident that Aquilino's books were not full of and padded with exhaustive psychological analyses of the characters, that they did not pay sufficient attention to the *interior world,* limiting themselves to beautiful exterior description without depth. Aquilino's books thus would not be *novels.* He would not be a novelist, but only a *prose writer.*

Alexandre Pinheiro Torres. Romance: O mundo
em equação (Lisbon, Portugália, 1967), pp. 190–91†

Primitivism/Civilization; Purity/Sin . . . rooted in the mountains of the Beira province are the principal lines that form the basis for the world of Aquilino's tales. This geographical area . . . will condition their definitive and unmistakable appearance.

Concerning ourselves with the meaning of these clashes in behavior and analyzing the creative process that transformed them into art, we attempted to show Aquilino Ribeiro as the last demiurge of an esthetic-social-spiritual cycle that . . . is defined by [Almeida] Garrett; acquires dramatic form in Camilo [Castelo Branco]; lyrical balance in Júlio Diniz; imbalance in Fialho de Almeida; lyricism with the neo-Garrettists and *saudosistas* [the nostalgic group]; and finally reveals in Aquilino the notable confluence of an end and a beginning.

Or more specifically in literary terms, the end of the omniscient narrator, creator of worlds, master of a Truth; and the birth of that being who has strayed (a product of our century), who no longer feels himself authorized to speak in the name of man, because the contours of reality have been dissolved, the certainties shipwrecked, because the truth is nothing more than a group convention and language itself has collapsed, since it shows itself impotent to express human existence.

At this threshold of worlds, the traditional one (which comes to an end with the war of 1914) and the contemporary one (which struggles to impose itself), Aquilino Ribeiro belongs to both. What his immense literary production shows us is that he never refused the role of a firm intermediary between the reality to be expressed and his reader. . . .

Aquilino Ribeiro belonged to a generation that received absolute values to serve them as orientation and guide in their lives' choices. He was one of the writers who had a Truth to offer, and they did it without shame nor hesitation. It is in this sense that we point to him as a "demiurge," the creator of forms, conscious of his mission and proud of it.

Nelly Novães Coelho. Aquilino Ribeiro (São
Paulo, Brazil, Quíron, 1973), pp. 163–65†

Although at very different levels of [linguistic re-creation], neither Aquilino's discourse nor that of [João Guimarães] Rosa is close to being a scrupulous register of popular speech. The original word is retaken by its root or its echo and withdrawn from its natural context. It is repeatedly decomposed and, also, recomposed; it is treated. A lower-class word assumes an erudite irony (it goes from spoken to written), or it appears in a literary game. The same thing happens with proverbs and sayings; they are separated from their conventional meaning or they are paraphrased in order to appear with a new force.

This treatment of expression evidently involves humor. Aquilino used to say, for example, that he liked [Camilo José] Cela's *The Family of Pascual Duarte* because being an "arid and sad novel" . . . it was full of humor.

There were, then, both geographical and generational differences between Aquilino and Rosa. . . . In spite of this, there are those signs of similarity: the transformation of popular speech . . . and above all a certain Franciscanism that is common to both in their treatment of the brotherhood between men and animals. A reader meanders through Guimarães Rosa's colorful, noisy *sertão* [backlands] and comes across the arara bird, the wildcat . . . and cannot help but think of Aquilino and the understanding with which he humanizes the hummingbird, the donkey, and the other creatures of our lesser kingdom. He even makes one of them—the so-called student, Wolf—the most important figure of a novel that brought him official excommunication [*When the Wolves Howl*].

José Cardoso Pires. Jornal de letras. Jan., 1984, pp. 2, 3†

RODRIGUES MIGUÉIS, JOSÉ. *See* MIGUÉIS, JOSÉ RODRIGUES

SÁ-CARNEIRO, MÁRIO DE (1890–1916)

Mário de Sá-Carneiro, along with Fernando Pessoa, is one of the two great renovators of Portuguese poetry. . . . Just as Antero [de Quental's] poetry appears to be regenerative, giving Portuguese poetry a rich metaphysical content and intellectual dramatics that counterbalanced the complacent traditional lyricism, the superficial sensibility, and the orientation toward exterior landscape descriptions, the poetry of Sá-Carneiro and Fernando Pessoa equally was able to illuminate unexplored regions, breaking into the immense horizon of interior reality. . . .

What is new in Sá-Carneiro's poetry involves neither ideas nor means of expression. It is not through formal innovation that he introduces something essentially new, since all the distortions to which he subjects the syntax and vocabulary only reveal the particular conditions of his own personality and do not really have the characteristic of stylistic advancement, since they are conditions that are his alone, and without them Mário de Sá-Carneiro would not be Mário de Sá-Carneiro. (1929)

> Adolfo Casais Monteiro. *Considerações pessoais* (Coimbra, Imprensa da Universidade, 1933), pp. 141–42†

Now attempting to descend a little into the core of Sá-Carneiro's singular poetry, we will state that its unquestionable domains are this life and the hereafter. That is, to reveal what has not yet been revealed, to express, or to suggest, the inexpressable about this life or the hereafter, everything about life that can be expressed directly, simply, and commonly—that is the most urgent tendency and the prime value of his art. Both sensual and voluptuous, Sá-Carneiro aims at transmitting to us the most elusive and distant sensations, the ones in embryonic form; or those which, owing to their perfection, almost escape the sphere of sensation. A metaphysician of the sentiments, he also aims at breaking down their barriers, at pursuing them, analyzing them in thunderbolts of lucid insanity, to the most profound depths of their innermost being. This is what his novels document, perhaps better than his poetry. But are the novels less poetic than the poetry? . . .

Read poems like "Dispersion," "False Statue," "Almost," "The Fall," in his first book; read any of the more subjective poems . . . and you will understand how this sense of being *incomplete,* which he calls

the pain of *almost-being,* torments him. Well, while he is conscious of
this degradation, while he makes a very humble confession about it, his
pride and his megalomania sate themselves through glorifying the demi-
god that he should have been, but never became. . . . And, not being
able to construct the auto-epic of a mutilating tragic destiny, and not
being able either to get rid of his crown of the vanquished prince, Mário
de Sá-Carneiro hovers in this twilight state of a dreamlike world in
which all transpositions are possible and all opposites adaptable.

José Régio. *Pequena história da moderna
poesia portuguesa* (Lisbon, Inquérito, 1941), pp. 92–93†

In *Traces of Gold,* published for the first time in 1937, the poems the
poet wrote between 1913 and 1916 are collected; some of these had
appeared in the first modernist magazines during the author's lifetime.
This book, in its language and its artistic content, continues the rhythm
of *Dispersion.* The poet's imagination is enriched, new visions strike
him, the linguistic juggling and daring are multiplied, incomprehensible
things accumulate, and at each turn the reader stumbles on apocalytic
verses that elude the analytic scalpel of reason. Mário de Sá-Carneiro
brought to Portuguese poetry—and this is precisely one of the extravagant revelations of his art—the irrational and the incomprehensible,
phantasmagoric hallucinations, the madman's dizziness and feverish
deliriums. . . .

It is in Sá-Carneiro's poetry that harmony, clarity, and the discipline of the faculties are intolerable, repudiated preconceptions, and,
for this reason, they are replaced by disorder, by the absurd, and by
chaos. . . . This means that in his poetry Sá-Carneiro became unin-
terested in the normalities of the exterior world and the arrangements of
real life; he descended to the core of consciousness and there came
upon not the light and beauty that at one time must have adorned this
moral region but rather a vast number of abnormalities and imbalances.

Feliciano Ramos. *Ocidente* (Lisbon). May, 1943,
pp. 27–28†

Like Minerva, who sprang full-grown and armed from the head of
Jupiter, Sá-Carneiro's poetry is born mature and in complete possession
of its resources. We do not find any development in it, in the sense of
progress. Of course, new forms will appear, the tone will change, the
dramatic aspect will be intensified, new themes will make an appearance, but what is essential in it—in material and form—is there
from the very first poem, "Departure." The title is already significant: it
translates the profound impulse of the poet: "to depart without fear,"
"to go up beyond the skies," drawn by the desire to find once again the
other side for which his soul is longing. But there is more: in these first
verses there is the revelation of the multiple facets, crests, and summits
of his personality: the desire to flee, the ideal search for beauty, the

delirium of colors, the sensorial acuteness, the certainty of being great and, for this very reason, alone. The words he will most use in his later writings, many of which are evidently a symbolist inheritance, are also found in these early writings: gold, crystal, ghost, halo, labyrinth, chimera, fog, timbre, etc. . . . .

Although he was a profoundly original poet, he did not remain completely free from the influences of his time, less because of voluntary imitation than intimate affinities. He is related to symbolism not only by the cult of the rare and euphonic word and rich rhyme, the use of allegorical capitalized words, but also, and above all, by the natural pleasure in what is precious—stones, metals, fabrics—the anxiety of capturing colors, forms, smells, sounds, which he merges into admirable synesthesias, the state of delirious semiconsciousness, the ability to suggest. . . . The futurist experiment by Sá-Carneiro is the poem "Manicure," which dates from 1915. Visibly influenced by Fernando Pessoa's "Maritime Ode" and "Triumphal Ode," the poet tries to identify himself in it with things of the present, to see with eyes "anointed by the New," those eyes that he calls "futurist, cubist and intersectionist," but which in truth are not.

Cleonice Berardinelli. *Mário de Sá-Carneiro: Poesia.* (Rio de Janeiro, Agir, 1958), pp. 9–10†

In "Manicure" Sá-Carneiro makes use of this game [the intersectionist style] with the aim of giving an idea of modern reality in the sense of futurism, which at many points in his prose works and letters is designated simply as "Europe": the modern European reality as a whole, which takes in, on one hand, technical civilization and, on the other hand, a set psychic predisposition to enjoy completely the multiple charms of this civilization. In no way does he create here a convincing sketch of modern life, as Fernando Pessoa did in "Triumphal Ode," written under the pseudonym of Álvaro de Campos. The noble free rhythms, with the verses added on in a parallelistic form, and the enthusiastic exclamations demand a certain monumentality of content, and do not fit in either with the limited atmosphere of a café, from which Sá-Carneiro observes life in "Manicure," or with the psychic intimacy that predominates here as well as in the rest of his poetry. And although this futurist experiment, which falls into unintentional ridiculousness, is a failure, one must consider the other attempt at making appear, in the midst of a chaotic futurist material and the sensations and associations provoked by it, that ideal of "fluid art," which, no matter how little importance it merits in his poetic achievements, is one of his most serious ideas, not very suitable for the cheap jokes of "Manicure." Be it intentional, as Fernando Pessoa has said, or not, the effect of "Manicure" is one of ridiculousness. It occupies a separate place in Sá-Carneiro's poetry. Without doubt, in the author's life the enthusiasm for the technical side of modern reality had a great deal of importance. Nevertheless, "Manicure" shows precisely how little the poet knew about using this material. [1960]

Dieter Woll. *Realidade e idealidade na lírica de Sá-Carneiro.* (Lisbon, Delfos, 1968), pp. 84–85†

It is easy to say that the succession of free images, with their own rhythms, threatens the flow of narration, and tends to make you forget that someone is trying to tell a story. But it becomes somewhat more difficult to indicate when this risk is occurring when what we are dealing with is an authentic poem in prose. . . . The designation "poetic novel" . . . in itself is a restriction, an indication of weakness in what the substance of fiction is. . . . What seems to me to be of interest and able to explain some of the term's weak points and lacunae is a second distinction in the term "poetic": the lyric tonality we accept as being of indescribable beauty and power, and what appears clumsy, out of date, and baroque in the negative sense. . . . Indeed, when faced with certain ways of saying things, with certain expressions, we have the impression of the unnecessary, of something that is excessive; perhaps this is a consequence of the language. . . .

This is the greatest restriction we can place on Sá-Carneiro's short stories, what can most damage their acceptability. It is no longer a question of the poetic stifling the novelistic; it is a question of the poetic stifling itself through the material that expresses it. The intervention of this material is enough for its existence to appear superfluous and troublesome—in a word, unsuccessful.

Maria da Graça Carpinteiro. *A novela poética de Mário de Sá-Carneiro* (Lisbon, Instituto de Alta Cultura, 1960), pp. 93–95†

In Lisbon, Sá-Carneiro published in the second issue of *Orpheu* his poem "Manicure," which Fernando Pessoa called a joke, but which contained no more nor less than the manifesto of the "modernist" school. In spite of the brevity of his creative life, the poet has exercised an incontestably profound influence on contemporary Portuguese poetry.

He wrote his first play, *Friendship,* in collaboration with Tomás Cabreira Júnior, who also later committed suicide, an act that greatly influenced Sá-Carneiro's final decision.

[José de] Almada-Negreiros remembers having heard two other plays read to him, besides *Friendship: Soul,* in one act, and *Brothers,* in three acts. These two plays have never been published and are considered lost.

It is necessary to recognize that Sá-Carneiro must have read a great deal of Dostoevsky, Gérard de Nerval, Baudelaire, Rimbaud (he translated "Le bateau ivre" and aspired, as did Rimbaud, "to the dissolution of all senses"), and Wilde (particularly "The Decay of Living"), all of which greatly influenced his work. In addition, Sá-Carneiro was a contemporary of Kafka, with whom he had a lot in common, even though he could not have known him, owing to the very late fame of the Czech author. But Sá-Carneiro's world is that of Dostoevsky and Kafka, and in my opinion, that of Proust.

H. Houwens Post. Neophil. Oct., 1965, pp. 302–3†

What one understands from [The Confession of Lúcio] is that something strange motivates the behavior of the characters, something they are not aware of. Only much later does Lúcio verify it, and he feels something inexplicable in not having immediately discovered the evidence of his absurdity. This process of conducting the narrative, allied with a concatenation of facts that is typical of the novel, in which the events become evident through their total interrelationship and progressive character, leads us to admit the possibility of seeing the passage of time in this novel as an expression of destiny. It is not specifically a question of chance relationships but one of a convergence of situations and details that will culminate in the final event and in this way give the narrator, who is far from the reality that he describes, a sense of motivation. It is not a question of a "weight" of fatality being felt by the character, since the relationships that could lead to this conclusion are almost always established a posteriori; in the meantime, the spirit organizes them and stirs, mistrusts, and doubts. Hence, the atmosphere of restlessness and even hallucination of the second part of the work and the narrator's conviction . . . that nothing can deter the course of events and of everything that was being prepared. It should be noted once again that the narrator here does not mean author but rather the character who is describing himself in the past. For this reason, the novel does not seem to be a mere false construction of causes and effects; it is not the author who orders his material in this way—it is the narrator-character who lets his sense of fate get out, although always in a veiled and non-explicit manner.

Maria Alzira (Seixo) Baranhona. Para um
estudo da expressão do tempo no romance
contemporâneo português (Lisbon, Centro de
Estudos Filológicos, 1968), p. 39†

"Rattletrap Jalopy" is a dramatic monologue in two voices. . . . The character [does not] present himself, [does not] limit himself to speaking about, but rather lives his situation with his whole body, although he continues to be two: He, the one who twitches, the one who suffers, and the Other, the one who sees the suffering and, in spite of everything, speaks in an ironical way about this suffering. . . .

The monologues that we consider a second phase of Sá-Carneiro's poetry thus appear to us to be on the threshold of dramatic language.

The language is no longer, as it was in the first phase, essentially narrative, it is not limited to describing the Other or making him into a metaphor—he treats him familiarly, he provokes him. . . , he spits out his contempt for him, he calls out to him, he makes fun of him (the active value of this language is recognizable in the vocatives, the apostrophes, the interjections, the verbal forms in the imperative and the present).

But Sá-Carneiro never managed, as did Pessoa, *to become another.* While for the latter the character was born into life through a complete act of creation, with the cutting of the umbilical cord, in the former, the creator and the creation were inseparable. . . .

The character of Sá-Carneiro is always an image of himself in a distorting mirror—a melancholic servant or a grotesque fool. . . .

Sá-Carneiro was not a dramatic poet like Pessoa because he never separated himself from that character: he lent him his body, since he did not have one—for life and for death. For this reason, like Ricardo of *The Confession of Lúcio,* upon attempting to kill the Other, his living shadow, it is in his very own body that death strikes the blow.

Teresa Rita Lopes. *Colóquio/Letras.* Dec.,
1971, pp. 24–26†

In Sá-Carneiro, manifestations of the supernatural are evidence of the element of mystery which is thematically a cornerstone of his writings. . . . The very frequency of the word *mystery* is evidence of his obsession with the concept. Therefore there are two levels: first, the narrative puzzle to be solved, a puzzle created by the intervention of the supernatural, and second, the idea of the unknown presiding over everything, which pervades Sá-Carneiro's thought and which the particular puzzles of the narrative represent. In the stories where there is no narrative puzzle, the emphasis falls directly on mystery with no intermediary, as it were. In *Beginning,* for example, we have psychological mysteries based on obsession, fear, sixth sense; [the critic] John Parker claims that all the themes of the stories "could be reduced to one central theme or attitude: "obsession," and he maintains that "this is true also of *The Confession of Lúcio* and *Heavens Ablaze.*" To all intents and purposes, the literary situation is the same in both types of story, for narrative puzzles are not really explained in those stories where they are a feature, and in those where mystery is investigated directly, without the metaphor of the question/answer device, we learn nothing. In fact, Parker sees the element of mystery as an end in itself, a means of escaping from everyday life: for Sá-Carneiro, "only the unknown is worth knowing." This is the philosophy of many of the Sá-Carneiro protagonists—for example, the hero of the short story in *Beginning,* "Page of a Suicide," who commits suicide because "the only interesting thing that at present exists in life is death." But here again the mystery is not solved, for the tale ends with the disappearance of the hero, and obviously the new experience that is his is not shared with the reader.

The third level on which the *contes fantastiques* of Sá-Carneiro can be taken is the one which reveals part of his own personality and problems, and it is on this level that we catch a glimpse of one of the causes of his personal tragedy and his suicide. It is, it seems to me, the uselessness of his "omniscience."

Pamela Bacarisse. *LBR.* Summer, 1975. p. 74

Sá-Carneiro's poetry, especially in *Traces of Gold,* is pregnant with descriptive words, and one can cite many examples of the poet's use of a highly suggestive vocabulary that calls to mind the kinds of techniques used by the "school" of Spanish American Modernists inspired by the *Azul* and *Prosas profanas* periods of Rubén Darío. These Spanish American Modernists, as does Sá-Carneiro, strive for a perfect synthesis of form and meaning in poetry. They both emphasize words and phrases evoking sensations and aesthetic and physiological "correspondences." Their use of synethesia is one example of this. The preoccupation with creating images which are full of light, colors, sounds, odors, and tastes is another common denominator. Just as the Spanish American Modernists struggled in their minds to reach exotic lands, so Sá-Carneiro longs to venture forth spiritually in order to find happiness. . . . Certain word-symbols relished by the Modernists in Spanish America, such as "iris," "princess," "palace," "gold," and "satin," are used to full advantage by Sá-Carneiro.

There are also certain psychological parallelisms between Darío's and Sá-Carneiro's works which are interesting to note: both needed to escape reality, albeit for different reasons, and both were destined to wake up to reality and find that they really preferred their self-fabricated worlds of non-reality.

William W. Megenney. Hispania. May, 1976, p. 263

SENA, JORGE DE (1919–1978)

With the exception of his last book, *Fidelity* . . . the poet brought together all his earlier volumes in *Poetry I.* . . . In this way, we can view for the first time the multiplicity of characteristics of a poetic personality. . . . Indeed, the essential aspects of the evolution of Jorge de Sena's poetry from *Persecution* to *Fidelity* are not evident in a clear line, but are dispersed in a restless and zigzagging search for meanings and expressions.

In *Philosopher's Stone* (1950), Jorge de Sena reaps the fruits of a path that, having passed through contradictory, passionate appeals and searches, some lived, some denied, opens out into a secure serenity and plenitude that gives the poet authority over himself and his language. This authority becomes evident in the clarity of many poems, which go beyond the tortured search so typical of his style. . . . The poet evolved to a certain classicism, not only in form but also at the heart of his poetry; this tendency was often revealed in his earlier books. . . . At the same time, the progressive *humanization* of Jorge de Sena's poetry . . . is projected into many of the love poems in this book, some of which possess a great sensual and erotic sensitivity and subtlety.

José Augusto Seabra. *Bandarra.* Summer, 1961,
pp. 22, 24†

Aside from two very notable translations of Eugene O'Neill . . . Jorge de Sena's theater to date is composed of a four-act tragedy in verse (*The Undesired One,* 1951—but according to the author written between December 1944 and December 1945) and four farces in one act (*Mother's Protection, Adulterous Ulisseia,* published in 1951 and 1952; *The Death of the Pope* and *The Eastern Empire,* the last one dating from 1964 and both unpublished). . . .

[Adolfo] Casais Monteiro has distinguished two constants in Sena's poetry, which at times appear separately and at other times are interspersed: surrealism and neo-Góngorism. In his plays these two tendencies are also present—but while the first is prevalent in the farces, the second is more common in the tragedies. . . .

The Undesired One is, as the author himself defined it, "the tragedy of a national conscience fighting the growing abstraction (and subjection) of its own destiny". . . . It is an existential tragedy more than a historical one, or perhaps a presentation of history in an existential perspective, and it is only through an error of judgement that anyone might find any indication of the resurrection of the historical drama, which was born and died with the romantic movement. . . . If we should want to discover any of its precedents in our national dramatic literature, we would not turn to the followers of [Almeida] Garrett . . . but to some rather singular works, such as the static dramas of António Patrício, *D. Carlos* by Teixeira de Pascoaes, or *King Sebastian* by José Régio.

Luís Francisco Rebello. *O tempo e o modo.*
April, 1968, pp. 321–22†

Art of Music (1968) by Jorge de Sena has become a major work of our poetry and our culture because, in addition to other reasons, no one has yet been able to say more, nor as much, about music in Portuguese poetry. It can be well understood that many of Sena's readers might have disliked this volume upon first reading it, or at least considered it inferior to *Metamorphoses* (1963), which forms a diptych with *Art of Music:* experiences of a music lover in one case and in the other those of a lover of the plastic arts. It is easier to accept hearing about painting or architecture than about music. . . . In addition, Jorge de Sena crosses all bridges to arrive at a happy relationship between poetry and music. If we except his spontaneous tendency toward the ten-syllable verse, and, to a lesser extent, the stanza groupings traditionally associated with this verse, the rhythm of *Art of Music* is notable for its simple, expressive syncopation in relationship to the normally expected syntactical pauses. Certain poems might appear to be prose because all their discursive, imagistic . . . and versifying organization has the purpose of little by little shaking poetic complacency. There are rhythms that put one to sleep; these serve to wake one up.

Óscar Lopes. *Modo de ler: crítica e*
interpretação literária/2 (Oporto, Inova, 1969),
pp. 42–43†

Jorge de Sena's translations of poetry in *Poetry of 26 Centuries* tell us something about the great poet that Jorge de Sena is. We now know that while he was producing his own poetic works, he was seeking his own artistic refinement, through matching himself up against his peers and through meditating, with his habitual and uncommon critical awareness, on the way to translate poets of past times. . . .

In one of Petrarch's songs—one of the most complex and demanding poetic forms—Jorge de Sena maintained the rhythm, certain assonant and even some consonant rhymes. Nonetheless, the problem of the structure of the song was without doubt one of the most difficult to resolve. Petrarch systematically maintained, in the *fronte* or in the *piedi,* the rhythmic scheme: a b c, b a c. And the translator was admirably able to conserve it in five of the seven stanzas that make up the song. . . .

This collection, the reading and rereading of which gives neverending spiritual delight, shows that Jorge de Sena is a translator in the class of [Boris] Pasternak and the legitimate successor to Fernando Pessoa. . . .

Luís de Sousa Rebelo. *Colóquio/Letras.* Jan.,
1973, pp. 58, 60†

Who are these people, *The Great Captains?* Where and when do they exist? . . . Who are they? Navy and army captains, soldiers and bureaucrats, military men and clerics? . . .

Where, when? In Portugal and Spain, bitter experiences of the 1930s to 1950s on the Iberian Peninsula. This volume is thus a fictional chronicle about a terrorist regime—a grayish one, Salazar's. The loneliness, the stifling of dream and desire, the pragmatism of despotism, the code of grayishness, the use/abuse of arbitrariness begin right there in the distant background of [the author's] infancy. . . .

Written in exile in 1961–62, these stories were set down with complete freedom and also with the extremely productive distance of someone who could not publish them at that moment in his homeland. Some scenes chronicle a country in a state of siege and are thus developed with all possible indignation, bitterness, and cruelty. The work is an attempt at recomposing through fiction, a world in complete decomposition. . . .

Realism, a phenomenological realism, is organized with great rigor in these seven narratives. Through an intensive stylistic experimentation a violent metaphor is produced: that of a concentration camp universe. . . ; that of a country evoked from the distance of exile and described with words such as "opaque-shadowy-livid-viscose-grayish"; a country . . . through which there pass "bodies" (a very significant word in these texts . . .). . . .

What kingdom is this? It was called Portugal. A Portugal joined with a Spain under "a protective laurel of fascists and the swastika"; that was our country—a monotonous existence, organized crime, a ferocity without limits, isolation at all levels, the horrors of war and fear.

Casimiro de Brito. *Prática da escrita em tempo da revolução* (Lisbon, Caminho, 1977), pp. 46–48†

Jorge de Sena's interest in the English language and curiousity about things British or American developed early and remained with him throughout his life. No doubt his admiration for Fernando Pessoa inspired his initial explorations. Like Pessoa, young Sena even composed one of his earliest poems in English. "Gentle Advice," despite its immaturity, is both revealing in what it tells us of his self-perceived strength of mind and character, and rather prophetic relative to his future battles and role as gadfly.

We cannot over-emphasize the importance of the *Cadernos de poesia* [Notebooks of Poetry] group in Portugal, to which Sena belonged. As the first generation of Portuguese writers to read and write English (rather than depend on French translations as others did, when and if they did take notice of an English-speaking author), it was peculiarly well suited—due to its members' intelligence as well as training—to introduce and subsequently foster in Portugal, an interest in twentieth-century British and American literatures to a nation which traditionally looked only to France for its cultural inspiration.

Besides translating, analyzing, reviewing and publishing the authors, Sena made the acquaintance of some and corresponded with others, such as Dame Edith Sitwell. Inspired both by what he read and by what he translated, Sena also composed a few more poems in English at this time. They remain in initial draft stage and in manuscript form. Some, like "The Blood Black" (October 5, 1948), are similar to the surrealistically oriented poems of the same period he published in his first two volumes.

Although he never published any of the English poems, save one ["Bilingualism"], and in truth he wrote relatively few when compared to his vast poetic output, still, they represent a curious fact of the complex personality of the poet. The impression one gets is that Sena attempted more poems in English than in any other language, save his own. It also seems clear that he had, over a long period of time, secretly harbored the desire to be regarded as an equally fine poet in English; but the language facility was lacking. No doubt he knew it, and that is why he never prepared the poems for publication. Of more than passing interest is the fact that on at least two occasions—and there is reason to believe there are more—a poem he had originally written in English was by him translated into Portuguese and published.

Frederick G. Williams. Introduction to *The Poetry of Jorge de Sena* (Santa Barbara, Cal., Mudhorn Press, 1980), pp. 26–29

SOROMENHO, FERNANDO MONTEIRO DE CASTRO (1910–1968)

In sum, *Calenga* deals with the narration of a legend of the blacks. It is the story of the appearance of the kingdom of Lunda, which resulted from the union of the Luba and Bungo tribes. Castro Soromenho, however, does not deal with the topic in light of any historical or ethnological criteria. Neither are we in the presence of a collection of folkloric elements. If we wanted to characterize the nature of Castro Soromenho's production, we might be able to say that it is one part of a *"black songbook."* And it is in this aspect that Castro Soromenho's creative achievement is found. The legend, which had been transmitted among the natives from generation to generation, was told to the author one day. To this necessarily cold and inexpressive narration, Castro Soromenho added his knowledge of the blacks, of their psychology, of their feelings, of their mentality. And he forged all this within his imagination, [and] created "medieval romance" of the African blacks. "Lueji and Ilunga in the Land of Friendship," which is the title given by Castro Soromenho to this legend, constitutes, for this reason, the use of native tales as a basis for re-creation with novelistic aims. We, the readers, do not realize it, but surely, not everything was told to the author. Without doubt, he improvised a great deal, he joined diverse facts together, perhaps he even included elements foreign to the legend; but everything was united into a perfect unit.

Franco Nogueira. *Jornal de crítica literária*
(Lisbon, Portugália, 1954), pp. 65–66†

The black man is the human material of the short stories and novels of Castro Soromenho. The jungle is his social ambience. And thus, until *Dead Land,* the writer's works had as characters forest flora and as the background the immense African jungle. Only later did Castro Soromenho bring together the two halves that had been separated until then—the white man and the black man. Beginning with the novels inspired by the problems that arise from the contact of the civilized white man with the native in his barbarous state, one can say, or at least in my opinion, that the author of *Turning Point* attained the peak of his narrative art. . . .

Castro Soromenho applied to his study and presentation of the black man a vision partially inspired by neorealism through his reading in Portugal of the first great novels by Jorge Amado. Thus . . . the blacks of the first books of the author of *Night of Anguish* suffer from an idealization that makes their presentation more poetic than truthful. . . .

Castro Soromenho, upon reorienting his work in this direction—that of the novel inspired by the conflicts and problems that result from the presence of metropolitan Portugal's representatives in the interior of the African jungle—found, in fact, the theme that his vigorous narrative art would seize upon. *Turning Point* is his best novel to date. [1958]

João Gaspar Simões. *Crítica,* Vol. III (Lisbon,
Delfos, 1969), pp. 53–55†

With the appearance of Castro Soromenho the colonial novel stops being the novel of the Portuguese traveler enticed by the call of the ocean or by the exoticism of foreign lands and who sends back to the "metropolis" a simple series of picturesque illustrated postcards, and becomes instead the novel of a man who set down roots in Angola, who was reborn there, and let himself be shaped by the steppe, by the solitude, by the sun, and by the two *batuques* [dances associated with the black African religious rites]—that of the black man in the slave quarters and that of the black gods unleashing thunderbolts and rains.

The fact that this writer . . . began his literary career with poetic novels and stories—*Gust of Wind, and Other Stories, Night of Anguish, Calenga,* and *Men without a Way*—might be surprising at first. . . . Castro Soromenho captures Angola—or, more exactly, a privileged area of Angola, that of the Lunda and Kioko tribes—in the exact moment in which the event that is to be narrated becomes disassociated from its concrete origins in order to change into song, to the beating of drums, when it changes from the banal to the African "thing." . . .

Castro Soromenho sings of his heroes' deeds as hunters, warriors, and witch doctors, and their meetings with the gods or their battles with hunger. And, in the style of the epic poet, he suddenly reaches the moments of great tension, placing himself less in the daily atmosphere than in the drama—the drama of hunger or of battle. Or, more exactly, the drama of man in the face of his destiny, a destiny that reveals itself through a series of catastrophes, when the violation of taboos results in a continuous rosary of crimes, insanity, illnesses, and droughts, until the final reconciliation with the supernatural through a blood sacrifice.

Roger Bastide. "L'Afrique dans l'œuvre de
Castro Soromenho," in Castro Soromenho,
Histórias da terra negra [*Stories of the Black
Land*] (Lisbon, Gleba, 1960), pp. iii–iv†

Castro Soromenho [in *Night of Anguish*] goes beyond anecdote in order to present the social functioning of an autochthonous tribe, which, as the reader will be able to verify, is not lacking in historical basis. What we have before us is a group of black men now entangled in the tight web of their social relationships, eminently class-conscious. The *soba* Xandumba represents, for all intents and purposes, the same thing that the suzerain represented in feudal society. The *sobeta* Salemo owes him vassalage, and Xandumba demands it from him. The tribal aristocrats behave in all their activities as blood nobles do, with their references to the family tree being frequent. Since all are linked by family ties, they fight for the exclusive right to the favors granted through the obvious nepotism of the *soba*. Muaquife, Xandumba's nephew, hatches a plot to put Salemo out of the running for the succession, and the events that take place as a consequence of this plot have clear points of resemblance to the complex machinations of Shakespearean characters. . . .

The primitivism of these men [the blacks] is obvious. Dominated by the terror of darkness, by the fear with which night fills them, by the power of witchcraft, their actions still offer a wide area of free will, of voluntariness, which indicates their relative psychological complexity. Ivenga is a woman dominated by passions, which in their dimensions imply a certain interior richness; the same thing happens with Muaquife and Xandumba, whose cautious actions, whose governing strategy show how the *soba* is a man who maneuvers with strictly psychological facts.

Alexandre Pinheiro Torres. *Romance: o mundo
em equação* (Lisbon, Portugália, 1967), pp. 208–9†

As is generally true of realistic writing, Castro Soromenho's works of fiction interest more because of their contents and the author's stated or implied attitudes than because of the style or technique of the narrative. Yet, his manner of writing differs from old nineteenth-century realism. For example, he is too much a child of our impatient age to waste time on describing exterior appearance in detail. . . . On the other hand, he is fond of the short lyrical paragraphs that can suggest a mood. . . . Considerable pain is taken to indicate and motivate the emotions, thoughts, actions of Africans, such as the feelings leading to suicide. Their beliefs and customs, even the harshest ones, like slavery, and the most repulsive ones, like cannibalism, are made understandable in the framework of tribal society. In this respect, Castro Soromenho's realism is modern, guided as it is by the objective methods of psychology, anthropology, and sociology.

Castro Soromenho used few flashbacks, and then only in his last novels. He scorns the modern fiction writer's tricks of the trade. We always know who speaks to whom. There is no flow of consciousness, no simultaneity of several actions, no circular movement or psychological time, and none of the toying with metaphysical problems of man's place in the universe with which the masters of contemporary fiction intensify the impact of their stories. Nor is there any experimentation with vocabulary or syntax, not even a suggestion of genuinely African ways of speaking, barring a few exceptions, such as the passage of the birth of the heart of the white man in *Dead Land*. At bottom, Castro Soromenho remained a journalist who sought out the facts, with a flair for the dramatic, yet unsentimental, stating them in correct, plain language, accessible to average readers.

Gerald Moser. Essays in Portuguese-African
Literature (University Park, Pennsylvania State
University Press, 1971), pp. 54–55

In Soromenho's view, African societies were victimized by their own state tribalism. His depiction of the superstition-bound, poverty-stricken "natives" gives evidence of his European prejudices towards Africa. Yet, his sense of the universal bonds of humankind and his attempts to capture cultural authenticity earned Soromenho the reputation, which spread beyond the borders of the Portuguese-speaking world, of a white man who understood the black man's soul. For all his understanding of and sympathy for the black subjects of his stories, Soromenho did cultivate the picturesque and the exotic, especially in his descriptions of traditional African customs. . . .

Since 1942, when he published *Men without a Way,* Soromenho had turned to the clash of cultures as his preferred theme. Even before modifying his language he had gained a new level of authenticity by treating his subject from within. In obvious reference to the rise of a new black consciousness, he told an interviewer that because of the contradictions of different realities he saw the necessity of adopting a new technique and style. . . .

In Paris Soromenho wrote for such journals as *Présence Africaine* and he aligned himself philosophically, if not actively, with the cause of African independence. His novelistic language only implicitly reached the level of Angolan nationalism, for his role was to dramatize that historical moment when exploitation had begun to reveal the emptiness of the adventure about which he had once written so grandiloquently. . . . The disintegration of the myths of manifest destiny . . . put his narrators into a frame of reference designed to jog a collective, Western conscience.

Russell G. Hamilton. *I&L*. Dec., 1976–Jan., 1977, pp. 40–41

TEIXEIRA DE PASCOAES (pseudonym of Joaquim Pereira Teixeira de Vasconcelos, 1877–1952)

Let us go on to extract Teixeira de Pascoaes's poetical philosophy from his last book, *The Shadows*. . . .

Even its title, *The Shadows*, is a discovery, and that is what I told him when he read it to me before he sent it to press in Amarante. The poetic philosophy of Teixeira de Pascoaes is a shadowy philosophy, not a gloomy one. Realities are diluted and dissolved into their own shadows, and the shadows are jelled and consolidated into realities. Dream and waking lose their boundaries, one melting in the other: wakefulness becomes dream and dream becomes wakefulness. And thus there results an infantile and ancient philosophy—of the infancy of man and of the infancy of humanity, of when the poet was something more sacred and spontaneous.

For Teixeira de Pascoaes, the work of man has more reality than man himself. . . . And this gives Teixeira de Pascoaes's poetry the vagueness that so characterizes it, and a certain wordiness that is its major defect. This is a defect without which his poetry would not be what it is, or be worth what it is worth. . . .

A naturalistic, vague, formless, instinctive rather than reflective, poetic rather than philosophical pantheism exudes from the best pages of this work. It is a pantheism that brings him to the love of animals, as can be seen in, among many poems, the very beautiful sonnets "The Eyes of the Animals" and "Buddha"—in which he narrates how Buddha, who came upon a dog full of worms, frees it from them; but then, feeling sorry for the worms, he turned around, cut off a piece of the flesh of his arm, and blessing them, fed it to them. . . .

Among the other compositions of Teixeira de Pascoaes's book there is one, "The Shadow of Pain," which is profoundly Portuguese. It is pain that has become a vast shadow, but, at the same time, soothed. . . . And this pain is what unites the past and future. [1908]

Miguel de Unamuno. *Por tierras de España y Portugal*, in *Obras completas, Vol. I* (Barcelona, Afrodisio Aguado, 1959), pp. 370, 372–73†

A Portuguese poet perhaps not widely known, certainly at least out of Portugal, is Teixeira de Pascoaes. He has the immense distinction in modern times of being a poet who is content to feel the poetry of Earth and Heaven without being haunted by the fear that he will be found deficient in rhymes and meters sufficiently clever to express it. He does not strain for originality; for him life is poetry, and hence his poetry is living. Those who demand of poets that their works should be of polished marble or aglitter with gems should beware of reading Teixeira de Pascoaes; those who can appreciate the true poetry of Wordsworth and William Barnes, of the *Imitatio* and the *Fioretti,* will probably read his poems and return to them with delight. . . .

The chief defect of Teixeira de Pascoaes is a constant tendency to diffuseness. The philosophy that sees no distinction between stone and flesh, Earth and Heaven, seems to have affected his poetry, depriving it of sharp divisions and definite shape. . . . His long poem in eighteen cantos, *Marânos* (1911) may be likened to a grey shadowland, a mountain mist, often lifting to reveal fair regions of noble verse. . . .

The *Marânos* is, in the phrase of Francisco de Mello, a quiet poem. . . . Throughout the poem the reader is reminded of the way in which, in Wordsworth's *Prelude,* some beautiful word-image or thought continually occurs to belie any feeling of weariness. In several beautiful passages (as in *Always* and *The Shadows*) the poet sings his home and the valley of the Tamega and the mountains of Traz-os-Montes [province]. . . .

The beauties of the poem are many and undeniable, but it is a pity that the author has allowed it to trail inordinately. Not only does this prolixity frighten away readers, to their own loss, but the effect is often inartistic, causing his Muse to crawl with broken wing.

Aubrey F. G. Bell, A águia. Feb., 1914,
pp. 58, 60, 62–63

Napoleon is the poetic interpretation of a man and of a decisive epoch in history—a poetic interpretation without formalist preoccupations about poetical genres; at its highest point [we see] the almost disdainful ease of a spirit who barely wants to relate in a multiform and varied soliloquy the impressions, the suggestions, the perspectives, the approximations, the emotions, the images, the desires, the ironies, the thanks, the deceptions, and the hopes that pass through his soul in the lived meditation of an extraordinary moment of human greatness.

Some may say that *Napoleon*—like *Saint Paul* and *Saint Jerome and the Thunderclap*—is nothing more than a chaotic work, without well-defined lines of construction, a simple agglomeration of unfinished material, embryonic sketches of heterogeneous compositions. I do not think so, but such judgments do not surprise me. . . .

Do not judge, however, that Teixeira de Pascoaes only reflects in *Napoleon* the animated projection of his spiritual meeting of poet with emperor. Teixeira de Pascoaes is never alone, and Napoleon always has a court that is more or less visible. Teixeira de Pascoaes is accompanied by his world of visions and ghosts, a world of anxieties, of frightening things, of shocks, of troubles, in a constantly variable atmosphere, passing suddenly through the most contrary states. This spiritual attitude cannot help but continually become clear in the literary expression of the work.

Whoever reads *Napoleon,* will accompany the Corsican from cradle to tomb, student, soldier, consul, emperor, in the splendors of the court or the turmoil of battle, in victory and defeat. But who will dare to give an idea of what happens to Teixeira de Pascoaes in Bonaparte's company?

A. F. Dias de Magalhães. *Brotéria.* May, 1941,
pp. 503–6†

Teixeira de Pascoaes thought about and attempted to reach the very heart of the Portuguese people through *saudosismo* [the nostalgia movement]. *Saudade* [nostalgia] is known as the union of remembrance and desire; *saudosismo,* the doctrine of *saudade,* was to give birth not only to an aesthetic, but also to a philosophy and to a religion. An unconscious creation—but one the poet made comply with the consciousness—of a people in whom the Semitic element came to take the place of the Roman element, *saudosismo* was destined in Pascoaes's spirit to reconcile all the antinomies that he embodied in Jesus and Pan, or in Mary and Venus. In this perspective, Pascoaes himself became one of the inspired *bards,* who revealed to the Portuguese race its own essence and was endowed with the power to recognize that same essence in the works of the great national poets of the present and the past. . . .

What distinguishes Pascoaes's poetry from all other poetry is a communion with nature of the type that has no precedent in our poetry; it is such a close and turbulent communion that it suppresses the boundaries between subject and object, between spirit and matter, between contemplator and the object of his contemplation. In the intermediate and vague zone where he hovers, Pascoaes identifies himself little by little with the mountains, with the trees, with the water, with the air, with the mist. . . .

In short, his supreme audacity is the drive to master the insurmountable distance that separates man from God and to invert the roles between the thing created and the Creator.

José Régio. *BEPIF.* 17, 1952, pp. 195–97†

For me one of [Teixeira de Pascoaes's] best works is *Ethereal Life* (1906), the most joyous of his volumes, almost all of which is a hymn to fecundity, to woman, to the material that was given life, that was made conscious, and that, through human beings, *creates* an unknown, beautiful future. For the first time, a Portuguese poet dignified in terms due them the companion of the male, with flatteries of a courting cock, seeing her as an equal, his true consort facing the destiny of the race. *The Shadows* (1907) has very dense and poetic moments. . . . It is, however, a book about the fall of humanism to the mystical extasis in the presence of the *shadows* of its cosmic past: the instinctive, vegetative rhythms, the hypnotic *mysteries* or *fears* of what existed before us. Similar is *Lady of the Night* (1909), that insinuating elegy, perhaps his best elegy. . . .

As we know, Pascoaes's poetry was predominantly elegiac, full of reticences, shadows, mists, howling of the wind, ghosts, and secret metaphysical correspondences that the *saudosista* school later explored to its fullest return and far past any poetic yield. . . .

Return to Paradise (1912) . . . was the last Dantesque canto that Portuguese poetry until today has shown itself capable of [producing]. Here the adult man breaks through in the very sad and miserable boy of Pascoaes's ancestral home, and elaborates a myth of a biblical basis in which the typical married couple (always wife and husband side by side!) advances, creatively, from sin to sin, from one level to a higher level of evil, from alienation to alienation, to an unknown objective, but, surely, beautiful, because it is a fruit of their effort, of their risks, of the evil they themselves cause to arise.

Pascoaes, as a doctrinarian, as a philosopher, was not able to reach the heights of his own poetic visions. They went beyond his own means—let's recognize it.

Óscar Lopes. *Vértice*. March, 1953, pp. 154–55†

The extreme seriousness of Pascoaes's works alternates constantly with unforeseen touches of irony—not urban or French irony, but transcendental irony of a Hispanic origin, pervaded by sarcasm and melancholy, by diabolism and anguish, like that of Camilo Castelo Branco or Cervantes. The duality of the tragic and satiric spirit is reflected in the poems themselves. . . . It is enough to look attentively through some of his fundamental works (such as *The Penitent, Napoleon, Saint Paul*, or *Saint Augustine*) to come face to face with the typical expressions of the poet's strange humor. In every instance, after a philosophical digression about life and death, about God or men, an unusual expression, a demoniacal suggestion, a commentary, or a definition of a terrible pungency appears. Sometimes the paradox fails. . . .

The poet understands that truth is in essence elusive and ironical. Like Pascal, he does not fear to state that authentic seriousness makes fun of seriousness. . . . And he provides an example, at times savagely ridiculing himself. At about forty years of age—a decisive age—Pascoaes felt himself at one of the most important points in his life. It was during this instant of deep bitterness and transcendental irony that he conceived and wrote *The Poor Fool*. What the poet hopes to convey in this monotonous and delirious work is the painful expression of his indefinable position of a man crucified in his own mockery and disgust, of a man who understands neither life nor death, who no longer knows what to say or what to do, who finally feels himself as an unoccupied being lost in a world of illusory shadows, a world empty of sense, unintelligible and gray. . . . After so many frustrated dreams, of such great delirium—what was to be done? Pascoaes sees himself, as never before, vanquished and ridiculed. It is then that he portrays himself as the ecstatic and perplexed ass in the middle of the old bridge of Amarante [in *The Poor Fool*]. . . .

> José Dionísio Sant'Anna. *O poeta, essa ave metafísica* (Lisbon, Seara Nova, 1953), pp. 65, 68–69†

After I reread *Elegies* by Teixeira de Pascoaes, a poetic work that is short but great and bountiful in lyric content and literary beauty, perhaps the most expressive of the style and esthetic belief of the poet of the Tâmega River, and of course the most spontaneous, our thoughts flew to a work by Rosalía de Castro—the poem whose first line reads "Era aplacible el día . . ." ["The day was tranquil . . ."]. Both works are based on the same theme—the death of a son—a theme of unfathomable human depth, and the most propitious to measure the spiritual reactions in writers of such a lively sensibility as are the two *saudoso* poets of the western part of Iberia.

Rosalía reflects in this poem the most varied and unrelated emotions, which sound like a deep, solemn, and painful chord in her soul: the grief and the consolation, the pessimism and the hope, the despair and the faith; spiritual reactions, very far from the one-chordic tone used by other authors. . . .

This work [*Elegies*] by Pascoaes . . . contains thirty-two poems, all dedicated to his nephew at his death. . . . The philosophical thoughts pulsate in such a faithful manner in the sap of *Elegies* that one could say that they were inserted in an ideological pattern: the love and death of the child cast light upon the pain he sings of in them and, in his song, the intimate forces of remembrance and hope, the accents of faith and pessimism vibrate all at the same time, in a varied and contradictory mood. This is the coincidence of thought and feeling that unites the poetic expression of Pascoaes with the poem of Rosalía.

> Sebastián Risco. *TPr.* No. 22, 1961, pp. 41–43†

I believe that . . . both writers [Pascoaes and Pessoa] treated each other unfairly; Fernando Pessoa was not a mere joker, although one who was a genius [as Pascoaes considered him]; nor did Pascoaes merit the disdain with which Pessoa arrogantly treated him on more than one occasion. Much to the contrary: spurred on by an incurable metaphysical anxiety, both translated it into superior poetry; and the coincidence of psychic states, the affinities in the conception of the world, not only result from irrepressible vocations but also from an identical historical-cultural situation. Their poetic works effectively document two alluring spiritual adventures, which, although unique, presuppose the shaking of traditional beliefs and, at the same time, the antirationalist reaction that began at the end of the nineteenth century. For this reason, the religious anxiety, the very necessity of a messianic faith, an antidote to the national "vile sadness," is debated against the walls of the absurd. . . . With a more optimistic tone in Pascoaes, a more depressing one in Pessoa, both, finally, submit themselves to the absurd: everything appears to them to be ambiguous, unstable, false and true at the same time. They are two masters of anxiety.

Jacinto do Prado Coelho. "Fernando Pessoa e
Teixeira de Pascoaes," *Aufsätze zur
Portugiesischen Kulturgeschichte* (Münster,
West Germany, Sociedade Científica de
Goerres, 1966), pp. 230–31†

An essential element in Saudosismo was of course Messianism—which in Portugal naturally means Sebastianism. [King] Sebastian figures in several poems of Pascoaes, but it is in "The Lusitanian Night" in *Obscure Verb,* a work written in poetic prose, that the poet has most successfully caught the essence of the Sebastianist myth and best conveyed it in poetic symbols. . . .

Obscure Verb . . . is in my opinion one of Teixeira de Pascoaes' most interesting experiments. Its greater economy of expression leads one to think that the poet may have taken to heart some of the criticism from such notables as Unamuno and Aubrey Bell, that he was prolix and diffuse. Its aphorisms serve to define rather closely a number of his poetic values. . . . Nor is *Obscure Verb* Pascoaes' only venture into the short, aphoristic composition. *Indecisive Songs* consists of fifty-nine poems, frequently of one quatrain, in which the poet is often content to fix a single image, concentrating on a single question. This same aphoristic quality he carried over to the last work that he was able to see published—*Poor Verses.*

While the poems of *Poor Verses* are uneven in quality, taken with *Obscure Verb* and *Indecisive Songs,* they add a new dimension to a poet best known for his tendencies toward poems of great extension. Yet it must be said in defense of the length of many of the poems of Pascoaes that the broad sweep of the themes of his poetry—such themes as the nature of God, Pantheism, Christ vis-à-vis the Greco-Roman deities, the meaning of Christian and pagan symbolism, the tragic destiny of man in this world and hereafter, the role of past and future in human life—lends [itself] to extended treatment, in fact almost demands it.

That the poet was able to embrace so much, and to find appropriate language and symbols to render his conceptions, is the true mark of his genius.

William H. Roberts. *JAPS*. Spring–Summer, 1975, pp. 12–14

TORGA, MIGUEL (pseudonym of Adolfo Correia da Rocha, 1907–   )

As the heroes in this book [*Animals*] Torga has creatures that he can easily dominate: dogs, horses, crows, roosters, sparrows, cats, and toads; and the only human being that appears is more an animal than a human being. Nothing is more significant, perhaps, and probably intentional than the choice of such an elementary human being as Madalena, who is so "animal-like," for the heroine of the only story that does not have an animal for its main character. . . . Miguel Torga, who rivals Aquilino [Ribeiro], and in some cases outdoes him, in the recreation of the primitivism of life in the mountain country, always invokes this type of life and the human types that represent it. . . .

What at first may seem paradoxical is another one of the evils from which the majority of these stories suffer; Torga's animals are almost always too humanized by the author. . . . "Nero" [is] the admirable story of a dog, the best paragraphs published in *Animals*. . . . In this story, even the style is obviously superior to that of the other stories. The other animals were themes treated by Torga as simple anecdotes, without love—without the love, without the feeling of brotherhood with which he speaks about the dog. [1940]

Adolfo Casais Monteiro. *O romance (teoria e critica)* (Rio de Janeiro, José Olympio, 1964), pp. 346–50†

This translation of [*Animals*,] a book of short sketches by the well-known Trás-os-Montes writer Miguel Torga, is welcome both in itself and as an interesting example of Portuguese fiction. . . . The animals (they are mostly animal stories) are meant for types of humanity, their situations for human predicaments. But those readers who prefer animal stories to be merely about animals can take them as such. They are touching and vivid and, in nearly every case, sad. Portuguese animals, one would gather, are unhappy. Or perhaps it is that the author dips into their lives at unfortunate moments. . . .

The best sketch in the book is of Miura the bull; the fight, vividly described, is an epitome of brutal tragedy. (It is, of course, a Spanish bull-fight, not the gentle Portuguese variety.) Here Senhor Torga uses a terse, vivid idiom, beautifully captured in his translator's English, to express the violent, agonising duel between man and beast, cheered and booed by a blood-lusting crowd, until the sword ends the bull's pain; a bull-fight from the bull's angle has never been so well described. In this story and in that of the faithful pointer Senhor Torga shows great imaginative sympathy and power; in many others there are touches of beauty, which remind us that the author is also a poet; as, particularly, in the story of the friendship, formed in the moonlit country night, between the old farmer and the toad, which has a quietly lyrical touch.

Rose Macaulay. Spectator. Nov. 3, 1950, p. 436

This transition [from psychological dramatic to historically and socially dramatic poetry] is the strong echo of the great human agonies that began again in the decade of the 1930s and whose voice has never stopped being heard. . . . *Punishments of Purgatory,* Miguel Torga's recent book of poetry, can be completely explained only in terms of the shadow of such a world. . . . It is *his* agony that is confessed here, but it comes from the roots that feed the agony of many. It speaks about *his* despair, but at the same time the contemporary despair of newer generations who are, like Torga, confronted by an identical world.

It is obvious that [despair] is more present than hope in *Punishments of Purgatory.* Hope is there a wish or a plea . . . , but despair is a palpable reality. Torga calls himself a "bird of hope" in the beautiful poem of the same name. . . .

Significantly, the poem entitled "Hope" is an undisguised confession of its impossibility. . . . There is no incarnation of hope here, but only the melancholy born from its absence.

Eduardo Lourenço. O desespero de Miguel
Torga e das novas gerações (Coimbra, Coimbra
Editora, 1955), pp. 28–30†

In his odes Torga recites the burden of the poetic vocation and the suffering that is inseparable from it. In *Nihil Sibi,* which contains the essence of his ideas on the poet and his mission, he celebrates the poet as mage and visionary. The poet as a youth is likened to a Quixote with ever new lances for new illusions and vain leaps over the abyss of madness and lyricism.

One of Torga's greatest gifts, and one that appears at its most excellent in his short stories, in his power of observation and analysis, assisted doubtless by his daily experience in the consulting-room. He insists on a frank and virginal approach to the phenomena of life, one that is devoid of all parti-pris and prejudice and that is free of all peering and prurience. He has almost a suspicion of the new gadgets which his profession [medicine] has taught him to use. He records his horror of old age and death, which can now be measured in the speed with which they advance upon us from within. Death is no longer an attack from without. . . .

Torga's lyrical power, which is controlled by the form of his verse, burst splendidly into the exuberance of his prose. Most of his short stories are great and arresting, chiefly by reason of his power to invest the moment and its circumstance with this lyricism. We may note particularly his power of evoking nature and its mood. He suggests the magic of a peninsular night with peculiar felicity. Night becomes brilliant; it reveals rather than hides. One is reminded of Lorca's use of the mood of night in [*The House of*] *Bernarda Alba*. . . .

Torga's gift of narrative is quite unique in Portuguese literature and the power of the stories is helped by a style that is equally unique. . . . He is master of the short terse sentence. A whole attitude or reaction to a dramatic situation may be summed up in one word—perhaps in a regionalism or an exclamation which has been invested with universality. The words roll like lava or like yeast, burning or fermenting the tiniest detail that they touch.

> Denis Brass. *Dublin Review*. Fourth Quarter,
> 1955, pp. 414–15

Is it necessary to name the story by Miguel Torga to which I allude? In its necessary and desirable concision, it has a dramatic power that makes it difficult to forget. It is the one that begins the volume *Stories of the Mountains*, and the title is "The Great Soul." We are in Riba Dal, "land of the Jews." Under the guise of a fervent Catholicism, the inhabitants hide their Mosaic faith behind their shutters. Just when they are at the point of death and in order for them not to betray the secret of the community, someone goes to get the "suffocator," whose name is Uncle Great Soul. The suffocator leans over the dying person, crushes his chest with his knee, and strangles him with his implacable hands. This sinister custom is accepted by all, and the resistance of certain ill people gets nowhere. It is thus that, as soon as Isaac finds himself near death, his wife Lia sends one of the children, little Abel, to bring Great Soul. That begins his horrible task. Isaac pleads and resists. The suffocator continues pitilessly. But suddenly he hears the bedroom door creak. Little Abel enters; he does not know the true mission of the suffocator, but there is a mystery that attracts and torments him. Disturbed by that innocent presence, incapable of acting before a witness, the Great Soul leaves after having spared the life of the suffering man. Isaac, contrary to expectations, gets better. But he does not forget. He is a Jew: his law is that of talion [an eye for an eye], and he plans his vengeance. One day, he meets the suffocator all alone, and he throws himself upon him and strangles him—under the eyes of little Abel, who witnesses the scene while hidden behind a rock. . . .

In short, the story of the Portuguese writer is a drama of three characters. Little Abel is as important as the two men. He plays a decisive role: it is his entry into his father's room that prevents the executioner from completing his task to the end, and which permits the cure, and then Isaac's vengeance. Furthermore, an interior drama takes place within him, parallel to the one that pitches the suffocator and his father against one another, and even more poignant because it mysteriously rends his innocent soul: he has doubts about the mission of Great Soul without understanding it completely, he has doubts about Isaac's vengeance without clearly knowing his intentions. He does not understand until he witnesses the fight and the murder.

Robert Ricard. *BEPIF.* No. 20, 1955,
pp. 211–12, 216†

[The poetry] that I like in Miguel Torga is that of the song of man who bet his permanence on the simple strength of being of the *here* and *now*.

And it is for this reason that, next to his poetry of protest or that of the purest discovery of life, I admire Torga above all as a short-story writer, or rather, his gift of pursuing, learning, and placing in his dramatic topics the most primitive and supreme animal and human courage, which is that of simply living, within a few pages.

And it of this that he wrote his best plays, in *Sea* and *Terra Firma*. . . . *Sea* and *Terra Firma* are two complementary dramas, but both, despite the second title, are dramas about the sea, a mythical sea where a siren who is the maternal lure of death sings. With the disappearance at sea of the protagonist of the first of these plays, and the interminable absence of the betrothed, who emigrated, in the second play . . . it is at sea that a certain poetic constellation of virility-seed-poetry always remains at a distance or hidden, so that the tragedy of expectant virginity pines away in our view, so that hope remains solely feminine, and barren, instead of fruitful, consummated. . . .

In truth, this *Sea* is a musical score of speeches and characters, where almost musical motifs cross and alternate; the virile silence of the fishermen; frustrated femininity (Mariana) and the femininity that waits (Rita); the baroque religious quality into which this frustration is transformed, in such a way that our comprehension and sympathy are raised (Cacilda); the adolescence seen again in the matured and radiant plenitude of the protagonist (Rapaz). The charm of the dialogues of this poetic world of family life is caught in the popular speech and lifestyle . . . .

Óscar Lopes. *Cinco personalidades literárias*
(Oporto, Divulgação, 1961), pp. 182–84†

"Mr. Ventura" is the story of a man from Alentejo province—a typical man of the province. Torga even assigns him a concrete village of origin: Penedono. And this man, Mr. Ventura, goes, like many other dyed-in-the-wool Portuguese, out into the world looking for fortune and adventure. In China this man joins up with some greedy Chinese. There he loves and later fervently hates, as the people of the Alentejo can, a Chinese woman. Later, fatally drawn by *saudade* [nostalgia], he returns to his village and begins to work as a laborer once again. He wants to die in the land where he was born. He works, destroying his health in order to make things grow. Later, hate makes him return to China to look for his unfaithful Chinese wife, and he dies there. But his son, who had been born in China and lived there for eight years, as if relentlessly fulfilling the destiny of his father's blood, stays in the Alentejo to tend the flock. . . .

Very well; Torga himself is something like Mr. Ventura of the novelette; eager to know about life and the world, about reality, but attached by a fatal flaw to his native land.

In *Vintage* we also have a stupendous picture of life in Portugal, in a rural farming community, with suffering men and women leading a hard life. The plot centers around the arrival of a group of mountain men to work in the grape harvest for two weeks. The protagonists are two socially antagonistic groups: workers and masters. Throughout the novel there are pain, love, hate, dances, and fights. . . . The masters reveal themselves as decadent; the workers, to the contrary, reveal a primitive and healthy strength. At the end, the grape pickers are confronted with the greed of the masters, who want to exploit the poor. But Torga, ultimately, gives a happy note to the return of the humble people to their mountain shacks.

Bernardino Graña. *Grial.* Jan.–Mar., 1964, pp. 46, 49†

Spain plays an important role in Miguel Torga's intellectual and emotional universe. Even the invention of his pseudonym, in 1934, shows us the importance that things Hispanic had for the then young writer. Well, while Adolfo Correia da Rocha changes his last name to Torga in order to symbolize with it the unavoidable obligation that, in his opinion, the artist has in presenting others with beauty, no matter how difficult the personal and historical circumstances in which one moves . . . , the choice of the name Miguel is a response to the aim of adding a new Lusitanian link to the Spanish chain (Miguel de Molinos, Miguel de Cervantes, Miguel de Unamuno) of combative and rebellious thought. . . .

Iberian Poems does not try to be a bouquet of compositions about Iberian themes, but rather the incarnation of all of Torga's theories about the Peninsula. . . . In "Earth," "Fate," "Life," "Bread," "Wine," and "The Illusion," the writer of the Trás-os-Montes province exalts what is hard and earthy on the Peninsula, the telluric limitations that gave strength and wings to the men of Iberia.

In the part of the book entitled "The Heroes," Miguel Torga offers the peninsular reader in search of his "I" a type of psychological X-ray of historical figures, writers, or artists both Spanish and Portuguese, whom he considers incarnations of national traits. . . . He sings not only about positive "heroes," but also about negative ones. . . .

Pilar Vásquez Cuesta. *RO*. 18, 1967, pp. 131–33†

Through his language, Miguel Torga has had a decisive influence on contemporary poetry in Portuguese: the concision and the precision of his poetic style—at times rough but always emotional and moving—began to play a very important role in an epoch in which there still persisted the sick remnants of hollow verbalism and the weak sentimentalism of the last generation of Symbolists; and, with the passing of time, his influence, instead of waning, has become even stronger, even among those [writers] who explicitly do not invoke him as their teacher.

On the other hand, with the title of one of his books of poetry—*Rebel Orpheus,* published in 1958—Miguel Torga symbolically gave us the best definition of himself; certainly, as I once had the occasion to observe, "he is, at the same time, a perfect example of the reincarnation of the mythic poet—the one who lives in the intimacy with the elemental forces (the land, the sun, the wind, the water) in order to praise them with his song—and a high example of constant rebelliousness, in an atmosphere that attempts to suffocate him." I said, in addition . . . , "Portuguese and European, regional but universal, and above all profoundly *Iberian,* torn between the cloudy Atlantic and the clear Mediterranean," Miguel Torga has assumed the inheritance of multiple cultural traditions, from Greco-Latin classicism to the unease of contemporary humanism, from Celtic messianism to Hebraic messianism—to both of which he feels equally indebted—to the problematics of the most recent ideological debates; and all these traditions he has untiringly integrated into an eminently Portuguese perspective, through which the knowledge that we have of ourselves is becoming decisively clearer.

David Mourão-Ferreira. *Colóquio/Letras.* Nov.,
1976, p. 63†

A full account of Torga's early life is given in his autobiographical work *The Creation of the World.* The first volume, *The First Two Days,* is divided into two major parts: "The First Day" describes T.'s childhood, which was spent in the mountains of the Trás-os-Montes province where he was born, and in a nearby city. "The Second Day" retells his adolescence, during which he worked on the plantation of wealthy relatives in Brazil in order to be able to continue his education. The second volume, *The Third Day of the Creation of the World,* treats, for the most part, the years at the University of Coimbra and his work as a country doctor. *The Fourth Day of the Creation of the World,* the third volume of the series, deals with his brief journey through Spain, Italy, and France at the time of the Spanish Civil War, his visit in France with

Portuguese émigrés, and his return to Portugal. Torga's auto-biographical writings reveal his struggle to be himself. With his out-spoken independence of mind, this means not only challenging the world as it is but life itself, its dependence on chance, its brevity and futility.

Since 1941 Torga has been publishing in installments his *Diary*. These diaries, which he started to keep in 1932, appear every few years. His thoughts on national and world problems are sometimes narrowly Iberian in spirit, but his work as a whole has universal appeal. These volumes contain insightful prose and the best of his lyric poetry. . . .

Torga's many volumes of poetry are filled with the despair of a humanist who loves mankind. In *The Other Book of Job* T. movingly laments man's insurmountable isolation in mass society. Although he sees this isolation as an evil to be struggled against, he defiantly proclaims it for himself. *Burning Chamber* is the expression of a Christian tormented by religious disbelief.

Elizabeth R. Suter. In *Encyclopedia of World Literature in the 20th Century,* Vol. 4 (New York, Frederick Ungar, 1984), pp. 456–57

WORKS MENTIONED

Listed here, author by author, are all works mentioned in the critical selections. Each writer's works are arranged alphabetically by the literal translation used uniformly throughout the book. Following each literal translation in parentheses are the title in the original language and the date of first publication. If a published translation of a work exists, its title, together with the city and year of first publication, is given after a colon. Collections in English translation of an author's poems, essays, plays, or stories that do not correspond to any specific collection in the original language are listed at the end of the author's works.

Spain

ALBERTI, RAFAEL

Concerning the Angels (*Sobre los ángeles,* 1929): *Concerning the Angels* (Chicago, 1967)
Fermín Galán (*Fermín Galán,* 1921)
Lime and Stone (*Cal y canto,* 1929)
Sailor Ashore (*Marinero en tierra,* 1925)
Sermons and Dwellings (*Sermones y moradas,* 1935)
The Uninhabited Man (*El hombre deshabitado,* 1931)

———

A Spectre Is Haunting Europe: Poems of Revolutionary Spain (New York, 1936)
Selected Poems of Rafael Alberti (New York, 1944)
Selected Poems (Berkeley, Cal., 1966)
The Owl's Insomnia (New York, 1973)
The Other Shore: 100 Poems by Rafael Alberti (San Francisco, 1981)

ALDECOA, IGNACIO

Great Sole (*Gran Sol,* 1957)
Lightning and Blood (*El fulgor y la sangre,* 1954)
Part of a Story (*Parte de una historia,* 1967)
Third-Class Waiting Room (*Espera de tercera clase,* 1955)
Vespers of Silence (*Vísperas de silencio,* 1955)
With the East Wind (*Con el viento solano,* 1956)

ALEIXANDRE, VICENTE

Destruction or Love (*La destrucción o el amor,* 1935): *The Destruction of Love,* in *The Destruction of Love, and Other Poems* (Santa Cruz, Cal., 1976)

549

Dialogues of Knowledge (*Diálogos del conocimiento,* 1974)
Final Birth (*Nacimiento último,* 1953)
History of the Heart (*Historia del corazón,* 1954)
In a Vast Dominion (*En un vasto dominio,* 1962)
Passion of the Earth (*Pasión de la tierra,* 1935)
Poems of Consummation (*Poemas de la consumación,* 1968)
Shadow of Paradise (*Sombra del paraíso,* 1944)
Swords Like Lips (*Espadas como labios,* 1932)
World Alone (*Mundo a solas,* 1950): *World Alone/Mundo a solas* (Great
    Barrington, Mass., 1982)

"Poems by Vicente Aleixandre," *Mundus Artium,* Summer, 1969, pp. 6–59
Twenty Poems (Madison, Minn., 1973)
The Destruction of Love, and Other Poems (Santa Cruz, Cal., 1976)
Poems-Poemas (Greensboro, N.C., 1978)
A Longing for Light: Selected Poems of Vicente Aleixandre (New York,
    1979)
*The Crackling Sun: Selected Poems of the Nobel Prize Recipient, 1977,
    Vicente Aleixandre* (Madrid, 1981)
A Bird of Paper: Poems of Vicente Aleixandre (Athens, Ohio, 1982)

ALONSO, DÁMASO

Children of Wrath (*Hijos de la ira,* 1944): *Children of Wrath* (Baltimore,
    1970)
Dark Message (*Oscura noticia,* 1944)
Final Dedication (The Wings) ("Dedicatoria final [Las alas]," 1944)
In the Shade ("En la sombra," 1944)
Insomnia ("Insomnia," 1944)
Love ("Amor," 1944)
Man and God (*Hombre y Dios,* 1955)
Man and God ("Hombre y Dios," 1955)
The Obsession ("La obsesión," 1944)
Pleasures of Sight (*Gozos de la vista,* 1955)
The Poetic Language of Góngora (First Part) (*La lengua poética de
    Góngora* [*Primera parte*], 1935)
Pure Poems: Short Poems of the City (*Poemas puros: Poemillas de la
    ciudad,* 1921)
Songs for Solo Whistle ("Canciones a pito solo," unpublished)
To Those Who Will Be Born ("A los que van a nacer," 1944)

ÁLVAREZ QUINTERO, SERAFÍN AND JOAQUÍN

Cancionera (*Cancionera,* 1924)
Concha the Pure (*Concha la limpia,* 1924)
The Daughters of Cain (*Las de Caín,* 1909)
Doña Clarines (*Doña Clarines,* 1909): *Doña Clarines,* in *Four Comedies*
    (London, 1932)

Fencing and Love (*Esgrima y amor,* 1888)
The Flowers (*Las flores,* 1901)
Fortunato (*Fortunato,* 1912): *Fortunato,* in *Four Plays of the Quinteros* (London, 1927)
The Galley Slaves (*Los galeotes,* 1900)
The Good Spirit (*La buena sombra,* 1898)
The Happy Nature (*El genio alegre,* 1906)
A Hundred Years Old (*El centenario,* 1910): *A Hundred Years Old,* in *Four Plays of the Quinteros* (London, 1927)
The Mad Muse (*La musa loca,* 1906): *Don Abel Wrote a Tragedy,* in *Four Comedies* (London, 1932)
Malvaloca (*Malvaloca,* 1912): *Malvaloca* (Garden City, N.Y., 1916)
The Patio (*El patio,* 1900)
The Women's Town (*Puebla de las mujeres,* 1912): *The Women's Town,* in *Contemporary Spanish Dramatists,* ed., C. A. Turrell (New York, 1919); *The Women Have Their Way,* in *Four Plays of the Quinteros* (London, 1927)

AUB, MAX

Battlefield of Almond Trees (*Campo de almendros,* 1968)
Closed Battlefield (*Campo cerrado,* 1943)
Desired (*Deseada,* 1950)
Geography (*Geografía,* 1929)
Green Fable (*Fábula verde,* 1933)
Heads and Tails (*Cara y cruz,* 1944)
Incomplete Theater (*Teatro incompleto,* 1930)
Jusep Torres Campalans (*Jusep Torres Campalans,* 1958): *Josep Torres Campalans* (Garden City, N.Y., 1962)
The Magic Labyrinth (*El laberinto mágico,* 5 vols., 1943–68)
Married Life (*La vida conyugal,* 1966)
Narcissus (*Narciso,* 1928)
No (*No,* 1949)
The Rape of Europa; or, Something Always Can Be Done (*El rapto de Europa; o, Siempre se puede hacer algo,* 1943)
San Juan (*San Juan,* 1964)
To Die by Closing Your Eyes (*Morir por cerrar los ojos,* 1944)

AYALA, FRANCISCO

The Bewitched ("El hechizado," 1944): "The Bewitched," in *Great Spanish Stories,* ed. Ángel Flores (New York, 1956)
The Bottom of the Glass (*El fondo del vaso,* 1962)
A Dog's Death (*Muertes de perro,* 1958): *Death as a Way of Life* (New York, 1964)
The Garden of Delights (*El jardín de las delicias,* 1971)
Hunter at Dawn (*Cazador en al alba,* 1930)
The Tagus (*El Tajo,* 1949)
The Usurpers (*Los usurpadores,* 1949): *The Usurpers* (New York, 1985)

AZORÍN

Angelita (*Angelita*, 1930)
Antonio Azorín (*Antonio Azorín*, 1903)
The Butterfly and the Flame ("La mariposa y la llama," 1929): "The Moth and the Flame," in *The Syrens, and Other Stories* (London, 1931)
Castile (*Castilla*, 1912)
The Castilian Soul (*El alma castellana*, 1900)
Cervantes; or, The Enchanted House (*Cervantes; o, La casa encantada*, 1931)
The Confessions of a Little Philosopher (*Las confesiones de un pequeño filósofo*, 1904)
Doña Inés (*Doña Inés*, 1925)
Félix Vargas (*Félix Vargas*, 1928)
The Guerrilla (*La guerrilla*, 1936)
The Licentiate Vidriera by Azorín (*El licenciado Vidriera por Azorín*, 1915)
The Nonpresent Gentleman (*El caballero inactual*, reissue of *Félix Vargas*)
Old Spain (*Old Spain* [title in English], 1926)
Salvadora of Olbena (*Salvadora de Olbena*, 1944)
Spanish Readings (*Lecturas españolas*, 1912)
Surrealism (*Superrealismo*, 1929)
To Ponder and Consider (*Cavilar y contar*, 1942)
Tomás Rueda (*Tomás Rueda*, reissue of *The Licentiate Vidriera*)
The Villages (*Los pueblos*, 1905)
Walking and Thinking (*Andando y pensando*, 1959)
White on Blue (*Blanco en azul*, 1929): *The Syrens, and Other Stories* (London, 1931)
The Will (*La voluntad*, 1902)

BAREA, ARTURO

The Broken Root (*La raíz rota*, 1955): *The Broken Root* (New York, 1951)
The Flame (*La llama*, 1951): *The Clash* (London, 1946)
The Forge (*La forja*, pub. in Spanish, 1951): *The Forge* (London, 1941)
The Forging of a Rebel (*La forja de un rebelde*, pub. in Spanish, 1951): *The Forging of a Rebel* (New York, 1946)

BAROJA, PÍO

Adventures, Inventions, and Mystifications of Silvestre Paradox (*Aventuras, inventas y mixtificaciones de Silvestre Paradox*, 1901)
The Cape of Storms (*El cabo de las tormentas*, 1932)
César or Nothing (*César o nada*, 1910): *Caesar or Nothing* (New York, 1919)
The City of Fog (*La ciudad de la niebla*, 1909)
The Errotacho Family (*La familia de Errotacho*, 1932)
The Fair of the Discreet (*La feria de los discretos*, 1905): *The City of the Discreet* (New York, 1917)
Hidden Kindness ("Bondad oculta," 1900)

The House of Aizgorri (*La casa de Aizgorri*, 1900)
The Legend of Jaun de Alzate (*La leyenda de Jaun de Alzate*, 1922)
The Lord of Labraz (*El mayorazgo de Labraz*, 1903): *The Lord of Labraz* (New York, 1926)
Medium ("Médium," 1900)
Memoirs (*Memorias*, 1944)
Paradox, King (*Paradox, rey*, 1906): *Paradox, King* (London, 1931)
The Quest (*La busca*, 1904): *The Quest* (New York, 1922)
Red Dawn (*Aurora roja*, 1904): *Red Dawn* (New York, 1924)
Road to Perfection (*Camino de perfección*, 1902)
Somber Lives (*Vidas sombrías*, 1900)
Songs of the Suburbs (*Canciones del suburbio*, 1944)
The Tree of Knowledge (*El árbol de la ciencia*, 1912): *The Tree of Knowledge* (New York, 1928)
The Visionaries (*Los visionarios*, 1932)
The Wandering Lady (*La dama errante*, 1908)
Weeds (*Mala hierba*, 1904): *Weeds* (New York, 1923)
Youth and Egolatry (*Juventud, egolatría*, 1917): *Youth and Egolatry* (New York, 1920)
Zalacaín, the Adventurer (*Zalacaín, el aventurero*, 1910): *Zalacaín, the Adventurer* (Cambridge, 1954)

BENAVENTE, JACINTO

Adoration (*Adoración*, 1948)
And It Was Bitter (*Y amargaba*, 1940)
The Angora Cat (*La gata de angora*, 1900)
Another's Nest (*El nido ajeno*, 1894)
Autumnal Roses (*Rosas de otoño*, 1905): *Autumnal Roses*, in *Plays of Jacinto Benavente*, Vol. II (New York, 1919)
Brute Force (*La fuerza bruta*, 1908): *Brute Force* (New York, 1935)
The Created Interests (*Los intereses creados*, 1907): *The Bonds of Interest*, in *Plays of Jacinto Benavente*, Vol. I (New York, 1917)
Field of Ermine (*Campo de armiño*, 1916): *Field of Ermine*, in *Plays of Jacinto Benavente*, Vol. IV (New York, 1924)
The Fire Dragon (*El dragón de fuego*, 1904)
The Governor's Wife (*La gobernadora*, 1901): *The Governor's Wife*, in *Plays of Jacinto Benavente*, Vol. II (New York, 1919)
The Grave of Dreams (*La losa de los sueños*, 1911)
The Hated Woman (*La malquerida*, 1913): *The Passion Flower*, in *Plays of Jacinto Benavente*, Vol. I (New York, 1917)
The Honor of Men (*La honra de los hombres*, 1919)
The Lady in Mourning (*La enlutada*, 1942)
The Lady of the House (*Señora ama*, 1908)
The Necklace of Stars (*El collar de estrellas*, 1915)
People of Our Acquaintance (*Gente conocida*, 1896)
Pepa Doncel (*Pepa Doncel*, 1928)
Saturday Night (*La noche del sábado*, 1903): *The Witches' Sabbath*, in

Masterpieces of the Modern Spanish Theater, ed. Robert W. Corrigan (New York, 1967)

The School of Princesses (*La escuela de las princesas,* 1909): *The School of Princesses,* in *Plays of Jacinto Benavente,* Vol. IV (New York, 1924)

Self-Esteem (*La propia estimación,* 1915)

The Unbelievable (*Lo increíble,* 1940)

We Are All One (*Todos somos unos,* 1907)

The Wild Beasts' Banquet (*La comida de las fieras,* 1898)

BENET, JUAN

Mazón's Other House (*La otra casa de Mazón,* 1973)

A Meditation (*Una meditación,* 1970): *A Meditation* (New York, 1982)

A Tomb (*Una tumba,* 1971)

A Winter Journey (*Un viaje de invierno,* 1972)

You Will Return to Región (*Volverás a Región,* 1967): *Return to Región* (New York, 1985)

BERGAMÍN, JOSÉ

Book of Spanish Aphorisms (*Disparadero español,* 3 vols., 1936–40)

The Burning Nail (*El clavo ardiendo,* 1974)

Deferred Rhymes and Sonnets (*Rimas y sonetos rezagados,* 1962)

Hermetic Thought in the Arts (*El pensamiento hermético de las artes,* 1928)

Infernal Frontiers of Poetry (*Fronteras infernales de la poesía,* 1959)

Little Somethings and Songs (*Duendecitos y coplas,* 1963)

Scatterbrain (*La cabeza a pájaros,* 1934)

The Statue of Don Tancredo (*La estatua de don Tancredo,* 1934)

BLASCO IBÁÑEZ, VICENTE

Among Orange Trees (*Entre naranjos,* 1900): *The Torrent* (New York, 1921)

The Big Vintage (*La bodega,* 1905): *The Fruit of the Vine* (New York, 1919)

Blood and Sand (*Sangre y arena,* 1908): *Blood and Sand* (New York, 1919)

The Cabin (*La barraca,* 1898): *The Cabin* (New York, 1919)

The Cathedral (*La catedral,* 1903): *The Shadow of the Cathedral* (New York, 1909)

The Dead Command (*Los muertos mandan,* 1909): *The Dead Command* (New York, 1919)

The Enemies of Women (*Los enemigos de la mujer,* 1919): *The Enemies of Women* (New York, 1920)

The Four Horsemen of the Apocalypse (*Los cuatro jinetes del apocalipsis,* 1916): *The Four Horsemen of the Apocalypse* (New York, 1918)

Mare Nostrum (*Mare Nostrum,* 1918): *Our Sea* (New York, 1919)

The Mayflower (*Flor de mayo,* 1896): *The Mayflower* (New York, 1921)

The Naked Lady (*La maja desnuda,* 1906): *The Naked Lady* (New York, 1920)

Reeds and Mud (*Cañas y barro,* 1902): *Reeds and Mud* (New York, 1928)

Rice and Covered Wagon (*Arroz y tartana*, 1895): *The Three Roses* (New York, 1932)

Sónnica the Courtesan (*Sónnica la cortesana*, 1901): *Sonnica* (New York, 1912)

BUERO VALLEJO, ANTONIO

Adventure in Gray (*Aventura en lo gris*, 1963)

Almost a Fairy Tale (*Casi un cuento de hadas*, 1952)

The Awaited Sign (*La señal que se espera*, 1952)

The Basement Window (*El tragaluz*, 1967)

The Concert at Saint Ovide (*El concierto de San Ovidio*, 1962): *The Concert at Saint Ovide*, in *The Modern Spanish Stage: Four Plays*, ed. Marion Holt (New York, 1970)

Dawn (*Madrugada*, 1953)

The Dream Weaver (*La tejedora de sueños*, 1952): *The Dream Weaver*, in *Masterpieces of the Modern Spanish Theater*, ed. Robert W. Corrigan (New York, 1967)

The Foundation (*La fundación*, 1974): *The Foundation*, in *Three Plays* (San Antonio, Tex., 1985)

In the Burning Darkness (*En la ardiente oscuridad*, 1950): *In the Burning Darkness*, in *Three Plays* (San Antonio, Tex., 1985)

Irene; or, The Treasure (*Irene; o, El tesoro*, 1954)

The Sleep of Reason (*El sueño de la razón*, 1970): *The Sleep of Reason*, in *Three Plays* (San Antonio, Tex., 1985)

Story of a Staircase (*Historia de una escalera*, 1949)

Today's a Holiday (*Hoy es fiesta*, 1956)

CASONA, ALEJANDRO

Ballad of Dan and Elsa (*Romance de Dan y Elsa*, 1938)

The Beached Mermaid (*La sirena varada*, 1934)

The Boat without a Fisherman (*La barca sin pescador*, 1945): *The Boat without a Fisherman*, in *The Modern Spanish Stage: Four Plays*, ed. Marion Holt (New York, 1970)

The Lady of the Dawn (*La dama del alba*, 1944)

Once Again the Devil (*Otra vez el diablo*, 1935)

Our Natacha (*Nuestra Natacha*, 1935)

Suicide Prohibited in Springtime (*Prohibido suicidarse en primavera*, 1937): *Suicide Prohibited in Springtime*, in *Modern Spanish Theatre*, ed. Michael Benedikt and George E. Wellwarth (New York, 1968)

The Third Word (*La tercera palabra*, 1953)

The Trees Die Standing (*Los árboles mueren de pie*, 1949)

CELA, CAMILO JOSÉ

The Family of Pascual Duarte (*La familia de Pascual Duarte*, 1942): *The Family of Pascual Duarte* (Boston, 1964)

The Hive (*La colmena*, 1951): *The Hive* (New York, 1953)

Jews, Moors, and Christians (*Judíos, moros y cristianos,* 1956)
Journey to the Alcarria (*Viaje a la Alcarria,* 1948): *Journey to the Alcarria* (Madison, Wisc., 1964)
ministry of darkness 5 (*oficio de tinieblas 5,* 1973)
Mrs. Caldwell Speaks to Her Son (*Mrs. Caldwell habla con su hijo,* 1953): *Mrs. Caldwell Speaks to Her Son* (Ithaca, N.Y., 1968)
Rest Home (*Pabellón de reposo,* 1943): *Rest Home* (New York, 1961)
Saint Camilo, 1936 (*San Camilo, 1936,* 1969)
Secret Dictionary (*Diccionario secreto,* 1969)
Songbook of the Alcarria (*Cancionero de la Alcarria,* 1948)
Tarts, Harlots, and Prostitutes (*Izas, rabizas y colipoterras,* 1964)
Toboggan of the Hungry (*Tobogán de los hambrientos,* 1962)
Treading on the Doubtful Light of Day (*Pisando la dudosa luz del día,* 1945)

CELAYA, GABRIEL

Basque Ballads and Sayings (*Baladas y decires vascos,* 1965)
Basque Rhapsody (*Rapsodia euskara,* 1960)
Ears of Corn (*Mazorcas,* 1962)
Elemental Movements (*Movimientos elementales,* 1947)
The Enclosed Solitude (*La soledad cerrada,* 1947)
Iberian Songs (*Cantos íberos,* 1955)
Letter to Andrés Basterra ("Carta a Andrés Basterra," in *Showing One's Cards*)
Night of Zungarramundi ("Noche de Zungarramundi," in *Basque Rhapsody*)
Poetic Objects (*Objetos poéticos,* 1948)
Showing One's Cards (*Las cartas boca arriba,* 1951)
Tide of Silence (*Marea de silencio,* 1935)
Verbal Apparatus ("Aparato verbal," in *Poetic Objects*)

The Poetry of Gabriel Celaya (Lewisburg, Pa., 1984)

CERNUDA, LUIS

The Clouds (*Las nubes,* 1943)
The Heath ("El brezal," in 2nd ed. of *Ocnos*)
Hymn to Sadness ("Himno a la tristeza," in *Reality and Desire*)
Invocations (*Invocaciones,* written 1934–35, in *Reality and Desire*)
Lazarus ("Lázaro," in *The Clouds*)
Like the One Who Awaits the Dawn (*Como quien espera el alba,* 1947)
Nocturnal Magic ("Sortilegio nocturno," in 2nd ed. of *Ocnos*)
Nocturne among the Little Insects ("Nocturno entre las musarañas," 1929)
Ocnos (*Ocnos,* 1st ed., 1942; 2nd ed., 1949; definitive ed., 1963)
The Piano ("El piano," in 2nd ed. of *Ocnos*)
The Poet and the Myths ("El poeta y los mitos," in *Ocnos*)
Profile of the Air (*Perfil del aire,* 1927)

Reality and Desire (*La realidad y el deseo,* 1st ed., 1936; 2nd ed., 1940; 3rd ed., 1958)
Variations on a Mexican Theme (*Variaciones sobre un tema mexicano,* 1952)
Written on Water ("Escrito en el agua," in 1st ed. of *Ocnos*)
Yankee Nocturne ("Nocturno yanqui," 1956)

The Poetry of Luis Cernuda (New York, 1971)
Selected Poems of Luis Cernuda (New York, 1977)

CUNQUEIRO, ÁLVARO

The Chronicles of the Wizard (*As crónicas do Sochantre,* 1956)
If Old Sinbad Were to Return to the Islands . . . (*Se o vello Sinbad volvese às ilhas . . . ,* 1962)
A Man Who Looked Like Orestes (*Un hombre que se parecía a Orestes,* 1969)
Merlin and Family (*Merlín e familia,* 1955)
School of Healers (*Escola de menciñeiros,* 1960)
Sea to the North (*Mar ao norde,* 1932)
The Seven Stories of Autumn (*Los siete cuentos de otoño,* 1968)
Treasures New and Old (*Tesouros novos e vellos,* 1964)
Ulysses (*Ulises,* 1960)
The Uncertain Mr. Hamlet (*O incerto señor D. Hamlet,* 1959)

DELIBES, MIGUEL

Diary of a Hunter (*Diario de un cazador,* 1955)
Diary of an Emigrant (*Diario de un emigrante,* 1958)
Faith ("La fe," 1970)
Five Hours with Mario (*Cinco horas con Mario,* 1966)
Long Is the Cypress's Shadow (*La sombra del ciprés es alargada,* 1948)
The Nativity ("La natividad," 1970)
Old Tales of Old Castile (*Viejas historias de Castilla la vieja,* 1964)
Parable of the Drowning Man (*Parábola del náufrago,* 1969): *The Hedge* (New York, 1983)
The Path (*El camino,* 1950): *The Path* (New York, 1961)
The Rats (*Las ratas,* 1962): *Smoke on the Ground* (Garden City, N.Y., 1972)
The Red Leaf (*La hoja roja,* 1959)
The Shroud (*La mortaja,* 1970)
Still It Is Day (*Aún es de día,* 1949)

DIEGO, GERARDO

Angels of Compostela (*Ángeles de Compostela,* 1940)
Chance or Death (*La suerte o la muerte,* 1963)
Human Verses (*Versos humanos,* 1925)
Image (*Imagen,* 1922)

Lark of Truth (*Alondra de verdad*, 1948)
Manual of Foam (*Manual de espumas*, 1924)
Poems on Purpose (*Poemas adrede*, 1932)
Soria (*Soria*, 1923)
The Surprise (*La sorpresa*, 1944)

ESPINA, CONCHA

The Girl from Luzmela (*La niña de Luzmela*, 1909)
The Nature of the Dead (*El metal de los muertos*, 1920)
Rear Guard (*Retroguardia*, 1937)
The Rose of the Winds (*La rosa de los vientos*, 1915)
The Sphinx of Maragata (*La esfinge maragata*, 1911): *Mariflor* (New York, 1924)
Sweet Name (*Dulce nombre*, 1921): *The Red Beacon* (New York, 1924)
A Valley in the Sea (*Un valle en el mar, 1950*)

ESPRIU, SALVADOR

Ariadne in the Grotesque Labyrinth (*Ariadna al laberint grotesc*, 1935)
Aspects (Narrations) (*Aspectes* [*Narracions*], 1934)
At Times It Is Necessary and Unavoidable . . . ("De vegades es necessari i forcos . . . ," in *The Bull's Skin*)
The Book of Sinera (*Llibre de Sinera*, 1964)
The Bull's Skin (*La pell de brau*, 1966)
Doctor Rip (*Doctor Rip*, 1931)
End of the Labyrinth (*Final del laberint*, 1955)
Holy Week (*Setmana Santa*, 1971)
Laia (*Laia*, 1932)
Mrs. Death (*Mrs. Death*, 1952)
The Walker and the Wall (*El caminant i el mur*, 1955)

———

Lord of the Shadow (Oxford, 1975)
Four Catalan Poets (New York, 1978)
Modern Catalan Poetry (St. Paul, Minn., 1979)

FELIPE, LEÓN

The Deer (*El ciervo*, 1958)
A Spaniard of Exodus and Lament (*Español del éxodo y del llanto*, 1939)

FOIX, J(OSEP) V(ICENÇ)

Alone and in Mourning (*Sol i de dol*, 1936)
Eleven Christmas Poems and One for the New Year (*Onze Nadals i un Any Nou*, 1960)
From the "1918 Diary" (*Del "Diari 1918,"* 1956)
Gertrudis (*Gertrudis*, 1927)
KRTU (*KRTU*, 1932)

Last Communiqué (*Darrer communicat,* 1970)
Practices ("Pràctiques," in *KRTU*)
What "The Vanguardia" Doesn't Say (Allò que no diu "La Vanguardia,"
    1970)
Within Reach (*Tocant a mà,* 1972)

———

Modern Catalan Poetry (St. Paul, Minn., 1979)

GANIVET, ÁNGEL

The Conquest of the Kingdom of the Maya (*La conquista del reino de maya,*
    1897)
Epistles (*Epistol ario,* 1904)
Finnish Letters (*Cartas finlandesas,* 1898): *Finnish Letters* (Philadelphia,
    1969)
Granada the Beautiful (*Granada la bella,* 1896)
The Labors of the Indefatigable Creator Pío Cid (*Los trabajos del inde-
    fatigable creador Pío Cid,* 1898)
Men from the North (*Hombres del norte,* 1905)
The Sculptor of His Soul (*El escultor de su alma,* 1904)
Spanish Idearium (*Idearium español,* 1897): *Spain: An Interpretation*
    (London, 1946)

GARCÍA HORTELANO, JUAN

The Caudine Forks ("Las Horcas Caudinas," in *People of Madrid*)
Mary Tribune's Great Moment (*El gran momento de Mary Tribune,* 1972)
New Friends (*Nuevas amistades,* 1959)
People of Madrid (*Gente de Madrid,* 1967)
Riánsarres and the Fascist ("Riánsarres y el fascista," in *People of Madrid*)
Summer Storm (*Tormenta de verano,* 1961): *Summer Storm* (New York,
    1962)

GARCÍA LORCA, FEDERICO

As Soon as Five Years Pass (*Así que pasen cinco años,* pub. 1937, pro-
    duced [in English] 1945): *If Five Years Pass,* in *From García Lorca's
    Theater* (New York, 1941)
Blood Wedding (*Bodas de sangre,* produced 1933, pub. 1935): *Blood Wed-
    ding,* in *Three Tragedies* (New York, 1947)
Book of Poems (*Libro de poemas,* 1921)
Buster Keaton's Promenade (*El paseo de Buster Keaton,* pub., 1928):
    Buster Keaton's Promenade, in *Accent,* Summer, 1957
The Butterfly's Evil Spell (*El maleficio de la mariposa,* pub. 1928, pro-
    duced 1920): *The Butterfly's Evil Spell,* in *Five Plays* (New York, 1963)
Chimera (*Quimera,* written 1928): *Chimera,* in *New Directions,* No. 8
    (Norfolk, Conn., 1944)
Doña Rosita, the Spinster; or, The Language of Flowers (*Doña Rosita, la
    soltera; o, El lenguaje de flores,* produced 1935, pub. 1938): *Doña
    Rosita, the Spinster,* in *From García Lorca's Theatre* (New York, 1941)

Gypsy Ballads (*Romancero gitano*, 1928): *The Gypsy Ballads of García Lorca* (Bloomington, Ind., 1953)

The House of Bernarda Alba (*La casa de Bernarda Alba*, pub. 1945): *The House of Bernarda Alba*, in *Three Tragedies* (New York, 1947)

Lament for Ignacio Sánchez Mejías (*Llanto por Ignacio Sánchez Mejías*, 1935): *Lament for the Death of a Bullfighter*, in *Lament for the Death of a Bullfighter, and Other Poems* (New York, 1937)

The Love of Don Perlimplín for Belisa in His Garden (*Amor de don Perlimplín con Belisa en su Jardin*, produced 1933, pub. 1938): *The Love of Don Perlimplín for Belisa in His Garden*, in *From the Modern Repertoire, Series One*, ed. Eric Bentley (Denver, 1949)

Mariana Pineda (*Mariana Pineda*, 1927): *Mariana Pineda*, in *Tulane Drama Review*, Autumn, 1962

Poet in New York (*Poeta en Nueva York*, 1940): *The Poet in New York*, in *The Poet in New York, and Other Poems* (New York, 1940); also *Poet in New York* (New York, 1955)

The Public (*El público*, written 1930, pub. 1974, produced 1978): *The Public*, in *The Public, and Play without a Title: Two Posthumous Plays* (New York, 1983)

The Puppets of Cachiporra: The Tragicomedy of Don Cristóbal and Doña Rosita (*Títeres de Cachiporra: La tragicomedia de don Cristóbal y la señá Rosita* (written 1928, produced 1937, pub. 1949): *The Billy-Club Puppets*, in *Five Plays* (New York, 1963)

The Shoemaker's Prodigious Wife (*La zapatera prodigiosa*, written 1930, revised 1935, pub. 1938): *The Shoemaker's Prodigious Wife*, in *Five Plays* (New York, 1963)

Songs (*Canciones*, 1927): *Songs* (Pittsburgh, 1976)

The Virgin, the Sailor and the Student (*La doncella, el marinero y el estudiante*, written 1928): *The Virgin, the Sailor and the Student*, in *Accent*, Summer, 1957

Yerma (*Yerma*, produced 1934, pub. 1937): *Yerma*, in *Three Tragedies* (New York, 1947)

Lament for the Death of a Bullfighter, and Other Poems (New York, 1937)
Poems (New York, 1939)
The Poet in New York, and Other Poems (New York, 1940)
Selected Poems (London, 1943)
The Selected Poems of Federico García Lorca (Norfolk, Conn., 1955)
Federico García Lorca: Some of His Shorter Poems (London, 1955)
After Lorca (San Francisco, 1957)
Lorca (Selected Poems) (Baltimore, 1960)
Tree of Song (Santa Barbara, Cal., 1971)
Lorca and Jiménez: Selected Poems (Boston, 1973)
Divan, and Other Writings (Providence, R.I., 1974)
Poems (San Francisco, 1979)
The Cricket Sings: Poems and Songs for Children (New York, 1980; bilingual)
Deep Song, and Other Prose (New York, 1980)

GIRONELLA, JOSÉ MARÍA

The Cypresses Believe in God (*Los cipreses creen en Dios*, 1953): *The Cypresses Believe in God* (New York, 1955)

A Man (*Un hombre*, 1946): *Where the Soil Was Shallow* (Chicago, 1957)

One Million Dead (*Un millón de muertos*, 1961): *One Million Dead* (Garden City, N.Y., 1963)

Peace Has Broken Out (*Ha estallado la paz*, 1966): *Peace after War* (New York, 1969)

The Tide (*La marea*, 1949)

GÓMEZ DE LA SERNA, RAMÓN

Autodeathography (*Automoribundia*, 1948)

The Bullfighter Caracho (*El torero Caracho*, 1926)

Contemporary Portraits (*Retratos contemporáneos*, 1941)

The Dead Men and Women and Other Phantasmagorias (*Los muertos, las muertas y otras fantasmagorías*, 1935)

Edgar Poe, the Genius of America (*Edgar Poe, el genio de América*, 1953)

The Gentleman in the Gray Bowler (*El caballero del hongo gris*, 1928)

Greguerías (*Greguerías*, 1917; definitive ed., 1960): *Some Greguerías* (New York, 1944)

Isms (*Ismos*, 1931)

Movieland (*Cinelandia*, 1924): *Movieland* (New York, 1930)

The Mute Book (*El libro mudo*, 1911)

New Contemporary Portraits (*Nuevos retratos contemporáneos*, 1945)

Quevedo (*Quevedo*, 1953)

The Rastro (*El Rastro*, 1915)

Softnesses (*Morbideces*, 1908)

Tapestries (*Tapices*, 1913)

The Theater in Solitude (*El teatro en soledad*, 1911)

The Unlikely Doctor (*El doctor inverosímil*, 1921)

GOYTISOLO, JUAN

The Circus (*El circo*, 1957)

End of the Fiesta (*Fin de fiesta*, 1962): *The Party's Over* (London, 1966)

Fields of Níjar (*Campos de Níjar*, 1960)

Fiestas (*Fiestas*, 1958): *Fiestas* (New York, 1960)

The Island (*La isla*, 1961): *Island of Women* (New York, 1962)

Juan the Landless (*Juan sin tierra*, 1975): *Juan the Landless* (New York, 1977)

Makbara (*Makbara*, 1979): *Makbara* (New York, 1981)

Marks of Identity (*Señas de identidad*, 1966): *Marks of Identity* (New York, 1969)

Sleight of Hand (*Juego de manos*, 1954): *The Young Assassins* (New York, 1959)

Trouble in Paradise (*Duelo en el paraíso*, 1955): *Children of Chaos* (London, 1958)

The Undertow (*La resaca*, 1958)
Vindication of Count Don Julián (*Reivindicación del Conde don Julián*, 1970): *Count Julian* (New York, 1974)

GUILLÉN, JORGE

Cántico (*Cántico*, 1928–62): *Cántico: A Selection* (Boston, 1965)
Homage (*Homenaje*, 1967)
Our Air (*Aire nuestro*, 1968)
Outcry (*Clamor*, 1957–63)

Affirmation: A Bilingual Anthology, 1919–1966 (Norman, Okla., 1968)
Guillén on Guillén: The Poetry and the Poet (Princeton, N.J., 1979)

HERNÁNDEZ, MIGUEL

Knowledgeable about Moons (*Perito en lunas*, 1933)
Last Poems (*Últimos poemas*, in *Cancionero y romancero de ausencias; El hombre acecha; Últimos poemas*, 1963)
The Lightning That Never Stops (*El rayo que no cesa*, 1936)
Man in Ambush (*El hombre acecha*, 1939)
The Shepherd of Death (*El pastor de la muerte*, 1938)
Songbook and Ballad Book of Absences (*Cancionero y romancero de ausencias*, written 1938–41, pub. 1958): *Songbook of Absences: Selected Poems of Miguel Hernández* (Washington, D.C., 1972)
Sons of Stone (*Los hijos de la piedra*, 1935)
Wind of the People (*Viento del pueblo*, 1937)

Miguel Hernández and Blas de Otero: Selected Poems (Boston, 1972)

JARNÉS, BENJAMÍN

Ariel in Flight (*Ariel disperso*, 1946)
Madness and Death of Nobody (*Locura y muerte de nadie*, 1929)
The Paper Guest (*El convidado de papel*, 1928)
Paula and Paulita (*Paula y Paulita*, 1929): *Paula y Paulita*, excerpt in *The European Caravan*, ed. Samuel Putnam (New York, 1931)
The Red and the Blue: Homage to Stendhal (*Lo rojo y lo azul: Homenaje a Stendhal*, 1932)
Saint Alexis (*San Alejo*, definitive version, 1934): "Saint Alexis," in *Great Spanish Stories*, ed. Ángel Flores (New York, 1956)
Stefan Zweig (*Stefan Zweig*, 1942)
Theory of the Top-String (*Teoría del zumbel*, 1930)
The Useless Professor (*El profesor inútil*, 1924)

JIMÉNEZ, JUAN RAMÓN

Animal of Depth (*Animal de fondo*, 1949)
Beauty (*Belleza*, 1923)

Poetry: (1917–1923) (*Poesía: (1917–1923)*, 1923)
Platero and I (*Platero y yo*, 1914); *Platero and I* (New York. 1956)
Sad Airs (*Arias tristes*, 1903)

Fifty Spanish Poems (Oxford, 1950; Berkeley, Cal., 1951)
Selected Writings (New York, 1957)
Three Hundred Poems: 1903–1953 (Austin, Tex., 1962)
Forty Poems (Madison, Minn., 1967)
Lorca and Jiménez: Selected Poems (Boston, 1973)

LAFORET, CARMEN

The Island and the Demons (*La isla y los demonios*, 1952)
The New Woman (*La mujer nueva*, 1956)
Nothingness (*Nada*, 1945): *Nada* (London, 1958); *Andrea* (New York, 1964)
Sunstroke (*La insolación*, 1963)

MACHADO, ANTONIO

Apocryphal Songbook (*Cancionero apócrifo*, 1926)
Bitter Oleander (*Las adelfas*, 1928, with Manuel Machado)
The Complementaries (*Los complementarios*, 1949)
Complete Poems (*Poesías completas*, 1973)
A Crazy Man ("Un loco," in *Plains of Castile*)
Fields of Soria ("Campos de Soria," in *Plains of Castile*)
From an Apocryphal Songbook (*De un cancionero apócrifo*, in *Juan de Mairena*)
Galleries ("Galerías," in *New Songs* [*1917–1930*]): "Corridors," in *The Penguin Book of Spanish Verse*, ed. J. M. Cohen (Baltimore, 1956)
Juan de Mairena: Epigrams, Maxims, Memoranda, and Memoirs of an Apocryphal Professor (*Juan de Mairena: Sentencias, donaires, apuntes y recuerdos de un profesor apócrifo*, 1936): *Juan de Mairena: Epigrams, Maxims, Memoranda, and Memoirs of an Apocryphal Professor, with an Appendix from an Apocryphal Songbook* (Berkeley, Cal., 1963)
Juan de Mañara (*Juan de Mañara*, 1927, with Manuel Machado)
La Lola Goes Off to Sea (*La Lola se va a los puertos*, 1929, with Manuel Machado)
The Land of Alvargonzález ("La tierra de Alvargonzález," in *An Anthology of Spanish Poetry from Garcilaso to García Lorca*, ed. Ángel Flores (New York, 1961)
New Songs (*Nuevas canciones*, 1924)
New Songs (1917–1930) (*Nuevas canciones* [*1917–1930*], in *Complete Poems*)
Plains of Castile (*Campos de Castilla*, 1912)
Praises (*Elogios*, in *Plains of Castile*)
Solitudes (*Soledades*, 1903)

Solitudes, Galleries, and Other Poems (*Soledades, galerías y otros poemas,* 1907)
Through Spanish Lands ("Por tierras de España," in *Plains of Castile*)
To the Great Zero ("Al gran cero," in *From an Apocryphal Songbook*)

———

Antonio Machado (New York, 1959)
Eighty Poems (New York, 1959)
Castilian Ilexes (New York, 1963)
Still Waters of the Air (New York, 1970)
Selected Poems (Baton Rouge, La., 1978)
The Dream below the Sun (Trumansburg, N.Y., 1981)
Selected Poems (Cambridge, Mass., 1983)
Times Alone: Selected Poems (Middletown, Conn., 1983)

MACHADO, MANUEL

Apollo (*Apolo,* 1911)
Ars moriendi (*Ars moriendi,* 1921)
Cadences of Cadences (*Cadencias de cadencias,* 1943)
The Evil Poem (*El mal poema,* 1909)
Folk Songs (*Los cantares,* 1907)
Museum (*Museo,* 1907)
Soul (*Alma,* 1902)

MARTÍN GAITE, CARMEN

The Back Room (*El cuarto de atrás,* 1978): *The Back Room* (New York, 1983)
Between Curtains (*Entre visillos,* 1958)
Inner Fragments (*Fragmentos de interior,* 1976)
The Spa (*El balneario,* 1955)
Threads of Discourse (*Retahílas,* 1974)

MARTÍN-SANTOS, LUIS

Apologues and Other Unpublished Prose (*Apólogos y otras prosas iné-ditas,* 1970)
Bullfighting ("Tauromaquia," n.d.)
Ramuncho's Complex ("El complejo de Ramuncho," in *Apologues*)
Time of Destruction (*Tiempo de destrucción,* 1975)
Time of Silence (*Tiempo de silencio,* 1962): *Time of Silence* (New York, 1964)

MARTÍNEZ SIERRA, GREGORIO AND MARÍA

All Is One and the Same (*Todo es uno y lo mismo,* 1910)
An August Night's Dream (*Sueño de una noche de agosto,* 1918): *The Romantic Young Lady,* in *The Plays of Gregorio Martínez Sierra: Vol. II* (New York, 1923)

The Cradle Song (*Canción de cuna*, 1911): *The Cradle Song*, in *The Plays of Gregorio Martínez Sierra: Vol. II* (New York, 1923)

Don Juan of Spain (*Don Juan de España*, 1921)

Fragile Rosina (*Rosina es frágil*, 1918)

Frost Flowers (Flores de escarcha, 1900)

The Kingdom of God (*El reino de Dios*, 1916): *The Kingdom of God*, in *The Plays of Gregorio Martínez Sierra: Vol. II* (New York, 1923)

A Lily among Thorns (*Lirio entre espinas*, 1911): *A Lily among Thorns*, in *Chief Contemporary Dramatists: Third Series*, ed. Thomas H. Dickinson (Boston, 1930)

Live Your Own Life (*Cada uno y su vida*, 1919)

The Lover (*El enamorado*, 1913): *The Lover*, in *The Plays of Gregorio Martínez Sierra: Vol. I* (New York, 1923)

Mama (*Mamá*, 1913)

Mistress of the House (*El ama de la casa*, 1910)

The Shepherds (*Los pastores*, 1913): *The Two Shepherds*, in *The Plays of Gregorio Martínez Sierra: Vol. II* (New York, 1923)

MATUTE, ANA MARÍA

The Abel Family (*Los Abel*, 1948)

The Dead Children (*Los hijos muertos*, 1958): *The Lost Children* (New York, 1965)

Fiesta in the Northwest (*Fiesta al noroeste*, 1959)

First Memory (*Primera memoria*, 1960): *School of the Sun* (New York, 1963)

In This Land (*En esta tierra*, 1955)

The Merchants (trilogy; *Los mercaderes*)

The Soldiers Cry at Night (*Los soldados lloran de noche*, 1964)

The Stupid Children (*Los niños tontos*, 1956)

Three and a Dream (*Tres y un sueño*, 1961)

The Trap (*La trampa*, 1969)

MIRÓ, GABRIEL

About Living (*Del vivir*, 1904)

The Angel, the Mill, the Lighthouse Snail (*El ángel, el molino, el caracol del faro*, 1921)

Book of Sigüenza (*Libro de Sigüenza*, 1917)

Complete Works (*Obras completas*, 1949)

Corpus, and Other Stories (*Corpus, y otros cuentos*, 1951)

Enriqueta's Feet and Shoes (*Los pies y los zapatos de Enriqueta*, 1934)

Figures of the Passion of Our Lord (*Figuras de la pasión de Nuestro Señor*, 2 vols., 1916–17): *Figures of the Passion of Our Lord* (London, 1924)

The Leprous Bishop (*El obispo leproso*, 1926)

Little Boy and Big (*Niño y grande*, 1922)

The Novel of My Friend (*La novela de mi amigo*, 1908)

Our Father San Daniel (*Nuestro Padre San Daniel*, 1921): *Our Father San Daniel* (London, 1933)

The Power of a Judge ("La potestad de un juez," 1917)

The Sleeping Smoke (*El humo dormido,* 1919): *The Sleeping Smoke,* excerpt in *European Caravan,* ed. Samuel Putnam (New York, 1931)

Years and Leagues (*Años y leguas,* 1928)

ORTEGA Y GASSET, JOSÉ

The Dehumanization of Art, and Ideas on the Novel (*La deshumanización del arte, e Ideas sobre la novela,* 1925): *The Dehumanization of Art, and Notes on the Novel* (Princeton, N.J., 1948)

History as System (*Historia como sistema,* 1936): *Toward a Philosophy of History* (New York, 1941)

Invertebrate Spain (*España invertebrada,* 1922): *Invertebrate Spain* (New York, 1937)

Meditations on Quixote (*Meditaciones del Quijote,* 1914): *Meditations on Quixote* (New York, 1961)

The Revolt of the Masses (*La rebelión de las masas,* 1930): *The Revolt of the Masses* (New York, 1932; new tr., Notre Dame, Ind., 1984)

The Spectator (*El Espectador,* 8 vols., 1916–34)

Studies on Love (*Estudios sobre el amor,* 1939): *On Love: Aspects of a Single Theme* (New York, 1957)

The Theme of Our Time (*El tema de nuestro tiempo,* 1923): *The Modern Theme* (New York, 1933)

OTERO, BLAS DE

And I Will Go Away ("Y yo me iré," in *Meanwhile*)

Doubling of Consciousness (*Redoble de conciencia,* 1951)

The Eternal ("Lo eternal," in *Fiercely Human Angel*)

Fiercely Human Angel (*Ángel fieramente humano,* 1950)

I Ask for Peace and a Chance to Speak (*Pido la paz y la palabra,* 1955)

In Castilian (*En castellano,* 1960)

Letters and Poems to Nazim Hikmet ("Cartas y poemas a Nazim Hikmet," in *In Castilian*)

Meanwhile (*Mientras,* 1970)

Orozco ("Orozco," in *Meanwhile*)

Speaking about Spain (*Que trata de España,* 1964)

———

Twenty Poems (Madison, Minn., 1964)

Miguel Hernández and Blas de Otero: Selected Poems (Boston, 1972)

PASO, ALFONSO

Aurelia and Her Men (*Aurelia y sus hombres,* 1961)

Call for Julius Caesar (*Preguntan por Julio César,* produced 1960, pub. 1961)

Careful with Serious People! (*¡Cuidado con las personas formales!,* 1960)

Dear Teacher (*Querido profesor,* produced 1965, pub. 1966)

Heaven in the House (*El cielo dentro de casa,* produced 1957, pub. 1958): *Blue Heaven,* adaptation (New York, 1962)

The Hunt of the Foreigner (*La caza de la extranjera,* produced 1965, pub. 1966)

Let's Tell Lies (*Vamos a contar mentiras,* produced 1961, pub. 1962)

Nero-Paso (*Nerón-Paso,* 1969)

Occupation: Suspect (*De profesión: sospechoso,* produced 1962, pub. 1963)

Papa's and Mama's Things (*Cosas de papá y mamá,* 1960)

The Poor Little People (*Los pobrecitos,* produced 1957, pub. 1958)

The Song of the Grasshopper (*El canto de la cigarra,* pub. 1958, produced 1960): *Song of the Grasshopper,* adaptation (New York, 1967)

There Is Someone Behind the Door (*Hay alguien detrás de la puerta,* produced 1958, pub. 1969)

You Can Be a Murderer (*Usted puede ser un asesino,* produced 1958, pub. 1959)

PEDROLO, MANUEL DE

Act of Violence (*Acte de violència,* written 1961, published 1975)

Anonymous II; or, On the Permanent Dimensions of the Triarchy (*Anònim II; o, De les dimensions permanents de la triarquia,* written 1970, published 1981)

Cruma (*Cruma,* written 1957, published 1958): *Cruma,* in George E. Wellwarth, ed., *3 Catalan Dramatists* (Montreal, 1976)

Full Circle (*Situació bis,* written 1958, published 1964): *Full Circle,* in George E. Wellwarth, ed., *3 Catalan Dramatists* (Montreal, 1976)

Men and No (*Homes i no,* written 1957, published 1960): *Humans and No,* in *Modern International Drama,* 10, 1 (1977)

Technique of the Room (*Tècnica de cambra,* written 1959, published 1964): *The Room,* in George E. Wellwarth, ed., *3 Catalan Dramatists* (Montreal, 1976)

PÉREZ DE AYALA, RAMÓN

A.M.D.G.: Life in Jesuit Schools (*A.M.D.G.: La vida en los colegios de jesuítas,* 1910)

Belarmino and Apolonio (*Belarmino y Apolonio,* 1921): *Belarmino and Apolonio* (Berkeley, Cal., 1971)

Darkness at the Heights (*Tinieblas en las cumbres,* 1907)

The Doctor of His Honor (*El curandero de su honra,* 1926): *The Doctor of His Honor,* in *Tiger Juan* (New York, 1933)

The Fall of the House of Limón (*La caída de los Limones,* 1916): *The Fall of the House of Limón,* in *Prometheus, The Fall of the House of Limón, Sunday Sunlight: Poetic Novels of Spanish Life* (New York, 1920)

The Flowing Path (*El sendero andante,* 1921)

The Fox's Paw (*La pata de la raposa,* 1912): *The Fox's Paw* (New York, 1924)

Honeymoon, Bittermoon (*Luna de miel, luna de hiel,* 1923): *Honeymoon, Bittermoon* (Berkeley, Cal., 1972)

The Masks (*Las máscaras,* 2 vols., 1917, 1919)

Mummers and Dancers (*Troteras y danzaderas,* 1913)

The Path of Infinite Variations (*El sendero innumerable,* 1916)

The Peace of the Path (*La paz del sendero,* 1903)

Poetic Novels of Spanish Life (*Novelas poemáticas de la vida española,* 1916): *Prometheus, The Fall of the House of Limón, Sunday Sunlight: Poetic Novels of Spanish Life* (New York, 1920)

Prometheus (*Prometeo,* 1916): *Prometheus,* in *Prometheus, The Fall of the House of Limón, Sunday Sunlight: Poetic Novels of Spanish Life* (New York, 1920)

Sunday Sunlight (*Luz de domingo,* 1916): *Sunday Sunlight,* in *Prometheus, The Fall of the House of Limón, Sunday Sunlight: Poetic Novels of Spanish Life* (New York, 1920)

Tiger Juan (*Tigre Juan,* 1926): *Tiger Juan* (New York, 1933)

The Trials of Urbano and Simona (*Los trabajos de Urbano y Simona,* 1923): *The Trials of Urbano and Simona,* included in *Honeymoon, Bittermoon* (Berkeley, Cal., 1972)

PÉREZ GALDÓS, BENITO

Ángel Guerra (*Ángel Guerra,* 3 vols., 1890–91)

Barbara (*Bárbara,* 1905)

The Bringas Case (*La de Bringas,* 1884): *The Spendthrifts* (New York, 1952)

Compassion (*Misericordia,* 1897): *Compassion* (New York, 1962)

Doña Perfecta (*Doña Perfecta,* 1876): *Doña Perfecta* (Great Neck, N.Y., 1960)

Electra (*Electra,* 1901): *Electra,* in *Modern Continental Plays,* ed. S. Marion Tucker (New York, 1929)

Fortunata and Jacinta (*Fortunata y Jacinta,* 1886–87): *Fortunata and Jacinta: Two Stories of Married Women* (Athens, Ga., 1986)

The Golden Fountain (*La fontana de oro,* 1870)

The Grandfather (*El abuelo,* 1904): *The Grandfather,* in *Poet Lore,* 21, 1910

Halma (*Halma,* 1895)

The Madwoman of the House (*La loca de la casa,* 1893)

Mariucha (*Mariucha,* 1903)

Miau (*Miau,* 1888): *Miau* (Baltimore, 1963)

National Episodes (*Episodios nacionales,* 1873–1912)

Nazarín (*Nazarín,* 1895)

Reality (novel: *Realidad,* 1889)

Reality (play: *Realidad,* 1892)

Torment (*Tormento,* 1884): *Torment* (New York, 1953)

Torquemada (*Torquemada,* 4 vols., 1889–95), comprising Torquemada in the Flames (*Torquemada en la hoguera,* 1889); Torquemada on the Cross (*Torquemada en la cruz,* 1893); Torquemada in Purgatory (*Tor-

quemada en el purgatorio, 1894); Torquemada and Saint Peter (*Torquemada y San Pedro,* 1895): *Torquemada* (New York, 1986)
The Unknown (*La incógnita,* 1888–89)

QUIROGA, ELENA

Blood (*La sangre,* 1952)
I Write Your Name (*Escribo tu nombre,* 1965)
The Last Bullfight (*La última corrida,* 1958)
The Mask (*La careta,* 1955)
North Wind (*Viento del norte,* 1951)
The Other City (*La otra ciudad,* 1953)
Sadness (*Tristura,* 1960)
Something's Happening in the Street (*Algo pasa en la calle,* 1954)

RIBA, CARLES

. . . And the Poems (. . . *Mes els poemes,* 1957)
Elegies of Bierville (*Elegies de Bierville,* 1942; enlarged ed., 1949; definitive ed., 1951)
Savage Heart (*Salvatge cor,* 1952)
Sketch of Three Oratories (*Esbós de tres oratoris,* 1957)
Stanzas (*Estances, primer llibre,* 1919; *segon llibre,* 1930)
Three Suites (*Tres suites,* 1937)

Poems (Oxford, 1970)

RODRÍGUEZ CASTELAO, ALFONSO

Always in Galicia (*Sempre na Galiza,* 1944)
Banterings (*Retrincos,* 1934)
A Glass Eye (*Un ollo de vidro,* 1922)
He Was a Little Butter Boy ("Era um menino de manteiga," 1926)
I'm Going to Tell You a Story ("Vou te contar uma historia," 1929)
Old People Should Not Fall in Love (*Os vellos non deben namorar,* 1941)
Pimpinela (*Pimpinela,* written c. 1935; third part of *Old People Should Not Fall in Love*)
Things (*Cousas,* 1926; 2nd augmented ed., 1929)
The Usual Two (*Os dous de sempre,* 1934)
We (*Nós,* 1929)

RUIBAL, JOSÉ

The Begging Machine (*La máquina de pedir,* 1969)
The Man and the Fly (*El hombre y la mosca,* 1968): *The Man and the Fly,* in *The New Wave Spanish Drama,* ed. George E. Wellwarth (New York, 1970)

SALINAS, PEDRO

Complete Poems (*Poesías completas,* 1971)
Complete Theater (*Teatro completo,* 1957)
Confidence (*Confianza,* 1956)
The Contemplated One (*El contemplado,* 1946): *Sea of San Juan: A Contemplation* (Boston, 1950)
The Director (*El director,* 1957)
Eve of Joy (*Víspera del gozo,* 1926)
Everything Clearer (*Todo más claro,* 1949)
Fable and Sign (*Fábula y signo,* 1931)
The Head of Medusa (*La cabeza de Medusa,* 1952)
The Incredible Bomb (*La bomba increíble,* 1950)
Jorge Manrique; or, Tradition and Originality (*Jorge Manrique; o, Tradición y originalidad,* 1947)
Nocturne of the Advertisements ("Nocturno de los avisos," in *Everything Clearer*)
Presages (*Presagios,* 1924)
Reality and the Poet in Spanish Poetry (Baltimore, 1940; pub. first in English)
The Saints (*Los santos,* written 1945, pub. 1954)
Sure Risk (*Seguro azar,* 1929)
The Telephone ("El teléfono," in *Fable and Sign*)
To Live in Pronouns ("Vivir en los pronombres," in *The Voice Because of You*): "To Live in Pronouns," in *To Live in Pronouns: Selected Love Poems* (New York, 1974)
The Voice Because of You (*La voz a ti debida,* 1933): *My Voice Because of You* (New York, 1976)
Zero (*Cero,* 1944): *Zero* (Baltimore, 1947)

Lost Angel, and Other Poems (Baltimore, 1938)
Truth of Two, and Other Poems (Baltimore, 1940)
To Live in Pronouns: Selected Love Poems (New York, 1974)

SÁNCHEZ FERLOSIO, RAFAEL

The Jarama (*El Jarama,* 1956): *The One Day of the Week* (New York, 1962)
The Projects and Wanderings of Alfanhuí (*Industrias y andanzas de Alfanhuí,* 1951): *The Projects and Wanderings of Alfanhuí* (West Lafayette, Ind., 1975)

SASTRE, ALFONSO

Anna Kleiber (*Ana Kleiber,* pub. 1957, produced 1960); *Anna Kleiber,* in *The New Theatre of Europe,* ed. Robert W. Corrigan (New York, 1962)
Blood and Ashes: Dialogues of Miguel Servet (*La sangre y la ceniza: Diálogos de Miguel Servet,* 1965)
The Blood of God (*La sangre de Dios,* 1955)
Condemned Squad (*Escuadra hacia la muerte,* 1953): *Condemned Squad,*

in *The Modern Spanish Stage: Four Plays*, ed. Marion Holt (New York, 1970)

Death in the Neighborhood (*Muerte en el barrio*, 1960)

Death Thrust (*La cornada*, 1960): *Death Thrust*, in *Masterpieces of the Spanish Theatre*, ed. Robert W. Corrigan (New York, 1967)

Every Man's Bread (*El pan de todos*, 1957)

The Gag (*La mordaza*, 1954)

In the Net (*En la red*, 1961)

Lugubrious Nights (*Las noches lúgubres*, 1964)

The Raven (*El cuervo*, 1957)

Red Earth (*Tierra roja*, 1954)

Sad Are the Eyes of William Tell (*Guillermo Tell tiene los ojos tristes*, 1955): *Sad Are the Eyes of William Tell*, in *The New Wave Spanish Drama*, ed. George E. Wellwarth (New York, 1970)

SENDER, RAMÓN J.

The Affable Hangman (*El verdugo afable*, 1953): *The Affable Hangman* (London, 1954)

Byzantium (*Bizancio*, 1956)

Carolus Rex (*Carolus Rex*, 1963)

Chronicle of Dawn (*Crónica del alba*, 1942): *Chronicle of Dawn* (Garden City, N.Y., 1944)

Chronicle of Dawn (*Crónica del alba*, 3 vols., 1966): Vol. I, comprising *Crónica del alba (Chronicle of Dawn), Hipogrifo violento (The Violent Griffin)*, and *La quinta Julieta (The Villa Julieta)*, tr. as *Before Noon* (Albuquerque, N.M., 1957)

The Equinoctial Adventure of Lope de Aguirre (*La aventura equinoccial de Lope de Aguirre*, 1964)

The Five Books of Ariadne (*Los cinco libros de Ariadna*, 1957)

The Golden Fish (*El pez de oro*, 1976)

In the Life of Ignacio Morel (*En la vida de Ignacio Morel*, 1969)

The King and the Queen (*El rey y la reina*, 1949): *The King and The Queen* (New York, 1948)

Magnet (*Imán*, 1930): *Pro Patria* (Boston, 1935)

A Man's Place (*El lugar del hombre*, 1939): *A Man's Place* (New York, 1940)

The Migratory Images (*Las imágenes migratorias*, 1960)

Mr. Witt in the Canton (*Mr. Witt en el Cantón*, 1936): *Mr. Witt among the Rebels* (Boston, 1938)

Night of the Hundred Heads (*Noche de las cien cabezas*, 1934)

Public Order (*O.P.* [= *Orden público*], 1931)

Requiem for a Spanish Peasant (*Réquiem para un campesino español*, 1960): *Requiem for a Spanish Peasant* (New York, 1960)

Saturnian Creatures (*Las criaturas saturnianas*, 1968)

Seven Red Sundays (*Siete domingos rojos*, 1932): *Seven Red Sundays* (New York, 1936)

The Shore Where Madmen Smile ("La orilla donde los locos sonríen," in *Chronicle of Dawn*, Vol. III, 1966)

The Sphere (*La esfera*, 1947): *The Sphere* (New York, 1949)
Tánit (*Tánit*, 1970)
Three Novels of Teresa (*Tres novelas teresianas*, 1967)
The Tontos of Conception Mission (*Los Tontos de la Concepción*, 1963)
The Wedding Song of Dark Trinidad (*El epitalamio del prieto Trinidad*, 1942): *Dark Wedding* (Garden City, N.Y., 1943)

TORRENTE BALLESTER, GONZALO

Don Juan (*Don Juan*, 1963)
Fragments of Apocalypse (*Fragmentos de Apocalipsis*, 1977)
Javier Mariño (*Javier Mariño*, 1943)
Lope de Aguirre (*Lope de Aguirre*, 1941)
Off-side (*Off-side*, 1969)
The Pleasures and the Shadows (*Los gozos y las sombras*, 3 vols., 1957, 1960, 1962)
The Return of Ulysses (*El retorno de Ulises*, 1945)
The Saga/Fugue of J. B. (*La saga/fuga de J. B.*, 1973)
The Voyage of Young Tobias (*El viaje del joven Tobías*, written 1936, pub. 1938)

UNAMUNO, MIGUEL DE

Abel Sánchez (*Abel Sánchez*, 1917): *Abel Sanchez*, in *Abel Sanchez, and Other Stories* (Chicago, 1956)
Aunt Tula (*La tía Tula*, 1921)
Book of Songs (*Cancionero*, 1953)
Brother Juan; or, The World Is a Stage (*El hermano Juan; o, El mundo es un teatro*, 1934)
The Christ of Velázquez (*El Cristo de Velázquez*, 1920): *The Christ of Velázquez* (Baltimore, 1951)
Life of Don Quixote and Sancho (*Vida de don Quijote y Sancho*, 1905): *Life of Don Quixote and Sancho* (New York, 1927); *Our Lord Don Quixote: The Life of Don Quixote and Sancho, with Related Essays* (Princeton, N.J., 1967)
Mist (*Niebla*, 1914): *Mist: A Tragi-comic Novel* (New York, 1929)
Nothing Less Than a Whole Man (*Nada menos que todo un hombre*, 1920): *Nothing Less Than a Whole Man*, in *International Short Stories*, ed. V. W. F. Church (Chicago, 1934)
Peace in War (*Paz en la guerra*, 1897): *Peace in War* (Princeton, N.J., 1983)
Poems (*Poesías*, 1907)
Saint Emmanuel the Good, Martyr (*San Manuel Bueno, mártir*, 1931): *Saint Manuel Bueno, Martyr* (New York, 1954)
Soliloquies and Conversations (*Soliloquios y conversaciones*, 1912): *Essays and Soliloquies* (New York, 1925)
Teresa (*Teresa*, 1923)
Three Exemplary Novels (*Tres novelas ejemplares*, 1920): *Three Exemplary Novels* (New York, 1930)
The Tragic Sense of Life (*Del sentimiento trágico de la vida*, 1913): *The*

Tragic Sense of Life in Men and Peoples (New York, 1921); *The Tragic Sense of Life in Men and Nations* (Princeton, N.J., 1972)

Perplexities and Paradoxes (New York, 1945)
Poems (Baltimore, 1952)
Selected Works of Miguel de Unamuno, 8 vols. (Princeton, N.J., 1967–85)

VALLE-INCLÁN, RAMÓN DEL

Altarpiece of Avarice, Lust, and Death (*Retablo de la avaricia, la lujuria y la muerte,* 1927)

Barbaric Comedies, 3 vols.: Heraldic Eagle, Ballad of the Wolves, Silver Face (*Comedias bárbaras,* 3 vols.: *Águila de blasón,* 1907; *Romance de lobos,* 1909: *Wolves! Wolves!,* Birmingham, England, 1957; *Cara de plata,* 1923)

The Captain's Daughter (*La hija del capitán,* 1927)

The Carlist War (*La guerra carlista,* 3 vols., 1908–9)

The Crusaders of the Cause (*Los cruzados de la causa,* 1908)

Divine Words (*Divinas palabras,* 1920): *Divine Words,* in *Modern Spanish Theatre,* ed. Michael Benedikt and George E. Wellwarth (New York, 1968)

The Dragon's Head (*La cabeza del dragón,* 1914): *The Dragon's Head,* in *Poet Lore,* Winter, 1918

Farce and License of the Native Queen (*Farsa y licencia de la reina castiza,* 1922)

The Farce of the Maid Who Loved a King (*Farsa de la enamorada de un rey,* 1920)

The Horns of Don Friolera (*Los cuernos de don Friolera,* 1921)

The Iberian Ring, 2 vols.: The Court of Miracles; Long Live My Master (*El ruedo ibérico,* 2 vols.: *La corte de los milagros,* 1927; *Viva mi dueño,* 1928)

Lights of Bohemia (*Luces de Bohemia,* 1924): *Lights of Bohemia,* in *Kenyon Review,* Nov., 1967

Marquise Rosalinda (*La marquesa Rosalinda,* 1913)

The Paper Rose (*La rosa de papel,* 1924)

Saintly Flower (*Flor de santidad,* 1904)

Sonata of Autumn (*Sonata de otoño,* 1902): *Sonata of Autumn,* in *The Pleasant Memoirs of the Marquis de Bradomin: Four Sonatas* (New York, 1924)

Sonata of Spring (*Sonata de primavera,* 1904): *Sonata of Spring,* in *The Pleasant Memoirs of the Marquis de Bradomin: Four Sonatas* (New York, 1924)

Sonata of Summer (*Sonata de estío,* 1903): *Sonata of Summer,* in *The Pleasant Memoirs of the Marquis de Bradomin: Four Sonatas* (New York, 1924)

Sonatas: Memoirs of the Marquis of Bradomín (*Sonatas: Memorias del Marqués de Bradomín,* 1902–5): *The Pleasant Memoirs of the Marquis de Bradomin: Four Sonatas* (New York, 1924)

The Tyrant Banderas (*Tirano Banderas,* 1926): *The Tyrant: A Novel of Warm Lands* (New York, 1929)

ZUNZUNEGUI, JUAN ANTONIO DE

Bankruptcy (*La quiebra*, 1947)
Chiripi (*Chiripi*, 1931)
The Greatest Good (*El supremo bien*, 1951)
The Happy Road (*El camino alegre*, 1963)
Life as It Is (*La vida como es*, 1954)
Oh . . . These Children! (*¡Ay . . . estos hijos!*, 1943)
The Ship Chandler (*El chiplichandle*, 1940)
The Ship's Rats (*Las ratas del barco*, 1950)
This Dark Flight (*Esta oscura desbandada*, 1952)

Portugal

BRANDÃO, RAUL

The Farce (*A farsa*, 1904)
The Fishermen (*Os pescadores*, 1923)
Humus (*Húmus*, 1917)
King Junot (*El-rei Junot*, 1912)
Memoirs (*Memórias*, 3 vols., 1919–33)
The Poor (*Os pobres*, 1906)
Story of a Clown (*História dum palhaço*, 1896)
The Unknown Islands (*As ilhas desconhecidas*, 1926)

CASTRO, JOSÉ MARIA FERREIRA DE

The Bend in the Road (*A curva na estrada*, 1950)
Black Blood (*Sangue negro*, 1923)
But . . . (*Mas . . .*, 1921)
The Easy Success (*O éxito fácil*, 1923)
Emigrants (*Emigrantes*, 1928): *Emigrants* (New York, 1962)
Famished Flesh (*Carne faminta*, 1922)
The Jungle (*A selva*, 1930): *The Jungle* (New York, 1935)
The Mission (*A missão*, 1954): *The Mission* (London, 1963)
The Supreme Instinct (*O instinto supremo*, 1968)
The Wool and the Snow (*A lã e a neve*, 1947)

FERREIRA, JOSÉ GOMES

The Daily Unreality: Stories and Inventions (*O irreal quotidiano: histórias e invenções*, 1971)
Imitation of the Days: An Invented Diary (*Imitação dos dias: diário inventado*, 1966)
Marvelous Adventures of Fearless John (*Aventuras maravilhosas de João Sem Medo*, 1963)
The Memory of Words (*A memória das palavras*, 1965)
Militant Poet (*Poeta militante*, 3 vols., 1977–78)

Poetry VI (*Poesia VI*, 1976)
The World of the Others (*O mundo dos outros*, 1950)

FERREIRA, VERGÍLIO

Apparition (*Aparição*, 1959)
Brief Happiness (*Alegria breve*, 1965)
Clear Void (*Nítido nulo*, 1971)
Coach J (*Vagão J*, 1946)
Pole Star (*Estrela polar*, 1962)
Rapidly, the Shadow (*Rápida, a sombra*, 1975)
The Road Is Long (*O caminho fica longe*, 1943)
Where Everything Was Dying (*Onde tudo foi morrendo*, 1944)

MIGUÉIS, JOSÉ RODRIGUES

Bread Does Not Fall from the Heavens (*O pão não cai do céu*, serial pub., 1975–76; book, 1981)
Happy Easter (*Páscoa feliz*, 1932)
It's Forbidden to Point (*É proibido apontar*, 1964)
Léah, and Other Stories (*Léah, e outras histórias*, 1958)
Nikalai! Nikalai! (*Nikalai! Nikalai!*, 1971)
Reflections of a Bourgeois (*Reflexões dum burguês*, 1974)
The School of Paradise (*A escola do paraíso*, 1959)
Third-Class People (*Gente de terceira classe*, 1963)
A Trip through Our Homeland ("Uma viagem por nossa terra," in *Léah, and Other Stories*)

Steerage and Other Stories (Providence, R. I., 1983)
Lisbon in Manhattan (Providence, R. I., 1984)

NAMORA, FERNANDO

A Bell in the Mountain (*Um sino na montanha*, 1968)
A Crime ("Um crime," in *Sketches of a Doctor's Life*, 2nd series)
The Clandestine Ones (*Os clandestinos*, 1973)
Earth (*Terra*, 1941)
Fire in the Dark Night (*Fogo na noite escura*, 1943)
The Migrant Workers' House (*A casa da malta*, 1945)
Mines of São Francisco (*Minas de São Francisco*, 1946)
The Night and the Dawn (*A noite e a madrugada*, 1950)
Reliefs (*Relevos*, 1937)
Sea of Sargassos (*Mar de sargaços, 1940*)
The Seven Regions of the World (*As sete partidas do mundo*, 1938)
Sketches of a Doctor's Life, 1st series (*Retalhos da vida dum médico*, 1ª série, 1949): *Mountain Doctor* (London, 1956)
Sketches of a Doctor's Life, 2nd series (*Retalhos da vida dum médico*, 2ª série, 1963)
Solitary City (*Cidade solitária*, 1959)

The Sun Worshippers (*Os adoradores do sol,* 1971)
Sunday Afternoon (*Domingo à tarde,* 1961)
The Wheat and the Chaff (*O trigo e o joio,* 1954): *Fields of Fate* (New York, 1970)

PESSOA, FERNANDO

The Anarchist Banker ("O banqueiro anarquista," 1922)
Antinous, 1918
Autopsychography ("Autopsicografia," in *Songbook*): "Autopsychography," in *Selected Poems* (Chicago, 1971); "Self-Analysis," in *Selected Poems* (Austin, Tex., 1971)
English Poems, 3 vols., 1921
In the Shadow of Mount Abiegnos ("Na sombra do Monte Abiegno," in *Songbook*)
Maritime Ode ("Ode marítima," in *Poetry of Álvaro de Campos*): "Maritime Ode," in *Selected Poems* (Chicago, 1971)
Message (*Mensagem,* 1934)
It's Night ("É noite," in *Poems of Alberto Caeiro*): "It's Night," in *Selected Poems* (Austin, Tex., 1971)
Oh Church Bell in My Village ("O sino da minha aldeia," in *Songbook*): "Oh Church Bell in My Village," in *Selected Poems* (Austin, Tex., 1971)
Poems of Alberto Caeiro (*Poemas de Alberto Caeiro,* 1946)
Poetry of Álvaro de Campos (*Poesias de Álvaro de Campos,* 1944)
Salute to Walt Whitman ("Saudação a Walt Whitman," in *Poetry of Álvaro de Campos*)
Songbook (*Cancioneiro,* 1942)
35 Sonnets, 1918
Triumphal Ode ("Ode triunfal," in *Poetry of Álvaro de Campos*)
Ultimatum ("Ultimatum," in *Poetry of Álvaro de Campos*)

Selected Poems (Austin, Tex., 1971)
Selected Poems (Chicago, 1971)
Selected Poems (Harmondsworth, England, 1982)
Fernando Pessoa: A Galaxy of Poets (1888–1935) (London, 1985)
Fernando Pessoa: The Surprise of Being (London, 1986)
The Keeper of Sheep (New York, 1986)
Poems of Fernando Pessoa (New York, 1986)

PIRES, JOSÉ CARDOSO

The Anchored Angel (*O anjo ancorado,* 1958)
The Ballad of Dogs Beach (*A balada da Praia dos Cães,* 1982): *Ballad of Dog's Beach* (London, 1986)
The Dauphin (*O delfim,* 1968)
Dom Quixote ("Dom Quixote," in *Games of Chance*)
Games of Chance (*Jogos de azar,* 1963)
Job's Guest (*O hóspede de Job,* 1963)

Most Excellent Dinosaur (*Dinossauro excelentíssimo,* 1972)
Primer for the Marialva (*Cartilha do marialva,* 1960)
Ritual of the Little Vampires ("Ritual dos pequenos vampiros," in *Games of Chance*): "The Ride," in *Mainstream,* Vol. II, No. 5, 1958)
The Surrender of the Heroes (*O render dos heróis,* 1960)
What Next, José? (*E agora, Jose?,* 1977)

REDOL, ANTÓNIO ALVES

The Boat with Seven Rudders (*A barca das sete lemes,* 1958): *The Man with Seven Names* (New York, 1964)
Clouded Horizon (*Horizonte cerrado,* 1951)
A Crack in the Wall (*Uma fenda na muralha,* 1959)
Eloquent Stories (*Histórias afluentes,* 1963)
The Forgotten Night ("A noite esquecida," in *Eloquent Stories*)
The Frightened Horse (*O cavalo espantado,* 1960)
Gaibéus (*Gaibéus,* 1940)
Grain Fields (*Fanga,* 1943)
Gully of the Blind (*Barranco dos cegos,* 1961)
Men and Shadows (*Os homens e as sombras,* 1951)
The Reinegros Family (*Os Reinegros,* 1972)
Tides (*Marés,* 1941)
The Tranquil Night ("A noite tranquila," in *Eloquent Stories*)
Vintage of Blood (*Vindima de sangue,* 1954)
Waterspouts (*Olhos d'água,* 1954)
The White Wall (*O muro branco,* 1966)
Why Am I Not Supposed to Believe in Felicidade? ("Por que não hei-de acreditar na Felicidade?" in *Eloquent Stories*)

RÉGIO, JOSÉ

Benilde; or, The Virgin Mother (*Benilde; ou, A Virgem Mãe,* 1947)
Black Hymn ("Cântico negro," in *Poems of God and the Devil*): "Hymn of Darkness," in John M. Parker, *Three Twentieth-Century Portuguese Poets* (Johannesburg, 1960)
Blindman's Bluff (*Jogo da cabra-cega,* 1934)
But God Is Great (*Mas Deus é grande,* 1945)
Christmas Story ("Conto do Natal," in *There Are Other Worlds*)
The Depths of the Mirror ("O fundo do espelho," in *There Are Other Worlds*)
The Diary ("O diário," in *Poems of God and the Devil*)
A Drop of Blood (*Uma gota de sangue,* 1945)
Foundations of Reality ("Alicerces da realidade," in *There Are Other Worlds*)
Mário or I Myself (*Mário ou eu-próprio,* 1957)
My Case (*O meu caso,* 1957)
The Old House (*A velha casa,* 5 vols., 1945–66)
The Paradoxes of Good ("Os paradoxos do bem," in *There Are Other Worlds*)

Picture ("Painél," in *Poems of God and the Devil*)
Poems of God and the Devil (*Poemas de Deus e do Diabo,* 1925)
Poem of the Flesh-Spirit ("Poema da carne-espírito," in *Poems of God and the Devil*)
The Prince with Donkey Ears (*O príncipe com orelhas de burro,* 1942)
The Roots of the Future (*As raízes do futuro,* 1947)
Suspended Hymn (*Cântico suspenso,* 1968)
There Are Other Worlds (*Há mais mundos,* 1962)
There Was in the City ("Havia na cidade," in *Suspended Hymn*)
Universality ("Universalidade," in *Poems of God and the Devil*)

RIBEIRO, AQUILINO

The Ass-Driver and His Ass ("O burriqueiro e o seu burro," in *House of the Scorpion*)
Battle without End (*Batalha sem fim,* 1931)
The Big House of Romarigães (*A casa grande de Romarigães,* 1957)
The Black Archangel (*O arcanjo negro,* 1947)
Garden of Torments (*Jardim das tormentas,* 1913)
House of the Scorpion (*Casa do escorpião,* 1964)
Lands of the Devil (*Terras de demo,* 1919)
Malhadinas (*O Malhadinhas,* 1922)
The Man of the Nave (*O homem da nave,* 1954)
The Man Who Killed the Devil (*O homem que matou o diabo,* 1930)
Maria Benigna (*Maria Benigna,* 1935)
The Marvelous Adventure of D. Sebastião (*A aventura maravilhosa de D. Sebastião,* 1936)
Mónica (*Mónica,* 1939): *Monica* (London, 1961)
Saint Bonaboião (*S. Bonaboião,* 1937)
Santiago Road (*Estrada de Santiago,* 1922)
Sentimental Geography (*Geografia sentimental,* 1951)
The Skin of the Bass Drum ("A pele do bombo," in *Garden of Torments*)
The Tale of the Fox (*O romance da raposa,* 1924)
Tungsten (*Volfrâmio,* 1944)
Village (*Aldeia,* 1935)
When the Wolves Howl (*Quando os lobos uivam,* 1958): *When the Wolves Howl* (New York, 1963)
The Winding Path (*A via sinuosa,* 1918)
You Have a Good Body . . . So Work! ("Tem bom corpo . . . que trabalhe!" in *House of the Scorpion*)

SÁ-CARNEIRO, MÁRIO DE

Almost ("Quase," in *Dispersion*)
Beginning (*Princípio,* 1912)
Brothers (*Irmãos,* unpublished)
The Confession of Lucio (*A confissão de Lúcio,* 1914)
Departure ("Partida," in *Dispersion*): "Departure," in John M. Parker, *Three Twentieth-Century Portuguese Poets* (Johannesburg, 1960)

Dispersion (*Dispersão,* 1914)
False Statue ("Falsa estátua," in *Dispersion*)
The Fall ("A queda," in *Dispersion*)
Friendship (*Amizade,* 1912)
Heavens Ablaze (*Céu em fogo,* 1915)
Last Poems (*Últimos poemas,* 1937)
Manicure ("Manicura," in *Last Poems*)
Page of a Suicide ("Página dum suicida," in *Beginning*)
Rattletrap Jalopy ("Caranguejola," in *Last Poems*)
Soul (*Alma,* unpublished)
That Other One ("Aqueloutro," in *Last Poems*)
Traces of Gold (*Indícios de oiro,* 1937)

SENA, JORGE DE

Adulterous Ulisseia (*Ulisseia adúltera,* 1952)
Art of Music (*Arte de música,* 1968)
"Bilingualism" (written in English, in *Exorcisms*)
"The Blood Black" (written in English, 1948, unpublished)
The Death of the Pope (*A morte do Papa,* unpublished)
The Eastern Empire (*O império oriental,* unpublished)
Exorcisms (*Exorcismos,* 1972)
Fidelity (*Fidelidade,* 1958)
"Gentle Advice" (written in English, unpublished)
The Great Captains (*Os grão-capitães,* 1976)
Metamorphoses (*Metamorfoses,* 1963)
Mother's Protection (*Amparo de mãe,* 1951)
Philosopher's Stone (*Pedra filosofal,* 1950)
Persecution (*Perseguição,* 1942)
Poetry I (*Poesia-I,* 1960)
Poetry of 26 Centuries (*Poesia de 26 séculos,* 2 vols., 1971–72)
The Undesired One (*O indesejado,* 1951)

———

The Poetry of Jorge de Sena (Santa Barbara, Cal., 1980)
England Revisited (Lisbon, 1986)
The Wondrous Physician (London, 1986)

SOROMENHO, FERNANDO MONTEIRO DE CASTRO

Calenga (*Calenga,* 1945)
Dead Land (*Terra morta,* 1949)
Gust of Wind, and Other Stories (*Rajada, e outras histórias,* 1943)
Lueji and Ilunga in the Land of Friendship ("Lueji e Ilunga na terra de amizade," in *Calenga*)
Men without a Way (*Homens sem caminho,* 1942)
Night of Anguish (*Noite de angústia,* 1939)
Turning Point (*Viragem,* 1957)

TEIXEIRA DE PASCOAES

Always (*Sempre*, 1898)
A Bird and the Poet ("Uma ave e o poeta," in *The Shadows*)
Buddha ("Budda," in *The Shadows*)
Elegies (*Elegias*, 1912)
Ethereal Life (*Vida etérea*, 1906)
The Eyes of the Animals ("Os olhos dos animais," in *The Shadows*)
Indecisive Songs (*Cantos indecisos*, 1921)
Lady of the Night (*Senhora de noite*, 1909)
The Lusitanian Night ("A noite lusíada," in *Obscure Verb*)
Napoleon (*Napoleão*, 1940)
Obscure Verb (*Verbo escuro*, 1914)
Marânos (*Marânos*, 1911)
The Penitent (*O penitente*, 1942)
The Poor Fool (*O pobre tolo*, 1924)
Poor Verses (*Versos pobres*, 1949)
Return to Paradise (*Regresso ao paraíso*, 1912)
Saint Augustine (*Santo Agostinho*, 1945)
Saint Jerome and the Thunderclap (*São Jerónimo e a trovoada*, 1936)
Saint Paul (*São Paulo*, 1934)
The Shadow of Pain ("A sombra da dor," in *The Shadows*)
The Shadows (*As sombras*, 1907)

TORGA, MIGUEL

Animals (*Bichos*, 1940): *Farrusco the Blackbird, and Other Stories* (New York, 1951)
Bird of Hope ("Ave da esperança," in *Punishments of Purgatory*)
Bread ("Pão," in *Iberian Poems*)
Burning Chamber (*Câmara ardente*, 1952)
The Creation of the World: The First Two Days (*A criação do mundo: os dois primeiros dias*, 1937)
Diary (*Diário*, 12 vols., 1941–77)
Earth ("Terra," in *Iberian Poems*)
Fate ("Fado," in *Iberian Poems*)
The Fourth Day of the Creation of the World (*O quarto dia da criação do mundo*, 1939)
The Great Soul ("O Alma-Grande," in *Stories of the Mountains*)
Hope ("Esperança," in *Punishments of Purgatory*)
Iberian Poems (*Poemas ibéricos*, 1952)
The Illusion ("A ilusão," in *Iberian Poems*)
Life ("Vida," in *Iberian Poems*)
Mr. Ventura (*O Senhor Ventura*, 1943)
Nero ("Nero," in *Animals*)
New Stories of the Mountains (*Novos contos da montanha*, 1944)
Nihil Sibi (*Nihil sibi*, 1948)
The Other Book of Job (*O outro livro de Job*, 1936)
Punishments of Purgatory (*Penas do purgatório*, 1954)

Rebel Orpheus (*Orfeu rebelde,* 1958)
Sea (*Mar,* 1941)
Stories of the Mountains (*Contos da montanha,* 1941)
Terra Firma (*Terra firme,* 1941)
The Third Day of the Creation of the World (*O terceiro dia da criação do mundo,* 1938)
Vintage (*Vindima,* 1954)
Wine ("Vinho," in *Iberian Poems*)

———

Open Sesame, and Other Stories from the Portuguese (London [?], 1960)

COPYRIGHT ACKNOWLEDGMENTS

583

Colóquio/Letras. For generous permission to use excerpts from numerous reviews and articles.

Columbia University Press. For excerpts from Demetrios Basdekis, *Miguel de Unamuno;* Robert E. Lima, *Ramón del Valle-Inclán.*

Comparative Literature. For excerpts from articles by Wilma Newberry on Gómez de la Serna reprinted by permission from *Comparative Literature,* Vol. 21 (1969), pp. 54–55; Helmut Hatzfeld on Alonso, reprinted by permission from *Comparative Literature,* Vol. 4 (1952), pp. 87–88.

Consejo Superior de Investigaciones Científicas. For excerpts from articles by Pablo Cabañas on Cela; José Hierro on Espina.

Constable and Company Ltd. For excerpt from article by John B. Trend on Baroja in *A Picture of Modern Spain: Men and Music.*

Contemporary Books, Inc. Reprinted from *Ortega y Gasset: Existentialism* by José Sánchez Villaseñor © 1949, used with permission of Contemporary Books, Inc., Chicago.

Contemporary Poetry/Poesis. For excerpt from David H. Rosenthal, "Salvador Espriu and Postwar Catalan Poetry," in *Contemporary Poetry: A Journal of Criticism,* Vol. 5, No. 1, © Contemporary Poetry, Inc., 1982.

Contemporary Review Company Ltd. For excerpts from articles by E. Allison Peers on Blasco Ibáñez in *The Contemporary Review;* Helen Granville Barker on Gómez de la Serna in *The Fortnightly Review.*

Cornell University Press. For excerpt from J. S. Bernstein's Introduction to Camilo José Cela, *Mrs. Caldwell Speaks to Her Son.* Copyright © 1968 by Cornell University.

Robert Creeley. For excerpt from article on Sender in *Black Mountain Review.*

Cuadernos Americanos. For excerpts from articles by Antonio Buero Vallejo on Aub; José Luis Cano on Cernuda; Paul Ilie on Zunzunegui; Maurice de la Selva on Felipe.

Cuadernos Hispanoamericanos. For generous permission to reprint numerous articles.

Curial Ediciones Catalanes. For excerpt from article by Joan Fuster on Foix in *Literatura catalana contemporánea.*

Andrew P. Debicki. For excerpt from article on Salinas in *Estudios sobre poesía española contemporánea.*

Miguel Delibes. For excerpt from Miguel Ángel Pastor's Prologue to Miguel Delibes, *La mortaja* (Alianza Editorial).

Dell Publishing Company. For excerpts from articles by Robert W. Corrigan on Sastre in *The New Theatre of Europe;* on García Lorca in *The Theatre in Search of a Fix.*

Magda C. De Moor. For excerpt from article on Ruibal in *Journal of Spanish Studies: Twentieth Century.*

DESTINO SOCIEDAD LDA. For excerpts from articles by Carmen Laforet on Quiroga, D. Ridruejo on Torrente Ballester, Antonio Vilanova on Espriu, Foix in *La Revista Destino;* Joan Teixidor on Espriu in *Cinc poetes.*

DIACRITICS. For excerpt from Interview with Camilo José Cela by Theodore Beardsley.

THE DOLPHIN BOOK CO., LTD. For excerpts from R. E. Batchelor, *Unamuno Novelist* (Oxford, Dolphin Book Co., 1972); Leo R. Cole, *The Religious Instinct in the Poetry of Juan Ramón Jiménez* (Oxford, Dolphin Book Co., 1967); John B. Trend, *Antonio Machado* (Oxford, Dolphin Book Co., 1953).

FRANCIS DONAHUE. For excerpt from article on Sastre in *Arizona Quarterly,* Autumn, 1973.

EDITORIAL DOS CONTINENTES. For excerpt from Delfín Carbonell Bassett, *La novelística de Juan Antonio de Zunzunegui.*

MRS. JOHN DOS PASSOS. For excerpts by John Dos Passos on Machado, Baroja, Benavente, Blasco Ibáñez, Unamuno in *Rosinante to the Road Again* (Doran).

DOUBLEDAY & CO., INC. Excerpt from *The Theatre of The Absurd* by Martin Esslin. Copyright © 1961, 1968, 1969 by Martin Esslin. Reprinted by permission of Doubleday & Co., Inc.

DUKE UNIVERSITY PRESS. Gustavo Pérez Firmat, "Idle Fictions: The Hispanic Vanguard Novel, 1926–1934," pp. 122–23. Copyright © 1982 Duke University Press.

E. P. DUTTON. From *Prometheus and Other Stories* by Pérez de Ayala. Copyright © 1920, by E. P. Dutton and Co., Inc. Reprinted by permission; *The Plays of Gregorio Martínez Sierra, I,* translated by John Garret Underhill. Copyright © 1922 by E. P. Dutton and Co., Inc. Reprinted by permission; *Conversions: Literature and the Modernist Deviation* by George P. Elliott. Copyright © 1971, 1970, 1969, 1966, 1965, 1964 by George P. Elliott. Reprinted by permission of E. P. Dutton.

GEORGE P. ELLIOTT. For excerpt from article on Sender in *Conversions: Literature and the Modernist Deviation.*

KEITH ELLIS. For excerpt from article on Francisco Ayala in *Hispania.*

ENCOUNTER. For excerpt from article by J. M. Cohen on Hernández.

EDITORIAL ESTAMPA, LDA. For excerpt on Redol in Augusto da Costa Dias, *Literatura e luta de classes.*

ESTRENO. For excerpts from articles by Frank P. Casa on Buero Vallejo; Barry E. Weingarten on Hernández.

PUBLICAÇÕES EUROPA-AMÉRICA, LDA. For excerpts from articles by José Palla e Carmo on Pires, Ferreira in *Do livro à leitura.*

FARRAR, STRAUS & GIROUX, INC. Excerpt from *My Belief: Essays on Life and Art* by Hermann Hesse, translated by Denver Lindley. English translation copyright © 1974 by Farrar, Straus and Giroux, Inc. Reprinted by permission of Farrar, Straus and Giroux, Inc.; excerpt from *The Selected Writings of Juan Ramón Jiménez,* translated by H. R. Hayes. Copyright © 1957 by Juan Ramón Jiménez.

EDWIN HONIG. For excerpt from *García Lorca* (New Directions).

HORIZON PRESS. For excerpt from article on Ortega y Gasset. Reprinted from *The Origins of Form in Art* by Herbert Read. Copyright © 1965 by permission of the publisher, Horizon Press, New York.

HOUGHTON MIFFLIN COMPANY. From book review by Archibald MacLeish on Guillén in *The Atlantic Monthly*, January 1951. Reprinted by permission of Houghton Mifflin Company; from article by John B. Trend on Manuel Machado in *Alfonso the Sage and Other Spanish Essays*. Reprinted by permission of Houghton Mifflin Company.

IRVING HOWE. For excerpt from article on Barea in *Partisan Review*.

THE HUDSON REVIEW. From "Ortega on Love," by Irving Singer. Reprinted with permission from *The Hudson Review*, Vol. IX, No. 1, Spring 1958. Copyright © by The Hudson Review.

HUTCHINSON PUBLISHING GROUP. For excerpts from J. M. Cohen, *Poetry of This Age;* Paul West, *The Modern Novel.*

IBEROROMANIA. For excerpt from article by Richard Cardwell on Alberti.

PAUL ILIE. For excerpt from article on Gironella in *Journal of Spanish Studies: Twentieth Century.*

IMPRENSA DA UNIVERSIDADE DE COIMBRA. For excerpt from article by Adolfo Casais Monteiro on Sá-Carneiro in *Considerações pessoais.*

ÍNDICE. For excerpt from article by Aurora de Albornoz on Bergamín.

INSTITUTO DE CULTURA PORTUGUESA. For excerpts from Maria Alzira Seixo (Baranhona) on V. Ferreira and Sá-Carneiro in *Expressão do tempo no romance contemporâneo português;* Maria da Graça Carpinteiro, *A novela poética de Sá-Carneiro.*

INSTITUTO DE ESTUDIOS ASTURIANOS. For excerpt from Esperanza Gurza, *La realidad caleidoscópica de Alejandro Casona.*

ÍNSULA. For excerpts from articles by Rabanal Álvarez on Rodríguez Catelao, July–August 1959; Vicente Aleixandre on Aub, October 1959; Antonio Buero Vallejo on Valle-Inclán, July–August 1961; José Luis Cano on Goytisolo, March 1955, on Matute, February 1949; Julio Cortázar on Salinas, November–December 1971; Biruté Ciplijauskaité, *Baroja, un estilo*, 1972; Ricardo Doménech on Martín-Santos, June 1962; José Domingo on García Hortelano, December 1967; R. de Garciasol on Martín Gaite, September 1955; Pedro Gimferrer on Benet, January 1969; Artur del Hoyo on Buero Vallejo, November 1949; Paul Ilie on Cela, January 1961; Juan Ramón Jiménez on Laforet, January 1948; Rafael Lapesa on Aleixandre, January–February 1979; Julián Mariás on Azorín, October 1953; José Ares Montes on Namora, May 1972, on Pires, July–August 1964, on Redol, July–August 1971; Rodríguez Padrón on Ruibal, September 1976; Luis Suñén on Torrente Ballester, March 1978; Juan Antonio de Zunzunegui on Pérez Galdós, October 1952.

INTERNATIONAL CREATIVE MANAGEMENT, INC. For excerpts from articles on García Lorca, Unamuno in Richard Burgin, *Conversations with Jorge Luis Borges.* As supplied by Holt, Rinehart & Winston.

Jacinto Benavente, copyright © 1924 Oxford University Press, Inc. Reprinted by permission.

PAPELES DE SON ARMADANS. For excerpts from articles by José Luis Aranguren on Riba; David Bary on Celaya; Sherman Eoff and José Schraibman on Martín-Santos; José María Castellet on Riba; Camilo José Cela on Matute; Leopoldo Panero on Alonso; Octavio Paz on Cernuda; María A. Salgado on Gómez de la Serna; Ricardo Senabre on Aldecoa; Gonzalo Sobejano on Cela; Sharon E. Ugalde on Celaya.

PAPERS ON LANGUAGE AND LITERATURE. For excerpt from Lynette Seator, "Alfonso Sastre, Committed Dramatist." *Papers on Language and Literature,* Volume 15, No. 2, Spring 1979. Copyright © 1979 by The Board of Trustees, Southern Illinois University. Printed by permission.

PARNASSUS: POETRY IN REVIEW. For excerpts from articles by Gregory Rabassa on Pessoa; Donald Sutherland on Alberti.

PARTISAN REVIEW. For excerpt from review by Irving Howe of Arturo Barea's *The Forging Of a Rebel* in *Partisan Review.* Copyright © May 1947 by Partisan Review.

ANTHONY M. PASQUARIELLO. For excerpt from Introduction to Alfonso Sastre, *Escuadra hacia la muerte.*

THE PENNSYLVANIA STATE UNIVERSITY PRESS. For excerpts from articles by Gerald Moser on Soromernho in *Essays in Portuguese African Literature;* George E. Wellwarth on Ruibal in *Spanish Underground Drama.* Copyright © 1971 and 1972 The Pennsylvania State University Press, University Park, PA.

MARCELINO C. PEÑUELAS. For excerpt from *La obra narrativa de Ramón J. Sender* (Gredos 1971).

A. D. PETERS & CO., LTD. For excerpt from article by V. S. Pritchett on Pérez Galdós in *Books in General* (Chatto & Windus Ltd.). Reprinted by permission of A. D. Peters & Co., Ltd.

ALLEN W. PHILLIPS. For excerpt from article on Antonio Machado in *Temas del modernismo hispanoamericano* (Gredos 1974).

PHILOLOGICAL QUARTERLY. For excerpt from article by Frances Weber on Pérez de Ayala.

EDITORIAL PLAYOR, S. A. For excerpt from John A. Catsoris, *Azorín and the Eighteenth Century.*

PLAZA & JANÉS EDITORES, S. A. For excerpts from José Luis Cano's Prologue to Blas de Otero, *País: Antología, 1955–1970;* article by Juan Ramón Jiménez in María de Gracia Ifach, *Miguel Hernández, rayo que no cesa.*

LIBRAIRIE PLON. For excerpt from André Malraux's Preface to José Bergamín, *Le clou brulant.*

POETRY. For excerpts from article by Edouard Roditi on Pessoa. The article first appeared in *Poetry,* copyright © 1955 by The Modern Poetry Association, reprinted by permission of the editor of *Poetry;* Wallace Fowlie on Guillén. The article first

Daniel P. Testa, eds., *Spanish Writers of 1936: Crisis and Commitment in the Poetry of the Thirties and Forties;* Derek Harris, *Luis Cernuda: A Study of His Poetry;* David Henn, *Camilo José Cela: La Colmena* (Grant & Cutler, Ltd.); Alan Hoyle on Gómez de la Serna in *Studies in Modern Spanish Literature;* David K. Loughran, *Federico García Lorca: The Poetry of Limits;* Ian R. MacDonald, *Gabriel Miró: His Private Library and His Literary Background;* Philip W. Silver, *"Et in arcadia ego": A Study of the Poetry of Luis Cernuda;* Alison Sinclair, *Valle-Inclán's Ruedo Ibérico: A Popular View of Revolution.*

TAURUS EDICIONES, S. A. For excerpt from Agnes Guillón, *La novela experimental de Miguel Delibes.*

MICHAEL D. THOMAS. For excerpt from article on Cunqueiro in *Hispania.*

TIMES NEWSPAPERS LTD. For excerpts from articles by J. M. Cohen on Aleixandre, Cela, Pessoa, Pires. Reprinted from the *Times Literary Supplement.*

TOPIC. For excerpt from article by A. Marquerie on Benavente.

LA TORRE. For excerpts from articles by Joaquín Casalduero on Miró; José María Castellet on Goytisolo.

ELISEO TORRES BOOKS. For excerpt from Rodolfo Cardona, *Ramón Gómez de la Serna.*

TWAYNE PUBLISHERS. For excerpts from Farris Anderson, *Alfonso Sastre,* © 1971; Patricia J. Boehne, *J. V. Foix,* © 1980; J. S. Bernstein, *Benjamín Jarnés,* © 1972; Mary Lee Bretz, *Concha Espina,* © 1980; Phyllis Z. Boring, *Elena Quiroga,* © 1977; Vicente Cabrera, *Juan Benet,* © 1983; Geraldine Clearly Nichols, *Miguel Hernández,* © 1978; Carl W. Cobb, *Contemporary Spanish Poetry: 1898–1963,* © 1976, *Antonio Machado,* © 1972; John Crispin, *Pedro Salinas,* © 1974; Santiago Daydí-Tolson, *The Post-Civil War Spanish Social Poets,* © 1983; Janet Díaz, *Ana María Matute,* © 1971, *Miguel Delibes,* © 1971; Rita Mazzetti Gardiol, *Ramón Gómez de la Serna,* © 1974; Kathleen Glenn, *Azorín (José Martínez Ruiz),* © 1981; A. Grove Day and Edgar Knowlton, Jr., *Vicente Blasco Ibáñez,* © 1972; Martha Halsey, *Antonio Buero Vallejo,* © 1973; Marion P. Holt, *The Contemporary Spanish Theatre: 1949–1972,* © 1975; Estelle Irizarry, *Francisco Ayala,* © 1978; Salvador Jiménez Fajardo, *Luis Cernuda,* © 1978; Roberta Johnson, *Carmen Laforet,* © 1981; Charles L. King, *Ramon J. Sender,* © 1974; G. Grant MacCurdy, *Jorge Guillén,* © 1982; D. W. McPheeters, *Camilo José Cela,* © 1969; Harold K. Moon, *Alejandro Casona,* © 1985; Patricia O'Connor, *Gregorio and María Martínez Sierra,* © 1977; Victor Ouimette, *José Ortega y Gasset,* © 1982; Walter T. Pattison, *Benito Pérez Galdós,* © 1975; Janet Pérez, *Gonzalo Torrente Ballester,* © 1984; Marcelino C. Peñuelas, *Jacinto Benavente,* © 1966; Marguerite C. Rand, *Ramón Pérez de Ayala,* © 1971; Kessel Schwartz, *Vicente Aleixandre,* © 1970, *Juan Goytisolo,* © 1970; Ronald Schwartz, *José María Gironella,* © 1972; Verity Smith, *Ramón del Valle-Inclán,* © 1973. All reprinted with the permission of Twayne Publishers, a division of G. K. Hall & Co., Boston.

THE UNIVERSITY OBSERVER. For excerpt from article by Arturo Barea on Ortega y Gasset, Winter, 1947. Permission granted on behalf of The University of Chicago.

INDEX TO CRITICS

Names of critics are cited on the pages given. Spanish critics are listed by their composite last names; Portuguese critics are listed by their last names.

ABBOT, James H.
  Azorín, 56

ADAMOV, Arthur
  Valle-Inclán, 441

ADAMS, Mildred
  Ortega y Gasset, 323

AIKEN, Conrad
  García Lorca, 191

ALARCOS LLORACH, Emilio
  Otero, 334

ALBERTI, Rafael
  García Lorca, 189; Hernández, 242

ALBORG, José Luis
  Aldecoa, 11

ALBORNOZ, Aurora de
  Bergamín, 95

ALEIXANDRE, Vicente
  Aub, 37

ALLEN, Rupert C.
  Jiménez, 262

ALONSO, Dámaso
  Diego, 163; A. Machado, 280; Otero, 334

ALONSO, J.M.
  Alberti, 9

ALONSO MONTERO, Jesús
  Rodríguez Castelao, 379

ALVAREZ, A.
  Guillén, 235

AMORÓS, Andrés
  Ayala, 45; Pérez de Ayala, 356

ANDERSON, Farris
  Buero Vallejo, 113; Sastre, 403

ANDERSON, Reed
  Buero Vallejo, 116

ANDRADE, João Pedro
  Brandão, 460

ANSELMO, Manuel
  Castro, 464

ARANGUREN, José Luis
  Riba, 374

ARJONA, Doris King
  Azorín, 48; Ganivet, 181

AUB, Max
  Alberti, 4; Felipe, 174

AUBRUN, Charles V.
  Baroja, 73; Buero Vallejo, 111

AYALA, Francisco
  Bergamín, 93; Laforet, 265; Ortega y Gasset, 331

AZORÍN
  Alberti, 3; Álvarez Quintero, 32; Baroja, 67

BACARISSE, Pamela
  Sá-Carneiro, 527

BACARISSE, Salvador
  Sánchez Ferlosio, 395

BALAND, Timothy
  Hernández, 246

BALLESTA, Juan Cano
  Hernández, 244

BALLINGER, Rex E.
  Zunzunegui, 453

BALSEIRO, José A.
  Azorín, 49

BAQUERO-GOYANES, Mariano
  Miró, 312

BARANHONA, Maria Alzira (Seixo)
  V. Ferreira, 472; Sá-Carneiro, 525

BAREA, Arturo
  Ortega y Gasset, 325; Unamuno, 425

BAROJA, Pío
  Ortega y Gasset, 320

BARRETT, William
  Unamuno, 430

BARROW, Geoffrey R.
  Otero, 337

603